Revolution and Its Narratives

CAI XIANG

Revolution and Its Narratives

CHINA'S SOCIALIST
LITERARY AND
CULTURAL IMAGINARIES,
1949–1966

EDITED AND TRANSLATED BY
Rebecca E. Karl and Xueping Zhong

Duke University Press   Durham and London   2016

© 2016 Duke University Press
All rights reserved

Typeset in Arno Pro by Graphic Composition, Inc., Athens, GA

Library of Congress Cataloging-in-Publication Data
Cai, Xiang, [date] author.
[880-01 Ge ming/xu shu. English]
Revolution and its narratives : China's socialist literary and cultural imaginaries, 1949–1966 / Cai Xiang ; edited and translated by Rebecca E. Karl and Xueping Zhong.
pages cm
"The Chinese edition was originally published by Peking University Press in 2010. This translation is published by arrangement with Peking University Press, Beijing, China."
Includes bibliographical references and index.
ISBN 978-0-8223-6054-4 (hardcover : alk. paper)
ISBN 978-0-8223-6069-8 (pbk. : alk. paper)
ISBN 978-0-8223-7461-9 (e-book)
1. Chinese literature—20th century—History and criticism.
2. Politics and culture—China. 3. Socialism in literature.
I. Karl, Rebecca E., translator. II. Zhong, Xueping, [date] translator. III. Title.
PL2303.C27913 2016
895.109'0051—dc23 2015029175

本作品原由北京大学出版社于2010年出版。
英文翻译版经北京大学出版社授权于全球市场独家出版发行。
保留一切权利。未经书面许可，任何人不得复制、发行。

The Chinese edition was originally published by Peking University Press in 2010. This translation is published by arrangement with Peking University Press, Beijing, China. All rights reserved. No reproduction and distribution without permission.

Cover texture: maxim ibragimov / Alamy.

CONTENTS

vii   A Note on the Translation

ix   Acknowledgments

xi   Introduction to the English Translation
Rebecca E. Karl and Xueping Zhong

1   INTRODUCTION
Literature and Revolutionary China

27   CHAPTER 1
The National/The Local: Conflict, Negotiation, and Capitulation in the Revolutionary Imagination

85   CHAPTER 2
The Mobilization Structure: The Masses, Cadres, and Intellectuals

145   CHAPTER 3
Youth, Love, "Natural Rights," and Sex

189   CHAPTER 4
Renarrating the History of the Revolution: From Hero to Legend

251   CHAPTER 5
Narratives of Labor or Labor Utopias

307   CHAPTER 6
      Technological Revolution and Narratives of
      Working-Class Subjectivity

357   CHAPTER 7
      Cultural Politics, or Political Cultural Conflicts, in the 1960s

403   CONCLUSION
      The Crisis of Socialism and Efforts to Overcome It

433   Bibliography

447   Index

A NOTE ON THE TRANSLATION

Several issues that have occupied us during the translation process should be noted. First, because of the length of the book in Chinese and some of its discursive tangents, we have trimmed and edited passages, sections, and discussions that seemed to us either too wordy or too specialized for the type of book we hope this to be in English. The outside readers for Duke University Press also urged us to trim passages cited from various literary texts. We have done as much pruning as we thought we could without depriving Cai Xiang's book of its flavor and textual richness. Those capable of reading Chinese will probably want to consult Cai's original alongside our translation. In the interest of readability and accessibility, we have not indicated in the text where we edited. Cai gave us total freedom to make these choices, and we took him at his word. No thematic material has been eliminated; what we have trimmed are repetitions and discussions of intricate plotpoints in and/or digressions about literary works that were not directly related to the discussion at hand. Some of this material has been summarized so as to provide appropriate segues, some has been paraphrased, and some simply has been eliminated.

Second, we have provided some assistance in the form of annotations for readers who may not be familiar with Chinese history, literature, or the multiple debates about them. Wherever in the text we deemed it necessary, we have added notes, with the notation "Tr." indicating our additions. So as not to add to the bulk of the book, we have kept these to a minimum. We have also trimmed Cai's notes, for the most part retaining only the information required for scholarly accountability. We would also like to mention here that a good number of the Chinese-language sources cited in Cai's book were missing page numbers. Where possible, we have tracked those down; many have been elusive. We have indicated in relevant places where we do not have proper pagination. In addition, Romanization systems for Chinese changed in the 1970s; for English-language translations, we cite in the system used at the time of the translation.

Third, again for the most part, we have not retranslated from Chinese back into English those passages that were originally written in English; nor have we retranslated other works whose original languages were not English, but which have already been translated into English. To the best of our ability, we have tracked down the existing English and dropped that into the text instead, with proper citation to the English-language versions. The Chinese versions are not cited in translation, unless we have been unable to find the existing English. We thank Xu Daoheng and Chen Xi for doing the bulk of that tedious but necessary work, as noted in the acknowledgments.

Fourth, we have tracked down and dropped into the text as needed citations from those originally cited works of fiction that have been translated into and published in English; these mostly include the Chinese novels of the 1950s. All other translations of Chinese works are our own.

The translators have each gone over all the chapters, in Chinese and in English, to ensure accuracy and unity in usage. All errors and translational choices are of course ours, and we take full responsibility for them.

ACKNOWLEDGMENTS

The translators thank Cai Xiang for being such a wonderful interlocutor and such a hands-off but helpful author through the translation process. We have talked much, eaten well, and drunk quantities of good tea together in the several years during which this project has come to fruition. Xueping and Rebecca also have each other to thank for an entirely enjoyable collaboration. The trust we all three had among ourselves made our endeavor one of comradely enthusiasms and learning experiences.

The translators are most grateful to Adrian Thieret for translating part of the conclusion for two different publications. We have completed the translation. As it appears in this volume, it is substantially different from its previously published form. We would like to note here, however, its previous incarnations: "The Crisis of Socialism and Efforts to Overcome It," in *Culture and Social Transformation: Theoretical Framework and Chinese Context*, edited by Cao, Zhong, Liao, Wang (Leiden: Brill, 2014), 241–62; and with the same title in *Debating the Socialist Legacy and Capitalist Globalization in China*, edited by Zhong and Wang (New York: Palgrave Macmillan, 2014), 85–108. We also are extremely grateful to Chen Xi at the University of Toronto and Xu Daoheng at Shanghai University for their editorial assistance. They tracked down citations, page numbers, and passages from English-language originals, essential labor that can be tedious but quite necessary to the process of producing a translated manuscript. Their seriousness of purpose and careful work made the preparation of this text less painful than it otherwise might have been. In addition, Lorraine Chi-man Wong from the University of Otago put in a number of weeks of work to help prepare the manuscript for submission for publication; and Mengran Xu, a graduate student in the History Department at New York University, compiled the bibliography. Zhu Qian did the index. Thank you! Wang Ban and two anonymous readers for Duke University Press were helpful, appropriately critical, and careful in their reviews. We are grateful for their exemplary work.

Ken Wissoker has demonstrated again that he is a most congenial and supportive editor, and we appreciate the entire crew at Duke University Press, a group that is as good as one can find and might hope for. The creative energy and intellectual acumen they all brought to this project have made it a pleasure to work with them. We want particularly to thank our copyeditor, Jeanne Ferris, whose painstaking work saved us from a number of inconsistencies and blunders. We would like to add our appreciation for the cooperation demonstrated by Peking University Press, the original publishers of Cai Xiang's book in Chinese, who provided speedy permission for the book's translation and assisted us as needed.

Finally, Xueping would like to thank the Faculty Research Awards Committee at Tufts University for a timely financial contribution, and Rebecca would like to thank Tom Carew, dean of the Faculty of Arts and Sciences, and Joy Connolly, dean of humanities, at New York University for their matching contribution. These combined funds helped us hire the assistants mentioned above, whose work was so essential to the manuscript's preparation. We are deeply appreciative.

INTRODUCTION TO THE ENGLISH TRANSLATION
REBECCA E. KARL AND XUEPING ZHONG

In 2010, Cai Xiang's *Revolution and Its Narratives* [*Geming/Xushu*] was published in China.[1] It immediately garnered positive reviews (as well as a few politically motivated attacks) and became one of the most talked about scholarly books of the year. Roundtables were organized to discuss its challenges to convential scholarship and workshops convened to explore its many strands of inquiry. The translators decided soon after that this was precisely the kind of book that is still quite rare in English-language scholarship on modern socialist Chinese literature. Its major topic—the relationship among Chinese narratives of revolution, modernity, and socialism in the Maoist period—generally has been dismissed in English-language studies of modern Chinese literature. In the few exceptions, the discussions often reduce the cultural to the political, neglecting the complex literary and aesthetic aspects of the work in favor of assumed transparently political-ideological readings, which amounts to the same thing as a dismissal. Cai Xiang's book argues otherwise and thus presents a potential map for future research. It is, in short, an entirely new

1. The literal translation of the title is *Revolution/Narratives*; we have been persuaded by outside readers and Duke University Press to slightly modify this title for the English edition.

theoretical meditation on the historical and aesthetic possibilities opened up by, as well as the ultimate impossibility of writing a literature adequate to, the socialist transformation of China in the 1950s and 1960s.

Since we undertook the translation of the book in the summer of 2011— it has taken several years to complete the work because each of us has been engaged in a number of other projects—a couple of studies on this general subject have been published and a slew of dissertations launched, with several doubtless already completed.[2] Indeed, after years of lying fallow, Chinese culture and cultural production of the 1950s and 1960s have become a rather trendy field of research, and as the period recedes into the past and becomes ever more historical, a newer research environment is without a doubt taking shape. Rather than completely initiating a trend in English, then, this book's English-language edition joins an ongoing scholarly conversation that increasingly takes seriously what Cai calls contemporary literature (*dangdai wenxue*) and what otherwise is usually known as socialist literature, or the literature of the seventeen years [1949–66]. Many of the individual literary works and some of the issues taken up in Cai's book have been raised in Chinese scholarship and U.S.-based studies of Chinese literature. Yet Cai's systematicity and his literary-historical dialectical mode of inquiry remain rare and lead in some startlingly innovative directions. Indeed, as Cai described the project in an interview we held with him in the summer of 2013 at a Shanghai coffee shop, his core problem in this book is how to take seriously the legitimacy of socialism and the experimental contemporary literature that was pioneered in its name—and the core difference between his work and that of others is that he does take that legitimacy seriously. As he indicated, even maintaining the legitimacy of the 1950s and 1960s (as compared to the left-wing literature of the 1930s) has become a matter of debate in discussions of modern China's history and contemporary literature. The highly politicized debate is not about theory but in the evaluation of socialist history and its literature and cultural

---

2. A partial listing of recent books would include Peter Button, *Configurations of the Real in Chinese Literary and Aesthetic Modernity* (Leiden: Brill, 2009); Alexander Cook, *Mao's Little Red Book: A Global History* (Cambridge: Cambridge University Press, 2014); Krista Van Fleit Hang, *Literature the People Love: Reading Chinese Texts from the Early Maoist Period (1949–1966)* (New York: Palgrave MacMillan, 2013); Richard King, *Milestones on a Golden Road: Writing for Chinese Socialism* (Vancouver: University of British Columbia Press, 2013); Wendy Larson, *From Ah-Q to Lei Feng: Freud and Revolutionary Spirit in 20th Century China* (Stanford, CA: Stanford Universtiy Press, 2009); Barbara Mittler, *A Continuous Revolution: Making Sense of Cultural Revolution Culture* (Cambridge, MA: Harvard Asia Center Publications, 2012).

imaginary, which are thus often dismissed. In these conflictual conditions, people often cannot forgive a certain seriousness in coping with the history of "the seventeen years" or its literary and cultural production.

We will have more to say about these issues in what follows. For now, suffice it to note that this introduction to the English translation of Cai's book is intended to situate the book in a context—English-language studies of literature produced under Chinese socialism—for which it was not originally intended. We thus hope to indicate what we believe is this book's importance not only for Chinese studies at the current juncture, but also for research on socialist and modern experimental literatures of the contemporary period more generally.

Our introduction proceeds in three parts. First, we situate Cai's discussion in the context of the Chinese historical turn in socialist new culture toward massification (*dazhonghua*) during the Yan'an period (1935–49) and after. If a previous emphasis in China on new culture focused on the May Fourth period and beyond (1915–1937) and located the source and catalyst of China's and the world's cultural renewal in the petit bourgeois urban literary sphere, then in the Yan'an period under Mao Zedong's directives and in the dual contexts of mobilizing for the national socialist revolution and the War of Resistance against Japan, the turn was toward the mass rural sphere (peasants) as source of and catalyst for social transformation and national unity. By the 1950s and 1960s, after the Chinese Communist Party came to power, having vanquished internal and external foes alike, the rural emphasis was joined, enhanced, and complicated by the revolutionary addition of the urban proletarian realm, symbolized by the problem of rural cadres' entering the cities from the villages in which the revolution had been developed and nurtured, and from which it had been launched. These successive and simultaneous turns posed sociological challenges, to be sure, but they also presented new possibilities for old-style (urbanized, petit bourgeois) intellectuals (*wenren*) and new-style (revolutionized and rusticated) cultural workers of the time. These challenges and opportunities were in large part articulated in and through Mao Zedong's important 1942 lectures, "Talks at the Yan'an Forum on Art and Literature" (hereafter, "Talks"). Following Cai's lead, we position his book's theoretical-historical contribution in this context.

Second, we locate Cai's discussion in the post-1980s global repudiation of all things socialist, and thus in the ascendant scholarly atmosphere in sociocultural analysis and wider society that Daniel Vukovich has called "liberal revenge."³ This atmosphere is even more prevalent in China than it is elsewhere. "Liberal revenge," in this case, resides most pointedly in the move from analyzing and taking seriously the political-cultural concepts of the masses (*dazhong*) and the revolutionary people (*renmin*) as the subject of history to primarily engaging the depoliticized ahistorical concept of the human (*ren*) or the individual (*geren*) not only as the subject of history but also as the measure of all worthwhile cultural, economic, and political endeavors. Cai addresses this question in the text at hand in his frequent evocations of the 1980s Chinese critiques of literature from the 1950s and 1960s. In this, we can see his insistence on retrieving the contemporaneous meanings and strivings of socialist literature from the detritus of recent historical-ideological erasure as one of the major goals of his study.

Third, we situate Cai's work in his attempt to answer the deceptively simple question: what happens culturally the day after the revolution?⁴ As Cai argues, a significant feature of the revolution was that it was an ongoing cultural narrative event, whose logic, tensions, localizations, and so on all needed to be worked out in concert with the economic building of socialism and the socialist transformation of everyday life. That is, the revolution was embedded in narratives just as it was narrativized in multiple different ways. These are not separable, according to Cai's analysis; indeed, he insists that the Chinese revolution was a cultural revolution from the very beginning in its intention to transform social consciousness. Rather than turn narrative into a function of revolution, then, Cai dialectically intertwines them. We conclude with a brief discussion of the ways in which Cai leads us from the literature of socialism toward the paradox of the Cultural Revolution (1966–76), which simultaneously strictly enforced various cultural dogmatisms while representing liberation from authority for many individual cultural workers.

The Yan'an Talks: How to Narrate the Revolution in Socialist Literature

One of Cai's major theoretical proposals derives from Benedict Anderson's discussion of imaginary communities as a nationalist narrative project and process. While for Anderson the implicit and explicit narrator of this project is the state, for Cai—reading Anderson through Mao, one could say—the

---

3. Daniel Vukovich, *China and Orientalism: Western Knowledge Production and the P.R.C.* (London: Routledge, 2012), 17–20.
4. "After the revolution" derives from Daniel Bell, *The Cultural Contradictions of Capitalism* (New York: Basic, 1976). See chapter 7 of this book.

narratives are written by novelists and fiction writers, who were tasked from the mid-1930s onward with inventing a socialist revolutionary literature. In this process, while the national imaginary and the socialist imaginary were often simultaneously narrated from the Yan'an period onward, and while they often drew upon common themes, Cai argues that neither of them can be dissolved into the other without some elision of the important ways in which the socialist imaginary departed from, enhanced, and embedded itself in society differently from the national one. This insight on the nonconflationary simultaneity of socialism and nationalism requires us to take the revolutionary nature of Chinese nationalism and socialism quite seriously. In other words, as Cai explains, socialist narratives had a revolutionary and thus socially transformative task: their explicit and ambitious goal was to embed themselves among the very audiences whose members were in the midst of transforming their own lives and the future of the nation. Thus, to embed itself in the countryside and among peasants, the socialist cultural narrative, or the narrative of socialist culture, often needed to strengthen local identities in typified ways by incorporating national transformations into traditional communal forms. This is what Cai calls the localization of the national imaginary through transformative social practice and imagination, a process that created socialist cultural content that itself mixed with and became a lived part of socialist everyday life.

The task of those who produced the literature and culture of the time was to create narratives adequate to this process—including the localization, socialist transformation, and multiple levels of cultural integration—with as much complexity and sympathy as possible. Thus, one of Cai's most important points in this regard is to elucidate how the relation of narrative to revolution in socialist literature was an integral part of socialist literary practice. Indeed, this was its very logic, rather than merely a political or ideological requirement imposed by the Party-State. Because of the internal relation demanded of narrative and socialism, Cai takes very seriously the attempts after 1949 (following World War II and what is commonly called China's "liberation") by a generation of major and minor literary producers to put into practice Mao Zedong's 1942 "Talks." He takes seriously the idea that this generation of writers were determined to produce socialist literature because of their own political commitments and social sympathies, and were striving very hard to achieve this goal both as writers—cultural producers—and as people who lived in and through the historical politics of the time. Retrospective denunciations or repudiations of this literature or these literary practitioners because of the supposed falsity of the ideological consciousness they espoused thus entirely miss the historical point. Indeed, what Cai demonstrates is how writers' political and social commitments led them to identify contradictions in socialist life, even while they were unable narratively to resolve those contradictions adequately.

Following Mao's indications in the "Talks" and elsewhere, then, narrative and narrativity became and remained effective, important, and necessary points of entry into socialism as a culturally, politically, economically, and socially generative lived system of ideology and social transformation aimed at revolutionizing the social relations of production and life in general. Cai reconfirmed this point in our summer 2013 interview, during which he emphasized that putting the ideas in Mao's "Talks" into practice demanded a high level of competency and self-reflection; that this endeavor was embraced by great writers of the time, and was essentially inaccessible to hacks; and that the effort was not merely to apply some theoretical or ideological yardsticks to existing writing, but rather, as in the spirit of Mao's "Talks," it was to create an entirely new literary form and content for the socialist transformation of life, culture, and China.

The difficulty of practicing what the "Talks" required thus stemmed in part from the fact that writers had to enter into a constantly changing social situation—everyday life, after all, is both routine and rife with transformative potential; narrating the resultant complexity required nimbleness so as to enhance the potential and ensure the proper direction of socialist transformation. As Mao observes in the "Talks," every transformation in the social relations of production requires the development of a new consciousness of and in society. For Mao, then, the task of socialist literature was not merely to reflect but to produce culturally this consciousness and this new society, for which the changing social situation became not merely the raw material for a crude representational practice, but also the ground upon which the cultural production of a socialist literature adequate to the ever-changing situation had to be engaged as a practice. The engagement, then, was to include the shifting political—as well as, and perhaps even more important, shifting cultural and social—consciousness of and in the masses for whom, by whom, and in whose name modern socialist literature was being created. The task that was taken on by the mostly elite intellectuals, who were literate and urban-educated, unlike the masses for whom they wrote and in whose idiom they strove to invent a new practice of cultural production, was not an easy one. It required that these intellectuals enter a rural or industrial lifeworld that was alien to them in many respects. And it required, as Cai pointed out in our interview, that intellectuals reform and reeducate themselves in conversation with peasants and proletarian workers. In this sense, the *renmin* (revolutionary people)—peasants and the proletariat—are the necessary interlocutors not only as a market (there is still a market consideration throughout the Maoist period), but primarily as an ethical principle of socialist literary practice. This was an ethics founded upon preexisting forms of sociality that needed to be embraced while also being transformed.

For this complex endeavor, Mao broke the tasks of cultural production in his "Talks" into five realms of creative consideration that he analyzed as the most important for the formation of a revolutionary national culture, a revolutionary cadre of culture workers, and a new culture of socialist revolution. The realms—each of which was autonomous and yet also dialectically related to the others—were class stand, attitude, audience, work style, and popularization (massification).[5] Cai's exploration into the creative potential in, as well as the impasses encountered by, contemporary literature refers to each of these realms specifically through an examination of the major literary figures of the late 1940s, 1950s, and early 1960s, including Zhao Shuli, Zhou Libo, Liu Qing, Yang Mo, Hao Ran, among others. For Mao—and for the writers who seriously attempted to put his social-literary analysis into practice so as to thereby invent a new socialist literature–the problem of class stand included not only a consciousness of where the cultural worker located himself or herself, but also and more important, it included a recognition that all works of art or culture embody a class stand. Just as socialist society in China was to be informed by and was intended to serve, while also strengthening, the peasant-proletariat alliance, socialist works of art needed to embody, create, and represent the class stand of these leading revolutionary classes. Those works of art had to narrativize the transformation of the former slaves of social production into masters of the state and nation.

If one took seriously the problem of revolutionary classes and the problem of class stand, then one's cultural attitude became an issue of paramount importance. Where, socially, did one locate oneself? Revolutionary works needed to help unite the socialist classes as well as encourage and promote revolutionary progress—whether in war, in urban and industrial construction, or in rural cooperation and collectivization; such cultural works needed

5. The "Talks" were delivered in May 1942 and published in revised form in 1943. Mao Tse-tung [Mao Zedong], "Talks at the Yenan [Yan'an] Forum on Literature and Art," *Selected Works of Mao Tse-tung* (Peking: Foreign Languages Press, 1967), 3: 69–98.

to criticize revolutionary enemies and laggards while praising and depicting positively revolutionary progressives. Yet these negative and positive depictions could not be cast in stone: they needed to provide hope and a method for change and social transformation. This needed to be done in a way that took the audience for such works seriously; that is, with due consideration for local and traditional forms and languages already loved and known by the masses, which were now to be integrated into a larger context of national-level socialist transformation and cultural production. The combination of attitude and audience, as Cai demonstrates, helped produce some very clear innovations in the uses of legend and myth, heroic narratives, romance, and other traditional oral narrative forms that were reconstituted into the modernist socialist novel, short-story, and narrative cinematic genres.

Creating works that were complex enough to grapple with the ongoing transformations in social life and yet direct enough to be understood and appreciated by a new proletarian and peasant audience required cultural workers to shift their work styles. Intellectuals were now encouraged to go forth from their petit bourgeois urban lives into the countryside and to industrial sites to learn the rhythms, languages, difficulties, and joys of the common people, and thus become better able to narrativize imaginatively and aesthetically the struggles and triumphs of regular folk. Intellectual high-handedness and pretension were to be traded for humble learning from the masses. The failures and foibles—the real life—of common people needed to be dealt with directly and yet also aestheticized and fictionalized. Tying the whole endeavor together, then, was the injunction to popularize or massify: to produce writing for the revolutionary masses and for a truly popular readership. This required not the dumbing down of literature, but the introduction of new narrative forms through the use of older oral story-telling forms; the conscious attempt to cater to a subaltern population, so that they could recognize themselves in the works as well as recognize how to transform themselves for the new society; and the participation of the masses themselves in the very creation of the works.

In tracing China's socialist literature movement to Mao's "Talks," Cai may be taking an unorthodox position on Chinese literary history. Many scholars, in fact, have understood China's socialist literature within a genealogy already produced in the Soviet Union through a Stalinist-inflected socialist realism and its major creations, such as Mikhail Sholokhov's *Virgin Soil Upturned*, Galina Nikolaeva's *Harvest*, and many others. These books and films were widely translated and read and watched in Maoist China. We cannot say with certainty why Cai decided to mostly ignore the Soviet influence (although we can note the fact that he disavows the problem of influence altogether), which may very well be a topic worth exploring in a different analytical idiom. However, we can speculate that Cai's point is to emphasize how socialism was nativized in and through China's modern experience with revolution and cultural production, for which Mao's "Talks" are far more important.[6]

As Cai demonstrates, in practice, the abstract idealism of Mao's philosophical "Talks" contained contradictions, which at first posed interesting narrative challenges but increasingly became amenable to simplified and eventually entirely rigid ideological solutions. It was in the Cultural Revolution that the requirements for literature finally were dogmatized; that the radicalism of the possibility of socialist literature was undermined; and that literary creation fell into the hands of lesser producers. This outcome was not inevitable, however. Indeed, Cai's book shows how revolutionary themes were opened into different types of narratives, creating the tensions and the possibilities that later were foreclosed by fiat.

"Liberal Revenge": How to Erase China's Socialist Literature after the Cultural Revolution

While challenges to the socialist cultural imaginary already existed within socialist practices during the Mao era, the wholesale repudiation of these practices emerging from the postsocialist period—dating domestically in China since the start of the reform and opening up of the late 1970s and, globally, from within the victorious capitalist West after the Cold War—has been overwhelming. This "liberal revenge," as Vukovich calls it, has mustered ideological forces from all corners to denounce the mistakes, disasters, and violence committed in the name of revolution and has, by extension, almost succeeded in relegating the socialist cultural imaginary to the dustbin of history. Vukovich argues that the "eclipse of Maoist discourse—its defeat in the discursive battle for hegemony within Chinese society—is one of the conditions for the rise/return of liberalism in China and abroad."[7] Starting in the late 1970s and throughout much of the 1980s, a good portion of what intellectuals pro-

---

6. We thank one of our anonymous readers for the Soviet works mentioned. We have disagreed with the reader's point, but it has helped us clarify another of Cai's contributions.
7. Daniel Vukovich, "From Charting the Revolution to Charter 2008," in *Culture and Social Transformations: Theoretical Framework and Chinese Context*, ed. Cao, Zhong, Liao (Leiden: Brill, 2014), 101.

claimed to be thought liberation in China's reform period was accompanied by such cultural movements as the new enlightenment and a culture fever, all of which were essentially responsible for casting doubt upon, if not completely delegitimizing, many of the socialist premises, practices, and accomplishments of the 1930s through the 1970s. The various short-lived but powerfully influential literary schools of writing, as well as critics who applied humanist theories in support of what they called new-era literature, paved the way for an abrupt ruptural cultural departure from the socialist cultural forms, content, and ideals that had been promoted during the Mao era. (Nonetheless, as Cai argues, what has been referred to as a rupture has not been as complete as some would claim.)

One of the best known voices advocating for the shift was that of Liu Zaifu, whose most influential 1980s writings include "On the Subjectivity of Literature," "Literary Studies Should Take Humanity as Its Central Focus," and *On the Composition of Literary Personality*.[8] Liu's major argument was that literature should not be understood as a political and ideological tool but as studies and representations of the subjective feelings and emotions of the individual. While Liu's central argument was highly political—and it was articulated in the midst of a denunciation of the political violence of the Cultural Revolution and its cultural expressions—his new theory was premised on a depoliticized and derevolutionized notion of the self or the human being, which is of course highly ideological.[9]

In a recent article titled "People's Literature: An Unfinished Historical Project," the Tsinghua University–based scholar Kuang Xinnian offers—by way of a brief discussion of Liu's 1989 article titled "The Loss and Return of the Enlightenment Spirit of 'May Fourth' Literature"—a clear reading of the ideological implications of Liu's argument for "human literature." Kuang points out that "Liu thinks that after the May Fourth . . . , Chinese society advanced directly into the modern world and quickly transitioned to a socialist society. And yet, according to Liu, in the process [of moving] toward a community of free individuals, a middle period—a commercial economic period in which material exchanges are emphasized—went missing. As a result, China lacked

---

8. Liu Zaifu, "Lun wenxue de zhutixing" (1985), "Wenxue yanjiu yingyi ren wei siwei zhongxin" (1985), and "Xinge zuhe lun" (1986).

9. For a postmodern critique of Liu's theory, see Jing Wang's *High Culture Fever: Politics, Aesthetics, and Ideology in Deng's China* (Berkeley: University of California Press, 1996).

a social form that would make human independence possible."[10] While actual May Fourth literature (1915–1927) was in fact more than humanistic and exhibited a potent mixture of urban petit bourgeois and revolutionary political and aesthetic experimentation, the post–Cultural Revolution realignment with the May Fourth New Culture Movement, as demonstrated by the writings of Liu and many others, downplayed the political message of May Fourth literature and reduced its content into a humanistic enlightenment movement.[11] This had the effect of presenting the 1980s return to humanism as a return to the unfinished project of the enlightenment. Such a realignment had the clear (and, in Kuang's view, pernicious) goal of negating the socialist literature that had questioned some of the May Fourth literature's narrower range of subjective voices and concerns; that is, the 1980s reform literature wished to erase and negate the socialist literature that had followed the Yan'an spirit in making efforts to create culture for, of, and by the people (or the massification of literature). The post–Cultural Revolution new enlightenment movement, by evoking its supposedly depoliticized version of the May Fourth spirit, thus managed to overthrow the revolutionary spirit that was already contained in the May Fourth literary scene and that had developed during the period of socialist literature's ascendancy, thereby derevolutionizing cultural forms—including literature—and negating the historical legitimacy of people's literature. What Liu assumed would objectively result from nonsocialist modernization was "a corresponding strong material foundation (a social form in which commodity exchanges are free and competitive)."[12] Upon this material foundation, a humanistic literature could grow, according to Liu. Yet, as Kuang argues, "what is essential in all of this development is the quiet and sure arrival of the capitalist market economy beckoned by and along with this discourse."[13] In other words, humanistic literature, far from being nonideological, is itself premised upon the arrival and development of capitalism.

---

10. Kuang Xinnian, "People's Literature: An Unfinished Historical Project in *Debating the Socialist Legacy and Capitalist Globalization in China*, ed. Xueping Zhong and Ban Wang (New York: Palgrave Macmillan, 2014), 269.

11. This type of ideological reduction was taken up by such American scholars as Vera Schwarcz and popularized in US-based China studies. See, for example, Vera Schwarcz's *The Chinese Enlightenment: Intellectuals and the Legacy of the May Fourth Movement of 1919* (Berkeley: University of California Press, 1986).

12. Quoted in Kuang, "People's Literature," 269.

13. Ibid.

In today's China, capitalist development has taught lessons about capitalism, but not in the way that Liu assumed would be the case. One of the lessons is none other than the fact that the modernization and humanistic literature imagined by Liu and others in the 1980s has proven irrelevant in face of the capitalist commercial tidal waves, which in fact have marginalized literature as a cultural form except as hot commodities on the market. Within this context, humanistic literature has also proved itself unable to contend with the development of capitalist social relations and the subalternization of the working people. The rendering of the masses as no longer a revolutionary people and the replacement of them with the depoliticized figure of the human—a cornerstone of the liberal discourse of the 1980s and beyond—has made unsustainable the utopian notion of the human despite its discursive hegemony in the cultural sphere. The marginalization of literature in today's China demonstrates that it is no longer a cultural form that people love, especially when it is not clear who constitutes the people today, who speaks on their behalf, and if and how they can speak for themselves.

This is where we believe Cai's study is particularly significant. In his challenge to liberal discursive hegemony, Cai presents us with a layered reexamination of socialist cultural practices—including the tensions and crises within those practices—that aimed at transforming a society and its people. That is, when Cai revisits the notion of *renmin* (the revolutionary people), he insists both on the humanist nature of the notion and the fact that in the socialist period, the revolutionary struggle for equality was constantly in danger of being hijacked by the newly formed state bureaucracy and the hierarchical impulses within it. *People* (*renmin*), therefore, is and was a concept fraught with impermanence; yet within the socialist cultural imaginary, as Cai's study indicates, this concept—especially as it was linked to "the people as masters of society"—was about the possibility for the weak to resist and transform themselves so as to construct a new society. It was also about the emergence of the "socialist new person," who represented the possibility and the potential of building a society in which economic equality and social dignity were central to the imagination of the present and a better future.

In this sense, Cai's discussion of the notion of *people* and the tensions within the concept echoes Maurice Meisner's musing on the "Yan'an spirit":

> The "Yan'an spirit" was in fact largely concerned with spiritual and moral matters and, more specifically, with the kinds of social and ethical values and life orientations once seen as essential to a continuing process of rev-

olutionary transformation. The values which Maoists derived from the Yan'an era, and which are attributed to that heroic revolutionary past, are essentially ascetic and egalitarian. They are the values of selfless struggle and self-sacrifice on behalf of the people, the values of hard work, diligence, self-denial, frugality, altruism, and self-discipline. . . . In the Maoist view, such values were not only responsible for the revolutionary successes of the past but remained essential to bring about the socialist society of the future.[14]

Where Cai differs from Meisner is in Cai's recognition of and emphasis on the dialectics in the "Yan'an spirit" when it comes to a mobilized and liberated people. That is, the literary texts Cai studies prove Meisner's argument that the "Yan'an spirit" would be carried over as the basis for China's socialist construction and cultural imaginary, but Cai's discussion helps break the rigidity in Meisner's evaluation, which is premised on a top-down perspective. Cai's argument lends credence to the importance of the liberation of a people as a force for the revolution and then a major social force for the socialist transformation of the old society and construction of a new social order, a revolutionary legacy that may be longer-lasting than most liberal scholars of today have been willing or able to recognize. Central to the Yan'an spirit and what Cai in this book calls the "mobilization structure" it motivated, in other words, is the attempt at the simultaneous social-cultural—and narrative—transformation and formation of a people. Such a practice was premised on what Cai refers to as "politics of dignity," through which people acquired not only political consciousness but sociopolitical agency as well. That is, they became masters of society. Despite—in fact, probably because of—the idealistic and utopian tendencies in such affiliated cultural imaginaries and practices, the "mobilization structure" functioned as a liberating force for a people, especially those at the lower rungs of society, to join society as fully political and social beings.

At the same time, in his typical dialectical fashion, Cai also critically reflects on the crises that emerged in the socialist cultural imaginary and its practices, crises in part occasioned by the very imaginary and practices themselves. As his discussion throughout the book demonstrates, the construction of the "new socialist person" also produced its negation. This leads to our third area of contextualization.

---

14. Maurice J. Meisner, *Mao's China and After: A History of the People's Republic*, 3rd ed. (New York: Free Press, 1999), 49.

What Happens Culturally the Day after the Revolution?

Within the Chinese historical context, the day after the revolution was also the beginning of the construction of a socialist nation. What happened culturally, therefore, happened in tandem with what the scholar Lin Chun has called the "socialist transformation" of China. Cai's study of 1950s and 1960s Chinese literature against the backdrop and as a contemporaneous narrative construction of the multilevel political, socioeconomic, and sociocultural lifeworlds of China's transformation restores a good deal of complexity to the cultural spheres. As Cai shows, each level of transformation was closely related to the others, giving rise not only to possibilities but often also to tensions and crises. Recognizing the uniqueness and also the dialectical domestic and international historical filiations of the literature of China's socialism forces Cai to grapple not only with the legacy of the revolution itself, as a newly narrativized historical form, but also with the social and cultural aporia contained within this narrative process.

Politically, in his discussion of the "mobilization structure," the notion of the people is divided into three categories: the masses, the cadres, and the intellectuals. What Cai reveals in his discussion of these three categories are the representations of the new type of village-level leaders who are not cadres in a bureaucratic or a hierarchical sense, peasants in a traditional sense, or intellectuals in terms of an educated urban elite. These leaders thus embody the ideal of the "new socialist person" that the mobilization-remolding movement wished to create. By grafting certain traditional or extant cultural forms onto the new socialist literary practices, these new local-level leaders could become narrators of a new socialist history in the making. Yet these new leaders (and the cultural forms from which they emerged) always were tinged with nonsocialist aspects. The challenge was to transform them adequately so that they were still recognizable and yet also new. This challenge also constituted a crisis for the literary production of new leaders.

In Cai's reading, the portrayals of new cadres—those progressive individuals who are peasants, instead of intellectuals—who emerged with such mass mobilization movements as land reform and the cooperativization in the 1950s are suffused with a moral and ethical ideal deriving from earlier literary, cultural, and social types that now also embodied the literary ideal of the "socialist new person." This moral and ethical ideal person—most typically depicted as a local villager—was someone with a politically progressive and socially forward-looking attitude and a free spirit who was willing to challenge old thoughts and tradition, even while his (and, rarely, her) ethics and morality gave voice to village traditions. Thus, as Cai points out, many of the moral and ethical ideals were local in their origins, and it was the political context of the socialist mobilization and transformation that breathed new life and meaning into those local values. In other words, the local was generalized. Writers such as Zhao Shuli, Zhou Libo, and Liu Qing were some of the literary practitioners and theorists who demonstrated a deep understanding of both the political need to mobilize and the cultural complexities involved in the mobilization practices.

At the level of socioeconomics, recognizing the question of what happens the day after the revolution is in effect recognizing a concern with specific visions, policies, and organizations of economic, social, and cultural life. In this regard, Cai focuses his discussion on well-known literary works that deal with land reform and the cooperativization movement or with industrial development in urban centers from the early 1950s through the mid-1960s. These works are socialist in that they represent peasants and workers as major protagonists. But Cai pushes the discussion further by uncovering the extent to which socialism on the economic level was filled with tension and the mobilization of people at times suffered from setbacks and pushbacks due to a range of factors internal to the transformations themselves. Still, Cai's analysis indicates that the socialist transformation and its associated literary forms could not have been possible without efforts to establish socialist economic relations. Without the latter, the former would have been entirely groundless, as was shown in the post–Cultural Revolution retreat from the Maoist socialist economic structure and practices and the defeat of such literary practices. Cai's discussions of the narration of labor and the working class as the new national subject and the long-neglected subject of history reveal at the same time a sophisticated modern socialist imaginary (based on structural changes in economic organizations, policies, and practices) and its powerful social-cultural literary instantiation. The constant difficulties posed by forces that resisted socialist transformation are likewise given their due.

These latter tensions are where Cai's study finds both the lifeworld possibilities and the everyday difficulties encountered in the course of socialist transformation. That is, as Cai demonstrates, the very point of transformation was quotidian: it was not merely abstract or beyond the arena of everyday life. As soon as large-scale policies and revolutionary mobilizations were brought to the narrative level of everyday life, problems and potentials emerged. As Cai foregrounds, the specific genre of strange tales of revolutionary heroes demonstrates the extent to which socialist literature relied on a mythification of revolutionary heroes, a mythification that was derived from certain earlier oral storytelling forms. In this genre, such lifeworld issues as love, sexuality, and desire were treated in a "transcendental" fashion to promote the revolutionary spirit in the context of the day after the revolution. But Cai also examines the contradictions emerging from within the impulse to continuous revolution, contradictions that produced their own desires and forces opposed to socialist transformation. In close readings of classical texts of contemporary literature—which is what Cai calls modern socialist literature—such as novels, short stories, plays, and films, Cai reveals what he refers to as the deterritorializing desires manifested in the representations of negative characters. He argues for the need to better understand such countercultural tendencies within the socialist context, and he does so based on his desire to search for ways that socialist literature attempted to overcome crises in socialism at the quotidian, cultural, social, and economic levels. This attempt, as he shows, was not successful, yet it is notable for its aesthetic, historical, and cultural innovativeness and vitality.

Concluding Remarks

We would like to end with an elaboration on this last point. As Cai makes clear, anyone who studies Chinese socialism and its culture must directly address antisocialist ideological challenges on the one hand, and examine the shortcomings, mistakes, and disasters in socialist China on the other hand. Citing in his introduction the early literary scholar Chen Yinque's notion of "understanding-based sympathy," Cai argues that "'understanding-based sympathy' is premised on the establishment of a particular kind of attitude toward history.... This attitude is both scholarly and political, for—at least with regard to contemporary Chinese history—there is no transcendent or pure scholarship. A historical attitude here must direct its attention to the problematics (*mingti*) of the 'resistance of the weak,' an issue that is both historically specific and theoretically challenging."

Cai does not evoke the "resistance of the weak" merely in a nationalist sense. "The weak" here refers primarily to the laboring people—the proletariat (including the peasantry)—who suffered the consequences of China's weakness at the hands of foreign imperialist aggressions and encroachment. Here, Cai echoes Lin Chun's point about the distinctiveness of the Chinese revolutionary formation, in which intellectuals as a social class were consitutively organic to the working class. As Lin observes, "after all, the rise of the social was not brought about by a burgeoning bourgeoisie, as in Europe, but rather by a peasant revolution led by communist intellectuals."[15] And, as Cai argues:

> Modernizing was the major goal of the revolution, to be carried out in political, economic, and cultural terms. Indeed, in contemporary [that is, socialist] Chinese literature, traces of modernity existed in the social form shaped by heavy industry in the modern organizational model of the nation-state, as well as in cultural expressions of radical pursuits for personal and individual freedom. Even at moments of radical debate on the form of literature, there continued to exist in-depth depictions of individual characters' inner thoughts or feelings. That was the case regardless of whether, in contemporary Chinese literature, such depictions took the form of a "socialist new person" or a "typical character in a typical environment."

In other words, the socialist cultural imaginary—informed by revolution and modernity—should be understood as both profoundly modern and uniquely Chinese due to its historical conditions. This basic understanding is the foundation for Cai's critical and dialectical exploration of literary works produced during the Mao era.

Central to Cai's study, then, is a consideration of how Chinese socialism was constructed culturally—that is, through narrative—in the context of what he calls the "after-the-revolution" (*geming hou*),[16] and how this cultural production struggled to sustain itself in the face of a range of international and domestic challenges. Cai notes that he "interpret[s] Chinese socialism as a historical process filled both with tensions of self-negation and impulses for continuous revolution." And the corresponding literary narratives address a wide range of questions central to China's revolutionary modernity. Those questions include why mobilization was key to after-the-revolution cultural reconstruction; how to understand the forms and structure of the mobilization; why certain traditional forms were retained and enlisted in modern so-

15. Lin Chun, *The Transformation of Chinese Socialism* (Durham, NC: Duke University Press 2006), 219. For Lin's further discussion on the issue of class in China, see her "The Language of Class in China," in *Transforming Classes: Socialist Register 2015*, ed. Leo Panitch and Gregory Albo (London: Merlin, 2014), 24–53.

16. We should point out that *after-the-revolution* is counterposed to and used along with *postrevolution*. *Postrevolution* treats the revolution as an event that ended in 1949; *after-the-revolution* makes clear that the work of the revolution begins after the seizure of state power in 1949. See Cai's introduction for more discussion on his usage.

cialist literature; how all of this helps explain the social-cultural characteristics of the Chinese revolution; what crises the practices of socialist culture generated; and how to understand the efforts, and their failure, to overcome the crises.

Thus Cai identifies the relationship between the multiplicity of narratives and revolution and the concept of revolution as multiple possible narratives, while exploring the tensions this relationship manifests and represents. The dual aspects of the people as both the agent and object of change inevitably informed and shaped various narrative forms—short stories, novels, plays, films—and the ways in which they were narrated. If the struggles for the success of the revolution were transformative, so were the establishment and construction of socialism, which was the goal of the revolution. But the transformations would prove even more challenging and difficult than the revolution itself. Cai's clear-eyed examinations of the various tensions manifested in modern socialist literature present us with a study based on a principled stance in favor of taking socialist revolution seriously and a willingness to critically explore the key question of what happens the day after the revolution.

Cai ends with the ways in which the Cultural Revolution both created a liberatory potential but also resubordinated everyone to other kinds of demands. In his summer 2013 interview with us, he said:

> The socialist period was about desires: how, in a relatively closed environment, to create desires that were both "healthy" and political? This closed environment made for a hothouse situation: once everything was opened up, there was no resistance to anything. Socialism before 1949 was about the creation of desires; after 1949, desire was gradually erased from the equation: this became a real problem. How to beckon to the young, [how to present] the everyday life aspects of desire and happiness as an embodied issue? This is where the Cultural Revolution felt like a liberation from the obedience and the lack of desire inherent in socialism.

However, the violence of the Cultural Revolution ultimately betrayed its utopian premises, and the scars that resulted led intellectuals in the 1980s to a full-scale reevaluation of socialism and, by the 1990s, to a wholesale repudiation of it. Today, by taking seriously and studying the modern socialist literature of the first seventeen years, a vital component part of what he calls contemporary literature, we can hope—as Cai mentioned to us—to be seen as advocating not a restoration of the past, but rather an understanding of its promises and legacies for our times. That is, as Cai said to us, "socialism requires narrative because it is creative; it is trying to re-create people's desires and aspirations; it is trying to transform existing relations and re-create a new narrative." Capitalism, too, has its narratives. In order to critique capitalism, one needs the creativity of socialism. The point of discussing socialism is, as Cai maintained, "not because one wants to return to that era, but to deal seriously with the possibilities and impossibilities of it" so as to deal with the possibilities and impossibilities of our current moment.

INTRODUCTION
Literature and Revolutionary China

I

In my opinion, the deep division within contemporary Chinese thought or theory does not mainly reside in how to understand and criticize existing social problems. Rather, major divisions exist more in the field of history. These divisions are not so much due to entanglements about the facts of any particular case, as historical materials can always be made to speak to different theories, and individual cases can also be exaggerated by anyone who wishes to present him or herself as an interpreter of history. Indeed, anyone can list a series of individual cases to pass judgment on history. Ideas, class-specific memories, positions, and even an individual's physical senses, hidden behind dazzling academic jargon and amid the sound and fury of self-delusional depoliticization, in actuality all manifest a strong political quest, regardless of whether or not one is willing to admit to it. Max Weber states that "you serve this god and you offend the other god when you decide to adhere to this position."[1]

---

1. Max Weber, "Part I Science and Politics," *From Max Weber: Essays in Sociology*, trans., ed., with an introduction by H. H. Gerth and C. Wright Mills (New York: Oxford University Press, 1958), 77–156.

In this sense, as I have suggested elsewhere, the sixty-year history of contemporary Chinese literature has in essence become a battlefield.

In his review of the first volume of Feng Youlan's *History of Chinese Philosophy*, Chen Yinque states that "for those who write about the history of Chinese philosophy, when it comes to the ideas of the ancients, they must not begin to write until they acquire a sympathy based on understanding. . . . They must learn to think and imagine so as to reach the same state of mind as the ancients, and, even if they do not share the same views, they must express a willingness to understand."² In recent years, many scholars in China have accepted Chen's "understanding-based sympathy," which has also become a scholarly approach in the study of the history of contemporary Chinese literature.

But what does such a sympathy mean? What is to be understood? And how to sympathize? According to Chen, sympathy is a kind of attitude. In this sense, then, "understanding-based sympathy" is premised on the establishment of a particular kind of attitude toward history. In my view, this attitude is both scholarly and political, for—at least with regard to contemporary [since 1949] Chinese history—there is no transcendent or pure scholarship. A historical attitude here must direct its attention to the problematics (*mingti*) of the "resistance of the weak," an issue that is both historically specific and theoretically challenging.

Throughout the twentieth century, this issue of resistance of the weak was Marxified—or, more specifically, Leninized —in China as well as in other parts of the world. According to [Alain] Badiou's succinct summary of the *Communist Manifesto*, communism

> means, first, that the logic of class—the fundamental subordination of labour to a dominant class, the arrangement that has persisted since Antiquity—is not inevitable; it can be overcome. The communist hypothesis is that a different collective organization is practicable, one that will eliminate the inequality of wealth and even the division of labour. The private appropriation of massive fortunes and their transmission by inheritance will disappear. The existence of a coercive state, separate from civil society,

---

2. Chen Yinque, "Feng Youlan zhexueshi shangce shencha baogao" [Review report on Feng Youlan's *History of Chinese Philosophy*, volume 1], in *Chen Yinque ji: jinmingguan conggao erbian* [Collected writings of Chen Yinque: Second publication of the jinmingguan collection] (Beijing: Sanlian Shudian, 2001), 279.

will no longer appear a necessity: a long process of reorganization based on a free association of producers will see it withering away.³

Supporters and detractors of this resistance of the weak debate among themselves not only the legitimacy of the Chinese revolution, but also issues of justice in the future. Different political positions tend to condition different historical attitudes, including different scholarly views. When positions and historical attitudes are completely opposite to one another, I have a hard time seeing the possibility of compromise and communication between different schools. Debates tend to result in friends becoming strangers and going their separate ways.

Once we have established our own historical attitude through which we emphasize the legitimacy of the Chinese revolution, we also recognize that this legitimacy was grounded in the [social foundation of the] resistance of the weak and in the demands of labor—that is, the laborers—to be liberated from a state of alienation. With this attitude, I do not believe I have any reason to interpret modern rebellion as any sort of illegitimate political pursuit.

At the same time, with this attitude there could be a scholarly or conceptual danger of interpreting our history as a garden of Eden, one that was serene and wonderful. Such an interpretation can evoke an original sin implication that not only might delegitimize the various kinds of exploratory ideas and resistances that existed in the socialist period, but also might dampen any courage and drive to imagine and create a new future. In fact, I agree more with Chen's further explanation of what he meant by sympathy based understanding: that "it is very easy for this kind of attitude of sympathy to fall into the bad habit of providing far-fetched interpretation" due to the fact that "the ancient materials either no longer exist in full or are too difficult to decipher; and, without a process of careful reading and comparison, there is no history of philosophy to speak of."⁴ In other words, when we use our own contemporary theories, knowledge, and attitude to reconstruct history, we are prone to making mistakes in which "the more systematized [our] theory is, the further we are from a relation to the essence of ancient thoughts and ideas."⁵

3. Alain Badiou, "The Communist Hypothesis," *New Left Review* 49, January–February 2008, 34–35.
4. Chen Yinque, "Feng Youlan zhongguo zhexueshi shangce shencha baogao" [Review report of Feng Youlan's *History of Chinese Philosophy*, volume 1] (Shanghai: Shanghai Guji Chubanshe, 1980), 247.
5. Ibid.

According to this logic, we ought not to remain only at the level of stressing the legitimacy of the Chinese revolution. On the contrary, besides the powerful empirical facts that the legitimacy of the revolution generated, I am more concerned with the irrationality to which this legitimacy also gave rise. What this means is that we should not take the simple route of being confined by our position and attitude; instead, we must return to the complexities of historical trajectories. Such complexities, additionally, are not a simple totality of specific cases and historical detail—too often we have seen certain specific cases and details being singled out and magnified from a particular narrative point of view, when in fact the self-proclaimed universal narratives embedded are quite ideological. Rather, the complexities here refer to structural issues and trajectories, as well as to the range of entangled logics within.

Badiou, in a resolute rhetorical style, expounds on the fate and work of the Left in the West:

> In many respects we are closer today to the questions of the 19th century than to the revolutionary history of the 20th. A wide variety of 19th-century phenomena are reappearing: vast zones of poverty, widening inequalities, politics dissolved into the "service of wealth," the nihilism of large sections of the young, the servility of much of the intelligentsia; the cramped, besieged experimentalism of a few groups seeking ways to express the communist hypothesis.... Which is no doubt why, as in the 19th century, it is not the victory of the hypothesis which is at stake today, but the conditions of its existence. This is our task, during the reactionary interlude that now prevails: through the combination of thought processes—always global, or universal, in character—and political experience, always local or singular, yet transmissible, to renew the existence of the communist hypothesis, in our consciousness and on the ground.[6]

On the whole, I tend to agree with Badiou. But the question is: how do we return to the nineteenth century? I believe there is no other way except by taking the legacies of the twentieth century with us—legacies that include the good and the bad and lessons from many failures—to probe and reexamine, so that we can better prepare for the arrival of another new century. Perhaps the new century is a long way away from us. Yet, as Zygmunt Bauman states, "by itself, knowledge does not determine which of the two uses we resort to. This is, ultimately, a matter of our own choice. But without that knowledge

---

6. Badiou, "The Communist Hypothesis," 41–42.

there would be no choice to start with. With knowledge, free men and women have at least some chance to exercise their freedom."⁷

Of course I do know that, within the context of contemporary Chinese literature, such a reexamination could be perceived as sounding lofty.

II

In this study, *revolutionary China* is largely a metaphorical term used mainly to draw a necessary line between it and traditional China or modern China. Many times and in many places distinctions among the three are not always clear. By *traditional China*, I refer to the ancient empire and the various cultural imaginaries and forms that existed within it. *Modern China* mainly denotes the period after China was forced into modernization in the late Qing Dynasty [1850s–1911] and the consequent Chinese pursuit, emulation, and imagination of Western classical modernity, which may be more simply identified as bourgeois modernity. Both traditional China and modern China, of course, are themselves figures of speech. *Revolutionary China*, needless to say, denotes the theoretical exploration, social revolution, and cultural practices of the twentieth century under the leadership of the Chinese Communist Party. In relation to this point, it is necessary to mention *Reinterpretation* (*Zai jiedu*), a book edited by Tang Xiaobing that was first published in Hong Kong in the mid-1990s and that, after publication, found various ways of reaching the mainland.⁸ The importance of this book exists not only in its generating a revolution (of sorts) in the methodological approach to the study of contemporary Chinese literature, but also in its Chinese interpretation of modernity that helped liberate the notion of the contemporary (*dangdai*) from the relational confines of the notion of the feudal (*fengjian*), a conceptual framework that had been established in the 1980s. Tang's book helped significantly broaden the scope of discussion. At the same time, however, too broad a discussion of modernity is likely to erase the difference between revolution and modernity, including how we explain the difference between capitalism and socialism.

I do not mean to suggest there are not explicit or implicit historical connections between revolution and modernity. On the contrary, in just about

---

7. Zygmunt Bauman, *In Search of Politics* (Stanford, CA: Stanford University Press, 1999), 2.
8. Tang Xiaobing, *Zai jiedu* [Reinterpretation] (Hong Kong: Oxford University Press, 1993). Tr.: In this volume, Cai Xiang cites from the second edition of the book which was published by Peking University Press in 2007.

every aspect, the Chinese revolution can be seen as the radical inheritor of the May Fourth New Culture Movement. Or we can say that revolutionary China is the child of modernity. As for identifying the Chinese revolution as a peasant revolution, that is no more than an empirical observation based on the fact that most of the participants in the revolution were peasants. Such an identification ignores the political modernity of the Party—the core of which was a collective of modern intellectuals—that led the revolution. The revolution's modern nature resides not only in the fact that the Party was an internationally active political organization, but also in the fact that modernizing was the major goal of the revolution, to be carried out in political, economic, and cultural terms. Indeed, in contemporary Chinese literature, traces of modernity existed in the social form shaped by heavy industry in the modern organizational model of the nation-state, as well as in the cultural expressions of radical pursuits for personal and individual freedom. Even at moments of radical debate on the form of literature, there continued to exist in-depth depictions of individual characters' inner thoughts or feelings. That was the case regardless of whether, in contemporary Chinese literature, such depictions took the form of a "new socialist person" or a "typical character in a typical environment" (*dianxing huanjing xia de dianxing renwu*).

In fact, such modern traces exist across the board in the narratives of revolutionary China. We can recall Liang Qichao's [1902] criticism of the "old historiography," in which history "was always written for the court and ministers but never for ordinary people" and which "was only cognizant of individuals but not [social] groups," "only good at describing but not prescribing," and "only about facts and not about ideals."[9] If we then recall a famous statement by Mao Zedong regarding his view of history, we realize that the latter did not come from nowhere: "History is created by people. But on the stage of old operas (and in all the old literature and art that had little concern about ordinary people), people were portrayed as dregs while their masters dominated the stage. Now you have reversed what had been turned upside down, returning history to its actual look. I congratulate you on turning a new page on the old opera."[10]

---

9. Liang Qichao, "Xin shixue" [New historiography], in *Qingdai xueshu gailun* [An overview of Qing Dynasty scholarship], ed. Xia Xiaohong (Beijing: Renmin Daxue Chubanshe, 2004), 232–34.

10. Mao Zedong, "Gei Yang Shaoxuan, Qi Yanming de xin" [Letter to Yang Shaoxuan and Qi Yanming], in *Mao Zedong wenji* [Collected Writings of Mao Zedong] (Beijing: Renmin chubanshe, 1996), 3:88.

It goes without saying that it is this kind of modern [impulse] that led to the strong antitraditional characteristics of revolutionary China. However, we must not equate the modernity pursued by revolutionary China with bourgeois modernity. First, we ought not to understand the Chinese revolution as purely a nationalist revolution (despite its strong national color). On the contrary, this revolution always had a strong internationalist tendency. Both during its early association with the Communist International and later, in the formation of the theory and practice of the Third World, there were clear indications of the international backdrop of revolutionary China. Second, such internationalism is proletarian in nature, which in turn conditioned the difference in value orientation between revolutionary China and modern China, with the former refusing to join the world capitalist system. The difference is primarily manifested in revolutionary China's attempts at transforming itself from a nation-state to a class-state, where the subalterns became the masters of the state with a newly promoted politics of dignity; where, among other things, the bureaucracy was constantly challenged and resisted; and where a new principle of relatively equal distribution was established. All of this revealed revolutionary China's "antimodern" characteristics that, according to Wang Hui, can be identified as a kind of "antimodern modernity."[11] Of course, there may be other identifications such as "alternative modernity" or "revolutionary modernity." At issue, however, is not what label to attach but in-depth analysis and discussion.

It is important to note that revolutionary China's challenge and resistance to modernity simultaneously carried with it a strong local color. I do not want, however, to place the discussion of the local quality within the framework of nationalism. I emphasize its localism to stress the fact that "any political experience is always local and unique."[12] But we must not assume that no universality can stem from local political experiences. This in fact explains why revolutionary China would later participate in the struggle for worldwide universality, even if the struggle was mainly confined to Marxist terms. This struggle does not have to do only with the legitimacy of one locale's political experience. Rather, it has everything to do with how to construct a vision for

---

11. Wang Hui, "Dangdai zhongguo de sixiang zhuangkuang yu xiandaixing wenti" [Contemporary Chinese thought and the question of modernity], *Tianya* (Frontiers) 5 (1997). Tr.: For English translation, see "Contemporary Chinese Thought and the Question of Modernity," trans. Rebecca Karl, *China's New Order*, ed. Theodore Huters (Cambridge: Harvard University Press, 2003), 139–87.

12. Badiou, "The Communist Hypothesis," 42.

the world that is both universal and diverse. It is in this sense that I believe that revolutionary China is one of the most important [conceptual and historical] legacies of the twentieth century.

Precisely due to this particular local political experience, which is also a particular local literary experience, there also exists a complex relationship between revolutionary China and traditional China. Similar to the entanglement between revolutionary and modern China in the literary sphere, in the political sphere the relationship between revolutionary and traditional China is often imbued with paradoxes. On the one hand, the Chinese revolution completely turned the traditional hierarchical order upside down; this included destroying the rural clan system. Such destruction demonstrates the modern characteristics of revolutionary China. On the other hand, revolutionary China also enlisted different aspects of traditional cultural resources and successfully transformed them into locally specific modern forms. Such a transformation is multilayered. For example, while the rural clan system was destroyed by the revolution, yet because contemporary China retained the natural village as an organizational unit across the rural regions, [post-1949] society was able to effectively use the governing model of the traditional clan. In literature, therefore, we find narratives about someone who leads or is the head of the house, such as Liang Baosheng in *The Builders*. These narratives are indications that traditional ethical politics may well have continued to exist even as they were being transformed in and by China's contemporary society.

As a matter of fact, the Chinese revolution offered creative and successful experiences and models for dealing with the complex relationship between modernity and tradition. How to understand all of this remains an important area for further study, including the question of how to study the politics of resistance in the socialist period. Obviously it is not difficult to focus on ostensibly dissident views, such as the relationship between [Aleksandr] Solzhenitsyn's Gulag system and Soviet communism. Rather, the difficulty lies in how to understand the fact that Chinese socialism retained within its own system a politics of resistance that provided it with a degree of legitimacy. Mass movements (including the "four bigs")[13] not only became a form of resistance from within the system, but they also contributed to the formation of the structure of feeling of socialist society in which antibureaucratism was

---

13. Tr.: The "four bigs" refer to "*daming, dafang, dazibao, dabianlun*," loosely translated as speaking out freely, airing views fully, holding great debates, and writing big-characters posters.

naturally legitimate, a legitimacy that allowed constant antisystemic movements to occur. I do not attribute such resistance to influence either from the West or from Chinese tradition, because such attributions tend to turn resistance into a natural part of elite intellectual history or the birthright domain of the Chinese peasants themselves, thereby channeling antisystemic resistance into the ideological framework of a capitalist—liberal capitalist, for example—interpretation. On the contrary, the antisystemic movements originated more from the support of the system itself (including the support of Mao Zedong), in the attempt, based on communist ideals and visions, to combat or resist certain concrete practices in socialism. I believe this constitutes the essence and complexity of the politics of resistance in the socialist period. What became a problem had to do with the fact that in the socialist period, the boundaries of the politics of resistance were difficult to delimit. On the one hand, the system hoped to use the politics of resistance to overcome systemic problems of its own. On the other hand, whenever such politics transgressed certain limits, the suppression of mass movements followed—the Anti-Rightist Campaign [1957] and the Cultural Revolution being two prominent examples. At the same time, however, such politics of resistance (mass movements) were considered legitimate within the system (supported by its ideology). Such legitimacy would allow this politics of resistance to move beyond the memories of a past suppression, to call on and attract new participants for inclusion.

That is to say, we must recognize that, even in the socialist period, this politics of resistance still presented a significant danger. Only with this dialectical understanding can we explain why, during the socialist period, there always existed antisystemic movements—regardless of their forms—and can we understand how they helped constitute a vital social force in that society. Even today they remain, in the form of a tradition that continues to influence us. At the same time, I have refused to describe modern Chinese history simply as a history of ideas of elite intellectuals. I prefer to treat modern Chinese history as a spatial domain, where different forces contend with one another for ideas and interests and where contingent political opportunities occur.

Meanwhile, we must also recognize that this particular local political and cultural experience has always existed within the conflict between certain universal ideas. This local experience, moreover, can, from time to time, be suppressed by such universality. For example, the process of the Chinese revolution created a political situation that was heterogeneous in nature, be it in the governing of the minority regions or the creation of rural and urban differences. Meanwhile, this state of heterogeneity inevitably faced two challenges, one in the domain of governance and one in terms of ideology. When it comes to the form of governing, the heterogeneity was challenged by the centralized state power in its modernization pursuits. Socialist ideology, by the same token, was universal and required a tendency toward homogeneity as opposed to heterogeneity. As a result, conflicts between homogeneity and heterogeneity ensued. Recognition of the local political experience created during and by revolutionary China must therefore be juxtaposed to recognition of the local conflict with universality. In this sense, we could say that the so-called new and creative form (including newly created system) of the first thirty years of the People's Republic of China (including the Cultural Revolution period) was in fact not new enough.

However, some newer ideas and concepts may have been articulated in literature. For this reason, therefore, when it comes to the study of the literature of this period, I would caution against a ready application of the notion of system unification (*yitihua*), a concept originally put forward by the scholar Hong Zicheng.[14] A literal interpretation of the concept could lead to treating the literature of the first thirty years as if it were an absolute and homogeneous system. To be sure, to go against that grain entails greater difficulties, for the object of the present study is not clearly defined: it can be described as part of the system, albeit mixed with antisystemic elements; or it can be identified as the antisystemic nature inherent in the system itself or as a system that is inherently antisystemic. Nevertheless, precisely because of such a lack of clarity, the present study provides the possibility for close textual reading of contemporary Chinese literature. It also challenges us to come up with a new methodological approach.

III

When discussing the legitimacy of revolutionary China, one inevitably encounters challenges and questions. Issues such as violence cannot be fully addressed by relying on a certain historical attitude only. Needless to say, like many other revolutions, including bourgeois revolutions, the Chinese revolution was accompanied with blood and violence. Few people, I believe, would praise violence just for its own sake. The real issue lies in how to examine

---

14. See Hong Zicheng, *Zhongguo dangdai wenxueshi* [History of contemporary Chinese literature] (Beijing: Beijing Daxue Dhubanshe, 1998).

revolutionary violence. One view stipulates that revolution is often forced and is therefore by nature violent. This description, however, does not offer an in-depth explanation of what constitutes revolutionary violence. While there exist a slew of studies on violence by the state or by the masses, when it comes to the specific violent forms of the Chinese revolution, few profound or historically sound studies exist. The factors that prevent in-depth study from occurring are very complex; some of those factors include criticisms based on memories informed by a particular class position, but more criticisms tend to be opportunistically motivated. For such critics, there is a ready resort to humanism whenever they wish to critique the violence of resisters. But when facing violence by the oppressors, they pretend neither to see nor to hear it, and their humanism is nowhere to be found. Of course one does not have to take such opportunistic criticism too seriously, but it is nevertheless the most difficult kind to deal with, for whenever we are prepared to seriously address it, it tends to quickly disappear into another system of logic.

Still, this does not mean that violence is not an important issue to address and debate. Quite the contrary. To a certain extent, violence is already not about violence itself, but a domain for debate. By entering this domain, not only can we delve more deeply into specific historical contexts, but we can also better grasp the structure of ideas in our own times. For example, among all criticisms of violence, land reform may figure as one of the most important [revolutionary] symbols. But many of the criticisms of land reform are mixed up with a positive imaginary of the traditional gentry-class structure and a tendency to resort to a moralistic discourse. Many such critics fail to realize that this rural social structure had already declined and disintegrated over a long period of time in history. After the mid-nineteenth century, the rise of the modern nation-state further demanded the establishment of a different social structure—the process of destruction of the old structure in early Chinese modern history had also given rise to landlords turning into local tyrants. The Chinese revolution was mainly to further carry out the historical trajectory and put it into practice. The scholar Du Runsheng summarizes the significance of the land reform in two points: (1) for the construction of a modern nation-state system, and (2) for the peasants to acquire their own class consciousness.[15] It goes without saying that such important historical events should not be interpreted only in moral terms. At the same time, I do not

---

15. Du Runsheng, *Du Runsheng zishu: Zhongguo nongcun tizhi biange zhongda juece jishi* [Du Runsheng remembers: Memories of the important decisions on China's village structural transformation] (Beijing: Renmin Chubanshe, 2005), 18–20.

agree with the violence that occurred after 1949, especially certain discriminatory violence that emerged from the simple fact that by then the proletariat had become power holders. So it should be clear that my understanding-based sympathy largely sides with the resistance of the weak. Only when we critically reflect on discriminatory violence can we better understand the significance of Yu Luoke's *On Family Origin* (*Chushen lun*) [which critiqued such a discriminatory basis for violence].[16] Meanwhile, however, I would still argue that even when it comes to discriminatory violence, our understanding should not remain at the level of morality alone. There are quite a few other factors to consider, including the international and geopolitical during the first thirty years after 1949.

So far as my study is concerned, I pay particular attention to criticisms from within China's own scholarly communities. One of those critiques stipulates that we return to modern Chinese history to find the origins of various strands of thought. From the very beginning of this history, there were already, albeit fragmented, thoughts and ideas akin to socialism.[17] The significance of these early ideas lies in the need for us to expand the resources for developing our own ideas by enlisting certain existing schools of thought in our thinking today. The truth of the matter is that the Chinese theory of socialism we discuss today tends to be too unilateral, oriented too much around Mao Zedong's words and ideas. Other communist theorists such as Zhang Wentian and Xie Juezai rarely enter our theoretical horizon. For this reason, I agree with the argument that we need to open our minds and expand our theoretical horizon further. At the same time, I do not take this argument as the politically correct point of departure in my study, because I do not subscribe to the same logic as those who foreground this view and argue that the problem with revolutionary history is that it veered off course from those early theorists' views. I prefer to examine theory within a specific historical context—which, in this case, is the context of the Chinese revolution, including all the historical experiences that created revolutionary China. I believe

---

16. Yu Luoke, "Chushen lun" [On family origins], *Wenhuadageming he ta de yiduan sichao* [The Great Cultural Revolution and its hereditary thought], ed. Song Yongyi (Hong Kong: Tianyuan Shuwu, 1997).

17. Tr.: See Arif Dirlik, *Origins of Chinese Communism* (New York: Oxford University Press, 1989) and *Anarchism in the Chinese Revolution* (Berkeley: University of California Press, 1992) for indications of early strands of radical socialistic thinking. Also see Lydia H. Liu, Rebecca E. Karl, and Dorothy Ko, eds., *The Birth of Chinese Feminism* (New York: Columbia University Press, 2013), general and historical introductions, for summaries of early radicalism and feminism.

it is only when we enter these experiences directly that we can actually enter contemporary Chinese history to learn from both its experiences and lessons. Only when we are clear about this particular twentieth-century legacy can we actually face the future, while knowing what socialist visions from modern history can be effectively enlisted for us today.

IV

As a matter of fact, the focus of my study is not entirely on revolutionary but rather also on postrevolutionary China. *Revolution* here refers to a specific historical practice in China, which we can define, in a form of shorthand, as a social-political practice that takes the form of a large-scale military resistance with the goal of capturing state power. Relative to this revolution, after 1949, China essentially entered a postrevolutionary period, which is of course a metaphorical reference. What I mean by *postrevolution*, then, differs from what Daniel Bell in *The Cultural Contradictions of Capitalism* refers to as "the day after the revolution."[18] I acknowledge the obvious symptoms of "the day after" that Bell identifies, but in China, there were numerous entanglements that on a fundamental level had much to do with Lenin's theory of "achieving socialism in one country."

The real issue may well lie in how to deal with one country's becoming socialist. On the one hand, the nation-state as a modern governing form, along with the strengthening of the state apparatuses and management, took center stage in the international geopolitical system. On the other hand, as one country in such a modern world, how can it exist as a pure socialist country as it carries out its own modernization construction (*xiandaihua jianshe*)? These domestic and global questions—including all their mutual contradictions, conflicts, and various resultant tensions—constituted the complexities of the postrevolutionary in China.

If revolutionary ideals—including the concrete political practice leading to the realization of socialism in one country—were the original motivation of the revolution, then postrevolutionary socialist China responded to this central problematic in its own creative way. In the present study, aside from treating socialism as a universal political idea, I also intend to explore socialism in practice by specifically focusing on the following three aspects.

---

18. Daniel Bell, *The Cultural Contradictions of Capitalism* (New York: Basic, 1976).

First, I interpret Chinese socialism as a historical process filled with both tensions of self-negation and impulses for continuous revolution. These tensions and impulses may have been given rise to by the characteristics of the specific historical period of the Chinese revolution—that is, the new democratic period (1940s and 1950s). But they may have even more to do with the anxiety generated by the tension between revolutionary ideals and the characteristics of the new democratic historical period. Let us take the notion and practice of the "united front" (*tongyi zhanxian*) for example. On a metaphorical level, the united front corresponds to [Antonio] Gramsci's notion of compromise, which in theory conditions the model of practice (including the form of governing by the state) for a socialism founded in a specific global and domestic historical moment. On a deeper level, however, I interpret this historical process as one in constant response to revolutionary ideals (the communist imaginary). To be sure, no political practice can be carried out without veering off the course of the framework of theory; there are always other factors at play (including various historical contingencies). What often results is a tension between grand and long-term ideals and specific local political experiences. The desire to overcome or negate the status quo, therefore, constituted an impulse for continuous revolution within [Chinese] socialism. Throughout this historical process of self-negation, there persisted a radical spirit of experimentation and endeavors to create a concrete new system, but all of this also disrupted and affected people's everyday life, a factor that led to the retrenchment that happened in the 1980s.

For critics, however, how to reenter this historical process for a fuller understanding remains one of the most important tasks. History cannot be hypothesized. Still, we can ask a hypothetical question: if there had not been such a self-negating history, what would China have become? For example, if there had not been the collectivization movement, what issues would rural China have faced? In the 1960s, the novelist Zhao Shuli made strong but sincere criticisms of the commune movement. But his criticisms were always premised on one key point—namely, that collectivization "stopped the rural reclassification that had started to occur after the land reform."[19] We might not have been able to fully comprehend what Zhao meant by this point thirty

---

19. Zhao Shuli, "Xie gei zhongyang fuze tongzhi de liang feng xin" [Two letters to comrades in the central government], in *Zhao Shuli quanji* [Complete collection of Zhao Shuli's writings] (Taiyuan: Beiyue Wenyi Chubanshe, 1994), 5:323.

years ago, but today we can. To be sure, as a revolutionary ideal, Chinese socialism could not just stay at the level of [ensuring] equality at the starting line; it also had to consider equality in the process and in outcome. So it had to be vigilant about the problems that occur in the process. The conceptual tensions revealed in Zhao's criticism are in fact highly valuable. Just this point alone, in my view, offers a concrete example of the importance of conceptual legacies of twentieth-century China.

Second, as mentioned above, I treat socialist (postrevolutionary) China in spatial terms, as a topological domain. This domain contains two levels of meaning. On the first level, socialist China was an international space in which China was located within the structure of global geopolitics. As Immanuel Wallerstein states, "geopolitics is about the structural constraints that govern, over a medium run, the interplay of the longer-term political and economic interests of the major players in the world-system. . . . An analysis of geopolitics is therefore an analysis of middle-run structures and trends. At any given moment, it is about a future that is uncertain."[20] If we remember the Cold War geopolitics between 1949 and 1966, we can understand what is meant by these structurally constraining factors. It is precisely the existence of these factors that partially conditioned the policy readjustments in socialist China. These readjustments exerted their influence not only in politics and economics but also in culture. For example, the accusations of peaceful evolution drummed up in the 1960s [by Mao and his supporters against Liu Shaoqi and other "capitalist roaders"] gave rise to anxiety inside China over issues of everyday life. Hence, at the same time as we consider any radical political experimentation inside China, we must also consider the presence and role of the international structurally constraining factors. Those factors constructed China as a socialist other in [Cold War] geopolitics.

On the second topological level, socialist China was at the same time a national space, constituted by the presence of different classes and groups and the struggles among them. Some classes were destroyed while many more continued to exist, including the bourgeois business class. The fact that these classes were able to "peacefully" enter the socialist stage seems to be one of the major characteristics of Chinese socialism. But the class memories of the extinguished classes and especially of the remaining ones did not readily dis-

---

20. Immanuel Wallerstein, "Northeast Asia and the World-System," *Korean Journal of Defense Analysis* 19, no. 3 (2007): 8–9.

appear. On the contrary, they may have just been temporarily buried, only to reappear when the time was right, asserting strong influence on people's lifeworlds. In this sense, we can say that ideological conflicts were more often than not conflicts between memories (including the writing of family history in the 1960s). At the same time, new social strata were also produced in this domain. These new social strata also participated in conflicts, fighting for their own interests. Indeed, social practices throughout the 1950s to the 1970s functioned like a battlefield for class struggle. This battlefield was without boundaries; it challenged not only the system of private property ownership, but also its culture and the collective memory shaped and informed by this culture. From a pessimistic and fatalistic perspective, we can admit that, when socialism was established in one country, this victory may have already determined the coming doom of its radical social practices. At the same time, a temporary failure does not necessarily entail a permanent one.

Third, China's postrevolutionary and systematized socialism can also be explained as a productive apparatus (*zhuangzhi*). This apparatus consists of highly complex mechanisms mixed, for example, with revolutionary ideals and their various and specific manifestations on the practical level, as well as modern forms of governing and managing models. This set of mechanisms simultaneously produced revolutionary ideals of equality and new social classifications and divisions; visions for [an alternative] political society and desires for a new lifeworld; concepts of the collective whole and of the individual; an emphasis on mass participation [in politics] and a bureaucratic management model; and so on. Combined, these contradictions constituted the complex panorama of Chinese socialism of the time. These contradictory elements were juxtaposed to one another in postrevolutionary socialist China, giving rise to various radical conflicts during this period. In this sense, I do not think it is enough to identify sources of contradictions in socialism as emanating only either from Chinese tradition or external threats. We must also enter and explore the structure within, or the apparatus itself, to look for the roots of the contradictions.

When contradictions abound, they cause crisis in a society. In this sense, we can say that socialism not only produced its supporters, it also produced its own opponents, and that the establishment of a socialist country does not mean the end of revolution. On the contrary, it could well mean the beginning of another revolutionary period. At the same time, however, we must carry out a careful analysis of who the opponents were. They could be supporters of revolutionary ideals, whose criticism may well have hinged on a refusal to accept the loss of these ideals. They could also be supporters of modernization ideals. How to understand the interpellation of the modern, especially technological modernization (which was upheld in the socialist period), is in this sense key to understanding both the socialist period and its aftermath.

V

In this study, I do not intend to offer yet another description of a particular history. I am mainly interested in what literature narrated throughout this historical period and how it narrated. Therefore, I do not entangle the issues on the level of factuality and the related conceptual framework of reflection theory. Despite the fact that, thirty years since the start of the post-Mao era, few people would resort to reflection theory to define literature, we nevertheless notice a rather strange phenomenon. There are critics who, to argue and prove the legitimacy of the present, stress the fictionality of literature. When they turn to history, however, they suddenly wish to stress whether or not literature realistically reflected life. It goes without saying that theory here becomes something equivocally employed only in a self-serving manner.

The literature I study in this book belongs to the period between 1949 and 1966, known as the seventeen-year literature. A few works will be from outside this period, such as some of the early works by Zhao Shuli written during the 1940s. As just mentioned, I am not interested in the issue of realistic truth. Instead, I am more interested in what imaginaries and concepts the literature of the time offered. Indeed, I am interested in the various ideas or concepts forwarded via literature. These ideas or concepts are both theoretical and emotional. The fact that we always construct our everyday life based on certain ideas means that literature, in this sense, is always useful. When studying this literature, one should not start by trying to separate it from politics. On the contrary, we must precisely situate it in relation to politics for an in-depth exploration. In this sense, I agree with [Gilles] Deleuze [and Félix Guattari]'s comment on Kafka: "Writing for Kafka, the primacy of writing, signifies only one thing: not a form of literature alone, the enunciation forms a unity with desire, beyond laws, states, regimes. Yet the enunciation is always historical, political, and social."[21] Literature is always situated against a certain kind of political backdrop; or, put differently, the political is always part of literari-

21. Gilles Deleuze and Félix Guattari, *Kafka: Toward a Minor Literature*, trans. Dana Polan (Minneapolis: University of Minnesota Press, 1986), 41–42.

ness. It can be a political act to discuss the state or a collective, but it can also be a political act to tell an individual's story.

Broadly speaking, the literature of the seventeen years mainly concentrated on themes such as nation-station/world, individual/collective, national [identity]/class, and so forth. The emphasis on nation-state, national identity, and class constituted the political characteristics of the literature of the time. Today, however, whenever the state is mentioned, the label of statism follows; when issues of national identity are evoked, it [national identity] is quickly labeled as nationalism; whenever the masses are evoked, it is viewed as no more than populism. This problem may very well itself be a fundamental cause in preventing certain critical views from coming to the fore. In fact, this problem pertains to more than literature, despite the fact that it is often manifested by way of discussing literariness. I do not deny that in the politicization of literature, some literary texts (including some of the good works) could become political mouthpieces and even serve to support certain policies; as such, in Deleuze [and Guattari]'s words, these works include the "inability to transcend the totality of the legal, state, and social systems." It is in this sense that I agree with the literary movement of the 1980s in its protest again using literature as a tool for class struggle. At the same time, what I do not agree with is the binarized or dichotomized way of understanding the relationship between the state and the individual. As a matter of fact, the perspective of state politics provided the literature of the socialist period with a narrative model through which to perceive the world in a profound way. I have called it a top-to-bottom narration. This way of narration was premised on concrete form[s] of experience, which manifested themselves not only in an attempt at narrating metahistory but also a particular political imaginary for the nation-state. If we reject outright the intervention of the political perspective of this metanarrative (which includes nation-state, history, and so on), we can well lose our political ability to have a dialogue with the world, including a corresponding ability to narrate [and tell stories about the world].

Even though the seventeen-year literature retained a close relationship with the politics of the state, we can still detect a certain form within that transcended this relationship. Several factors contributed to this form. On the one hand, when the politics of the state and writers shared a consensus, there was no conflict between the two. But as soon as the conflict between the politics of the state and an individual writer arose, the relationship could become murky. One typical example is Zhao Shuli. With reference to the existing discussions of this writer, my argument is that, while it is certainly important to explore "the Zhao Shuli path," what is equally important is to explore the question of why this path ended. There are multiple reasons for the end. To be sure, there was direct interference by the state (for example, the 1960s criticism of the middle character [that is, a character who was neither purely good nor purely evil]). But the end of this path could also be related to another modern Chinese intellectual tradition that, as the scholar Luo Gang [of East China Normal University] has put it, can be described as the radical urban intellectuals' romantic imagination of the world. In addition, to what extent Zhao (or whether or not he) exerted a strong influence on contemporary Chinese literature remains a debatable question. The truth of the matter is that much of the seventeen-year literature was a variation on the Western bildungsroman model, and Zhao's fiction does not fit that model.

On the other hand, what is perhaps more important, within the close relationship between literature and politics, is how we explore a more invisible way of writing that "transcends the totality of the legal, state, and social systems." This way of writing stemmed from valuing egalitarianism (*pingdeng zhuyi*), which emphasizes the sharing of mutual interests. In this kind of writing, the individual is always examined by being placed in the context of a collective. While such narration expressed strong disapproval of extreme individualism (which is often interpreted as part of the rule of the jungle), it is also against any form of oppression. This explains why antibureaucracy and antiprivilege were always major themes in the seventeen-year literature. In terms of form, this way of writing provided an opportunity for writers to develop an ability to tell other people's stories well. I believe that how to tell other people's stories well was not only a challenge to a writer's personal experience and his or her own values, but it was even more a challenge to their narrative skills. Obviously, this kind of equality-oriented ideal and respect for lower-class people could not easily be understood by anyone upholding an extreme individualist view. Precisely because of the presence of such ideals, regardless of whether one applauds or condemns this literature, it is difficult to resort to the "totality of the legal, state, and social systems" for a full interpretation.

There are many difficulties in analyzing literature of this period. On the one hand, the quality of works is not even (just like in any historical period). On the other hand, we must not separate literature and politics in a rash manner. Instead, we must examine literature and its history in the context in which literature actively interacted with politics. And we must do so by reading and analyzing the texts closely and carefully.

VI

This book has seven chapters.

Chapter 1 is titled "The National/The Local: Conflict, Negotiation, and Capitulation in the Revolutionary Imagination." This chapter mainly examines the relationships between the state and the local and between the knowledge of modernity and local knowledge in the context of the postrevolutionary socialist period. While there was an emphasis on centralized control by the central government, the local and local knowledge nevertheless persisted. To a certain extent, I do not agree with the view that Chinese socialism was totally antitradition. In actuality, that could not have been possible. Revolutionary China inherited China's traditional territorial space and, inevitably, its corresponding knowledge of various places. The key for us is how to understand tradition in a dialectical manner. I am of the opinion that so-called tradition tended to exist largely in the form of local knowledge or, put differently, existed as localized tradition. This tradition must be understood differently from that of the elites (in the form of a canon). In this sense, modernity and tradition constituted a relationship that mutually enlisted one another. For example, when natural villages were retained as the basic administrative units for the socialist state, parts of the traditional culture and power relations in these villages inevitably were retained. What was retained could on the one hand lead to ideological conflicts, but [on the other hand] it could also be used by modern knowledge. For instance, in literature, the leader-like characters (*dairouren*) are often portrayed with a high moral overtone (such as Liang Baosheng in the novel *The Builders*). Such a depiction cannot be explained by the model of modern technocrats but can be better understood if we search for the ideal type in the traditional kinship system. By extension, it is important to realize that the village constituted one of the most important spatial units in the seventeen-year literature and was more important than the family.

Chapter 2 is titled "The Mobilization Structure: The Masses, Cadres, and Intellectuals." It mainly discusses the so-called mobilization structure and the relationships between different groups within this structure. Strictly speaking, this structure was a social organizational form that was not systematized. Yet there is no question that it played a particularly important role in political and cultural life in China. The implication of mobilization no doubt had a Leninist slant to it—namely, imposing class consciousness from outside. But its importance to the Chinese revolution lies in the fact that it helped address the problem of China's lack of a large number of industrial workers and a corresponding lack of theoretical guidelines [for implementing Marxist revolution in a rural context]. Via mobilization, the proletarian class could be created as a kind of political proletariat. This political intervention led to the formalization of the class struggle in China and helped identify the embodiment of the proletariat class—namely, the military. If we look more closely at the image of demobilized soldiers portrayed in that literature, we can have a clearer idea of what the political proletariat class meant and how its implication also pointed to the importance of the practice of individual reform. At the same time, this social organizational form also emphasized the creative spirit of the masses on the premise that ordinary people had a natural inclination toward socialism. It therefore also emphasized a respect for the masses with the belief that they were the subject and agent of the revolution. By extension, it gave rise to promoting the masses as the embodiment of social morals and a belief that the new socialist person could be portrayed through them [the masses as the embodiment of social morals]. It goes without saying that, even within the mobilization structure itself, there were layers of contradictions and various expressions.

Chapter 3, "Youth, Love, 'Natural Rights,' and Sex," focuses on the relationship among these concepts. What I would like to add here is that revolution requires passion, but postrevolutionary socialism also needs the production of passion. If passion was once being produced via a slew of representations of sex and romantic love as well as of war (including sacrificing one's life), in the postrevolutionary socialist era in which individualism (including personal romantic love and sexuality) was deemphasized, the production of passion was increasingly transferred to the domain of literature. How to produce passion that corresponded to socialist politics thus became a major question. Otherwise, we cannot explain why revolutionary China's politics could have bestowed so much attention on literature. In this sense, we can assume that various kinds of efforts at the popularization of literature (such as the new popular lyrics movement) had something to do with the endeavor of producing passion. In producing passion, literature also produced youth, or literary youth. I briefly touch on the issue of literary youth again in chapter 7, but the topic requires a more extensive exploration. On the one hand, the literary youth, symbolized as the new socialist persons, were the agents of the socialist future. On the other hand, they were also a major antiestablishment force. As such, the phenomenon of literary youth, together with layers of various related issues, presents itself as an important subject for further exploration. This is not only about the first thirty years of the socialist period but is also related to the thought liberation movement of the 1980s.

Chapter 4, "Renarrating the History of the Revolution: From Hero to Legend," focuses on why, in the postrevolutionary socialist period, there was a constant retelling of revolutionary history and how it was retold. A modern nation is first of all a political entity, but such an entity needs cultural support. How best to tell the history and the legendary construction of this modern nation constitutes an important issue of narration. In this narration, the most important task is to establish a collective value system, for the purpose of forming political identity within a nation. Such an identity is both political and historical. In this sense we can see why a depoliticization process must begin with dehistorisization.

Chapter 5 is titled "Narratives of Labor or Labor Utopias." In the narration of revolutionary China, *labor* was always one of the most important concepts. The narratives about it were not only political but also (in Zhao Shuli's words) full of understanding or *qingli* [emotion and reason]. Labor as a concept was premised on the basis of understanding or qingli, a premise that contributed not only to the configuration of a particular kind of structure of feeling but also to the establishment of a sense of social justice. The positive valuation of labor brought a sense of dignity to the laboring masses. In this sense, we can say that the Chinese revolution was also a revolution in winning dignity for the masses, or, put differently, the revolution was itself a social practice based on the politics of dignity [for the masses].

Chapter 6 is titled "Technological Revolution and Narratives of Working-Class Subjectivity." For quite some time, we have been discussing the demarcations between socialism and capitalism. Often, we find the boundaries are not always that clear. Still, boundaries that differentiate the two have always existed, manifested in the distinction between the different historical contexts of revolutionary China and modern China. The demarcation lies in the issue of who is considered the master. Even though during the socialist period the promise for workers and peasants to become masters was not fully realized, efforts to realize this ideal nevertheless never ceased. And such efforts were always echoed in literature. In the representations of labor, we can see manifestations of modern tensions, mainly between circles of experts and the participation of the masses [in various endeavors]. The latter's participation was more than in politics; it was present in knowledge production as well. In the process of mass participation, democratization was also gradually transmitted from the political arena to that of economics. The so-called Anshan Constitution was one such example. To be sure, to what extent the masses were able to participate, and what kind of social crisis was caused by repression from management, are some of the questions that merit further and separate discussions. The issue that I am concerned with here is, if the subjectivity of the masses can be realized and established only through their own participation, once such participation comes to a halt, what accompanies this end would be the disappearance of the subjectivity of the subalterns.

Chapter 7 is titled "Cultural Politics, or Political Cultural Conflicts, in the 1960s." By the 1960s, I refer specifically to the first half of the decade, before the outbreak of the Cultural Revolution. The importance of this period lies in the fact that the city and its corresponding importance had steadily increased during this period, generating a series of challenging issues—such as the problem of the individual, desire, and consumption—that the Chinese revolution had to confront. We ought not to assume that because Chinese socialism emphasized the collective, the individual had in turn disappeared. On the contrary: in producing the collective, socialism was also producing the individual. The problem was that this individual produced in socialism did not acquire a corresponding legitimacy. While on the one hand, socialism produced more and more individuals, on the other hand, it tried to contain the individual by way of criticizing individualism. As a result, not only were there increasing tensions and conflicts between the individual and the collective, there was also tension and conflict in how to understand the relationship between individualism and the individual. To a certain extent, incidentally, this tension can explain the political demands for the restoration of the individual in the 1980s. To contain this individual, especially individual desire, class struggle became the political form and method through which this tension was addressed. Yet at the same time, behind class struggle there were demands for the formation of an obedient personhood capable of controlling selfish desire. An immediate challenge that this new person faced, in addition, was whether or not she or he was capable of shouldering the mission of the continuous revolution. Continuous revolution demands a politically decisive ability to challenge and subvert, while it also requires a mode of production that can continuously turn out passion. We can find all of these tensions in the film *The Young Generation*, for example, especially the issue of how the literary youth were enlisted in political terms. In this sense, I tend to agree that the outbreak of the Cultural Revolution was, in part, intended to overcome the obedient society produced in the 1960s and the corresponding crisis in the continuous revolution.

In "Conclusion: The Crisis of Socialism and Efforts to Overcome It," I reiterate my overall historical attitude. On the one hand, we must in earnest summarize the positive experiences and lessons of the Chinese revolution. On the other hand, I also make efforts to explore [the various factors that caused] crises in socialism. My examination addresses the socialist production apparatus, practices to overcome crisis, and the resources employed to do so. If we view the various attempts to overcome the crisis as historicized, we can say that its [overcoming crisis] earliest manifestation occurred in the Anti-Rightist Campaign in 1957, followed first by the call to never forget class struggle in the 1960s and then by the Cultural Revolution; it ended in the 1980s. With that, the entire twentieth century also came to an end [in its revolutionary sense]. This chronology reflects the conceptual characteristics of China's antiestablishment movement on the one hand. On the other hand, it also demonstrates efforts made to search for new conceptual resources. This search revealed uncertainties in socialist theory about conceptual resources for overcoming crisis. It also implies that, when in the 1980s such a search turned to the West (which is the topic of my next project), it would produce much bigger social crises. I do not, however, believe that this search has ended. It will continue until we create a new socialist form.

VII

When literature, as Hayden White puts it, "pretends to let the world speak for itself,"[22] there already exist differences between imagination and practice and between fiction and facts. But between imagination and fiction, we can still discern a kind of historical discourse of narrative that is influenced and conditioned by a range of factors. Some of the influences and conditions seem obvious, while most come from the political unconscious of a particular historical period. The key question I want to explore is, why write this way? I therefore focus on issues related to the intertextuality between literature and social politics. This is my methodology, even though I do not believe it is the only correct one. As a matter of fact, I cannot believe there is only one cor-

---

22. See Hayen White, *The Content of the Form: Narrative Discourse and Historical Representation* (Baltimore: Johns Hopkins University Press, 1987).

rect methodology. Nor do I believe mine is the best research method, but it is the most suitable one for me. What interests me more is the fact that, in the study of contemporary Chinese literature, we must pay attention to the question of methodology, especially how a particular one can be pushed to a point where a narrative model of our own can be formed. Needless to say, as we push our point, shortcomings in our methodology are revealed that in turn can prompt us to find a way to address and overcome them. In this sense, I do not deny that there are limitations in my methodology, and I also respect those employed by other scholars.

In the final analysis, however, the issue of methodology is not the most important one. What is important is that I hope to reestablish a kind of narration in which, regardless of how the world changes, falls or fails, I still want to respond to the manifested revolutionary ideal of equality—that is, the "communist imaginary," in Badiou's words. And once again, we can only bring with us the conceptual/theoretical legacies of the twentieth century to return to the nineteenth century.

1

THE NATIONAL/THE LOCAL
*Conflict, Negotiation, and Capitulation
in the Revolutionary Imagination*

When I use the word *local* here, it is a spatial concept that I counterpose to the centralized power of the national state. Of course, this concept cannot be delimited by the position of a local administrative entity, nor can it be contained in some naturalized geographical description. Rather, my interest is more on the multiple elements that comprise this space, such as systems, mores and customs, social groupings, the disposition of the population and its languages (or dialects), as well as those deep accumulated cultural modes that are hidden in the heart of these spaces. It is these multiple elements and their inner cultural modes that comprise what we will call the local or even local knowledge.[1]

---

1. Concern with the Chinese local, whether by historians, sociologists, or anthropologists, has already produced a good number of works, such as Fei Xiaotong's *Economy of River Towns*, which is an example of a classic from Chinese sociology while it could also be seen as a profound narrative of modern China's local (especially the local of the Jiangnan region). Prasenjit Duara's *Culture, Power, and the State* takes northern Chinese villages as its narrative object and describes in detail how, in the course of modernization, a local government gets formed and altered in relation to rule and religion. And in Yang Nianqun's edited volume, *Space, Memory, Social Transition*, we also see how this concept of the local has in myriad ways entered the research

Naturally, one could unconsciously evoke the local as if it were a self-regulated or self-sufficient space; but I rather tend to see the national and the local in relations of mutual constitution. For the nation-state not only deploys myriad forms—as well as systemic methods—to effectively incorporate into itself local knowledge (for example, the ancient system of collecting folk songs); but at the same time, it deploys different methods to deeply implant its own political vision, its own quest for power, and its own forms of knowledge into the local (for example, the form of traditional storytelling). This is so much the case that the nation-state has become a sort of dominating ideological form.

It is precisely because of the complex interactive relationship between the state and the local that, in the process of China's modernization, the transformations in China's ruling power have never been simple substitutions of one kind of power for another kind. Rather, at the same time, these transformations have always also implied changes in the nation-state structure and its ideologies. It is precisely because nation-state ideology is in an instructional position with relation to the local that the disintegration of older national ideologies usually spreads to the local, even producing great instability and disorder in the local order. In certain historical descriptions—for example, in *Zheng Chaolin's Memoir* (*Zheng Chaolin huiyilu*)—we can see that popular disorder in Xiangping villages began only four or five years after the Xinhai Revolution [of 1911]. In these four or five years, "in order to express certain differences with and to alter despotic dynastic rule, the name of the administrative position of 'general inspector [*zongdu*]' was changed to 'provincial military inspector [*dudu*],' and 'county magistrate [*zhixian*]' [was changed] to 'provincial governor [*zhishi*].'" Gradually, "the second-grade district government was abolished," and at the same time "the centuries-old system of 'hometown avoidance' was eliminated." In other words, "somebody from this province could become the district administrator of this same province." Behind the systemic transformations were profound alterations in the forms of knowledge and ideologies. Indeed, in the narrative of *Zheng Chaolin's Memoir*, there are two details that stand out. One is that "the former official in office from the previous dynasty had more sway than the official in office for the current dynasty," and he doesn't even speak one word of the dialect local

---

perspectives of new social history and how it has received massive research funding support, and so on. Here, my narrative target is mostly concerned with the rural in contemporary Chinese fiction from 1949 to 1966; I have discussed the urban elsewhere.

people can understand. The second is that "the fact that there is no more emperor is something that the common people in Zhangping County cannot in any way grasp. How can the world not have an emperor? There has been an emperor ever since Pan Gu established the earth."[2] I think what this explains, or at least partially explains, is that the local, at least in the cultural or ideological sense, cannot exist outside of the control of the state.

From the late Qing [1880s] onward in China, a so-called unprecedented historical transformation was occasioned due to the arrival of Western modernity; this transformation was rooted in the emergence of the so-called modern nation-state. According to [Benedict] Anderson, the modern nation-state is "an imagined political community—and imagined as both inherently limited and sovereign."[3] In the course of this imaginative process, the individual is at the same time imagined as a citizen and his rights and obligations are not subject to racial, religious, ethnic, or class restrictions; rather, all can enjoy equally the resources society offers. Because of this, inherent to this concept is the political implication of participation in national sovereignty, and thus the modern system of participatory politics.[4] [Kōjin] Karatani also believes that "the so-called nation should be understood as being composed of a community of individuals (urbanites) who have separated themselves from blood- and race-based characteristics." That is to say, the nation is "formed out of urbanites, who were freed from the shackles of feudalism."[5] As a consequence, in the process of building modern nation-states, the reform of the individual—how to turn the obedient subject of feudal society into a citizen in the modern sense—became one of the greatest tasks of modern political culture. It is thus that we can see the derivation of, for example, Liang Qichao's advocacy for the new citizen [in 1902] or Lu Xun's reform of the national people [in the 1920s].

Through this process, the local, or the local knowledge therewith associated (for example, religions, superstitions, political systems, modes of production, and so on), is usually seen as a spatial obstacle to the realization of modernization. Such a perspective is in some measure evident in Lu Xun's early sto-

2. Zheng Chaolin, *Zheng Chaolin huiyilu* (Beijing: Dongfang Chubanshe, 2004), 5–10.
3. Benedict Anderson, *Imagined Communities: Reflections on the Origin and Spread of Nationalism* (London: Verso, 1983), 6.
4. Partha Chatterjee, "Community in the East," *Economic and Political Weekly* 33, no. 6 (1998): 277–82.
5. Kōjin Karatani, *The Origins of Modern Japanese Literature*, trans. and ed. Brett de Bary (Durham, NC: Duke University Press, 1993), 3.

ries, such as "Madman's Diary" [1918] or "New Year's Sacrifice" [1924].[6] In particular, when the older state system is in the process of being dismantled, its national knowledge or ideology will have been disseminated to the local, there to be preserved or even to become itself an important element of local knowledge. As a result, the national and the local, in the sense of knowledge or culture, are sometimes difficult to distinguish from one another. But this is only one part of the problem. Another part resides in the fact that "'nation' is not composed only of the rational aspects of an urban social contract; it must also be implanted in the sympathy that informs the mutual interactions and dependencies between kin or ethnic communities. We could go so far as to say that nation is the product of the expansion of capitalist market relations and the consequent destruction of ethnic communities, which forced people to use imagination so as to restore the lost reciprocity of that type of mutual dependence." That is to say, "in this process, that ideal community of rural village communities was destroyed, and that ideal condition of mutual dependence and mutual reward had to be restored anew through imagination."[7]

Even though Karatani himself has a provisional attitude toward his own explanation ("whether or not this can be linked up to the concept of the nation is not yet determined"[8]), we can feel the seriousness of his attitude toward community as well as the importance of tradition manifested within those communities in nation-state building. In reality, modern Western social theories of modernity do not all merely trace one path of liberal individualism; the fact that this factor is singled out and exaggerated has to do with other complex social historical conditions. In any case, in China's modern history, including modern literary history, the critique of the local always follows a rediscovery of it. This rediscovery is manifested not only in the stories and novels by Shen Congwen [1930s] and others. It is also tangled up in Lu Xun's works, such as his story "Hometown" [1921]. In other words, critique and sentimental attachment are often mutually entangled.

After 1949, conflicts of modern nation-state building were included in the Chinese socialist imaginary as well. For this reason, some important issues of concern in [pre-1949] modern intellectual history were extended into this period. This is one reason that in the literary narration of the 1949–66 histori-

---

6. All of the short stories by Lu Xun referenced in this book can be found in Lu Xun, *Diary of a Madman and Other Stories*, trans. William A. Lyell (Honolulu: University of Hawaii Press, 1990).

7. Karatani, *The Origins of Modern Japanese Literature*, 3.

8. Ibid.

cal period within the nation-state there always lurks the intention to reform and remold the local. At the same time, the local is always being rediscovered and in various ways is being appropriated into national knowledge or modern knowledge. A complex sociocultural form eventually came into being from all of this.

I. Narratives of Local Landscape and the Bewildered Reconstruction of Landscape

The analytical model for what I want to discuss with the topic of landscape is Karatani's "discovery of landscape" in his *Origins of Modern Japanese Literature* and certain discussions by [Stuart] Hall. In Karatani's view, the description of the object (landscape) is not merely a simple attempt to represent the natural world; to the contrary, this so-called object only exists in narrative, and so-called narrative can only ever be subjective. Put differently, the object does not exist prior to the [narrating] subject but rather is the product of the subjective narration. By the same token, in Hall's theory of cultural structuralism, things do not derive meaning from material manifestation, but rather "it is by our use of things, and what we say, think and feel about them—how to represent them—that we *give them a meaning*." That is to say, meaning "is also produced . . . when we weave narratives, stories—and fantasies—around them" and for this reason, "one of the privileged 'media' through which meaning is produced and circulated is language."[9] Yet a follow-up question has to be how this "we" or subject is produced. It is precisely here that Karatani introduces the concept of *installation* [*zhuangzhi*]. In Karatani's view, the subject or subjectivity can never be posited as a priori existence but rather is a continuous process of construction. In the course of this process, the flood of national, social, systemic, political, and ideological forces enters; precisely only with the entrance of these multiple forces can there be the productive formation of an installation. The production of this installation is actually the construction of the subject and of subjectivity; correspondingly, this produces and constructs the narrative materials of the subject. For this reason, the so-called object—namely, the material of the subject's narrative—always retains some sort of concealed link to the subjectivity of the narrator. In other words, what we see is possibly only what we wish to see. To emphasize this

---

9. Stuart Hall, introduction to *Representation: Cultural Representations and Signifying Practices*, ed. Stuart Hall (London: Sage, 1997), 3–4.

point, Karatani uses the concept of landscape to explain the signifying importance of the discovery of the landscape. In analyzing the story "People Hard to Forget," Karatani writes: "Landscape is intimately linked to the inner core of solitude. This character experiences a feeling of 'not me/not him' towards a random person, but at the same time this feeling exhibits a certain coldness towards the 'other' who is right before him. In other words, landscape is discovered only when the 'inner person' has no concern for those around him. Landscape is discovered by someone who does not see 'outside.'" For Karatani, this "inner person" is precisely a product (as individual, self, and subjectivity, and so on) of Japanese modernity since the Meiji Restoration [1868]. For this reason, the actual discovery of landscape is "a product of a particular system."[10] The point of Karatani's analysis is to argue that "what I am referring to as 'landscape' is an epistemological constellation, the origins of which were suppressed as soon as it was produced."[11]

What interests me here are not the specifics of Karatani's analysis of landscape in Japanese literature. I borrow this concept and the theory that informs it merely to explain that I do not consider landscape in contemporary Chinese literature (1949–66) simply as a description of the natural world. Rather, I wish, through an analysis of landscape, to explore how, after 1949, under the imperative of China's modern nation-state formation, the discovery of landscape was introduced into [modern socialist] contemporary literature[12] and how, hidden within, were complex relations between nation and the local. In addition, I wish to elucidate how, with the entry of class politics [in the socialist period], the reestablished local landscape became particularly difficult to narrate and how its narrative produced an internally paradoxical discourse.

---

10. According to Karatani's translator, Karatani's so-called 'system' or literary system implies two levels: one is that of economics, law, politics, education, and such external material systems; the other indicates modes of thinking that are consolidated and do not change or systems of interiority.

11. Karatani, *Origins of Modern Japanese Literature*, 22.

12. Tr.: Cai uses the term "contemporary literature" most often to refer to the literature of the 1949–66 period. This is distinguished by him from the more common usage of the term "socialist literature" (1949–76) or "modern literature" (1920s–1940s, resumed in the 1980s–1990s). All of these terms are highly politicized and debated. The significance of calling the literature of 1949–66 "contemporary"—or modern socialist contemporary literature—is to emphasize that this literary production cannot be seen as aberrant and outside of the history of modernity and contemporary life, but rather must be treated as integrally constitutive of it.

In her essay on the transformation of *White-Haired Girl*,[13] Meng Yue uses a case study of the drama to discuss the "process of cultural-political production in the liberated areas" and the "unpolitical dimensions of political literature" in this "production process." What Meng means by "unpolitical dimensions" perhaps points to how, under politically discursive narrative conditions (for example, "the old society turned people into ghosts, [the] new society turns ghosts into people"), there were still concealed certain "unpolitical narrative conventions akin to folk artistic patterns." That is to say, "the narrative mechanisms of the opera *White-Haired Girl*, even though its major theme was molded out of political discourse, were not completely controlled by it"; "rather, to some extent, its plot is structured around a certain folk lifeworld, ethical order, and moral logic."[14] Within this narrative construction, the landlord, Huang Shiren, does not exist merely to represent a class enemy; he also exists as "an enemy of the folk ethical order." As Meng Yue proceeds to point out, in the opera *White-Haired Girl*, "the function of a folk ethical logic and its mutual relation to political discourse is expressed in the following way: the stability of the folk ethical order is the legitimizing premise for political discourse. Only as an enemy of the folk ethical order can Huang Shiren also be a political enemy."[15] Meng Yue's explanation here is extremely significant for research into contemporary literature, for not only does the intruder become a relatively common structural element in contemporary literature, but at the same time a multiplicity also exists in Yan'an cultural practice and, to a great extent, persists through the socialist literary-cultural imaginary from 1949–66 as well.

There are complex reasons for the existence of multiplicity, but here it may have to do with certain implicit connections to the specificity of the Chinese revolution. The Chinese revolution was not only profoundly rooted in rural villages and for this reason usually maintained a certain respectful and compromising posture vis-à-vis rural ideals, but at the same time, because of the stagist quality of the Chinese revolution (for example, national revolution/

---

13. Tr.: *White-Haired Girl* is a classic Chinese folk tale that saw multiple revisions in different media through the socialist period and even before.

14. Meng Yue, "Some Comments on the Evolution of *White-Haired Girl*—A Discussion of the multi-vocality of Yan'an Culture," Wang Xiaoming, ed., *Ershi shiji zhongguo wenxueshi lun*, [On the history of twentieth-century Chinese literature], ed. Wang Xiaoming (Shanghai: Dongfang Chuban Zhongxin, 2003), 2.

15. Ibid.

class revolution, new democracy/socialism,[16] and so on), even though the politics of class were from the beginning a dominant desire, this politics could never completely eliminate other political desires and their related literary-cultural imaginaries. For this reason, within a heterogeneous political discursive space, the so-called other was not always the same; indeed, sometimes there were many others [national, class, and so forth]. And the political subject constructed from the stipulations of these many others bore the particularity of multiplicity. Of course, this is not to say that the multiplicity existed in a relation of equality or in some state of calm; to the contrary, this multiplicity precisely animated and informed a sharp ideological-cultural struggle. It is only because of this type of multiplicity and struggle that political discourse was able to establish itself as hegemonic. For this reason, so-called reeducation (*gaizao*)[17] or self-remolding was informed by multiplicity in political discursive space and in fact foreshadowed the possibility of self-negation or continuous revolution. However, this multiple political discursive context in some sense also brought about the posture of compromise in the Chinese revolution. Often modern knowledge (political discourse) either proactively or passively incorporated and transformed local knowledge (folk ethics) into its own narrative resource. Needless to say, this process of incorporation was filled with contradiction and conflict.

To understand the multiplicity inherent in China's revolution, perhaps most helpful to us will be not to take Hong Zicheng's theory of the "unification" (*yitihua*) of contemporary Chinese literature[18] at face value, but rather to see this so-called unification as in some sense the contradiction- and conflict-laden process of the construction of contemporary Chinese literature.[19] At

---

16. Tr.: In the 1930s and 1940s, Mao Zedong undertook a thorough theorization of the ways in which the Chinese revolution would need to unfold, given the global and domestic situations at the time. His classic statement of the two-stage nature of the revolution is contained in "On New Democracy," delivered as a speech in 1940 and later worked into a widely read essay.

17. Tr.: *Gaizao* is a difficult term to translate into English. It means transformation, reeducation, remolding with the goal of reorienting the self toward the socialist project and standpoint. At different times, we translate it as any of the above three words in line both with its contextual meaning and more common English usage.

18. Hong Zicheng, *Wenti yu fangfa* [Problems and methods] (Beijing: Sanlian shudian, 2002).

19. Tr.: Cai here is arguing against a prominent post-1980 literary analysis that posits the unified hegemony of state (political) discourse as the necessary interpretive angle through which to view Mao-era Chinese literature. His emphasis on multiplicity and conflict is precisely aimed at disputing the unitary nature of the political-state hegemony.

the same time, the characteristics of the multiplicity of the Chinese revolution also in turn brought about the complex structuration of contemporary Chinese literature and its multi-perspectival narrativization or, that is, its diversity. For example, from a certain perspective of class politics, local landscape is perhaps difficult to represent. Li Liuru writes in his *Sixty Years of Transformation* (*Liushinian de bianqian*) that, after the failure of the Great Revolution [1924–27], the protagonist Ji Jiaoshu takes a boat to Shanghai: "the closer the ship approaches the shore, the more those countless tall buildings and bright lights appeared like gigantic beasts silently squatting there, flashing their gaze, ready to devour people."[20] There, none of the so-called fine day and enchanting scenes [of classical local literature] can be represented. Apparently, in this political perspective the so-called local is a dark analogy to old China, which is the target of revolution. Its landscape naturally in turn must stay invisible. Yet if we cast our concern toward other principal sources of revolution, such as the perspective of the nation, then it is not only possible to narrate the local landscape, but in the complex and heterogeneous political discursive context, there can also emerge an alternative landscape formation.

Among contemporary authors, Sun Li is particularly good at writing landscape. In his [1944 short story] "Lotus Creek" ("Hehua dian"), for example, the story begins as follows:

> The moon had risen and the little courtyard was delightfully fresh and clean. The rushes split during the day were damp and supple, just waiting to be woven into mats. A woman was sitting in the yard plaiting the long soft rushes with nimble fingers. The thin, fine strands leaped and twisted in her arms. . . . The young woman in the yard was plaiting a mat, seated on a long stretch of it already accomplished where she seemed enthroned on virgin snow or on a fleecy cloud. From time to time she strained her eyes towards the creek, another world of silver white. Light, translucent mist had risen over the water, and the breeze was laden with the scent of fresh lotus leaves.[21]

This realist technique of writing landscape is also seen in Sun's other works and has been praised by many critics. In *Stormy Years* (*Fengyun chuji*) he writes of Qiufen's residence: "Qiufen grew vegetables round their hut. After dusk she

---

20. Li Liuru, *Liushinian de bianqian* [Sixty years of transformation], 3rd ed. (Beijing: Renmin Chubanshe, 2005), 3.
21. Sun Li, "Lotus Creek," in *Lotus Creek and Other Stories*, trans. Gladys Yang (Beijing: Foreign Language Press, 1982), 8–9.

put a lamp in the small window facing south to guide the boats. On the frame before the window she trained loofah gourds and loofahs, when full grown, hung down through the thick leaves nearly to the ground. At the southwest corner, overlooking the river, she planted a row of sunflowers, ready to welcome wanderers far from home."[22] And he writes of Chun'er: "At that time Chun'er was sound asleep on her kang,[23] unaware a young man was thinking about her. She did not hear her sister tossing and turning or murmuring endearments in her dream. A green grasshopper on the trellis outside the window drank its fill of dew and set up a joyful shrilling. The gourds heavy with moisture drooped, and dew-drops rolled down the tender bloom on their skins. A large white flower on a long stem was reaching up from the trellis to the sky. Chirping away, the grasshopper crawled slowly up it."[24]

Due to the Japanese invasion of China, this beautiful local scene is in imminent danger of being destroyed, and in the novel's next narrative passage we see a different type of scene, which is due to the war: "That night, the refugees slept sprawled out by the embers of the bonfires. The river ran fast and savagely pounded the bay, sucking away clods of earth. Moonlight fell on a boundless expanse of misty water, on ruined crops lashed by the waves. All the villagers far and near were gripped by panic. Many were sleepless that night in their despair. A child's ear-splitting cries filled Old Gao's hut. 'Damned Japanese!' Curses drifted through every small village window, muttered even by those tossing restlessly in their dreams."[25]

We recall here what Meng Yue concluded from her study of *White-Haired Girl*: the narrative structure intrusion/destruction—which often introduces an alien element—became a common phenomenon in contemporary Chinese fiction. It is just that in [the writing of] Sun and other such works with the anti-Japanese war as the background—such as Yuan Jing and Kong Jue's *New Heroic Sons and Daughters* (*Xin ernu yingxiong zhuan*) [1949]—this alien element mostly emerges in the form of the national enemy. In this structure, landscape, especially local landscape, usually takes on an important role in the narration. And the construction of the local scenes depends upon the intrusion/destruction structure determined by the political discourse of an

22. Sun Li, *Stormy Years*, trans. Gladys Yang (Beijing: Foreign Language Press, 1982), 6.
23. Tr.: A *kang* is a conventional piece of northern Chinese household furniture: a masonry or earthen platform under which a fire can be built for warmth. An all-purpose surface, it is used as a bed, a table, and so on.
24. Sun Li, *Stormy Years*, 12.
25. Ibid., 34–35.

other. In addition, because of the violent integration of national discourse, the control of political discourse in some ways starts to loosen, and the local (folk ethics, the ideals of village life, and so on) not only does not become a mechanical target of revolution or reform, but rather it becomes the homeland in need of protection and defense within the same political discourse.

To a certain extent, the local in this discursive context, has already gradually been transformed into an analogy for native soil. According to Karatani, the constructing of a nation-state that merely relies upon the articulation of a social contract is far from sufficient; rather, one must use the imaginary to build some sort of common feeling or to restore that "lost mutual assistance and reciprocity." However, this common feeling in a modern nation-state already cannot rely upon blood origins, so "it might as well rely upon 'geography'" and complete its articulation through the discovery or the extolling of landscape.[26]

It is evident that with the support of national discourse, the local not only can become analogous to native soil, but also narrating local landscape can build a common feeling in a community. However, the articulation of the nation-state that relies upon geography conceals the danger of class reconciliation. For traditional Marxists, this danger not only exists but, through the articulation of the nation-state, it can also lead to the subversion of class discourse. For example, with regard to the truth or falsehood of the Paris Commune Wall, the "Paris Commune Friendship Society" answered a letter from a particularly curious girl; in its response, the Society very clearly stated its own position: "Dear Friend: You have made of the large statue in the Place Gambetta near Père Lachaise Cemetery a martyr's wall for the Commune. This statue is the work of M. Wauthier and it depicts a zealous woman—France—signifying a unification between Communards reconciled in death with elements from Versailles. The guiding principle of our Society is to preserve the glorious memory of the Commune martyrs, so we have always rejected the type of symbolism that would reconcile the 30,000 Parisians murdered with their murderers."[27] It is clear that under the strictures of class discourse, what is asked is always: "whose country is this country?" This question requires the rejection of any form of class reconciliation under the nation-state's symbol such as "woman of France."

---

26. Karatani, *The Origins of Modern Japanese Literature*, 5.

27. Shen Dali, "*Bali 'gongsheqiang' kaobian*" [Investigations on the Paris "commune wall"] in *Balishengyin* [Voices and traces of Paris] (Beijing: Beijing chubanshe, 1989).

However, in socialist countries, national discourse and class discourse have always coexisted, and this clearly stems from the experience of Leninist socialist revolutions, which went from world revolution to national revolution. Socialism had to continue the form of the nation-state project. Anderson notes "the fact that since World War II every successful revolution has defined itself in national terms—the People's Republic of China, the Socialist Republic of Vietnam, and so forth—and, in so doing, has grounded itself firmly in a territorial and social space inherited from the prerevolutionary past."[28] For this reason, Anderson supports Eric Hobsbawm's observation that "Marxist movements and states have tended to become national not only in form but in substance, i.e., nationalist. There is nothing to suggest that this trend will not continue."[29] At the same time, Anderson still uses the example of the national bourgeoisie to express his own doubts: "Why is this segmentation of the bourgeoisie—a world class insofar as it is defined in terms of the relations of production—theoretically significant?"[30] This phenomenon leads Ernst Gellner to his bold statement: "Marxists basically like to think that the spirit of history or human consciousness made a terrible booboo. The awakening message was intended for *classes*, but by some terrible postal error was delivered to *nations*."[31]

In the experience of the Chinese revolution, class discourse was a strong presence, and it maintained a constant vigilance with relation to the development of national discourse. Whenever national discourse strayed from its designated post, class discourse would wage struggle with it. For example, after the 9/18 incident [when Japan bombed Shanghai] in 1931, the Nationalist state apparatus promoted a nationalist literature movement. Their [the Nationalists'] confused notion of official nationalist literature was immediately met with the unrelenting critique and sharp sarcasm of Lu Xun, Qu Qiubai, and other left-wing writers.[32] At the same time, the struggle [surrounding nationalist literature] always was widespread within left-wing literature—for example, the conflict between "national defense literature" and "mass literature of the national revolutionary war," which is known as the struggle between the "two slogans." This concrete experience of the Chinese revolution rendered the

---

28. Anderson, *Imagined Communities*, 2–3.
29. Quoted in ibid., 3.
30. Ibid., 4.
31. Ernest Gellner, *Nations and Nationalism* (London: Basil Blackwell, 1983), 129.
32. Kuang Xinnian, "Minzu zhuyi, guojia xiangxiang yu xiandai wenxue" ["Nationalism, nationalist imaginaries, and modern literature"] in *Shanghai Wentan*, 2007, 2.

situation unlike what Gellner proposed: that the message was erroneously sent to the nation when it had been addressed to class. To the contrary, "in China, the postmaster seems to have delivered the awakening message to class and nation at the same address."[33]

Related to all of this is the fact that class discourse participated in the narrative of local landscape and thereby formed a relatively complex narrative structure. Strictly speaking, even in the sense of the national discourse of native soil, it is hard to say if local landscape in contemporary Chinese literature is entirely a product of modernity. In reality, when landscape is analogized to the idea of missing the old country, it already exists in ancient literature. For example, we can see this in Qiu Chi's "Letter to Chen Bo" ("Yu Chen Bo zhi shu") [dating from 506]: "March, late spring. The grass is long in Jiangnan. Various flowers are in bud, flocks of birds fly about wildly. When I see the national flag flying, I remembered the past."[34] I tend, however, to think that the so-called actual discovery of landscape in contemporary Chinese literature relies upon the emergence of the perspective of the subaltern. That is to say, the narrator relies upon the perspective of the subaltern (laboring) people to rediscover local landscape. And it is precisely within this type of landscape narration that national discourse and class discourse achieve a degree of tacit and higher-level unity.

Actually, in Sun Li's "Lotus Creek" we already begin to feel the existence of this subaltern perspective, but because of the limitations of short stories or because of the time of writing (1945), his narrative still is regulated by the "anti-Japanese united front line," and as a result the class discourse did not clearly surface.[35] At the same time, the fact that the subaltern perspective is still hidden rather deeply contributed to the story's artistic quality. After 1949,

---

33. John Fitzgerald, *Awakening China: Politics, Culture, and Class in the Nationalist Revolution* (Stanford, CA: Stanford University Press, 1996), 316.

34. Qiu Chi, "Yu Chen Bo zhi shu" [Letter to Chen Bo], in *Guwen guanzhi xinbian* [New edition of the best of classical literature], ed. Qian Bocheng (Shanghai: Shanghai Guji Chubanshe, 1988). Tr.: Qiu Chi is known in studies of ancient Chinese literature as a landscape writer. Here Cai is following Karatani in marking landscape as a conceptual tool rather than a descriptive device.

35. Tr.: The anti-Japanese united front was a political and cultural strategy of Mao's Yan'an period, to unify the country against the Japanese invasion; in this national unity discourse and strategy, class struggle was relegated to the back burner, although never completely ignored. This strategy is clearly indicated in Mao Zedong's 1942 lectures, "Talks at the Yan'an Forum on Art and Literature." This item is cited in the bibliography as Mao Tse-tung, "Talks at the Yenan Forum on Literature and Art," in *Selected Works of Mao Tse-tung* (Peking: Foreign Language Press, 1965), 3:86.

class discourse began to dominate cultural and political strategy, including in the renarration of revolutionary history. By then, the local landscape had to be presented anew from a class perspective. We can now see that, for example, in Sun's *Stormy Years*, there is the following landscape description: "In the due north of the village there was a large mausoleum complete with a wall and a courtyard. At the left side were residences, three courtyards one after another . . . all painted in a greyish color. Seen from a distance, it looked like an evil mountain. On the right was a big yard along which were farmhands' rooms, animal barns."[36] This landscape consists, on one side, of "farmhands' rooms" and, on the other side, of the landlord's residence that looks like an "evil mountain." This differentiation is due to the fact that the "large mausoleum" belongs to the landlord, Big Blind Tian, who, "at the time, . . . owns three to four large plots of fertile land worked by four or five long-term farmhands."[37] This type of landscape narrative is clearly filled with the demand for class discourse. But in this kind of narrative, what really needs to be accomplished is an integration of national and class discourses. That is to say, the enemy of the nation must at the same time be the class enemy; or, put differently, the class enemy inevitably becomes the enemy of the nation. For this reason, a relatively common narrative model is that this kind of enemy has a bloody history of suppressing peasants or being anticommunist, and during the national war of course naturally collaborated with the [Japanese] invaders. No matter whether in *Stormy Years* or other similar stories, such as Liang Bin's *Keep the Red Flag Flying* (*Hongqi pu*) or *Spreading the Fire* (*Bo huo ji*), this narrative mode was resolutely implemented. And for this reason, in anti-Japanese war–themed stories, the description of the invader is usually not at all complex. It is usually collaborators or [native] traitors who receive more narrative attention, and, as a general rule, they all have the dual identity of being enemies of the nation and class enemies as well.

As soon as one encounters this kind of landscape treatment, intrusion/destruction pertains not only to the nation but also to class. For example, in *Spreading the Fire*, Liang Bin writes of a thousand-li dyke:

> The crops were covered in dew, on the grass tips were drops of moisture, the dyke embankment was filled with little red and white flowers. . . . The water buffalo ate his way along the dyke embankment, all the way to the well in the east of the village, where the thousand-li dyke took a sharp turn.

---

36. Sun Li, *Stormy Years*, 6–7.
37. Ibid., 8.

Yan Ping felt tired; she ran to the top of the embankment and looked along the river to the east, across the red horizon, and glimmering on the surface was a red lake of fire. The cottony clouds in the sky seemed multicolored. She felt happy so she ran to the dyke, leaping up and calling in a high voice: "Chunlan, Chunlan, come!" Chunlan tied the water buffalo's rope to a tree and climbed up, saying: "What are you up to? What happened?" Yan Ping pointed to the river and then to the sky, and said: "Look at how beautiful this is!"[38]

Later, this kind of landscape is destroyed because of the intrusion of [the landlord] Li Decai. Clearly, in *Keep the Red Flag Flying* and its sequel, *Spreading the Fire*, the father Feng Laolan, along with his son and the murderers Lao Shantou, Li Decai, and others, are exactly the kind of intruding antisocial forces of which Meng Yue speaks. Yet at another level, national discourse simultaneously enters this narrative of the local scene as the Japanese invade: the Japanese provide an even larger force of intrusion/destruction into the landscape. For this reason, the peasant revolution in central Hebei Province during the 1930s had a dual implication: it was a class revolution, and at the same time, it was a national revolution. This implies that the landlord class already is incapable of leading the national revolution and even has already become an enemy of the nation. In this way, the narrative of local landscape was supported by both class and national discourses.

In the realm of national discourse, local landscape is often transformed into native soil; and in the realm of class discourse, this landscape indicates the people; while in the folk ethical order, landscape more often than not implies some sort of rural ideal. In the course of the Chinese revolution, these three narratives were effectively unified into one, forming the basis of a certain imagined vision. This vision was rooted in China's rural society, contributing to the rendering of land as the core of the revolutionary formation. For example, in *Keep the Red Flag Flying* the treasured land of Yan Zhihe's family constitutes one important narrative plot in the story: "The soil here was black, with a fresh, rich tang. It raised fine crops, thanks to the work grand dad had put into it. He had tilled it, handled it, trampled it. Now grand dad had gone, but left it to his children. Father had tilled it, Yuntao had tilled it, and now Jiangtao was tilling it."[39] Inherent in this landscape is some sort of common

---

38. Liang Bin, *Bo huo ji* [Spreading the fire] (Tianjin: Baihua Wenyi Chubanshe, 1963), 40–41.
39. Liang Bin, *Keep the Red Flag Flying*, trans. Gladys Yang (Beijing: Foreign Language Press, 1961), 70.

feeling of blood relations between peasant and land; for this reason, when writers turned the great land into a symbolic representation of the national-state, they had to keep the peasants in mind. It is also for this reason that China's land revolution [of the 1940s and 1950s] was not only supported by objective peasant interests, but also was supported by the rural ideals of the peasants themselves.

By the same token, the Chinese revolution, including class discourse, was composed of many complex elements, and revolutionary historical novels often mix together a number of different discursive sources. For example, in *Keep the Red Flag Flying*, there is the following landscape narrative:

> He leaned closer to Chunlan, whose great black eyes were gazing at him tenderly. At this time in her life a girl feels unutterably happy. Chunlan was no longer lonely when she worked. Her eyes were laughing all day; her lips were curving in a perpetual smile. Her heart was like a full moon surrounded by countless stars in the boundless sky, looking down on the world and finding all in it lovely. As she sewed alone in the melon field, she would lean back and think of the time when the revolution would succeed and the forces of darkness in the village would be overthrown. She and Yuntao would be married then. They could do as they pleased and talk all day long as they tended the pear trees together.[40]

This type of man sows/woman weaves life scenario clearly evokes certain rural ideals. But more important, it also had received legitimating support from the May Fourth [1920s] enlightenment discourse (such as free love, free marriage) while also garnering a guarantee for the promise of happiness fulfilled from the revolution ("when the revolution is successful, the evil forces in the village will be overthrown").[41] We can also see how successfully the modern imaginary incorporated local village ideals. In short, in the narrative of local landscape, the Chinese revolution effectively assimilated multiple discursive sources. At the same time, it rediscovered the local even as it also completed the relational interaction between the duality, national/local.

Yet there is a danger concealed in these kinds of narratives. If we say that the treasured land used to analogize the legitimacy of China's (land) revo-

---

40. Ibid., 121.

41. Tr.: Here Cai is making clear that certain revolutionary narratives were continuations of, rather than departures from, May Fourth traditions. This is a counterargument to a certain prominent strand in literary analysis that claims Maoism is a rupture with May Fourth enlightenment ideals.

lution, then how can we grasp anew the 1950s agricultural cooperatives movement? If we say that rural ideals had been effectively absorbed into political discourse, then how might we understand Mao Zedong's proposition that the small peasant economy and its associated ideology had to be transformed along with corresponding political practices? Clearly, socialism in China was not some determinate or static notion, but rather a long revolutionary process. Moreover, in this process, the Chinese revolution never stopped presenting its own negation and hence exhibiting its associated special characteristic, which was permanent revolution.

The socialist reeducation (*gaizao*) movement in the 1950s pointed not merely to intellectuals but also to peasants; it did not point only to urban areas but also to the expanse of rural villages. If we say that the local landscape had been rooted in certain rural ideals, then at this time, as socialism was taking new steps forward, the narratives of this local landscape encountered new obstacles. At this point, precisely the local landscape that had the natural economy as its main content became the target of revolutionary transformation. The previously concealed new citizens or the reeducation of national character undertaken after 1949 were introduced as important elements of national knowledge or modern knowledge and were mobilized to vigorously support the revolutionary experiments in socialist transformation. In this discursive context, the local simultaneously became the target of national transformation; in some sense the local was to be named anew by the nation. For this reason, the local landscape returned to its early role in revolutionary narrative. It was no longer beautiful, flourishing, and self-sufficient but rather was represented as containing abject poverty, coldness, and ignorance. It was only in the landscape narratives of this type of local that socialist transformation and revolutionary experiments could gain legitimacy and support. If we say that in revolutionary historical novels the local landscape is composed of a number of discursive sources, and to some extent the narratives can appear a little tentative, then in the discourse of socialist reeducation this local landscape was fundamentally rewritten.

For example, in Chen Dengke's *Feng lei* (*Storm*) we read the following depiction of landscape:

> The more the snowflakes in the sky fluttered the bigger they got; the wind blew harder and harder. Soon there was more than a half inch of snow on the ground. It was cold; the roads were slippery, and it was hard to take one step after another. He bowed his head, faced the wind, and in one effort,

walked five or six li in these conditions. . . . The thick snow did not fall directly upon his head, but rather came from the left and pelted his neck. . . . He looked around at and saw in front of him a blanket of white, not one house. Seeing a broken wall nearby, he walked over there to shelter away from the snow a bit, smoke a cigarette, rest his legs and then proceed.[42]

This "he" is the novel's protagonist, Zhu Yongkang, who has been demobilized from the military and is being transferred to the north Anhui region. Before he left the military, the [Communist] Party commissar had said to him: "Our Party's current task in the villages is primarily to lead the peasants onto the path of rural cooperatives to build the new socialist villages."[43] What this suggests is that, in the design of the new socialist village, the [previously understood] local would correspondingly be treated as an old village. This old village is naturally the "blanket of white" in front of his eyes, with "not one house." Indeed, in similar novels, what fills the local are landlords, rich peasants and bad elements, middle peasants who dream of getting rich, cadres whose revolutionary views are corrupted, and so on. Any sort of beautiful natural scene is concealed, and what replaces it is a kind of wasteland such as the [empty] grasslands in *Feng lei* or the terminal southern mountain in Liu Qing's *The Builders*. Human affairs and nature all accordingly compose the landscape narrative in these novels, and such narratives are precisely conditioned by the revolutionary practices of socialist transformation and remolding.

II. The Local in Narratives of Mobilization and Reeducation [*Gaizao*]

In 1949, with the success of the Chinese revolution, a reconstruction of the modern nation-state began along with large-scale socialist transformation and modernization development. A number of related imaginations about China's future gradually started to emerge in the works of Party and state leaders; these informed a number of official documents so as to guide and constrain the numerous concrete projects of national revolution and development. Among these, the most pronounced was the socialist transformation movement. This transformation continued the demand for modernity begun in the late Qing period; for this reason it was supported at the time by a majority of intellectuals.

42. Chen Dengke, *Feng lei* [Storm] (Beijing: Zhongguo Qingnian Chubanshe, 1964), 17.
43. Ibid., 23.

In the course of this movement, rural society and the rural ideals rooted within it that had supported the Chinese revolution now became the targets of socialist transformation. In a different sense, this meant that the nation started to regulate the local and to appropriate it vigorously into its own imaginary. The cooperative movement was the concrete social practice of this transformation, although a detailed consideration of this movement is outside the scope of my present discussion. What I want to focus on here is the imaginary represented in contemporary literature against the cooperative movement backdrop; how this imaginary was specifically developed in textual terms; and, of course, the various forces constraining this imaginary and the ways in which these forces intervened in local social narratives.

Mark Selden, in looking back at the history of the process of China's land revolution, has the following discussion: "Mao Tse-tung [Mao Zedong], who stood at the pinnacle of party leadership from 1935, had long favored a relatively moderate land policy stressing preservation of the interests of middle and (at times) even rich peasants and was himself criticized for rightism throughout the Kiangsi [Jiangxi] period. With the memory of the defeat in Kiangsi still fresh, Mao sought a land policy which would elicit broad peasant support with a minimum of dislocation in the primitive rural economy upon which the Red Army depended for supplies and the peasantry for its livelihood."[44] The primitive peasant economy precisely refers to the traditional natural economic formation; it is the primary material of which the local is composed, at the same time as it also supported the local power structure and cultural formation. For this reason, we could also say that China's land revolution was an incomplete expression of modernity. The flexible and ever-changing revolutionary transformative strategy in actuality was another expressive form of the united front. This expressive form also to some extent determined the conciliation between the Chinese revolution and the local.[45] This conciliation preserved not only the local natural economic formation, but also the village ethical order and customary outlooks, along with their deeply embedded rural ideals. What all of this generated was precisely the characteristic multiplicity of revolutionary culture of which Meng Yue writes.

Yet the conciliation originating from the flexibility and changeability of revolutionary strategy could not completely replace the ultimate political de-

---

44. Mark Selden, *China in Revolution: The Yenan Way Revisited* (New York: M. E. Sharpe, 1995), 80.
45. Ibid., 21–22.

mands of the Chinese revolution, including the demand for modernity embedded within it. One such conflict, for example, was that which emerged between the socialization of mass production [in urban industry] and the traditional small peasant economy. At the same time and in addition, it was precisely this flexible and changeable conciliatory strategy of the Chinese revolution that not only produced the real need for the permanent revolution, but also lent both urgency and difficulty to the efforts at socialist transformation.

For this reason, in 1951, in the course of the Party debates about the Shanxi peasant cooperatives, even though [Vice Chairman] Liu Shaoqi maintained a consistently oppositional view [to that of Mao Zedong], he was not opposed to the socialist transformation in its entirety. To the contrary, the debate was largely limited to the questions of timing and strategy.[46] Actually, the cooperative movement was a continuation from the Yan'an period, when Mao Zedong noted in a speech: "Among the peasant masses a system of individual economy has prevailed for thousands of years, with each family or household forming a productive unit. This scattered, individual form of production is the economic foundation of feudal rule and keeps the peasants in perpetual poverty. The only way to change it is gradual collectivization, and the only way to bring about collectivization, according to Lenin, is through co-operatives."[47] By the same token, another major reason for [majority] support for the cooperative movement stemmed from the fact that, after the land reform, there emerged a new differentiation between rich and poor and from the consequent deep concern over the possibility of the emergence of a new exploitative class along with its ideology. For example, at the end of 1950, the Northeast Region Central Party Strategy Research Bureau in Heilongjiang Province carried out an investigation in three villages in Baicheng County. The investigation indicated that middle peasants already comprised 63.8 percent of the three villages' households and 67.3 percent of the population; they possessed 87.5 percent of the farm animals and 75.7 percent of the land. From this it was apparent that middle peasants had become the majority of the peasantry and played a very important role in rural production. At the same time, the purchase and sale of village land along with the phenomenon of hired labor had reemerged, such as in Tiande District of Shulan County in Jilin Province, where in 1950, 14.67 *xiang* [1 *xiang* equals 15 *mu*; 1 *mu* equals roughly 1.6 acres] of land changed

46. Luo Pinghan, *Dangdai lishi wenti zhaji* [Records of contemporary historical issues] (Guilin: Guangxi Shida Chubanshe, 2006), 2:35.

47. Mao Tse-tung [Mao Zedong], "Get Organized!," in *Selected Works of Mao Tse-tung* (Peking: Foreign Language Press, 1965), 3:165.

hands, of which 73.2 percent was sold by hired laborers, 12.3 percent by poor peasants, and 15.5 percent by middle peasants. The reasons for selling land were numerous: some peasants moved back to China proper [inside the Great Wall]; some sold because of a lack of productive materials and labor to cultivate land; some sold inferior land in exchange for better land. New rich peasants also began to appear. In the aforementioned three villages in Jilin Province, 4 rich peasant households emerged, comprising 0.5 percent of the 581 total households.[48] In this way, "the sprouts of land concentration and rich-poor differentiation emerged, leading people to wonder about the following question: after the overthrow of feudalism in the countryside, could it be that a new exploitative class would emerge? The result of the poor peasants becoming middle peasants might further lead to rich-middle peasants becoming (new) rich peasants. Should this development be permitted or restrained? This became a major problem of the latter part of the land reform process."[49]

The question of how to evaluate this type of rich-poor peasant emergence [in 1950] did not receive a unified answer from within the Party at the time.[50] In his discussion of the [earlier] Yan'an cooperative movement, Selden has a passage that could perhaps draw our attention in this regard. He says: "One of the ironic consequences of the land revolution in [the Communist base area of] Shen-Kan-Ning was to reinforce the pattern of autonomous family farming and to reduce the traditional practice of cooperative labor."[51] This relative disincentive to cooperation did not directly lead to the cooperative movement; however, the so-called mutual support and mutual aid [of the Yan'an period] is in fact a very important narrative theme of novels that deal with the [1950s] cooperative movement, and it constitutes an important ethical resource within those narratives. Another passage of Selden's is also important. After his analysis of the mutual aid movement in the Yan'an period, he explains:

> In Mao's vision, the cooperative served as an intermediary between the state and the family. Rather than the government directly taxing the peasantry, cooperatives would eventually contribute assessments for their members; when funds were required locally for schools or the militia, the

---

48. Luo, *Dangdai lishi wenti zhaji*, 2:15. Tr.: Please note that the percentages do not quite add up here, but we are not correcting Luo's math.

49. Ibid.

50. See ibid., 2:37; Bo Yibo, *Ruogan zhongda juece yu shijian de huigu* [Remembering certain major decisions and events], 2 vols. (Beijing: Zhongyang Dangxiao Chubanshe), 1:198.

51. Selden, *China in Revolution*, 187.

government would avoid direct imposition on the people inasmuch as funds could be channeled from the cooperative surplus. The potential of the mutual-aid teams and cooperatives lay in providing effective popular channels for directing the economic, social, political, and military life of the community. The locus of the power and the key to rural development lay neither in the individual family farm nor in state management but in the cooperative community.[52]

Since the late Qing, because of the retreat of the gentry there was in reality a rupture in certain aspects of the national/local power structure. Mao's whole discussion of the cooperative movement actually was bound up with his plans for the future of China's political structure and methods of governing the local. In actuality, the large-scale cooperative movement of the 1950s and the people's communes that followed can be seen as different stages of the realization of Mao's political plans. Clearly, the cooperative movement was composed of many complex elements and sources: direct and indirect, obvious and concealed, economic (mode of production) and ideological reasons (to eliminate differentiations), ethical (mutual aid) and political (power structure). In some sense we could also say that these four aspects actually comprised the entirety of the special political characteristics of the socialist transformation. They also comprise four major narrative themes in contemporary literature. Naturally, there were always conflicts—sometimes paradoxical ones—within and among these four themes. Yet by the same token, the cooperative movement was a concentrated expression of the political characteristics of the socialist transformation. This seems to explain why contemporary literature paid it continuous attention. This movement already constituted a sort of imagined political community, and for this reason in the narrative sense, it transcended the experiential level to articulate intellectuals' imaginary of the nation/future.

Despite this, I do not entirely agree [with much contemporary scholarship] that we should see the seventeen years of literature as a mere mouthpiece of politics. Despite the fact that the literature of this period exhibited a high level of political content, it also was a continuation of the May Fourth political imaginary, albeit with added narrative aspects of socialism. For example, at the end of March 1951, the Party Committee of Changzhi Prefecture in Shanxi Province held a regional meeting for representatives of mutual aid teams; there they discussed issues regarding the establishment of coop-

---

52. Ibid., 196.

eratives. At the meeting, Party Secretary of Changzhi Prefecture Wang Jian reported upon the cooperatives' experiments: "The general policy direction should be to unify cooperative organization with new scientific techniques. . . . To overcome the current dispersed mood of peasant thinking and to raise and transform peasant producers to a higher level of progress; in addition, to allow us to move another step along the path of peasant collectivization, the foundation of our current organizational work should be to experimentally put in place a type of form that is higher than the current mutual aid groups—this would be rural production cooperatives."[53] This is a typical expression of modern intellectuals' imaginary.

Moreover, we can see that this expression manifests many similarities with the imaginaries of certain [earlier] intellectuals, such as Liang Shuming. Later in his life, Liang thought that China lacked two things; one was group organization, and the other was scientific technology. Since the May Fourth [New Culture Movement], science and democracy were one aspect [of intellectual concern], while organization and science were another. In modern China's historical practices, these two aspects consistently informed one another. For this reason, while seeing the ways in which politics guides literature, we should also recognize that behind intellectuals' identification with politics, there lies an important preexisting conceptual [theoretical] support. Indeed, these imaginaries already developed from within the imaginary indicated by the slogan of the peasant cooperatives themselves for large-scale production methods: the imaginary of elimination of differences, of mutual aid, and of political structure. In relevant literary works, these have all been assimilated into what I call the mobilization-transformation narrative.

This mobilization-transformation narrative structure was launched by land reform novels [of the late 1940s] (for example, Ding Ling's *The Sun Shines over the Sangan River*), and in the literature narrating the 1950s cooperative movement this narrative structure not only is extended but also becomes one of the more important compositional forms. Noting this may be important: it might imply the importance of the masses possessing truth, and it might imply that the so-called mobilization-transformation narrative structure has been hidden within the support [for land policies] lent by mass legitimacy.

Moreover, this mobilization-transformation narrative structure precisely mirrors the contemporary Chinese social-political structure. In their discussion of Chinese politics, James Townsend and Brantly Womack have expressed

---

53. Quoted in Luo, *Dangdai lishi wenti zhaji*, 2:29.

doubt about the focus in Chinese studies on the model of centralized power in China: "The theories (of totalitarianism) developed largely from studies of Nazi Germany and Stalinist Russia, leaving the Soviet Union as the principal model of totalitarianism in the postwar years." However, one reason for this reluctance [their doubt about using the totalitarian model to assess China] was the emergence of important discrepancies between the People's Republic and the model. In Townsend and Womack's view, in China, Mao's leadership of the Chinese Communist Party was not comparable to the dictatorship of Hitler or Stalin, as controls [in China] rested much more on psychological pressures of indoctrination and persuasion and on close personal supervision by cadres rather than on police terror; central bureaucratic planning and controls were less salient, especially after 1957, than in the Soviet Union. Moreover, theorists of totalitarianism had identified the phenomenon as a reaction against or perversion of the modern Western state, one that "could have arisen only within the context of mass democracy and modern technology." While the Chinese revolution occurred in such a context in the global sense, it was not directly aligned with this particular historical pattern.[54]

Even though Townsend and Womack tend to sound idealistic at times and we actually do find some characteristics of centralized power in Chinese politics, nevertheless in general, I am still interested in the alternative model through which Townsend and Womack introduce Chinese politics, which places China in the context of developing countries.[55] While it appears that Townsend and Womack do not completely agree with assimilating research on China into the "developing countries" model, they also do not completely neglect the concept of mobilization. In their Chinese model narrative, they emphasize the multiplicity of the Chinese political system and its changes but also give political mobilization a very large share of their attention. Actually, mobilization and transformation precisely coincide in their emergence within Chinese literary textual sources as core concepts, so even if we do not treat systems of mobilization as China's normal social model, it is nevertheless true that this model effectively became a literary narrative structure.[56]

Among novels of this variety, Zhao Shuli's *Sanliwan Village* (*Sanli wan*) is perhaps an exception. In this work, we cannot see the same narrative structure

---

54. James R. Townsend and Brantly Womack, *Politics in China*, 3rd ed. (Boston: Little, Brown, 1986), 17–18.

55. Tr.: We have omitted the Townsend and Womack quote here, as it appears in chapter 2, in a more appropriate setting.

56. For more on mobilization, see chapter 2.

as is evident in *The Builders* or [Zhou Libo's] *Great Changes in the Mountain Village* (*Shanxiang jubian*). But the fact of the matter is Zhao uses an even more internalized mode to narrate the story of cooperatives. For this reason, the novel begins with the following abbreviated scene: "At the southeast tip of Sanliwan Village are two connected courtyards known as Flagstaff Compound."[57] In the author's well-paced telling, we begin to understand that the thing called a flagstaff was not something that "every landlord . . . could fix . . . up, though. You had to be a 'provincial graduate' at least."[58] And "Sanliwan's provincial graduate was one of the Liu family, but no one knows how long ago he lived. Liu Lao-wu, who worked for the Japanese, did say the Liu family records showed that the provincial graduate came eleven generations before him. But no one else in the family had seen those records, and after Liu was seized and shot for helping the enemy no further interest was taken in that matter."[59]

This kind of narrative can easily remind us of what Meng Yue identifies as a "reading of history." According to her analysis, starting with the May Fourth generation, intellectuals' "reading of history" became a common "socially symbolic behavior": "the 'readers of history' and their relationship to the history that they manage to produce through reading is very much like the relationship between writers of new literature (*xin wenxue*) [May Fourth literature] and their works. It seems that it is this very relationship that constitutes the new literature's most important tradition: fictional narratives were really always narration 'about' history and 'about' the survival of the nation."[60] Yet, as a history reader, Zhao Shuli's purpose is to make this history hang in midair (as in "but other than Liu Lao-wu, no one in the Liu family has seen the genealogy album").

As here exemplified and generally speaking, history or legend usually supports the power structure of the local, or even constitutes one of the more important elements of local knowledge. For this reason, the unsettledness (or deconstruction) of history implies some sort of liberation for the local from a certain power structure or its narrative. It also contains the political implications of doing away with superstitions. In Zhao's novel, this liberated local

---

57. Zhao Shuli, *Sanliwan Village*, trans. Gladys Yang (Peking: Foreign Language Press, 1957), 5.

58. Tr.: Provincial graduate is one of the ranks in the imperial civil-service examination system, which was discontinued in 1905.

59. Zhao, *Sanliwan Village*, 5.

60. Meng Yue, *Lishi yu xushu* [History and narrative] (Xi'an: Shaanxi Renmin Jiaoyu Chubanshe, 1988), 18.

forms a space urgently in need of reorganization and even renaming. To wit: "After [old Liu was shot]—this happened in 1942—the county government let the village take over [Liu's compound], and most of the rooms became offices: the village office, the local militia, the primary school, the peasants' night school, the reading room, the club, and the supply and marketing co-op all moved into the two courtyards."[61] The renaming of space here is extremely important. In his memoirs of the land reform, Du Runsheng writes:

> In the past, when we spoke of the importance of land reform, we tended to emphasize land distribution. In fact, in rural China, there wasn't a lot of land to be distributed. The land occupied by landlords and rich peasants perhaps was about 50 percent of the total, not the rumored 70–80 percent. Recently, several scholars have reexamined the investigations of land since the Republican era and have discovered that landlords occupied less than 40 percent of the land with a population of 5 percent of the total. The results of the reform were that peasants received an insignificant plot of taxed land.[62]

If this indeed was the case, then, what was the meaning of the land reform? Du believes that "because there was a scarcity of land, there was the need to fulfill the peasants' desire for land and to break the landlords' monopoly on land and to stimulate the development of a commodity economy so as to prepare the conditions for national industrialization. This cannot be underestimated." Yet an even more important meaning resides in the following:

> The Chinese Communist Party's land reform was not a political favor bestowed [upon the peasants], but rather was designed to overthrow feudal ruling power and to install a ruling force dominated by the villages' peasant masses so as to raise the self-consciousness of the peasants, instigate class struggle, and promote the self-liberation of the peasant masses so as to realize the goal of "land back to the family." This demand was unlike the "dynastic cycle" of yore, or any previous imperial or official method of bestowal, such as "evening out land, containing the rich and powerful," or promoting some kind of "conciliatory policy." Rather, [land reform] was intended to destroy the old reactionary rule and substitute for it mass rule;

---

61. Zhao, *Sanliwan Village*, 6.
62. Du Runsheng, *Du Runsheng zishu: Zhongguo nongcun tizhi biange zhongda juece jishi* [Du Runsheng remembers: Memories of the important decisions on China's village structural transformation] (Beijing: Renmin Chubanshe, 2005), 18–20.

to overthrow root and branch the old village order so as to allow China to complete its twentieth-century task: "reorganizing the grass roots" so as to better integrate the upper and lower levels of society as well as the central and the local [governments]. This allowed the central government to obtain a huge organizational mobilizing capacity and [gave it], among other advantages, the ability to unify and pass down political directives. With regard to an agrarian nation that had previously been seen as a "plate of loose sand," the significance of all this was enormous.[63]

In particular with regard to politics, we can certainly see the cooperative movement [of the mid-1950s] as a continuation of the land reform [of the early 1950s], as a "reorganization of the grass roots." This relates back to Zhao Shuli. In describing the space of the flagstaff courtyard, Zhao specifically notes: "In 1951, the village established a rural production cooperative; meetings and bookkeeping all happened in this compound, as if it had become the cooperative's offices."[64] In addition, the politics of Sanliwan Village also unfold and are completed in this socially symbolic space.

For his part, even Liang on the one hand was critical of the cooperative movement, saying for example that "there was too much interference of higher-level cadres in the form of commandism"; yet, on the other hand, he praised highly the political implications inherent in this movement: "Previously, the Chinese peasantry was extremely disorganized and scattered, with everyone looking out only for himself and his own family. There was no organization. . . . Now the peasantry is truly organized. . . . Everything is completely organized. Economics and politics are joined together. The People's Commune is by no means purely an economic organization."[65] For these and other reasons, peasants' organizing themselves is primarily a political act, and the mobilization-transformation sociopolitical structure inaugurated through land reform and continued in the cooperative movement had to rely upon the organizational system of this power. This vision consolidated and controlled the political imaginary and writings of contemporary Chinese authors from 1949 to 1966.

In this regard, it is not hard to understand why, in these types of novels, scenes of conflict often are written around the issue of cadres. In *Sanliwan Village*, conflict is established and centered on the village leader, Fan Deng-

63. Ibid., 18–20.
64. Zhao, *Sanliwan Village*, 2. Tr.: Gladys Yang's English translation is missing this passage. We have translated it from the Chinese provided in Cai's text.
65. Shuming Liang and Guy S. Alitto, *Has Man a Future? Dialogues with the Last Confucian* (Berlin: Springer, 2013), 195–96.

gao, and in Liu Qing's *The Builders*, this image of conflict is embodied in the director of lower Fort Village, Guo Zhenshan. Both Fan and Guo ascended the stage of village government in the wake of the land reform, yet both subsequently become obstacles to the progress of the village cooperative movement. We should say that in comparison with later publications like [Hao Ran's] *Sunny Days* (*Yanyang tian*), Zhao's and Liu's treatment of such characters is still quite mild: Fan hires labor to peddle goods, engaging in a type of village commercial activity; Guo's family has some members working "on the outside" while "others can still tend the land," desiring to be rich like the middle-rich peasant Guo Shifu.[66] This is unlike the conflict of Xiao Changchun and Ma Zhiyue in Hao Ran's writing, which is defined as an intra-Party class struggle. However, Zhao and Liu still place Fan and Guo in the realm of the spontaneous eruption of capitalism in the villages and see them as exemplifying a type of Party member who engages in unacceptable individualistic behavior. Liu's attitude seems more radical, as he locates Guo with the rich peasant Yao Shijie.

The characterizations of Fan and Guo were based on some historical evidence. In the beginning of the 1950s, after the land reform in villages in the Northeast, there emerged some evidence of Party members' hiring workers to get rich. Surrounding the question of whether Party members should get rich or not, there were internal debates in the Party; all theoretical questions were resolved in the wake of Mao's clarification of his attitude.[67] To be sure, these were ideological issues. But in the narratives of *Sanliwan Village* and *The Builders*, it is represented more as an issue of village political power. Only when we place this kind of contradiction in the historical context of "reorganizing the grass roots" can we understand it most fully. In other words, what the narratives regarding the conflicts and contradictions surrounding Fan and Guo ultimately address are issues concerning the reorganization of the rural political structure after land reform.

After such a reorganization of power, the peasant cooperatives (including the subsequent communes) are no longer merely political organizations, but rather are a new model for village political structures. This model was effectively assimilated into the system of mobilization and began to undertake the

66. Liu Ching [Liu Qing], *The Builders*, trans. Sidney Shapiro (Peking: Foreign Language Press, 1964), 41.
67. For example, at the time Liu Shaoqi said: "Those who think that Party members cannot exploit is a form of dogmatism." It was said that Mao's "face was livid so dissatisfied was he with Liu's statement" (Luo, *Dangdai lishi wenti zhaji*, 21).

task of national organizing and mobilizing for modernization. For this reason, in narratives of rural cooperatives, we can also see how the concept of the nation forcefully intrudes into the local and helps complete the transformation of the local, which entails the constructing of a new socialist village. These new villages are no longer self-sustaining local spaces of their own but an effective element of the nation-state.

To be sure, in its representation of reality, this literature intentionally or unintentionally avoids or glosses over some harsh realities, such as how, from 1949 to 1966, Chinese villages became the targets of the extraction of resources for national modernization. There were certainly elements of political control, but by the same token, we should still recognize that rural cooperatives (including the subsequent people's communes) became the mediator between individual peasant families and the state. This mediation effectively moderated any direct conflict between the interests of individual peasant families and the state, which perhaps is another reason for the glossing of reality.

In these narratives, additionally, the nation in effect shoulders the responsibility of the symbolic task of [imagining] some sort of futurity. In symbolic terms, by way of narrative transformation, rural cooperatives become a kind of beckoning structure: a type of futurity that beckons people. For this reason, in the narratives of mobilization-transformation, the act of organization is a particularly important concept. This concept is not only relevant to village power structures, but it also indicates a mode of production and even a type of ethical attitude.

Ultimately, one of the problems rural cooperatives needed to solve was how to move from the conditions of a small-scale peasant economy toward large-scale modernized rural production. In some novels, this large-scale modernized rural production appears in some sort of mechanized (scientifically technologized) fashion. However, this production form is not often seen in the novels that specifically narrate rural cooperatives; of course, this was due to the reality of most rural villages in China.[68] For this reason, at that time this production formation more often appeared in a different type of novel,

68. The foundation for this was Liu Shaoqi's directive: "first nationalize industry, then collectivize agriculture." That is, collectivization needed to await machines, since without machines, it was not suitable. Rural collectivization needed to be established on the premise of industrialization offering machines. And Bo Yibo, wrote an article in the June 29, 1951, *People's Daily* titled "Strengthen Party political work in the rural areas—in memory of the 30th anniversary of the Chinese Communist Party," in which he emphasized that without large and strong nationalized industry, there was no possibility for a full scope of rural collectivization. See Luo, *Dangdai lishi wenti zhaji*, 33–34.

such as Bai Wei's *Reclaiming Wasteland* (*Kenhuang qu*) or Xu Huaizhong's *We Sow Our Love* (*Women bozhong aiqing*). These novels are situated on [state] farms or farming stations. In some sense we could say that they offer a vision of a meaningful other (future) to China's village (now). Actually, they also became a modernized goal beckoning to the rural cooperative movement.

In those novels that narrate rural cooperatives, the modernized mode of rural production is usually transformed into forms of collective labor, which in turn are highly praised. On the title page of *The Builders*, Liu Qing cites a rural saying: "Household property should be divided among the brothers; labor should unite villagers." Labor, needless to say, is collectivized labor. What is interesting is that in these novels, different types of natural formations emerge one after another, such as the green grass lake of *Storm* or the Terminal Southern Mountain of *The Builders*, and so on. Nature is that which has to be subjugated and transformed. Marshal Berman identifies such subjugation and transformation of the natural world as an attitude characteristic of modernity.[69] But in China this attitude did not lead to [what Berman calls] the trend in modernity of "individuals daring to find their individuality"; rather, it was appropriated by the ideals of socialist collectivity. For this reason, in *Feng lei*, each time Ren Weiqun seeks to transform the green grass lake through his own efforts, he runs into all sorts of obstacles; whereas in *The Builders*, Liang Shengbao and Gao Zengfu, through the deployment of collective labor, successfully transform Terminal Southern Mountain into a living and productive resource. Perhaps this organized and collective labor does not quite exhibit modernized agricultural production forms; however, this formation reveals a possible path toward a modern imaginary and garners great enthusiasm.

In *Sanliwan Village*, the twenty-fifth chapter is titled "Three Pictures." There are captions for all three pictures: the first is "today's Sanliwan Village," the second is "Sanliwan Village next year," and the third is "Sanliwan Village under socialism." Under the latter [third picture] we see this description:

> The hills and Sandy Creek were thickly wooded now, and a little way up the hillside, not far from the flats, was a highway running north from the village. There were trucks on this road, and telegraph-poles beside it. Trees grew inside and all around the village, but nestling among them you could glimpse new rooftops. The farming now was on a much larger scale—on half [of] the Lower Flats waved golden wheat, while the other half was di-

---

69. Marshall Berman, *All That Is Solid Melts into Air* (New York: Penguin, 1988), 1.

vided into two parts, one for autumn crops, one for vegetables. The Upper Flats were given over to autumn crops. In the wheat field on the Lower Flats combines were reaping the wheat, a cultivator was weeding the Upper Flats.[70]

Zhao's ensuing description is perhaps even more important: "All conditions are similar to those of the state farms."

Actually, almost all of these novels locate their narratives of the villages and village cooperative movements in the discursive realm of state modernization. That is to say, the local in reality has already been assimilated into the national imaginary of modernity. For example, in *Storm*, Chunfang is depicted as follows:

> Chungfang had not been to the city already for a long time. As soon as she got there, she was terribly surprised at all of the great leaps of development! Before Liberation, what this city had been like, she had no idea because at that time she'd never been to the city. After Liberation, the first time she'd entered the city she was unclear about where the streets were and she didn't see what the buildings were like; all she'd seen was the broken pieces of things all over and bomb craters in the ground. The second time she'd entered the city, she saw buildings and roads being built on the land where she had seen bomb craters. The third time she went to the city, she not only saw new buildings but also needed to lift her head to see some soaring chimney stacks.[71]

Once collective labor is situated in this discursive context, the cooperative movement takes on a very important modern significance, a significance that pertains to the future, or an imaginary that is guided by the radical goals of futurism. For this reason, the mode of production of collective labor is perhaps properly seen as signifying a form of utopia. While this imaginary in its own historical context was not fully realized, still we have no right to sneer at the huge enthusiasm for this utopian imaginary that once saturated contemporary Chinese literature.

Inherent in the idea of collective labor is concealed a certain ideological intervention centering on the strong conflict between individual enrichment and collective enrichment, a conflict that has permeated the entirety of con-

70. Zhao, *Sanliwan Village*, 194–95.
71. Chen, *Feng lei*, 283.

temporary Chinese history.[72] However, in the historical and discursive context of the 1950s, if we consider the symbolic significance of the terms *exploitation* and *oppression*—that is to say, the fact that these terms directly sparked the Chinese revolution and became the ultimate purpose of the revolution (to abolish exploitation)—then it is not hard to imagine how the tremendous inertial force of the revolution (the political search for egalitarianism) was extended into the 1950s and determined the imaginary mode of contemporary Chinese literature. This is something known in political science as "leaning to one side." Regardless of how later generations judge it, we should recognize how Chinese authors at the time resolutely maintained their ideals and extended them into their literary narratives. In this historical and discursive context, collective labor as a new form of production was able to offer to the Chinese revolution a mode of practice. This mode of practice, at the same time, was appropriated in contemporary literature to become a huge enthusiasm for utopia. It hence took on an ideological significance.

For example, Liu Qing in *The Builders* describes the following two scenes filled with spatial implications: one revolves around the middle-rich peasant Guo Shifu, who "built a house in front of the tiled courtyard of Sanhetou" where "he would separately invite the artisans, those gift-bearing kinsmen, and those neighbors who assisted [him] to pay their respects in the back courtyard; from there emanated the fragrant scent of stewed and fried pork as well as the strong smell of the fermented wine." The second scene concerns Liang Shengbao and Gao Zengfu, who invited "twenty-odd people who had been long-suffering workers and itinerant workers to gather together and discuss whether or not they could organize themselves." These two scenes are radically different and at the same time they express a certain disquiet. This disquiet discloses an anxiety and unease about the possibility of the reemergence of class divisions in the rural villages. Whether or not Liu's or others' disquiets were exaggerated[73] is a question; yet behind these narrated disquiets is nevertheless a certain ideological legitimacy.

In this narrative of disquiet we can see middle-rich peasants becoming a kind of symbol that signifies a tendency toward becoming rich peasants. What

72. In 1980, with the "production to the household, labor to the household" policy and the attendant dismantling of the people's communes, this conflict was declared resolved; individual wealth became legitimized and supported in state policy. But this is just at the level of social experience; it does not mean that this conflict has been resolved in the discursive realm of the ideological imaginary.

73. Bo has a rather detailed account and memory of this (*Ruogan zhongda juece yu shijian de huigu*, vol. 1).

is interesting is that in these novels middle-rich peasants are not only described as shrewd and capable, but also as selfish, cold, miserly, and so on. I think the real meaning behind various narrative details about those characters resides in the emptying out of the moral legitimacy of the process of becoming rich peasants. What Meng Yue summarizes as those "unpolitical, folk cultural forms and narrative conventions" once again are concealed within political discourse and at the same time provide support for this discourse. That is to say that the behavior of the confused people [who want to become rich] is an affront to the "cultural signifying system of rural ideals" manifested in mutual aid and assistance. This cultural signifying system is at the same time also an ethical signifying system reanimated by collective labor and the rural cooperative movement that supported this form of labor.

Hence, when Liu writes of Liang Shengbao, he usually writes that he is "purely kind and full of sympathy." For example, "Shengbao felt very sympathetic to these hard-up peasants who couldn't even plough unless they worked with others." So he organizes mutual aid teams to go to Terminal Southern Mountain to cut bamboo and "now Shengbao's idea was to switch them to bamboo felling also, and put the needy peasants from all the other wards on to the porters' work. In this way every needy peasant in the village could be given a gainful employment and part of the problem would be solved."[74] In this type of narrative, the rural cooperatives attained a certain ethical legitimacy, which is also rooted in the rural ideals of mutual aid. In other words, Liang Shengbao, "a Communist Party member with a deep sense of responsibility towards assisting the masses in trouble," makes it possible for the rural ideal to be transformed into a modern ideal.

In the mobilization-transformation narrative structure and through these types of cultural, political, ideological, and moral imaginaries, the rural cooperatives attained legitimacy among the villagers along with a huge injection of utopian enthusiasm from them. These imaginaries were appropriated into the entire national modernization construction project, with the local simultaneously integrated into the modern mobilization-transformation program. At the same time, this modern vision was also narrated as a spontaneous demand from the masses. The mobilization-transformation was not narrated as a top-down movement but more as a bottom-up movement of the masses, and it was because of this rural cooperative movement that village politics acquired a modern expression. In this political narrative, the local was assimilated into

74. Liu Ching, *The Builders*, 164.

the national command-implementation structure. This is a quintessentially classical developmentalist mode of narrative.

In some way, the local also often harbored within it the meaning of social group. In [Partha] Chatterjee's view, "it would appear then that Western political theory does not deny the empirical fact that most individuals, even in industrially advanced liberal democracies, lead their lives within an inherited network of social attachments that could be described as community." However, in theories of modernity, "not all communities are worthy of approval in modern political life. In particular, attachments that seem to emphasize the inherited, the primordial, the parochial or the traditional are regarded by most theorists as smacking of conservative and intolerant practices and hence as inimical to the values of modern citizenship." At the same time, they are seen as "a collection of backward *gemeinschaften* lacking the internal dynamic to transform themselves into modern industrial nations."[75] In even more radical types of narratives, such as Wang Wenshi's *Heifeng*, the types of social groups "lacking the internal dynamic to transform themselves into modern industrial nations" are concretely expressed in the figures of backward/conservative peasants. To transform the thinking of these backward/conservative peasants—that is to say, to liberate the local or "conservative and closed" societies from their "primitive, subaltern, or traditional relations of subordination"— one must rely upon certain intruding outside forces. In novels, these forces are often specified as youth. Hence, in Wang's narrative, [the titular character] Heifeng not only implies the future of the local, but this future, because of the "grand forging of steel," is effectively assimilated into the national articulation of modernization. Simultaneously, she shoulders another narrative task, which is to engage in conceptual struggle with conservative/backward elements. In the eyes of her second uncle, Ding Shichang, Heifeng "strives for unconventionality," and once she returns to the countryside, she "spends all day finding this wrong, that problematic, finding bones in the eggs; she organized a wall newspaper, and in her column she made no distinction between old and young, big and small things, all day she just nitpicked away, so that the whole village population was in a constant state of distress." However, Heifeng believes this second uncle of hers "is accustomed to going through the motions of the traditional calendar and calmly goes about tending his crops. She thinks that the mass movement has startled her second uncle out of his

---

75. Chatterjee, "Community in the East," 277–82.

routine and confused him.... This second uncle, who has no thought of the future other than to tend his crops without fail, suffers mightily from not being able to keep up with the demands of the times." He is an "old conservative" and is part of the "faction of retreat."[76]

The backdrop of Heifeng is obviously related to the 1958–61 Great Leap Forward. In the novel, this movement is largely transmitted as an imaginary of national modernization that is also bound up with the dreams, enthusiasms, and future-oriented ideals of the youth. The treatment of youth as a modern force is of course one tradition of modern Chinese literature. It is directly and indirectly related to Liang Qichao's [early twentieth-century] narrative imaginary in "The Young China" ("Shaonian Zhongguo shuo"), while at the same time [it is] related to the particular characteristics of youth as a category. This categorical characteristic includes dedication to radical new ideas along with commitment and loyal devotion to new endeavors. Yet according to Selden's analysis of China's northwestern regions, "veneration of the elderly as well as a predilection for stability contributed to the traditionally low status of youth in China. Among leaders, both in the bureaucracy and the local elite, age was an important determinant of prestige and power."[77] The revolution first liberated those lowly Chinese youth, and it did so by turning them into significant forces of the Chinese revolution. In novels, they are represented as mediators who bring modernity to the local.[78]

At the same time, we have no evidence for the claim that the definition and narration of youth in the 1949–66 years is informed by the theory of evolution. To the contrary, in practically every novel that touches upon this theme, youth is placed in the progressive/conservative narrative frame. And what differentiates progressive from conservative is neither individual personality nor the level of cultural cultivation. An even more important force that figured in the representation of youth is something we may identify as education. Wang writes of Heifeng: "From when she could stand to when she could walk and run, she'd not once left her mother's side.... Up until around ten years of age, if she did not have her mother or father nearby, Heifeng wouldn't have dared to leave the village to play or do anything." But "because of an accidental opportunity, something changed in Heifeng's heart." This "lucky oppor-

76. Wang Wenshi, Heifeng (Beijing: Zhongguo qingnian chubanshe, 1964), 56–57.
77. Selden, China in Revolution: The Yenan Way Revisited, 77.
78. In the novels of this period, young/old is often narrativized as progressive/conservative. I will discuss this question in chapter 7.

tunity" came from the intrusion of her second maternal uncle (a revolutionary soldier) and a female revolutionary soldier. "Second uncle, with his short gun holstered at his waist, and that female fighter who drank water from the big bowl under the almond tree" form a sort of "tableau," and for Heifeng, the tableau's image has a dual meaning: it implies modern women's liberation ("women... can do anything! When you grow up, you can do whatever you want!"), and it also contains a revolutionary promise for the future ("after the war, uncle will take you away for school"). Ultimately, revolution/woman is effectively embodied by the female revolutionary soldier ("all those stories of revolutionary female soldiers—are so very lively and touching").[79] Here, education takes on a certain ideological function of persuasion and training.

Hence, narratives of youth imply a theme of growth and, in the course of that growth, revolution or revolutionary ideology is usually embodied in the novels by a character who functions as a guide. We find examples in a number of novels, including *Keep the Red Flag Flying* and [Yang Mo's] *Song of Youth* (*Qingchun zhi ge*). From these examples, we can see how the Chinese revolution extended the May Fourth modern imaginary of enlightenment. Education, or the persuasion-training ideological function taken on by education, renders the course of growth into a simultaneous self-transformation; this self-transformation is also an overcoming of the self or of an object, in the course of which the construction of subjectivity will have been completed.

Because of the introduction of the concept of education, environmental factors are made more visible. In *Sanliwan Village*, Zhao writes of the Ma family's courtyard:

> The Ma family had its own peculiar custom. Sanliwan had been liberated early, and after the land reform there was no more stealing, so a lot of houses had no gate at all, while those that did simply fastened the catch at night as a precaution against wolves. The Ma household was the only one to make a point of closing and bolting the gate. As soon as dusk fell, no matter how many family [members] were still out, the gate had to be latched, then opened each time anyone came home. The last one back had to bolt it with two bolts, and put up a bar as thick as your arm, which was wedged in place with a lozenge-shaped chunk of wood. And a tree-stump torn up by its roots was propped against the gate. Moreover, the fact that they had very little to do with anyone but Tienzheng's family or their mutual-aid team—no one else ever called—had made their big brown dog very surly.

79. Wang, *Heifeng*, 15–17.

It used to bite all strangers. All but Tianzheng's family or the members of their team.[80]

One wing-room[81] of the house is described as follows: "It was too dark inside to see him at first. . . . There had been two windows behind Yu-yi's bed giving on the open country, but Muddlehead had nailed the boards over them and piled up bricks inside as a precaution against thieves. It was hard in the gloom to see what was in here."[82] Zhao repeatedly describes the Ma family's courtyard. Besides situating it outside the order of rural life [because of its isolated self-sufficiency], thereby providing further support to the cooperative movement, his descriptions manage to construct a space in which a conservative, backward, and self-enclosed family resides. This narrative clearly inherits the modern Chinese literary theme of antifeudalism.

At the level of knowledge, we can also say that on the question of youth, there is simultaneously a conflict between different kinds of knowledge: a conflict between modern and local knowledge. Households with wing-rooms are treated here as backward, conservative, and closed spaces. Hence all local knowledge about kinship (inheritances or obeyances) would be seen as outmoded or backward. For this reason, a revolution in the wings is a form of legitimacy for modern knowledge. Of course, on the question of what is modern knowledge, there has been a never-ending heated conflict in the realm of ideology, particularly when the ideology of the socialist revolution was challenged from the position of modern knowledge (for example, scientism, professionalization, and so on). Ideology was able to stage a heated reaction, and this was not only experienced in the Great Leap Forward, but it also had a direct impact on the totalistic evaluation of 1949–66 education during the Cultural Revolution itself.[83] However, in the 1950s, on the question of mod-

---

80. Zhao, *Sanliwan Village*, 40–41.
81. Tr.: A "wing-room" refers to an addition in the courtyard home that could house different branches of an extended family. As Cai makes clear later in this paragraph and in subsequent ones, this architectural feature becomes a symbol of backwardness because of its connection to housing for an extended family or clan.
82. Zhao, *Sanliwan Village*, 186.
83. This totalistic evaluation, the so-called two appraisals, was broached in a meeting on national education work held in August 1971. This meeting's summary was revised by Yao Wenyuan, with Zhang Chunchao's final edits and Mao Zedong's approval. Of the two appraisals, one was that the seventeen years of education prior to the Cultural Revolution consisted of the bourgeoisie dictating over the proletariat, it was the "black line of dictatorship"; the other was that the basic worldview of most intellectuals was bourgeois, and thus they were bourgeois intellectuals (Xu Qingquan, *Wentan boluan fanzheng shilu* [Documenting bringing order out of chaos in cultural domains] [Hangzhou: Zhejiang Renmin Chubanshe, 2004], 62).

ern knowledge, Chinese authors maintained a relatively moderate attitude. For example, in *Sanliwan Village*, Zhao on the one hand believes that when Ling Zhi "was looking for a husband on the basis of an incorrect hypothesis that book-learning came before everything else,"[84] this is a "wrong way of thinking," thus indicating the subordinated position that thought or knowledge now occupies. Yet on the topic of the relations between Ling Zhi and Yu Sheng, Zhao also intentionally includes such details as Ling Zhi "felt she ought to lend him (Yu Sheng) the geometry set she had used at school—compasses, protractor, set, square, and metric ruler,"[85] and Yu Sheng says to Ling Zhi, "if we could do mathematics, I needn't have spent so long on making that model!"[86] In these details, Zhao illustrates an approval of and praise for scientific knowledge; clearly this corresponds to the construction of national modernization in the 1950s.

Through this kind of narrative, the local begins to become an organic component of the nation's vision of modernization. For example, Heifeng imagines her own village along this line: "She had a strong desire to return to her village to realize her revolutionary ideals, to transform the old appearance of the village. She had so many plans in mind: in the future in her new-style village there would be innumerable tall steel stacks horizontally filling the sky, along with electric wire poles, tractors, combines, irrigation canals, running water, like a small city teeming with houses." An even more radical narration emerges in *Heifeng*: in the Ya'er Mountains where steel is forged, peasants are reorganized in a sort of militarized formation (battalion, company, platoon) thus replacing the old local (village or clan) connections.[87]

The Great Leap Forward of the late 1950s—including what it offered to novels in its backyard forging of steel, its construction of large-scale irrigation, and so on—was a form of organization and mobilization. This imaginary was precisely controlled by the totalistic nature of the modernization project for the nation and the individual, which glossed over or did not notice the actual results of this movement. In some sense, this kind of modernity can be explained through Anthony Giddens's theory of "disembedding": "the 'lifting out' of social relations from local contexts of interaction and their restructuring across indefinite spans of time-space."[88] These social relations—modern

---

84. Zhao, *Sanliwan Village*, 146.
85. Ibid., 192.
86. Ibid., 66.
87. Wang, *Heifeng*, 55–56.
88. Anthony Giddens, *The Consequences of Modernity* (London: Polity, 1990), 21.

or revolutionary—cut through what is visible in the local and structured a new site for the staging of the modern nation-state. But in this type of imaginary or narrative, has the local really disappeared or [has it simply] been concealed? Or does it escape the city?

III. Escaping the City, On Location, and Preserving the Local, or the Transformation of Modernity

Zygmunt Bauman once analogized modernity as a force of "fluidity": "Configurations, constellations, patterns of dependency and interaction were all thrown into the melting pot, to be subsequently recast and refashioned; this was the 'breaking the mould' phase in the history of the inherently transgressive, boundary-breaking, all-eroding modernity."[89] What this fluidity leads to is precisely what [Friedrich Engels and Karl] Marx wrote of in [the] *Communist Manifesto*: "All that is solid melts into air." In some sense, perhaps it is this "migratory modernity" [as Giddens calls it] that called into being Giddens's notion of "escape from the city." At the level of social practice, this migratory modernity has usually depended for its realization upon the free movement of populations as well as the international system of free trade.

Yet how are we to understand this "escaping the city" or "migratory modernity" in the context of China's contemporary history? On December 19, 1957, *People's Daily* published a Central Party and State Council document passed the day before titled "Declaration on Controlling the Blind Movement of Village Populations." It said: "Last winter and this spring, there were large numbers of people from the villages who blindly moved into the cities, and although various local governments tried to stop this and sent them home, the problem is still not completely under control. . . . The large numbers of village populations who are leaving not only leads to a scarcity of rural labor power, which prevents the development of rural production and the consolidation of rural cooperatives, but it also leads to an increase in the numbers of unemployed in the cities and will bring new difficulties to urban management."[90] This is also the linguistic origin of the term *mangliu* (blind movement). And on January 9, 1958, the "People's Republic of China Household Registration Regulation" was published [in *People's Daily*], and this law confirmed the principle of one family, one registration, thus using legal means to control and

89. Zygmunt Bauman, *Liquid Modernity* (London: Polity, 2000), 6.
90. "Declaration on Controlling the Blind Movement of Village Populations," *People's Daily*, Dec. 19, 1957.

limit the movement of village populations to the cities.⁹¹ This change in the legislative mode of population movement also seems to have had an impact on contemporary novelistic narratives. For example, in *The Builders*, a member of the Youth League, Wang Yamei, says to Gaixia: "Industrial construction requires people: that is a fact. Young people participate enthusiastically in economic construction: that too is a fact. However, it appears that the majority of unmarried girls are not happy in the villages and are not willing to marry young villagers.... The Central Party and State Council has issued an instruction to educate village youth about not blindly moving to the cities; it has just arrived in our county yesterday."⁹² The novelistic narrative reflection of this change of the mode of population movement was not limited to such direct explanatory passages.

One actual result of the rural cooperative movement was to liberate village peasants from the local—if by the local we mean [what Chatterjee calls] the traditional "informal power structure based on kinship and community elite with a formal administrative system and the bureaucracy of cadres" or, really, the "cultural influx of power" (of the family, clan, social area, and so on). The mode of liberation was realized by having the individual or even the family join national policy, thereby creating a new social space for the individual.⁹³ But, after all, what is this new social space? Is it a strange place or the land of the hometown? In *The Builders*, there is a scene of Gaixia departing, when she "determinedly leaves for the national industrial front"; yet in the concrete historical context of the population policy [underpinned by the hukou system], ultimately Gaixia's departure is an exception.⁹⁴

There is also another narrative model implied—for example, in *Sanliwan Village*. The narration of revolution in the wings on the one hand extends the May Fourth antitradition theme, but on the other hand, it abandons the May Fourth narrative ideal of departure [from the village]. As a result, revolution in the wings takes the form of dividing the family to achieve the goal of entering the society of the cooperative. Entering the cooperative actually indicates some sort of national political sphere, as the individual can enter only that

91. Tr.: We have omitted the short history Cai provides here of the *hukou*, or household registration system, in which he notes that legislation on the issue had begun to be formulated in mid-1951, but that it was not until January 1958 that the system was fully inscribed in law.

92. Liu Qing, *Chuangye shi* [The builders] (Beijing: Zhongguo Qingnian Chubanshe, 2009), 593.

93. Yunxiang Yan, *Private Life under Socialism: Love, Intimacy, and Family Change in a Chinese Village, 1949–1999* (Stanford, CA: Stanford University Press, 2003), 231.

94. Liu Qing, *Chuangye shi*, 564.

national political sphere to attain legitimizing support from the collective, including support for love. But now the way to join is on location, through the division of the family.

A discussion of this question is perhaps of some importance. On the one hand, national politics liberated the individual, by way of cooperatives, from a certain cultural influx of power. Yet on the other hand, several concrete national policies, such as the household registration system [hukou], restricted the free movement of populations and in some sense restored as well as consolidated the family system [in the villages]. Hence, individual transformations were constrained and contained by these limits. That is to say, the construction of modernization in Chinese socialism from the outset took a very different path from that of the West—namely, the separate administering of town and country. The impact of the restrictions on population movement is far greater than merely on the legal level, in that it conditioned the "on location" characteristics of China's modern imaginary. Actually, this "on location" nature forced China to inherit the old space of the local—with all of its forms of tradition, including the family—in which the modern escape from the city was to be realized. Subsequently, these "on location" characteristics also restricted the modern imaginary of the future in many novels, where perhaps the most extreme expression is found in *Sanliwan Village*, in the hopes expressed by Ling Zhi and Yu Sheng who imagine their new family formation: "Let's go home to talk it over with our people, and not register as a separate household if we can help it. Your work-points can still be marked up to your family, and my work-points to mine; but we'll be together at night. If that won't do, the mess-hall is opening the day after tomorrow, and after registering as a new household we can eat there."[95] But even in this extreme imaginary, the old family form persists; when departure is no longer an option, then conflicts within a given space will appear especially intense, and this is one reason that mobilization-transformation could exist for such a long time in socialist China. However, we can also say that these conflicts are relatively moderate, as the transformation of tradition also implies an extension of tradition.

This special "on location" characteristic of Chinese socialism also rendered possible a quasi-natural extension of various cultural forms that existed in the local, including mores and customs, perspectives, kinships, ethical relations, and so on. In some sense, this phenomenon aroused a degree of vigilance in novel narratives. At the end of *The Builders*, we read the following passage:

95. Zhao, *Sanliwan Village*, 276.

"The third day after Shengbao, Yuwan and Ren the Fourth returned from the county seat to Frog Flat, a new name—'Lighthouse Agricultural Producers' Co-operative'—flew like the wind through the hundreds of large and small villages dotting the area of the Tang Stream."[96] This is a classic example of how national politics renames local space. One implication of this renaming could be that through naming—a socially symbolic act—the local is assimilated into the universality of the nation and into some version of its modern imaginary.[97] But no matter whether in social practice or in novelistic narrative, I doubt that the phenomenon was widespread and common.[98] For example, in Hao Ran's's *Sunny Days*, what we find is that the East Mountain Slope Commune is named after its own natural geography. What we see here is a compromise between the nation and the local through naming.

Actually, it is difficult to find any purely modern aspects in China. Anderson, in discussing modern nations, focuses on the concept of simultaneity: "a simultaneity of past and future in an instantaneous present."[99] This type of simultaneity is "measured in the interstices of clock time and calendrical time, and it is their unification." For this reason, it is "certainly connected, in ways that have yet to be well studied, with the development of the secular sciences."[100] It is precisely this simultaneity that forces events that may have no relation to one another or no cause-effect relation to be put into a connected relationship. In this understanding of simultaneity, Anderson has even discovered "the obscure genesis of nationalism,"[101] in particular in the novels of Balzac. For, in Anderson's theory, novels and newspapers are extremely important forms for the nationalist imaginary. Anderson here discovers some sort of "homogeneous, empty time" to articulate the design of simultaneity. That is to say, it is a sort of "a complex gloss upon the word 'meanwhile.'"[102] And "the idea of a sociological organism moving calendrically through homo-

---

96. Liu Qing, *Chuangye shi*, 569.

97. The most radical form of renaming was during the Cultural Revolution—for example, when "street names and shop names were changed, and the new names were intentionally crude, such as 'anti-revisionism' or 'red sun' or 'struggle'" (Wang Anyi, *Qimeng shidai* [The enlightened era] [Beijing: Renmin Wenxue Chubanshe, 2007], 1).

98. This renaming did indeed exist, such as the Four Seasons Youth Park in the Beijing area. It was hence not completely empty. Yet it is hard to say whether this was common. When I was sent down to Huai River region, the local people's communes all had their old local names. Usually, the people's communes adopted the local geographic name as their own.

99. Anderson, *Imagined Communities*, 24.
100. Ibid.
101. Ibid.
102. Ibid., 25.

geneous, empty time is a precise analogue of the idea of the nation, which also is conceived as a solid community moving steadily down (or up) history."[103] This European sense of temporality gradually spread into the world's other spaces with the global expansion of capitalism. In this modernity, the sense of temporality is one of the most important elements. It is precisely that type of progressive, developmental, and changing sense of time that profoundly influenced and transformed modern China.

The shared sense of simultaneity between one local and another also helped construct some sort of connection between localities. For example, in Wang Wenshi's *Heifeng*, the character Heifeng tries to persuade Li Yueyan of the Yangli Brigade to join the production labor team of Ding Wang Village: "Please think about it . . . now, 600 million people all over the nation—from the top of the Central Party Committee to the grannies and boys in the villages—are busy building the country; everyone is working their hardest day and night! Wherever they go visiting, many people bring tools with them! Of course we don't need you to bring your own furniture with you! It's just that you've been visiting here for a few days now; you must be terribly bored, aren't you? Come on, let's work together, there's no need to be polite."[104] In Heifeng's telling, the nation is absolutely not some static essence; to the contrary, it is conceptualized as a historical subject, a stable and substantial community that is steadily moving upward. In her entire life, Heifeng will never know the vast majority of the 600 million from the "Central Party Committee to the grannies and boys in the villages." Yet she is "completely convinced about the fact that each and every one of them is stably and consistently active."[105] For this reason, in Heifeng's narration, there is no host/guest [subject/object] division.

Of course, in China's system of mobilization, that type of simultaneity must rely upon some event (politics or a political movement) to structure it; and supporting this structure is a certain notion of totality. In the structure of this kind of simultaneity, politics is not external to the individual but rather is an internal understanding and demand: every individual is a political subject. Hence, between the individual and the nation is a relation of recognition. At the end of part I of Hao Ran's *Sunny Days*, the novel articulates the views of the masses this way: "Party Secretary Xiao was correct: one should not forget the nation when there is a bumpy harvest. We can eat a bit more, keep a bit

103. Ibid., 26.
104. Wang, *Heifeng*, 23–24.
105. Ibid., 55.

more grain, but we should also sell a bit more surplus grain."[106] This kind of narrative can be a bit dangerous, however, for it could easily lead to an impression of pure modernity [in which the rural supports the urban in a national totality].

Yet to dispel this impression, we could well ask how we can explain the fact that after 1949, China's villages preserved an alternate calendar (a concept of temporality)—namely, the rural calendar (or lunar calendar)? This calendrical mode used to unite traditional China's sense of time, but in the modern era, rural time retreated from the time of the nation, although, through the local (villages), it attained an alternative mode of continuation, and even today it continues to organize productive labor and quotidian life, despite the fact that this kind of traditional temporality is often challenged by modern temporality. Nevertheless, this traditional temporality continues to be common in the everyday lives of the villages. This temporality not only is the origin of any given individual (birthday time), but it is often also used to organize village social group activities, such as local markets.[107] And beyond national or local time, there is another individual (natural) time. Perhaps because in the villages clocks were scarce, people still used the natural rising and setting of the sun or moon to organize their own personal time. For this reason, in novels of this era, we often read such notions of time as *shangwu* [noon, in dialect] or *bangwan* [evening]. To use a crude generalization, we can say that people use national (modern) time to organize their political or public lives; they use local (traditional) time to organize their quotidian and labor lives; [and] they use natural (individual) time to organize their individual family or personal lives. The overlapping of these times illustrates the persistence of the local or traditional forms and the fact that there is no pure modern life in China's rural society.

While this temporal overlap organized, through compromise, the complex forms of rural life under socialism, it certainly could not erase the tense relations between different types of temporalities. Even though we do not see in the novels of the 1949–66 period a deep narrative treatment of such temporal issues, we do see the treatment of issues regarding the entry of national (modern) time into and its transformation of local (traditional) and individual (natural) time and how this irruption is usually illustrated in spatial terms. In Wang Wenshi's stories, the periodic market days often indicate a certain

106. Hao Ran, *Yanyang Tian* [Sunny days] (Beijing: Zuojia Chubanshe, 1964), 670.
107. Where I went as a sent-down youth, markets were still held according to the rural calendar: every fifth day a small market, every tenth a big one, and so forth.

narrative space. For example, in the beginning of "The Master Carpenter" ("Da mujiang")[108] there is a passage about the big village meeting, which is in fact a market day usually scheduled according to local (traditional) time. This form of social life preserves traditional customs and mores, so "the management committee of the agricultural co-op had decided to make it a holiday. Horses were hitched to ten strong carts to take the co-op members to town for a good time."[109] Such markets function to fulfill the quotidian life needs of the villagers: "all the villagers had some private business to attend to.... Some went to town for oil or charcoal, others were out to buy cotton cloth, and the opera lovers headed straight for the theatres. Young lovers walked blissfully to the photographers and young suitors went with match-makers to their chosen one's house to meet their parents-in-law for the first time."[110] The narration of this everydayness is extremely lively and provides evidence that in this period, it was legitimate to narrate the existence of private life. Yet there is also tension within this everyday life represented in traditional temporal and spatial terms. For example, in Wang Wenshi's "The Master Carpenter," we can perhaps say that the modern perspective of the carpenter—which is both political and moral[111]—supports the spread of the concept of modern knowledge precisely by borrowing local or traditional forms.

Li Yang, in discussing the methods of spreading modern knowledge, argues that,

> The borrowing of "folk" or "tradition" is precisely the classic mode through which modern knowledge is spread. Modern politics is a collective identity established through a shared value system, history, and symbolic expressions. Therefore, there is no modern politics that does not have its own popular mythology and cultural tradition. Within the structuring of "nation-states" or "class"—these collective "imagined communities"—traditional modes of identification such as ethnicity, religion, ethics, language, and so on all function as important resources. Only when these "imagined communities" are, without exception, explained as having long

---

108. In Wang Wenshi, *Fengxue zhi ye* [The night of the snowstorm] (Beijing: Renmin Wenxue Chubanshe, 1977), 164–89.

109. Wen-shih Wang, "The Master Carpenter," in Wen-shih Wang, *The Night of the Snowstorm* (Peking: Foreign Language Press, 1961), 141.

110. Ibid., 141–42.

111. The "moralization of politics" is, in Li Yang's analysis, a particular concept of the "literature of the 1950s–70s" (*50–70 niandai Zhongguo wenxue zai jiedu* [Rereading 1950s–1970s Chinese literature] [Jinan: Shandong Jiaoyu Chubanshe, 2003], 146).

historical and mythological roots and unquestionable common origins can their legitimacy not be impugned. It is also precisely through such molding that modern politics become interiorized as part of people's psychological structure, emotions, and structure of feeling.[112]

Whether or not this mode of spreading modern knowledge actually operates "without exception" is dubious. Nevertheless, in China's contemporary novels, political narration certainly does borrow from folk or traditional forms and resources.

Early in the Yan'an period—for example, in the opera *White-Haired Girl*—this type of borrowing from folk and traditional forms was already quite evident. The third scene of the fourth act of *White-Haired Girl* depicts the entry of the Eighth Route Army into the village:

> LI (showing amazement): Quick! Quick! I was just coming in from the fields, when I saw troops coming down the Southern Hill!
> ALL (alarmed): What! Troops?
> FIRST PEASANT: Could it be the Japanese?
> LI: No, they didn't look like Japanese. They're Chinese troops!
> SECOND PEASANT: Ah, they must be retreating.
> LI: No, they don't look like retreating either. You look. (All stare in the direction he points.) They are in good order, heading briskly due north.
> ALL (looking): Ah, there are so many of them!
> LI: Ha! That's a funny army! They're all youngsters, wearing big straw hats, and with no puttees, only shoes. And there's a figure "eight" on their sleeves.
> ALL (in union): Oh, they must be the Eighth Route Army!
> (The martial music grows louder.)
> (They watch anxiously.)
> SECOND PEASANT (suddenly catching sight of them): Ah! Here they come! Here they come!
> (An army man's voice offstage: "Hey! Countryman, countryman!")
> (They all take cover in fright.)
> (Enter DASUO, ragged and unkempt, leading a soldier who proves to be DACHUN.)
> DASUO: By calling out like that, Dachun, you frightened them all away! Say, Dachun, just now there was someone who looked like Uncle Zhao.

---

112. Ibid., 288.

DACHUN: Let's call him then.
DASUO: Uncle Zhao! Uncle Zhao!
DACHUN (calling too): Uncle Zhao!
(After a pause, ZHAO and others enter; but the sight of the soldier makes them fall back a few steps in fear.)
DACHUN (advancing): Uncle Zhao, don't you know me? I'm Dachun!
DASUO: I'm Dasuo!
ALL (incredulously): What? Dachun! Dasuo! (After a second, they recognize them, and are overjoyed.) Well! Well! Dachun! Dasuo! You've come back! (Other peasants crowd in.)
(They sing happily in union):
A clap of thunder,
And then a sunny sky!
The stars in heaven
Are falling from so high!
Dachun! (Some: Dasuo!) You've been away so long,
Who could tell you would come home today!
(Enter a peasant: "Dachun! Your mother's coming!")
(Dachun goes to meet her.)
ALL (following Dachun to meet her, sing):
Now mother and son will meet,
And be together from now on!
All we country folk are happy too;
All we country folk are happy for you!
(AUNTY WANG, calling "Dachun! Dachun!," runs in.)
DACHUN (shouts): Mother!
WANG (unable to believe her eyes, hesitates, then rushes forward, crying.): Dachun! My boy!
DACHUN: Mother! (He breaks down too.)
SOME PEASANTS (comfortingly): Aunty Wang......
SOME PEASANTS (singing): Don't take on so.
OTHERS (singing): Don't be so upset, Dachun!
ZHANG: Don't make your mother sad, Dachun!
ZHAO (wiping his eyes): Don't take so on, Aunty. Dachun's back, isn't he?
WANG (wiping her eyes): Oh ... I'm not ... not sad. (Cries again.)
ZHAO: Well! (singing)
You waited day after day so many years,

Now Dachun's here, isn't he?

ALL (singing): Isn't it grand that he's back!

ZHANG: Your day of rejoicing has come, Aunty!

ZHAO: Tell us, Dachun, how did you come back?

DACHUN and DASUO: Right!

DACHUN: Mother, Uncle!

DASUO: Aunty Zhang, neighbors!

DACHUN and DASUO (singing): When we left that year/ Landlord Huang!

DACHUN: Drove me out with nowhere to go!

DASUO: Threw me into the county jail!

DACHUN: I fled to Shanxi Province/ And joined the army there.

DASUO: Life was misery in that jail!

DACHUN: Today our troops have come to the front/ Determined to fight the Japanese invaders!

DASUO: They stormed the county town and opened jail doors/ Letting us out after all we'd suffered!

BOTH: So we came back together/ To see our old neighbors!

ALL (to DACHUN): What army do you belong to then?

DACHUN (singing): I'm in the Eighth Route Army!

DASUO (simultaneously): He's in the Eighth Route Army!

ALL (delighted, crowding around him): Oh, so you joined the Eighth Route Army then!

ALL (singing): The Eighth Route Army! The Eighth Route Army! You came from the west! It was you who won the battle of Pingxing Pass/ You're the army with the super officers and men!

DACHUN: Yes, the Eighth Route Army, led by the Communist Party, is like one family with the common people. Do you remember, Uncle Zhao, you used to talk about the Red Army? The Red Army is the present Eighth Route Army!

ZHAO: Eh? What's that you say? The Eighth Route is the same as the Red Army? (Wildly happy, to all.) Ho! Have you all forgotten the Red Army that came to Zhao Village on the thirteenth of the fifth moon that year, the day the War God sharpened his knife? . . . It's too good to be true! It's too good to be true! Everything will work out all right now. The Red Army's come back again!

DACHUN (correcting him): The Eighth Route Army—the Eighth Route Army's come back!

ALL (in union): The Eighth Route Army—the Eighth Route Army's come back! Now there'll really be a chance for the better!
(Laughter.)
(The "Eighth Route Army March" sounds loudly offstage.)
(All go to meet the troops.)[113]

This passage is brilliant: it goes from doubt to acceptance. While there is the unquestioned Red Army as origin, for the Eighth Route Army to be turned into "our troops" requires the appearance of Dachun. Of course this is part of the structural need for drama, but behind this form we can still sense that for the Chinese revolution to truly enter the villages, it required the local resources of the "community where everyone knows each other."[114] This community is a personalistic but also an ethical one. For this reason, the narrative retains traditional ethical modes of address, such as "Uncle" and "Brother" and so on. Only when the revolution acquires the support of village ethics can it become "ours." We may call it the ethicalization of politics.

The ethicalization of politics also means acknowledging and respecting the local order of the villages. This acknowledgment or respect in turn implies an inheritance of the space of the local. We see a similar type of depiction in, say, Liu Qing's *The Builders*. When Guo Zhenshan in the end is excluded from the list of cooperative leaders, it renders "the stubborn Guo Zhenshan unable to control the tears welling up in his big eyes." What causes his "embarrassment" is not just being excluded from the village power structure, but also the fact that this "retirement" would mean a loss of the [interpersonal] trust based in rural ethics.[115] By the same token, Liang Shengbao gives Old Liang San "a new set of cotton padded clothes, fulfilling the old man's dream," thus restoring support for the village ethical system: "When the peasants waiting in the queue discovered that the old man was the father of chairman Shengbao of the Lighthouse Co-op, they invited him to go to the head of the line and buy his bean oil. He was getting on in years; his legs would ache if he stood too long."[116] In rural China, respect is always an extremely important ethical relationship.

113. He Jingzhi, Ding Yizhi, *Baimao nü* [White-haired girl] (Jinan: Shandong Xinhua Shudian, 1949), 90–93.
114. Tr.: This is a social category (*shuren shehui*) that the sociologist Fei Xiaotong used in multiple works to characterize China's rural communities (as opposed to the alienated impersonal urban spaces).
115. Liu Qing, *Chuangye shi*, 774.
116. Ibid., 572.

Because of the modern inheritance of old tradition and the local space supported by the tradition, descriptions of everydayness became the narrative arena of many 1949–66 novels, constituting one important source of the so-called flavor of life (*shenghuo qixi*). Indeed, we ought not deny, just because of politics, that everyday life existed. In fact, the political conflicts in everyday life illuminate the "on location" characteristics of Chinese modernity, which—once again—has to do with the modern legacy of tradition and the local space supported by the tradition. Because of this, the so-called local and local knowledge entered novelistic narratives in multiple ways and constructed relationships that overlapped, conflicted, struggled, and compromised with one another.

Amid this multiplicity, language remained an extremely important factor. In the 1950s, there was a discussion in contemporary Chinese literature about the use of dialects [local languages]. For example, the first issue of the second volume of *Wenyi xuexi* [Study of literature and art] published in Tianjin on August 1 [1951] carried the essay by Xing Gongwan titled "On 'Dialect Literature.'" This article subsequently drew a good bit of attention and instigated a discussion in the *Wenyi bao* [Culture news]. On March 10, 1951, the editorial statement of the tenth issue of volume 3 of *Wenyi bao* specifically introduced the content of this essay:

> The major argument of this essay is to point out that in his speech of remembrance about "May Fourth" at the literary soiree held in Tianjin on May 3, 1948, [Comrade Xing Gongwan] himself had referred to the problem of "dialect literature." At that time, he reinforced the views of Comrade Mao Dun on the topic; the gist of what Xing Gongwan said was: . . . [for Mao Dun] dialects are the vernacular languages of particular localities; there is in theory no way to leave dialects out of the vernacular and in reality, this cannot occur, . . . a national language that is theoretically also a mass language does not exist today; what we have today are mass languages that are the dialects of people of particular localities. To deploy these real mass languages which are the dialects of local people into literature, this is "dialect literature." However, subsequently, after he [Xing] had read Stalin's essay on "The Question of Linguistics and Marxism," he considered his previous views "in need of reinvestigation." He pointed out that the theory of dialect literature had at least two mistaken tendencies. First, the slogan for dialect literature was not to lead us to look forward but rather led backward; nor was it something that would lead toward unity, but rather toward

division. Second, the slogan for dialect literature was formulated only out of the superficial forms of Chinese language, not formulated out of any understanding of the innate foundations of Chinese language.[117]

From today's vantage, we can see that Xing's arguments about dialects—for example, that dialects could lead to a backward direction or could lead to division—already pointed to the important relationship between language and the modern nation-state.[118]

This perspective provoked some different opinions at the time. The same tenth issue of volume 3 of *Wenyi bao* published a critical essay by Liu Zuocong titled [Some more comments on "dialect literature"]. Liu's criticism was based on Lu Xun's point that "when applying old forms, there must be deletion; with deletion, there must be addition. This is how a new form emerges." Liu's point was to emphasize gradual change or promote tolerance, mainly to argue for the legitimacy of using dialects in literature.[119] In the same issue, Xing published a piece called [Additional views on "dialect literature"]. It responded from the angle of history and reality:

> In the past, during the beginning phases of the war of liberation, the majority of combatants were peasants, and the revolutionary bases were in the villages; for this reason, cultural activity most reflected peasant activity, and the modes of literary expression used were local dialects with rich local color. At that time (and even after we first entered into large cities), we had to undertake struggle in the cultural arena in the very areas occupied by the Guomindang [the Nationalists]. We needed to introduce peasants, introduce villages, because that was in fact introducing the revolution itself. And so, on the question of modes of expression, we proffered the slogan of "dialect literature," and from the perspective of that phase [of the revolution], this was not at all wrong. That is because this slogan was one weapon in the struggle against counterrevolutionary rule and was revolutionarily significant. After the revolutionary forces of the Chinese people liberated many larger cities, it [the slogan] quickly achieved a full victory. The tasks of the Chinese people is to complete the new democratic

---

117. "Bianjibu de hua" [A word from the editors], *Wenyi Bao*, March 10, 1951.

118. The relationship between language and the nation-state is one of the questions given most attention by literary and historical scholars. See, for example, Anderson, *Imagined Communities*, chapter 5; Karatani, *Origins of Modern Japanese Literature*.

119. Liu Zuocong, "Wo dui 'fangyan wenxue' de yidian yijian" [Some more comments on "dialect literature"], *Wenyi bao*, March 10, 1951.

revolution at the level of politics, economy, and culture and to achieve the unification of the people and national independence, to transform itself from an agricultural country to an industrialized one. In particular, today after the convening of the People's Consultative Congress we can say that our country is now independent, democratic, peaceful, and unified and has embarked on the road to becoming a rich and powerful nation. In this circumstance, today, should we create works using a unified national language (that is to say, in our works, should we appropriately avoid local vernaculars), or should we use dialects to create such works (that is to say, in our creative works, should we intentionally use local vernaculars and even emphasize such usage)? When the revolutionary forces had not yet entered the big cities or had only just entered them, the slogan for "dialect literature" was entirely correct; now that the revolutionary forces have attained a full victory over all of China, requiring creative works to be done in the still-developing national common language (language of the whole people) is also correct. These two different slogans pertain to two different eras, but they are also mutually contradictory, and asking them to be not contradictory is impossible.[120]

Xing's "national common language (language of the whole people)"—in other words, *guoyu* [national language]—was subsequently consolidated under the form of *putong hua* [common speech; Mandarin Chinese].

If we suppose that the modern nation-state is in fact an imagined community, then the issue of a national common language (language of the whole people) inevitably pertains to the state, politics, or even ideology; for this reason, the debate over dialect [local languages] inherently touches upon the national/local question, including the conflict between unity and division. However, when it comes to literary creative writing, this language issue was not that simple. Zhou Libo published his essay "Discussing 'Dialect Literature'" in the same issue of *Wenyi Bao*. In Zhou's view, there never had been any such thing as a slogan for "dialect literature" ("according to what I know no one in the past or the present formally put forward the 'dialect literature' slogan"), and he emphasized the nature of language as a tool ("I can go, the invader can go too"). Thus, what Zhou points to is the expressive capacity of

---

120. Xing Gongwan, "Guanyu 'fangyanwenxue' de buchong yijian" [Additional views on "dialect literature"], *Wenyi bao*, March 10, 1951.

dialect in literature—for example, "deploying dialect ... so as to render [the speech] more proximate to the real life of the people."[121] Of course, this "real life of the people" is also political, and for this reason, inherent in the debate between the national common language and dialects is in essence a kind of ideological conflict.[122] With a few examples, Zhou emphasizes the possibility of turning dialects into part of written language (thus, the national common language). It echoes what Mao Zedong in his "Talks at the Yan'an Forum on Art and Literature" emphasized: the relation between "people" and "truth."[123]

In his "On Literary Language," published a few years later, Tang Tao extended Zhou's view, pointing out that the political stance that "emphasizes learning from people's spoken language, especially their accuracy, sharpness, and vividness," acknowledges the legitimacy of using dialects, local sayings, and proverbs.[124] Of course, opposing views also existed. For example, Mao Dun emphasized:

> We cultural workers should make strict demands on ourselves, and our works should serve the purpose of spreading the standardization of language. We should consider the study of putong hua—that is, the study of the standardization of Mandarin—not only as a requirement for the betterment of our capacity to write, but also as a political task. However, there are those writers who, for whatever reasons, use a lot of dialects and vernacular expressions. One of their reasons is to enrich their works with local color. We have no objection to works having local color, and in particular for certain special themes in which local color is inevitable. Still, the achievement of local color cannot simply depend upon the use of dialects

---

121. Zhou Libo, "Tan 'fangyan' wenti" [Discussing "dialect literature"], *Wenyi bao*, March 10, 1951.

122. Tr.: Cai is evoking a long modern history of debate over the status of "local languages"—dialects—in relation to some unitary language called "Chinese." These debates had begun in the late nineteenth century—among Chinese as well as foreign linguists and philologists—and continued mostly unabated until the late 1950s, when they were settled by state fiat: there would be but one common spoken and written language in the public sphere. This did not and still does not regulate what language people speak in their everyday lives. The question has been reopened today and prompted an animated and passionate discussion.

123. For example, "the people's vocabulary is rich, vigorous, vivid and expressive of real life" (Mao Tse-tung, "Oppose Stereotyped Party Writing," in *Selected Works of Mao Tse-tung* [Peking: Foreign Language Press, 1965], 3:60).

124. Tang Tao, "Guanyu wenxue yuyan" [On literary language], *Wenyi yuebao* [Culture monthly] vol. 8, 1959, n.p.

and local expressions; rather, it must rely on depictions to highlight the typicality of local life and mores, so as to create that special environment.[125]

Yet what we actually see in novels of 1949–66 is the continued existence of dialect, despite the fact that this existence is limited (for example, only seen in dialogue between characters). For this reason, we can understand the coexistence of putong hua and dialect as a compromise, resulting from debates like these. The presence of local language indicates the extent to which the local or local knowledge was preserved, albeit with limitations, in literature.

In short, we can say that in many senses—temporal, spatial, everydayness, ethical relations, and even language—the conflict between nation-state and local often appears in the form of a compromise. This compromise means that the socialist imaginary of this period did not completely detraditionalize [itself]; rather, at times, it recalled tradition by occasionally treating the local (tradition) as a resource for its own imaginary. What happens in this process is that the local (tradition) also acquires the possibility of being transformed into a certain form of modernity. For this reason, I argue there is no such thing as something that is purely modern.

Conclusion

The contradictions and conflicts between the nation-state and the local under the pressure of various interventions often emerge in some form of compromise. On the systemic level, we cannot underestimate the important function of the united front and the political consultation processes. These compromises to some extent indicate the modern nation-state's capacity to accommodate and encompass the spheres of the popular. Of course, this is a new form of popular encompassing. It was constructed only after the expulsion of the comprador bureaucratic class and the feudal landlord class. And this new people of the nation passed through the phase of new democracy [1949–1957] to acquire its legitimacy. In fact, what Xing Gongwan's essay indicates is the explicit connection between language and politics, when he says that in a new democratic society "the task of the Chinese people should be the political, economic, and cultural completion of the new democratic reforms, imple-

125. Mao Dun, "Guanyu yishu de jiqiao—zai quanguo qingnian wenxue chuangzuozhe huiyishang de baogao" [On the techniques of art—Report at the all-China young literary workers' conference], in *Ershi shiji Zhongguo xiaoshuo lilun ziliao* [Documents on twentieth-century Chinese theories of the novel], ed. Hong Zicheng (Beijing: Beijing Daxue Chubanshe, 1997), 161.

menting national unification and independence, and transforming [China] from an agricultural to an industrial nation," and from this premise he emphasizes the importance of a type of new national common language (language of the whole people).[126] However, strictly speaking, there is a difference between Mao Dun and Xing on the question of a national common language. Indeed, in the subsequent process of the standardization of Mandarin or putong hua, what was more in evidence was a consciousness of the nation-state (Party-state) and its ideological control. This is the historical reason that led to the subversion of language in the 1980s [once ideological control had been lifted to some extent]. In the background to the conflicts over language lay the struggle over the power to interpret or the discursive power about the modern nation-state; at the same time this struggle was also precisely about the inherent conflict between new democracy [a multiclass united front] and socialism [rule of the peasant-proletarian alliance].

Meanwhile, this conflict proceeded within the framework of the Party-state. According to Wang Hui's interpretation, the increasing transformation and normalization of state power is precisely "a process of the state-ification of the Party," while at the same time "it is inevitably also a process of Party-fication of the state. However, this process of Party-fication has an entirely different significance from that of the early period of the expansion of the Party."[127] This process of "state-ification of the Party" or "Party-fication of the state" at the same time has left behind many possible paradoxical spaces. For example, in terms of language, from the perspective of the "state-Party," there is a demand for the standardization of language, and from this demand emerges the rejection of dialects. However, from the perspective of the "Party-state," it seems impossible to deny the legitimate existence of dialects as the languages of the people. This paradox is not limited to the problem of language alone, but rather is a common issue in the historical socialist experience of China from 1949 to 1966. Recognizing this paradoxical historical experience, I think, will allow us to open up many explanatory spaces.

It thus follows that a more radical narration would always attempt to break through the temporarily balanced narrative mode that emerges from various compromises. In some sense, we could even say that what it tries to break through is precisely the limited framework of the modern nation-state. This radical narration would refuse the possible legitimacy of the local or local

---

126. Xing, "Guanyu 'fangyanwenxue' de buchong yijian."

127. Wang Hui, *The End of the Revolution: China and the Limits of Modernity* (London: Verso, 2009), 1.

knowledge and would exhibit the radical stance of an absolute break with tradition. In this era, in other cultural arenas, such as in the May 1964 Conference on Model Opera Performances held in Beijing, where the opera *The Red Lantern* (*Hong deng ji*) was performed, this symptom of a radical break was particularly clear. Li Yang manifestly recognizes that a new model structure emerges in *The Red Lantern*: "the basic relations that compose the 'family' are not at all kin blood or kin relations, but rather they are abstract 'class' relations; the three protagonists are not mother/son or father/daughter relations but rather are revolutionary 'war comrades,'" and "of particular note is that in this revolutionary era those ties built from blood or kinship—those flesh and bone relations—became an 'abstract' concept while 'class feeling' became a concrete emotion. This is without a doubt a complete overturning of traditional ideology." The emergence of this structural model can help explain "that in the middle of the 1960s, the essence of 'class' in an opera such as *The Red Lantern* was constructed. It did not need to rest upon either kinship or love to substantiate itself; to the contrary, kinship and love became the 'other' of 'class feeling' and hence the targets of the revolution. From this we can see the rapid momentum of the development of the revolution and its force that led to self-revolution." What is more, in *The Red Lantern* "other than the opposition between 'class identity' and 'kinship identity' another highly significant modern opposition pops up, and that is the transcendence of the 'nation-state identity' by 'class identity.'"[128] Li Yang's observations and narrative here are quite correct.

At the same time, however, the individual in the midst of this class identity cannot possibly completely transcend nation and family. In fact, an individual continues to deploy the forms of the nation and the family, and what this individual tries to separate himself from is the relations of dependence within a social group. The question is, once the individual is constructed as one who has no existing structurally dependent ties to a social group, then is it possible to substantiate interiority? And how can the genuine amplitude of interiority be developed? Here, what we actually see is that the state or the nation becomes the largest and sole political social grouping. What *The Red Lantern* and other similar types of works extend is still the national-state narrative mode, except that the nation is gradually being replaced by class. In this type of narrative, the individual has been determined to be a particular sort of political subject who is ready at any moment to sacrifice herself for the nation

---

128. Li Yang, *50–70 niandai zhongguo wenxue jingdian zai jiedu*, 235–40.

(class). Yet the individual also at the same time faces the danger of her subjectivity being hollowed out. This is one reason why *The Red Lantern* and subsequent Cultural Revolution literary works are criticized by later generations.

The individual constructed out of this exchange of family or nation for class, having completely broken away from tradition and simultaneously disentangled himself from all dependent ties on social groups, still belongs to the nation and to a class, which are the biggest and sole political entities. Such an individual, however, is in danger of not disengaging from his unidirectionality as a person. In some sense, this type of person must rely on three supports and their corresponding discourses: (1) state power, (2) moral ideals, and (3) the possibility of political subjectivity and of political participation. After the 1980s, with the retreat of the state from the social arena and with the gradual dissolution of moral ideals (ideology)—and, even more important, with the process of what Wang Hui calls depoliticization—the position of the individual as a political subject was lost, and the prospect of political participation became impossible. With all this, the individual became an individual in the formal sense only (this individual in the formal sense is still a result of liberation by the Chinese revolution from older political-cultural relations), and in this sense faces the prospect of being renamed by various political, economic, and ideological forces. These are the real historical origins of the individualizations of the 1980s and after.

2

THE MOBILIZATION STRUCTURE
The Masses, Cadres, and Intellectuals

In contemporary Chinese political documents, *mobilization* (*dongyuan*) is one of the most frequently used terms. It also often appears in contemporary literature, helping constitute what I call the mobilization-reform (*dongyuan-gaizao*) narrative structure.[1] The fact that a political concept enjoyed such a prominent presence in literature, influencing especially its narrative structure, undoubtedly indicates the close and complex (even troubled) relationship between literature and politics in contemporary [socialist] literature.[2] It also explains the importance of mobilization in the political life of the [socialist] era, and the fact that, after the 1950s, mobilization moved into the domains of society, culture, and thought. It even directly affected political and organizational forms during the Cultural Revolution.

In this chapter, I explore how mobilization became a kind of invisible political and cultural structure, how such a structure was represented in contemporary literature, and how it conditioned creative writing of the time. Addi-

---

1. I briefly discuss this narrative structure in part 2 of chapter 1 of this book.
2. Tr.: As we note in the introduction to the English edition of this book, Cai's use of "contemporary literature" mostly refers to the seventeen-year literature, or literature of the socialist period.

tionally, by placing the masses, cadres, and intellectuals within this structure, I explore and analyze how they are represented in fiction and the various paradoxical relationships among them.

I. The Structure of Mobilization

Zhou Libo's *Great Changes in a Mountain Village* (*Shanxiang jubian*) begins as follows: "It was an afternoon of gentle breeze amid warm sunshine, early in the winter of 1955, at a county town on the lower reaches of the River Tzu in Hunan Province. Over a thousand men and women with bedding-rolls and umbrellas on their backs poured jostling out of the office of the county committee of the Chinese Communist Party and scattered into the rough stone-paved high street. They walked along in groups of three or four or five, smoking, talking, and joking. At the crossroads, they all shook hands, nodded, and exchanged good wishes or good-natured abuse by way of farewell. Then some went north, some south across the river to the various districts and townships that were their destinations."[3] These "over a thousand men and women" are cadres. A major character in the novel, Deng Xiumei, is one of them. Their task is none other than to go to the countryside and carry out the mobilization and reformation (*gaizao*) for the agricultural cooperative movement (*nongye hezuohua yundong*): "The provincial Party committee had convened a district secretaries' conference and afterwards the county committee had called a nine-day three-level cadres conference. They had discussed Chairman Mao's article and the decisions of the Party's Central Committee, and heard a report by Secretary Mao of the county committee. Both theory and policies were much clearer now. The county committee had also explained to them in detail how to start work in the townships."[4]

This opening easily reminds us of another of Zhou's novels, *The Hurricane*, in which the work-team leader, Xiao, and his coworkers go to Yuanmao Village to mobilize the land reform movement. To a large extent, we can say that the mobilization-reform narrative structure started with land-reform fiction (for a further example, see Ding Ling's *The Sun Shines over the Sanggan River*).[5]

---

3. Zhou Libo, *Shanxiang jubian* [Great changes in a mountain village] (Beijing: Renmin Wenxue Chubanshe, 2005), 3. Tr.: Translation adapted from *Great Changes in a Mountain Village*, trans. Derek Bryan (Peking: Foreign Language Press, 1961), 1.

4. Tr.: Adapted from *Great Changes in a Mountain Village*, 4–5.

5. Ding Ling, *The Sun Shines over the Sanggan River*, trans. Gladys Yang and Yang Xianyi (Beijing: Foreign Languages Press, 1984).

When it comes to the literature about the cooperative movement, this structure would soon become one of the major narrative structures. Examples include Liu Qing's *The Builders*, in which the only difference is the identity [background] of the main character, Liang Shengmao. Instead of being a cadre from outside, Liang is a local peasant. This particular difference in *The Builders* may have directly influenced Hao Ran's 1964 novel *Sunny Days* (*Yanyang tian*), as in Hao Ran's work the main character, also a cadre of peasant origin, is given a major narrative function in the mobilization-reform narrative structure. It is important to note this change in characterization, for it may be indicative of the relationship between mass support for and the political legitimacy of the mobilization-reform narrative structure.

To a certain extent, the mobilization-reform narrative structure paralleled the Mao era's social and political structure. In their discussion of Chinese politics, James Townsend and Brantly Womack state:

> China also corresponds to a system that appears in nearly all typologies of developing countries, variously referred to as mobilization system, movement regime, neo-Leninist mass party system, or radical or totalitarian single-party system. The type varies in its definition by different writers but contains the following core elements: a single political party that monopolizes political power and penetrates all other politically significant organizations; an explicit official ideology that legitimizes and sanctifies revolutionary goals; a determination to politicize and mobilize the citizenry, characteristically through party-led mass movements. The mobilization system, to use David Apter's phrase, clearly has something in common with the totalitarian model, but it places the dominant political party in a significantly different context. Whereas the totalitarian model projects an image of an impenetrable, monolithic, bureaucratic and technologically competent regime, the mobilization system operates in a fluid, unresolved struggle to transform a "transitional" society. The latter seems closer to Chinese reality, identifying the social context more accurately and emphasizing the open struggle to mobilize the population behind the radical, futuristic goals of elites.[6]

Townsend and Womack did not seem eager to study China within the model of a "developing country." At the same time, they did not abandon the con-

---

6. James R. Townsend and Brantly Womack, *Politics in China*, 3rd ed. (Boston: Little, Brown, 1986), 20–21.

cept of mobilization either. In their so-called Chinese model, they both emphasize the multiplicity (*duoyang xing*) and change in Chinese politics and pay close attention to political mobilization.

At the same time, however, the notion of mobilization, especially when it became a signifier for a social system or political structure, often appeared rather unclear and could be arbitrarily interpreted. What we must therefore ask are the following questions: Why does a society need mobilization? Who are the mobilizers, and what are the purposes of mobilization? What are the supporting forces for such mobilization and, what are the factors that facilitate the acceptance of such mobilization on the part of the masses? Lastly, was the mobilization really structured? To answer these questions, we of course must return to the specific historical context.

Within the so-called structure of mobilization, the concept of *the masses* is the most important. Recognizing the importance of the masses has to do both with the key revolutionary ideal of serving the people and with the wartime need for mass support. The Chinese revolution in essence was a revolution for political power. The so-called Jingangshan path (of military struggle and military basis) was in effect a manifestation of the endeavor to nationalize party politics through the state. Undoubtedly it was precisely the participation of the masses and the quality of their participation that determined who would win and who would lose in the Civil War (1945–49). In addition, the participation of the masses meant more than providing manpower and material support; it was a process through which the masses evolved into a political subject—that is, masters of the state. Put differently, we can say that the process rendered the revolution the business of the masses themselves. Indeed, even as early as the era of the Red Army [1930s], Mao Zedong emphasized that "at this moment, the Red Army is not an entity for fighting only. Its major task (or function) is to mobilize the masses. Fighting is only a means."[7] It is precisely mass participation in the revolution that made it possible for contemporary literature to establish the people as its major narrative theme, a theme that permeates almost all revolutionary-history novels (*geming lishi xiaoshuo*). It was through the masses as a major signifier that the Chinese revolution provided legitimacy for the Party-state and its politics.

---

7. Mao Zedong, "Hongjun disijun qianwei gei zhongyang de xin" [Letter from the Front Committee of the Number Four Red Army Group to the Central Party Committee), in *Mao Zedong wenji* [Collected writings of Mao Zedong] (Beijing: Renmin Chubanshe, 1993), 1:57.

Based on this understanding alone we can begin to reread such land-reform novels as *The Hurricane* by Zhou Libo. To be sure, this and other such novels (Ding Ling's *Sunshine over the Sanggan River*, for example) deal with quite a few political issues, including the relationships between revolution and violence and between land policies and the modernization of the nation, and those regarding the reorganization of the rural power system. But in literature or the literary imagination, the positive values and ideas that the mobilization motif helped establish remain a major underlying signifier in these novels. In this sense, then, the most melodramatic scene in *The Hurricane* may be the episode about the distribution of horses (*fen ma*), but the most important, or perhaps the most ideologically conceptualized (*gainian hua*) scene may be the chapter titled "Joining the Army" at the end of the novel. Led by Guo Quanhai, director of the Village Peasants Association, the Yuanmaotun villagers begin to express their enthusiasm for joining the People's Liberation Army (PLA). In the words of Old Sun, "We have beaten all small Chiang Kai-sheks in this village. Now we're going to beat the big Chiang Kai-shek. Then we can come back and live in peace." Liu Deshan, another character, wants to join up as well: "I'm a middle peasant and have a place in the sun. I'll go to the front."[8] Conversations constitute the major components of this chapter; many of them, to be sure, appear ideologically determined.

At the same time, however, criticism of such ideologically driven narrative should be employed with care, especially in analyzing novels. Sometimes, the so-called conceptualized (or symbolized) characters or narration may precisely be the most imaginatively rendered or most tension-filled. The daoist and the monk in the traditional novel *Dream of the Red Chamber* are good examples. They tend to appear highly symbolized, yet without these two characters, the rich implications of the novel cannot be fully conveyed. A creative writer often lingers between the world of everyday life and that of his imagination. What such a writer does most is perhaps none other than finding a way to connect the two worlds, or to reveal the structural relationship between the two. We thus should not hastily reject conceptualization or symbolization without due consideration. Novels have their own variety of narrative forms that transform everyday life into imagination, through which a fictionalized world gets created. It is in this sense that we can say that what the

---

8. Zhou Libo, *The Hurricane* trans. Xu Mengxiong (Beijing: Foreign Language Press, 1981), 442.

chapter "Joining the Army" attempts to depict is how the land reform enables the masses to gain political subjectivity and consciousness; and, in the terminology of the time, it was about how the poor turn themselves over (*fanshen*) to become masters of the country.

Obviously, mobilization did not simply refer to looking for manpower and material support. In the context of the Chinese revolution, the more important task was how to enable people to become masters of the country (*dangjia zuozhu*) or, in other words, the political subject of the nation. At the level of literary narration, at least, this intended task began to inform the imagination in creative writing. What this imagination embodied was the structural model (*jiangou moshi*) of revolutionary China, rather than the model of the modern nation-state. In this sense, we can say that this imagination was geared toward the future, or a utopian orientation. Different forms of utopia have existed throughout human history (Shangri-la in traditional China being one of them). But the difference between traditional utopias and modern utopias resides in the following: in the former, a utopia exists only as an imagination of another world, while in the latter, all efforts are meant to be made for the realization of a utopia in this world. In Marxism, especially, the constant emphasis is on how to change the world rather than on how to interpret it. The introduction of such a this-worldly utopia helped liberate people's imagination and their ability to act. And this imagination often has a connection to a future-oriented attitude. In this sense, Marxism's critique of utopian socialism is not about the goal but about the latter's lack of proper means to reach the goal; or, put differently, it is about the unwillingness to acknowledge both the constraints imposed by history and the possibilities offered by it. This, of course, does not demonstrate that Marxism in essence is not utopian. If anything, today many people tend to accept the well-circulated blaming of utopia for all kinds of human disasters, assuming a cause-and-effect connection between a utopia and totalitarian politics. Maurice Meisner questions such a connection and insists that "in the case of modern Chinese history, the pronounced totalitarian character of the Kuomintang regime . . . clearly was never associated with any utopian ideology—nor, for that matter, even with any serious program for social change."[9]

It was precisely the existence of a utopia, or the presence of a future-oriented attitude that was made possible via the existence of utopian striving,

---

9. Maurice J. Meisner, *Marxism, Maoism, and Utopianism* (Madison: University of Wisconsin Press, 1982), 19.

that constituted the driving force and the narrative characteristics of contemporary literature. What is more, this utopian imagination not only supported the political concept of mobilization, it also conditioned the inner drive (*neizai dongyin*) of the people who accepted this kind of mobilization. The importance of a utopia did not exist only in the content material that it promised to offer, but [also and even] more in how the masses responded to it—namely, in the ways in which how "the motivation of the minority is turned into the belief of the majority of a people."¹⁰

The content of the utopian imagination in the narratives of revolutionary China was rich and varied, but the most important narrative was about how to construct a new "imagined [political] community," a term that Benedict Anderson deploys to refer to the modern nation-state. But between the state and people, especially people of the lower classes, this state could not remain at the level of an abstraction only; it had to be transformed into an affective and tangible social form closely related to people's everyday life. Only in this way could such a state be turned into "the belief of the majority of a people."

When the opera *White-Haired Girl* chose for its theme how "the old society turned humans into ghosts, and the new society turned ghosts into humans" [a line in the opera] it in effect provided the narration of revolutionary China (*geming Zhongguo de xushu*) with an exceedingly crucial mediating concept—namely, the "new society."¹¹ Of course, what exactly is the new society? To date, I have not come across a singular authoritative and all-encompassing theoretical definition. Nonetheless, the notion is scattered throughout various narratives, including literary ones. In the 1962 novel *The Spring of Battle* (*Zhandou de qingchun*), for example, the character Gao Tiezhuang states his ideal this way: "My hope for the future is that, after we defeat the Japs, I can first have a few meals of *jiaozi* [dumplings] filled with meat. Then I'll pick up that little manure basket of mine to take care of my four-*mu* vegetable garden [1 *mu* equals 0.1647 of an acres]. Of course, the landlord must unconditionally return that piece of land to me; after that, when I finish working in the summer, I'll sleep on a new straw mat placed under the big willow tree by the river and do so without having to have anyone on guard. When I wake up, I'll just jump into the river for a bath. Oh, isn't that [wouldn't that be]

---

10. Ibid.

11. I had a brief discussion with Wang Hongsheng, a professor at Tongji University, about this chapter. His excellent interpretation of the notion of the "new society" was particularly enlightening. I thank him very much for sharing his thoughts with me.

nice."[12] Here the new society is a pastoral poem. In such a poetic pastoral, people are equal to one another; exploitation is not only overthrown as a system, it is also completely devoid of any legitimacy on an ethical level (as stated in Zhou Erfu's *Morning of Shanghai* [*Shanghai de zaocheng*]). Also in this pastoral, men are not allowed to bully women, men and women are free to determine whom they want to marry, and the cadres must "serve the people" heart and soul. Paternalism is overthrown, young people have an unprecedented right to speak, and profiting for oneself is viewed as immoral behavior and as harmful to one's dignity. This new society is unprecedentedly clean and moral, without such social ills as prostitution. In short, the new society reconstructs the relationship between individuals, or reconstructs a political and economic commonwealth, based on the principle of equality. More important still, this commonwealth is at the same time an ethical one, whose core value resides in emphasizing mutual support and assistance. Underlying the political, economic, and moral expressions related to this, above all, is none other than the cultural imagination of serving all under heaven (*tianxia wei gong*).[13]

Ironically, however, it is hard to say that this is a brand-new socialist imagination, for within it we can detect traces of traditional culture. For this reason, the new society, thus conditioned, though full of vitality was at the same time somewhat conservative. Of course, with no support from history, a purely future-oriented attitude might not be attractive enough. This is why we can say that the expressions of this new society, especially during the 1950s, may have actually awakened deeply embedded historical memories that helped strengthen its attraction.

At the same time, of course, this new society did not intend to return to the past. On the contrary, its imaginary insisted on a future-oriented attitude that inevitably required the addition of new narrative elements. Women (*funü*) thus became one of its most important symbols.

Zhao Shuli's 1945 short story, "Meng Xiangying Stands Up" ("Meng Xiangying fanshen") is a good example. It is what Zhao refers to as a "true story"

---

12. Xue Ke, *Zhandou de qingchun* [The spring of battle] (Beijing: Renmin Wenxue Chubanshe, 2005), 448.

13. Tr.: *Tianxia wei gong* (all under heaven) is an old saying. In modern Chinese political discourse, it was a Republican-era ideal articulated most clearly by Sun Yat-sen. It wasn't exactly socialist in Sun's version, but as appropriated by Mao and the Chinese Communist Party, it became a socialist ideal, more often promoted as "serving the people."

(*xianshi gushi*) that reads like reportage.¹⁴ It depicts Meng's unhappy marriage in relation to the regional custom in which men do not want to appear henpecked if they are not known as wife beaters. In Meng's case, more specifically, in the eyes of her mother-in-law, her family, her personality, and her big feet [feet not bound] are all causes for her to be beaten by her husband. The story, however, does not focus on Meng's love life. The author does not even bother to tell us what happens to her marriage in the end.¹⁵ What Zhao focuses on, instead, is Meng's life not related to love, but things like how she becomes a village cadre, how she participates in mobilizing the villagers, how she leads women in the village to participate in agricultural production, and how she eventually becomes a model worker. Obviously, this story about Meng Xiangying is not about love; for Zhao, unless women actively participate in social or public political affairs, their position at home or in society cannot be elevated. And this social participation is also one of the major paths to women's liberation, a path made possible by the establishment of the new society. In this sense, Zhao not only offers another mode of interpretation for women's liberation, originally promoted by the May Fourth New Culture Movement (1915–27), but this new mode would also directly influence post-1949 literature.

In fact, post-1949 literature devoted much energy to representing how women actively devote themselves to social affairs or public politics, thereby gradually forming their own subjectivity. Work is an important intermediary that links women and social affairs, making it possible for women to step outside of the home (*zouchu jiating*), which became a central theme in literary and artistic expression. The new society found its own answer to the question Lu Xun had posed years before—"what happens to Nora after she leaves home?"¹⁶ Working is a process of socialization as well as a process of politici-

---

14. [The quote is from the story, in] Zhao Shuli, "Meng Xiangying fanshen" [Meng Xiangying stands up], *Zhao Shuli wenji* [Collected writings of Zhao Shuli] (Beijing: Gongren Chubanshe, 1980), 1:195.

15. Ibid., 1:210.

16. Tr.: Here Cai is referring to a famous debate of the early 1920s. With the translation and popularization of Henrik Ibsen's *A Doll's House* during the May Fourth period, Nora, the protagonist, became the icon for the new woman who would seize her life in her own hands and walk out into the world to find her fortune and forge her own path. Lu Xun at the time poured cold water on these enthusiasms, by posing the question: what happens to a Chinese Nora when she leaves home? With this, Lu Xun indicated that Chinese society was still not developed enough to give Chinese Noras any real options in life.

zation. In that process, women not only become social subjects but also political subjects, active supporters of the new society.

If symbols govern our imagination, the appearance of a new symbol, then, can also liberate our imagination (at least to an extent). Conflicts within the domain of symbols may therefore manifest fundamental political conflicts. In this sense, the word *nüxing* [female][17] is representative of the political imagination of the time, an imagination that also manifested itself in literary imagination. To me, what this word symbolizes is precisely a close relationship between the new society and the subaltern [group] that included women. In a stricter sense, this indicates a relationship of recognition, or a politics of recognition. It is within this recognition that people obtained unprecedented subject and social positions. Moreover, by way of the new society's everyday life, people came to strongly identify with revolutionary China, which in turn helped lay a wide social foundation for mobilization. In China, therefore, mobilization was not entirely a series of external commands; it also contained a degree of popular emotional response, such as a sense of dignity or honor brought about by being masters of the nation. Cornelius Castoriadis, his sarcasm and implicit criticism of "homogeneity" notwithstanding, states that, in praising revolutionary China, Simone de Beauvoir "admired the fact that China could mobilize every ordinary person to pick up a fly trap to combat flies."[18] Behind the seeming homogeneity, however, is often a series of complex historical and contemporaneous issues that can be overlooked by simplistic criticisms of homogeneity. What we should focus our discussion on is precisely why mobilization tended to take various forms of political movements and why those movements enjoyed strong foundational support from the masses, none of which is fully explicable by the term *authoritarian politics* (*jiquan*). What made all of this possible may well have been the workings of the politics of recognition (*chengren de zhengzhi*) that manifested and expressed itself on the everyday level in the new society. We can say that, to some extent, the politics of recognition constituted the popular foundation of what the historian Benjamin Schwartz terms "ethical politics."[19] It goes with-

---

[17]. Tr.: Cai uses *nüxing* (female) here in place of *funü* (woman) without knowing the debates among feminist scholars about the difference between these two terms. For the debates, see Tani Barlow, *The Question of Women in Chinese Feminism* (Durham, NC: Duke University Press, 2004).

[18]. Cornelius Castoriadis, "Mao zhuyi yu faguo zhishi fenzi" [Maoism and French intellectuals], *Ershiyi shiji pinglun* [Twenty-first century review], no. 36 (August 1996), 26.

[19]. Benjamin I. Schwartz, *Chinese Communism and the Rise of Mao* (Cambridge, MA: Harvard University Press, 1996), 189–204.

out saying that, when devoid of the identification, support, and participation of the masses, mobilization and movement would indeed degenerate into a homogeneous or power-enforced formality. Such degeneration was one of the root causes of the failure of the Cultural Revolution.

Still, this is insufficient for a full understanding of mobilization. One can well limit the significance of mobilization to the level of a kind of social movement in compliance with state policies. Indeed, during the socialist period, the fulfillment of many tasks from the state level all the way down to the level of the work unit was not solely dependent on bureaucratic management but often depended on the mobilization mechanisms that radiated from Chinese Communist Party (CCP) members, Youth League members, and model workers, all the way to the ordinary masses. We may identify such a mobilization method as an invisible bureaucratic system. I will return to the relationship between this form of mobilization and bureaucracy.

However, if we understand mobilization only on this level, we miss the larger political context. Let us recall a point made at the beginning of this chapter: how do we understand the real purpose of Deng Xiumei in Zhou Libo's *Great Changes in a Mountain Village* when she goes to the village to mobilize the peasants? Deng's task is not only to mobilize the masses but also to reform (*gaizao*) the township's Party branch. The subtext of the novel lies precisely here: the task of Deng and her cohorts is not just to mobilize and change those individuals with backward viewpoints but also to mobilize and transform those who constitute part of the lowest-level organization of the CCP (the township Party branch). The subtext has to do with the real-life political struggle between "Chairman Mao's article and the Party's resolutions" and those "rightist opportunists in the Party" (during the Cultural Revolution the struggle was dubbed the inner-Party line struggle). In contrast to those rightist negative forces are the majority of the people—including progressive individuals, lower-middle-class peasants, and middle-of-the-road individuals who can be won over. They are thought to have a vast reservoir of enthusiasm for socialism. Once such enthusiasm is mobilized, nothing can stop the force that explodes from the reservoir. Looking more widely at the literature of the time, [we can see that] this subtext and corresponding representations of characters exist in other novels, including *The Builders* and *Sunny Days*. Indeed, this subtext constitutes the narrative model of mainstream literature of the time.

If the novels touched on this political theme mainly in an implicit way, it was Mao whose writings made explicit the intraparty political struggle and the related political thinking on the struggle. In "On Agriculture Co-Operation" ("Guanyu nongye hezuohua wenti"), Mao ridiculed "some of our comrades, [who,] however, are tottering along like a woman with bound feet, complaining all the time about others, saying: [You're] going too fast, [you're] going too fast" on the one hand, and highly praised the enthusiasm for socialism among the masses, on the other hand, predicting that "a high tide in the socialist mass movement will soon sweep across the rural areas throughout the country," and therefore "we should treasure and not thwart any small bit of socialist enthusiasm on the part of peasants and cadres."[20] Meanwhile, Mao stated with frustration: "Yet, as things stand now, it is the mass movement that is running ahead of the leadership, and the leadership is unable to catch up with the movement. The situation must be changed."[21]

For the time being, let us set aside the question of how to judge, historically, the implications of Mao's criticism. Let us focus instead on the statements themselves. There we can see that, starting from the 1950s, mobilization began to move toward the political domain and acquire other types of significance and function that can be described as a kind of politics of pressure that came into being by way of mobilized mass political movements. The targets of this politics of pressure ranged from the bureaucratic system to official bureaucracy, [reformist] conservatism, and inner-Party dissidents.

Mao's strong belief in the masses and his distrust of organization (*zuzhi*) may be indicative of his subconscious belief that people share a common hope and are naturally inclined toward socialism. It is precisely in this sense that some Western observers have noted a difference between Maoism and Leninism, in that they believe that Mao was naturally a populist.[22] We can also identify this difference as a conflict between the Yan'an path and the Soviet model. The former is rich in implications. One of its major expressions is the political enthusiasm of the masses in participating in various activities (such as those organized in the name of a united front)[23] and another is the corresponding affirmation of the political subject position of the masses. What all of this potentially differs from is precisely the modern characteristics of the Soviet model in the latter's emphasis on specialization, professionalization

20. Mao Zedong, "On Agriculture Co-Operation," in *The Writings of Mao Zedong, 1949–1976*, ed. Michael Y. M. Kau and John K. Leung (Armonk, NY: M. E. Sharpe, 1986), 1:591, 595.

21. Ibid., 1:591.

22. The differences include issues of organization, peasants, and professionalism. For a detailed discussion, see Meisner *Marxism, Maoism, and Utopianism*, chapter 3.

23. Such as the *San san zhi yuanze* at the time. Tr.: This refers to the one-third principle in the distribution of power during the War of Resistance against Japan (1937–1945).

(*keceng hua*), and bureaucratization.[24] The reasons for the formation of the Yan'an path are historically complex; it also took a rather long period of time. In his article titled "The Importance of Commemorating the Paris Commune" ("Jinian bali gongshe de zhongyao yiyi"), first published in 1926, Mao Zedong stated that there were two reasons for the failure of the Commune, one being the lack of leadership provided by a centralized and well-disciplined party, and the other being too much compromise and being too charitable to the enemy.[25] In this article, the influence of Leninism is obvious. When it came to the commemoration of the ninety-fifth anniversary of the Paris Commune in March 1966, the emphasis then fell on the Commune's election system (that is, the principle of people's rights to vote for, to supervise, and to get rid of Commune officials), people's spontaneous revolutionary spirit (as shown in the saying "the self liberates the self"), and so on. Despite the fact that these commune principles would later be scaled back (*daotui*) as time went on, thereby revealing the paradox and schizophrenia in Mao's political ideals and political practice (which harks back to issues related to the history of the Cultural Revolution and, as such, exceeds the scope of this discussion), we can nevertheless still recognize in this critique some of the major characteristics of the Yan'an path or the Chinese model.

The emphasis on mass participation is obviously related to another theoretical model, having to do with how we understand the notions of proletariat and proletarian consciousness. Meisner writes:

> For Maoists, "proletarian dictatorship" was not exercised by the proletariat as such but rather by those deemed to possess "proletarian consciousness." While the cluster of beliefs and values which constitute this "consciousness" has been defined and redefined in Maoist ideology, its particular social carrier is not so easy to identify. "Proletarian consciousness" was neither an attribute of a specific social class (as Marx believed), nor, for that matter, did it reside in a specific institution (the Communist party, as Lenin insisted). Although the claim was made that Mao developed and enriched the experience of Paris Commune, the social and political content of the

---

24. For more information, see Shintani Akinoku, *Sulian shi shehuizhuyi guojia ma?* [Is the Soviet Union a socialist country?], translated from Japanese by Yu Yiqian (Hong Kong: Xianggang Sanlian Chubanshe, 1970).

25. Mao Zedong, "Jinian bali gongshe de zhongyao yiyi" [The importance of commemorating the Paris Commune], in *Mao Zedong wenji* [Collected writings of Mao Zedong (Beijing: Renmin Chubanshe, 1993), 1:35.

Maoist version of the "dictatorship of the proletariat" remained vague and unfulfilled.[26]

The uniqueness of Maoism also conditioned its internal contradictions.[27] That is why in "On Agriculture Co-Operation," while Mao recognized the fact that "there are still rich peasants' capitalistic ownership and a sea of private ownership by individual peasants in the countryside," he still emphasized the need "to treasure even just a tiny sense of socialist class consciousness among the peasants and cadres." Mao argued that "for them [peasants and cadres], there is no way out other than socialism." This is why he insisted on seeing the small amount of peasant enthusiasm as indicating that "the majority of the peasants share an enthusiasm for socialism," through which, he predicted, "the imminent arrival of the high tide of the new socialist mass movement."[28] Here, the so-called enthusiasm for socialism is implicitly expressed as a natural desire on the part of the peasants. Such a natural desire in turn becomes the foundation on which to raise proletarian consciousness. But for the raising of proletarian consciousness to be possible, there must be Party leadership, which consists not only of "Chairman Mao's articles and the Party's resolutions" but also of concrete activities to educate, mobilize, and reform the masses. In this sense, the so-called active participation of the masses was not in a strict sense a spontaneous mass movement. Rather, it was a political movement that relied on mobilization that resulted in a [social] restructuring (*chongxin jiegouhua*). This is also why in *Great Changes in a Mountain Village*, for example, the author spent extensive narrative time on the activities of the propaganda team led by Sheng Shujun and on the specific differences between being progressive and backward. I will return to this issue below in the section on the masses.

After 1949, the CCP became a ruling party. Not only did the Party's Central Committee have to take on the responsibility of governing the country,

26. Meisner, *Marxism, Maoism, and Utopianism*, 151–52.
27. For example, when Mao introduced Chen Yun at the third meeting of the Seventh Plenum of the Seventh CCP Party Congress where the issue of setting positions for vice president of the state and general secretary of the CCP was discussed, he said that "he [Chen] is from a working-class family. To those who say that there is a small portion of working-class members, I'd say not small. Among five of us, chairman and vice chairman of the state, there is one working-class member." There, Mao seemed to be emphasizing the proletariat nature of the CCP. See Mao Zedong, "Guanyu zhonggong zhongyang she fuzhuxi he zongshuji de wenti" [On the question of setting positions for the vice chair and general secretary for the CCP Central Committee], in *Mao Zedong wenji* [Collected writings of Mao Zedong] (Beijing: Renmin Chubanshe, 1999), 7:110.
28. Mao, "On Agriculture Co-Operation," 1:591–95.

but its grassroots-level organizations had to take even more of a direct role in governing and organizing economic activities.²⁹ In *Great Changes in a Mountain Village*, for example, the district Party secretary, Zhu Ming, is depicted in exactly this double role: not only attending to the cooperative movement but also responsible for all the production activities in the district. What this indicates is that, as a ruling party, the function or role of the CCP is also changing, a change that signaled the danger of bureaucratization of the Party. The historical context of such an imminent change has to do with the fact that, in the 1950s as China began to entertain the dream of industrialization and modernization, it inevitably had to use various forms of modernity, ranging from the modern nation-state to modern administrative organizations. And the basic characteristic of all of these modern organizations is their tendency toward specialization (*zhuanye*). This tendency not only leaned toward excluding the participation of the masses but also could lead to a restratification of society.³⁰ And the key issue above all was the danger of revolutionary China falling under the sway of [and] being assimilated by modern China. Issues concerning the day after the revolution, therefore, would not only manifest themselves in campaigns against bureaucracy but also in the agricultural cooperative movement.³¹ It is within this context that mass mobilization, or mass participation, began to be geared toward the political domain, and that the politics of pressure came into existence and began to be applied (albeit in varying degrees). Only when we recognize this context can we begin to explore the "Let a Hundred Flowers Bloom" campaign in 1956 (even though it was stopped by the Anti-Rightist Campaign [in 1957]) and the political visions and the various corresponding mass-participant political movements mobilized prior to the campaign. Also only in this way can we further consider the following seeming paradox: while stories that critically engaged with contemporary life (*ganyu shenghuo*) caused writers such as Liu Bingyan and

---

29. In 1950, for example, Mao stated that Party officials "must themselves be in charge of treasury, finance, and economy related work," untitled piece in *Mao Zedong wenji* [Collected writings of Mao Zedong] (Beijing: Renmin Chubanshe, 1999), 6:59.

30. For a theoretical study of specialization, see Alvin Ward Gouldner, *The Future of Intellectuals and the Rise of the New Class* (New York: Seabury, 1979).

31. Daniel Bell explains "the day after the revolution" as the time "when the mundane world again intrudes upon consciousness, and one finds that the moral ideas are abstract against the intractable desire for material incentives or to pass privileges on to one's children. Thus one finds a revolutionary society itself becoming bureaucratic or being enmeshed ceaselessly in the turmoil of permanent revolution" (*The Cultural Contradictions of Capitalism* [New York: Basic, 1976], 29).

Wang Meng to be severely criticized, themes of antibureaucracy and anti–special privilege continued in the literature of the time (such as Ai Wu's *Steeled and Tempered* [*Bailian chenggang*] and Cao Ming's *Chengfeng polang* [Riding the wind and waves], and films such as *Duo Yin* [Seize the seal]). In other words, contemporary literature in fact did not forgo being critically engaged with society. This paradox, though attributable to an array of complex factors, undoubtedly must count as one of the major conditioning factors of mass participation and the politics of pressure.

Of course, mass participation does not mean that there was a lack of Party leadership. If anything, just the opposite is true. Whether from the actual situation on the ground between 1949 and 1966 or from Mao's own writings, we find that the Party's leadership position remained strong and unbreakable. It goes without saying that Mao was a Marxist strongly influenced by Lenin, especially the latter's vanguard-party theory. Yet Mao's own contradiction is that, on the one hand, he strongly believed in mobilizing the masses and tried to check the bureaucracy by way of mass criticism and mass movements. On the other hand, he also believed that only under the correct leadership of the Party could China move forward into socialism. Thus, in various narrations, the Party is split into two images: an abstract one endowed with absolute political correctness (represented by things like "Chairman Mao's articles and the Party's resolutions"), and another one in the form of concrete organizations that often consisted of the Party's own dissidents (such as the rightist opportunists) and bureaucracy and that required oversight, criticism, and even reform by the masses. The former—the abstract image—not only constitutes the highest political principles but also embodies what Schwartz refers to as "ethical politics."[32] Schwartz's term, though vague, can be nevertheless understood in Gramscian terms of hegemony that, in essence, refer to discursive power and can help explain Schwartz's observation as to why, despite the fact that the Party's organizations were temporarily paralyzed during the Cultural Revolution, China remained highly unified. He believes that a crucial factor has to do with the competitive survival of revolutionary discourse. While much of the power of that discourse comes from "Chairman Mao's articles and the Party's resolutions," there was also undeniably a strong element of the cult of personality embedded in this ethical politics.

32. See Benjamin I. Schwartz, "Essential Features of the Maoist Strategy," *Chinese Communism and the Rise of Mao* (Cambridge, MA: Harvard University Press, 1951), 189–204.

However, it is in fact difficult to draw a clear line between the two images—that is, between what is correct and what is wrong about the Party. Even Mao often oscillated between the two. What is more, the Party's highest principles, or political ideals, still needed the Party's organizational support, not to mention [the fact] that it is often not always clear how the masses were best to participate and to criticize. To determine where the line was supposed to be, or whether or not mass participation was correct, such efforts were either constrained by the politics of the day (such as the Anti-Rightist Campaign) or they even led to political persecutions.[33] From all of this, we may be able to realize why, in contemporary literature, many important themes of criticism (such as antibureaucracy and anti–special privilege) are often embedded in certain kinds of politically correct narration. And this is precisely what we need to treat and analyze with care.

The political participation of the masses was thus often closely related to mobilization by the Party (or its leader). Put differently, what such participation manifests first and foremost is the Party's (or its elite's) imagination of the state and its corresponding structural design. For this reason, we should understand that a structure of mobilization like this did not require that the social movements of the masses be spontaneous happenings; in many ways they were largely contained within the paradigm of party politics. This explains why, without the Party's permission and without them [the Party] offering certain forms of expressions—including the four bigs: speaking out freely, airing views fully, writing big-character posters, and holding great debates—the masses would not have had any way to participate politically.

At the same time, however, this does not mean that this mobilization structure was completely bound by the Party's interests or will. On the contrary, mobilization also contained within it a strong will often spontaneously expressed by the masses. In our understanding, therefore, we should not deny the overlap between the interests of the masses and party politics, for otherwise we cannot fully comprehend the foundation of mass support for mobilization. Yet the masses could also use the political legitimacy offered by the

---

33. Even Mao could at times be restricted by this paradox. A typical example pertains to his comments on Wang Meng's story "Zuzhibu xinlai de nianqingren" [A young man arrives at the organization department], which still was not enough to change what subsequently happened to Wang [Wang was labeled as a "rightist" during the 1957 Anti-Rightist Campaign]. See Mao Zedong, untitled piece in *Mao Zedong wenji* [Collected writings of Mao Zedong] (Beijing: Renmin Chubanshe, 1999), 7:255.

Party-state to express their own political views, wishes, and interests. Mobilization, in other words, was not simply a politics of manipulation. The political participation of the masses compelled the mobilization structure after the 1950s to take on the function of exerting political pressure. This is why, while mass movements often appeared in the form of various political movements, mixed with them were also elements of social movements. In this sense, we may be able to understand why the masses actively participated in various political movements through which they also expressed themselves (the most extreme form of which was the so-called self-denunciation [*ziwo kongsu*]).

To be sure, any attempt to directly or mechanically employ the political reading above to interpret contemporary literature is dangerous. Still, I believe that it is only by way of this kind of political reading that we are able to reach the interior of the texts produced during that period. It is true that critics have long criticized the blatantly political nature of the literature, but if we find a different angle from which to reenter it, we will be able to recognize more complexities in the relationship between politics and literature. From the mobilization structure analyzed above we can recognize the grassroots political enthusiasm of the masses. The political enthusiasm expressed in literature was in many ways generated by the mobilization structure that correspondingly helped construct a forward-looking utopian imaginary. What this imaginary encouraged was precisely that literature should actively intervene in (*ganyu*) everyday life (including political and social issues). Of course, such active interventions were often impeded by the politics of the day or even manipulated by it. Our task, difficult as it may be, is to find a way to differentiate between where literature and politics collude and where they differ.

Even though I often quote Mao's individual writings, it does not follow that I intend to locate contemporary Chinese politics and literature within his narrative paradigm alone. On the one hand, there was a complex array of political forces and political ideas that influenced contemporary society and literature; by refusing to recognize this point, we run the risk of severely simplifying contemporary Chinese history and literature. Challenging as it may be, I believe in the significance of analyzing those complexities. On the other hand, we must also acknowledge the fact that Mao's own writings profoundly influenced and had a great impact on contemporary politics and literature, especially with regard to issues of the power of leadership. For this reason, I also find it undesirable to ignore Mao's writings when studying contemporary Chinese history and literature.

In the final analysis, however, I do not intend to idealize the mobilization structure and the political participation of the masses that was enabled by it. The fact is that, no matter whether [we consider] political expressions and practices or literary narratives, all of them are full of contradictions and paradoxes. In what follows, I focus on how, with much difficulty and often paradoxically, the mobilization structure dealt with the complex relationship among the masses, cadres, and intellectuals.

II. The Masses

It goes without saying that in contemporary [socialist period] Chinese political documents and literary narratives, *the masses* (*qunzhong*) is a very important concept. At the same time, it remains a difficult task to define clearly what it means. The fact is that for a long time this concept appeared vague and unclear. Related to *the masses* was another concept, *the people* (*renmin*). The two terms were often used interchangeably, but they did not always mean the same thing. When they were interchangeably used, they both meant the populace—that is, the majority of the people. The difference lies in the fact that *the people* was usually employed in relation to a political system. The most classic example is Mao's definition of the people in "On the People's Democratic Dictatorship": "Who are the people? At the present stage in China, they are the working class, the peasantry, the urban petit bourgeoisie and the national bourgeoisie."[34] The people in this definition corresponded to the "people's democratic dictatorship" of new democracy.[35] At the same time, the definition of the people is not fixed, with an immanent core. It could change along with changes in the political system. This is likely what Mao meant by "at the present stage." Compared with *the people*, the concept of *the masses* tends to be used as a social category referring to the majority in a society. At the same

---

34. Mao Tse-tung, "On the People's Democratic Dictatorship," in *Selected Works of Mao Tse-tung* (Peking: Foreign Language Press, 1961), 2:417.

35. Tr.: New democracy, in Maoist thought, was a phase between semicolonial or semifeudal China and socialist China. It encompassed a cross-class unity under the Party, which guaranteed the interests of the proletarian class as the leading class in sociopolitics and guaranteed that the direction of China's development would be toward socialism and not capitalism. In terms of the oxymoron *democratic dictatorship*, then, in the conditions of new democracy, the revolutionary people enjoy democracy while the nonrevolutionary remainder must submit to dictatorship. The classical statement of this theory is in Mao, "On the People's Democratic Dictatorship."

time, however, in terms of participation, it is a highly political concept. It denotes the majority but does not equate with the meaning of *citizen*. In the political context of the time, the notion was often constrained by the concept of *class*, while also enjoying a broader connotation than any one example of the latter. To some extent, we can understand the masses to be a sociological category manifesting the political notion of the united front. Hence, in terms of population, it overlaps with the concept of *the people* in constituting the legitimacy of the political system. In terms of political participation, however, the meaning of *the masses* can be constrained by a range of factors that function to determine who can and who cannot participate in sociopolitics. It is precisely this latter characteristic that constituted the discriminatory mechanisms within the masses and helped produce a corresponding concept: *the revolutionary masses*.

Therefore, it is one thing to discuss the notion of *the masses*, including the mobilization structure and political participation in the abstract, but it is quite another to analyze it in conjunction with its varied connotations in specific historical contexts. I do not object to discussing the concept in abstract terms, for it is precisely in the abstract that the term managed to acquire a discursive imaginary whose expressions were both political and literary. Theoretically speaking, therefore, we can understand the notion of *the masses* as a constructed imaginary (*xugou*) but not as a fabrication (*xujia*). Understanding it as fabrication would easily lead to a simplistic way of understanding history; it would eliminate the possibility for debate and discussion. The significance of the constructed imaginary, in contrast, lies in the fact that such a formulation helped establish identity and legitimacy, which in turn functioned to mobilize the masses' enthusiasm for political participation; and, at least in name or at a formal level, this imaginary also helped the masses acquire a political subject position. While critics have noted the importance of form to a political community, equally important is to delve into specific issues and to fully explore and understand them. It is precisely on the concrete level that we see the schism between the imaginary and practice, and even contradictions within the narratives about what is imagined. At the same time, the existence of these contradictions leaves gaps (*lie hen*) in various texts, providing opportunities for us to enter, or reenter, those texts for in-depth exploration. What is more, much of the literature from the 1949–66 period was created within the framework of realism, making it difficult for narration to be carried out on an abstract (and self-oriented) level only. And as soon as a story or novel touches on the everyday life of individuals, it is compelled to return to issues related to the quotidian. It is in moments of such returns that gaps often occur in a text.

In chapter 16 of Qu Bo's *Linhai xueyuan* [*Tracks in the Snowy Forest*; originally published in 1957], there is the following scene: The new government sends relief [supplies of] grain, winter clothing, and weapons to the people of Jiapigou Village. Shao Jianbo [the leader of the military brigade] "shouted excitedly, 'The Kuomingtang, the Eagle, they rob us, they ruin our work, they take our guns away, they think they can starve us to death. But now the government has given us grain, it's saved us, and it's opened up the road for us to earn a living. That's why we must protect our grain, protect our home, protect our right to work unmolested.... 'Clean out the root of our trouble first,' shouts from the agitated villagers interrupted. 'Give us guns, commander. We'll go into the mountains and wipe out those bandit sons of bitches like we'd kill a pack of wild boars.'" In this same scene, however, we find a critical response from one of the main characters, Li Yongqi [Li Yung-chi]: "This remark seemed to have raised the floodgate on all Yung-chi's grievances. 'It's no use to twitter like sparrows and scatter at the first report of a gun. Last time when the Eagle was taking our weapons away, we didn't stick together,' he roared. 'There were mice who couldn't resist a little fragrant bait; they were all caught in the bandits' rat trap. And there were rabbits who got scared and ran.'"[36]

In this scene, in effect we find three discourses, or three images. One is Shao Jianbo. He shoulders the responsibility of persuading and mobilizing the masses with a specific ideology. Shao, in other words, is an embodiment of party politics. The second figure is Li Yongqi. As a member of the masses whose consciousness has been raised earlier than most of his fellow villagers, he is a progressive individual. Compared with the members of the military team [sent to Jiapigou Village to mobilize the masses], however, Li is supposed to be one degree lower in terms of his political consciousness. Nevertheless, he functions as an important connecting point between the Party and the masses. The third figure is the masses [the villagers]. As a group of people, they remain nameless, yet they harbor a strong revolutionary enthusiasm with a recognition that the revolution is on the side of their own interests. At the same time, they are not fully conscious of their interests and still need [political] education, consciousness-raising, and guidance. In essence, this scene manifests

36. Chu Po [Qu Bo], *Tracks in the Snowy Forest*, trans. Sidney Shapiro (Peking: Foreign Language Press, 1962): 215–16.

the precise logical relationship among the Party (and its politics), progressive individuals, and the masses that constitutes the mobilization structure.

Although the novel *Tracks in the Snowy Forest* shows traces of the influence of the traditional martial arts novel—in which there is a strong heroism and a kind of unconscious disdain toward the masses—nevertheless, in other novels, such as *Great Changes in a Mountain Village*, we find a similar setup of character representation—namely, a similar three-layered characterization. In the latter novel, surrounding Deng Xiumei are such progressive individuals as Liu Yusheng, Chen Dachun, and Sheng Qingming. Surrounding Liu Yusheng and Chen Dachun are the secondary progressive individuals, including Sheng Jiaxiu, Sheng Shujun, and Chen Mengchun. Outside of this circle, we find Ting Mianhu, Chen Xianjin—followed by Ju Xiaojin and Qiu Sigua—who are naturally representatives of the backward masses (*luohou qunzhong*) in need of education and reform. Unlike the villagers in *Tracks in the Snowy Forest*, however, the masses in *Great Changes in a Mountain Village* all have names and are represented in quite a vivid manner. What is more, the [latter] novel also designs complex relationships among and between these characters, and many of these relationships are not defined by class or political relations. In representing these relationships, the novel is able to depict vivid scenes of everyday life. Still, the three-pronged relationship—[among the] Party, progressive individuals, [and] the backward masses—is clearly discernible in the novel's complex web of relationships among the characters.

After 1949, criticisms of bureaucracy never ceased. Embedded in the criticisms was a political vision in which the state (and the Party) and its administration would be under the critical supervision of the masses, while at the same time the Party's political power and its leadership would not be weakened. In this sense, we can [once again] see the strong influence of Leninism on China and a strong similarity between Maoism and Leninism. The difference in the Chinese case, though, lies in its emphasis on the fact that the Party was more often required to perform a correct type of politics [as compared to the Soviet case, in which such considerations were not as important]. For this reason, in the literature of the era, there existed contrasting images of Party politics, which was represented in the comparative images of one leader who is [politically] correct and another one who is not. This kind of contrast offered an opportunity, at least in theory, for the political participation of the masses, although at the same time the ultimate control of mass movements was in the hands of the Party. In various narratives, the Party's and masses' interests are treated as exhibiting a high degree of agreement with one another:

the Party represents the real interests of the masses. It is for this reason that the masses are still considered to be in need of mobilization. Without this understanding, we could easily mistake the political participation of the masses as spontaneous social movements.

When the masses are surrounded by the Party (that is, politics), there inevitably appear groups that can be labeled progressive or backward. In literature, this particular political content is made specific. In *Great Changes in a Mountain Village*, for example, the narrative centers on the issue of joining the cooperative. However, the more general theme in this context pertains to each individual's political attitude, suggesting that it is one's attitude that determines one's political stance and where one is situated among the masses. This point is worth noting: emphasizing attitude denotes the importance given to the subjective will of the individual; the subjective will is believed to be something capable of being reshaped and transformed. The progressive individuals in the novel, then, shoulder one narrative function in that they help educate and reform the backward masses—the belief is that the socialist enthusiasm palpable in the masses needs to be transformed from being spontaneous to exhibiting a more self-aware political consciousness. And the only way for such a transformation to be possible is through education and learning. Meanwhile, since the State cannot be the sole player in educating the masses, it needs a variety of mediators to perform such a role. One such mediator is found in the progressive individuals among the masses. This method of [having] the masses educate the masses reveals a tendency to believe in an all-powerful politics, whose origin can be traced to the reform idlers (*gaizao erliuzi*) movement during the Yan'an period.[37] The masses educate the masses model is a successful case of an all-powerful politics, which is also a classic example of the fact that the socialist-reform movement (*shehui zhuyi gaizao yundong*) did not target intellectuals only; it had the whole people (*quan min*) in mind, with its aim of constructing the so-called new socialist human beings. The belief was that only when such new human beings were constructed could political and economic issues be solved. It goes without saying that, in this political imagination, revolutionary China was not to rely on the management model of modern bureaucracy but, rather, was to depend directly on the

---

37. For additional information on this movement, see Zhu Hongzhao, *Yanan richang shenghuozhong de lishi (1937–1947)* [History of Yan'an's everyday life (1937–1947)] (Guilin: Guangxi Shida Chubanshe, 2007), 57–65. In extreme political situations— for example, during the Cultural Revolution—"masses educate the masses" could turn into "masses fight the masses." Additional research is needed to further explore this topic.

development of socialist consciousness among the masses. Thus, this model is highly moralistic in its tendencies and quite panpolitical in its structure. Without a doubt, it is an extremely idealistic vision.

Because this future-oriented political vision tended to be presented as encompassing the core interests of the masses, even though the masses were being educated and reformed, elements of interests did not completely disappear from the mobilization-reformation model. Again, in *Great Changes in a Mountain Village*, when Liu Yusheng tries to mobilize Sheng Jiaxiu, he uses a kind of accounting, listing a number of concrete items [of particular importance to peasants] such as forests, land, labor power, and water buffalo and manure to make a comparison between [the effectiveness of] individual family farming and cooperation so as to emphasize the advantage of socialism. Here, it is important to note that in this novel political attitude is not emphasized in a simplistically correct manner. Instead, it is by way of moral persuasion, or affect, that the political theme gets transmitted. The resort to moral persuasion is bound up with [Mao's concept of] internal contradictions among the people (*renmin neibu maodun*). This concept renders it difficult for the novel to categorize the masses completely by class, or entirely to politicize the masses. During the 1950s, revolutionary narration was relatively gentle when it came to representing the masses, but the tendency already was to moralize mass-related issues. This tendency led to the widespread [use of a] narrative framework that contrasted the new person and new things with the old-style person and old-style things.

Taking *Great Changes in a Mountain Village* as an example again, we find that such new-person individuals as Liu Yusheng and Chen Dachun not only represent [what was] then political correctness, but more important, they represent a certain kind of moral ideal of rural society. For example, Liu is willing to sacrifice his own family interests for the good of the larger community, and, though short-tempered, Chen is a man of integrity with a clear sense of right and wrong. To be sure, an overemphasis on personal morals that appeared in subsequent works did result in abstraction, while generating a sense of moral pressure in the reader. Still, the fact is that the emphasis on morality became a necessary force in narration. The other side of the coin is the fact that backward individuals have to be morally deficient. The character Wang Jusheng (nicknamed Juyaojin), for example, is depicted as someone who, although frugal and hardworking, is nevertheless shrewd and, like another character [Zhang Qiusheng] nicknamed Qiusigua, is one of those hard-to-deal-with rural folks. The way Wang mistreats the family of Uncle Man [Manshu], especially, makes it appear that his real aim is to take over the latter's family property, thereby directly violating a taboo in rural society. Also violating the taboo are characters like Qiusigua and Fu Jiangeng. Similar characters appear in other works. All of them share another defect, in that they are licentious, lusting after women. In Liu Qing's words [in *The Builders*], such men "can truly scare a good girl."[38] In contrast, correct characters all tend to be slightly overly reserved in front of women. Ironically, the restraint on the part of these male characters is often shown to be particularly attractive to young women.

Representations of men like this are reminiscent of those found in traditional novels such as *The Water Margin*, but they are also reminiscent of traditional rural views of what a good man is. It goes without saying, then, that such literary representations are not only informed by the politics of the day but also by the cultural resources of traditional rural morality and traditional aesthetics.

What we see by now is that, in representing the widespread phenomenon of mobilization of the masses, these novels rely on the model of masses educate the masses, rather than on showing a direct intervention by power from above. But this model also indicates that mobilization is at the same time a politics of pressure that, as the novels demonstrate, comes from orienting the narration around the majority of the masses. In the second volume of *Great Changes in a Mountain Village*, there is a chapter titled "Competition." It tells of the moment at which the cooperative and Juyaojin's family compete to transform low-yield land. Obviously, the contest here far exceeds the usual meaning of competition and takes on strong political implications as a competition between the collective and individuals, between socialism and capitalism. The notion of the majority here has multiple meanings: the political will of the people; the collective and the better realization of economic goals; and, more important, the rise of a new community that is not just a political and economic one but is also bound by feelings and emotions informed by traditional ideals in rural China that promote mutual aid. What it also implies, at the same time, is that staying outside this community is not only politically and economically hopeless but can also result in isolation and lack of aid from others. It is precisely the last point that jolts Chen Xianjin and Juyaojin out of their individualist mind-sets. In *The Builders*, we also find that this mode of pressure makes the character Guo Zhenshan realize with apprehension that what he may lose is not just a political future but also the kind of respect nec-

---

38. Liu Qing, *Chuangye shi* (Beijing: Zhongguo Qingnian Chubanshe, 2009), 188.

essary for him to function in a rural community. While there is an exclusionary mechanism in this form of pressure that can cause a few in the masses to be isolated, the fact that it puts emphasis on competition as opposed to struggle as a form of self-reform by the masses indicates that the literature of the 1950s not only assumed a gentle attitude but also manifested a political and cultural self-confidence.

All of this denotes a strong desire to construct the new socialist person as well as an urgent need to reform the entire society. The purpose of such reform was not just so that the individual would obey the collective, but, in a much deeper sense, to quickly establish an identity with the modern nation-state. The collective in this sense functioned as a medium between the individual and the state, thereby making the individual-collective-state an integral whole. It does not mean, of course, that the notion of class disappeared from the masses. We see its traces in the relationship between the progressive and the backward. For example, when it comes to the desire to become rich, we see little difference among those (backward) characters who desire it, other than the fact that some of these characters are poor peasants while others are rich middle[-class] peasants. According to the Chinese version of class analysis, the former have a natural tendency to lean toward socialism, while the latter naturally tend toward capitalism. Characters like Tingmianhu [in *Great Changes in a Mountain Village*] then, though tending to be selfish, are considered to incline more toward socialism and therefore to be more acceptable both politically and morally. The significance of such characters has to do with the fact that their depictions help offer a glimpse into the details of the everyday life of rural society of the time. Many of the subsequent representations of the so-called middle character, such as the old man Liang San in *Chuangye shi* (The builders), originated from this model.[39]

Further discussion should focus on characters like Qiusigua in *Great Changes in a Mountain Village*. Zhou Libo, the author, is relatively balanced in his representations of Wang Jusheng (nicknamed Juyaojin) and Zhang Qiusheng (nicknamed Qiusigua). While the former insists on going it alone (rather than joining the cooperative), he stays away from politics. Qiusigua,

---

39. For additional discussion on this point, see Shao Quanling, "Zai Dalian 'nongcun ticai duanpian xiaoshuo chuangzuo zuotanhui' shang de jianghua" [Speech at the "forum on the rural-themed short story" in Dalian], in *Zhongguo dangdai wenxue shi: shiliaoxuan* [History of contemporary Chinese literature], ed. Hong Zicheng (Wuhan: Changjiang Wenyi Chubanshe, 2002), 2:501–11.

in contrast, exhibits stronger political tendencies. He is shown to have once been a member of the army riffraff, but the author does not depict him in a clear-cut manner. While in certain parts of the novel Qiusigua is shown to have been pulled into the enemy camp represented by a character named Gong Ziyuan, who is an underground special agent for the Nationalists, the novel nevertheless consistently assumes his problem to be part of the internal contradictions among people and celebrates his eventual decision to join the cooperative. This kind of narrative treatment indicates a hesitance on the part of the author in judging what belongs to internal contradictions among people and what belongs to contradictions between us and the enemy. Such hesitance, at the same time, indicates that the author is still confined to the framework of class analysis. Similar examples are found in Liu Qing's treatment of Guo Zhenshan [in *The Builders*] and Zhao's of Fan Dengao [in *Sanliwan Village*]. The novel that ended such narrative uncertainty was *Sunny Days* by Hao Ran, in his representation of Ma Liben. There, the author not only directly identifies Ma Liben as a class enemy within the Party but also depicts him as morally degenerate—that is, a bad person. This narrative shift corresponded with the emergence of another narrative model: good people and good deeds versus bad people and bad deeds. This narrative model signified that, in the 1960s, the class struggle would extend to individuals like Ma Liben.

The changes signaled by representations of Qiusigua and Ma Liben indicate the changes in how the notion of class was understood: *class* began to change from being defined as a social category to being defined as a person's political position and even political attitude. This change implied that when one changed one's political stance or attitude based on one's own interests, one's original class position, stance, or attitude could very well change also. Redetermining an individual's class position based on his or her political stance or attitude, as opposed to his or her original class position, was a major characteristic of Chinese-style class struggle.[40] At issue is not only that this new and strongly subjective definition of class pushed its way into the category of the masses, thereby effectively blurring the line between internal contradictions and contradictions between ourselves and the enemy, but also the fact that the right to define who are the enemies was in the hands of

---

40. For example, among the five black types [*hei wu lei*] of landlord, rich peasant, counterrevolutionary, bad elements, and rightist, the latter three are obviously more political in nature.

those in power.⁴¹ Such was also one of the root causes of the broadening of class struggle during the Mao era (1949–76). Today when we discuss again the political culture of the first thirty years of the socialist period, I believe it is not easy to overthrow the consensus, reached during the 1980s, about the problems regarding the broadening of class struggle.

Despite all of this, I would still like to highlight the kind of utopian vision generated from the notion of the masses. In contemporary Chinese history, this notion acquired a political legitimacy that made the masses' participation in political activities more than just a theory. What is more, because the mobilization structure often took the form of a political movement, it made it possible for the masses to find a way to express themselves. However, under the socialist historical conditions, the redefinition of the notion of class led to the broadening of class struggle on the one hand, but on the other hand, it also paradoxically ignited the political enthusiasms of the masses and the possibility for them to change their own conditions. This paradox was particularly palpable at the beginning of the Cultural Revolution. Only when we have a good grasp of this point can we better understand the context in which Yu Luoke wrote "On Family Origins" in 1967.⁴² Political attitude, a strongly subjective criterion, ironically led to a theoretical possibility for the masses to make their own choices. In the final analysis, therefore, despite the fact that there was clearly Party-controlled politics in the mobilization structure, the masses had the potential to break out of this controlled political framework. That explains why, in almost all the political movements [during the Mao era], even when the Party and the masses were on the same page, there still could be tensions and even conflicts between the two. How to adjust those

---

41. To some extent, at the beginning of the Cultural Revolution, some of the rebels rose with the precise intention of overthrowing the class or political labels that had been imposed on them.

42. Tr.: Yu Luoke's "On Family Origins" was written in 1967 to counter the then-ascendant theory of blood lineage. This theory basically held that a son's or daughter's status was inevitably bound up with his or her father or mother, summarized in the pithy slogan: "father a revolutionary, son a hero; father a capitalist, son a bastard." Yu objected to this blood theory of class and instead supported a theory of political consciousness and the mutability of class. As Cai is depicting it, in the 1950s, the gentle version of class is far closer to Yu's version than the 1960s version heralded by Hao Ran, which is more rigid and feeds eventually into the Cultural Revolutionary blood lineage theory that Yu contested. Yu was attacked, jailed, and executed in 1970. For original text, see Yu Luoke, "Chushen lun" [On family origins], *Wenhuadageming he ta de yiduan sichao* (The Great Cultural Revolution and its heretical thought trend), ed. Song Yongyi et al. (Hong Kong: Tianyuan Shuwu, 1997).

tensions and conflicts was also one of the major problems confronting each political movement.

III. The Cadres

There is one scene in [Xue Ke's 1961] novel *The Spring of Battle* (*Zhandou de qingchun*) that goes like this: the district team of the Zaoyuan District spends a night in the open. The Party secretary of the district, Xu Feng, "quietly walks around tucking in the three young women with overcoats. Looking up, she sees Li Tie, who has just returned from doing the rounds of the guard posts, also helping tuck in others with overcoats."[43] Tucking someone in with overcoats (*gai mianpao*) is in fact not a small detail made up by writers. Similar occasions are described in historical documents. In the "Resolutions of the Ninth Representative Conference of the Fourth Red Army Group of the CCP," for example, there is one resolution that stipulates: "army officers, especially those at the company level, should frequently check up on the wounded, bring them drinking water, tuck them in well at night. If the wounded feel cold, they [the officers] must look for ways to help them [the wounded], including borrowing clothes from others. These should be made into rules for caring for the wounded. If we routinely implement them, this is the best way to win over the masses."[44] From being part of a political vision to [being] its systemic practice and its fictional narration, this specific gesture became a literary trope. Even though people from different positions interpret it differently, we nevertheless find in this trope a particular image of a cadre who is to be a new kind of manager of revolutionary China.

It is hard to underestimate the impact and attraction this image and its practice accumulated over the process of revolutionary history. Its power lies in the mobilization structure in which the cadres are the force who carry out the Party's tasks to mobilize and reform the masses. Within this structure, the role of the cadres is a prominent one, not to be understood in the usual sense of bureaucrats or managers. Some historians have studied the Chinese documents obtained by the U.S. military during the Korean War, documents

---

43. Xue Ke, *Zhandou de qingchun*, 337.
44. Mao Zedong, "Zhongguo gongchandang hongjun disijun dijiuci daibiao dahui juyi an" [Resolutions of the Ninth Representative Conference of the Fourth Red Army Group of the CCP], in *Mao Zedong wenji* [Collected writings of Mao Zedong] (Beijing: Renmin Chubanshe, 1993), 1:112.

that were lost in battle and belonged to the twenty-sixth and twenty-seventh armies of the Chinese People's Volunteer Army. Those documents consisted of official files and soldiers' private letters and diaries. Among them were a few companies' statistical tables of political quality, which showed that one-third of the soldiers who had previously been captured from the Nationalist army in the Civil War [1945–49] had begun to change their minds to become more Communist. Despite the fact that there were deserters among those captured from the Nationalist army, those constituted only 1 percent of the total military. There was a soldier who had joined the Nationalist army at the age of fifteen. He explained his change this way: "When I was in the Nationalist army, we were told that the PLA would kill us so I was really afraid. But when I got liberated and came to this side, I was well treated. I had ham to eat every day and was issued new clothes and two pairs of shoes, more than the old comrades had. I felt this was a very good policy. . . . When we were fighting in the southwest region, we listened to the lectures by our political instructor, who told us that this army was the poor people's army. That got me thinking; I'm from a poor family. In the future when we distribute land to the peasants that will be a kind of revolution against the landlords. I came to understand what revolution meant a bit more." Another solder offered a similar account of how his mind changed, saying that "in the battles against various kinds of bandits, I personally witnessed the special treatment of the military families and how the people's government helped the poor to better their lives. That helped further raise my class consciousness."[45] These documents demonstrate that what helped heighten military morale, in addition to the fact that the government helped the poor with land reform and gave special treatment to military families, was the equal relationship between soldiers and officers and [the fact] that the cadres cared for the masses.

What led to this particular notion of the cadre and its corresponding practice is a mix of complex factors, but the major factor was always the pursuit of equality. In contrast to the social hierarchy of traditional China, the revolution aimed to first smash the political or patriarchal clan structure that upheld such hierarchy. At the same time, to prevent the appearance of a new bureaucratic system, emphasis fell on imagining a new type of cadre. Literature, accordingly, was to join the imagining of these new types by offering its own new narrative codes and stories.

45. Quoted in Yang Kuisong, *Kai juan you yi* [Reading is always beneficial] (Nanchang: Jiangxi Renmin Chubanshe, 2007), 150–51.

Great Changes in a Mountain Village depicts the first day Liu Yusheng becomes the director of the cooperative. In addition to the many things that await his attention, "he is surrounded by a crowd of women, some holding their kids, some holding their needle work, who noisily press upon him their demands or ask questions. 'Director, I've lost a chicken; what should I do?' 'Director, someone has stolen the eggs laid by my black hen. I know who did it; he's going to die a bad death for doing that. But Director, please help me punish this thief...' 'Director Liu, that shameless SOB of mine didn't come home again last night and was with that bitch of his....'"[46] What is interesting about this narrative moment is that it shows that Liu Yusheng not only has to deal with the important matters of managing the agricultural cooperative, he also has to deal with various small family matters. In fact, this is a recurrent theme in the literature of the time. There are similar images of such cadres in many novels and stories. What they demonstrate is that a cadre has first to earn legitimacy by caring for the poor and then, through ability, must lead the poor out of poverty and toward a better life. This corresponds to the revolutionary tradition that strictly demands that cadres care for the lives of the masses. Caring for people's lives not only helped establish the legitimacy of the Party but also helped extend the political into the private domain of people's lives.

This phenomenon helps explain why, during the socialist period, there was no clear demarcation between the public and private domains; the two spheres were in a constant motion and mutually acting on one another. And it was the cadre who functioned as the intermediary force, actively connecting the two domains. On the one hand, the cadres embodied the power of the state's capacity to penetrate into the private domain of people's lives. This extension undoubtedly manifested the desire for political control. On the other hand, cadres also embodied the concern of the state for the ordinary people. Ignoring or overemphasizing either of these two aspects renders the entirety of that historical period and its complexities invisible.

It is also erroneous to interpret the role and meaning of cadre as equivalent to [those of] officials in a modern bureaucracy. The image of the cadre on the one hand denotes the revolutionary destruction of [the role and image of] traditional government officials; on the other hand, this image also carries with it a certain traditional imaginary about good officials in the notion of

---

46. Li-po Chou [Zhou Libo], *Great Changes in a Mountain Village*, trans. Derek Bryan (Peking: Foreign Language Press, 1961), volume 2.

xun li, [a lawful and reasonable official], such as Xiao Yunxian depicted in the traditional novel *The Scholars* [by Wu Jingzi], for example. As early as during the Red Army period (1928–37), Mao began to emphasize that "the soviet form of government is the organizer of people's lives. Only when this government tries its utmost to help solve people's life concerns and helps change their lives for the better can it win people's faith, can it mobilize the people to join the Red Army and to defeat the enemy's encirclement." In the same article [report], Mao goes on to offer a design through which "every month a peasant can have on average five days of (various kinds of) meetings, which can function as a time for them to rest."[47] It goes without saying that during the Mao era proper, the political was never an abstract term; not only was it manifested in wars and political movements, it also penetrated into the small things of people's everyday life.

Another type of detail is also worth noting. From Zhou Libo's 1948 *The Hurricane* to his 1958 *Great Changes in a Mountain Village*, a shared narrative element is that, after the work team finishes its task of mobilizing and reforming, it hands over the responsibility for managing the villages to local cadres. This transfer of power is based not just on political trust but also on a tacit understanding between those in political power and rural society. As Mother Sheng in *Great Changes in a Mountain Village* says to Deng Xiumei: "It's all thanks to your hard work in selecting a group of reliable individuals to lead us. Once the cooperative was set up, everybody went to ask for work and food from the director. A roomful of people wanting to eat but only one person doing the work. Without someone like Director Liu who's willing to give all he's got to lead, we would not feel reassured."[48] Individuals in the image of Liu Yusheng who is "willing to give all he's got" can be found in the characters Liang Baosheng in *The Builders* and Xiao Changchun in *Sunny Days*. This willingness to give all he's got implies such virtues as selflessness and the sacrifice of one's own family for the good of all families. I believe this was not

---

47. Mao Zedong, "Changgang Xiang diaocha" [Investigative report on Changgang Township], in *Mao Zedong wenji* [Collected writings of Mao Zedong] (Beijing: Renmin Chubanshe, 1993), 1:298. Tr.: The Red Army period refers to the time from the 1927 White Terror and the escape of some members of the Communist Party to the countryside to the end of the War of Resistance against Japan (1937–45), when the Red Army was renamed the PLA. This was when Mao's peasant-centered revolutionary strategy was worked out and when the soviet form of government—a communal form of governance—was pioneered and established in the various base areas outside Nationalist territory.

48. Li-po Chou, *Great Changes in a Mountain Village*, vol. 2.

only the Party's expectation for its own members, but with the localization of cadres, it also represented the transformation of social functions formerly performed by the clan or family. In other words, revolutionary politics made effective use of the traditional ideal of a clan leader and transformed it into a new image of someone who leads. Thus, this kind of leader tended to have an easier time earning the trust of their rural community. It is a known fact that, in contemporary China, rural cadres are not strictly categorized as state officials, and yet the state has had to rely on them to manage rural communities for those communities to function effectively within the structure of a unified nation-state.

In the cities, a similar structural transformation based on the image of an ideal leader was also taking place. For example, in Zhou Erfu's *Morning of Shanghai*, the author narrates that "after the construction of the Caoyang Workers Residential Area (*caoyang xincun*), the Hujiang Textile [Factory] was given four [housing] units" and Yu Jing, the Party secretary and chairman of the workers' union, "was also given one unit. But she refused to take it, insisting that the fine spin [*xisha*] workshop had a large number of workers who should be given one unit. After some discussion, one unit was given to Mother Qin."[49] In so doing, Yu Jing wins the workers' trust. What also wins their trust is revolutionary politics. Indeed, it is evident that, in the political visions of revolutionary China, the spirit of sacrifice on the part of the cadres was the first force to be relied on; it was based on this that the state succeeded in reorganizing and restructuring the grassroots administrative level.

What was considered most important when it came to cadres was whether or not they had a heightened political consciousness. Such consciousness was the key criterion for measuring whether or not a cadre was good. In all the literature of the time, the corruption of a cadre was attributed to the loss of political belief. Cadres in Zhao's *Sanliwan Village* and in [Liu Qing's] *The Builders* exemplify this. In a theoretical sense, the molding of this kind of cadre is in fact highly modern—indeed, a product of modern party politics that was not reducible to any local or group interest. An emphasis on caring for people's lives could sometime lead to conflicts between local interests and those of the state. But the state's interest always had to be paramount. The cadre Lu Ren, in the 1959 novel by Luo Dan, *The Storm of Dawn* (*Fengyu de liming*), for example, in telling the story of the Anshan Steel Mill before liberation,

---

49. Zhou Erfu, *Shanghai de zaocheng*, 3:140.

repeatedly emphasizes the danger, or the destructive nature, of localism to the revolution.⁵⁰

Cadres constituted an extremely important element in the mobilization structure; they not only shoulder the political task of mobilizing and reforming the masses, but they are also responsible for guiding the masses into the political vision of the State. Representing good cadres became an important task for the literature of the time. The classic image that most symbolized the good cadre, of course, did not appear until the journalistic report depicting the life (and death) of Jiao Yulu.⁵¹

If by representing good cadres—as people who take the lead on the road to socialism—the literature of the socialist period offered its vision for newstyle officials of revolutionary China who are shown to be a major force in the reconstruction of the basic level of Chinese society, it is only natural that the other task of this literature is to criticize another kind of cadre. Such criticism constituted the antibureaucracy and anti-special-privilege theme in literature.

As mentioned above, the CCP was a modern political party with a very well organized system. It demanded that the individual obey the collective (*geren fucong zuzhi*) and the entire Party follow the leadership of the Central Committee (*quan dang fucong zhongyang*). Any form of interest group, including regionalist ones, would encounter severe criticism. The aforementioned novel *The Storm of Dawn* tells of the chaotic state of affairs in the Angang Steel Mill shortly after liberation. What causes the chaos has to do precisely with different sections (interest groups) in the factory taking apart and moving around machines and facilities based on their own needs. The novel depicts the opposition, conflict, and struggle between Song Zezhou and Yi Qiufan on one side and Lou Kunhua and Zhang Chong on the other side. It celebrates the political ideal of serving all under heaven. But more often than not, literary representations of localism or local interests at the time tended to shift the blame onto individual officials who were pursuing their own personal interests; this theme tended to depict local interest groups as political factions that either represented the wrong political line or were the work of class enemies

---

50. Luo Dan, *Fengyu de liming* [The storm of dawn] (Beijing: Zhongguo Qingnian Chubanshe, 1959).

51. Tr.: Jiao Yulu (1922–64) was a cadre in Henan Province who became known for assisting his villagers through what turned out to be the great famine of the Great Leap Forward. He died of liver cancer in 1964 and was lionized by the press at the time as an honest and caring local Party official.

within the Party. That is to say, most such literary representations are ideologically or politically oriented. In addition to possibly direct political reasons for such depictions, the narrators (authors) were themselves much motivated by the idealistic impulse to oppose bureaucracy and special privileges. Such an impulse was not informed only by the political quest for equality, but also by the imaginary of a united nation that included the socialist form of the state and its associated political life.

In 1979, the Shanghai Literature and Arts Publishing House published a book titled *Flowers Reblooming* (*Chong fang de xianhua*) that collected twenty short stories that had been major targets of criticism during the 1957 Anti-Rightist Campaign.[52] Among them, twelve pieces touch on the relationship between cadres and the masses. In 1957, then Shanghai Party Secretary Yao Wenyuan published an article titled "On Revisionism in Some Cultural and Creative Tendencies" ("Wenxue shang de xiuzheng zhuyi he chuangzuo qinxiang"). Yao specifically criticized antibureaucratism, especially the related views held by the prominent intellectuals Feng Xuefeng and Xu Maoyong. In Yao's estimation of Xu's writings at the time, Xu was said to emphasize that "so long as there is still bureaucracy, we should not wait for the bureaucrats to step down to enjoy democracy. The democratic form that we are fully enjoying now is none other than struggling against bureaucracy. Without necessary struggle, bureaucracy would not itself choose to disappear."[53] This emphasis was said to be unnecessarily negative. In this vein, Yao also mentioned a number of other antibureaucracy stories including [works] by Wang Meng, Liu Binyan, and Liu Shaotang. In his article, Yao deliberately conflated antibureaucracy with expose literature, thus harking back to the Yan'an debate on whether literature and arts should praise or expose. He accused Feng and Xu of relying too much on exposing.

Yet what is more worth noting is another passage in Yao's article:

If in our socialist society there is still a "dark side," then that is where the hidden counterrevolutionaries, rightists, hooligans, thieves, and other class enemies, who harbor a hatred toward socialism, carry out their sabotage activities. The next in line are the bourgeois ideas that still dominate some individuals' hearts. That darkness in their heart is where the social-

52. *Chong fang de xianhua* [Flowers reblooming] (Shanghai: Shanghai Wenyi Chubanshe, 1979).

53. Yao Wenyuan, "Wenxue shang de xiuzheng zhuyi he chuangzuo qinxiang" [On revisionism in some cultural and creative tendencies], *Remin wenxue* [People's literature], no. 11 (1957): 110.

ist sunshine cannot reach. For literature to help people rid themselves of these dark shadows in their lives, it must uphold the Party's principle when exposing the ugly essence of the enemies of socialism, to show that their shadowy activities will not escape the fate of being exposed as socialism develops. It should also criticize their bourgeois individualism. Of course we should criticize bureaucraticism. We have always encouraged the spirit of self-criticism with which to expose the shortcomings in our work. We also oppose nonconfrontation [appeasement] attitudes. But bureaucracy is not a product of the socialist system nor does it occupy a dominant position [in it]. Therefore, we should not demonize those who have been bureaucratic, nor should we describe bureaucraticism as a dominant force as if our society is at the mercy of the bureaucracy with no room to breathe.[54]

Here, Yao limits the legitimacy of exposing to being about struggles outside of socialism—having to do with such elements as "counterrevolutionaries, rightists, hooligans, thieves, and other class enemies" who hate socialism. At the same time, he interprets bureaucraticism as a kind of remnant of the old ideology and old working style and not a product of the socialist system. Yet whether or not bureaucraticism is a product of socialism and whether or not things like bureaucraticism can be reproduced in socialism, these questions touch on an important theoretical problematic. If it is not possible for socialism to produce bureaucraticism, the continuous revolution would have no theoretical foundation. Even though how far a theory and practice of continuous revolution can go is contingent on a specific political situation, what is implicit in this theory is the question of "alienation," a problem that came to be debated only during the 1980s. (I will discuss later in the book how this issue was discussed in the 1960s in conjunction with the political slogan "never forget class struggle." For it was within that context that the notion of the bureaucratic class was brought to the fore. I argue that behind the notion of class struggle was a kind of anxiety over modernity, including managerial technocracy, which is characterized by two things—namely, bureaucratization and specialization.)

The top CCP leaders never stopped worrying about bureaucraticism; neither did many writers, despite the political pressure that confronted them. The political quest for equality as a literary theme was a shared one throughout the works of Chinese writers at this time. Indeed, one of the characteristics of the literature of the socialist period was that, even though the anti-

54. Ibid., 111.

bureaucracy and anti-special-privilege theme was severely criticized in the 1957 Anti-Rightist Campaign, and many writers were persecuted because of that critique, this theme continued in various forms and eventually became part of mainstream writing.

If we place certain texts included in the 1979 anthology *Flowers Reblooming* in the larger context of socialist literature, the criticism of bureaucraticism in them appears relatively mild. Many of them treat bureaucracy as a problem of work style, which is viewed as part of the problems brought on by the bureaucratization of the administrative system. We see this treatment in Wang Meng's and Liu Binyan's stories of the later 1950s. The phenomenon of the cadres gradually cutting themselves off from the masses is also treated as part of the new historical conditions. Liu Shaotang's and Li Guowen's stories of the time belong to this category. As a whole, however, these "exposés" of the "dark side" (in Yao Wenyuan's words [from the same article]) still followed the spirit of cure the sickness to save the patient (*zhibing jiuren*) that strictly confined the issues within the framework of internal contradictions among the people. In other words, in the theoretical terms of the time, these were issues resolvable within socialism itself.

After 1958, however, many novels began to treat cadres' problems as more than an issue of working style or of bureaucraticism. Indeed, works exposing the "dark side" not only did not stop being produced, but rather they increased in number, especially in the 1960s. The theme was even elevated to the level of class struggle. In Zhao's *Sanliwan Village* and Liu Qing's *The Builders*, we find representations of two cadres, Fan Denggao and Guo Zhenshan, respectively. As both novels proceed, we learn that the two characters were once active participants in the revolution in the countryside. Because of that, they become leaders of the [new] rural political power structure but also soon become individuals with their own vested interests in that structure. Those interests are both political and economic. In *Sanliwan Village*, Zhao, the author, humorously relates that the cadre Fan Denggao "has turned his life around so high that people call him *fan de gao* [literally: turn up high; almost a homonym for his actual name]." In response, Fan's wife remarks that, "well, actually not that high; he just got a few *mu* of good land and people then talk a bunch of rubbish."[55] In fact, in some earlier stories, Zhao had already begun to address the issue of these kinds of cadres who had become individuals with

---

55. Zhao Shuli, *Sanliwan Village*, trans. Gladys Yang (Peking: Foreign Language Press, 1957), 59.

vested interests in the rural revolution, suggesting that there was a high likelihood that they would become a group of new oppressors in the countryside. In *Sanliwan Village*, the author pushes the issue one step further by connecting Fan's vested interests with the fact that these interests have assisted him in realizing a primitive accumulation of capital. In the words of another character, Ma Youyi, with regard to the two mules Fan uses for commercial activities, "at the time, it was not [that] no one wanted them. It was just that no one could find enough money. Why was Uncle Denggao able to find money? Well, was it not because the good land helped him yield good crops for him to save enough money?"[56] The primitive accumulation of capital and its continuation could very well lead to these individuals' forming a new interest group in the countryside, turning their backs on continuous revolution. To a certain extent, the appearance of this new interest group began to cause fissures in the mobilization structure. Indeed, in *The Builders*, the author Liu Qing repeatedly depicts how, when it comes to the character cadre Guo Zhenshan, political directives lose their effectiveness. The main reason has to do with the fact that Guo "has gone on to live his own life" and has over time lost the trust of his rural community.[57]

Zhao's and Liu's worries were not groundless.[58] This kind of "problem cadre" could directly affect the integrity of the mobilization structure. This, then, was no longer a question of one's working style but a larger question of whether or not the Chinese revolution could produce individuals with their own vested interests, who would go on to form new bureaucratic interest groups.

In the literature of 1949–66, the land reform and cooperation topic was a repeatedly told story about history and reality. The constant retelling of this kind of story has to do with the fact that they [such stories] encompassed too many complex aspects of the Chinese revolution. First, these stories touch on

56. Zhao, in *Zhao Shuli wenji*, 2:379.
57. Ibid.
58. The reality at the time showed there was a capitalist tendency among cadres. As early as the late 1940s, there were incidences in which Party members employed and exploited workers [poor peasants]. And there were also debates within the Party's top leadership regarding the issue of Party members getting rich. For a further discussion on this issue, see Luo Pinghan, *Dangdai lishi wenti zhaji* [Records of contemporary historical issues] (Guilin: Guangxi Shida Chubanshe, 2006), vol. 2. One key question was where the original capital came from for those Party members to exploit workers. This had to do with land distribution in the land reform movement. Zhou Libo touches on this issue in *The Hurricane*. At issue, in other words, is the fact that in distributing the fruits of victory in land reform, cadres, Party members, and active participants often had the right to choose first.

the transition from the new democratic revolution to socialism [in the late 1950s] and the corresponding self-negation (*ziwo fouding*) in that transition. Second, this self-negation further brought about various internal tensions; oppositions; contradictions; conflicts; and feelings, on the part of many individuals, of uncertainty, depression, and loss. At issue, in other words, was how liberated individuals faced new challenges and found a way to respond. This latter theme had actually already existed in earlier modern literature. Lu Xun's question "What happens to Nora after she leaves home?" is a classic expression related to this very complex issue. In the literature of the socialist period, the renewed response to this modern problematic focused on collectivization and, by extension, on the various related challenges faced by cadres. It goes without saying that the mobilization structure was not a fixed concept. As the political content of mobilization changed, it required the structure of mobilization to change accordingly. This may explain why even after the Anti-Rightist Campaign in 1957, the antibureaucracy theme continued to appear and even became increasingly radicalized. To some extent, we can take *Sunny Days* to be a sequel to *The Builders*. In the former, the story is set at the time when the early agricultural cooperative movement had evolved into a more mature stage (advanced cooperatives) [1955–56]. But the story itself centers on the conflicts and struggles surrounding dividends on land share in the village of Dongshanwu. Similar narrative details are found in the 1963 movie, *Duo Yin* [Seize the seal], such as the incident of distributing the rice seeds privately (*sifen daozhong*). The issue at the heart of these narrations is that of distribution. And the redistribution of wealth was indeed one of the major issues in revolutionary China. It is an issue that not only concerns the restructuring of the system but, more important still, involves ideological confrontations. We should note, of course, that in these stories the issue of distribution is treated as one that must first meet the interests of the state. As some scholars have pointed out, from 1949 to 1976, China's need for various modernization endeavors led to a disproportionate appropriation of resources from the countryside and, within this process of appropriation, localistic [regionalistic] interest groups would be met with severe criticism. As part of this process, the cadre issue, especially with regard to rural cadres, was repeatedly mentioned due to the fact that this problem encompassed more than whether or not political directives could be fully implemented; it also concerned the issue of constructing a commonwealth and who should have the power to lead it. The distribution problem that confronts the aforementioned village of Dongshanwu in *Sunny Days* reveals the possibility of internal divisions in the newly constructed commonwealth. In the novel, such a division is manifested spatially between the north side and the south side of the village.

At the same time, the conflict between rural villages and the state is just one narrative aspect. Another aspect has to do with the class conflict surrounding the issue of how to divide land shares [in the village], including the related ideological conflicts between capital (land) and labor (manpower). These two aspects were directly related to the larger political issues of the time, but it was rather difficult for literature to deal with the implications of these issues in an in-depth manner. In novels, there was a tendency to overemphasize the interests of the state accompanied by a near-total neglect of the interests of the masses.[59] This limitation can be attributed to more than the writers' own understandings of the issues; rather, it also came from the historical context of the time. To elaborate, in what follows I will focus mainly on the character named Ma Zhiyue, in *Sunny Days*, whose representation is related to the issue at hand.

If we place Ma Zhiyue within the genealogy of characters like Fan Denggao and Guo Zheshan, we realize that the creation of this character in effect means that the notion of class struggle has now come to be considered a problem within the cadres as a group. For this reason, the conflict between Xiao Changchun and Ma Zhiyue is not just one of bureaucratic working style or of personal interests; nor is it one of incorrect political ideas (issues that are the focus of earlier novels like *Sanliwan Village* and *The Builders*). In *Sunny Days*, the conflict between Xiao Changchun and Ma Zhiyue is a highly political one, focusing on their struggle for power. Unlike another character by the name of Ma Lianfu (who is head of a production team) who supports "dividing of land shares ... so that every family on the north side can have more grain," Ma Zhiyue is more ambitious, aiming at establishing a form of control centered on his leadership. Ma Zhiyue's ambition in essence denotes a rural power structure oriented around local bureaucratic politics. In an earlier story, Zhao had started to ponder whether, after the elimination of rural landlords, there would emerge a new self-interest-oriented and oppressive ruling group, and whether such a new ruling group could well be constituted by a bureaucratic system (*guanliao zhengzhi*). This demonstrates the highly prophetic quality of Zhao's thinking and his works, which explains why Zhao continues to occupy an important position in [our understanding of] socialist literature.

59. Zhang Yigong's "Fanren Li Tongzhong de gushi" [The story of the prisoner Li Tongzhong] (*Shouhuo*, November 1980, 1) is a subversive rewrite of the issue of distribution (of food). I will discuss this issue further elsewhere.

The contribution that Hao Ran, in *Sunny Days*, made was that he extended Zhao's speculation into a new historical context. In this new historical context, be it the agricultural cooperatives or later people's communes, the traditional community still retained the form of villages. The Chinese socialist movement did not steadfastly nor completely eliminate tradition—a characteristic of the so-called Chinese model—but retained the traditional community form, which left the possibility for the appearance of new local bureaucratic power groups. The latter could find different ways to use various resources, including resorting to the not completely dead clan structure or traditional cultural mentality. In *Sunny Days*, therefore, we can detect traces of clan conflict in the narrative framework of class struggle (for example, the spatial conflict between the north and south and family conflicts between the Ma, Han, and other families). Here, Hao Ran's concern has to do with whether or not the socialist system (along with its various organizational forms) could produce new bureaucratic interest groups. But frankly speaking, Hao Ran does not push very deep in thinking about this question. Or maybe he was avoiding it. His interpretation for the formation of these groups largely relies on historical reasons.

In chapter 6 of the first volume of *Sunny Days*, for example, the narrator details Ma Zhiyue's personal history and explains why, because of this history, Ma is not even a fellow traveler of the revolution: "Ma Zhiyue has never had any revolutionary ideals nor, therefore, is there a question of whether or not he should continue to carry out the revolution to the end."[60] In this regard, there is an essential difference between Ma Zhiyue and Fan Denggao in *Sanliwan Village*, or Guo Zhenshan in *The Builders*, or even Xie Qingyuan in *Great Changes in a Mountain Village*. Ma Zhiyue's personal history conveniently allows the narrator to define him as an enemy who has sneaked into the revolutionary ranks, while also permitting the narrator to exaggerate the external factors embodied in the [former] landlord Ma Xiaobian. Indeed, it is the Ma Zhiyue–Ma Xiaobian linkage that makes this narrative a "class struggle" story. The Xiao Changchun–Ma Zhiyue conflict, in turn, naturally becomes an extension of class struggle in a historical sense. While such an interpretation of the process of land distribution is simplistic, rigid, and devoid of in-depth thinking, Hao Ran's interpretive model still went on to become a major narrative model for this type of literature in the 1960s.

60. Hao Ran, *Yanyang tian* (Beijing: Zuojia Chubanshe, 1964), 1:77.

The March 1963 issue of the magazine *Juben* [Drama scripts] published the script of a seven-act play of the Yangzhou opera [a local opera from a northern Jiangsu Province area] titled *Seize the Seal*, which was later made into a film with the same title. This publication implicitly corresponded to the socialist education movement (also known as the four clean-ups movement) that was taking place at the time.[61] In the play, Chen Guangqing, leader of a production brigade, is portrayed as a cadre corrupted by class enemies because of his strong self-interest. This type of character was increasingly found in various creative works at the time. In the play, the mediating role between the revolution and the establishment of a comfortable personal life for an individual is played by someone named Chen Jingyi who states that "in this village, on the surface Chen Guangqing is the brigade leader, but in actuality I'm the one in control."[62] The play narrates how Chen was "a good helper to the landlord" in the past but, after liberation, "he quickly changed himself and actively participated in all kinds of activities," which earned him a position in the brigade committee.[63] He became a core member of the village. Here, we can see a shared narrative structure between the novel *Sunny Days* and this play: the so-called corrupt cadres plus hidden enemies, with the enemies sometimes identified as members of former enemy classes (such as Ma Xiaobian, the former landlord in *Sunny Days*) and sometimes identified as alien class elements (such as Ma Zhiyue, Chen Jingyi, and others). Within this narrative structure, certain types of cadres are shown to be the representatives of the landlord or bourgeois classes within the Party, while the class enemies are harboring evil intentions toward the new society. The two forces collaborate with one another, thereby forming a particular kind of political situation. In this way, the importance of power was foregrounded through a kind of crisis-oriented narration.

Let us set aside the question of whether or not it is possible for someone like Chen Jingyi to enter the core leadership in the first place and whether or not this kind of story is based on any kind of reality. Such crisis-oriented narration, in its tendency to exaggerate the presence of the residues of the landlord class (or bourgeois class) as dangerous external forces, in effect avoided

---

61. Tr.: The four clean-ups movement was launched in 1963 to cleanse the realms of ideology, politics, and organization of their capitalist tendencies, which were supposedly exhibited after the rehabilitation of Deng Xiaoping in 1961—which in turn was a restoration of the status quo before the Great Leap Forward and its great famine.

62. Li Yaru et al., "Duo yin" [Seize the seal], *Juben* [Drama scripts], no. 3 (1963): 6.

63. Ibid.

addressing the truly important question of whether or not it is possible for the socialist system to become alienating to itself. Or at least such a tendency turned a potentially important theoretical question into a simplistic one. It is important to point out that such exaggerated narration about crisis at the lowest level of power not only became a major literary mode of narration but also a major model in social practice. It can be found in the four clean-ups movement as well as in the Cultural Revolution and can be said to be responsible for broadening the scope of class struggle and various degrees of persecution.[64]

Relative to the narration by literary writers, political thinkers had deeper and broader theoretical visions. For example, from late 1960 to 1961, Mao used the term *dead bureaucratists* (*si guanliao zhuyi zhe*) when he talked about problems regarding cadres.[65] The article "Is Yugoslavia a Socialist Country?," first published in September 1963, mentioned the "bureaucratic bourgeoisie" (*guanliao zichanjieji*); "On Krushchev's False Communism and Its Lessons in World History" (*Guanyu heluxiaofu de jia gongchanzhuyi jiqi zai shijie lishi shang de jiaoxun*) put forward the concept of "the privileged stratum" (*tequan jieceng*). When these notions and analyses were applied to the domestic context, they became "capitalist roaders" (*zou ziben zhuyi daolu de dangquanpai*), as found in the "Twenty-Three Articles" (*Er shi san tiao*) passed in January 1965.[66] In 1970, an editorial [in *Renmin ribao* (People's Daily), *Jiefangjun bao* (PLA Newspaper), and *Hongqi zazhi* (Red Flag) a magazine] titled "Leninism, or Social Imperialism" (*Lienin zhuyi, haishi shehui diguo zhuyi*) went even further and coined the term *bureaucratic monopoly bourgeoisie*.[67] All of these culminated, in 1975, into a conceptualization of "bourgeoisie within the

64. See "Zhonggong zhongyang guanyu muqian nongcun gongzuo zhong ruogan wenti de jueding (caoan)" [Draft of the Party Central Committee's resolution on contemporary issues in the work in rural regions], in *Gongheguo dang'an* [Archives of the republic], ed. Jiang Shan (Beijing: Tuanjie Chubanshe, 1997), 199.

65. Zheng Qian, "Dangdai shehuizhuyi gaige yu zhongguo de 'wenhuadageming'" [Contemporary socialist reform and the "Cultural Revolution], in *Huishou "wenge": Zhongguo shinian "wenge" fenxi yu fansi* [Reexamining the "Cultural Revolution": Analyses of and reflections on China's ten-year "Cultural Revolution"], ed. Zhang Hua and Su Caiqing (Beijing: Zhonggong Dangshi Chubanshe, 2000), 219.

66. Tr.: The 1956 Hungarian call for socialism with a human face as well as the Titoist critique of the bureaucratic new class in Yugoslavia all posed challenges to Mao and the CCP. Mao wrote on these issues in the essays Cai notes. January 1965, when the twenty-three articles were passed, was the first time the enemy was identified as being in the Party itself.

67. Tr.: Lenin's phrase is *monopoly capital bourgeoisie* and pertained to the world of the 1910s and 1920s; Mao repurposes this phrase to indicate that the class struggle is now no longer between capitalists and socialists but within socialism itself and, in fact, within the "monopoly bureaucratic Party"—that is, the CCP.

Party."⁶⁸ There are multiple reasons that led Mao to theorize these issues. One of them was the challenges from the economic reforms started in the 1950s by the Soviet Union and Eastern European countries (these reforms were later depicted as revisionist waves), including the Soviet Communist Party's program (*sugong gangling*) passed at the twenty-second Congress of the Soviet Communist Party in October 1961. This program promoted economic stimulation, giving more autonomy to enterprises and making good use of commercial and monetary relations and other economic incentives that were to strengthen economic-oriented reforms.⁶⁹ Another reason for these theorizations had to do with Mao's own vigilance against a market economy, despite the fact that at a meeting in Zhengzhou in November 1958 Mao criticized Chen Boda's leftist argument for a complete elimination of the market economy. Mao stated at that time that "some self-styled Marxist economists promote elimination of the market economy and replacing it with distribution of commodities (*chanpin diaobo*). This idea is wrong and violates objective laws (*weifan keguan guilü*)." He further pointed out that "ours is a country with underdeveloped commodity production. Commodity production should not be confused with capitalism. The fear of commodities is no more than the fear of capitalism. . . . I believe that now that we have communes, we should further develop commodity production and exchange."⁷⁰

On a theoretical level, however, Mao never treated the commodity economy as a necessary characteristic of a socialist economy but rather saw it as the legacy of capitalism, as part of bourgeois rights, and therefore as something that had to be kept in check. That is why he had a negative view of relying on prices as a way to regulate social production. At a meeting in Wuchang

---

68. Zheng Qian, "Dangdai shehui zhuyi gaige yu zhongguo de 'wenhua dageming'" [Contemporary socialist reform and the "Cultural Revolution"], in *Huishou "wenge": Zhongguo shinian "wenge" fenxi yu fansi* [Reexamining the "Cultural Revolution": Analyses of and reflections on China's ten-year "Cultural Revolution"], ed. Zhang Hua and Su Caiqing (Beijing: Zhonggong Dangshi Chubanshe, 2000), 213.

69. Ibid., 213. Tr.: These reforms are what Mao called economism, or the reliance on economic incentives rather than revolutionary fervor and consciousness, for development and industrialization. This represents the high tide of Mao's anti-Sovietism, which had taken a quantum leap following the Sino-Soviet split of the late 1950s and early 1960s.

70. Quoted in Du Pu, "'Zuo'qing lilun yu shehui zhuyi quzhe renshi de guanxi" [The relationship between "left-leaning" theory and the complex understanding of socialism], in *Huishou "wenge": Zhongguo shinian "wenge" fenxi yu fansi* [Reexamining the "Cultural Revolution": Analyses of and reflections on China's ten-year "Cultural Revolution"], ed. Zhang Hua and Su Caiqing (Beijing: Zhonggong Dangshi Chubanshe, 2000), 200–201.

in November 1958, in addition to once again criticizing those who rejected commodity production, Mao further suggested that China could have a commodity economy for as long as thirty years, or at least fifteen years more.[71] An article published in *People's Daily* on February 2, 1975, conveyed Mao's deep worries over the commodity economy by stipulating that "our current system is a commodity one. We even have an unequal wage system, eight different levels, and all. These must all be put under the control of the proletarian dictatorship. Otherwise, it will be easy for the likes of Lin Biao to start a capitalist system if they come into power."[72]

In addition to these theoretical issues, the distribution system established after the founding of the People's Republic of China, especially with regard to the income distribution for cadres, was another major problem in socialist economics. Known as a system that was transformed "from the supply system to the system of salary/wages based on ranks" starting from the 1950s, this issue, according to Yang Kuisong, has come under scholarly scrutiny in recent years.[73] From the point of view of recent studies, although the supply system was tightly connected to the wartime environment, there was also a strong ideological factor related to the Communists' own reasons and ideals for starting this revolution in distribution: it was to transform the severely unequal system of wealth distribution and establish a society in which all people are equal. These are ideals compatible with the principles of Marxism and Leninism. To be sure, the supply system itself was not absolutely egalitarian. Embedded in it were hierarchical differences whose formation had to do with a number of complexities, including different needs for different work

---

71. Tr.: This all pertains to the question of what a socialist economy should be: one based on commodity production and commodities sold through markets that were regulated by prices or one based on state-centralized distribution of commodities produced not for a market or for market circulation but for state industrialization and/or people's daily needs. The issues were hotly debated from the late 1950s into the 1960s. The famine and its aftermath briefly interrupted the debates, which then resumed in the late 1960s and lasted into the 1970s, only to be revised in the Deng Xiaoping era.

72. Quoted in Du, "'Zuo'qing lilun yu shehui zhuyi quzhe renshi de guanxi,'" 200–201.

73. The historian Yang Kuisong has conducted extensive studies of the transformation of the system. His studies are a major source for my discussion here. For a detailed discussion, see Yang Kuisong, "Cong gongjizhi dao zhiwu dengji gongzi zhi—xin zhongguo jianli qianhou dangzheng renyuan shouru fenpei zhidu de yanbian" [From the supply system to the system of salary/wages based on ranks: Changes in income distribution system for party and state officials shortly before and after the founding of the PRC], *Lishi yanjiu* [History research] no. 4 (2007): 111–37.

and special considerations generated by the united front policies for attracting and retaining a range of individuals.[74] Influence from the Soviet model was yet another important factor that caused the existence of different levels in the supply system. Not only did the top leaders [of the CCP] enjoy a supply of goods at a level three times higher than average cadres, but this difference later also became systemic. Such a policy generated strong criticisms, with the best-known case being Wang Shiwei's open criticism at the beginning of the Yan'an rectification movement in the spring of 1942. Wang published an article arguing that the [new] regulations on the different levels of supply were paramount to a hierarchical system that divided people into "three styles of outfits and five types of food."[75] Yet this type of hierarchy at the time was highly limited. And the supply system kept individuals much closer to the collective, making it easier for the Party to implement its rules and regulations and keep the cadres relatively honest. That is why Mao more than once praised the system. Additionally, before the CCP and its troops entered the cities in 1948, Zhu De[76] stated that: "We have come to this point through the supply system. No one is paid to fight; no one has to pay to eat. The success of our revolution depended on this system." He even predicted that "we're also going to depend on this system to build a new country." But the "new country" would soon abandon this system and switch to the salary/wage system based on ranks.

There were many complex reasons for this switch, and the Soviet model was a major factor. Also according to Yang Kuisong, as soon as Soviet advisors went to the northeastern region [of China], they implemented a wage system in which they divided the wage earners into thirteen types and thirty-nine levels. The difference between the highest and the lowest wages was a factor of nine. When the CCP and its troops later occupied much of the northeast region, they followed the Soviet model and started a wage system. In the name of rewarding progressives, they began to borrow and put into place the salary/wage ranking system practiced by the Soviet state bureaucratic system.

Marx and Engels once suggested that, under proletarian rule, all public employees would work for low salaries so as to avoid the ills caused by a system of

74. For example, during the Yan'an period, a number of well-known writers enjoyed a higher-level supply within the supply system. See Zhu, *Yanan richang shenghuozhong de lishi*.

75. Tr.: Wang Shiwei was an important intellectual in the 1930s and 1940s. He was later imprisoned and executed for his criticisms. This incident is often recalled as one of the earlier manifestations of Mao's ideological rigidity.

76. Tr.: Zhu De was one of Mao's most trusted generals and comrades in arms. Indeed, before the Red Army was given that name, it was called the Zhu-Mao Army, so central was Zhu to Mao's leadership until their deaths months apart in 1976.

hierarchy.[77] European countries have experimented to different degrees with versions of this idea. But the ranking system established in the Soviet Union far exceeded the salary differences among European and American public employees. Due to the fact that there was a widespread belief that the distribution system in the Soviet Union was the most reasonable and was socialist in its characteristics, it then followed that the new Chinese system would also widen the difference between various levels. Only in that way would the new system fit the supposedly reasonable model of the Soviet Union. Consequently, the salary standards for new cadres issued in 1955 showed that the highest level was more than 31.11 times greater than the lowest level. Also copied from the Soviet model were some of the fringe benefits, including the provision of guards, secretaries, cars, and housing.

We can see that the implementation of the Soviet-style ranking system was closely related to issues of modernity. When new China made modernization (industrialization) its goal, it inevitably resulted in the adoption of a model of technocratic management. This model, in turn, naturally required a corresponding division of social levels, and the salary ranking system was a response, in distribution terms, to this tendency toward bureaucratization. The problem is that this model of distribution was in contradiction to Marxist theory, resulting not only in an internal conflict between modern China and revolutionary China but also one between the Soviet model and the Yan'an model. These differences became worrisome not only because cadres could end up separating themselves from the masses but also because the differences could lead to the creation of a new privileged stratum. This latter point especially caused Mao much worry, so he repeatedly tried to remind [the Party] that "if there is a higher-paid level, there would be a lower-paid level," and the latter would be the majority of the society; as a result "it is dangerous for a society to have higher-paid strata."[78]

The open letter [by the Chinese Communist Party] to the Soviet Central Committee, which Mao himself had read in its final version, clearly stated that "we must not implement a higher-paying system for a minority of individuals. Instead, we must gradually reduce the differences in personal income between public employees who work for the Party, the state, the various enterprises, the communes, and the masses. We must prevent public employees

---

77. Karl Marx, "Falanxi neizhan" [French civil war], *Makesi Engesi xuanji* [Selected works of Marx and Engles] (Beijing: Renmin Chubanshe, 1995), 3:55.
78. Quoted in Yang, "Cong gongjizhi dao zhiwu dengji gongzi zhi," 137.

from using their power to gain privileges."⁷⁹ Whether or not Mao's methods for limiting the development of the privileged class were reasonable is one issue, but the related issue in his thinking and writings nevertheless touches on some of the key theoretical issues concerning whether or not the socialist system itself can have alienation (in the Marxist sense).

In the 1960s, the aforementioned views by Mao did not find their way into the literature of the time. There were of course many complex reasons for this, but what this fact can remind us of is that when we discuss the literature and politics of the Mao era, we ought not to use Mao's writings as our sole source for interpretation. At the same time, we ought not to overlook the 1957 Anti-Rightist Campaign's lingering negative impact on writers, either. Due to this negative impact, writers had given up thinking about the question of alienation in socialism. Still, coming back to an earlier point, literary attention to the crisis at the grassroots level did lead to an abandonment of exploring deeper problems at the systemic level and turned to the remnants of the landlord class (or bourgeois class) as the major source of crisis, thereby significantly simplifying what should have been a crucial theoretical issue of socialism's own production of unevenness.

At the same time, when the cadres at the basic level came to embody the narration of crisis, there was a tendency to generalize the existence of crisis. Indeed, many lower-level cadres did not enjoy pay much higher than the workers. In 1956, some were paid even lower wages than average workers. Many township-level cadres were not recognized as state employees until 1955, while the production-team level cadres were never recognized as such.⁸⁰

Of course, I do not mean to suggest that the novels mentioned above are devoid of actual significance. If anything, they touched on the real issues of the day regarding the crisis that was occurring in various rural communities. And these issues were closely related to the question of how to redistribute wealth. Due to the fact that village-level cadres were excluded from the ranks of state employees, their income would then be closely correlated with that of average peasants. When they worked to accumulate wealth, then, that would directly threaten peasants' interests in the community. When accumulation of wealth came to be associated with a highly concentrated power structure (communization), that is, this combination could lead to the creation of a new

---

79. Quoted in Yang, "Cong gongjizhi dao zhiwu dengji gongzi zhi," 135–36.
80. Ibid., 137.

privileged class in the countryside that, in turn, could lead to a split in the imagined new commonwealth. But the most important issue at hand was still the concentration of power as the result of specialized technocracy. This concentration of power was also closely related to the high pay and privileged benefits, which would lead to further bureaucratization of the political system. The bureaucratization of the political system would ultimately threaten the nonsystemized mobilization structure, including the political enthusiasm of the masses and the theory of demanding a continuous revolution.

IV. Intellectuals

Of the various kinds of commentaries and narratives about intellectuals, the most influential one is probably Mao's notion of skin and hair (*pi/mao lilun*)—that is, "without the skin, how can hair grow?" (*pi zhi bu cun, mao jiang yan fu ye*).[81] This metaphor not only directly canceled out intellectuals' subject position but also either directly or indirectly resulted in the Party's (or the state's) continuing efforts at reforming, criticizing, and even struggling against intellectuals. In his analysis of this issue, Nan Fan depicts a new but invisible (*yin xing de*) binary structure in which the masses became the subject of revolution while intellectuals were cast in "a role that is awkward and even dangerous."[82] In the 1980s, the fate of Chinese intellectuals in modern Chinese history became the focus of various writings, including fiction. Many theoretical discussions also appeared. But what I would like to focus on here is the intellectuals' position in the mobilization structure and the related discussions on the issue of knowledge.

If we conclude that the Chinese revolution despised intellectuals and was anti-intellectual, and if we do so based mainly on the fate of the intellectuals, especially their political fate, this conclusion is only a partial one. For starters, in various publicized political documents, we find a palpable politeness on the part of the revolution toward intellectuals, and a sense of urgent need for intellectuals. For example, on December 1, 1939, Mao wrote a resolution on be-

---

81. Tr.: Here Mao was presumably paraphrasing the *Zuozhuan*, a classic Chinese text. The phrase suggests that intellectuals are like hair; without skin—the people—they cannot exist. This metaphor was included in a number of 1957 speeches and texts in the context of the Anti-Rightist campaign.

82. Nan Fan, *Hou geming de zhuanyi* [Postrevolution transference] (Beijing: Beijing Daxue Chubanshe, 2005), 16.

half of the Central Committee in which he emphasized that "the Communist Party must be good at winning intellectuals, for only in this way will it be able to organize great strength for the War of Resistance, organize the millions of peasants, develop the revolutionary cultural movement and expand the revolutionary united front. Without the participation of the intellectuals victory in the revolution is impossible." Therefore, we must "recruit large numbers of intellectuals."[83] Objectively speaking, in wartime the Party was quite successful in accepting a large number of intellectuals. Additionally, during the Yan'an period, the rationing system gave special treatment to [people with] certain talents for the purpose of keeping them there. Even after the founding of the People's Republic, during the various political criticism movements against intellectuals, the state did not eliminate the relatively favorable material treatment of intellectuals, especially high-level ones. Meanwhile, in the same 1939 article, Mao also emphasized that "the creation of the proletariat's own intellectuals cannot be done without the help of the existing intellectuals."[84] Here, [use of the two phrases] "the proletariat's own intellectuals" and "existing intellectuals" already implied some important political distinctions between the two. The existing intellectuals may be considered as fellow travelers of the revolution, which we can interpret as hinting at a lack of political trust [on the part of the Party]. So as a large number of intellectuals joined the revolutionary forces, the task of reforming the "existing intellectuals," including their self-reform, would become one of the major tasks of the revolution. All of this culminated and reached a full expression in Mao's Yan'an talks ["Talks at the Yan'an Forum on Art and Literature"] in 1942. While there is a wide range of content regarding intellectuals' reform and their self-reform, one of the central issues addressed in all of these debates is the debate on what is real or useful knowledge.

In "Oppose Stereotyped Party Writing," Mao mentions the problem of knowledge: "A few years ago a slogan appeared on the Yenan [Yan'an] city wall which read, 'Working men and peasants, unite and strive for victory in the War of Resistance Against Japan!' The idea of the slogan was not at all bad, but the character '工' [*kung*, meaning working] in '工人' [*kung jen*, meaning working men], was written as '工,' with its perpendicular stroke twisted into a zigzag. How about the character '人' [*jen*, meaning men]? It became '人,'

---

83. Mao Tse-tung, "Recruit Large Numbers of Intellectuals," in *Selected Works of Mao Tse-tung* (Peking: Foreign Language Press, 1961), 2:301.

84. Ibid.

with three slanting strokes added to its right leg."[85] According to Zhong Ling, the person who wrote the slogan, in 1951 in Beijing:

> We were with Chairman Mao in the Haiqinzheng Hall in Zhongnanhai. Wang Dongxing mentioned to Chairman Mao that Zhong Ling was the one who wrote those characters that Mao criticized in his speech "Oppose Stereotyped Party Writing." Because I had not expected Wang would mention this, I got quite nervous. But Chairman Mao laughed loudly, asking me, "Do you still write this way?" I replied, "After your criticism, I wouldn't dare to write that way any more. Not only do I not write that way, but even the *lishu*-style calligraphers have changed their way of writing these characters." On hearing this, Mao fell silent for a moment, and then said, "That won't do. *Lishu* style is *lishu* style. No need to change. The extreme cursive hand style or the *xiaozuan* style, they're even harder to recognize. But that's the art of calligraphy. We should still respect tradition. I criticized you not because you wrote the characters wrongly. It was because I felt that if such slogans were meant for the masses as part of our propaganda work, they should not be written in a style difficult for the masses to recognize. Please explain on my behalf when you see friends in the field of calligraphy. Whatever style they write in, be it *lishu* or *zuanshu*, they should continue to do so. No need to be affected by that article of mine. Of course, sometimes they may need to see who their audiences are. So long as they understand my original intention, that's good enough." Chairman Mao's words put me at ease. I no long feel like I have been misunderstood again.[86]

Whether or not, or to what extent, this informal conversation with Mao had any impact on contemporary art and literature is not what I would like to explore here. Rather, for me the more important key concept relevant to this discussion is "propaganda" (*xuanchuan*). In the mobilization structure, to mobilize and organize the masses was always the most important political task. To do so, one had to start with propaganda and education. The impor-

---

85. Mao Tse-tung, "Oppose Stereotyped Party Writing," in *Selected Works of Mao Tse-tung* (Peking: Foreign Language Press, 1965), 3:58–59. Tr.: The point here is that the characters were written in a stylized way that would have made it difficult for barely literate people to read them. Mao is emphasizing the need to write in readily legible form.

86. Zhou Hangsheng, "Ta ba shufa xie shang tiananmen hongqiang—yu zhumin shufajia, yishujia Zhong Ling duihua" [He brought calligraphy to the red walls of Tiananmen: A conversation with the famous calligrapher and artist Zhong Ling], *Dang'an chunqiu* no. 5 (2006): 16. Tr.: The various styles of calligraphy referred to here are well-established art forms in the Chinese writing tradition.

tance of propaganda work was always a key aspect of the revolution.[87] At the same time, to propagandize requires the support of culture and knowledge. That is why Mao once stated that "an army without culture is a dull-witted [*yuchun*] army, and a dull-witted army cannot defeat the enemy."[88] Meanwhile, such propaganda was also highly political and highly instrumentalized. Any knowledge that was incorporated into the mobilization structure had to be politicized. Mao made this point quite clearly in his "Talks at the Yan'an Forum on Art and Literature": "In the world today all culture, all literature and art belong to definite classes and are geared to definite political lines. There is in fact no such thing as art for art's sake, art that stands above classes or art that is detached from or independent of politics." [Mao also said:] "Proletarian literature and art are part of the whole proletarian revolutionary cause; they are, as Lenin said, cogs and wheels in the whole revolutionary machine."[89] Defined this way, it would be difficult for knowledge to exist as personal subjectivity or autonomy expressed in literature and art within the mobilization structure. The reestablished central theme, instead, was "issues that concern the masses and issues that are about how to help the masses."[90] It is not my task here to reevaluate the historical implications of Mao's "Talks," but we should recognize the following: On the one hand, the politicization of knowledge and its instrumentalization did not result in an overly narrow understanding of knowledge and literature and art. On the other hand, in the historical context of the time, such politicization and instrumentalization effectively succeeded in politically mobilizing the masses. Chen Dengke, another revolutionary writer, for example, remembered when the *Yanfu People's Paper* was first published in April 1943, "it was a bimonthly. Two hundred pages per issue, no subscription, all were distributed for free." When the central theme of the paper became "to tread the path of the worker-peasant-soldier and to face the worker-peasant-soldier,"

---

87. In his summary of the importance of the Long March, for example, Mao referred to the Red Army as a "propaganda team" (*xuanchuan dui*]). See Mao Zedong, "Lun fandui riben diguozhuyi de celüe" [On strategies against Japanese imperialism], *Mao Zedong xuanji* [Selected works of Mao Zedong] (Beijing: Renmin Chubashe, 1964), 1:149–50.

88. Mao Tse-tung, "The United Front in Cultural Work," in *Selected Works of Mao Tse-tung* (Peking: Foreign Language Press, 1965), 3:235.

89. Mao Tse-tung, "Talks at the Yenan Forum on Literature and Art," in *Selected Works of Mao Tse-tung* (Peking: Foreign Language Press, 1965), 3:86.

90. Zhu, *Yanan richang shenghuozhong de lishi*, 120.

we would receive around 1,700 to 1,800 submissions and about five hundred [readers'] letters. Every issue was around five thousand copies. The bimonthly was also changed to weekly and later [was published] every three days. In the countryside, even the seven- to eight-year-old kids knew about *Yanfu Masses*. Every time the paper arrived in a village, elementary school teachers or the village committee members in charge of culture work would copy the poems from the paper onto the outside walls of peasants' [houses]. Those poems were copied all over different villages.... The paper also published short stories, reports, and teaching materials for winter learning in the countryside.... Hundreds of worker-peasant-soldier reporters wrote for the paper.[91]

I will return to this at a later point.

When knowledge is politicized or instrumentalized, new definitions of knowledge must be offered. This is what Mao offers in "Rectify the Party's Style of Work": "What is knowledge? Ever since class society came into being the world has had only two kinds of knowledge, knowledge of the struggle for production and knowledge of the class struggle. Natural science and social science are the crystallizations of these two kinds of knowledge, and philosophy is the generalization and summation of the knowledge of nature and the knowledge of society. Is there any other kind of knowledge? No."[92] In Mao's perspective, those who have only book knowledge are not complete intellectuals. Here, we clearly hear echoes from Mao's theoretical views found in his philosophical text "On Practice."[93] The significance of emphasizing "practice" lies at the heart of the political context of the time: that is, to address the question of whether or not "Marxism can exist deep in the mountains" [whether Marxism is suitable for China], which also pertains to the issue of political legitimacy of the Yan'an path. In "Rectify the Party's Style of Work," Mao clearly states that "there is only one real theory in the world: theory that stems from objective reality and that is also proven by objective reality." At the same time, he finds further support for this point from Stalin: "Stalin once said that the-

---

91. Chen Dengke "Tongzhi, laoshi, zhanyou—yi Qian Yi" [Comrade, teacher, comrade in arms—remembering Qian Yi], in *Hongqi piaopiao* [Red flags are fluttering] (Beijing: Zhongguo Qingnian Chubanshe, 1957), 1:136.

92. Mao Tse-tung, "Rectify the Party's Style of Work," in *Selected Works of Mao Tse-tung* (Peking: Foreign Language Press, 1965), 3:39.

93. Mao Tse-tung, "On Practice," *Selected Works of Mao Tse-tung* (Peking: Foreign Languages Press, 1965), 1.

ory detached from material reality is empty theory; empty theory is useless, incorrect, and should be discarded."[94] All of this constituted a major point in the Yan'an rectification campaigns.

This definition of knowledge cast a long shadow on the Chinese revolution, then and after. Emphasis on the practiced aspects of knowledge is not totally meaningless: it not only can broaden intellectuals' spectrum of knowledge, but it also can compensate for the limitations in their existing knowledge (book knowledge). Most important, it can stimulate activity so as to break the uncritical superstition concerning the sufficiency of certain kinds of classical knowledge as well as the monopoly of such knowledge on social life. And it offers strong intellectual support for the proletariat's (including proletarian intellectuals') subject consciousness and confidence. Indeed, the widespread mass-level technological innovation and creation after 1949, and even the creative writing by worker-peasant-soldier writers, are in one way or another related to this approving focus on the practice aspects of knowledge. The negative effect, of course, is the pragmatist tendency in understanding what knowledge is and a contempt for and even criticism of other forms of knowledge (book knowledge).[95]

Within the mobilization structure, the demand that knowledge serve, which led to the politicization and instrumentalization of knowledge and a redefinition of what knowledge was, inevitably generated requests to reform those who were knowledgeable—namely, intellectuals. Such reform would consist of two dimensions, theory and feelings. The former is determined within classical Marxism and Leninism, while the latter promotes the fact that only when intellectuals "experience a change in feelings would they complete the process of a change from one class to another."[96] No matter whether in terms of theory or feeling, the key point pertains to issues of worldview. And issues of worldview were not just political ones; they were also issues of morality. Throughout the mobilization-reform process, some intellectuals were successfully transformed, although not, I argue, simply as a result of coercion. Indeed, when considering the real-world problems in China, Marxism definitely offered a certain powerful analysis. Without this understanding, it would be difficult for us to comprehend why, among the various modernity discourses that actively competed with one another starting in the late Qing, Marxism as a latecomer could have won out over all others. This fact is not

94. Mao Tse-tung, "Rectify the Party's Style of Work," 40.
95. For detailed discussion of this point, see chapter 6.
96. Mao Tse-tung, "Talks at the Yenan Forum on Literature and Art," 3:73.

something that can be easily brushed aside with an explanation that stops at the level of power politics. The coexistence of the political pursuit for equality, a utopian vision of an egalitarian society in the future, and corresponding social practices aimed at realizing that vision all could have been determining factors in the change in position for some intellectuals. Other intellectuals who showed discomfort, confusion, and even resistance did not do so purely for political reasons. Most opposition would have stemmed from their different interpretation of what knowledge was—namely, their stubborn preservation of knowledge as book knowledge. In some ways, book knowledge constitutes a certain kind of intellectual tradition known as schools of learning. Such a tradition in fact consists of more than just knowledge; it also includes lifestyle, mentality, taste, conventions, and emotions. Some intellectuals still hoped to find ways to study and live their own lives outside the mobilization structure. Examples can be found, among others, in Yang Jiang's story "Baptism" ("Xizao"), in which she vividly remembers the details of the lives of this kind of intellectual during the reform movement in the 1950s.[97]

In his reinterpretation of the historical significance of Mao's "Talks," Qian Liqun argues that in the context of the wartime environment, intellectuals

> had a particularly strong sense of powerlessness and uselessness as individual knowledge holders, so they strongly desired to group themselves with people who had strength so as to become part of the fighting community. That is why, when Mao Zedong issued a call "for intellectuals to integrate themselves with the workers, peasants, and soldiers," he could win heartfelt support from the intellectuals due to the latters' own experience and reflection.... But when the intellectuals were treated as targets for an "inside out" reform, which required them not only to emulate workers and peasants in terms of appearance but also to change their mentality, thoughts, emotions, life's habits, and lifestyle accordingly, the result of such change would be a disappearance of intellectuals.... Consequently, the "integration of workers and peasants with intellectuals" as a historically legitimate problematic dissolved into a mere issue of reforming the intellectuals and of the relationship between intellectuals and the populace of workers and peasants—namely, one of reform versus to-be reformed and one side "consuming" (*hua diao*) the other side.[98]

97. Yang Jiang, *Xizao* [Baptism] (Beijing: Renmin Wenxue Chubanshe, 2004).
98. Qian Liqun, *Wo de jingshen zizhuan* [An autobiography of my spiritual life] (Guilin: Guangxi Shidao Chubanshe, 2007), 102–3.

On the whole, I find this is a relatively balanced argument.

It goes without saying that only within the mobilization structure can we fully understand the unique historical reasons, significance, and specifics of the Party's or the state's demands on knowledge and knowledge holders. Such demands have their own historical significance, in effect denoting the importance placed on knowledge and intellectuals. To be sure, there was a utilitarian purpose attached to this importance, in that the intellectuals were expected to take on the tasks of propagandizing, educating, and mobilizing the masses and to do so within the framework of the mobilization structure. At the same time, however, in addition to this historically reasonable interpretation, this demand also brought about various kinds of negative impacts. Besides the kind described by Qian, the emphasis on the practicality of knowledge could easily narrow the classical definition of knowledge as being exclusively biased toward book learning/knowledge. There was a strong instrumentalist tendency in this definition. Moreover, the expectations for proletarian intellectuals would inevitably lead to reform and would criticize and even politically discriminate against "existing intellectuals," a tendency that would result not only in an extremism in education reform in 1949–66, but also in the basic assessment of the education carried out during the period.[99]

But the most crucial of all is that within the structure of mobilization, despite the fact that intellectuals' own thinking did not completely disappear, such thinking could be expressed only implicitly or in politically acceptable ways, thereby constituting textual ambiguity (*wenben de yinbi xing*). The disappearance of the independence of the intellectuals—in education, the elimination of the autonomy of the university—would lead to a retreat of cultural politics. Yet, according to Lu Xun, who stipulates in his "On the Knowledge

---

99. This is the basic content of the education revolution, indeed what [Mao's 1966] "May 7 Directive" emphasized: "Students' major obligation is to study, but they have to study other subjects, too. They have to study culture as well as learn about industry, agriculture, and military affairs. And they have to criticize the bourgeoisie. The number of school years should be reduced. Education needs revolution. The situation in which the bourgeoisie gets to control our school should not and cannot go on" (Gucheng Li, *A Glossary of Political Terms of the People's Republic of China* [Hong Kong: Chinese University of Hong Kong Press, 1995], 489). The resolution of the national meeting on education held in August 1971 offered two assessments: (1) the seventeen-year [period of] education before the Cultural Revolution had been dictated by the bourgeoisie—"black-line dictatorship (*heixian zhuanzheng*)," and (2) the worldview of the majority of intellectuals was bourgeois and therefore they were bourgeois intellectuals. For additional information, see Xu Qingquan, *Wentan boluan fanzhen shilu* [Documenting bringing order out of chaos in cultural domains] (Hangzhou: Zhejiang Renmin Chubanshe, 2004), 62.

Class" (*Guanyu zhishi jieji*), [members of] the real knowledge class must always integrate themselves into actual social movements and should never be satisfied with the status quo and should forever be critics.[100]

Conclusion

I would like to reiterate that the mobilization structure was in effect an informal political model. At the same time, it had a strong political and social energy. On the one hand, it functioned as a supplement to the political-social system. On the other hand, it constituted a strong pressure on the system and at times even became an oppositional force to the system, especially when the system turned more bureaucratic and specialized and when its administrative structure became an obstacle to the ideal socialist visions or to continuous revolution. When the latter happened, the mobilization structure functioned to restructure society and provide structural support for a counterpolitical movement. The fundamental significance of the mobilization structure lies in the fact that it provided theoretical support for the political participation of the masses. It affirmed the political subjective position of the masses.

I have always believed that the importance of this theory and its corresponding political vision should not be underestimated. For while it could function as a powerful support for mass political participation, as historical conditions changed, it could also become an empty shell. Yet this emptiness implies a new moment for the reinterpretation of the legitimacy of this mobilization theory. In other words, only when we understand this theory and its related political imaginary can we enter history to further understand what the political enthusiasms of the masses and intellectuals might be, even despite the latter's alienation and the criticism leveled against them during specific political movements. Such political enthusiasms continued to exist; they are a text, urgently waiting to be studied. Put differently, we should try to understand further the implications of the continuing political enthusiasms on the part of the masses through this period and beyond.

At same time, we ought not to understand the mobilization structure as a kind of spontaneous popular political or social movement. The dominant position in this structure was always occupied by dominant politics. The Party, or its leader's personal will, constituted the major component of that domi-

---

100. Lu Xun, "Guanyu zhishi jieji" [On the knowledge class], *Lu Xun Quanji* [Complete works of Lu Xun] (Beijing: Renmin Wenxue Chubanshe, 2005), 8:223–31.

nant politics. Yet we should not then conclude that under this dominant politics, the social movement had to die an untimely death or could never actually exist. The irony in all of this lies in the fact that often the political movements offered legitimacy for the masses to openly or implicitly express their own interests and demands.[101] We know that class- or society-level oriented demands are a major characteristic of a social movement. In China, therefore, not only did this complex and often implicitly present characteristic find a legitimate way to express itself, but its expression also depended on the existence of this mobilization structure.

To be sure, politics is the fundamental method and way used to solve social conflicts. In this sense, we should not overestimate or exaggerate the significance of a social movement. However, without the support of social movements and concrete demands from the masses with regard to their own interests, politics would become an abstraction and consequently lose its popular foundation. This is why I argue that the mobilization structure went through a radical as well as an extreme development during the Cultural Revolution, leading to a high degree of abstraction of the political. This abstraction not only led to a societywide political fatigue but also to a decrease in the masses' enthusiasm for political participation. Such a decrease further led to apathy on the part of the populace toward politics. And that was one of key historical reasons for the "depoliticization" of Chinese society after the 1980s.

When this mobilization structure was not systemic but remained a supplement to the system, it had a tacit relation to the system. But when it became a system itself, especially as an oppositional force to a rigid system, a split and conflict between the mobilization structure and the dominant system became

---

101. During the rectification campaign in 1957—before the start of the Anti-Rightist Campaign, for example—some workers put forward demands of their own. A certain factory's chronicle of events offers the following: "On May 9, some workers, influenced by the free airing of views, occupied the apartments not yet assigned. Workers had a lot of complaints about livelihood and welfare. Many of them were quite emotional, while the factory leaders were not well prepared to deal with such discontent. As a result, both the masses and the cadres felt quite confused about the situation. Throughout the month, the Party committee [members] focused their work on 'the correct handling of internal contradictions among the people.' The committee members changed their working style and became more proactive by listening to the opinions of the Party members and non-Party members. Afterward, they worked to solve such major problems as housing, child care, shower facilities, transportation, and so on. Their work helped stabilize the workers' mood" ("Shanghai erfangji dangshi dashiji" [Chronicle of events: Shanghai no. 2 textile machinery factory], internal publications, 151). During the Cultural Revolution, some mass organizations even made collective demands based on their own interests. Such activities were the so-called evil economism trend (*jingji zhuyi yaofeng*).

inevitable. The problem lies in the fact that, due to the wrongheaded policies on intellectuals, the oppositional force did not originate from a certain kind of politics of culture but continuously turned into the form of a political movement. Yet the mobilization structure lacked the possibility of becoming a system; despite constant political movements, it did not lead to the creation of a new system, the Cultural Revolution notwithstanding. On this point, Qian argues that "seen from another perspective, the Cultural Revolution was no more than a movement to 'dismiss officials' (*baguan yundong*) with no restructuring of a system of any kind. As a result, any establishment of a 'red power' would inevitably turn bureaucratic. When the rebels entered this system and became power holders, they unfailingly became corrupt and 'new aristocrats.'"[102]

It is important to point out that the reasons for such a development were highly complex, be they the conflict between ideals and reality or a split between content and form. The root cause of it all, however, is that it is an issue of modernity. That is, on the one hand, the dominant ideology struggled to overcome the limitations of modernity, while on the other hand, the design of the entire [new] social system was a modern one, not only taking the form of the modern nation-state but also [using] its governing and technocratic model. Within this paradigm, it is in fact very difficult to create a new system. Still, I argue that the unresolved issues regarding social movements, cultural politics, and innovations in the system must be part of the issue when we continue to think about China's path to solve its problems.

To some extent, the mobilization structure implicitly bolstered the narrative mode in the literary representations of mobilization-reformation of the socialist period. But this mode was an unstable one. This instability makes it possible for various texts to have fractures in them. The presence of these fractures urges us to move beyond our own biases to reopen these texts for further exploration.

---

102. Qian, *Wo de jingshen zizhuan*, 46.

3

YOUTH, LOVE, "NATURAL RIGHTS," AND SEX

In Chinese literature between 1949 and 1966, we find a significant number of representations and narrations about youth. They manifest a particular kind of literary imaginary. It goes without saying that such an imaginary originated from the historical practices of the Chinese revolution, in which countless numbers of young people participated and for which they sacrificed their lives. It was this kind of contribution that led to the success of the revolution.[1] We can say that the history of the Chinese revolution was fueled by youthful passion, and that the narratives about this history and related literary representations are very much informed by such an imaginary about youth. By

---

1. Mark Selden writes: "Virtually every observer of the communist movement during the Kiangsi and Yenan period has remarked on the predominance of youth from the lowest ranks up to the leadership. Shensi partisans from 1927 were led by young men, most of them in their early twenties and who at the time of the arrival of soldiers completing the Long March were barely thirty years of age. The party's highest-ranking leadership was dominated by men who had been students at the time of the May Fourth movement of 1919. On the eve of the outbreak of war with Japan, after more than a decade of leadership, they were still only in their mid-thirties or early forties. Edgar Snow reported that the average age of the rank and file of the Red Army in 1936 was nineteen, while that of its officers was twenty-four" (*China in Revolution: the Yenan Way Revisited* [Armonk, NY: M. E. Sharpe, 1995], 76).

the same token, this imaginary of youth as a literary subject helped shape the strong futuristic character of the literature of that period.

Yet this literary subject is not simply about youth, or the remembrance of youth and the expressions of their emotions. For behind the various kinds of emotional articulations, which did constitute a major form of literary writing of the time, resides a demand for constructing a [new kind of] subjectivity. This subjectivity denotes youth as a sociological group but at the same time also symbolizes the revolution and the state. In its quest for subjectivity, this literature is political in nature: for the youthful imaginary is not only a historical one but also futuristic. When we place youth in the revolutionary political context, we can clearly see how the quest for this subjectivity was realized and in what ways; during the process, personal emotions, including love and sex, were mobilized as revolutionary motivation as well as a form of political expression.

I. Youth, or the Politics of Youth

On February 10, 1900, Liang Qichao published "Young China" ("Shaonian Zhongguo shuo") in *Qingyi bao* [Journal of pure critique]. In this essay, Liang for the first time set up a binary opposition between the young and the old. He identified conservatism—holding on to conservatism, pessimism, fearfulness, and willingness to live with the status quo—as symbolizing the old, while associating the future, hope, progressiveness, constant change, adventurousness, and creativeness with the young. That is to say, Liang did not discuss the old-young binary in a biological sense but rather in a symbolic and rhetorical one, as a metaphor related to China as a country. He states that "there are old and young among humans, so it is with a country as well."[2] Here, Liang was, in David Wang's words, "imagining China" (*xiangxiang Zhongguo*), an imagination that was characterized by a strong futuristic tendency. Liang states:

> Therefore, responsibilities of the present all fall on the young. When the young are wise, the nation will be wise. When the young are rich, the nation will be rich; when the young are strong, the nation will be strong; when the young are independent, the nation will be independent; when the young are free, the nation will be free; when the young are progressive,

---

2. Liang Qichao, "Shaonian Zhongguo shuo" [Young China], in *Liang Qichao xuanji* [Selected works of Liang Qichao]), ed. Wu Jiaxun and Li Huanxing (Shanghai: Shanghai Renmin Chubanshe, 1984), 127.

the nation will be progressive; when the young are better than Europe, the nation will be better than Europe; when the young surpass the earth, the nation will surpass the earth.... Oh, my beautiful young China, forever as young as heaven (*yu tian bu lao*); oh, our strong youth, forever live as long the nation."[3]

To some extent, we can say that Liang's young China imaginary deeply influenced and changed twentieth-century Chinese history. The significance of its influence is not only in how it liberated [the category of] youth from traditional political and cultural power structures, but also in how it revealed the sharp opposition between traditional and modern China. Liang's imaginary also introduced into modern China a narrative element for telling stories about the future. What is more, in narrating stories about the future, the major conflict would no longer be confined within the traditional power structure in which one individual/group struggles to replace another. In modern fiction, a classical example of this narrative change is undoubtedly found in Ba Jin's *Family* (*Jia*).[4] What supports Juehui's—the protagonist's—desire for revolution is none other than the imagined future of China signified by youth.

That is, despite the fact that the desire is expressed by way of the first person, "I" (or the individual), the repeated expression in the novel by Juehui, "I am a youth! Yes, I am a youth!" transcends this individual character. With the introduction of the modern temporal notion of the future, the contrast between the young and the old inevitably expanded into a spatial divide between a "narrow cage" and the "broad world." Along with this logic, *Family* cannot but end with Juehui's leaving home. His departure is at one with his destination: the "broad world" that denotes the future and hope, the death of the old and birth of the new. Thus, *Family* differs from *Dream of the Red Chamber* in a crucial way: the modern contains a destination while the traditional is without destination. Upholding this distinction, I might add, is the ideology of modern developmentalism.

In modern Chinese history, in particular, this developmentalism tended to manifest itself, or tended to be expressed, as a form of a spatialization of time, in which time and space were superimposed onto one another and in which space also functioned as the destination of modern politics. For example, from the Red Army era (1940s) slogan "smash the old world and establish a

3. Ibid.
4. Ba Jin, *Jia* [Family] (Shanghai: Shanghai Kaiming Shudian, 1933).

new world" to the ending of Cao Yu's well-known play *The Sun Rises* (*Richu*),[5] there always existed a destination that beckoned.

[Michel] Foucault argues that such an impulse to leave home and the rapture over a new destination inevitably leads to "a break with tradition, a feeling of novelty, of vertigo in the face of the passing moment," and he wonders "whether we may not envisage modernity rather as an attitude than as a period of history." By "attitude," Foucault states, "I mean a mode of relating to contemporary reality; a voluntary choice made by certain people; in the end, a way of thinking and feeling; a way, too, of acting and behaving that at one and the same time marks a relation of belonging and presents itself as a task."[6] This "relation of belonging" and its task of representation are both modern and political. Indeed, in his study of Ba Jin's trilogy—which includes *Family*—the literary critic Huang Ziping argues that it is important to understand his depictions of social and cultural activities organized by such Beijing-based newspapers and magazines as *Xin shu bao* [Journal of new books] and *Liqun zhoubao* [Liqun weekly], and [the character] Juehui's letters and articles sent from Shanghai, as organic components of the novel: "All that is lost from 'family' can be found in these new places, including friendship, love, youthful vitality, life's meaning, and purposeful struggle. Ba Jin is said to have wanted to name his [unwritten] fourth novel *Qun* [crowd, mass, or group]. If that is true, we can say that all those activities depicted in the trilogy function as a prelude to the transformation from 'family' to 'the masses.'"[7] What *qun* denotes here is none other than modern Chinese [mass] politics.

Beckoned by the modern sense of the future, youth and the themes surrounding it—such as family, romantic love, youthful energy, life's meaning, and purposeful struggle—were constantly politicized. However, as Huang also states, "the repetition of these signifiers—youth, life, happiness, love, beauty, new era, future—managed to acquire a sense of excitement precisely due to their having become empty signifiers. They acquired a strong interpretive power due to abstraction, helping formulate a modern ideological mythology in the 1930s."[8] In my view, what made this set of signifiers "exciting" with "strong interpretive power" was its form of affective representation, which

5. Cao Yu, *Richu* [The sun rises], *Wenxue yuekan* [Literary monthly], vol. 1, no. 4 (1936).

6. Michel Foucault, "What Is Enlightenment?," in *The Foucault Reader*, ed. Paul Rabinow (New York: Pantheon, 1984), 37.

7. Huang Ziping, "Mingyun san chongzou: Jia yu 'jia' yu 'jia zhong ren'" [Life's ensemble of three: *Family*, family, and family members], in *Geming· lishi ·xiaoshuo* [Revolution history fiction] (Hong Kong: Oxford University Press, 1996), 137.

8. Ibid., 135.

helped politicize emotions. Conversely, we can say that politics also became affective. The politicization of emotions and affected politics, in short, originated from Liang's "Young China" and became one of the major forms of representation in the romanticist narration characteristic of the May Fourth New Culture Movement.

It is also safe to say that China's leftist revolution, including its literature, was also part of this tradition. Left-wing writers as well as left-wing political leaders such as Mao Zedong were deeply influenced by the narrative mode related to this May Fourth tradition. For example, on November 25, 1919, Mao published an article titled "The Question of Love—Young People and Old People." In the main, he applied Liang's oppositional dichotomy between the young and the old: "I often feel that in matters of all kinds, old people generally take a position of opposition to young people. From such things in daily life as eating and dressing, to feelings about society and the nation, and attitudes toward mankind in the world at large, they [old people] are always drearily, rigidly, and coweringly passive. Their views are always ingratiatingly humble. Their position is always negative."[9] For Mao, interestingly, what caused the opposition between the old and the young was sexual desire:

> (What we call sexual desire, or love, involves not only the satisfaction of physiological urge of fleshly desire, but the satisfaction of a higher order of desires—spiritual desires and desires for social intercourse.) The slave's work of making tea and cooking is a result of capitalism. . . . In short capitalism and love are in conflict with one another. Old men are in conflict with love. Thus there is a tight bond between old men and capitalism, and the only good friends of love are young people. Wouldn't you say that old men and young people are in conflict with each other?[10]

In this example of Mao's early thinking, we can detect the presence of the emotive pattern mentioned above. Indeed, the notion of developing the future persisted through Mao's revolutionary practices. While Mao often consciously or unconsciously repressed romanticism, from time to time this tendency surfaced in his own expressions. For example, in concluding his important 1930 political analysis "A Single Spark Can Start a Prairie Fire," he states: "It is like a ship far out at sea whose mast-head can already be seen from the shore; it

---

9. Mao Zedong, "The Question of Love—Young People and Old People: Smash the Policy of Parental Arrangement (November 25, 1919)," in *Mao's Road to Power*, ed. Stuart R. Schram [Armonk, NY: M. E. Sharpe, 1997), 1:439.

10. Ibid., 1:440.

is like the morning sun in the east whose shimmering rays are visible from a high mountain top; it is like a child about to be born moving restlessly in its mother's womb."[11] Here, future, hope, and new birth—words Liang earlier had associated with the young—received a revolutionary reinterpretation, despite the fact that they belonged to the same intellectual genealogy as that of Liang and of twentieth-century China more generally.

This intellectual genealogy not only profoundly influenced twentieth-century literature but also constituted one of the political characteristics of the Chinese revolution. This revolutionary characteristic, to reiterate, while signifying future, hope, and new birth, identified tradition as representing the past, conservativism, and death; as an obstacle to China's modernization [and] development; as an object of intense revolutionary resistance and struggle. It is in this sense that I treat China's revolutionary politics as one of youth politics. It is also in this sense that I argue that, it is the revolutionary movement, including its theoretical expressions, led by the Chinese Communist Party that should be recognized as the heir to China's quest for modernity since the late Qing.

The notion and the discourse of young China opened a way for emotive expressions of the individual, or of the young. Charles Taylor identifies the force that generates such emotions as "the ideal of authenticity."[12]

This "ideal of authenticity" contains within it "moral significance." As Taylor indicates, "before the late eighteenth century, no one thought that the differences between human beings had this kind of moral significance"; this "ideal of authenticity," therefore, constitutes an important part of modern consciousness, indicating that each individual has their unique way of being human: "It greatly increases the importance of this self-contact by introducing the principle of originality: each of our voices has something unique to say. Not only should I not mold my life to the demands of external conformity; I can't even find the model by which to live outside myself. I can only find it within."[13]

Taylor's point echoes the notion of self/individual that we have consistently been discussing. When the self/individual is expressed by way of youth,

---

11. Mao Tse-tung, "A Single Spark Can Start a Prairie Fire," in *Selected Works of Mao Tse-tung* (Peking: Foreign Language Press, 1965), 1:127.

12. See Charles Taylor, "The Politics of Recognition," in *New Contexts of Canadian Criticism*, ed. Ajay Heble, Donna Palmateer Pennee, and J. R. (Tim) Struthers (Peterborough, ON: Broadview, 1997), 98–131.

13. Ibid.

its demand for liberation from the hierarchy of traditional society or the associated political and cultural domains can at the same time be naturalized. In other words, the temporal and biological content attached to youth made it possible for their political pursuits to acquire a naturalized and moralized legitimacy. Such an ideal of authenticity or principle of originality can apply not only to the self or individual but also to a nation (*minzu*). Like an individual, a nation also must be loyal to itself, its ideals, and its path to the future. In Liang's writings, while the young are in opposition to the old, China nevertheless came to be in line with the world. There, the young and China were identified with one another, an identification that made it possible, in a political sense, for one to stand in for the other. We can conclude that, from the start of modern Chinese discourse, youth signified China and was associated with political and social movements. Youth, in this sense, is not entirely an individual-based concept. At the same time, with the support of youth, China and various related political and social movements also functioned to denote individuals, again replete with a naturalized and moralized legitimacy. This legitimacy would become a powerful emotive and moral force and would constitute the revolutionary form of youth.

To be sure, within the politics of the Chinese revolution itself, there was a built-in need for the construction of subjectivity. Within different historical contexts, the constitutive discourse of subjectivity changed in relation to policies and tactics, ranging, for example, from class to nation, united front, and political consultation.[14] Of course, among these rather complex expressions, class politics was always the dominant political orientation; namely, it was what Mao had always insisted on: "never forget the long-term interests of the working class."[15] Nevertheless, we can still detect a connection between the construction of subjectivity in class politics and the narratives produced in the May Fourth Movement. That is, the self or individual did not completely disappear. Instead, it reentered revolutionary politics and its storytelling as part of the class/nation discourse. Just as Taylor insists, the notion of the ideal

14. Tr.: These are all possible collective modes of identification. Class and nation are explicated throughout the book. "United front" pertains to the period of the War of Resistance against Japan through the New Democratic period (1937–45); "political consultation" pertains to the existence of multiple political parties, all of which are allowed to exist conditional on their acceptance of the dominant leadership of the Chinese Communist Party, a system that was inaugurated formally in 1949 and persists to this day.

15. Mao Zedong, "Zhuan fa Zhu De gei zhonggong zhongyang xin de piyu" [Remarks on Zhu De's letter to the Party's Central Committee], in *Mao Zedong wenji* [Collected writings of Mao Zedong] (Beijing: Renmin Chubanshe, 1996), 5:46.

of authenticity applies both to categories of the individual and of the nation. And from this perspective, we find that youth/future discourse has always been part of the underlying structure of the revolutionary story.

Even in the most canonical revolutionary text, *White-Haired Girl*, we can see the youth/future element at work. As far as much of the story goes—the young lovers Xi'er and Dachun are forced apart by Huang Shiren, the landlord—it may not be something new; in some ways, it was retelling an old and traditional story like *Southeast the Peacock Flies* (*Kongque dongnan fei*).[16] What was new was the introduction of class politics that offers a modern interpretation of the old story. In this modern interpretation, the future was not just an empty signifier or symbol. Rather, the intervention by the new (Communist) political power helps make the future visible and also realizable in the present. Ding Yi, one of the authors of the play *White-Haired Girl*, wrote in the introduction to the 1949 edition of the play that "the peasants who had always been oppressed finally came upon their own army. From then on, they have had power and hope."[17] Along these lines, we find on the cover of the republished play the words "new opera" (*xin geju*), a term not only referring to a new form of art but also indicating that it was a new interpretation of an old story. If we take the play as the main text, the term *xin geju* then is the subtext, and it is the intertexuality between the main text and the subtext that powerfully transmits the modern significance of *White-Haired Girl*.[18] In the new interpretation, emotions were politicized. The grand reunion between Xi'er and Dachun, therefore, was not simply a popular way to end the story. Rather, only with this grand reunion can the possibility of the future, realized in the present, be forcefully made clear. The temporal notion of now in turn helped indicate that utopia was not just a mere imagination but something

16. In Ouyang Shan's novel *San Jia Xiang* [*Three family lane*] [first published in 1959], which is set during the May Fourth Movement, the author essentially retells this old story [*Southeast the Peacock Flies*, a long narrative poem believed to be written around the late Han Dynasty (196–220 A.D.), original author unknown]. Through narrating how the protagonist Zhou Bin and his cohorts revise and restage this play, the novel helped connect the May Fourth Movement with the Chinese left-wing revolution.

17. Ding Yi, "Bai Mao Nü Zaiban Qianyan" [Introduction to the republication of *White Haired Girl*] (Jinan: Shandong Huadong Xinhua Shudian, 1949), 2.

18. I would like to thank She Danqing (of East China Normal University), whose PhD dissertation (2007) titled "Zhou Libo xintan" ("A new study of Zhou Libo") uses the French theorist Gerard Genette's theorization of subtext in his study of the vicissitudes of the different kinds of publications of Zhou Libo's works. I would like to acknowledge She Danqing's study for helping me think about this issue.

that could be applied to human social and political activities. What is more, this narrative structure informed by youth/future was also highly affective. Directly catering to the emotive sentiments of the audience, it enabled the new society to acquire a strong emotional and moral power that was at the same time inspirational.[19]

In short and to reiterate, from a political perspective, we can sense the presence, or retaining, of the self/individual—individuality—as a core component of Chinese revolutionary politics and literature.

In addition to youth/future as a temporal dimension of narration, such narration also effectively mobilizes the body of the individual. Indeed, in revolutionary narration, the body always functioned as a powerful motivator—such as the notion of *fanshen* that William Hinton used in his narrative of China.[20] Even after 1949, storytelling connected the body with youth or future. In Wang Meng's "A Young Man Arrives at the Organizational Department," for example, the female protagonist, Zhao Huiwen, says to her male friend, Lin Zhen:

> It's a very beautiful night, isn't it? Can you smell the fragrance of the locust tree? The little white blossoms, though ordinary, are neater and more refined than peonies, and stronger and more fragrant than the blossoms of peach and plums. Can't you smell them? What a pity! Goodnight. Until early tomorrow morning when we meet again, when we both once more throw ourselves into the great but troublesome work. Afterward, in the evening, come to me and we'll listen to the 'Capriccio Italien.' Then I'll boil you water chestnuts and we'll throw the peels all over the floor.[21]

In this romantic narrative, the young body, including its physical senses, is fully mobilized, precisely so that it can better serve the temporal youth/future narration. At the same time, of course, such youth-oriented narration was highly political.

---

19. Reportedly, during the Yan'an period, every staging of *White Hair Girl* was a populist event. Some people climbed onto rooftops to watch it, while others walked dozens of miles to see the play. See Ding Ling's "General Introduction" to *Yan'an wenyi congshu* [Series on Yan'an art and literature] (Changsha: Hunan Wenyi Chubanshe, 1984), 6.

20. William Hinton, *Fanshen: A Documentary of Revolution in a Chinese Village* (New York: Vintage, 1968).

21. Wang Meng, "A Young Man Arrives at the Organization Department," in *Literature of the Hundred Flowers*, ed. Hualing Nieh (New York: Columbia University Press, 1981), 510.

This kind of subjective articulation inevitably called for a corresponding style of expression. What resulted was lyricism.[22] Poetry and music were the best forms of lyrical expression. This may explain why, even in the most hardship-ridden and difficult wartime environment, the Chinese revolution never excluded romantic forms of expression. Indeed, romantic expressions were more often than not associated with youth and songs. In describing Yan'an, for example, He Qifang offers the following lines: "The gate of Yan'an is always open. Every day, young people from all over the country enter the gate, carrying with them their luggage as well as their burning hope. They study; they sing; their life is exciting and lively. When it is time for them to depart, they do so in groups, in uniform and with burning enthusiasm, moving out toward different directions."[23] Zhou Libo also wrote in a poem ["Yige zaochen de gezhe de xiwang" ("The hope of an early morning singer")]: "I want to sing my song loudly and repeatedly, because I believe my song celebrates beauty, like the sun that believes in its warmth, like the violin that trusts its well-tuned strings, like youth that believes in a pure and sincere dream, like a piece of floating cloud that dashes away freely and lightly."[24] Whether or not these depictions were realistic, underlying these lyrics were the intellectual resources traceable to Liang's imaginary of young China. And they also demonstrate the extent to which the ideal of authenticity was simultaneously manifested on the level of both the individual and the nation; that is, the lyrics about the individual signified the nation, and those about the nation implied the fate of the individual. Thus, they constitute a classical mode of expression for youth/China.

In the socialist literature of 1949–66, such expressions not only continued to exist but also ascended to the level of being identified as the national literary mode of writing, or "the method that combined revolutionary realism and revolutionary romanticism."[25] During the 1950s, this lyricism was widespread, manifesting a strong politicization of individual subjectivity. When singing—lyrical expression—became a requirement, youth inevitably came to be a recurrent object of narration. At the same time, with the intervention of revolutionary politics, along with its interpretive power and force of action,

---

22. In modern Chinese literature, both in terms of its form and language, lyricism is a modern phenomenon, one closely related to the pursuits of the modern subject.

23. He Qifang, *He Qifang wenji* [Collected writings of He Qifang] (Shijiazhuang: Hebei Renmin Chubanshe, 2000), 2:39.

24. Quoted in She Danqing, "Zhou Libo xintan."

25. Tr.: This method was promoted in the late 1950s for creating proletarian literature and art.

the future no longer existed in imagination alone but also became a realizable now. Thus, this particular kind of now helped relieve the tension between the present and the future, causing the lyricism of that period to exude an optimistic spirit.

In the political documents of twentieth-century China, the concept of youth is frequently encountered. But compared to other concepts, it remains a group-related one without having clearly delimited lines of definition. If, for example, notions like worker, peasant, and soldier denote either a profession or class, what does youth signify exactly? To which category does it belong? It is perhaps due to this lack of clarity that Huang Ziping designates youth and other related notions like the young, love, and life as a set of empty signifiers. Yet without clearly defined boundaries, youth as a concept nevertheless occupied a powerful position in Chinese politics and literature. On the one hand, it implies the complexity of the Chinese revolution and Chinese politics, in that youth could suggest a kind of united front that constitutes an imagined community composed of a diverse array of social groups. On the other hand, for this blurred-boundary conceptual category to enter the intellectual or political discursive spectrum, its emotive quality had to be supported by a new kind of theoretical interpretation.

Lu Xun once offered his interpretation of youth in biological terms based on evolutionism. He states: "The way I understand it now is rather simple. Based on phenomena in the biological world, it is about (1) maintaining life, (2) continuing life, and (3) developing life—or evolution. If organisms can do that, fathers can surely do the same."[26] Influenced by evolutionist ideas, Lu Xun harbored strong hope, both culturally and politically, for youth. During the 1930s, however, Lu Xun declared that his evolutionary thinking had been completely destroyed.[27] During the same period, Mao offered his definition and interpretation of youth along the lines of revolutionary politics; he did so in his well-known articles "The May Fourth Movement"[28] and "The Orientation of the Youth Movement." In these two articles, Mao proposed the notion of "main force" (*zhuli jun*):

26. Lu Xun, "Women xianzai zenyang zuo fuqin" [How can we be fathers today?], in *Lu Xun quanji* [Complete collection of Lu Xun's works] (Beijing: Renmin Chubanshe, 2005), 1:135.
27. Lu Xun, "San Xian Ji xuyan" [Introduction to *San Xian Ji*], *Lu Xun quanji* [Complete collection of Lu Xun's works] (Beijing: Renmin Chubanshe, 2005), 4:5.
28. See Mao Zedong, "Wusi yundong" [May Fourth Movement], *Mao Zedong Xuanji* [Selected Works of Mao Zedong] (Beijing: Renmin Chubanshe, 1991), vol. 2.

> What then is the main force? The workers and peasants. Our young intellectuals and students must go among the workers and peasants, who make up 90 percent of the population, and mobilize and organize them. Without this main force of workers and peasants, we cannot win the fight against imperialism and feudalism, we cannot win it by relying only on the contingent of young intellectuals and students. Therefore, the young intellectuals and students throughout the country must unite with the broad masses of workers and peasants and become one with them, and only then can a mighty force be created.[29]

Here, Mao makes two distinctions: one is to concretize the notion of youth into "young intellectuals and students" and incorporate them into categories of class/social strata for analysis, thus rejecting any discussion of youth as an abstract category. The other distinction is the notion of "major force," which essentially means main political subject. Defining "broad masses of workers and peasants" as the major political subject in and of the Chinese revolution helps define the position of the "young intellectuals and students" in relation to them, including what the youth's actions should be (namely, unite and become one with workers and peasants). The notion of integration (*jiehe*) played a significant role in the relationship between intellectuals and the Chinese revolution. I will discuss this issue at some point in the future. In this chapter, I am mainly concerned with the ways in which Mao's definition and interpretation of youth exerted influence on the literary narration of contemporary socialist Chinese literature.

I would like to borrow Edward Said's notion of "structure of attitude and references" to address the issue. The structure of attitude and references is an important concept found in Said's *Culture and Imperialism*. Unfortunately, Said did not offer enough theoretical elaboration. What we can discern is this notion's affinity with Raymond Williams's "structure of feelings" and the influence [on Said] of [Antonio] Gramsci's theory.[30] Said's concept contains two key elements—experience and geography—and through his discussion of the nineteenth-century British novel, we can recognize what he meant by "structure of attitude and references." This structure is experience-based and also

---

29. Mao Tse-tung, "The Orientation of the Youth Movement," in *Selected Works of Mao Tsetung* (Peking: Foreign Language Press, 1961), 2:245.

30. According to Said, Gramsci "thought in geographical terms ... in the Hegelian tradition, which is organized around the temporal scheme. The geographical, or spatial, scheme is quite a different one; the spatial is much more material" (quoted in *Power, Politics and Culture: Interviews with Edward W. Said*, ed. Gauri Viswanathan [New York: Pantheon Books, 2001], 195).

consists of geopolitical implications. What interests me specifically are the two key elements—experience and geography—and the discussion of how the subject gets extended into the building of subjectivity in different geographical, political, and cultural relations. For my own purposes, I am going to lift Said's concept of the structure of attitude and references out of his context and use it as an abstract notion for my discussion of contemporary Chinese literature.[31]

I believe that, in Mao's earlier emphasis on the educated and student youth integrating themselves with the worker and peasant masses, the notion of integration also contained within it a geographical implication. It demanded that the educated and student youth delve deeper into revolutionary space; this space could be the countryside, factories, or the military, all of which constituted the center for the revolution. Related to these geographical designations is the issue of attitude—that is, a revolutionary attitude, which in specific terms had to do with the attitude of the educated and student youth toward the masses of workers and peasants, who were the revolution's major force. What Mao tried to address in his "Talks at the Yan'an Forum on Literature and Art" was also this issue of attitude. To Mao, "attitude" was not just about one's political stance but also about issues of sentiment or feeling, learning, reform, and self-reform. He used himself as an example:

> At that time I felt that intellectuals were the only clean people in the world, while in comparison workers and peasants were dirty. I did not mind wearing the clothes of other intellectuals, believing them clean, but I would not put on clothes belonging to a worker or peasant, believing them dirty. But after I became a revolutionary and lived with workers and peasants and with soldiers of the revolutionary army, I gradually came to know them well, and they gradually came to know me well too. It was then, and only then, that I fundamentally changed the bourgeois and petty-bourgeois feelings implanted in me in the bourgeois schools. I came to feel that compared with the workers and peasants the unremoulded intellectuals were not clean and that, in the last analysis, the workers and peasants were the cleanest people and, even though their hands were soiled and their feet smeared with cow-dung, they were really cleaner than the bourgeois and

---

31. Tr.: Said's original concept pertains to the ways in which the colonial erupts—albeit obliquely—into mainstream nineteenth-century British fiction, such as Jane Austen's *Mansfield Park* and other such novels. See, in particular, the chapter on Austen in Edward W. Said, *Culture and Imperialism* (New York: A. A. Knopf, 1993).

petty-bourgeois intellectuals. That is what is meant by a change in feelings, a change from one class to another.[32]

Here, we find that "workers and peasants" not only attain political legitimacy but also moral and aesthetic legitimacy.

Assuming the [correct] attitude was naturally accompanied by a corresponding geographical reference, which entails in literary practice not only a change in the object of representation but also an author's self-examination and reform. This change would obviously cause a narrative structural change in contemporary Chinese literature. The "broad world" was not only to be made specific but also politicized into a world worthy to be hoped for, which in turn helped establish the structure of attitude and references. This political restructuring of literature in essence meant that fiction writing was to become part of the expansion of the revolutionary and its geography.

In this sense, Yang Mo's *Song of Youth* (*Qingchun zhi ge*) is a quintessentially representative work.[33] In this novel, space is the expressional form of the structure of attitude and references. Space not only exists in Yang's memory, it is also used to spatialize history. After the novel was published, Yang wrote an article titled "The Red Tower in Beijing's Shatan: Why I Set *Song of Youth* with the Backdrop of Beijing University."[34] She states that it was at Beijing University that she witnessed modern Chinese intellectual history:

> In many of the tiny apartments around the Shatan area, countless revolutionary youth came and went. As they worked and struggled day and night for the liberation of the Chinese nation and for the ideals of communism, they suffered from hunger and cold and risked the danger of being arrested or killed by the enemy. At the same time, in the red tower, a different group of people existed: they went to study in the library or worked in the lab. The nation, society, and serving the masses: what did any of that have to do with their own self-interest? . . . Deep down, they were mainly concerned about their own professional success and ascendance.[35]

32. Mao Tse-tung, "Talks at the Yenan Forum on Literature and Art," in *Selected Works of Mao Tse-tung* (Peking: Foreign Language Press, 1965), 3:73.

33. Tr.: Yang Mo's *Qingchun zhi ge* [Song of youth] (Beijing: Renmin Wenxue Chubanshe, 1960) was first published in 1958. In the second edition, published in 1960, the author made rather extensive revisions and offered explanations for the revisions in her "Epilogue." Subsequent republications of the novel were based on this second edition.

34. Quoted in Li Yang, *50–70 niandai Zhongguo wenxue zai jiedu* [Rereading 1950s–1970s Chinese literature] (Jinan: Shangdong Jiaoyu Chubanshe, 2003), 102.

35. Quoted in ibid.

In contrast, the novel, especially the second edition, sets up the countryside of Hebei Province as a counterbalance [to the city]. It is there that Lin Daojing, the female protagonist, goes through a real transformation and rebirth. In this sense, her personal growth is not only a historical and temporal one but also a geographical and spatial one. In the specific historical context of the Chinese revolution, by extension, "the countryside encircling the cities" (*nongcun baowei chengshi*)[36] was not a mere military term; it also had the implication of the political and cultural geographical expansion of the revolution. Put differently, it is a kind of spatialization of the future. In the literature of 1949–66, this particular structure of attitude and references existed implicitly or explicitly in various narratives. Through Said's notion, we can see how hegemony was narrated and constructed via geography, and how this geography was not a natural one but a political one.

Still, we need to explore, within this structure of attitude and references, what kind of intersubjective relationship was established between the educated and student youth and the worker and peasant masses. Taylor argues that "there is no such thing as inward generation, monologically understood." On the contrary, the "crucial feature of human life is its fundamentally *dialogical* character." In this sense, "the genesis of the human mind is . . . not monological, not something each person accomplishes on his or her own, but dialogical. . . . [W]e understand the formation of identity and the self as taking place in a continuing dialogue and struggle with significant others."[37] Despite the fact that, in the Chinese context, the "significant other" is designated by the revolutionary party, we should not simply negate the dialogic components within the revolutionary party itself. In fact, it is precisely such a dialogue that enabled intellectuals to genuinely enter China. On the one hand, this process repressed an excessive expansion of intellectuals' subjectivity, including their exaggerated narrative and lyrical style and language. On the other hand, through such repression, the intellectuals came to an equal recognition of other classes, especially the legitimacy and rationality of workers' and peasants' politics and culture. I argue that this is also a kind of subjectivity, except it no longer exists in monologue but is formed by "continuing dialogue and struggle" between subjects (*zhuti*). Without fully understanding this point, we cannot fully understand the educated and student youth in socialist China.

36. Tr.: A concept, developed by Mao as early as in the 1920s, was later fully theorized by Mao in 1936 in his "Zhongguo geming zhanzheng de zhanlue wenti" [Strategic issues in Chinese revolutionary war] and practiced in the CCP-led revolution.

37. See Taylor, "The Politics of Recognition," 98–131.

Even during the Cultural Revolution, with the educated population being relocated on a large scale (such as during the rustication movement), such dialogic relations never stopped. And it is precisely within these dialogic relations that a generation of intellectuals quietly transformed themselves, learning to tightly connect their lives with those of the people and to move beyond their own stories. It is also only when we understand this point that we can fully understand why, since the 1990s, groups of Chinese intellectuals have begun to demand anew the telling of people's stories.

At the same time, we must also explore another aspect of the issue. That is, throughout the history of the Chinese revolution, this dialogic relationship did not constitute the entirety of the aforementioned intersubjective relationship. More often than not, the dialogue was one that proceeded between the imitator and the imitated. In literature, specifically, when it came to the unresolved issue raised in the "Talks at the Yan'an Forum on Literature and Art" of celebrating versus [critically] exposing [a person, event, or situation], implicit in [the demand for] celebrating is none other than a demand for the narrator to imitate a different but more meaningful life. Also implicit in the celebration is the narrator's self-criticism and self-reform, and an attempt at a perfect combination of moral integrity and the people. In Kang Zhai's "My Two Landlords" (Wo de liangjia fangdong), for example, the story narrates precisely a "different but more meaningful life" of the young.[38] While it is perfectly fine for the people's story to become part of one's narration, problems arise when such narration overly emphasize imitation and repress the narrator's own story. Surely we should not completely negate the legitimate elements in intellectuals' own stories. In this sense, what is really significant in Xiao Yemu's "Between My Wife and Me" ("Women fufu zhijian") is its attempt at correcting this one-dimensional narrative tendency by constructing some dialogue.[39] There are quite a few dialogic elements behind "I," the narrator, and his wife, such as those between the worker and peasant masses and the intellectuals, city and countryside, and civilization and nature. Unfortunately, within the then-prevalent structure of attitude and references, the necessity for such a dialogue was either overlooked or criticized.

The difficulty we encounter is how to understand the relationship between dialogue and imitation within the larger framework of the structure of atti-

---

38. Kang Zhai, "Wo de liangjia fangdong" [My two landlords], *Kang Zhai xiaoshuo xuan* [Selected stories of Kang Zhai] (Changsha: Hunan Renmin Chubanshe, 1984), 100–22.

39. Xiao Yemu, "Women fufu zhijian" [Between my wife and me], *Renmin wenxue* [People's literature] 3 (1950), 37–45.

tude and references. What I want to insist on is a dialectical approach to uncover heterogeneous narrative elements in what appears to be homogeneous narration.

As long as a party or a country mobilizes its politics within the narrative framework of new birth/future, it is impossible for them [the party or country] to completely give up telling stories about youth. This was especially true in China during the 1950s. In the epilogue to his novel *Long Live Youth* (*Qinchun wansui*), Wang Meng's reminiscences offer glimpses into the lives of the young (in cities, of course) during the 1950s. On the one hand, "we learned to waltz; we addressed our high-school and college teachers as *xiansheng* [a respectful term for teachers of both genders]; and we referred to student dormitories as *zhai* [as in "*shu zhai*," or study]. Among the interactions between male and female students, there were budding natural feelings in need of good guidance." On the other hand, "there was promotion of rounded personal development and for making progress in both revolution and study [literally, in both being red and expert], for lively and colorful collective activities that were organized by classes or the youth league, friendships and mutual help between classmates that reflected the new social relationships among people, establishment of a new kind of relationship between teacher and students and strong feelings among this generation of youth toward the party, Chairman Mao, and the socialist country."[40] We have no reason to doubt the authenticity of Wang's memories. On the contrary, it is precisely the coexistence of varied, old, and new cultural elements here that allowed the notion of youth to acquire a renewed abstraction that would constitute an ideological force to intervene in the real historical situation. Indeed, to one extent or another, many novels of the time—such as Liu Qing's *The Builders*, Zhao Shuli's *Sanliwan Village*, Zhou Libo's *Great Changes in a Mountain Village*, and Wang Wenshi's *Heifeng*—used youth as a collection of images to complete their grand narratives of socialist reform. In these novels, youth was once again defined as representing the future, hope, reform, and the new China, while elders were also once again depicted in association with tradition, conservatism, unwillingness to change, the old social order, and the lack of internal drive to change themselves for the construction of a modern industrial country.

40. Wang Meng, *Qinchun wansui* [Long live youth] (Beijing: Renmin Chubanshe, 1979), 346–47.

At the same time, however, this does not mean that, because of this, contemporary literature returned to the May Fourth tradition. Despite the reabstraction of youth as a category, youth was fairly strongly lodged in the interpretive structure of the revolution. That is why, in these novels, youth still belongs to the objects that need to conform to revolutionary necessity (*bei guifan de*). And strictly speaking, in these novels, it is not the conflict between the young and the old that constitutes the central conflict, but rather the conflict between the young and the middle-aged that does. Such a conflict implies a new kind of power struggle, in which the party is unfailingly on the side of the young. It is important for us to recognize the highly politicized and highly organized structure of attitude and references in which contemporary Chinese literature existed. For even Lin Zhen, the main character in Wang Meng's "A Young Man Arrives at the Organization Department," ultimately resorts to asking for help from the Party secretary of the district. At the same time, however, we must not conclude that intellectual subjectivity completely disappeared from this hegemonic political structure. What we need is probably a different kind of interpretation or understanding. This interpretation stipulates that we recognize that, in actual writings, intellectuals [writers] often quietly but surely transferred their own wishes and ideas to their characters, especially those who are workers and peasants, to express their own subjective will. One example comes from a new folk song so popular in the 1950s that it was included in [elementary school] Chinese textbooks. Its lines go as follows: "there is no Jade Emperor in heaven/there is no Dragon King on the ground/I am Jade Emperor/I am Dragon King/Shouting my order to the lofty mountains/I am here."[41] Who is to say that this is a poem of the workers and peasants? Who is to say that it has no implicit connection to May Fourth literature such as Guo Moruo's poem "Tiangou" [The heavenly hound]?[42] The truth of the matter is that intellectuals had always participated in the construction of the subjectivity of the workers and peasants and of revolutionary politics.

In the process of this construction, intellectuals experienced a degree of suppression of their own subjectivity on the one hand, but also the transference of their own subjective will onto their object, on the other hand. This, I believe, constitutes the unique significance of this literature both in terms of

---

41. *Gaoji xiaoxue keben: yuwen* [Advanced elementary school textbook: Chinese] (Beijing: Renmin Jiaoyu Chubanshe, 1958), 3:33–34.

42. Guo Moruo, "Tiangou" [Heavenly hound], in *Guo Moruo xuanji* [Selected works of Guo Moruo] (Beijing: Renmin Chubanshe, 1997), 1:38–39.

form and narration. In this vein, Wang Meng has stated that he thinks "Mao Zedong's formula of combining 'revolutionary romanticism with revolutionary realism' is better than the Soviet Union's 'socialist realism.' The former allows leeway and more space for creating art."[43] What the combination of "revolutionary romanticism and revolutionary realism" allows, in other words, is a middle space in which intellectuals express their subjective feelings and do so via monologue and lyricism. This explains why we find, in the politicization of literature, certain heterogeneous elements that coexisted, even if they were often expressed in a seemingly homogeneous fashion. In this sense we can say that the youth/future narrative element also existed in revolutionary literature and art and continued to inform the future-facing revolutionary modernity of the Chinese revolution.

However, this particular kind of "long live youth" lyricism did not last too long. Despite conforming to revolutionary politics, the renewed temporal and biological significance of youth had a tendency to expand beyond the tolerance of the political powers that be. When that happened, the political powers that be—especially when society was stabilized and when the new state needed to reconstruct its own myths and new traditions and norms—would redefine youth and redraw the boundaries for its narratives in the name of revolution. The difficulty, however, resided in the choice of whether to let youth continue its narrative function as figuring youth/future or to allow youth to figure revolution/rebellion, or, yet again, whether to construct youth as the heir and protector of the new tradition—namely, as the successor to the revolution.

In 1963, the October-November double issue of *Juben* [Drama script] published a play titled *Wish You Good Health*,[44] which was later renamed *Never Forget* (*Qianwan buyao wangji*). The play's major theme of never forgetting class struggle manifested an anxiety about how to define youth. Throughout the play, the character Ding Shaochun is positioned as someone to be educated, while his father (Ding Haikuan) and his grandfather are positioned as educators. Compared with many previous literary works, here we see a reversal of the positions of the young and the old. This reversal was symptomatic of the political character of the time: in the newly established tradition, efforts to affirm and maintain the present coexisted with an anxiety about the future.

43. Wang Meng, *Wang Meng zizhuan* [Wang Meng's autobiography] (Guangzhou: Huacheng Chubanshe, 2006–7), 2:62.
44. Cong Shen, "Zhu ni jiankang" [Wish you good health], *Juben* [Drama scripts], 1963, 10 and 11: 4–45.

This anxiety was not about destroying or subverting the present, but rather about how to continue the current (new) tradition of revolution. The responsibility that narration had to shoulder, in other words, was to protect what had been accomplished, not to destroy it. If we place this reversal in the larger context of the mid-1960s, what this play manifested, despite the radical politics at the time (chiefly expressed in the ideological debate between China and the Soviet Union) and despite its ostensible class-struggle narrative theme, was that revolution was in fact in danger of being deconstructed.[45] That is why, during the 1960s, in addition to this play penned by Cong Shen, there were other similar works such as the play *The Young Generation* (*Nianqing de yidai*) by Chen Yun[46] and the story "Family Problems" ("Jiating wenti") by Hu Wanchun.

Yet interestingly, efforts to maintain the status quo, on a different level, contradicted Mao and the radical political force Mao represented that promoted self-negation and insisted on continuous revolution. This contradiction culminated in the Cultural Revolution, launched in 1966, when Mao's quotation about youth was popularized and came to function as a powerful theoretical reason for mobilizing the youth again: "The world is yours as well as ours, but ultimately, it is yours. You young people are full of energy and vitality, just like the morning sun. Hope is placed on you."[47] In this context, revolution and rebellion once again emerged as the dominant way forward into the future.

After the Cultural Revolution, in the late 1970s, youth was also mobilized as an important political and literary narrative resource, in opposition to the Cultural Revolution, to negate it. Wang Meng's novel *Long Live Youth*, which had been written in the 1950s, was finally published in 1979, with its first printing numbering 170,000 copies. The *Guangming Daily* [a national newspaper catering to the educated class] quickly followed by publishing Wang's epilogue [which was included in the published novel]. In Wang's memory, "[the publication] was really unexpected—I didn't submit my manuscript to the publisher; they came to me and asked for it.... And shortly after the novel

---

45. For a detailed discussion of the play and the political characteristics of the 1960s, see chapter 7.

46. Chen Yun, *Nianqing de yidai* [The young generation], *Juben* [Drama scripts], 1963, 8. Tr.: *The Young Generation* became much better known after it was adapted into a film by the same name. *Nianqing de yidai* [The young generation], dir. Zhao Ming (1965).

47. Tr.: This is a quote from a speech Mao gave to Chinese students studying and professionals working in the Soviet Union on November 17, 1957, Moscow. *Mao Zhuxi zai sulian d yanlun* [Chairman Mao's speeches in the Soviet Union] (Beijing: Renmin Ribao Chubanshe, 1957), 14–15.

was published, Liu Guosheng, an editor from Shanghai Film Studio, immediately contacted me to discuss its adaption."[48] Not long after the film version of the novel (directed by Zhang Xuan) was released, it was also met with strong and popular reception, yet another example that characterizes the significance of the issue of youth in the 1980s.

For more than one hundred years, Liang Qichao's young China has continued to play an important role in the modern Chinese imaginary, helping construct the youthful characteristics of Chinese politics. At the same time, however, when revolution mobilized the young, it also tried to make them conform while training and disciplining them about, among other things, love and sex.

II. Love, or Stories of Love

Revolution plus love was a popular mode of writing left-wing literature of the 1930s. In his 1935 article "'The Revolution' plus 'Love' Formula" ("Geming jia 'lianai' de gongshi"), Mao Dun criticized this phenomenon.[49] He pointed out that the "'revolution' plus 'love' formula" had become a fashion. The basic formula is as follows: the writer begins by dramatizing the conflict between the revolutionary mission and romantic love; the writer ends by calling on the protagonists to devote themselves to the revolution and to forgo personal feelings. What follows this conflict formula is the mutually beneficial formula, in which the writer does not portray revolution as an obstacle but rather as an attraction that encourages the couple in love to work together for the revolution. In the end, this mutually beneficial formula developed into a formula in which revolution transcends all: revolution is no longer the precondition for love, but love itself.[50] At that time, in 1935, Mao Dun's criticism had a particular target in mind: Jiang Guangci and writers who wrote in a similar idiom.

Yet there are reasons to raise questions about Mao Dun's criticism. David Wang, for example, has this to say: "Mao Dun's criticism must lead us to the question: wasn't Mao Dun himself among the practitioners of revolution plus love fiction he attacked? His first two novels, *Eclipse* and *Hong* (Rainbow, 1930), both deal with young men and women's struggle with the ever-entangled re-

---

48. See Wang Meng, *Wang Meng zizhuan* [Wang Meng's autobiography] 2:31, 41.
49. Mao Dun, "'Geming jia 'lianai' de gongshi" [The "revolution" plus "love" formula], in *Mao Dun quanji* [Complete collection of Mao Dun's works] (Beijing: Renmin Chubanshe, 1990), 20:317–52.
50. Ibid.

lations between revolution and love."⁵¹ Obviously, Wang traces the origin of the "'revolution' plus 'love'" narration to Mao Dun's early works by following the very line of this argument. To be sure, Wang differentiates between Mao Dun and Jiang Guangci: "whereas revolution plus love is for Mao Dun a symptom of a larger social malaise, for Jiang Guangci it serves as a treatment for the malaise."⁵² I think this distinction can help us better understand Mao Dun's early novels.

But our questions do not stop here. The fact is that during the May Fourth period, love was represented in connection with many other issues: politics, society, and the liberation of the individual. Even Mao Zedong, as we recall in his article titled "The Question of Love" (1919), argued that "capitalism and love are in contradiction with one another." Is this not yet another different version of the "'revolution' plus 'love'" formula? A different piece of information provided by Wang may actually help us better explore this issue:

> Significantly enough, the revolution and love issue did not concern only leftists. As early as April 1928, *Geming yu lianai* (Revolution and love) was published under the aegis of the Nationalist Party. Its author, Hong Ruizhao, a sociologist and cultural critic, began his study by observing that romantic love had become the most "worrisome problem" within the Nationalist revolutionary campaign. The problem was intensified, as Hong observed, by the boom in literature dealing with "modern-style love": "The conflict between revolutionary fever and romantic passion has become such a serious issue that it demands an immediate solution." Hong then pointed his finger at the Communists affiliated with the Wuhan government, accusing them of promoting a dubious reconciliation between one's romantic instinct and revolutionary commitment. For Hong, although the Communists cautioned the revolutionaries on the harmful consequences of romance, they secretly encouraged sexual desires among revolutionary youth so as to undermine their political convictions. He therefore called for a more engaged Nationalist Revolution, which he believed promised genuine freedom and equality in economy and education, and a total emancipation of the force of love.

Wang continues to point out that,

51. David Der-wei Wang, *The Monster That Is History* (Berkeley: University of California Press, 2004), 89.
52. Ibid., 91.

He nevertheless suggested that at a time of national crisis, a strong revolutionary must subordinate his personal yearning to the public good; he must modulate his desires, avoiding the pitfalls of either stoicism or promiscuity, so as to facilitate a successful revolution. "For those who do not wish to be trapped by lack of sexual fulfillment, they had better heighten their desire to a love for truth, good, and beauty, to a love for family, society, and nation, so that they will contribute to academic construction and Nationalist Revolution."[53]

We can clearly see that, at the time, both the left and the right originated from the same tradition that we call the modern.

One of the benchmarks of the modern is the so-called awakening of the individual (*geren juexing*), as this awakening relates both to the imagination of the modern nation-state and to what Anthony Giddens refers to as "emancipatory politics."[54] For Hannah Arendt, of course, the core of any modern revolution is freedom, because "it may be a truism to say that liberation and freedom are not the same; that liberation may be the condition of freedom but by no means leads automatically to it."[55] In China, this emancipatory politics liberated the individual from the yoke of tradition and returned the individual, we may say, back to an existence as an atomized being. The relationship that can be most quickly reestablished between such individual beings seems to be one between the sexes. It was in this new kind of sexual relationship that romantic love was rediscovered and upheld as a symbol for individual freedom and social emancipation. Views on love were expressed not only in literature but also in politics;[56] even love in traditional literature received a new interpretation. In short, from the very beginning, narratives about modern love were never purely about romantic love alone, but rather, they have been streamlined into specific social and political symbolic systems. What is more,

---

53. Ibid., 90.
54. Anthony Giddens writes: "Emancipatory politics involves two main elements: the effort to shed shackles of the past, thereby permitting a transformative attitude towards the future; and the aim of overcoming the illegitimate domination of some individuals or groups by others" (*Modernity and Self-Identity* [Stanford, CA: Stanford University Press, 1991], 210–11).
55. Hannah Arendt, *On Revolution* (New York: Penguin, 1990), 29.
56. For example, on November 14, 1919 when a Hunanese woman named Zhao Wuzhen committed suicide in rejecting her arranged marriage, Mao Zedong published a series of ten articles, including "Duiyu Zhao nüshi zisha de piping" (Commentary on the suicide of Miss Zhao). See Mao Zedong, "Commentary on the Suicide of Miss Zhao," in *Mao's Road to Power*, ed. Stuart R. Schram [Armonk, NY: M. E. Sharpe, 1997], 1:421–22).

in the modern Chinese historical context, the individual, from the very beginning, already functioned to embody the state; by extension, romantic love as social symbol also already carried with it the meaning of the state. This is why it is not difficult for us to understand that, in Yu Dafu's "Sinking" ("Chenlun") [a short story published in 1921], for example, the protagonist's sexual depression is so "unnaturally" entangled with a desire for a strong nation.

It is in this context that romantic love, something that belongs to the private domain of personal feelings, was mobilized for the revolution. In the words of the literary scholar Steven Chan [Chen Qingqiao], "if 'love can be considered the inner, emotional symbol for an eternal, social revolution, then Eros in this sense may be taken to signify the Life-energy that propels the wheel of the ultimate Revolution.'"[57] Similar types of articulations can be found even in the literature of the 1949–66 period.

While the individual always existed in Chinese revolutionary politics and was an important object of mobilization for the revolution, when the politics of class entered the picture, the structure of Chinese politics and culture inevitably underwent a further transformation. Within this new structure, the existence of atomized individuals had to be renarrated into a story about the [intertwining of] individual, class, and revolution. For the same reason, the story about love and revolution also had to be recoded. It is against this backdrop that Mao Dun's view of revolution plus love as a social ill was in part more acceptable than Jiang Guanci's view, in which revolution plus love was upheld as good medicine for social ills. Many years after this 1930s debate, Chen Lide published a novel titled *Pioneer* (*Qianqu*), which retold the love story of two May Fourth youth, Li Jian and Yao Yuhui.[58] For the two protagonists, literature is the medium of their love. Their pure love "makes Yao Yuhui feel that she is like a caged bird and oppressed by her family; she desires to break out of the cage and fly high into the vast and boundless sky."[59] Later, with the help of Qi Yuan, the two protagonists succeed in doing precisely that. Here, we can see the partial reappearance of May Fourth love stories in contemporary literature. However, this love story is interrupted by the revolution. In the midst of the revolutionary tidal waves, the two protagonists each begin to enter other people's stories. And it is from within those other people's stories that they "feel ashamed about their past, in which they were wallowing in their own decadent ideas, neuroses, unnamable sadness, and pessimistic

---

57. Quoted in D. Wang, *The Monster That Is History*, 80.
58. Chen Lide, *Qianqu* [Pioneer] (Beijing: Zuojia Chubanshe, 1964).
59. Ibid., 75.

spirit," and that renders them "now determined to devote their faith to the party and [commun]ism, ready to shed their last blood for the tens of millions of suffering people."[60] This recoded love story is bolstered by the theoretical notion of the "small self/big self."[61] Even though, as a concept, the dichotomy of small self/big self feels somewhat crude, it is nevertheless still applicable when we try to decode love stories in contemporary literature [of the socialist period].

It is not my task here to discuss modern love stories; my interest continues to be in how these stories were retold in contemporary Chinese literature. I largely agree with David Wang's point on love in literary narration: "revolution plus love functioned both as a literary trope, titillating and sustaining a society's desire for self-reform, and as a political mandate, calling for the redisposition of the social body in both public and personal spheres."[62]

To some extent, Zhao Shuli's "Xiao Erhei Gets Married" ("Xiao Erhei jiehun") offers a different type of love story for contemporary Chinese literature.[63] Despite the attention paid to some of the story's minor characters in a few recent studies, here I would like to return the focus to its main characters—Xiao Erhei and Xiao Qin. Through the free love (*ziyou lianai*) between the two main characters, Zhao expresses his view on love and marriage. And, frankly speaking, there is nothing particularly new in his view. Free love is everywhere in May Fourth literature, for which there is also a range of different interpretations. To some readers, the attraction of Zhao's story lies in its portrayal of Xiao Erhei and Xiao Qin. In Zhou Yang's words, for example, it [the story] is about "a young and handsome peasant, an excellent sniper, who is in love with a beautiful peasant girl."[64] But in what ways is this "talented man and beautiful woman" story different from the traditional scholar-beauty dynamic? Perhaps

---

60. Ibid., 242.
61. Tr.: In the modern Chinese context, the "big self" usually refers to the collective while the "small self" refers to the individual. The earliest appearance of the two terms is believed to be in Sun Zhongshan's "Shehui zhuyi de fasheng yu paibie" [The emergence of socialism and its different schools]. See Sun Zhongshan, *Sun Zhongshan wenji* [Collected writings of Sun Zhongshan], ed. Meng Qingpeng (Beijing: Tuanjie Chubanshe, 1997).
62. D. Wang, *The Monster That Is History*, 80.
63. Zhao Shuli, "Xiao Erhei jiehun" [Xiao Erhei gets married], *Zhao Shuli quanji* [Complete collection of Zhao Shuli's works] (Taiyuan: Beiyue Wenyi Chubanshe, 1986), 1:154.
64. Zhou Yang, "Lun Zhao Shuli de chuangzuo" [On Zhao Shuli's creative work], in *Zhao Shuli wenji* [Collection of Zhao Shuli's writings] (Beijing: Gongren Chubanshe, 1980), 4.

what we have here is an organic integration of the May Fourth spirit and urban popular culture. But we know that the Mandarin Duck and Butterfly fiction of the 1930s had already worked toward such an integration, whether in Zhang Henshui's *Fate in Tears and Laughter* (*Tixiao Yinyuan*) or in Liu Yunruo's *Apricot Flower Flaming out over the Wall* (*Hongxing Chuqiang*). To a certain extent, the formation of modern popular literature in the 1920s and 1930s was significant not only for the formation of the modern urban class but also for the formation of a modern national people. In his discussion of late Qing fiction, Li Oufan [Leo Lee] raises the issue of a "community of readers" in relation to "the community of urban fiction readers, whose world is precisely that in which this fiction unfolds": "in this world, [writers and readers] created an imagination that culminated in 1930s Shanghai and constructed a Chinese vernacular modernity."[65]

My point here is that by the 1940s, this "Chinese vernacular modernity" in effect bifurcated and went in two different directions. One is in the direction of Eileen Chang, and the other direction was manifested in Zhao and other writers from the liberated regions. Zhao's genealogy of reading, I might add, contained elements of the aforementioned 1920s and 1930s popular culture. Indeed, to some extent, we can say that Zhao rewrote the love story by using this Chinese vernacular modernity for rural areas. However, the poor peasants in rural areas also managed to rewrite this Chinese vernacular modernity in that the typical urban-style negotiation in a love relationship disappears and is replaced by the love exemplified in the love story between Xiao Erhei and Xiao Qin.

To me, however, the real significance of Zhao's "Xiao Erhei Gets Married" lies in its happy ending—or, more specifically, when the district head appears. To be sure, this district head is largely a political symbol, but without this character, the happy ending would be impossible and the story would be no more than a rural version of modern [as opposed to traditional] popular literature. The appearance of the district leader completely recodes this popular love story, thereby placing the story in the political genealogy of the Chinese revolution. There, revolution is not only political, economic, and military but is also emotive, capable of directly entering the private domain of personal feelings. Revolution not only supports poor peasants to turn over (*fanshen*) politically and economically, it also resolutely supports them to liberate their

65. Li Oufan, "Wan Qing wenhua, wenxue yu xiandai xing" [Late Qing culture, literature, and modernity], in *Liwa he pan lun wenxue* [Discussing literature by Liwa River], ed. Chen Zishan and Luo Gang (Shanghai: Huadong Shifan Daxue Chubanshe, 2006), 59.

love. This narrative mode became widely adopted in contemporary literature. By way of this popular form, Zhao succeeded in transposing the modern notion of romantic love from the city to the countryside, from the urban to the peasant, and from the elite to the subaltern.

Still, this is just the first step. What is truly significant is that the writing of the love story makes revolutionary politics the supporter and liberator of private feelings. In the process of supporting and liberating private feelings, revolutionary politics also manages to win legitimacy on an emotional level. In these transformations, politics comes to be naturalized and revolution is also transmitted into an individual's natural rights. What is more, when love is closely related to politics, the political significance of the old trope of "talented young man and beautiful young woman" becomes more salient, in that the Chinese revolution is now shown to be a supporter of beauty. Thus, politics is also aesthetically promoted.

Zhao's "Registration" ("Dengji"), written in 1950, is in some ways a revised version of "Xiao Erhei Gets Married." But perhaps because of its strong advocacy of specific policies of the new marriage law, this story exhibits less political tension than "Xiao Erhei Gets Married," though it is still quite a lively read. But what interests me more about this story is what it aims to satirize: at the district's marriage registration office, every couple repeats the same lines:

> QUESTION: Are you both willing?
> ANSWER: Yes, we are willing.
> QUESTION: Why do you want to marry her?
> ANSWER: Because she works hard![66]

What is significant about this formulaic mode of registration is how it indicates the extent to which an antifeudal modernist theme has now been systemized by the state via a form of law. Years later, Yan Yunxiang, an anthropologist, discovered in his fieldwork that young people in rural China place importance on whether or not they have something to talk about with one another (*you hua shuo*) when they look for love. He noted that "the contemporary emphasis on youhuashuo, to a great extent, derives from official propaganda regarding marriage reforms during the first three decades of socialism, in which having 'common language' (gongtong yuyan) was promoted as one

---

66. Zhao Shuli, "Dengji" [Registration], *Zhao Shuli quanji* [Complete works of Zhao Shuli], 2:149.

of the main criteria in mate choice."⁶⁷ By way of imagination, narration, and the state system, revolutionary politics simultaneously stimulated a romantic revolution in the countryside and significantly changed the emotional life there. On this front, it is very different from the way Fei Xiaotong once depicted rural China.⁶⁸

What is most important in all of this is how, by narrating love stories, politics came to be naturalized. It was no longer an external order but an internal emotional need, which in turn is represented as the inner expectation of an individual. Thus, when the individual is constructed into a political subject, he or she is simultaneously narrated as an emotional subject. In the mutual interaction between these two subjective dimensions, the political story is simultaneously told as a love story, and vice versa. In this sense, the narrative mode of the love story created by Zhao and his colleagues from the liberated zones in the 1930s and 1940s exerted a different influence on love-story writing in 1949–66 literature, in which love is not only a literary metaphor but also a political one.

In his memoir on the leftist advance (*zuoqing maojin*) during the early agricultural cooperative movement, Du Runsheng recalls what happened in Daming in Hebei Province as an example. In 1952, he states, local officials there placed two tables on the street, told the masses that the tables each represented two paths, and asked the masses to choose between "the socialist road and the capitalist road. . . . If you want to choose the socialist road, you come to that table and sign your name to join the cooperative. . . . Anyone who doesn't want to join, that means they want to join the path with the landlords, rich peasants, bourgeoisie, and America."⁶⁹ The successes, failures, and

---

67. Yunxiang Yan, *Private Life under Socialism: Love, Intimacy, and Family Change in a Chinese Village, 1949–1999* (Stanford, CA: Stanford University Press, 2003), 74.

68. In his book *Xiangtu Zhongguo*, Fei Xiaotong describes the emotional life in rural China quite differently. Tr.: Essentially, Fei notes that marriages in China's rural areas are not based on romance or love and thus are more enduring, for while love and romance fade—leading to instability—in modern urban society, in rural China, feelings grow deeper because of the lack of love and romance. Fei's notes were made in the 1940s. See Xiaotong Fei, *From the Soil: The Foundations of Chinese Society: A Translation of Fei Xiaotong's "Xiangtu Zhongguo,"* with an introduction and epilogue by Gary G. Hamilton and Wang Zheng (Berkeley: University of California Press, 1992).

69. Du Runsheng, *Du Runsheng zishu: Zhongguo nongcun tizhi biange zhongda juece jishi* [Du Runsheng remembers: Memories of the important decisions on China's village structural transformation] (Beijing: Renmin Chubanshe, 2005), 37.

lessons of the cooperative movement have continued to be studied by many scholars; what interests me here is how this movement is represented in literature. Even though literary narration is fictional, that does not mean that what is narrated is not real. According Clifford Geertz, fictional narration does not fundamentally differ from any other narrative activity in that all narratives are essentially "creative activity."[70] At the same time, however, I would add that imaginative activities are nevertheless conditioned [and constrained] by all kinds of political and cultural factors and are carried out under particular conditions. Coming back to what Du remembered: while we do not read in fictional texts what Du remembered he had seen during the cooperative movement, what we do read in fiction are stories of love against the backdrop of the cooperative movement.

Indeed, what we read in many love stories provides strong support for the legitimacy of the cooperative movement. Examples include Zhao Shuli's *Sanliwan Village* and Zhou Libo's *Great Changes in a Mountain Village*. But the stronger intention lies beyond the love stories themselves. Just like Zhao's "Xiao Erhei Gets Married," love stories at the same time function as literary or political metaphors. That is, in these narratives, the cooperative movement is not simply a political and economic event but also an emotional event; the so-called political and economic commonwealth is at the same time an emotional commonwealth. What people gain through this [cooperative] movement cannot be counted as merely political and economic benefits, but [the gains] also include love and happy marriages. By way of such narration, the cooperative movement manages to transcend the level of political economy and extend into the private domain of emotions; it gets internalized as part of the natural rights of young men and women in love.

In China, the meaning of a particular political event is always exceedingly complex, for it often evokes different responses from different corners of society, while also producing numerous unexpected consequences. In literature, when the narration incorporates all kinds of complex factors, its implication in essence exceeds the sociopolitical event it depicts, thereby acquiring symbolic meaning and significance. In literary representations of the cooperative movement, for example, we find that the narration succeeds in associating a social group (such as youth) or a social class (such as poor peasants) with an

---

70. Clifford Geertz writes about "fictions, in the sense that they are 'something made,' 'something fashioned'—the original meaning of *fictio*—not [in the sense] that they are false, unfactual, or merely 'as if' thought experiments.... But the one is as much a *fictio*—'a making'—as the other" (*The Interpretation of Cultures* [New York: Basic, 1973], 15–16).

imagined community. Equally important is how revolutionary politics found its way into the private domain of emotions by way of love stories, thus powerfully stimulating the interaction between the public and the private. Put differently, when revolution became an organic part of human natural rights, the legitimacy of the revolution, in turn, could not exist only in the domain of politics. It also came from individuals' emotional demands, which helped constitute an imagined community both in political and emotive terms. With this understanding as a backdrop, we can grasp why Xu Huaizhong's novel published in 1957 was simply titled *We Sow Our Love* (*Women bozhong aiqing*).[71] The expansion of this model of narration into other artistic domains such as cinema, for example with the production of films like *Young People in Our Village* (*Women cunli de nianqingren*) demonstrates this point. What these and other examples indicate, once again, is a characteristic in socialist narration—namely, a simultaneous rendering of the political emotive as emotions are politicized. Youth in these love stories are shown to be mobilized, to acquire a political identity, and to become an important collective component of the socialist revolution. It is precisely in such narration that politics is transformed into a kind of romanticized revolution. The importance of highlighting this point has to do with the fact that it is precisely this romantic nature of the Chinese political revolution that helped effectively mobilize youth as a social group, while also continuing to exert influence on the Chinese socialist literary and cultural imagination.

Yet simply creating a love story as a political metaphor can in many ways appear rather crude. Particularly for ordinary readers, interest may only lie in the love story itself as opposed to any political implications. Indeed, if we find that the love stories published between 1949 and 1966 exhibit such characteristics as purity, reservation, and bashfulness, they are in part related to the targeted readers—subalterns—of these writings. Meanwhile, we also sense the presence of the individual in the narratives' application of various aesthetic tools. In fact, once we analyze modern love stories, we inevitably encounter young male and female characters being treated as individuals. As mentioned above in this chapter, one characteristic of the Chinese revolution is its need to first represent the individual as an independent entity so as to

---

71. Xu Huaizhong, *Women bozhong aiqing* [We sow our love] (Beijing: Renmin Chubanshe, 1960).

liberate him or her from traditional politics and culture; the next task is to organize these [new] individuals into a brand-new, modern, and imagined political commonwealth. Without this political process, Chinese socialism would have had no way to begin its trajectory. While the Chinese revolution always emphasized its antifeudal cultural thematic, it was in essence a class revolution, which was demonstrated by its class discourse. In this sense, we can say that the political characteristic of the Chinese revolution, from the very beginning, embedded a paradox in the revolution: while it produced the individual, it also produced the collective; while it produced the collective, it also produced the individual. This individual and collective entanglement, as a result, was also always entangled in the socialist literary and cultural imaginary and its inner tensions.

Such internal tension inevitably existed in the narration of love stories. If in narrating romantic love, the writer was bound to narrate the individual, the challenge was how to make sure that this individual was always correctly positioned in a political sense. Another challenge had to do with the fact that, when the political was naturalized in revolutionary discourse to legitimize the revolution's support for the individual's freedom to love, it may well have followed that romantic love came to be interpreted as naturalized and independent of politics. In this case, a love story, then, could stand on its own without having to be part of any political context. What difference, if any, would such a love story exhibit from that of a petit bourgeois one? To avoid this danger, in the narration of socialist literature we see blatant politics at work to make clear what constitutes correct love and what does not. What such blatantly political messages manifest, however, is the perennial tension between the individual and the collective.

In contrast to stories by Zhao Shuli and others—whose treatments of the relationship between love and politics helped provide an emotional legitimacy to the Chinese revolution and especially to its rural revolution and, as a result, were well received—there were other works that did not enjoy the same recognition. In the July 1957 issue of *People's Literature* (Renmin wenxue), Zong Pu published a short story titled "Red Beans" ("Hong dou").[72] It told another kind of love story and as a result was criticized. In some ways, Zong Pu's story shared a theme with other love stories of the era: the protagonist, Jiang Mei, breaks up with her lover, Qi Hong, thereby also breaking away from her own old self. Penned by a woman writer, this story succeeds in pay-

---

72. Zong Pu, "Hong dou" [Red beans], *Renmin wenxue* [People's literature], (1957), 7:17–28.

ing detailed attention to the complex entanglement among the historical era, the revolution, and the individual. Its narration, while showing the revolution ultimately overcoming the individual's emotions, nevertheless leaves room for alternative interpretations. For example, the story spends time portraying how Jiang Mei feels about Qi Hong. On the one hand, Jiang can say why she does not like the kind of callousness he has, but on the other hand, she cannot explain why she also feels intoxicated by his love. It is this deeply entangled and inexplicable emotional complexity that constitutes Jiang Mei's sentiments. And such inexplicable emotion exceeded the boundaries of the political discourse of the time. Incidentally, other stories—such as Zhang Xian's "The Representative from Party A" ("Jia fang daibiao") and Deng Youmei's "On the Cliff" ("Zai xuanya shang")[73]—all exhibited similar kinds of emotional entanglements or ambivalences.

Identified as petit bourgeois, the sentimental emotions expressed in these works were deeply politically inappropriate. But in a larger interpretive context, we must carefully explore such sentiments and ask why they were not acceptable as components of the revolutionary love story. I argue that, aside from being identified as petit bourgeois, such sentiments had to do with the conflict at the time between language and nonlanguage and between rationality and irrationality. As I noted in chapter 1, I do not identify and treat Chinese socialism as a totalitarian model of governing, because in many ways the Chinese socialist state relied mainly on political mobilization and ideological persuasion and training. Within this political structure, the function of ideology was emphasized and exaggerated. Meanwhile, ideological persuasion and training inevitably depend on language, making the role of language salient and important. Only with this understanding can we explain why stories of the socialist era all had clear themes and emphasized clear and straightforward narration, while rarely resorting to narrating and depicting ambivalent and sentimental feelings. And also only in this way can we understand the fact that love stories of the time were inevitably part of this discursive practice and of the common language that had a clear political connotation. The goal of this common language was to construct a new political commonwealth in which love and marriage constituted basic building blocks. That is why any ambivalence and sentiment that exceeded the common language might have weakened ideological persuasion and training by potentially allowing the formation

---

73. Deng Youmei, "Zai xuanya shang" [On the cliff], *Wenyi xuexi* [Literature and art studies] (1957), 1.

of a different kind of relationship between individuals. As a result, the stories mentioned above, with their expressed sentiments possibly opening [the way] for alternative interpretations, were deemed politically unacceptable.

Now, if Zhao's love stories tend to overemphasize the political—in "Xiao Erhei Gets Married," for example, we read hardly any depiction of the love relationship between the two young lovers—in stories by Zong and others love tends to be placed outside the political. Yet between revolution and youth, love is in fact an important medium. Only a well-told love story can make revolution have a strong summoning power for youth. This is why the mode of narrating a love story was consistently explored in contemporary literature.

With this in mind, let us now take a look at Yang Mo's novel *Song of Youth*. Scholars of the novel have shown that its publication was warmly welcomed. Repeatedly republished, the total number of copies in circulation exceeded five million.[74] It was translated into about twenty languages for overseas readers. The Japanese translation was published in 1960 and by 1965 had been reprinted twelve times, for a total of 200,000 copies. The Communist Parties in Japan and Indonesia made the novel required reading for their members. Many young Japanese youth are said to have wanted to join the Communist Party after reading the novel. Inside China, national leaders such as Zhou Enlai, Peng Zhen, Zhou Yang, and Mao Dun praised the novel, and the Central Communist Youth League issued a call for young people to study the novel.[75] Here, however, I am not interested in how well received the novel was but rather in what kind of love story Yang told.

To a certain extent, the relationship between the two main characters, Lin Daojing and Yu Yongze, in *Song of Youth* is not that different from the one between Jiang Mei and Qi Hong in "Red Beans." In both stories, the female characters succeed in achieving self-reform with the help of the revolution, and both authors depict a transformation from an old self to a new self. The length of Yang's novel, of course, helps with the depiction of the transformation in a more detailed way. The key difference between the two texts lies in something else: that the character type named Xiao Su [a young revolutionary male friend of the main female character Jiang Mei] in "Red Beans" is replaced in *Song of Youth* by another type represented by Lu Jiachuan (a student turned revolutionary) and Jiang Hua (a revolutionary with a working-class

---

74. Li Yang, *50–70 niandai Zhongguo wenxue zai jiedu*, 133. These figures come mainly from Yang Mo's "Zibai—Wo de riji" [Confession: My diaries], in *Yang Mo wenji* [Collection of Yang Mo's writings] (Beijing: Beijing Shiyue Wenyi Chubanshe, 1994), vol. 6.

75. Li Yang, *50–70 niandai Zhongguo wenxue zai jiedu*, 133.

background). This difference not only affects the difference in the narrative structure of the stories but it also affects the way in which the relationship between revolution and love is dealt with.

It is difficult to claim that Lin Daojing and Yu Yongze never loved one another. The novel in fact says that Lin Daojing "loved Yu Yongze very much." It's just that she "didn't want to marry him right away." The novel also recounts that the two of them once had had a "common language" when they talked about Tolstoy, Hugo, Heine, all the way to Cao Xueqin, Du Fu, and Lu Xun. Because of this shared language, "aside from her gratefulness and excitement about having found a soul mate, Lin Daojing also admired Yu Yongze as a comrade."[76] Problems occur when another character, Lu Jiachuan, appears in Lin's life. Lu causes her to rethink her love for Yu Yongze. This rethinking is in essence a transformation from one language or discourse to another. In this process, how Lin feels becomes articulable; that is, once her feelings can be articulated, they can no longer be fertile ground for the old ideology. In other words, when Lin experiences the dissolution of her old love, she does not experience ambivalence and entangled sentiments similar to Jiang Mei's in Zong Pu's story. Rather, for Lin, everything is clear. What that means is that, in Lin's case, revolutionary discourse succeeds in providing a language through which she can experience the process of love and reform. She learns to repudiate the sentiment of gratefulness and to forgo the old common language she had with Yu. Narratively, this process of transformation into revolutionary discourse is portrayed via a depiction of love. That is, there is a strong discursive force that accompanies her love-related experiences. This force not only offers a justifiable reason for her to leave Yu, but also offers an explanation for the difference between Lu Jiazhuan and Jiang Hua, including why "a Bolshevik like Jiang Hua is worthy of her deep love."[77] What does being "worthy of her deep love" mean? Behind the notion of worth, there is a kind of value criterion. Moreover, we also see that when male revolutionaries like Lu Jiachuan and Jiang Hua are objects of her love, revolution itself becomes love; the political is embodied in the image of these male revolutionaries.

Their image is not only political but also aesthetic. The novel describes Yu Yongze as having a "thin face and dark complexion" and "small eyes," whereas Lu Jiachuan "has charisma that easily attracts people to him," and Jiang Hua "is a tall and strong young man with a dark complexion."[78] We can understand

---

76. Yang Mo, *Qingchun zhi ge* [Song of youth] (Beijing: Renmin Chubanshe, 1960), 160.
77. Ibid., 610.
78. Ibid., 56, 263.

these descriptions as symbolizing Lin's deepening understanding of the revolution. If Yu Yongze represents a past age, Lu Jiachuan is someone in between, who retains something familiar to Lin while bringing something powerfully new to her. As for Jiang Hua, he represents a brand-new but surpassingly meaningful other. His success in complete self-transformation [into a revolutionary] embodies something that Lin hopes to achieve for herself. This is the fundamental reason why, while Lin feels that Jiang Hua is unfamiliar, she is constantly attracted to him. This reason is political, aesthetic, and moral and helps explain the way the scene at the end of the novel is depicted: in the midst of the violent suppression of student demonstrations against the Japanese invasion, Yu Yongze "stood in a leisurely way on the stairs ... watching, appreciating her swollen face and the blood oozing out of her nose."[79] In the epilogue to the first edition of the novel, Yang Mo writes that "many characters and things in the book are based on real events."[80] As a result, her depiction of Yu Yongze, who is modeled on Zhang Zhongxing, a real person, predictably generated Zhang's displeasure.[81] Whether or not what Yang represents was once real, the depiction of Lin's separation from her old self marks the fundamental difference between *Song of Youth* and "Red Beans."

In the literary and cultural imagination of 1949–66 literature, there always existed an intense struggle over aesthetics. From the discussion on aesthetics in the 1950s to the radical view of aesthetics in Yao Wenyuan's article "Aesthetics in a Photo Shop" ("Zhaoxiangguan li chu meixue"),[82] the focus was on asking and answering the question, "what is beauty?" [or "what is beautiful?"]. In the fiction of the time, beauty was redefined through love stories and through the relationship between youth and revolution. Thus, by rewriting love stories, [revolutionary] politics succeeded in acquiring legitimacy on moral, emotional, and aesthetic levels simultaneously.

As the discussion above indicates, Zhao's "Xiao Erhei Gets Married" is aimed at naturalizing politics and winning legitimacy for young people's emotions. When it comes to *Song of Youth*, the emphasis is on repoliticizing emotions; the goal of this repoliticization was to construct the new person. In this sense, this new person was neither an atomized individual nor a citizen

79. Ibid., 666.
80. Yang Mo, "Chuban houji" [Epilogue to the first edition], [republished in] *Qingchun zhige* [Song of youth] (Beijing: Renmin Wenxue Chubanshe, 1977), 625.
81. Zhang Zhongxing, *Liu nian sui ying* [Fleeting years and fragmented shadows] (Beijing: Zhongguo Shehui Kexue Chubanshe, 1997), 754.
82. Yao Wenyuan, "Zhaoxiangguan li chu meixue" [Aesthetics in a photo shop], *Wenhui bao* (Wenhui daily), May 8, 1958.

(*guomin*) in a nationalist sense; rather, this new person was a new individual who belonged to and in a socialist political context. The appearance of this new person consequently helped reduce the individual versus collective tension in socialist culture.

However, in this design, especially when a love story was employed to accomplish the design, there existed an unstable factor, one that was capable of obstructing the realization of the design. This unstable and potentially obstructive factor was none other than sex/sexuality.

III. Sex/Sexuality, or the Narration of Sex

What I discuss here is not sex/sexuality but the narration of sex. Sex as a human behavior never stops in any historical period; the socialist period is of course no exception to this general observation. What is exceptional, however, is the significant decline in the narration of sex—including sexual desire, sensual pleasure, and pornography, which filled the pages of early modern literature—during that period. The question I raise and explore here is: what caused such a decline?

Among the behavioral and political writings of early Chinese communists, sex/sexuality was in fact not a taboo subject.[83] On the contrary, whether in private life or political activities, sexual desire was a highly important concept. While the new culture promoted by the May Fourth Movement strongly influenced early Chinese communists, in struggling against the power structure of the traditional society, sexual desire also exerted a strong political and cultural attraction. As such, it even extended into the land revolution period in the liberated zones (1927–37). In Mao Zedong's "Xunwu diaocha" [Report from Xunwu] of 1930, we can see that during the Red Army period, the slogan was "to overthrow feudal power" and to "attack the landlords and distribute land."[84] Embedded in the slogan of "overthrow feudal power" is the

---

83. In his memoir, Zheng Chaolin mentions the rather open private lives of some early Chinese communists (*Zheng Chaolin huiyilu* [Zheng Chaolin's memoir] (Beijing: Dongfang Chubanshe, 2004), 2:61–65.

84. Mao Zedong, "Xunwu diaocha" [Report from Xunwu], in *Mao Zedong wenji* [Collection of Mao Zedong's writings] (Beijing: Renmin Chubanshe, 1993), 1:240–43. All the quotes in the rest of this paragraph come from this item. Tr.: This report was one of several that Mao produced in the early years of the rural embedding of the Chinese revolutionary troops (1928–35). The report is famous for its detailed account of rural and village life, almost anthropological in its detail and yet revolutionary in intent: the depictions were not to serve a static purpose, but to serve as the basis for the revolutionary transformation of everyday life.

notion of "freedom to divorce and marry." The issue of new orders by the [Red Army's] soviet government significantly liberated women from feudal marriages; these women in turn became strong supporters of the revolution. Women also acquired a strong self-awareness. As Mao wrote in his Xunwu report, "starting with the establishment of local township governments, women were the ones who asked for divorce." In addition to issuing new regulations and laws, the local governments also announced a "prohibition for capturing adulterers." As a result, young men and women "went up to the mountains to openly 'free' themselves," which in turn caused some men to complain that the "revolution is now cutting wives loose." Meanwhile, "almost in every village, there were married men who found new lovers," which "generated protests from the wives." [The report continued:]

> In February this year, the county revolutionary committee held an expanded meeting where a "resolution on chastity" (*zhencao wenti*) was passed. It stipulates that "no married men and women should have sex with other men and women. Violators will be seriously punished." At the same time, they also issued another rule on marriage that was against polygamy and polyandry. "No one was to be allowed to marry a new spouse without having had a divorce. Anyone who has made a mistake must immediately correct it by obtaining a divorce and be married to only one person." ... After the resolution was passed, disputes stopped ... and people were able to turn their attention to the aggression from the enemy.

Even though similar problems occurred later, Mao's vivid reporting offers a glimpse into a moment when the traditional rural social order was disrupted by sexual desire.

The fact is that throughout the history of the Chinese revolution, sex/sexuality existed in two ways, one helping young men and women gain individual awareness, and the other being destructive of the existing social order. I am always of the opinion that the Chinese revolution had a flexible ability to compromise. The same was true on the issue of sex/sexuality. During wartime, for example, it was necessary for the revolutionary forces to consider the need to respect the rural ethical system. The resultant compromise may have contributed to producing constraints on the literary narration of sex/sexuality.

The Chinese revolution was not merely tasked with destroying; it had a clear general social and political goal. That is, the Chinese revolution was in fact a constructive force. This in-built pursuit for political construction also functioned to constrain the role of sex/sexuality in literary imagination. What is more, in literary imagination, family always functioned as a relatively stable factor as well as the destination for sexual/love relationships. Placing importance on that destination may be yet another element of constraint in the narration of sex/sexuality, and explains why the emphasis in "Xiao Erhei Gets Married" is on "marriage" and in "Registration" is on the final act of marriage registration. The premise for establishing a new family is freedom to love, a theme inherited from the May Fourth antifeudal struggle. At the same time, due to the family factor, freedom to love was constrained, and the emphasis tended to be put on faithfulness. As a result, when a sexual relationship was narrated, it was always represented within a love relationship, and this love relationship was also confined to the direction of marriage [because the assumption usually was that the couple was to get married]. Promiscuous behavior in love was often criticized. In [Xue Ke's] *The Spring of Battle* (*Zhandou de qingchun*), for example, Xu Feng and Hu Wenyu break up largely due to Hu Wenyu's relationship with Xiaoying. In this sense, contemporary Chinese literature tended to be influenced more by traditional and modern popular literature [the latter refers to popular literature of the early twentieth century]. During the 1950s, there were stories about extramarital affairs, and most of them treat such affairs critically in their narration. Sun Qian's "A Strange Divorce Story" ("Qiyi de lihun gushi"), for example, tells the story of a cadre named Yu Shude who, after entering the city, wants to leave his country wife and find a new love. In the end, however, the city love fails, he gets demoted at work, and his country wife divorces him.[85] Dong Zhilin calls the story "a contemporary version of the traditional opera *The Execution of Chen Simei* (*Zha mei an*)."[86]

Deng Youmei's "On the Cliff" also tells the story of an extramarital affair. But there, despite some moralistic and ideological preaching, we sense in the narration of the sexual relationship the presence of an important concept: innate nature. We can find the presence of the notion of innate nature in the narration of sex/sexuality as a rather active signifier. In modern Chinese literature, innate sexual nature is used to symbolize human life and individual awakening, and to release socially repressed political emotion. When it comes to contemporary literature, we cannot say that this kind of narration completely disappeared. In the film *Hongse niangzijun* [*The Red Detachment of*

---

85. Sun Qian, "Qiyi de lihun gushi" [A strange divorce story], *Changjiang wenyi*, no. 1, 1956.
86. Dong Zhilin, *Jiu meng xin zhi: "Shiqinian" xiaoshuo lungao* [Old dream, new knowledge: Writings on the "seventeen-year" fiction] (Guilin: Guangxi Shifan Daxue Chubanshe, 2004), 93.

Women],[87] for example, through the narration of Honglian's sad life and the camera lens that captures the "wood-made dummy" [in her bed, meant to symbolize her dead husband], the film vividly demonstrates the connection between sexual repression and political or class oppression.[88]

A more detailed depiction of innate sexual nature is found in Feng Deying's novel *Bitter Flowers* (*Ku cai hua*). Among other things, the novel tells the story of Xingli's mother's marriage to Wang Jianzhi, a man who studies in the city where there are lots of seductive women. The mother lives like a widow "all year long, alone in this large and empty compound.... Gradually, she begins to notice the young workman in the house, Changsuo, and peers through windows and door cracks at his strong body and the bulging muscles on his arms and legs.... Bit by bit, driven by the wild and burning desire inside her, she makes her moves."[89] Such bold narration of innate sexual desire is rarely found in the literature of 1949–66.[90] Even in this novel, Xingli's mother's adultery with the workman is legitimized when the novel shows her husband, Wang Jianzhi, to be a collaborator (with the Japanese) and a spy. There, the same sexual/political connection is still at work.

Unlike in *Bitter Flowers*, the narration of sex/sexuality was much diminished in many other works of contemporary literature. Part of the reason for that may be due to innate nature's being considered unstable or even dangerous. Revolutionary literature did not recognize innate nature, or libido, as capable of shouldering important revolutionary tasks or of being contained within revolutionary boundaries. The workman Wang Changsuo in the aforementioned novel, *Bitter Flowers*, for example, is forced to knuckle under to the husband, Wang Jianzhi, in exchange for his continued sexual pleasure. However, Marxism never interprets the proletarian revolution as one based on innate impulses. Rather, there are clear rational guidance and principles for the revolutionary movement that, as a class-related ideology, is viewed as scientific. Indeed, traditional Marxism is consistently political-economic oriented, not psychoanalytically inclined. And in the historical context of socialism, the

87. *Hongse niangzijun* [The red detachment of women], dir. Xie Jin (1961).
88. In the ballet version of *The Red Detachment of Women*, this scene was excluded. This may help explain the puritanical attitude toward sex/sexuality in Cultural Revolution politics. See *Ba da yangbanxi* [Eight model plays], ed. Li Hui (Beijing: Guanming Ribao Chubanshe, 1995).
89. Feng Deying, *Ku cai hua* [Bitter flowers] (Beijing: Jiefangjun Wenyishe, 1958).
90. According to the author, during the Cultural Revolution, novels like *Ku cai hua* were labeled as "big poisonous grass that promotes love and has pornographic depictions . . . and were banned" (Feng Deying, "Xie zai xinban 'san hua' qianmian" [Preface to the new publications of the "three flowers"] (Shenyang: Chunfeng Wenyi Chubanshe, 2003), 3.

individual was constrained by the higher principle of the revolution: whenever innate nature sought to exceed this higher principle, it would be repressed in narration.[91]

As we can see, in the narration of sex/sexuality in question, there was a constant moralistic intervention. Or, to put it more accurately, such narration was constantly trying to balance sex/sexuality with morality. We can trace this characteristic to Mao Dun's *Midnight* (*Ziye*)[92] in which the negative meaning of Wu Sunpu's class position is demonstrated through his rape of a maid. Following this logic, in contemporary literature, acts of sexual indulgence are usually assigned to negative characters. Among such characters, women are often shown as licentious seducers. Such representations and the moral judgments inherent in them are undoubtedly male-centric, an issue I will discuss below. When acts of sexual indulgence are assigned to negative characters, when it comes to narration of sex/sexuality for the positive, especially female, characters, the task becomes difficult.

As a result, narrating sex/sexuality in a positive way becomes difficult and its representations appear sexually repressed. However, such difficulty also led to a style, where depictions were somewhat reserved and indirect. One example is the way the love relationship between Xu Wenxia and Zhang Jun is depicted in Lu Wenfu's story *Deep within a Lane* (*Xiao xiang shenchu*). Xu and Zhang often study together in the evening. From time to time, Xu would make Zhang take a break by "walking over to him, gently pulling his ears and scratching the back of his head," or, after a while, Zhang "would walk over to her and fetch the small knife in her pocket and proceed to peel an apple."[93] These little gestures imply some kind of seduction. And sure enough, after "such back and forth, the two of them didn't feel like continuing with their studying." But after they put away their books, all they do is "chat away" about the future. And "when they are talked out, they take a walk on the street hand in hand." Part of the reason for this reserved depiction can be explained by the fact that the story has already assigned to Xu the role of sufferer, as a former prostitute, in contrast to the ugly sexual behavior of men who visit brothels. As the story narrates, in Xu's memory, sex is "full of shame, insult, and tears," and the ugly face of men who abused her body. Situated against this [ugly]

---

91. Of course, "innate nature" does not just belong to sex/sexuality. I will discuss the ambivalence and hesitancy in contemporary (socialist) literature regarding innate nature elsewhere.

92. Mao Dun, *Ziye* [Midnight] (Shanghai: Shanghai Kaiming Shudian, 1933).

93. Lu Wenfu, "Xiaoxiang shenchu" [Deep within the lane], *Mengya* [Sprouts] October (1956), 21.

other, the love between Xu and Zhang can be represented only in the acts of "talking" and "walking."

What needs to be further explored is that, aside from the aforementioned reasons that made narrating sex/sexuality so difficult in contemporary Chinese literature [of the socialist period], we should not overlook the presence of the image of women. In contemporary literature, the Chinese revolution underwent a process of constant purification that, to a certain extent, was realized via the purification of women. In *Song of Youth*, for example, Lin Hong (a Communist) is described as "having a beautiful marble-like face," while in Lin Daojing's mind, this "staunch experienced Bolshevik" resembles a holy goddess.[94] In fact, such a female image is not uncommon in contemporary literature. At issue is [the fact] that, with the creation of such a purified image of women, literary narration of sex/sexuality also is repressed. In many ways, narration of sex/sexuality is informed by, or grounded in, male-centrism. Within this male-centric discursive system, the male-female relationship is unequal, with the latter [female] being dependent on the former [male]. With women's liberation, especially when that discourse helped foster the creation of the holy female image, when it comes to the issue of sex/sexuality, the still-male-dominant narration of sex/sexuality found itself in a difficult position: it had trouble accounting for the shattering of [traditional] male fantasies. This difficult position is already manifest in the eighteenth-century novel *Dream of the Red Chamber*. There, Jia Baoyu, the major male protagonist, is paired with Lin Daiyu, his real love, but Jia is prevented from marrying Lin by his family. In contrast to the representation of his relationship with Lin, which is depicted as an innocent albeit at times temperamental one, the novel places Jia as having sexual intercourse with Qin Keqin [his sister-in-law] in one of his dreams and in a secret sexual relationship with Xiren, his personal servant. Whether intended or not, representing women as pure or respectable leads to repression in the male narration of sex/sexuality.

Such repression, needless to say, is male-centric, coming from a male perspective in which the man still holds the dominant position. In the novel *Tracks in the Snowy Forest* [by Chu Po], for example, despite frequent gestures of interest from Bai Ru, a female protagonist, Shao Jianbo, the major male protagonist who is interested in Bai Ru, holds back. His holding back is in some way an indication of the loss of sexual expression on the part of men (his sexual fantasies can unfold only in his diary). In fact, it is not an exagera-

---

94. Yang Mo, *Qingchun zhige* [Song of youth], 390.

tion to suggest that in contemporary Chinese literature, there is never a successful construction of an equal sexual relationship between men and women. When male sexual discourse stays repressed, it also represses female narration of sex/sexuality. Our understanding of this particular gender politics gives us a highly significant perspective with which to study the narration of sex/sexuality in contemporary literature.

On a more fundamental level, however, the constraints on the narration of sex/sexuality originate from the fact that Marxism has never treated sexual desire as a fundamental revolutionary force. Marxism is still geared toward the study of political economy and relations of economic exploitation. Yet human desires, including sexual desires, continue to exist, which inevitably requires us to understand the narration of sex/sexuality. The irony that I find in my reading of contemporary literature, therefore, is that, while revolution is represented, in Huang Ziping's terms, as a "sexless body,"[95] nevertheless sexual enlightenment is realized through the narration of sex/sexuality of negative fictional characters. What this paradox results in is the strong counterrevolutionary currents in the 1980s, when the [supposed] repressed human nature was mobilized as a strong response to subvert revolutionary narration, making it possible for sexual desire to be exaggeratedly used to interpret history. Within this process of subversion, we witness psychoanalysis chase off political economics and occupy the dominant position in the intellectual discourse of the postrevolutionary era.

Concluding Remarks

When youth becomes a profound literary metaphor, the notion itself still requires all kinds of exploration. In such explorations, the political must deal carefully with various kinds of related experiences, including love and sex/sexuality. All kinds of narration ultimately touch on the sensitive domain of the body. It is in fact difficult for us to claim that, in the story of the Chinese revolution, the body is completely marginalized or, even worse, driven out of its territory. The fact of the matter is that, from the very beginning, Chinese revolutionary modernity brought the human body into its social system of political mobilization. This body contains the antifeudal theme of the May

---

95. Huang Ziping, *Geming, lishi, xiaoshuo* [Revolution, history, fiction] (Hong Kong: Oxford University Press, 1996), 56.

Fourth period and is also directly inscribed as a political-economic being. It is in this sense that we find some of the most commonly used revolutionary terms are often related to the body: oppression (*yapo*) and turning over (*fanshen*) are two ready examples.

When the Chinese revolution inherited Liang's modern imaginary of young China, it also inherited the dual—temporal and biological—meaning of the notion of youth. In Liang's imaginary, time has already acquired modern characteristics as linear, progressive, and developing. And it is the acceptance of this modern concept of temporality that made it possible for the Chinese revolution to acquire its future-facing narration. As for biology, it was even more directly applied to the human body, in that this body denotes the body of the individual, a designation that helped establish the concept of the individual. It was based on this concept that the Chinese revolution was able to liberate the individual from the traditional power structure and to construct a new imagined political community. From this perspective, we can also see the ways in which the Chinese revolution, directly and indirectly, inherited the legacies of the May Fourth New Culture movement.

At the same time, in the specific historical context of the Chinese revolution, revolution and body began to fracture and come into conflict with one another. The cause of the conflicts between the two is not entirely due to the revival of traditional ethics. Rather, it is due to the fact that, be it in theory or in practice, the Chinese revolution was always constrained by a certain kind of totality, and this totality constituted the basic backdrop of revolutionary ideology. Within the theoretical imaginary of this totality, a particular higher principle was established, a principle that all individuals were expected to obey. As a result, within the theoretical imaginary of this totality, the individual and the body of the individual both had to be reidentified. Not only was youth reidentified or turned into a class concept, but love was also expected to be narrated anew with the goal of establishing a kind of genuine love. But the problem is that in this process of reidentification, sex/sexuality, or innate nature, was always an unstable element and was also capable of breaking the imaginary boundaries defined politically or by the totality [of the revolution]. As a result, the narration of sex/sexuality remained a highly sensitive area.

This totality is modern and is supported by an optimistic rationalism. It believes that humans can control nature and also themselves. The power of control stems from the belief that humans can create a brighter future by way of this control. From control of nature and of humans—all of these are traces of modernity guided by an Enlightenment rationality. When such optimism and rationality themselves encounter a crisis—and this is the premise upon which we are to understand the decade of the 1980s—the totality inevitably faces the danger of being deconstructed. To some extent, we can say that it is precisely at the level of innate nature or desire that the decade of the 1980s began its dismantling of this total theoretical imaginary, including by exaggerating the role of sexual desire in human history. The individual was liberated again through this process of dismantling but paid other prices for this liberation.

In the end, we come face to face with another important question: how to maintain a necessary tension between the collective and the individual, or between political economics and psychoanalysis, and by extension how to reinterpret totality. Needless to say, this will be a story for and of a different era.

4

RENARRATING THE HISTORY OF THE REVOLUTION
From Hero to Legend

Some scholars have used the concept of "revolutionary popular literature" (*geming tongsu wenxue*)[1] to discuss novels written in the 1949–66 period. This concept applies not only to such contemporaneous materials as *White-Haired Girl*, but it also includes romantic stories such as *Tracks in the Snowy Forest* [by Qu Bo (Chu Po)]. I think in the deployment of this concept what needs to be clarified is not merely the structural genre of the novel, but also—even more important —what touches on the author's narrative attitude. We could say that this attitude is a nonmodern elite intellectual attitude, a topos that in large part is derived from Mao Zedong's 1942 "Talks at the Yan'an Forum on Literature and Art." Indeed, it is only due to these talks that the concept of the masses could irrupt into literary formulations and that multiple transformations in these formulations could result from this irruption. One piece of superficial symbolic evidence for this transformation is precisely the trend

---

1. Li Tuo, "1985," *Jintian* [Today], nos. 3–4 (1991): n.p. This concept has been used by Meng Yue to analyze *White-Haired Girl*; it can also be seen in Li Yang's analysis in *50–70 niandai Zhongguo wenxue zai jiedu* [Rereading 1950s–1970s Chinese literature] (Jinan: Shandong Jiaoyu Chubanshe, 2003).

toward the popularization of what I call contemporary literature.[2] Yet revolutionary popular literature is a retrospectively designed concept. In practice, from 1949 to 1966, contemporary literature had no rigid division between elite and popular categories that could have yielded some properly defined category called revolutionary popular literature. The question we need to pursue, then, is: how, in this period, could revolutionary popular literature become national literature or national mainstream literature, and how could it become a kind of guiding narrative method? Moreover, in a different respect, this type of novel mostly narrated stories concerned with revolutionary history or a performative history of the revolution. Huang Ziping's concept—"novels of revolutionary history"—combines these issues and opens a way to analyze and evaluate this type of novel.[3] Below, I mainly address not only how revolutionary popular literature could become mainstream national literature, but also what, ultimately, is the significance of this kind of renarration of the history of revolution as well as why this type of renarrated revolutionary history could emerge in popularized form.

The popular (*tongsu*) not only bears within it an original signification of the heroic, but it also includes the narrative characteristics of legend. Indeed, in contemporary Chinese literature, the passage from hero to legend is usually understood as a process of moving from the real to the romantic, while also connoting a type of distinction between the common and the fantastic. Yet it is precisely this latter distinction that opens anew the imaginary arena of the new and the strange. According to Meng Yue's explanation, the imaginary arena of legend always implies a certain neither/nor subject.[4] What requires clarification is the question of what compelled contemporary literature to rely on legend as the new imaginary arena.

---

2. Tr.: As mentioned in the translators' introduction and elsewhere in the book, "contemporary literature" is Cai's designation for the socialist literature he discusses in the book. He uses the term to cover 1949–66 literature *as well as* the post–Cultural Revolutionary literature of the present moment. An unconventional usage, we have retained it here as it is also a theoretical wager as well.

3. Huang Ziping, *Geming, lishi, xiaoshuo* [Revolution, history, fiction] (Hong Kong: Oxford University Press, 1996).

4. Meng Yue, "Zhongguo wenxue de 'xiandaixing' yu Zhang Ailing" [The "modernity" of Chinese literature and Zhang Ailing], in *Ershi shiji zhongguo wenxueshi lun* [On the history of twentieth-century Chinese literature], ed. Wang Xiaoming (Shanghai: Dongfang Chuban Zhongxin, 2003), 2:105.

I. Ordinary Sons and Daughters, Collective Heroes

If for the moment we put aside the question of whether or not the concept of popular revolutionary literature can be constituted as a legitimate analytical object—including which specific literary works this category might include and what precisely is meant by the trend toward popularization—then I think we need to first address the emergence of this phenomenon in the culture of the liberated zones (*jiefang qu*) [1935–49].[5] It was precisely in this era that popularization and massification not only received full support from the politics of revolution, but at the same time, that the culture produced from these movements was designated as occupying the politically legitimating position of new literary classics. This legitimacy was explained by Zhou Yang by way of the "Zhao Shuli path" as "a victory for the creativity of Mao Zedong's theory of literature and art."[6] The most important component in the process of this literature's becoming classical was the support derived from Mao's "Talks at the Yan'an Forum on Literature and Art."[7] Yet we cannot ignore the fact that even before the publication of the "Talks," lurking in the background were prior discussions concerning the relation of national form[8] to the war of resistance.

---

5. Tr.: The liberated zones were those areas of China under Chinese Communist Party rule from after the Long March (1935) until the end of the Civil War (1949). These zones were mostly in northern China. After 1949, they came to be called the "old liberated zones" (*lao jiefang qu*).

6. Zhou Yang, "Dui jiuxingshi liyong zai wenxueshang de yige kanfa" [A perspective on using old methods for new literature], cited in Wang Yao, *Zhongguo xin wenxue daxi (1937–1949)*. *Xu* [preface to The encyclopedia of new Chinese literature (1937–1949)], (Shanghai: Shanghai Wenyi Chubanshe, 1990): 1:9.

7. For example, in 1941, Zhao Shuli joined the editorial board of *Wartime life* [*Zhanshi shenghuo*] and, along with Wang Chun, Lin Huo, and others, established a group to research the problem of popularization. They serially published such essays as 'Introduction' to Popularization," "Popularization and 'Bogging Down,'" and so on, but they did not manage to get a campaign going. It was not until Mao's "Talks at the Yan'an Forum on Literature and Art" that the problem of popularization and massification of art and literature became main currents of the era. Just as Zhao Shuli noted, the "Talks" affirmed his direction and made permissible his idea that literature should go in the direction of popularization and massification. See Cai Rongtian, ed., *Shanxi wenxue wushinian zongheng lun* [A complete discussion of fifty years of Shanxi literature] (Taiyuan: Shanxi Renmin Chubanshe, 2000), 65.

8. Tr.: National form refers to the problem of how to designate "Chinese culture" as a national (as opposed to imperial or ethnic) entity. This relates to a series of prewar debates that ranged over problems of the relationship of language to writing, of politics to literature, of the past to the present, and so on. As Cai is preparing to discuss here, the problem of national form is reopened with the posing of the problem of socialist culture and the culture of socialism. As he notes, these are intimately related, but cannot and should not be conflated.

The importance of this historical background resides in the fact that the outbreak of the war led to the large-scale geographical migration and movement of intellectuals [from Shanghai and Beijing inland, to the wartime Chinese Communist Party capital, Yan'an]. This geographical movement brought to literature a new sense of space. As Zhou Yang put it,

> one new influence on literature provided by the war was the encounter between advanced literature and art and the backward villages, between artistic and literary people and the vast masses, in particular the peasants. The war of resistance changed the environment for literature and art, as the previous centers of new literature and art were lost in the wake of the loss of the urban areas [to the Japanese]. The vast peasant villages and the innumerable small towns became almost the exclusive new environment for new literature.... The former cultural centers were transformed into regions of darkness, and the question now was how to transform formerly backward places into cultural centers. This was a responsibility placed on new art and literature by the war of resistance.[9]

According to Wang Yao's explanation, this change in spatiality

> provided the majority of authors with a discovery that was both worrisome and pleasant: on the one hand, they experienced in person a serious gap and estrangement between the new literature and art since May Fourth and the life of the common people, particularly of the peasants, who make up the majority of the Chinese population. This was a wake-up call to the writers, who had assumed their duty was to enlighten and mobilize the masses through literature. It forced them to engage in critical reflection [on their previous petit bourgeois practices]. On the other hand, writers also genuinely experienced the strength of the Chinese peasants, their intelligence, and in particular their urgent requirements with respect to new literature and art, new thought, and new culture. Thus, Chinese peasants truly—and not merely superficially or rhetorically—became recipients and targets of a new literary expressivity. At the same time, writers discovered the creative energy of folk culture embodied in the peasantry as well as the hidden mystical power of traditional Chinese literature, which had long been neglected and slighted by the writers of new literature. Because of the ac-

9. Quoted in Wang Yao, *Zhongguo xin wenxue daxi (1937–1949). Xu* [preface to The encyclopedia of new Chinese literature (1937–1949)], (Shanghai: Shanghai Wenyi Chubanshe, 1990), 1:9–10.

cidental discovery of folk culture, writers of new literature could not help but be shaken out of complacency.

Wang Yao continues:

> These two discoveries led to rapid adjustments and transformations in the self-awareness required of post–May Fourth new literature: they structured and blanketed the discussions of this era on the question of "national form" and provided a profound backdrop and internal motivation to the Yan'an rectification movement [beginning in 1942]. The adjustments and transformations in May Fourth new literature were concentrated mainly in two arenas: readjustment to the relation between new literature and traditional culture, particularly the former's relation to folk culture, so as to promote the further nationalization (*minzu hua*) of new literature; and readjustment of the relation between new literature and peasants so as to promote the massification of new culture. These two aspects constituted the discussions of the question of national form and informed the basic contents of the Yan'an rectification movement as well as its major goals and demands.[10]

I think that Wang Yao's explanation offers an excellent entry into understanding the popularization and massification of the culture of the liberated zones. Indeed, the process of establishing the correctness of the "Zhao Shuli path" did not derive solely from political support, but more important, it also exhibited a certain hope for the self-adjustment and reform of new culture itself. It is this hope that forms the core aspiration for the establishment of a new classical literature [of the liberated zones], which also comprises a certain continuation of new culture while in no way being a negative response to old culture. I think this is a premise for any understanding of the popularization and massification of the culture of the liberated zones; perhaps it is even a point of departure for those who theorize revolutionary popular literature, even if this latter concept still is capable of giving rise to certain misunderstandings.

In addition to the question of form, I want to emphasize a certain narrative attitude that is not merely about the reconstruction of a new subjectivity for the culture of the liberated zones but that also concerns the narrative perspective of novels, including the renewed explorations into the multiplicity of forms that this exploration entails. It is precisely the renewed exploration into form that determined the experimental nature of contemporary litera-

10. Ibid., 9–10.

ture—which is to say that contemporary literature in the new discursive context never actually abandoned cultural experimentalism, including experimentalism with the novel's form, language, character development, and so on. Indeed, it is clear that this experimentalism began with the culture of the liberated zones. Of course, in the process of experimenting, contemporary literature paid an incalculable price that, at times, led to an almost crude cultural formation. Yet it is also true that in any process of literary experimentalism, this kind of crudeness or even imperfection in cultural formation is unavoidable, including during the very beginning of the May Fourth New Culture Movement.

In the process of the formulation of this narrative attitude, politics was without a doubt an important core component, and in concert with the changes in [class] perspective, object of work, study, and so on, politics inevitably led to the discussion of the problem of attitude. According to Mao Zedong, "from one's [class] stance there follows specific attitudes towards specific matters."[11] The narrative attitude that can exist under this type of political regulation naturally has severe limitations; nevertheless, in another sense, this narrative attitude brought with it another set of changes that, in retrospect, not only led to the workers and peasants becoming a significant other and entering into the culture and literature of the liberated zones, but also led to the formation of a type of dialogic relation [between peasants/workers and intellectuals/authors]. Naturally, in this dialogic relation, the subjective transformation of the national character was somewhat rewritten, and at the same time as workers and peasants were politicized, they also were moralized.[12] By the same token, and even more important, is the narrative angle demanded by politics that implies some sort of imaginary totality of the construction of national sovereignty. In any event, this led to a sort of grand narrative. What this imaginary was supposed to offer was a top-down narrative perspective. I think we need not reject entirely the legitimacy of this political angle as one basic source of China's modern historical transformation, precisely because one feature of it was the emergence of a new state power. Sociologists have already observed that, to strengthen themselves, modern states vigorously absorb capital resources from grassroots society; undoubtedly, the development of this process in China forced an unprecedented amount of change on China's rural society, as it not only altered the relations, activisms, and roles of

11. Mao Tse-tung, "Talks at the Yenan Forum on Literature and Art," in *Selected Works of Mao Tse-tung* (Peking: Foreign Language Press, 1965), 3:70.
12. See chapter 3 for more on this dialogic relation.

various groups in society, but at the same time also disrupted the traditional role of local elites in totalizing the social order.[13]

In some sense, then, the political angle in literature also assisted cultural workers of the liberated zones to observe China's rural order more closely. For example, several works of the time (including Zhao Shuli's *Changes in Li Family Village* and the opera *White Haired Girl*, among others) exhibited the phenomenon of evil and hegemonic landlords collaborating with reactionary government officers as narrative content. The emergence of this phenomenon is the result of the modern rupture in the Chinese gentry structure—namely, the rupture of the tradition of limited local autonomy. In the telling of this story, it turns out that the culture of the liberated zones drew extensively on narrative resources from traditional novels (for example, *The Water Margin*). Yet in basic ways, this narration was also no longer similar to the old traditional novels. This dissimilarity resided in the following: because of the entry of modern politics, what was being examined was not a [local] particularity, but rather some sort of universal structure of political power in village society; what this political power was dedicated to was not merely some pure ridding society of tyrants and bringing peace [as in traditional novels], but rather, political power was dedicated to delivering a profound revolution [in social structure more generally]. This revolution demands not merely the alteration of the political power structure of village society, but also the construction of national sovereignty as well as the necessity for village society to be completely united with the demands for this national construction. Hence, in these works there is a very clear and strong modernist political desire. It is also for this reason that these works are modern and not traditional; they are revolutionary and not just popular. And precisely because this modern political angle regulates these works, there is a consistent narrative focus on the collective over and above any descriptive strength devoted to the individual.

However, embedded in this regulatory regime, we can still find an obvious continuation of the May Fourth spirit. Even in the memoir material of the writers of the liberated zones, the existence of this modern genealogy can be felt.[14] For this reason, those theorists who trace the origins of the spirit of

13. Zhang Jing, *Xiandai gonggong guize yu xiangcun shehui* [Modern public rules and rural society] (Shanghai: Shanghua Shudian Chubanshe, 2006), 3.

14. For example, according to Cai Rongtian, Zhao Shuli, when he was studying at the Changzhi Shanxi Provincial Normal School, already was reading a large number of the new cultural works of the May Fourth movement and in 1929 he wrote a May Fourth–type novel titled *Hui* [Regret]. See Cai Rongtian, ed., *Shanxi wenxue wushinian zongheng lun* (Taiyuan: Shanxi renmin chubanshe, 2000), 35. Yet Ma Feng, who went to Yan'an after 1940, while he was at the Lu

these liberated zone writers to the May Fourth era new culture are, for the most part, not wrong, I think.[15] This continuation of May Fourth culture was also supported by the politics of that time, at least in theory and in form.[16] One implication of the so-called May Fourth spirit is a concept of the modern individual as the basis [of narrative]. In 1941, Zhao Shuli wrote in a short essay that "humans are always human, and only if one can master one's own life, is life worth living."[17] This is one major aspect of so-called cautionary literature (*quanren wenxue*).[18] Under the influence of this modern concept, praise for the freedoms, happiness, and dignity due to individuals constitutes one of the more common narrative components of these works, including Zhao's "Xiao Erhei Gets Married" ("Xiao Erhei jiehun") and Kang Zhuo's *My Two Landlords* (*Wode liangjia fangdong*), among others. The narrative concern with the individual's (and that means the peasant's) freedom, happiness, and dignity was in concert with the main antifeudal subject of revolutionary Chinese literature. I think the antifeudalism theme is a key point of entry into studying the cultural form of the revolutionary base areas. And the incorporation of peasants into the narratives of the antifeudal theme—as a form of individual liberation—is not only an important contribution of the culture of the liberated zones [to contemporary literature], it is also an important political desire of the Chinese revolution. This is so because only when peasants are liberated

---

Xun Institute began to read works of the Chinese new culture era as well as famous works from abroad, including Alponse Daudet's *The Last Class* (1873), Alexander Serafimouvich's *Iron Flow* (1924), Alexander Alexandrovich Fadeyev's *Destruction* (1927), Mikhail Sholokhov's *Virgin Soil Upturned* (1932), and others. See Gao Jie, ed., *Ma Feng, Xi Rong yanjiu ziliao* [Ma Feng, Xi Rong research materials] (Taiyuan: Shanxi Renmin Chubanshe, 1985), 1.

15. Some theorists believe that the cultural materials, spiritual sources, and origins of Zhao Shuli's writing are in the May Fourth new culture, although Ma Feng and others drew their cultural and spiritual materials from the cultural formation of the base areas [liberated zones] rather than from the May Fourth new culture formation. To counterpose the base area cultural formation to the May Fourth new culture formation is a product of the 1980s intellectual formation and requires new discussions.

16. For example, Mao Zedong in his essay "The Orientation of the Youth Movement" reiterated the targets of the Chinese revolution—"imperialism is one target and feudalism the other"—and noted that for that moment, "nothing we do goes beyond the bourgeois-democratic revolutionary scope" (Mao Tse-tung, "The Orientation of the Youth Movement," in *Selected Works of Mao Tse-tung* [Peking: Foreign Language Press, 1961], 2:242).

17. Zhao Shuli, "Minyi yu 'jiao piao'" [The people's convenience and banknotes], in *Zhao Shuli quanji* [Complete collection of Zhao Shuli's writings] (Taiyuan: Beiyue Wenyi Chubanshe, 1994), 5:126.

18. Tr.: This is a category of literature proposed by then-Cultural Commissar Zhou Yang in the Yan'an period for culture in the liberated zones.

from traditional feudalistic constraints and are transformed into modern individual subjects is it possible to reconstruct the basis of social relations upon a new political collectivity.

In these works, therefore, there is always an imaginary and a desire for the "glorious, new-born things" of which Zhou Yang spoke.[19] Indeed, these indicate a new world, new life, and new knowledge, where the so-called new knowledge is not only expressed through the mass literacy movement (winter schools, night schools, erasing illiteracy, and so on), it also permeates the didactic function—to educate and to caution against—in these writings. In this sense, in the movement for saving the nation [from the Japanese], the quest for enlightenment was in fact not disrupted; it was merely developed in a different form in China's grassroots (village) society. Yet as enlightenment entered village society, it underwent changes; it became part of the coordinated development of modernity in village culture, where modernity preserved the May Fourth idea of the individual and yet even more clearly incorporated narrative resources from traditional folk culture, including now the influence of an urbanite culture that always had depended upon modern popular novels for its propagation.[20] For this reason, this village-level enlightenment bore far more strongly the markings of nativism, including the quest for ethicality that, due to traditional and folk influences and its containment of the radical posturing of May Fourth new culture, contained a degree of conservatism.

Yet from a different perspective, this village enlightenment also affirmed the importance of the collective—an affirmation, I think, that not only stimulated a new discussion about the relationship between the individual and the collective but also provided for the post-1949 so-called liberated individual a new path for the consideration of collectivization (helping address the old question of what happens to Nora after she leaves home).[21] For this reason, in popularization and massification are embedded the possibilities for the introduction of modernity into the villages, especially in the context of a war that had led to certain social fissions and fissures and that had forced intellectuals into a form of active or passive reeducation, but that also had included what Wang Yao calls "the readjustment and reform [*gaizao*] of new May Fourth culture." This readjustment and reform were articulated in the language of the novel, although not merely through a complete acceptance of the incorpora-

19. Zhou Yang, "Lun Zhao shuli de chuangzuo" [On Zhao Shuli's creative work], in *Zhao Shuli wenji* [Collection of Zhao Shuli's writings] (Beijing: Gongren Chubanshe, 1980), 1:580.
20. See chapter for additional discussion of this issue.
21. See chapter 2 for more on this issue.

tion of peasant oral speech or old literary usages, but also by including the vernacularizations of the May Fourth period (which included to some extent a Europeanized language) in its mutual intertwining with and mutual transformation of mass spoken language. As this was articulated in concrete works, on the one hand it emphasized the legitimacy of dialects [local languages];[22] yet on the other hand, it opposed the extreme use of dialects. As Ma Feng clearly stated, "we need to avoid the use of remote regions' native vernaculars; if we don't, then people from a lot of other places will not understand the writing." So "we need to find a universal mode of speech."[23] For this reason, since the vernacularization undertaken during the May Fourth period had already become a sort of universal speech, it entered these novels, even while it underwent a certain alteration. In reviewing *Chronicles of the Lüliang Heroes*, Yuan Ke had already noted this phenomenon.[24]

This alteration [*gaizao*] precisely is what subsequently constituted the refined language (the written language) of contemporary literature. Even in the 1980s, while this type of language was subverted and deconstructed on the one hand, on the other hand, this language tradition not only continued but was also further perfected. In other words, literature since the 1980s has never returned to the May Fourth new culture mode; rather, it has continued to be written in the language structure and tradition already forged by [revolutionary] contemporary literature, even if writers have never stopped promoting a return to the May Fourth. Behind this language is precisely an attitude toward narration that includes a set of values and a cultural stance. It is just that this attitude has entered into a sort of political unconscious: this is the concealed link that connects what I would call the sixty years of contemporary literature together.[25]

If what politics offered was a type of top-down perspective, it made possible for Zhao Shuli and others to become keen observers of grassroots Chinese society. What intellectuals offered was a narrative perspective that went from outside in, through which they developed a cautionary literature filled

---

22. See chapter 1 for more discussion of this.

23. Ma Feng as quoted in *Ma Feng, Xi Rong yanjiu ziliao*. Tr.: There is not a specific page here.

24. Yuan Ke, "Du Lüliang yingxiong zhuan" [Reading *Chronicles of the Lüliang Heroes*], in *Ma Feng, Xi Rong yanjiu ziliao* [Ma Feng, Xi Rong research materials], ed. Gao Jie (Taiyuan: Shanxi Renmin Chubanshe, 1985), 129.

25. Tr.: That is, it connects the first thirty years (1949–79) to the later thirty years (1979–2009), despite the fact that many intellectuals declared an absolute rupture between the Maoist first thirty years and the post-Maoist later thirty years.

with enlightenment spirit. But we must also note that the writers of the liberated zones—including Zhao, Ma Feng, Xi Rong, and others—had an alternative identity as peasants. I think this peasant identity offered these writers a narrative perspective that was internal and bottom up. In other words, this peasant identity does not merely indicate the long experience of living in the rural villages of these writers and the abundant resources this life experience offered them; and it does not merely point to their custom of oral storytelling, including their enthusiasm for traditional stories and local operas and related folk cultural forms. While this is all clearly important, and to different extents all of it influenced their narrative modes, also of great importance is the narrative attitude that this peasant identity afforded them. In other words, their peasant identity often determined how they observed, experienced, and thought about village communities. For this reason, they not only "breathed with and shared the fate of" the peasants,[26] but they were somatically suffused with the life of rural villages. The emotive force of this type of internalization of rural life, along with their experiences, observations, and thoughts about it, genuinely penetrated into the core content of what was called the China question. In this sense, the implications and the significance of these novels and stories cannot be completely appropriated by the category of Party-state narrative. In fact, this is where the real value of these works, in particular those of Zhao, resides.

This type of narrative attitude is expressed in a particular fictional form that became known as narratives of the quotidian (*shenghuohua xushi*). Zhou Yang, in his discussion of Zhao Shuli's *The Rhymes of Li Youcai*, held up Zhao's depictions of the environment and atmosphere as a model [of such narratives]. As Zhou put it, in offering detailed depictions of the items in Li Youcai's cave, Zhao "succeeds in rendering Li Youcai's identity and personality through these depictions." But what Zhou really meant was that writers should alter their stance and emotional investments in their narratives so as to oppose "isolated descriptions in narrative, in which how to write of scenery or people is somehow entirely encapsulated within the world of the writer, who could just as well be writing of the moon or ghosts, using beautiful phrasing and terms with deep meanings, none of which would have anything to do with the people and places of which he is writing and which are entirely unsuited to the situations." In Zhou's estimation, what is behind such empty writing is precisely a petit bourgeois view and emotional investment, and be-

---

26. Tr.: This is a reference to Mao's "Talks at the Yan'an Forum on Literature and Art."

cause of this, the realm of narrative "needs a sweeping cleanup."²⁷ Whether or not Zhou's critique is justified is not our concern here. What he clearly raises is the particularities of Zhao's style of narration, a style that enters into human life, or really represents life. While this style led to an absence of scenic descriptions, the scenic nevertheless awaits renewed discussion, one that is not restricted to the level of technique.²⁸

This kind of narrative particularity that represents details of life was extended through all of contemporary literature. I think that these narratives of the quotidian, in particular representations of subaltern life, were not unique to the literature of the liberated zones at the time. The [earlier] works of Shen Congwen and Ai Wu already contained such narrative characteristics, called the breath of life (*shenghuo qixi*). Actually, contemporary Chinese literature did not extend in toto the inheritance of left-wing literature, for while in plot structure, contemporary literature was relatively similar to popular modern literature (such as that of Zhang Henshui), yet at the level of narrative (including language), it tended far more in the direction of Shen, Ai Wu, and others in its treatment of subaltern society.²⁹

This combined structure comprised of multiple narrative perspectives led to a particularity of the culture of the liberated zones, its polyphony.³⁰ This polyphony contained elements of mutual reinforcement as well as internal structural conflicts, all of which were part of the artistic and political strengths of works of this type. This strength demonstrated the intention of contemporary literature to construct among and between the legacies of new May Fourth

27. Zhou Yang, "Lun Zhao shuli de chuangzuo" [On Zhao Shuli's creative work], in *Zhao Shuli wenji* [Collection of Zhao Shuli's writings] (Beijing: Gongren Chubanshe, 1980), 1:585.

28. On the question of scenery, see Kōjin Karatani, *Origins of Modern Japanese Literature*, trans. and ed. Brett de Bary (Durham, NC: Duke University Press, 1993).

29. In the 1980s, with the rediscovery of Shen Congwen and Zhang Ailing, people found it extremely easy to enter their works because, in some sense, their writing had not been all that unrelated to the narrative traditions of contemporary literature. Of course, this is mere speculation. Tr.: These are post–May Fourth 1920s and 1930s distinctions: Shen Conwen, Ai Wu, and Zhang Ailing were not known as left-wing writers; meanwhile, Zhang Henshui was a best-selling author and was known as a writer for the mass market, not a writer for the masses in the revolutionary political sense. Cai Xiang is arguing here that in the liberated zones of northern China during the Yan'an period and the War of Resistance against Japan, these distinctions—which had been sharp and defining during the 1920s and 1930s—became blurred in the forms and languages of novels of the time.

30. Meng Yue, "*Bai maonü* yanbian qishi—jianlun Yan'an wenyi de lishi duozhixing" [Notes on the evolution of *White-Haired Girl*—A brief discussion of the multiplicity of the history of Yan'an art practices]. In *Ershi shiji zhongguo wenxueshi lun* [On the history of twentieth-century Chinese literature], ed. Wang Xiaoming (Shanghai: Dongfang Chuban Zhongxin, 2003), 2:193.

culture, traditional literature, and even folk culture the possibility for a new type of subjectivity.

I repeatedly emphasize this new narrative attitude so as to explain how it structured the compositional context for the totality of the culture of the liberated zones, including the textual composition of heroes. Under the constraints of this context, the political nature of the hero was particularly evident. At the same time, this hero was also a common person, a member of the masses, and for this reason could flourish even more. To use Guo Moruo's evaluative language, these were "ordinary sons and daughters, heroes of the collective."[31] It is this [juxtaposition of] the ordinary and the heroic that suppressed the legendary elements in such narration. In the culture of the liberated zones, those works that can be incorporated into the category of the heroic are perhaps Ma Feng and Xi Rong's *Chronicles of the Lüliang Heroes* [Lüliang yingxiong zhuan] along with Yuan Jing and Kong Jue's *New Heroic Sons and Daughters* [Xin ernü yingxiong zhuan]. In my discussion below of the heroic in this period, I focus my analysis on these two novels.

The story of the composition of *Chronicles of the Lüliang Heroes*, according to the novel's foreword and afterword, goes as follows: In 1944, at a meeting celebrating heroes in the border area, 124 heroic people's militiamen were chosen to be honored. Among them was a man called the explosives king, another the handgun expert, yet another the model of traitor elimination, and so on. The *Jinsui Mass Paper* of the time needed to report the "stories of these heroic militiamen in fighting against enemies." But "because there was limited space in the newspaper and there were many hundreds of heroic militiamen and stories, there is no way to introduce them one by one." So the newspaper editorial collective decided to let an author "choose some rather typical types and turn the material into a serialized story."

> At the time, there was no plan to turn these stories into a book, so there was no overall outline; all we thought to do was to use a few people to link together all of these battle stories, to write a segment at a time and publish a segment at a time. We did not write it in one fell swoop, and for this reason, in etching out the personalities of each figure, we never really spent any time considering how each part would fit into an overall book structure or as elements in plot development. In this way many holes and insufficiencies remain.

31. Guo Moruo, "*Xin ernü yingxiong zhuan. Xu* [preface to New heroic sons and daughters], rev. ed. (Beijing: Renmin Chubanshe, 2005), n.p.

The *Jinsui Mass Paper* serially published ninety-five episodes. After the authors incorporated the opinions of reviewers and critics, "they found a bit of time and revised the whole thing once." Thus it became the best-selling "eighty-episode edition."[32]

In this foreword by the authors, we find that in the border regions of the time, *hero* was a high honor and title. Also, these heroes burst forth from the masses and became heroes of the masses. Thus, these gatherings of heroes of the masses did not just celebrate the heroes but also became a place for gathering materials about heroes. A good number of works, including the subsequent novel by Zhi Xia, *Guerrillas on the Railways* [Tiedao youji dui], had their materials collected this way.[33] To emphasize the mass nature of heroes was not only a systemic requirement of the time, but it also bore a strong political significance. In a general sense, heroes can be only a small fraction of the population who dare steel their bodies to resist their surrounding environment. The behavior of this small number of people, because they secretly embody the heartfelt desires of the majority, can turn them into leaders. At the same time, when turning these figures into symbols, people will consciously or unconsciously place their own fate in the hands of the heroes. For this reason, in the process of narrating these heroes' deeds, there is always the potential to include a sort of power designation. Illustrating the problem, Sidney Hook has written: "A democracy should contrive its affairs, not to give one or a few the chance to reach heroic stature, but rather to take as a regulative ideal the slogan 'every man a hero.'"[34]

China's revolution as a modern revolution had as its goal to mobilize people to steel themselves in resistance to their surrounding environments. For this reason, the revolution inevitably demanded heroic types, and in narrating their stories, a sort of model was formulated. Yet the task of revolution was

32. For the above several quotes, see Ma Feng, Xi Rong "Foreword," and "Afterword," to *Lüliang yingxiong zhuan* [Chronicles of the Lüliang Heroes] (Beijing: Renmin wenxue chubanshe, 1952), n.p. Also see "*Lüliang yingxiong zhuan* de xiezuo jingguo" [The process of writing *Chronicles*] in Gao Jie, ed., *Ma Feng, Xi Rong yanjiu ziliao* [Ma feng, Xi Rong research materials] (Taiyuan: Shanxi Renmin Chubanshe, 1985), n.p.

33. Zhi Xia, *Tiedao youji dui* [Guerrillas on the railways] (Shanghai: Shanghai Wenyi Chubanshe, 1978). According to Zhi Xia, the first time he met the guerrillas on the railways and came to understand their story was in the beginning of the summer of 1943, when he was on the Shandong front at a meeting called to interview provincial heroes and models of the war. See Zhi Xia, "*Tiedao youji dui* de chuangzuo jingguo" [The process of writing *Guerrillas on the Railways*] (Beijing: Xin wenxue ziliao, 1987), vol. 1.

34. Sidney Hook, *The Hero in History: A Study in Limitation and Possibility* (New York: John Day, 1943), 239.

not to be undertaken by a small number of people: it required the participation of the broad masses. For this reason, heroes could not monopolize the revolution; rather, they had to originate in the participatory possibility that everyone can be a hero. The heroes of the masses resolved doubts about the modernity of the Chinese revolution—which is to say, in this conceptualization, that heroes were both ordinary and collective. So Mao Zedong on the one hand used the image of Zhang Side to affirm the ordinary nature of a hero.[35] On the other hand, Mao demanded that "subsequent heirs to the title of heroic model must diligently engage in learning and guard against arrogance; only in this way can they become models forever."[36] In my view, guarding against arrogance implies a caution against the dictatorial tendency in heroes. And guarding against the dictatorial tendency is precisely Mao's political demand for his personal staff. We could say that already embedded in these demands for the heroic were elements of modern democratic society, and for this reason, in narratives these demands are intimately connected to the Chinese political structure of mass mobilization.

If we enter *Chronicles of the Lüliang Heroes* or *New Heroic Sons and Daughters* through this perspective—that is, the potential for everyone to become a hero—we will discover the unlegendary quality or color of such novels. The plot of *Chronicles of the Lüliang Heroes* concerns how the Kangjia Village people's militia takes up arms during the War of Resistance against Japan in the Lüliang mountainous region, and it narrates the militia's struggle to protect their families and village. What is important here is that the people's militia is really just a bunch of armed peasants.[37] This type of peasant identity can also be seen in the characters of Niu Dashui and Yang Xiaomei from *New Heroic*

---

35. Mao Tse-tung, "Serve the People," in *Selected Works of Mao Tse-tung* (Peking: Foreign Language Press, 1965), 3:227–28. Tr.: Zhang Side (Chang Szu-the) was born a common peasant. When the Red Army arrived in his Shaanbei hometown in 1937, he joined the army; by 1943 he had become one of Mao's bodyguards. In 1944, while Zhang was participating in the elimination of stashes of opium collected from villages under CCP control, a bonfire exploded and he was killed. Mao participated in his funeral and specifically noted his sacrifice in a eulogy subsequently published as his famous September 1944 essay, "Serve the People."

36. Mao Zedong, "Dui yingxiong mofan xu qinjia jiaoyu" [We must diligently educate heroic models], in *Mao Zedong wenji* [Collection of Mao Zedong's works] (Beijing: Renmin Chubanshe, 1996), 3:246.

37. There was some commentary on the Internet about the movie that was made from this novel in 2005. Netizens complained that the movie should be called *Kangjiazhai minbing zhuan* [*The Chronicles of the Kangjia village militia*] rather than *Lüliang yingxiong zhuan* [Chronicles of the Lüliang heroes]. Clearly, the more contemporary definition of *hero* here comes from a different kind of legendary writing, such as Jin Yong's martial arts novels.

Sons and Daughters. Indeed, in the post-1949 era, even with the increasingly legendary casts in novels such as *Tracks in the Snowy Forest*, the main figure is clearly said to have been born a hired farmhand. This identity makes these novels entirely distinct from the hugely popular novels of knights-errant of the late Qing and after. Indeed, the emphasis on the peasant identity of these heroes on the one hand derives from the demands for the class struggle; yet on the other hand, it offers an attractive way to mobilize the masses, as it allows every ordinary son and daughter to see himself and herself as a potential hero.

The demonstrated potential to participate in politics on the part of the masses is part of the novel's modern narrative perspective, as—in a modern democratic society—the standard dream is that everyone can become a hero. This standard dream at the same time restrains the depiction of a hero as possessing superhuman capacity, precisely the capacity that structures elements of legendary hero narratives from ancient to early modern times. Hence, the Lüliang heroes actually are just some regular peasants, who have no martial arts abilities and who, in the beginning of the novel, also lack even the most basic military knowledge. In the thirtieth chapter of the novel, for example, the Kangjia Village people's militia "lured the enemy to step on land mines": "the people on the mountain saw the enemy run away, and with Meng Erzhu at their head, they ran pell-mell down the mountain in hot pursuit into the valley to grab trophies. Lei Shizhu was afraid that the enemy would counterattack, so he shouted that someone should stay behind as rear guards. But hardly anyone heeded him and all shouted and screamed their way down to the bottom of the valley."[38] Such descriptions are not uncommon in the novel, reflecting the peasant habits of these heroes, or their ordinariness.

Observing these habits from some modern perspectives also points to the deficiencies of peasant heroes. In other words, they are also a bunch of deficient heroes. For example, they like drinking and playing drinking games, they gamble, they loaf about a good deal, and so on. These deficiencies await redress, not only by the war but, more pointedly, by political education. For example, because the Kangjia Village people's militia fought a few victorious skirmishes, they become arrogant and proud; they are unwilling to plant their crops. This tendency immediately is criticized by Lao Wu. What Lao Wu criticizes is not only the phenomenon of their separating themselves from

---

38. Ma Feng, Xi Rong, *Lüliang yingxiong zhuan* [Chronicles of the Lüliang heroes] (Beijing: Renmin wenxue chubanshe, 1952), n.p. Tr.: We have not been able to identify the page numbers for all the quotes Cai has from this novel.

the masses, but also the possibility that separation embodies a heroic type who could isolate himself [and place himself above the masses]. Here, we can perhaps grasp why in these types of novels individualistic heroism is always criticized and even suppressed. Yet the embodied deficiencies of these heroes allow the reader to develop a feeling of intimacy with them, which not only derives from a shared ordinariness but also allows for the affirmation of a political recognition that offers the possibility for one's own maturation. In this sense, *Chronicles of the Lüliang Heroes* also contains in it the theme of maturation, a topic that gains far more expressive clarity in Yuan Jing and Kong Jue's *New Heroic Sons and Daughters*.

Under the constraints imposed by the idea that everyone is a potential hero, the heroic person was mostly articulated as a sort of ordinary son and daughter; at the same time, he or she was also a collective hero. Supporting this articulation perhaps was a social truth that could create social ideals. Today we see these as works in the idiom of legend, but at the time they were merely stories of current events. These stories not only demanded the use of materials that bore a certain relation to truthfulness, they also demanded a descriptive truthfulness—that is, they had to be based upon real people and real events. This demand for truthfulness on the one hand restrained the fictitious nature of novels—which is to say, the move from [real] story to novel does require a certain fictitiousness; for this reason, many authors were troubled by the demand for a basis in reality.[39] Yet on the other hand this basis offered a certain possibility for narratives of the quotidian. We should say that within the convention of this narrative mode, the breath of real life in *Chronicles of the Lüliang Heroes* is quite robust. Strong scenes of the quotidian often enough irrupt into the novel's descriptions of battles and heroism. These narratives of the quotidian without a doubt represent a common world; at the same time, they represent a world that is also quite new. Depictions of a real and ordinary world in some sense effectively constrained legend—that is to say, they suppressed depictions of the supernatural commonly found in legends. We should say that this commonness in the narrative of the quotidian also entered into the cinematic and other performances of heroic roles after 1949 and formed a type of popular literature that was an alternative to martial arts novels. I think this is another meaning of revolutionary popular literature.

---

39. For example, Zhi Xia at the time was troubled by the problem of "truth in life and truth in art," which was "how to avoid the constraints of real people and real events ... to more freely engage in artistic creation." See Zhi Xia, *Tiedao youji dui* de chuangzuo jingguo, n.p.

But *Chronicles of the Lüliang Heroes* is after all a novel and a long one at that; it is not just some tale of current events. Moving from such tales to a novel not only requires fabrication, it also requires the inclusion of plots, characters, and so on that need to be structured and imagined anew. In particular, when *Chronicles of the Lüliang Heroes* deploys a quasitraditional episodic form, the form itself might demand its own kind of legend.

I understand the elements of legend in the episodic-novel form as narrative enchantment, a tumbling into a maze of scenes. In this sense, it is hard to deny the legendary quality of *Chronicles of the Lüliang Heroes*. The existence of these elements probably comes from two sources. As we already know, *Chronicles of the Lüliang Heroes* started out as a story told in serial form published in *Jinsui Mass Paper* in daily installments. In the creation of modern novels, the print media is both an important constraint and a leading force as the development of modern popular novels is intimately related to the modern form of communication that is newspapers, and especially the serials column.[40] With the introduction of the print media in the form of newspapers, the concept of the modern reader (urbanites) gradually began to take shape. To attract readers, stories not only had to fulfill the expectations of these readers, but at the same time they also had to manufacture never-ending suspense and climaxes. For this reason, the plots or the legend aspects of the plots became important structuring factors in the novel.

We should say that *Chronicles of the Lüliang Heroes* did in fact attract a large number of readers. According to the readers' reactions of the time, because *Chronicles* was serialized in *Jinsui Mass Paper*, it made "people who usually pay no attention to newspapers urgently wish to read the paper" and it made people "afraid that there might not be another issue forthcoming and if the newspaper arrived late, people would miss it like missing their own mother." However, we must also note that the literacy rate in the villages at the time was quite low, and oral storytelling became an important form for the transmission of newpaper content. At the time, not only did teachers read to their students ("ever since *Chronicles of the Lu Liüliang Heroes* began to be serialized, I turned it into supplementary course materials for the citizen classes and read it aloud to the students ... it attracted student interest and attention"), but at the same time students also read to adults ("when students returned to their homes and got under the covers to sleep, they told the adults [in their

---

40. See Ye Hongshen, *Shushan jianxia pingzhuan* [Critical biography of the Shu mountain swordsman] (Taipei: Taiwan Yuanjing chuban gongsi, 1982), 290.

families] about the stories of heroes"); leaders, also, read to the masses ("This time, when I went to the countryside, there happened to be a big meeting of the people's militias and everyone asked me to read *Chronicles*; therefore, I read a couple sections and everyone listened attentively"), and so on.[41] To satisfy this oral transmission form, not only did the story need to enchant, it also needed to take into consideration the popularization of language. I think that in the course of the formation of revolutionary popular literature, oral transmission was a very important market element. I will continue this discussion in a moment.

But from another angle, in the process of writing a novel, the author's memory from his own reading often plays a very important role. That is to say, in the process of the composition of a text, there are always traces left behind of other texts. In the case of the *Chronicles*, this intertextuality derives from two places. One is Ma Feng's and Xi Rong's memories of their own reading in the past. The other, which emerged in the course of the [1930s–1940s] debate on national form, is Chinese classical novels.[42] For example, Zhou Libo chastised himself for "when I taught in the Lu Xun Institute of Art [in Yan'an] a course on 'classic works,' I selected too few Chinese materials to read," and he further thought that "precisely because Chinese classical novels were never fully accepted by the Chinese literati, nor, for this reason, were they properly canonized, they were able to reflect the lives of people at the time."[43] Later, he also summarized three major virtues of Chinese classical novels: (1) the story is complete; (2) typical characters are written in creative ways; and (3) the novels are written in vernacular language. He believed that "the authors of episodic novels were genuine artists who were multitalented, serious, not chasing after fame."[44] In some sense, what these explanations offer is political legiti-

---

41. The previous several quotes all derive from Zhou Wen, preface to *Lüliang Yingxiong zhuan, Xu* [preface to Chronicles of the Lüliang heroes], in *Ma Feng, Xi Rong yanjiu ziliao* [Ma Feng, Xi Rong research materials], ed. Gao Jie (Taiyuan: Beiyue Wenyi Chubanshe, 1994), 107–9.

42. Tr.: This was a discussion that began in the late 1930s and lasted into the 1940s. Its point of departure was the May Fourth repudiation of all things ancient and classically Chinese, a radical position that was rethought and rediscussed in the context of the war, the popularization of literature, and the need for new forms of writing and reading that accorded with the times and with the masses' desires.

43. Zhou Libo, "Shenghuo, sixiang he xingshi" [Life, thought, and form], in *Zhou Libo wenji* [Collected works of Zhou Libo], (Shanghai: Shanghai Wenyi Chubanshe, 1985), 5:285.

44. Zhou Libo, "Dushu zhaji" [Reading notes], in *Zhou Libo wenji* [Collected works of Zhou Libo], (Shanghai: Shanghai Wenyi Chubanshe, 1985), 5:514.

macy for the return to tradition. And in *Chronicles of the Lüliang Heroes*, there are many traces of traditional narrative.

There were also critical opinions focused on the episodic form. For example, Xie Qing believed that "the heroes in the work, even though they are all members of the masses and all possess the mannerisms of common people born and raised on the soil, and there is no fabrication of unlikely situations or strange happenings, however, these heroes are individuals who stick out, whose behaviors are secretive and whose manners are unrefined, and can easily remind people of the good fellows and heroes of Liangshanbo [in *The Water Margin*].... [In addition], the heroes in the novel even compare themselves to those characters of Liangshanbo."[45] There were also those who criticized the language used in the novel: "the phrases and words are too casual and lacking in feeling."[46] In these critiques, we can sense a critical attitude toward old novels originating in the May Fourth new culture tradition and continuing to this day. The critical discourse from the new culture tradition wished to restrain some of the elements of legend in these novels. The subsequent [postserialization] eighty-chapter bound book of *Chronicles of the Lüliang Heroes* to some degree incorporated these critical opinions.

In addition, some new culture authors paid attention to certain modern subjects or themes rather than to the popularization or massification of the novels. For example, even though Mao Dun thought that the depictions in *Chronicles* were "crude and unrefined," nevertheless he believed it had a very important "educational significance" that resided, on the one hand, in the fact that readers could "recognize themselves in this mirror, could examine themselves, affirm themselves, and lift themselves up a little." On the other hand, through the novel's depiction of "the people's" [*renmin*] maturation, readers could also "overcome their backward notions of 'fate.'"[47] In other words, in Mao Dun's summary there is a certain modern bildungsroman theme that is a political subject, because the maturation is completed only when the subjects recognize that only through organization can there be strength. Clearly, it is

45. Xie Qing, [Book reviews of *Chronicles of the Lüliang Heroes*] in *Ma Feng, Xi Rong yanjiu ziliao* [Ma Feng, Xi Rong research materials], ed. Gao Jie (Taiyuan: Shanxi Renmin Chubanshe, 1985), 114.

46. Yan Wu, [*Chronicles of the Lüliang Heroes* and *Xiao Erhei Gets Married*], in *Ma Feng, Xi Rong yanjiu zhiliao* [Ma Feng, Xi Rong research materials], ed. Gao Jie (Taiyuan: Shanxi Renmin Chubanshe, 1985), 117.

47. Mao Dun, [Concerning *Chronicles of the Lüliang Heroes*], in *Ma Feng, Xi Rong yanjiu ziliao* [Ma Feng, Xi Rong research materials], ed. Gao Jie (Taiyuan: Shanxi Renmin Chubanshe, 1985), 120.

only this subject of maturation that lends the novel its ability to open up new ideas along with the possibility to attract readers to the idea that everyone has the potential to be a hero. In my opinion, this is an impeccably modern critical requirement.

Guo Moruo, in his preface to *New Heroic Sons and Daughters*, articulated this critical requirement quite clearly:

> The characters here are all ordinary sons and daughters, and yet they are all collective heroes. It is their ordinary qualities that allow us to feel close to them, and it is their heroic bearing that allows us to respect them. This seamlessly educates the readers to recognize the most genuine aspects of Communist Party members. Readers can receive a good deal of encouragement from this in their efforts to reeducate and improve themselves. Is it possible that most men could not become like Niu Dashui? And that women could not become like Yang Xiaomei? Makes no difference that you're ordinary, backward, or even illiterate without knowledge; all you need is self-awareness, a desire for progress, a spirit of self-sacrifice, a loyal desire to realize Mao Zedong thought, and everyone can become foundational bricks in building a new society.[48]

When Guo wrote this preface, what he had read was what the author had sent him, which was the compiled version of *New Heroic Sons and Daughters*, similar to the compilation of *Chronicles of the Lüliang Heroes*. Indeed, *New Heroic Sons and Daughters* was also originally published in serialized form in newspapers. However, *New Heroic Sons and Daughters* was a little bit more new culture–like. If we can say that *Chronicles* mostly focuses on depictions of groups, then *New Heroic Sons and Daughters* concentrates on describing the two main characters, Niu Dashui and Yang Xiaomei, including their process of maturation. For this reason, in contrast to Mao Dun's critical comment that the depictions in *Chronicles of the Lüliang Heroes* were "crude and unrefined," Guo thought that in *New Heroic Sons and Daughters* the "characters were rendered skillfully, as were the narratives of incidents, the renditions of nature, and the use of the mass language of the common people."[49] I think that these comments are related to the structure of *New Heroic Sons and Daughters*, which, with a smaller cast of characters, naturally allows for fewer digressions.

48. Guo Moruo, preface to *Xin Ernü yingxiong zhuan* [New heroic sons and daughters] (Beijing: Renmin Chubanshe, 1956), n.p.
49. Ibid.

In their afterword to the bound book version of *Chronicles*, Ma Feng and Xi Rong summarized the "deficiencies and holes" in their novel; among them is that there is "no emotional growth," which can be understood as a type of undeveloped subject of maturation, leading to the impression that there "is no process" in the novel and that there are "even some contradictory aspects between the beginning and the end." In contrast, there is relatively more emphasis on emotional growth in *New Heroic Sons and Daughters*, for example in the scene of Niu Dashui attending the district-level training course. Because he is smoking a cigarette, he is criticized by the comrades, and he feels incredibly aggrieved. First he fulminates, then he snorts, but then after he has gone through the training, his "breathing is regulated and his heart is at peace," and he "laughingly ... in the Party conference" guarantees that he will never again "lose his bull-like temper."[50] One of the more important reasons for the process of this emotional growth is membership in the Communist Party. For a common peasant at the time, to be a member of the Party was not only a personal identity, it also brought with it a certain respect and honor. These lead to Niu Dashui's emotional growth.

This process is also the process of a person's maturation. The basic narrative emphasis of the novel is precisely on how two completely ordinary individuals, Niu Dashui and Yang Xiaomei, mature into heroes of the collective. This story line, beginning with *Chronicles* and moving through the extravagance of *New Heroic Sons and Daughters*, gradually structures a type of writing model in which the legendary factors gradually faded. If *Chronicles* still bears a good deal of the narrative trace of classical fiction, then *New Heroic Sons and Daughters* tends more toward the new culture psychologizing requirements of writing. In addition, it is both more ordinary but also more romantic. Niu Dashui and Yang Xiaomei's new culture story of revolution plus love not only gets extended in this novel, but depictions of transcending nature also basically disappear completely from the story lines. In this way, revolution plus ordinariness plus romance came to structure a completely revolutionary and modern popular story. What this story led to is a possibility for the masses to emulate; that is, all men should be Niu Dashuis and all women should be Yang Xiaomeis.

In these novels, the elements of legend inherent in popular fiction often were consciously or subconsciously suppressed for various reasons. What re-

---

50. *Xin Ernü yingxiong zhuan*, n.p.

quires further discussion is why, after 1949, these elements were liberated and came to structure a new heroic form of storytelling.

II. Legends and the Travels of a Story

In the summer of 1943, a provincial conference of battle heroes and models was convened in the Shandong Military District. At this meeting, Zhi Xia came to know Xu Guangtian, a railway guerrilla team member. Zhi Xia was deeply attracted to the battle stories Xu told of the team's activities. And even though this conference was attended by all sorts of famous battle heroes from the entire province of Shandong, the stories Xu told of the railway guerrillas' activities were "evaluated unanimously by everyone there as outstanding heroic stories of battle." This unanimity cannot but be related to the legendary status achieved by the railway guerrillas. Later, when Zhi Xia got deeply involved in interviewing the railway guerrillas, he discovered that "these heroic figures are all enthusiastic and courageous, they behave like knights-errant and are somewhat similar to the legendary itinerant fighters of yore." At the same time, "the battle incidents they create" all have a certain legendary quality. Despite this quality, Zhi Xia, in his afterword to *Guerrillas on the Railways*, emphasizes repeatedly that "all of the battle incidents in this book are real events."[51] These real events can be understood as a form of information, a basic structure for the foundation of a good number of revolutionary historical novels. That is to say, these novels repeatedly emphasize that their narratives are fragments of real revolutionary history. Not only do *Chronicles of the Lüliang Heroes* and *Guerillas on the Railways* conform to this requirement, but Qu Bo also insisted that *Tracks in the Snowy Forest* was based upon his personal experience. He particularly explained that [his main protagonist] Yang Zirong was a real person and because of this, Qu emphasized that the novel was no fabrication.[52] This issue of real people and events was not only incorporated into the concept of fiction writing at the time, but it also was very important for providing evidentiary legitimacy for the renarration of revolutionary history. I will say more about this in a moment.

---

51. For the several quotes above, see Zhi Xia, *Tiedao youji dui* [Guerrillas on the railways] (Shanghai: Shanghai Wenyi Chubanshe, 1978), afterword.

52. Qu Bo, *Linhai xueyuan* [Tracks in the snowy forest], rev. ed. (Beijing: Renmin Wenxue Chubanshe, 2005), n.p.

Zhi Xia, unlike Ma Feng or Xi Rong, did not immediately write a novel out of the information he gathered. Rather, he wrote some newspaper reportage and essays for media outlets, because what he really wished to do was "to use a novelistic form to reflect" on his materials. Before he finished his story in the form of a novel, Zhi Xia "used his mouth to speak, like a regular oral storyteller," and "everyone loved to listen and was deeply moved."[53] Qu Bo did the same: before he finished writing his novel, he had already "narrated orally innumerable times the stories of the *Tracks in the Snowy Forest*, and particularly the heroic deeds of Yang Zirong, all of which deeply touched the comrades listening, who were greatly surprised and seemed to gain strength from the stories."[54]

This communicative process constitutes a story's travels. In the course of such travels, information gradually turns into transmission. This transmission is where narrative or the creative process enters. In Zhang Ailing's words, it becomes a sort of "gossip." By tracing the travels of true stories, we can begin a discussion of how these stories gradually become legends.

The fifth chapter of *Guerrillas on the Railways* concerns the political commissar, Li Zheng, who, before leaving the mountain, has heard various transmitted accounts about railway guerrillas: "Stories circulated among the troops regarding how these guns came to hand and how Lao Hong hijacked a train and killed the 'ghosts' [Japanese]. These stories bore a certain whiff of mythification in their retelling." This "whiff of mythification" structures a type of challenge to those ordinary sons and daughters—that is, it is possible that mythification could shed doubt on the regulating ideal that everyone could become a hero. Furthermore, "the battalion commander was a courageous fighter in the mountain areas and had great leadership skills. It was said that, on the train the guerrilla team stole arms from the enemy, and when the commander thought of the situation on that train, even he shook his head and thought it was really difficult." The problem is the narrator believes that the narrative attitude itself is quite difficult: if he narratively establishes these "whiffs of mythification," then how can he deal with so-called reality? Yet if he doesn't recognize this mythic story, then how can he possibly explain the exploits of the guerrilla team on the train? So Li Zheng, on the one hand, is made to disbelieve all myths, and on the other hand, "he is nevertheless moved by these stirring exploits."[55] Li Zheng's attitude is precisely that of the narrator. On

53. Zhi Xia, Afterword to *Guerillas on the Railways*.
54. Ibid., n.p.
55. Ibid., n.p.

the one hand, what supports the real is the commonness of the world. Only within this world can politics mobilize the broad participation of the masses and establish the principled ideal that everyone can become a hero. This ideal is precisely a type of modern narrative attitude. The decrease of supernatural elements in narration is symptomatic of the modern progress of secularization. It is this narrative attitude that guided the writing of such novels as *Chronicles of the Lüliang Heroes*.

On the other hand, in a secular world supported by its ordinariness, there is simply no way to complete an imaginary of the hero and its narration. This is because there is no way to explain that a hero always emerges from a minority of people, even despite the fact that the regulating ideal that everyone can be a hero reduces the distance between common people and heroes. That is to say, to make it so that everyone could become a hero would turn modern society into an open society, yet modern society requires and indeed never ceases to create [exceptional] heroes. The aim of this fashioning resides in the fact that modern society wishes to borrow this mode to demonstrate how the impossible becomes the possible, and a minority of people—heroes—are precisely those who are able to first symbolize this transformation of the impossible into the possible. It is also this small number who will then be able to evoke the strong attraction of modernity, which bears within it a good deal of mythic magic. For this reason, one paradox within modernity is the contradiction and conflict between the narrative of heroes and that of democracy.

If we define the Chinese revolution as a modern revolution, then it too faces this paradox of modernity. What it needs to do most urgently is to offer a rational explanation for the relationship between the ordinary and the mythical. This explanation in Li Zheng's character is precisely the narrator's perspective, which is "under the leadership of the Party, wisdom added to courage is the origin of all victories."[56] Behind this narrative is a theoretical explanation of the transformation from impossible to possible as well as the political legitimizing support for this myth. Only through this understanding can we grasp why, after the railway guerrillas enter the mountains, these modern grassroots heroes are invited by every battalion to make reports and are enthusiastically received. Clearly, the process of making a report is another form of narrative mythmaking as, in this process, the revolution produces through legend the mythic strength of the transformation from impossible to possible. This strength does not prevent the reader from being moved

56. Ibid., n.p.

by these stirring stories, and it also firms up one's confidence in whatever work one is undertaking. For this reason, in the travels of the story, politics represents the entry of elements of the modern and plays an important role in the formation of the legendary. I think that the burden borne by this modern legendary story itself comes close to being a form of religious rhetoric.

However, support for this legend narrative clearly also derives from an exploration of an experiential impossibility. If we define the legendary as "a new type of experience . . . outside the realm of traditions of common sense which are hypotheticals or even fantasies," then writing this legend can also be said to be "a sort of imaginary performative leaping over of known experience."[57] The fourteenth chapter of *Guerrillas on the Railways* borrows the speech of a certain "old grandpa," who expresses his views on trains:

> When you talk about these trains, it sure seems like it could be a really destructive thing! The guys in my village all say that a bull is large, and yet ten, a hundred, a thousand bulls don't come close to the size of that thing. It is so big that one of its carriages has four or five compartments, and one train can have several dozen carriages; it can be as long as a hundred to two hundred compartments; something like half a mountain of coal can be loaded up in it. You only have to hear it once—choo-choo choo-choo—and in a blink of an eye, it'll pass by. It sure is speedy! It can go a thousand *li* in one day. Those people from big places really are something! I've heard such a huge thing requires only one person to drive it.

In this kind of articulation, the modern (industry) becomes for tradition (agriculture) an imaginary realm of the new and strange; that is, it becomes a narrative resource for legend making. Subsequent to the old grandpa's speech, Peng Liang, as he is introduced by Xiao Po ("This comrade of ours . . . can drive a train!"), becomes the leading figure in the legend ("Comrade, you really have some talent!"). But the story's travel is not yet finished, as Xiao Po says: "He not only can drive a train, he can also battle ghosts [Japanese]. . . . When he sees a ghost train, he leaps with his whole body onto this giant. He kills the ghost driver, and he drives the ghost train wildly down the tracks."[58] In Xiao Po's telling, Peng Liang not only is modern, he is also antimodern: he has a sort of strength that transcends and resists the modern. Clearly, in different experiential narratives this alien imaginary realm is both modern and

57. Meng Yue, "Zhongguo wenxue de 'xiandaixing' yu Zhang Ailing," 2:105.
58. Zhi Xia, *Tiedao youji dui* [Guerrillas on the railways] (Shanghai: Shanghai Wenyi Chubanshe, 1978), chapter 14.

antimodern; the one without the other is impossible. The combining of the modern and the antimodern into one is where the particularity of the Chinese revolution resides, and the hero's courage and ability to resist is one of the more important elements of the structuring of the basic foundations of the legend. For this reason, with Xiao Po's speech, "the heads of the elders did not stop shaking, and they all declaimed: 'Our Eighth Route Army fellows sure are something!'"

In its travels through different experiential realms, this story gradually is structured around what Meng Yue has called the imaginary realm of new alien things. This realm at the same time marks the entry into the narrative space of the audience (the listeners or readers), which is the only thing in the end determining the essential elements of the story's legend. In my view, what the travels of the story within the text of *Guerrillas on the Railways* represent is the process of the author's storytelling in his creative life, just as with Qu Bo before he wrote *Tracks in the Snowy Forest*, who already "narrated orally innumerable times the stories of the *Tracks in the Snowy Forest*." This oral communicative process indicates that the reader's position is incredibly important, as the entirety of the "whiffs of mythification" is produced in the reaction of the reader. For this reason, in novels such as *Guerrillas on the Railways* or *Tracks in the Snowy Forest*, the reader actually is ushered urgently into the creation of the novel. This is a form of postincident writing: the re-creation of the story after its telling. That is, the novel writing already sub-consciously anticipates the expectations of the listener (reader), which is precisely a narrative feature of the oral form of traditional storytelling in China. In this sense, the railway guerrillas' "whiffs of mythification" exist not only in the circulation of the legends everywhere, but, in a reversal, these legends in the text have already influenced the narrator's expressive mythic attitude toward the railway guerrillas. Or, rather, this story is really the result of the prior circulation of the legend.

I want to continue here with my discussion of the structuring role played in these writings by the reading resources of the author—including the genealogy of knowledge constructed by these reading resources. We have already grasped that memory plays an important role in writing; yet this memory is not formed only from the life experiences of an individual, for actually in individual memory reading is quite an important element. If we analogize this reading memory to a library, then in some sense we could say that what is happening is a type of library writing, which is characterized by the fact that the process of writing is also a process of imitating. To formulate a target of imitation is precisely why we read. In this imitative process, we might wish to transcend the target, or challenge it or revise it; it is also possible to accept or identify with it. Regardless, it always exists and is the premise for any writing. At the same time, it is the intertextuality that is created in our writing at any given moment. But the number of books in a library is large; thus, like our reading memory, we have all sorts of reading experiences to structure our thoughts. The question becomes, what path into that library do we take? And how quickly can we find the one book collected there that we wish to reread? That is to say, how do we reopen our reading memories?

I think insofar as novels are concerned, form is a very important aspect. The choice of form is related to our reading experiences; at the same time, it also invites us to reenter the library of our memories. And this time when we enter it is for reading, but it is even more for research. In this sense, we can say that form is a key to unlock the memory library.

A discussion of Zhi Xia's *Guerrillas on the Railways* and its creative process can serve as an example to further explore this problem of form. According to Zhi Xia, we know that in the summer of 1943 there was a big conference of the Shandong military area's battle heroes and models, where the famous battle heroes of the whole province gathered. Among so many battle heroes, why did Zhi Xia take such a huge interest in the railway guerrillas? I think this is related to literature. From the very beginning, Zhi Xia was unsatisfied about using the form of reportage to describe the exploits of these heroes. Rather, he determined to "reflect on them through literature," and he created all of the conditions necessary for him to write this literature.[59] Zhi Xia's process was very different from that of the [more contingent] creation of *Chronicles of the Lüliang Heroes*, insofar as Zhi Xia had a very clear idea about form. Wherein does the literariness reside? In Zhi Xia's estimation, first it resides in the fact that "the heroic figures of the railway guerrillas were enthusiastic and courageous, they behaved like knights-errant and had a tinge of itinerant fighter of yore about them"; second, "they often penetrated deeply into enemy ranks, so as to conveniently complete their tasks in one fell swoop, and they frequently had encounters with enemy troops and always emerged victorious; third, their battles on the railways lent themselves to storytelling because they were complicated."

It turns out that these three features are precisely the basic narrative foundations of old Chinese traditional stories of knights-errant. Any story of knights-

---

59. Zhi Xia, *Tiedao youji dui de chuangzuo jingguo*. All subsequent references are to this piece, so I will not cite them separately.

errant is the combination of the knight and martial combat.[60] These three elements also were the basic foundational structures for the special characteristics of mythic narratives in revolutionary popular literature (for example, *Tracks in the Snowy Forest, Steel Meets Fire* (*Liehuo jingang*) [by Liu Liu], *Behind the Enemy Lines* (*Dihou wugongdui*) [by Feng Zhi], and so on). In some sense, we can also say that Zhi Xia's selection was guided by his choice of reading—or, behind his selection of form for this novel already stood the originary textual experience of the knight-errant novels. So from the very beginning, Zhi Xia "prepared to use the folk cultural form of writing that the masses already liked to hear and read, thus to narrate the battle exploits of the railway guerrillas in episodic story form."

I have already discussed how, after the publication of Mao's "Talks at the Yan'an Forum on Literature and Art," China's traditional novel forms attained the stamp of political legitimacy; this is what Zhi Xia calls "those folk cultural stories the masses love to hear and see." Episodic chapter forms were an important formal aspect of ancient Chinese novels and literary works. Indeed, researchers have already noted that embedded in revolutionary popular literature were the shadows of folk formations. For example, in *Guerrillas on the Railways*, the descriptions of many major characters bear within them the narrative structures derived from *Romance of the Three Kingdoms*. This type of derivative form in revolutionary popular literature is quite common. In addition, the revenge subject [characteristic of older literature] underwent an efficient political revision and found a new narrative location in these novels.[61] It is thus clear that the origins of the derivative style were complex, and they included ancient Chinese narratives as well as the gradual formation of modern popular literature from the late Qing onward; all of this had formed a kind of modern cultural imaginary for urban readers.[62] Naturally, in the course of reviving the episodic form, all sorts of derivative story lines that pertain to this form were also revived; these were both old and modern. I think this de-

---

60. For more on knights, see Cai Xiang, *Xia yu yi—wuxia xiaoshuo yu Zhongguo wenhua* [Knights and meaning—stories of knights-errant and Chinese culture] (Beijing: Shiyue Wenyi Chubanshe, 1993).

61. See Li Yang, *50–70 niandai Zhongguo wenxue zai jiedu*, chapter 1 (regarding the novel *Tracks in the Snowy Forest*).

62. Li Oufan [Leo Oufan Lee] has used the concept of "the modernity of revolutionary popular literature" to discuss this problem ("Wan Qing wenhua, wenxue yu xiandai xing" [Late Qing culture, literature, and modernity], in *Liwa he pan lun wenxue* [Discussing literature by Liwa River], ed. Chen Zishan and Luo Gang [Shanghai: Huadong Shifan Daxue Chubanshe, 2006], 59).

rivative nature accounts for the transformation [in popular revolutionary literature] from witnessing to transmission [in narrative style and form].

Yet it remains to explain why, even if the revival of stories from the derived forms is complex, some derivative forms entered revolutionary popular literature and others got eliminated. Zhi Xia, in his essay on the process of writing *Guerrillas on the Railways*, has a detailed discussion of how real people and events troubled him greatly even though the real people and events writing style was on the ascendant at the time in the base areas. Zhi Xia's doubts were not raised only because, when he had spoken to some of the railway guerrillas, they had always reminded him not "to forget to write about my story"; more important still was the fact that most of the railway guerrillas with whom he had become rather close were all quite imperfect heroes. Among them, Xu Guangtian, the first with whom Zhi Xia became acquainted, subsequently was revealed to have many imperfections; indeed, Xu ended up actually surrendering and defecting to the enemy. The figure on which Li Zheng's character was modeled was a political commissar named Du Jiwei who insisted on carrying on a love affair with a young woman. Because this woman's older brother "had joined the enemy and had subsequently been killed by the railway guerrillas," the guerrillas' leaders, for fear that she might avenge her brother's death, disapproved of the love affair. Yet "when Du was transferred to the mountains to receive some political training at the Party school, he secretly brought the young woman with him." And then there was the figure on whom Sister Fanglin was modeled: after the sacrifice of [her lover] Lao Hong, this figure "had intimate relations with a number of the railway guerrillas," and because of this "she attracted the derisive dissatisfaction of many, so that most of her comrades actually had nothing but contempt for her." Even the figure who served as the model for [the hero] Lao Hong, a battalion commander named Hong Zhenhai, "exhibited an explosive temper, so that every time he encountered a difficulty, he exploded like thunder."

These people and incidents were the biggest obstacle to Zhi Xia's writing. Thus, the incident that led to Xu Guangtian's betrayal actually freed Zhi Xia to feel he was "even more able to write the novel *Guerrillas on the Railways*." This is because "I could finally just free myself from the real people real events constraint and use real people and true stories as a foundation to more freely create and compose my novel. In the process of composition, I could just eliminate those trivial, repetitive, and inessential things by combining the most important features of a hero and boldly fashioning them into characters." In this artistic fashioning, the question of the derivative aspect of the novel disappears.

The above account of the creative process provided by Zhi Xia can explain a lot about the problem of realism. That is to say, realism is absolutely not naturalism, because the real is a truth that has been fashioned anew as it undergoes the process of annotation and conceptualization. According to [the literary critic] Wang Hongsheng's analysis, "any realism is actually the combination of the real and conceptualization."[63] Realism is thus a subjective product of reality plus conceptualization, and its creative principle is essentialism or typicality. Even though this conceptualization implies a clear political element, it also provides a certain individual imaginary space for creativity, including how to deal with the problem of legend. In the post-1949 period, this creative mode came to be explained as the combination of revolutionary romanticism and revolutionary realism. According to [the cultural critic and novelist] Wang Meng, this mode "is better than Soviet socialist realism, for at least it provides a bit more creative space."[64]

In the thirtieth chapter of *Guerrillas on the Railways* there is an account of the guerrilla team going up into the mountains to retrain themselves. On that night, "headquarters had specially organized for them a welcome party, where the cultural troops of the military area put on a performance." Part of the performance consists of a spoken drama that is based upon the battle exploits of the railway guerrilla team. According to the description of this performance in the novel, the effectiveness of the transformation from story to stage is entirely dependent upon a representation of truth: "He never even saw the stage sets: if it said it was nighttime, the lights on the stage immediately were dimmed and there really was a star-filled sky." Clearly, the form of spoken drama provided a type of representational realism that no traditional opera could attain.

Now, we can also imagine that these guerrilla team members at the time were quite shocked. They sat below the stage, while on the stage is another them who are "real." They are looking at themselves: "These scenes one after another reminded Xiao Po that he really had been a few days before in an urgent battle situation." Naturally, what they see is just a fragment of them-

---

63. Wang Hongsheng, "Shirun de xushu: Bo'er yu Chen Yinsong" [Humid narratives: Bauer and Chen Yingsong], *Shucheng zazhi* [Journal of the book city] 11 (2007).

64. Wang Meng, *Wang Meng zizhuan* [Wang Meng's autobiography] (Guangzhou: Huacheng Chubanshe, 2006–7), 2:62.

selves exaggerated for artistic purposes. Yet this becomes their mirror image, through which their selves as well as their lives and subjectivities could be formed. This is the effect of a narrative of essence. This narrative of essence is also a process of eliminating all that is alien. For this reason, even though "it was already quite late by the end of the performance," nevertheless "everyone was so excited no one could sleep."

This excitement is something requiring further discussion. In some sense, in the stimulation of excitement, the imaginary of the self gradually emerges from the process of the narrative of essence. This represented and emergent self becomes a more real self, a better self. In [Slavoj] Žižek's terms, this is also the "sublime object of ideology."[65] When the members of the railway guerrilla team are "so excited" that they cannot sleep because of the discovery of this new self, they also begin to become the mirror image of the whole battalion: "On the second day, a representative of the guard troops from headquarters arrived and asked the comrades from the railway guerrilla team to deliver a report to the troops, to talk about their exploits in battle on the railroad: this was the desire of all the troops." At every report, "it wasn't clear just how many times there was applause." In the process of narrating these reports, the narrative itself strengthens the power of the mirror image. So Lin Zhong loudly proclaims: "Today, I finally feel like a person, a real person, the glory of being a person."[66] This sublime becomes a summoning that not only beckons the troops but also the railway guerrillas themselves; indeed, this ideal self has already been turned by the narrative into the real self. The narrative thereby precisely avoids the defects of real people and real events.

Clearly, form here is not merely a matter of technique; rather, it harbors a number of implications that are at once ideological and emotionally individual. For this reason, form can revive some originary models even while rejecting others.[67] And thus, in the process of turning heroes into legends, form is quite significant. It does not matter whether the conscious narrative quest is

65. Slavoj Žižek, *The Sublime Object of Ideology* (London: Verso, 1989).
66. Zhi Xia, *Tiedao youji dui* [Guerrillas on the railways] (Shanghai: Shanghai Wenyi Chubanshe, 1978), chapter 30.
67. For example, in the revival mode, there are some very clear masculine characteristics, particularly those related to military fighting and those related to the heroic that emerge from armed battles For this reason, Leoi Oufan Lee's summary of male and female plots that feature "strong women, weak men" can be thoroughly disproved, or it never entered into this particular form of literature ("Wan Qing wenhua, wenxue yu xiandai xing," 56). For more on this point, see chapter 3. Similar plots can also be found in Yang Mo, *The Song of Youth*, trans. Nan Ying (Peking: Foreign Language Press, 1964).

for the story to be transmitted orally or in episodic form; all of it has a certain implication for the legendary, which itself is a form of narrative of essence.

Aside from legend and form, then, it is necessary to discuss yet another element, which is the problem of the reader and the market.

III. The Reader and the Market

In the beginning of this chapter, I noted that the concept of the masses was powerfully inserted into the structure of contemporary Chinese literature through Mao's "Talks at the Yan'an Forum on Literature and Art." This led to great changes in the patterns of consumption of literature. One symbol of these changes is the tendency toward popularization in literature. Yet it is very difficult to use the political concept of the masses to discuss a good number of the questions raised by and through the category of literature. For this reason, I am more inclined to substitute for this category that of the reader.

An important feature of contemporary literary history is that the concept of the reader is not entirely produced through the process of communications media. On the contrary, the concept of the reader was first constructed through politics, which is to say it derives from the political concept of the masses. Hence, it not only bears a clear implication of a demographic group, but it also contains the idea of a majority of the people, which includes workers and peasants and soldiers.[68] In the culture of the liberated zones, this majority or the concept of the reader mostly indicated the peasants in the villages, although obviously after the People's Republic of China was established, it also included the urban classes. Yet this is only one aspect of the issue. Another aspect: not only does this concept of the reader come from a political process of legitimation, it also has its own traditional self-constituting elements. That is to say, the transmission process of some traditional cultural forms—ancient literature, folk oral storytelling, folk music, and others—had already created some sort of reader out of Chinese grassroots (rural and urban) society. These readers could perhaps be called an imagined cultural community.

---

68. Tr.: Workers, peasants, and soldiers (*gong, nong, bing*) is the triad that primarily constitutes the masses or the people as political concepts, although at different times during the Mao era, the concept of the masses could expand or contract depending on political requirements. By the Cultural Revolution, this triad was the most privileged in rhetoric and often in practice. Of historical significance for intellectuals, this triad usually did not include them, thus often casting them out of political favor.

In Benedict Anderson's research, we can already see the intimate linkage between an imaginary and a modern sovereign nation; in his terms, "modern nation-state" or "the imagined political community."[69] However, [the literary scholar] Leo Oufan Lee believes that one needs to add to the process of this construction the extremely important concept of the reader, in which different types of readers allow for the possibility of "multiple modernities."[70] Indeed, novels make readers and readers make novels; there is a mutual construction or even a dialectical relationship.

For this reason, when the political concept of the masses came to be transformed into the literary concept of the reader, what contemporary literature needed to face then was not only the masses from China's subaltern society, but also the fact that these masses as a cultural community already had literarily constructed tastes. It was the members of this cultural community who were to be readers of the new literature. In this sense, the reading subjects contemporary literature needed to face were in fact quite ambiguous. On the one hand, as a political concept *the masses* is a revolutionary subjectivity; contemporary literature not only has to serve the masses, it also must accept reeducation from the masses. Yet on the other hand, as a cultural concept *the reader* is a product of some sort of traditional culture that not only is not charged with meeting some political demand but also departs widely from the May Fourth notion of the reader. Hence, the reeducation of the reader was one of the major tasks of contemporary literature, and its intention was to fashion a new type of reader from this reeducation process. This is to say, the task was to fashion a new cultural community that was political and cultural at both an emotional and a moral level. Only with this understanding are we able to enter the core of contemporary literature: in some sense, contemporary literature was always entangled with the masses and the reader in its efforts to reform and be reformed. In this process we can see the recalibration of forces.

An example will help explain the function of reeducation more clearly. In discussing the culture of Yan'an, many researchers have noted the *yang'ge* form.[71] As Zhu Hongzhao has noted, "the traditional yang'ge was to be 'vented' [*nao*] . . . to vent the yang'ge was to discharge wild village sexual passion. . . .

---

69. Benedict Anderson, *Imagined Communities: Reflections on the Origin and Spread of Nationalism* (London: Verso, 1983). See in particular chapters 2 and 3.

70. Li Oufan, "Wan Qing wenhua, wenxue yu xiandai xing," 56.

71. Tr.: The *yang'ge* is a northern form of folk song. In the Maoist period it became a type of loyalty dance. But in the Yan'an period, it was one among many folk forms of singing and dancing collectively.

In comparison to the 'wildness' of traditional yang'ge, revolutionary yang'ge was 'civilized.'"[72] We can perhaps understand this civilized nature in two ways. First is that it eliminated any hint of sex, including the way performers move their bodies. Eliminating pornography was one basic demand for reform that politics made of popular culture. Second, the narrative content of the yang'ge was increasingly related to reality, which helped to attract audiences. Most of the audiences at the time had been trained in the old-style yang'ge; that is to say, they were produced by the old form [of cultural consumption]. The question that interests us is, how were they retrained to become readers for new culture? On the one hand, the government here played a major role in its monopolization of the market, which was one of the major reasons for the success of this retraining. On the other hand, the new narrative content also very possibly produced a certain effect of estrangement, which allowed these readers to embrace enthusiastically a new take on older styles. These reasons will be addressed more fully in my discussion of the market below.

Yet such simple forms as that of the yang'ge cannot really explain completely the problem of the reader; in some more complexly structured forms, such as a novel, the reader can become far more ambiguous. That is, in the end was it contemporary literature that reeducated the reader, or was it the reader who reformed contemporary literature? As we have seen above in the discussion of the creative process that informed the writing of *Chronicles of the Lüliang Heroes* and Zhi Xia's *Guerrillas on the Railways*, the readers' transformation meant that certain aspects of legend from older literary traditions were suppressed; yet by the same token, the revival or liberated resurrection of the legendary in texts also is related to changes in the readers. This change was a result of time, and it was also related to space. What I mean by time is the fact that after 1949, the war started to become part of revolutionary history and was no longer a current event. When history becomes an object of consumption, it naturally comes to be related to the introduction of the reader, which after 1949 means the urbanite.

The formation of modern Chinese urban society in some sense is related to the transmission of popular literature from the late Qing period onward. That is to say, this popularized literature created its own readers, and at the same time these readers also constructed modern popular literature and offered it a sort of Chinese pedestrian-level imaginary of modernity. China's

---

72. Zhu Hongzhao, *Yan'an—Shenghuo zhong de lishi* [Yan'an: History in everyday life] (Guilin: Guangxi shida chubanshe, 2007), 123–53. Subsequent citations are to this page range.

urban and rural people already had a certain blood-level relationship with one another, one of whose symbols was the fact that they all shared an enjoyment for literature. This is what we often call popular literature, which fashioned an urban and rural audience identity out of local operas, spoken storytelling, text reading, and oral transmission. So when *Chronicles* was serially published in 1945 in Chongqing's *New China Daily* [Xinhua ribao] it produced a huge impact. One reason was because of the episodic form, which not only awakened the reader identity of rural people but also awakened this identity in urban people. Hence, in the process of reading popular literature, both rural and urban people not only shared an enjoyment for "scholar and beauty" stories, but also for heroic knight-errant narratives.[73] After 1949, the flourishing of revolutionary popular literature was intimately related to the prior creation of this reader.

However, with regard to contemporary literature, how do you differentiate between a person's political and cultural identities? Or how do you deal with the relationship between the masses and readers? This has been a very difficult issue to unravel. Xiao Yemu's short story, "Between My Wife and Me" ("Women fufu zhijian"), was a relatively early work that took on this question. One of the wife's anxieties is that those things she thinks belong to bourgeois society—such as permed hair, lipstick, and so on—at the same time are embraced by the proletariat ("Among those female workers, quite a few wore makeup and lipstick, and many also had their hair permed in a 'bird nest style.'"[74]) These workers in some sense also have a different type of shared identity, which is as readers. They not only read revolutionary literature, they also read bourgeois and even traditional literature. In this sense, it is actually impossible to differentiate between the cultural identities of the so-called worker and urbanite. For this reason, how to alter a person's cultural identity—that is, as a reader—was a question that was taken up consistently by and in Chinese revolutionary cultural production, particularly after the revolution[ary forces] entered the cities. What this was related to, of course, was the problem of hegemony.

After 1949, there emerged, particularly in the cities, a large-scale readjustment of the market that also announced the entry of the state into the urban

---

73. Tr.: "Scholar and beauty" is a type of narrative popular in the Ming and Qing dynasties. As its name suggests, it tells tales (which usually have a happy ending) of the romantic love between a scholar and a lady, who after overcoming many obstacles end up together.

74. Xiao Yemu, "Women fufu zhijian" [Between my wife and me] (Peking: Renmin wenxue, 1950) 1, 11:37–45.

areas. This readjustment—for example, in Shanghai—first was expressed as a cleaning up of the entertainment industries, including the elimination of brothels.[75] At the same time, this readjustment started to extend to the reading market. For example, in 1955 the state formally issued a document titled "State Council Instructions on How to Deal with Antirevolutionary, Obscene, and Preposterous Books, Magazines, and Pictures." In these instructions, the state not only clearly stipulated the manner in which the market should be readjusted ("it must proceed through the combined efforts of political mobilization and administrative implementation"), but it also stipulated the appropriate measures to be taken, such as banning, clearing, and preserving. Insofar as each type of content was concerned, "those books and journals that are extremely antirevolutionary, or those pictures that depict sex acts must all be banned." However, those martial arts materials that concern revenge, outlandish things, and so on also should be cleared away—which actually just meant they could no longer be published. And naturally, "those general descriptions of good knights-errant" should be preserved and kept.[76] This document was quite obviously the product of multisided negotiations that included new culture intellectuals. It concerned all types of literature that had flourished from the late Qing onward, including such modern popular genres as what was called butterfly fiction.[77] Actually, already in 1948 Guo Moruo had included [for elimination] "sexy, mystical, martial art, and detective" fiction in "the general category of pornographic culture" and "the standard feudal literature ... which appeals only to base tastes and for profit making."[78]

Opinions varied about how to evaluate popular novels of the early twentieth century, including those written in episodic form. On July 11, 1945, Zhang Henshui published an article titled "Martial Arts Novels and Subaltern Society" [Wuxia xiaoshuo yu xiaceng shehui] in the *New China Daily* in which,

---

75. Xiong Yuezhi, Zhou Wu, eds., *Shanghai—A History of the Years of Transformation of a City*, (Shanghai: Shanghai shudian chubanshe, 2007), 515.

76. "Guowuyuan guanyu chuli fandongde, yinhuide, huangdande shukan tuhua de zhishi" [State Council instructions on how to deal with antirevolutionary, obscene, and preposterous books, magazines, and pictures], in *Zhongguo dangdai wenxueshi. shiliao xuan* [Contemporary Chinese literature, selected materials], ed. Hong Zicheng (Wuhan: Changjiang Wenyi Chubanshe, 2002), 1:280.

77. Tr.: Butterfly fiction was a designation given in the 1920s and 1930s to mass-appeal fiction that was, from the perspective of elites, deemed less worthy, less culturally important, and thus less relevant to true literature. It is equivalent in many ways to what is called low-brow fiction.

78. Guo Moruo, "Su fandong wenyi" [Sweep away antirevolutionary culture] in *Zhongguo dangdai wenxueshi. shiliao xuan* [Contemporary Chinese literature, selected materials], ed. Hong Zicheng (Wuhan: Changjiang Wenyi Chubanshe, 2002), 1:97.

on the one hand, he expressed deep dissatisfaction with the state of martial arts novels—for example, their feudal thinking was quite overwhelming; their fantasies departed too much from reality, and so on. Yet on the other hand, he also noted that martial arts, mystical, and historical novels were all quite popular among subaltern groups, even though love stories were only popular in women's circles. In Zhang Henshui's opinion, martial arts novels only trained people in an "obscure version of heroism," while at the same time they "spouted about the inequalities among people." Of course, Zhang's attitude was very clear; he maintained that even if these novels were "the hobbies of subaltern groups," they nevertheless needed to be "thrown into the trash heap" because they distracted from "educating the masses." What is raised in Zhang's article is precisely the question regarding the relationship between the nature of the episodic novel and the nature of popular literature.[79]

On September 5, 1949, the *Literature and art newspaper* [*Wenyi bao*] held a forum to which they invited writers from the Beijing and Tianjin area who used to write episodic novels published in newspapers in installments. The summary notes from the forum on the topic of "petty urbanite readers" were published in the first issue of the first volume of the paper. The forum on the one hand firmly supported the new culture direction of popular revolutionary literature, criticized the base taste and crudeness of old vulgar literature, and so on. On the other hand, Zhao Shuli indicated, "we should use whatever form can be accepted and enjoyed by the masses," so "we must preserve the good things from the old, create new forms, be sure that all topics are related to current reality, and educate the masses." Ding Ling's critical attitude was even more acute, but she also emphasized that it was necessary to "do research on the interests of the readers," because doing so means "keeping the masses in mind." On the question of how to create new popular literature, there was no unanimity at the forum; it was decided that "in the future more wide-ranging and deeper discussions are needed."[80] The problem of the masses and readers clearly continued to trouble the selection of narrative form in post-1949 contemporary literature.

Another aspect of this issue revolves around the state's consolidation of the market, which, even by 1950, elicited a certain amount of dissatisfaction on the part of readers. Ding Ling's article, "Stepping into the New Era: On the Former Interests of Intellectuals and Worker-Peasant-Soldier Culture"

---

79. Zhang Henshui, "Wuxia xiaoshuo yu xiaceng shehui" [Martial arts novels and subaltern society], *New China Daily*, July 11, 1945.

80. Editorial statement, *Wenyi bao*, vol. 2, November 1950.

[Kuadao xinde shidai lai—tan zhishifenzi de jiu xingqu yu gongnongbing wenyi] was in essence a reply to the readers' letters addressed to *Wenyi bao*.[81] In her article, we can observe that the majority of readers complained that worker-peasant-soldier culture was monotonous, dry, lacking in cultural sensibility, and too anxious, to the point that most workers did not like to read it. They even thought that "these books are merely for entertaining the tastes of the progressives." What they wanted was to "read a few relaxing books"; they "like[d] Ba Jin's novels as well as those of Feng Yuqi and Zhang Henshui; [they] enjoy[ed] cartoon books that depict scenes of engagements in battle," and so on. Ding Ling's response of course was meant to plead the case for worker-peasant-soldier literature and art, yet she also did not avoid the fact that these works "were not yet very mature." In Ding Ling's ideal, contemporary literature needed to reject "the vulgar and outmoded butterfly literature style" while also distancing itself from "the revolutionary culture of the immediate past, as well as Europeanized styles." The new form needed to be more like *Chronicles of Lüliang Heroes, Rhymes of Li Youcai, New Heroic Sons and Daughters, Wang Gui and Li Xiangxiang*; "those forms that were sloughed off from older ones and were then elevated." And DingLing did not forget the existence of readers—this expansive group, which included not only "the strata of petty urbanite" but actually also included the worker-peasant-soldier category. Behind this reader stood the masses, an entity that lent legitimacy to the politics of the time. In this sense, on the question of form, contemporary literature already indicated a willingness to compromise with readers.

Thus the reader was from the outset an important conceptual constraint on contemporary literature: on the one hand, readers needed to be educated; on the other hand, readers' reading preferences needed to be respected. This of course brings in the problem of the market. We often deal with socialism as if it were an antimarket state form; to be sure, on the question of culture, the state continuously was deeply involved and even often interfered in the market. However, the consolidated market was still a market, and for this reason the state still needed to offer cultural products that would sell on the market.

At the time, there was another opinion on this matter. For example, in July 1963, the editorial comment included in the first issue of the new journal, *Story Time* (*Gushi hui*), noted "these stories are written in easy-to-understand language, so they are more suited to the tastes of the masses. With these easy-

---

81. Ding Ling, "Kuadao xinde shidai lai—tan zhishifenzi de jiu xingqu yu gongnongbing wenyi" [Stepping into the new era: On the former interests of intellectuals and worker-peasant-soldier culture], *Wenyi bao*, vol. 2, November 1950.

to-read materials, we help expand space for spreading socialist ideas." If we render this opinion in different words, we might say that contemporary literature was a type of antimarket product that affirmed its own marketability.

In reality, after 1949, there was a very widespread mass culture in China that not only received systematic support (such as through mass cultural palaces, and so on) but that also created varied cultural forms. These forms included local operas, storytelling, and so on. To take *Story Time* as an example, the first issue in July 1963 sold over 200,000 copies, and from 1963 to 1964, there were over twenty-four issues published that sold over 6.12 million copies.[82] It is clear that the huge group of readers that includes subaltern groups structured the existing market of the time. For contemporary literature to enter this market ("to expand space for spreading socialist ideas," as *Story Time* put it), the reading habits of these mass readers needed to be respected. That meant a popular form was needed to tell one's story. At the same time, literature inevitably also became an object of consumption. I think this is one big reason for the rise of revolutionary popular literature. Because of the consolidation of the market by the state, heroic legends became a primary form for revolutionary popular literature. As for detective, historical, mystical, and romantic literature, and so on: none of these completely disappeared, but rather, elements from them entered into heroic legends in one way or another. Actually, in novels such as *Tracks in the Snowy Forest* and in *Guerrillas on the Railways*, it is easy to find traces of these latter narrative forms.

This is not to say that, due to the influence of the readers, contemporary literature was thoroughly popularized or marketized. Educating the masses was still an important task: not only was this a state ideological demand, but it was also the desire of intellectuals to transmit new culture. For this reason, in reality, revolutionary popular literature became a site of negotiation and compromise for a number of different social forces. These included state ideology as well as intellectuals' new culture. At the same time, such literature also included the desires of the masses or readers.

Supplementary to and beyond the problem of popularized form was the occasional emergence of various traditional tastes. For example, in traditional Chinese narratives, the bandit is a historically murky and unclear concept. The bandit is not only entangled with the forests, but this figure is also of-

---

82. Shen Guofan, *Jiedu "Gushi hui"—yiben zhongguo qikan de shenhua* [Reading Story Time: A Chinese journal legend] (Shanghai: Shanghai Shehui Kexue Chubanshe, 2003), 20.

ten intertwined with the knight-errant.[83] For this reason, cases of extralegal justice [pursued by bandits] are often thoroughly part of the conditions for knightly deeds [to be accomplished], even while dynastic court figures and itinerant bandits sometimes jointly and sometimes separately pursue action. This type of narrative particularity is undoubtedly bound up with the identity of readers. Once those who read are able to distance themselves from their own environments, the rivers and lakes [where bandits roam] could become an arena for legends and novelty, through which a sort of never-never land imaginary could be fulfilled. However, once the reader returns to his or her everyday life—in the village or the city—quotidian life could feel threatened by bandits. This complex identification not only might lead to an ideological revision of the meaning of the bandit, but the bandit figure itself, in the process of this ideological revisioning, could also be fragmented into several identities: bandit, dweller in the green forests, knight-errant, kidnapper, and so on. From this fragmentation, the reader might derive a certain margin of safety.

But when we get to the articulation of Chinese revolutionary history, the matter becomes even more complicated. This complexity resides in the way in which class struggle structured the core of all ideology; using this type of perspective to narrate Chinese history, the characters in *The Water Margin* obviously became the models for peasant uprisings and were easily incorporated into the narration of Chinese revolutionary history. This view was thoroughly expounded by Mao in his "Letter to Yang Shaoxuan and Qi Yanming" ("Gei Yang Shaoxuan, Qi Yanming de xin").[84] Moreover, in the unfolding of the Chinese revolution, land bandits had already been incorporated into the chapters on revolutionary history, with the most famous of these being the Wang Zuo and Yuan Wencai gangs of the Jinggangshan period.[85] Actually, some of the

---

83. Gong Pengcheng has offered a fairly detailed study on the different uses of the notion of *xia* (knight-errant) in classical literature (*Da xia* [The great knight-errant] [Taipei: Taiwan Jinguan Chunbanshe, 1987]).

84. Mao Zedong, "Gei Yang Shaoxuan, Qi Yanming de xin" [Letter to Yang Shaoxuan and Qi Yanming], in *Mao Zedong wenji* [Collection of Mao Zedong's writings] (Beijing: Renmin chubanshe, 1996), 3:88.

85. Mao Tse-tung, "Struggle in the Chingkang Mountains," in *Selected Works of Mao Tse-tung* (Peking: Foreign Language Press, 1965), 1:84–85. Tr.: Jinggangshan was an early base for Mao's faction of the Communist Party after the 1927 White Terror that split the Party from the Guomindang (GMD, the Nationalist party) and that led to the retreat of the Communists from the urban areas. It was known as a bandit-infested area, and the Wang Zuo and Yuan Wencai gangs became famous for providing succor to Mao and his followers.

most noted leaders of the early Chinese Communist Party—such as Mao, Li Dazhao, Peng Pai, Liu Zhidan, and others—recognized the important function of secret societies in rural society and defied Central Committee decisions of the time by incorporating these various and complex forces into the revolutionary project.[86] However, the clarity of this concrete experience cannot explain why, after a gap of several decades, contemporary literature took up the problem of the narrative and imaginary of bandits.

Perhaps it is precisely because mainstream culture of the time (state political and new cultural) suppressed martial arts novels that some core elements of this type of novel then quietly infiltrated revolutionary popular literature, successfully allowing bandit and knight-errant figures to attain a new culturally explanatory resonance. In this explanatory presence, the bandit figure was split into two and to different degrees entered Party politics: one type was the evil hegemon, such as Xu Damabang and Zuo Shan Diao in *Tracks in the Snowy Forest*, who terrorized the mountains and who, in fact, had already become members of the Guomindang antirevolutionary faction. The struggle with this type of bandit in essence just continued the "cases of extralegal justice" type of stories popular from traditional narratives. Another type of bandit was closer to the *Water Margin* heroes and good guys, such as Li Shuangsi in [Liang Bin's] *Keep the Red Flag Flying* [Hongqi pu]. This latter type of bandit was the only type that became a real narrative object of revolutionary popular literary.

This type of bandit took some features from traditional forest outlaws who might evoke reading memories in some readers (and authors); at the same time, with the entry of ideological factors, the bandits' particularities of class resistance as identifying or behavioral markers were strengthened, all of which gave these new characters an intimate relationship to contemporary readers. From this amalgam was structured a simultaneously traditional and modern reading practice, which also regulated the margin of safety between the space of the narrative and the place of the reader.

Some researchers have spoken of this phenomenon in terms of the incorporation of these characters into traditional folk culture and have determined that the artistic attractiveness of these characters derive from sources in the folk grass roots.[87] This is not incorrect. However, we should at the same time

---

86. Mark Selden, *China in Revolution: The Yenan Way Revisited* (New York: M. E. Sharpe, 1995, 1971), 26–27.

87. Chen Sihe, "Minjian de fuchen: Cong zhanzheng dao wenge wenxueshi de yige jieshi," [The resurrection of the folk: An explanation of literary history from the war to the Cultural

see that characters of this kind—whether Liu Baye of *Bitter Flowers* [Ku caihua] or Li Shuangsi of *Keep the Red Flag Flying*, or Wu Qi of *The Little Town in the Spring and Fall* [Xiaocheng chunqiu]—are not in any sense the main protagonists of the novels; they are at most second-level heroes who need to be led and reeducated. So if we see the novel as a totality, then inside the text itself there is an intertextuality between stories and among characters that structures all sorts of complicated productive relationships with one another. It is only within these complex relationships that meaning of the characters and the stories can be mutually produced.

Surrounding these characters are always some more top-level types of heroes. Liu Baye in *Bitter Flowers* is always seen as a model from folk culture, and indeed, in contrast to Liu, the novel's other hero, Yu Dehai, is far more murky. However, Liu Baye is after all just a passing figure in the novel; to pluck this character out of the totality of the novel clearly cannot explain either the success or the failure of the narrative. Moreover, in the novel, the genuine success, or that which strikes one most about the depiction of Liu, comes in the episode on the execution of the platoon leader Ma. In the narrative of this episode we can see how politics reeducates the bandits—that is, it is only in the text about Yu that Liu's textuality can also be produced. If we leave Yu aside, then Liu's significance cannot be constituted autonomously. For this reason, the narrative success of Liu can only be accomplished in his mutual interactions with Yu, that is, intertextually.

It is unnecessary to discuss this issue within the ever-expanding abstract concept of the folk. On a more concrete level, we perhaps can see this intertextual phenomenon as a complex entanglement between revolutionary politics and vagabond culture. From one angle, Chinese revolutionary politics never abandoned the incorporation of vagabond culture into its mobilizational compositions and intentions. From another angle, it also never abandoned its goal of reforming this vagabond culture, a reform that was an extension of a traditional political desire for centralization, on the one hand, and was also part of the goal of organizing China into a modern society, on the other hand. It is therefore both traditional and modern. In addition, when revolutionary politics began to appropriate vagabond culture into its own mobilizational compositions, it inevitably was forced to put on display the full and flourishing range of elements of this culture so as to awaken the readers'

Revolution," in *Ershi shiji Zhongguo wenxueshi lun* [On the history of twentieth-century Chinese literature], ed. Wang Xiaoming (Shanghai: Dongfang Chuban Zhongxin, 2003).

interest. Yet when revolutionary politics tried to reform this culture, it would also need to meet the approval of readers: that is, it had to awaken in readers a certain rejection of the threat of bandits. This fear and rejection at the same time also subconsciously constituted another expectation on the part of the reader. This expectation is twofold: full of interest while containing rejection. This dual reader expectation is precisely the tactic used by traditional cases of extralegal justice and knight-errant narratives.

To reread this type of literature is to discover that reform [*gaizao*] is full of narrative tactics. The characteristic of these tactics is that the reformer and those being reformed are always under the control of the same cultural or reader expectation. In these types of narratives, it is extremely easy for the reformer to enter into the reader's view, and because the reformer is always stronger than those being reformed, reform itself is legitimated. However, the danger of such narration is that reform can be controlled by the culture of those being reformed, leaving it impossible for reform to completely communicate where its own significance or goals might lie. Hence, one avenue of possible subversion of revolutionary popular literature occurs in the new explanation of the figure of the reformer. This is where the significance of the character Teacher Jia in *Keep the Red Flag Flying* resides. Jia Xiangnong as a character is neither like Yu Dehai of *Bitter Flowers* nor the same as Lao Wu in *Chronicles of the Lüliang Heroes* because Jia is an intellectual, and therefore he is entirely outside the control of the cultural system of those being reformed. That is to say that Teacher Jia's strength derives not only from some sort of abstract theory of reform, but also and more important, it derives from the fact that he is already modern [by virtue of being an intellectual]. Hence, he is not only a reformer, he is also the one who summons others to be reformed; in being summoned, those awaiting reform themselves can experience a process of maturation. Therefore, other characters are all constrained as secondary figures in the novel by having their stories demoted in relation to Jia's. In this way, popular revolutionary literature can become a sort of substitute for the old-style bildungsroman. Indeed, the reformer/reformed narrative model of *Keep the Red Flag Flying* gradually became a mainstream model, such as in the subsequent Peking opera, *Azalea Mountain* [Dujuan shan].

It is obvious that the process of narrating the bandit is also one in which different forces are shown to be competing with one another. In this process, the reader and the market are both extremely important factors. Because of these factors, contemporary literature continually searched for popular narrative methods, which both were within the discipline of narratology and fit in a revival of tradition. At the same time, efforts in contemporary literature to reform the popular novel never stopped. Here, then, in revolutionary popular literature, revolution and popularity were functions of one another. At the same time, they also were in antagonistic struggle with one another. When popularity overwhelmed revolution, the flavor of old novels would come streaming out; a typical example of this was Ouyang Shan's *Three Family Lane* [Sanjia xiang] or *Bitter Struggle* [Kutou]. Yet when revolution suppressed popularity, a different sort of narrative method needed to be found. This is where the origin of *Keep the Red Flag Flying* can be seen as a precise portent of the return of contemporary literature to its May Fourth new culture traditions. This is of course not to say that this return to May Fourth traditions completely erased the popular aspects of revolutionary literature; to the contrary, the traces of the popular were impossible to erase, and this is where one major difference between modern [May Fourth] and contemporary literature lies.

IV. Why or How to Renarrate Revolutionary History

The materials for revolutionary popular literature are overwhelmingly fashioned from the renarration of revolutionary history. Huang Ziping has proposed that we substitute the concept of revolutionary historical novels for the concept of revolutionary popular literature because these novels are concerned with "telling history."[88] Naturally, the extension of Huang's concept is wider in scope, as a number of novels—such as *Keep the Red Flag Flying*—that are impossible to incorporate into the revolutionary popular literature category are central to Huang's category of revolutionary historical novel.

My interest, however, is in why, after 1949, the renarration of revolutionary history became such an important creative trend. This trend was evident not only in the production of novels, but also in the appearance of the narrative form of revolutionary memoirs, which indexed the high level of importance placed on this issue by state politics by its direct intervention in this publishing trend. The process of the writing and publication of many of the revolutionary memoirs makes clear that the ones published earliest had the greatest impact. The earliest, then, started to be published in continuous serial form in May 1957 by the journal *Red Flag Flying* (*Hongqi piaopiao*).[89] The publication of *Red Flag Flying* was not only due to the fact that "there are authors who

---

88. Huang, *Geming, lishi, xiaoshuo*.
89. This publication instigated a huge fashion for the publication and writing of revolutionary memoirs.

enthusiastically embrace revolutionary struggle and heroic figures, who have not had sufficient time to write their works; but also, because the writing of a relatively complete chronicle or novel of heroic figures or to reflect upon the revolutionary struggle all require a certain amount of time to accomplish." For this reason, *Red Flag Flying* is "a journal that specializes in the description of heroic figures and works on the revolutionary struggle . . . ; we publish long or short articles of indeterminate length. We publish chronicles, stories and novels, memoirs, and general interviews."[90]

More important, this publication satisfied state political requirements in a timely fashion. The May 1957 editorial statement in the first issue of the magazine, in fact, very appositely cited an April 8 editorial published in the *People's Daily*: "Before the triumph of the Chinese revolution, Chinese Communist Party members and many revolutionaries were unafraid of being executed or of being imprisoned; they left their homes and roamed all over the country, not to seek fame and fortune and not for enjoyment and entertainment: their only concerns were the survival of the nation and the catastrophe visited upon the people. In pursuit of revolutionary success, they sacrificed themselves; they were diligent and they suffered, and when those in front fell, those behind immediately stood to take up the fight. If the revolution failed, they picked up the banner and raised it high again."[91]

This type of political description of revolutionary history in actuality came to define the standard form for writing the orthodox history of the revolution. In their statement, the editors of *Red Flag Flying* explained further the importance and current significance of this type of history:

> In the revolutionary history of our people, there is much to sing of and much to cry over, many traces of things that light the earth and the ghostly tears that soak it. But all of this is quite unfamiliar to the youth of today. Hence, they need to become acquainted with the revolutionary history of our people and to derive some spiritual strength from the heroic figures of this history so as to construct a beautiful socialist project and protect our great nation. For this, we need to preserve the indomitable spirit that dares to overcome difficulty and that possesses boundless loyalty to the people's revolutionary project.[92]

90. Editorial statement, *Hongqi piaopiao* [Red flag flying], May 1957, 1.
91. Ibid.
92. Ibid.

Adding "Chinese" or "the people's" to modify "revolution" clearly is the result of a carefully thought out and calculated grammatical structure. In this grammar, class interests have been transformed into the people's interests, while the revolutionary war has also been transformed into a national war—which at the same time marks the significance of the contrast between justice and injustice, which in turn is transformed into the structurally required legitimizing of this particular form of nation-state.

The grammatical secret of this requirement was already embedded in Mao Zedong's September 30, 1948, text, written for the inscription on the Monument to the People's Heroes [to be erected in Tian'anmen Square]: "Immortal Glory to the People's Heroes who have given their lives over the last three years in the People's War of Liberation and the People's Revolution! Immortal Glory to the People's Heroes who have given their lives in the last thirty years in the People's War of Liberation and the People's Revolution! Immortal Glory to the People's Heroes who, since the year 1840s, have given their lives in the many struggles to resist the enemy, domestic and foreign, to strive for the independence of the nation and the freedom of the people!"[93] In this chronological narrative, the Chinese revolution is neither three years old nor thirty, but is actually one hundred years old, which precisely coincides with the temporality of China's modern (*jindai/xiandai*) history.[94] Hence, in this temporal narration of history not only are a class, the people, the nation, and the state efficiently conflated, but the revolution that was instigated from this combination of forces is evidence of its modernity. More important still, the universal significance of the revolution and the new society born thereof is effectively structured from within this type of historical narrative. This universality not only guarantees the power that emerges from the legitimacy of this historical narrative, but it also guarantees that this new China is not only revolutionary but also national and historical. This grammar cannot be seen merely as the

---

93. Mao Zedong, "Draft for Inscription on the Monument to People's Heroes," in *The Writings of Mao Zedong, 1949–1976*, ed. Michael Y. M. Kau and John K. Leung (New York: M. E. Sharpe, 1986), 9.

94. Tr.: Conventionally, *jindai* (meaning modern) spans the Opium Wars (1840) through 1919, the beginning of the May Fourth period; *xiandai* (also meaning modern) covers the period from 1919 to 1949. The point Mao makes, and that Cai is underscoring, is that the century from the 1840s to the 1940s is an anti-imperialist revolutionary century. This periodization has been brought into question in recent discussions of Chinese history that attempt to separate imperialism, capitalism, the West, and other such hegemonic categories from the understanding of China and modernity.

class calculus of the power of new democracy; to the contrary, it consolidates and preserves national elements in the revolution. Actually, of all the renarrations of revolutionary history, the majority—whose influence were largest—were those novels on the War of Resistance against Japan. Clearly, this is related to their popularity among readers.

However, these historical narratives were not merely a way to commemorate happy and sad incidents. All nation-states have to renarrate or restructure their establishment myths, which always include some version of an origin story (that provides legitimacy to the national state); at the same time, this myth needs to become the common sense of the people or a deep national spirit and the symbol of the truth of the nation. This is the modern myth, which accords with the people's memories of history and at the same time resides in the historical unconscious.[95] This modern myth can never avoid the intervention of state politics or state ideology. The dual aspect of the modern myth—memory and ideology—demonstrates the complex demands upon the nation-state of a variety of national imaginaries. On the one hand, the national people must be political; that is, they must be a people in the political sense, for only then can they structure an imagined political community. On the other hand, this national people must also be historical; that is, they must be a people in the cultural sense. Hence, in the imaginary, there is a necessity to revive the people's memories of history, from which can be derived their historical or cultural identity. The process of producing this modern myth clearly is a story that must be articulated by any modern nation-tate. It is only in the articulation of this type of story that "I" or "we" can be represented as having a shared modern history.

In this sense, China's revolutionary history is obviously a basic element in the modern myth of China. For this reason, the renarration of revolutionary history was aimed at re-creating this modern myth, in the process of which revolutionary history was not only romanticized and allegorized but also highly ideologized. This myth was thus not only modern, it was national; that is, it was a national myth or a myth of the nation. This myth expressed a certain national truth or a state truth. And through this narrativization, not only did state power derive legitimacy, but it also effectively restructured the imagined political community. Clearly, the modern ideological significance of this myth—including the imaginary of the modern system it projected—to one

---

95. James Oliver Robertson, *American Myth, American Reality* (New York: Hill and Wang, 1981), 3.

degree or another attempted to vigorously structure the people in a political sense, so that even in many novels and stories written by [non-Han] minority peoples there are such ideological traces, albeit perhaps to a smaller degree. Examples of the latter include Xu Huaizhong's novel *Our Young Love* [Women bozhong aiqing], or Li Qiao's novel *The Smiling Jinsha River* [Huanxiao de jinshajiang].

The process of renarrating revolutionary history also helped incorporate the articulation of male and female heroes. In the narratives of revolutionary popular novels, or the novels of revolutionary history, we can see that the stories are not just about heroes, but also that the fashioning of heroes is the most important concern. The emergence of these fictional or historical heroes turned revolutionary history into a formalistic exercise that exhibited all the marks of stereotypicality. More important, it turned historical literature into a symbol that could more easily take up the burden of creating metaphors of truth for the nation. The serial creation of hero figures was thus not merely about readers' consumption or to satisfy the desires of readers for imaginaries of legends of justice and new realms of experience; more important, this creation could take up the responsibility for propagating the national truth for an entirely new era.

In this sense, if we see 1949–66 as China's era of industrialization (an era of industrialization that insinuated itself into every possible arena of society, including rural villages and their cooperatization movements), then in Jean Baudrillard's terms, this is an era that requires the large-scale production of heroes: "the painful, heroic Age of Production."[96] To "derive spirit and strength from the figures of heroes" was, [in the words of the editorial statement of the *Red Flag Flying*], aimed at "constructing the beautiful project of socialism and protecting our great nation. For this, we need to preserve the indomitable spirit that dares to overcome difficulty and that possesses boundless loyalty to the people's revolutionary project." This "beautiful socialist project" clearly included modernization, which was the industrializing quest of the state. I think that many Chinese cultural imaginaries are connected in one degree or another to the features of this industrializing era, and many issues in contemporary China are at different levels connected to the imaginaries of this era of industrialization.

However, the modern myth produced in the process of the renarration of revolutionary history also has another and perhaps even more important

---

96. Jean Baudrillard, *The Consumer Society: Myths and Structures* (London: Sage, 1998), 83.

narrative function, which we can understand as a narrative about the significance of human existence. When Anderson's discussion of nationalism entered Chinese historical discourse, it incited a large number of debates. His discussion of the relation of the nation-state to the "rebirth" of the individual can help open a new space of discussion: "With the ebbing of religious belief, the suffering which belief in part composed did not disappear. Disintegration of paradise: nothing makes fatality more arbitrary. Absurdity of salvation: nothing makes another style of continuity more necessary. What then was required was a secular transformation of fatality into continuity, contingency into meaning."[97] Actually, already in 1944, Mao, in his eulogy for [his bodyguard] Zhang Side, articulated the problem in this way: "All men must die, but death can vary in its significance. The ancient Chinese writer Szuma Chien [Sima Qian] said, 'Though death befalls all men alike, it may be weightier than Mount Tai or lighter than a feather.' To die for the people is weightier than Mount Tai, but to work for the fascists and die for the exploiters and oppressors is lighter than a feather. Comrade Chang Szu-teh [Zhang Side] died for the people, and his death is indeed weightier than Mount Tai."[98]

In the discourse of China's contemporary history, the state, revolution, and the people are usually one concept with three components. This is why the kind of densely teleological modern linguistic prepositional structure indicated by "for (*wei*) . . ." was so temporarily fashionable in China's mainland: in this structure is embedded the ethical response to and proof of the significance of death and revival [for the state, revolution, and the people]. Naturally, this death is not limited to any one individual's physical being or significance; rather, it serves to suppress temporarily at least any practical desire or need that could arise from the individual. So the April 8, 1957, *People's Daily* editorial had to specifically emphasize:

> Before the triumph of the Chinese revolution, Chinese Communist Party members and many revolutionaries were unafraid of being executed or of being imprisoned; they left their homes and roamed all over the country, not to seek fame and fortune and not for enjoyment and entertainment: their only concerns were the survival of the nation and the catastrophe visited on the people. In pursuit of revolutionary success, they sacrificed themselves; they were diligent and they suffered, and when those in front

97. Anderson, *Imagined Communities*, 11.
98. Mao Tse-tung, "Serve the People," 3:227.

fell, those behind immediately stood up to take up the fight. If the revolution failed, they picked up the banner and raised it high again.

This political statement is at the same time an ethical one; even more pointedly, it is a description of the existential significance of death and rebirth. After becoming the inscription to the Monument to the People's Heroes, this formula of death and rebirth could effectively be narrativized. At the same time, through the telling of stories, one could locate the significance of the relationship between the individual and the nation-state.

For example, in Sun Jingrui's novel *Planting the Red Flag on Damen Island* [Hongqi chashang Damendao], there is the following description: a small atoll called Damen Island, because it is on the front lines of the [Taiwan] straits, has attracted the concern and attention of the whole country. It thus continuously receives "sympathy letters and packages from people all over our country." In one of these packages, there is a "transistor radio that is made ingeniously." With this radio, not only is Damen Island connected to the state-owned Pioneer Steel Factory on the mainland, but it also connects Damen Island to the Korean War's Battle of Triangle Hill. This spatial connection is a perfect metaphor for the linkages between individuals and the nation-state, as it is in this type of metaphor that the individual's death or rebirth attains significance. This is quite evident in the speech given by the novel's battalion leader, Xu Wenlie: "Even though we are stationed as guards on this tiny ocean island, we are nevertheless absolutely not isolated; behind us there is the strength of 600 million others."[99] This kind of detail—which is really a narrative method—is certainly not coincidental in the literature of the 1949–66 period. I think it forces us to consider why in this period the concept or problem of isolation had to be forcefully suppressed in the stories of the time. What was behind this suppression? Was it the formalistic narrative force of the national imaginary?

At the time, state politics absolutely realized the significance of death and rebirth, and for this reason, heroes gradually moved from history into the present. In 1965, China Youth Publishers put out a series of booklets titled *Stories of Young Heroes*, which collected the stories of eleven "young heroes for the present." In Luo Ruiqing's view, these "young heroes for the present" had "through the war era demonstrated qualities similar to those heroes [of the war era], they are all the most outstanding sons of daughters of our Chinese

---

99. Sun Jingrui, *Hongqi chashang damendao* [Planting the red flag on Damen Island] (Shanghai: Wenyi chubanshe, 1958). Tr.: Page numbers are not given.

people." Although these "young heroes have already died, which of course saddens us incredibly, yet the demands of the people's revolution for sacrifice are many. Nevertheless, their heroic images will live on in our hearts forever, and will tower in front of us. Their communist spirit is worth studying everywhere and forever." The significance of death and rebirth was in this way repeatedly evoked, and in this particular case, there was always the element of [heroes for the] state, revolution, and the people. Luo continues: "Let those imperialist beards have their daydreams! Let them shoot their sugar-coated bullets and play their games of peaceful evolution! History has already proven and will continue to prove that it will absolutely not be imperialism, the oppositional factions, modern revisionism, or other ghosts and snake spirits that will 'evolve' China's youth; rather, it will be China's youth, along with the world's revolutionary youth, who will, one by one and group by group, overthrow all corrupt people and reactionary fellows on this globe!"[100]

The earliest selection of the form for the renarration of revolutionary history by revolutionary popular literature was conditioned (or constrained) by the political nature of the masses, which required a popular method of articulation to complete the mobilization of subaltern society for the revolution. At the same time, this was also a product of the market and the readers, who demanded stories written in the form of legends to fulfill their consumption desires.

Yet in the process of renarrating revolutionary history, revolutionary popular literature very quickly exposed some discrepancies within state politics, or the modernity of the state. For example, in addition to the popularized forms of these stories, there were traditional elements that often consciously or unconsciously fashioned solitary heroes on whom readers could pin their traditional ideas of knights-errant, who seemed now to be resurrected. This is of course one reason revolutionary popular literature could be part of the consumer market for books. Yet in the discourse of Chinese literature from 1949 to 1966, simply depending on these old-style knights-errant was insufficient for the narrative purpose of completing the modern legend of the revolution. Not only could such old-style heroes revive a sort of individualism (often called heroic individualism), but this revival could very well pose obstacles to the realization of the rhetoric of collectivism. The conflict in rhetoric between the individual and the collective had already instigated a cer-

100. Luo Ruiqing, "Zhenzheng geming, chedi geming de yingxiong" [Real and complete revolutionary heroes], in *Qingnian yingxiong de gushi* [Stories of young heroes] (Beijing: Zhongguo Qingnian Chubanshe, 1965), 2:4.

tain vigilance in modern narratives, and for this reason, the narratives often provided a rational leader to guide these heroes so as to preserve the political correctness of their behavior and actions. The existence of these leaders thus is usually a form of constraint upon the greenwood heroes, even if the air of the grass roots in the stories can punch through the political constraints to become the primary protagonist for the consuming pleasure of the readers.

In his discussion of *Tracks in the Snowy Forest*, Li Yang quoted a critic of the time, whose opinion can give us the historical flavor of the conflict in rhetoric between the individual and the collective:

> We should understand that the most enthusiastic readers of *Tracks in the Snowy Forest* are the youth (this is true of the movie as well). Young people are in the process of growing, enhancing their knowledge, and the whole world to them is new and strange.... Yet, precisely for this reason, deficiencies in books (such as exaggerating the role played by any given individual; describing as an individual achievement what was really the achievement of those who relied upon the Party's leadership and the strength of the collective; depicting what was a struggle of the masses as merely an individual intervention) can give readers a mistaken sense through artistic persuasion of individual heroism in the place of the correct spirit of the times and of the expected new content. This is especially true for young readers. We should recognize that some of these deficiencies can incite a certain "superman" type of desire among some readers, which is of course not anywhere near the new spirit and new content we require.[101]

From today's vantage point, this critique appears crude and dogmatic. But the issue is that this crudeness and dogmatism derive from modernity, which not only emerges from state ideological political considerations but at the same time is rooted in the forms of industrialized society itself. Indeed, it is only in the environment of a large industrial society or a society seeking industrialization that there could be such a strong demand for organization. Hence, when we note the Chinese revolutionary rhetoric of realizing collectivism, aside from noting its relation to state politics and ideology, we must also see it as a product of modern industrialized society.

Of course, the problem does not end here. What a legend intends to open up is a realm of the new and the strange that at the same time becomes formalistic because of frequent use of a melodramatic story or plot. This realm

---

101. Quoted in Li Yang, *50–70 niandai Zhongguo wenxue zai jiedu*, 31.

of newness and strangeness and formalism satisfies the consumption desires of readers and also, in the reading process, can help shape the imaginary and self-recognition. But viewed from a different angle, this realm can also lead to the reseparation of ordinariness and strangeness. Because of the imaginary and self-recognition formed through reading, it is also possible to be attracted by an individual heroism that is potentially in great conflict with revolutionary history. That is to say, revolutionary history could very possibly be understood to be the task of a minority. Hence, how to turn the renarration of revolutionary history into a quotidian everyday? Or how to recombine the ordinary with the strange? These are the questions that contemporary literature was forced to face. Indeed, it is only in the everydayness of history that it is possible to genuinely articulate a national truth from which a powerful mobilizing and summoning force could be produced for the vast majority of the people.

More important still: the revolutionary popular literature that drew resources from old stories was also the pioneer in fashioning an essence for new heroes; this essence (or capacity) becomes evident at the first appearance of the character in the story. The environment or surroundings are merely the arena for the characters' demonstration of this essence (or capacity): it is merely a sort of stage. This type of articulation of an essence clearly cannot depict the growth or maturation of the individual or the nation, yet it is precisely this growth that modernity, including May Fourth new culture, needs to have as its narrative subject. This subject at the same time inevitably will also be of great concern to state politics because the growth of the individual or the nation can happen only under the required ideological educational tutelage, which in turn is informed by a certain historical consciousness. Under no circumstances can this happen in an autodidactical way. Hence, not only do the legendary aspects of revolutionary popular literature need to be dialectically readjusted, but those episodic stories that depend on fragments and units and that are mainly structured narratively in spatial terms clearly are rendered incapable of taking on the burden of narrativizing the education and maturation of individuals and the nation in historical time.

Actually, as early as 1954, Zhou Yang had already articulated a relatively complete but still somewhat murky plan for Chinese literature. In his ideal, contemporary literature could not just be a sort of traditional literature; rather, socialist realist literature needed to develop May Fourth literature, [and] it needed to continue the May Fourth new culture tradition to become an entirely new modern literature.¹⁰² Yet in fiction and particularly in novels, what in fact constituted the May Fourth tradition? Some scholars of modern literature, such as Wang Hui, have indicated that what can be called the Mao Dun tradition actually was more influential in the subsequent development of Chinese literature than Lu Xun, who is usually held up as being the most influential. The "Mao Dun tradition" in novel writing, according to scholars, includes the fact that novels "should be written in the vernacular and must have a certain modernity implied within them. At a narrow level of ideology, these were seen as ultimately becoming revolutionary literature or national literature, and they undertook to express the history of the people's liberation and to depict the great suffering entailed in this task." This was also how these novels became classics or canonized, which was an extremely complex process. Aside from various ideological and political reasons, this process "was related to the dominant position of the new literature both in theoretical discourse and in education."¹⁰³

In December 1957, the novel *Keep the Red Flag Flying* was published. It clearly satisfied the new demands for the renarrativization of revolutionary history. Some reviewers highly praised its political subject: "This novel vividly depicts the forces of history in the great new democratic revolution led under the banner of the Communist Party, with the peasants as the main force in alliance with the united army." These reviewers also made comparisons between *Keep the Red Flag Flying* and *Tracks in the Snowy Forest*: "The image of Zhu Laozhong [in *Red Flag*] offers a history of the development of the personality an old Chinese revolutionary peasant; Yang Zirong's image [in *Tracks*] offers a legendary story of one moment in the life of struggle of a revolutionary combatant."¹⁰⁴ This sort of discussion lends political affirmation for the type of narrative in which "a person matures in history."¹⁰⁵

The author of *Keep the Red Flag Flying*, Liang Bin, introduced the process of the novel's creation and his own thinking:

---

102. Zhou Yang, "Fayang 'wusi' wenxue geming de douzheng chuantong" [Developing the tradition of struggle of the "May Fourth" literary revolution] *Renmin wenxue* [People's literature], March 1954, n.p.

103. Chen Jianhua, *Geming yu xingshi—Mao Dun zaoqi xiashuo de xiandaixing zhankai* [Revolution and form: The depiction of modernity in Mao Dun's early writing] (Shanghai: Fudan Daxue Dhubanshe, 2007), 2, 6.

104. Li Xifan, "Geming yingxiong dianxing de xunli" [A pilgrimage towards typicality of revolutionary heroes], *Wenxue pinglun* [Literature critique] 1 (1961): n.p.

105. On the theme of maturation in *Keep the Red Flag Flying*, see Li Yang, *50–70 niandai Zhongguo wenxue zai jiedu*, chapter 2.

> In the process of composition, I considered how to imitate and develop a form that was more abbreviated than that of Western novels but more detailed than was usual in Chinese stories. The result of this experiment is the form that was published. I did not consider the problem of using the episodic form, but I did think about the ways in which sentences and phrases are arranged in Chinese stories, and in the end I concluded that this could not be arranged in the manner of new-style stories, so it came out the way it is now. I think if I'd only considered the issue of episodic chapters, I wouldn't have been able to use folk language that had been well developed, and I'd not have been able to include the life customs and habits, the spirit and the outward appearances of the folk and the people. Thus, in not using the episodic form, the work still could become a novel in the national form.[106]

If we look at this closely, then we can see that the Western novels of which Liang Bin writes refer to nineteenth-century European literature, in which a historical consciousness is prominent. This European literary tradition deeply influenced new-style literature of the May Fourth period, as exemplified by Mao Dun, especially in the realm of the writing of novels. Hence, this reference to Western novels does not merely indicate a formal level; rather, it also refers to a type of historical consciousness expressed in the dualistic oppositional categories of light/dark, revolution/reaction, progress/backwardness, and so forth. These oppositional categories were of course constitutive of progressive history as a perspective. In particular, when politics becomes the perfect representative of this progressive historical consciousness, *Keep the Red Flag Flying* can easily be read as "vividly demonstrating the forces of history in the great new democratic revolution, led under the banner of the Communist Party, with the peasants as the main force in alliance with the united army."[107] For this reason, the developmental history of a character, which is precisely the developmental process in historical time of national liberation, is also inevitably political. To criticize Chinese contemporary literature for being politicized is obviously not difficult; however, what is more necessary is to look for complex historical processes within this politicization. This includes the awareness of how politics informs a theoretical recognition of historical consciousness that derives from some sort of modernity.

106. Liang Bin, "Mantan *Hongqi pu* de chuangzuo" [Speaking of the creative process for *Keep the Red Flag Flying*], *Renmin wenxue* [People's literature] 1959, 6.
107. Ibid.

However, another aspect of this return to the new culture tradition of the May Fourth period can be found in the extension of the general tradition of Chinese fiction. But what is this tradition? It is hard to say. Perhaps, according to Liang Bin's articulation, it is "that which has been tempered by folk language ... including the living customs and habits as well as the spiritual lives of the folk and the people," and for this reason "even if the episodic chapter form is not used, it can still become a novel in the national form." Even though this articulation is still quite murky, I believe it is important. These "customs and habits, as well as the spiritual aspects of life"[108] possibly indicate the parameters of that which permeates everyday life and is lifted out of that life by the living language of the elite, so as to be fashioned into some sort of grassroots culture—which then gets reabsorbed and penetrates into the lifeworlds, habits, dialects, leisure times, and even folk tunes of the people. The representation of this grassroots culture cannot be completed within historical time. Hence, representation must always rely on the existing forms of timeless spatiality.

Here, then, lies the genuine significance of the liberated zones' cultural tradition of the quotidianized narrative form pioneered by Zhao Shuli and others. And this may also explain why the spatial form of the village is so revered in contemporary Chinese literature. It is only in the space of the village where the limits of the historical consciousness of modern times can be surmounted; it is also only from the village that those very details of everyday life repeatedly thrown aside by modernity can be salvaged. This is where the cultural implications of this literature and form reside. And it turns out this grassroots culture was supported by the masses—that politically legitimizing concept—because it incorporated some sort of national truth. Hence, an individual's maturation did not entirely depend upon temporality; rather, spatiality remained an extremely important element. This is because it was precisely in space that the masses and politics, as well as tradition and modernity, gained their legitimizing foundations. In this sense, the Hebei village narrative aspects added into the revised edition of *The Song of Youth* depict a wanderer returning to his proper place—or to his roots—through which he can soak up the appropriate political and cultural nutrients. This process is obviously also a process of being educated and reformed, but it is already quite different from the Western form of bildungsroman.

108. Ibid.

Liang Bin's discussion of Western fiction and general Chinese fiction is quite symbolic of the process through which the renarration of revolutionary history proceeded: on the one hand, at issue was how contemporary Chinese literature would once again split off from tradition, a splitting that announced yet again a return to the May Fourth new culture spirit; and on the other hand, at issue was also how in practice the traces of popular culture—that is, the national form—could not be eradicated. This national form was precisely the arena in which the residual aspects of the everyday life of the subaltern masses could be salvaged in and for contemporary Chinese literature. And in this sense, the circularity formed by the interaction between Western fiction and general Chinese fiction is precisely where the characteristic features of contemporary Chinese literature were created. It is in this nativist space that the discovery of historical consciousness could find its primary location, a location that dictated where the re-creation of language and form of literature would take place. This is true not only of *Keep the Red Flag Flying*, but also of *The Builders*, *The Song of Youth*, and so on. And this tradition continues to this day to influence the writing of contemporary Chinese fiction.

Conclusion

On February 14, 1949, Zhou Libo published a short piece in the Shenyang-based *Northeast Daily* [*Dongbei ribao*]. The piece was titled "[A Small Guide to *Folk Stories*]" ("*Minjian gushi* xiaoyin"). This was supposed to have been the preface to a book titled *Folk Stories* (*Minjian gushi*) that collected twenty-one stories, all of which "had been orally told by the peasant group of the Hejiang's Lu Xun Literature and Art performing group." The reason I mention this piece is because of my interest in Zhou's account of these folk stories. According to Zhou, we know that these stories were mostly written "before the land reform . . . about the everyday relations between feudal landlords and laboring people." These everyday stories were "stories about the never-ending everyday conflicts between the people and the landlords," and to some extent, these everyday stories "were an expression of the important contradictions in the rural villages before land reform."[109] These stories are mostly about how landlords played ever more elaborate tricks to further exploit the labor power of peasants. The stories all have similar structures, which, crudely stated, fol-

---

109. Zhou Libo, "*Minjian gushi* xiaoyin" [A small guide to *Folk Stories*], in *Zhou Libo wenji* [Collected writings of Zhou Libo] (Shanghai: Shanghai Wenyi Chubanshe, 1985), 5:290.

low the pattern of the landlord contravenes the old rules, the peasant resists. This is a shared narrative model for a large number of folk stories.

Zhou Libo and those like him became interested in this folk story model; many literary works, even those like *White-Haired Girl*, absorbed this structure into their storytelling.[110] However, we can sense that in these folk narratives the old rules invoked were of course quite idealized; rather, they appear as some sort of timeless pastoral poetic. Meng Yue has described this kind of pastoral poetic as "the ethical order of a harmonized everyday life," from which was formulated a cultural system, moral logic, and aesthetic narrative resource. In this regard, what genuinely moved audiences about the opera *White-Haired Girl*, aside from its political subject, was the folk/antifolk moral conflict: when the landlord, Huang Shiren, "appears on stage, he immediately represents an evil type of violence against the folk ethical order." By the end of the opera, the subject of the villagers' chorus is "the sun has appeared," which demonstrates that the "white-haired girl" can once again "lead a human life."[111]

In this sort of narrative structure, the landlord, Huang Shiren, represents a figure who has broken the old rules—rules that, through the revolution, have been revived. In this narrative model for folk stories we could of course deploy in a new way a Hegelian theoretical discourse, such as the negation of the negation or a spiral development and transcendence. Indeed, behind the explanations offered by Yan'an intellectuals of these folk stories, we can sense to some extent the influence of the [infamous] Marxist five-stage theory of historical narrative and development (primitive society→slave society→feudal society→capitalist society→communist society). Yet as everyone already knows, this five-stage theory is a product of European modernity and the typical narrative structural model of the Enlightenment. In China, by contrast, modernity and nativism passed through the mediation of the revolution to form a highly synthesized narrative model.

However, a problem remains: the old rules, which have been narratively transformed through a nativist discourse that has been worked over by the European medieval era/modern renaissance model, still conceal a pastoral poetic that could become the teleology of the Chinese revolution. This tele-

---

110. Another example is the metaphorical description of "the coppery clock" in Liang Bin, *Keep the Red Flag Flying*, trans. Gladys Yang (Beijing: Foreign Language Press, 1961).

111. Meng Yue, "*Baimao nü yanbian de qishi*—jianlun yan'an wenyi de duozhixing" [Notes on the evolution of *The White-Haired Girl*—A brief discussion of the multiplicity of the history of Yan'an art practices], in *Ershi shiji zhongguo wenxueshi lun* [On the history of twentieth-century Chinese literature], ed. Wang Xiaoming, 193.

ology stands in internal narrative contradiction to the political and cultural attitudes and tasks faced by the future of the Chinese revolution. Because to establish a political attitude about the future, it is important to specify what sort of intimate relationship it would have with our own history. That is, if we say that Mao Zedong narrated Chinese revolutionary history as beginning in the 1840s, then we have to figure out what the prehistory of revolutionary history—that is, pre-1840s history—might have been. Thus, how to speak of this prehistory became not only a literary narrative problem, but also an urgent problem for historical research.

In 1949, Mao provided the following materialist account of Chinese history: "Classes struggle, some classes triumph, others are eliminated. Such is history, such is the history of civilization for thousands of years. To interpret history from this viewpoint is historical materialism; standing in opposition to this viewpoint is historical idealism."[112] This perspective in actuality became a basic principle of post-1949 historical research and literary narrative. What we can still discuss is that this struggle produced a tendency toward a historical developmental process that would inevitably, albeit temporarily, suspend the poetic pastoral outside of historical time. And then the important question becomes: What can civilization salvage out of this process of historical movement entirely monopolized by class struggle? Or how do we tell this historical story? On January 9, 1943, after Mao Zedong saw the Peking opera *Driven to Join the Liangshan Rebels* [Yushang Liangshan], he wrote a letter to the editor: "People make their own history, and yet in older operatic pieces (in all old cultural and literary products that depart from the people), people become the dregs on a stage ruled by the elites; this sort of reversal of history requires that you now stand it properly on its feet, to restore to history its proper aspect, from which new facets of old dramas can be revealed. You should be congratulated."[113] Four years later, Mao revisited this perspective: "in regular dramas, the elites constitute a world in which poor people have no place."[114] This view of history, actually, can be traced back to Liang Qichao's early-twentieth-century work "New Historiography" ("Xin shixue"). However, the difference is that, if Liang's intention was to narrate from scratch a new history of the citizenry (*guomin*), Mao wished to narrate a history of the

---

112. Mao Tse-tung, "Cast away Illusions, Prepare to Struggle," in *Selected Works of Mao Tse-tung* (Peking: Foreign Language Press, 1961), 4:428.
113. Mao Zedong, "Gei Yang Shaoxuan, Qi Yanming de xin," 3:88.
114. Mao Zedong, "Gaizao jiu yishu, chuangzao xin yishu" [Reform old culture, create new culture], in *Mao Zedong wenji* (Beijing: Renmin chubanshe, 2004), 4:326.

[revolutionary] people (*renmin*). In the telling of this history of the people, the problem of how to allow the subaltern to speak was an urgent and important narrative task. On this point, a history of the people is not entirely the same as a bourgeois national historical narrative. Indeed, we can say that after 1949, whether in the field of history or in the field of literature, scholars strove in their research into the peasant wars of the older and more modern eras to rewrite history in the idiom of people's history in contrast to that of imperial or colonial histories.

Another relatively ignored element could be that the kind of history shaped out of the people as a historical subjectivity forms a type of radical political/cultural national identity, and thus in the multiethnic formation of the Chinese nation, the dominant political/cultural identity can avoid the worst of the Han-centric (elite cultural) narrative dangers. Yet it remains true that this type of historical or subaltern narrative is clearly completely dominated by ideological and political tendencies, and with only slight slippage, it can become very reductive. This was the point of departure for the 1980s critiques [of revolutionary popular literature]. Hence, the question is not entirely about the prehistorical history narrative form, but rather about how this form suppressed other forms of historical writing. That is, just as the doors of history were thrown open and new air came flowing in, the doors of history also were slammed shut.

More important still, in a writing of history where peasant wars shape the historical prehistory, an important aspect of what in elite discourse is called "cultural China" may be relatively neglected in historical representation. Yet the absence of cultural China leads to a crisis in national identity. This crisis was inherited in subsequent eras and continues to unfold explosively today. In the sixty-year history of contemporary China, what we can sense is none other than the complex contradictions between modern, revolutionary, and traditional China, and the many historical conflicts and entanglements within this period. But that already takes us far from the topic of this chapter.

5

NARRATIVES OF LABOR OR LABOR UTOPIAS

When we describe the modern world in which we are embedded, we cannot help but note the presence of technology. Technology has completely transformed our modes of being, to the extent that it has entirely re-created our living environments. One sort of possibility [created by this transformation] and the imaginary derived from it is experiential activity, which has constructed and redrawn the parameters of the ideology of the modern. The boundaries of these imaginaries along with their interpenetration are murky: everything that used to be settled on one shore of the world's imaginary has become the large motivating factor that unsettles and transforms that very world. Utopias emerged from their encapsulation by religion and were transformed into this-worldly constitutions of secular empires of possibility. *The impossible* was a special term in the ancient world; yet in modern times, everything has become possible and is being dreamed into existence through large-scale technologies.

It is precisely in the midst of this technological illusion that man awakens to rationality and at the same time constructs a form of epistemology of strength. This strength is about humanity and also about labor. Evidently, in this epistemology, man receives a different type of explanatory significance:

that is, laboring man. The attention to labor clearly transforms thinking man's structure of feeling toward the world.

From any perspective, Marx remains the most profound thinker on the questions of labor. Not only does Marx's deep analysis of labor and the production process explore the intimate relation between capital and surplus value, but at the same time his labor theory of value proposes that the proletariat alone is the subject of history. Clearly, only when the concept of labor emerges can the revolutionary topic of who is the genuine architect of the world be raised. This topic had a profound impact on twentieth-century China.

In the course of the propagation of Marxism, pioneering modern Chinese thinkers of the twentieth century began, to one extent or another, to be influenced by the labor theory of value. However, it is worth pointing out that in their concrete articulations on labor, there already was some form of nativist content. That is to say, they did not discuss labor only from some application to China of the modern abstraction of productive relations, nor did they think of labor merely as pertaining to the proletariat alone. Even though Li Dazhao was an early exponent of Marxism, yet he specifically said: "The victory of laborism will be the victory of the common people," because "the capacity for labor is possessed by every person and labor can be done by everyone."[1] Cai Yuanpei, for his part, said: "The world after this is a world of labor." But for Cai, this concept of labor was quite complex and broad: "When I say labor, it refers not merely to metal workers, carpenters, and so on, but to all those who transform matter for the advantage of human beings, no matter whether they employ manual labor or mental labor. This is all labor."[2] As for Chen Duxiu, he included in his notion of labor all manual laborers—that is, China's subalterns, "those who sow the fields, work with cloth, fashion wood, move earth, do petty labor, work with steel, work with clay, operate machines, labor on boats, pull rickshaws, are hands at sea, do transport work... and so on"—were positively evaluated by him: "In my view, those who do work are the most useful and the most valuable." Meanwhile, he also predicted the future of China's political structure: "Ancient Chinese used to say 'those who work with their minds rule people; those who work with their hands are ruled by others.' Today, we need to turn those words on their head: 'those who work

---

1. Li Dazhao, "Shumin de shengli" [Victory of the common people], in *Wusi yundong de wenxuan* [Selected essays from the May Fourth Movement] (Beijing: Sanlian Shudian, 1979), 176.
2. Cai Yuanpei, "Laogong shensheng" [The sacredness of labor], in *Wusi yundong de wenxuan* [Selected essays from the May Fourth Movement] (Beijing: Sanlian Shudian, 1979), 185.

with their hands rule people; those who work with their minds should be ruled.'"³ Even though there were different takes, the shared point fell on what Cai Yuanpei emphasized: to recognize the value of labor and what was often called the sacredness of labor. This type of valuation does not emerge entirely from political economy; rather, it implies something more elementally emotional, almost of an ethical or aesthetic nature.

The reason I want to emphasize these early endeavors at the nativization of Marxism lies in the fact that these theoretical discussions of labor are not entirely contained in and by the antagonistic duality of the categories of bourgeoisie and proletariat; rather, they expand to cover the entirety of the social subalterns, that concept indicated by Li Dazhao's "common people." Subsequently, the course of the concrete realization of the Chinese revolution and its intellectual expression was intimately related to this notion of common people. At the same time, it is worth pointing out that, in the texts of the ancients and practices of the literati [in traditional China], there was always attention paid to the importance of manual labor.

Of course, the sacralization of labor, in particular of manual labor, along with powerful support for the transformation of the proletarian-peasant alliance into the revolution's "main force," was the product of Mao Zedong's important theoretical discussions. In his essay "The Orientation of the Youth Movement," Mao noted the concept of the "main force (*zhuli jun*)": "What then is the main force? The workers and peasants."⁴ Meanwhile, in the section on "the problem of attitude" in his "Talks at the Yenan Forum on Literature and Art," attitude not only is linked to [class] stand and target, but it also is related to feelings and even to aesthetic ideas. Mao takes himself as an example [when he narrates the story of his own class awakening and transformation].

The concept of labor serves as evidence for Mao's discussion of personal transformation. This labor concept was even pushed to the level of epistemological knowledge, a central point in Mao's "Rectify the Party's Style of Work": "What is knowledge? Ever since class society came into being the world has had only two kinds of knowledge, knowledge of the struggle for production and knowledge of the class struggle."⁵ These relevant portions of Mao's

3. Chen Duxiu, "Laodongzhe de juewu" [The awakening of laborers], in *Wusi yundong de wenxuan* [Selected essays from the May Fourth Movement] (Beijing: Sanlian Shudian, 1979), 356–57.
4. Mao Tse-tung, "The Orientation of the Youth Movement," in *Selected Works of Mao Tse-tung* (Peking: Foreign Language Press, 1961), 2:245.
5. Mao Tse-tung, "Rectify the Party's Style of Work," in *Selected Works of Mao Tse-tung* (Peking: Foreign Language Press, 1965), 3:773.

theoretical discussions imply a biased view against mental labor (including corresponding forms of knowledge and even intellectuals); even in his later years, Mao continued to express an intense criticism of the Confucian ideal of the bookish person who is divorced from manual labor. Meanwhile, in his strong recognition of labor was the implication that therein concealed was a great force for liberation. It was only from within this type of radical theorization or requirement (including the biased denunciation of mental labor), that the subjectivity of China's subalterns, including the dignity of this subjectivity, could be confirmed sufficiently. In this sense, the common people cannot be fully encapsulated by the notion of people-centeredness (*minben*); rather, they are constituted through a certain form of the logical extension of Marxism.[6]

Clearly, in the twentieth-century left-wing Chinese imaginary, labor is one of the most important concepts. In Marxism, one major import of labor is its attachment to the concept of the proletariat, which opens imagination and practical activity to a national and a global politics of power. At the same time, this concept efficiently indicates the subject position of those who labor, a position that is not only political and economic but also is ethical and emotional. This is a position that demands the creation of a new lifeworld. As a type of challenge and also an echo, contemporary literature relies upon this concept to organize its own narrative activity. Below, I explore four fictional works to discuss how labor entered the lifeworld of imagination and creativity.

I. "The Land" (*Diban*): Political Debate and Rationalization of Law

On April 1, 1946, Zhao Shuli published his short story "The Land" ("Diban") in the second issue of the first volume of *Journal of Literature and Art* [*Wenyi Zazhi*]. Among Zhao's works, "The Land" cannot be considered a major opus, but if we consider his corpus of work from "Xiao Erhei Gets Married" ("Xiao Erhei jiehun") to *Changes in Li Village* [*Lijiazhuang de bianqian*] and others, I think it is an important turning point. The sign of this turning point is that Zhao more deeply than previously expresses his opinions about Chinese poli-

---

6. Tr.: *Minben* refers to an imperial-era ideology of an obedient and docile people, who are the paternalistic subjects of an imperial dynastic polity. Cai is differentiating here between the central role of subalterns as historical subjects in China's Marxism and the centrality of the people (*min*) as subjects of the state during imperial times.

tics. There is clearly a very intimate relation between his politics and the Party.[7] Research that separates Zhao from politics is irrelevant. Indeed, we ought not to dismiss offhand his profound insights into politics, including party politics and about the world. Rather, I believe, only when a strong political perspective is introduced does the depth of Zhao's own politics come through. Additionally, the profound observations by Zhao of China's village society also lend his political narratives their freshness, uniqueness, and fullness.

In this sense, the politics of "The Land" not only affords us a research perspective on Zhao, it also gives us an opportunity to study the emerging literary relationship between land and labor, in effect pointing toward the question of who can claim the power to create the world. This is one question that twentieth-century politics in general and Chinese revolutionary politics in particular resolved to address. It must be explained anew today.

Even though "The Land" cannot be considered a major opus, that does not mean there is nothing to be said about it; to the contrary, "The Land" provides a very illuminating mode of narrative debate. This mode not only is deployed more specifically in Zhao's subsequent works (for example, *Sanliwan Village*), but it became a common powerful narrative ploy in much contemporary literature, such as Liu Qing's *The Builders* and Zhou Libo's *Great Changes in the Mountain Village*, among others. It is hard to say whether it was Zhao's work that influenced others' works. Rather, it was the major incidents and turning points of socialism itself that simultaneously stimulated huge debates in both the political and artistic spheres. And these debates were not among intellectuals alone but also penetrated into the everyday lives of the masses. For this reason, when literary works take up the lifeworlds of this era, they naturally also take up the debates as a narrative way to explain the huge transformations and turning points of the era as well as the various intellectual struggles and conflicts of interests derived therefrom. This debate narrative mode extended all the way to works produced in the Cultural Revolution, such as *Niu tian yang* [Niu Tian Yang] or *History of Line Struggles in Hong Nan* (Hong

7. According to Zhao Shuli himself, he was originally a "propagandist in the countryside," and only later did he become a professional writer while retaining the particular characteristics of the task of coordination with contemporaneous politics. Of course, on the one hand Zhao believed that this type of requirement was correct, and on the other hand he also recognized the limitations imposed on writers by the required relationship between literature and politics. However, Zhao also recognized that this limitation was not absolute: it could be overcome. See Zhao Shuli, "Foreword to *Sanliwan Village*" [*Sanli Wan xu*], *Zhao Shuli quanji* [*Zhao Shuli's Collected Works*] (Taiyuan: Beiyue Wenyi Chubanshe, 1999), 4:282.

Nan zuozhan shi) [written by a Shanghai collective and published in 1972], although these latter ones were more ideological still. Startlingly, this mode abruptly ended in the 1980s.

The debate in "The Land" about land and labor does not take place between landlords and peasants—unlike many of the land reform novels with which we are familiar. Rather, it occurs within the landlord class itself. This is clearly a product of some mature considerations on Zhao's part. The story begins with the reduction of rent in Wang Family Village.[8] Although the landlord, Wang Laosi, has "set the rent rates according to the law," he is nevertheless dissatisfied. His dissatisfaction is not with the law ("reducing rents according to the law, I have no complaints with that"); rather, it is the so-called logic in which "everyone says that rice is produced by labor power, not by land." "If you want to speak of logic, I won't stop you from speaking about whichever logic you wish. If he wants to use labor power to produce, let him return the land to me and go produce rice in midair!" Evidently, there are two forms of logic in conflict here. Zhaoi is very attentive to the conflict between the logics; he even uses the slogan of the chair of the Peasant Associations to express it: "The law is established based on reason."[9] Zhao's differentiation between "law" and "reason" implies a very sophisticated politics. In the scheme of the entire story, Zhao never specially recognizes that which departs from common knowledge (reason) by validating law. To the contrary, the foundations of law are supposed to be reason: only law that accords with common feelings and common reason can become a certain contract form. In this sense, "The Land" is an extended debate about contract law.[10] The introduction of reason allows the law to be debated in a cultural and ideological sense in that, for law to garner popular support, it must be subjected to the process of persuasion and debate.

In other words, politics cannot merely rely upon law for support; it must garner support in the realms of popular sympathy and ethics. Thus, politics

8. Tr.: Rent reduction was part of the Chinese Communist Party's land reform policies during the War of Resistance against Japan; it was paired with a reduction in interest on loans.

9. Zhao Shuli, *Diban* [The land], *Wenyi zazhi* [Journal of culture and literature], vol. 1 (1946): n.p. Tr.: All citations in the text are to this story; we have no page numbers to provide. The story is not translated into English, thus all translations here are from the text in Cai's book.

10. This relationship between law and reason drew a large amount of commentary and debate from legal scholars in the 1990s, set off by Zhang Yimou's film *The Story of Qiu Ju* [Tr.: A more literal translation of the Chinese title (*Qiu Ju daguangsi*) would be *Qiu Ju Brings a Lawsuit*]. See Su Li, *Fazhi yu qi bentu ziyuan* [Rule by law and its nativist sources] (Beijing: Zhongguo Zhengfa Daxue Chubanshe, 1996).

cannot be experienced merely through legal regulations; rather, it must also be turned into a form of feeling and ethics, even into a type of moral politics. This political imaginary explains why from beginning to end Zhao is attentive to the relationship between (political) law and (mass) reason. For once this relationship is ruptured, the author encounters real problems, which is why in 1964 Zhao said at a meeting that "the contradictions between state interests and the interests of the collective are the most problematic ... in places where the task of purchase requisitioning is completed at the expense of alienating the masses."[11] He also said that he did not have the guts to add more idealism in his writing. The truth Zhao was always willing to see and hear was clearly some form of the actual state of existence of the peasant masses that he believed to contain reason. Because of this, Zhao also said: "Only when you really settle down [in a village] can you truly comprehend the situation from house to house and door to door. When you are invited to a wedding celebration, the conversations you overhear there—that is real."[12]

However, in novels written in 1945, at least so far as Zhao was concerned, law and reason were highly compatible with one another. In other words, the new law was established upon a form of reason that Zhao affirmed. So what was this affirmed form of reason?

"The Land" first gives voice to the landlord Wang Laosi's version of reason: "My rent is taken in exchange for my land," as without land (soil) the producers can "go produce in midair." Frankly, this reason is precisely that encoded in the phrase "exploitation is reasonable," and it structures the legitimacy of the ideology that capital creates or produces the world. So, Wang Laosi asserts: "I cannot understand this," and "not in a thousand years will I be able to understand your thinking." Yet this reason cannot be encapsulated only in capitalist explanatories; to the contrary, it also expresses thousands of years of ideological support for the foundational property regime of Chinese villages. A few years later, Hao Ran's *Sunny Days* (*Yanyang tian*) rehearses how in the transition to what the novel calls the "Higher Agrarian Cooperative of Dongshanpo" there was another episode of excited debate over the distribu-

---

11. Tr.: Purchase requisitioning was a state policy requiring collectives (all forms of peasant collective productive activity) to provide to the state a set amount of produce at a set price, for the state's redistributive purposes. In the wake of the Great Leap Forward (1958–61) and the great famine, purchase requisitioning was a very hard sell, even though it was a cornerstone of state policy.

12. Zhao Shuli, "Zai Zhongguo zuoxie zuojia, bianji zuotanhui shang de fayan" [Speech at the conference of the authors and editors of the Chinese Writers' Association], in *Zhao Shuli quanji* [Complete works of Zhao Shuli] 4:631.

tion of dividends according to land or labor.[13] It is clear, then, that debate over which was the correct reason remained a major issue in Chinese villages. The strong presence of Wang Laosi's reason actually suppresses Zhao Shuli's own reason. The two forms of reason are in a conflict and struggle structured by that which suppresses and that which is suppressed. In the story, this struggle is expressed in the form of a debate.

It is worth noting that Wang Laosan, the elementary school teacher in the story, is also a member of this landlord class, and it falls to him to represent the debate's other side, which clearly has an indirect narrative effect in the novel. Wang Laosan says that he himself "is of the family that has long owned the land," and that the "old contract" includes in the holdings some deserted mountain land. Yet "beginning from the time when the rent was given to Old Chang's grandfather, there were about ten years during which more than 30 *mu* of good land was opened up. Later, when Old Wang and Old Sun arrived, all three families constituted a village. By Old Chang's generation, the three families together could just about sow one *qing* [a little over sixteen acres] of land. I don't know how much rice they could reap, but at least they have given me cash rent in the amount of 60 taels a year."

In this narration, land is in effect divided into two concepts: "deserted mountain" and "good soil." The deserted mountain pertains to the old contract. Even if one tacitly accepts the legitimacy of this old contract (pertaining to the old property regime), the deserted mountain is nothing but a state of nature and itself cannot be the basis for the creation of a lifeworld. On the contrary, it is only in the course of the application of the labor power of Old Chang's grandfather and subsequent generations that this deserted mountain could be transformed into good soil. In this sense, the land (soil) is precisely that which is produced through labor power. That is to say, it already contains labor power in its meaning. Only due to the presence of this factor of labor power does the question of whom the rice belongs to even arise. From deserted mountain to good soil: it is precisely here where the debate over nature and labor lies—a debate that pointed to the importance of labor, which raises the most basic question of who creates the world (rice).

In the course of the debate over the central question of who the creating subject is, the narrator (Wang Laosan) employs a self-reflective mode of speech and in this mode successfully turns reason into a situation where sym-

---

13. Tr.: A higher agrarian cooperative was one of several forms of collective production and administration in the Maoist years. Dividends distribution (*fenhong*) was the mode in which peasants divided the fruits of collectivization.

pathy manifests itself. He first discusses man-made catastrophes ("the Japanese along with their bandit collaborators created chaos"), then he talks of natural disasters ("then there was a huge drought, and for two seasons there was no rain; the earth turned red"); as a consequence, "in the village, of more than 200 families there were those who died, those who fled—in all, up to 30–40 families disappeared." "Old Wang and Old Sun," Wang Laosan's peers, "were starving to the point that they collected their family members and fled the drought district." Old Chang came to borrow rice but, as Wang Laosan declined to give him any, he "starved to death, and his wife took their three kids to Lin County, even though in that village there was not a soul." Of course, afterward, "when he [Wang Laosan] thought of it, he regretted it; he could have given folks some rice." In this narrative, class relations in a Chinese village are thoroughly exposed; what is more, these class relations are shown to be not only irrational but also devoid of sympathy: the producers of rice are precisely those from whom rice has been expropriated.

Not only are there natural disasters that create human hardship, but even more disastrous are the cruelty of class expropriations. The result is that the land yielded nothing and for Wang Laosan, "naturally no one paid rent." But it is not until Wang Laosan's family "larders, overflowing with rice and grain, had all been emptied" that Wang Laosan can finally recognize the principle of labor and sweat as being where rice comes from. When Wang Laosan himself is forced to work the soil, he begins to feel the hardship of labor and, even more pointedly, he begins to experience the creative relationship between labor and rice (the world). All of this would later, when labor became a form of reeducation, be the source of certain ideas that affirmed the subject position of the laborer.

From deserted mountain to good soil and again to "a deserted mountain somewhere," the final result of the debate is that "we mustn't again claim that land can be exchanged for rice . . . rice ultimately is the exchange for labor." This is Zhao's reason, which, in the debate staged in "The Land," is positioned as a form of natural presence. That is to say, this reason is not a product of the Chinese revolution, but rather it is a natural fact that has existed in the world forever: it is just that it has been exposed through the juxtaposition of another type of principle (Wang Laosi's reason). Thus, the only thing that the revolution needs to accomplish is to take this newly exposed reason and liberate it anew, even while it is institutionalized (as law). This is a very typical form of nativizing of Marxism. In this sense, Zhao seems to believe that the significance of the revolution is not that it comes from outside, but rather that it has grown, albeit ambiguously, from within this world of sympathy or reason. I will return to this point to further explore the quality of this ambiguity; I will argue that it is an extension of the conflict of the encounter between modernity and tradition.

The importance of labor power as highlighted in "The Land"—including its sacralization—is a form of modern expression that also transcends the narrative paradigm of bourgeois modernity. This is so because at its very foundation are none other than the basic modern revolutionary ideals of Marxism. After the October Revolution in Russia, these ideals turned toward establishing a polity based upon a proletariat-peasant alliance. These ideals powerfully influenced China's revolution. Yet in China, these ideals even more directly overturned the traditional ideological legitimacy of "those who do mental labor rule, those who do manual labor are ruled"[14] (which includes Wang Laosi's reason). In this sense, they also transcend the duality of tradition and modern and offer a grand utopia, from which a brand-new world can be fashioned, a world that includes state sovereignty just as it does a brand-new cultural disposition. This, too, is Marxist, and in particular it is where the most important social experiments of Leninism reside. In this regard, we cannot ignore the importance of contemporary literature. When literature can really provide witness to and actually participate in the fundamental transformation of human cultural society, its importance cannot be evaluated only on its literariness (its technique).

When labor was cited by this modern revolutionary force—even if this citation is, in the Benjaminian sense a violent one—we must acknowledge the enormous liberatory mechanism embedded in it. In the very process of this liberation, the laborer (the worker or peasant) not only gained an enduring legitimate political and economic status, but more important, she or he was able to attain a certain type of dignity. This dignity was comprised of what Zhao Shuli articulates as being the sympathy between labor and the created lifeworld. Actually, a good number of contemporary literary works also participated in the narrative process marked by this reason or sympathy. For example, in Zhi Xia's *Guerrillas on the Railways* [*Tiedao youji dui*], the political commissar, Li Zheng, teaches a class on politics to the members of the railway guerrilla group. In Li Zheng's narrative, some abstract notion of coal mining is turned into a concrete thing that one can feel: coal. It is only in the face of this concrete thing, coal (a thingness it shares with Zhao's rice), that one can

---

14. Tr.: This is a traditional mode of thinking that derives from Confucius.

confront the problem of creative production. Li first describes a scene in the coal mining village where there is a "tall pile of coal accumulated by the coal mining company." Right after this description, the question posed is naturally where does this "mountainous pile of coal" actually come from? Li's answer is very clear: "This mountain of coal is what we black-faced coal miners, enduring hardships that are beyond endurance, have hauled up from underground with our sweat and blood." Precisely because "there is this daily growing mountain of coal, a railway is being constructed by the village so that one car at a time, it can be transported away and exchanged by capitalists for untold riches; with this mountain of coal, our village has gradually grown larger and more coal factories are located here; every day, there are more people whose lives depend upon coal, while the streets now have general stores and restaurants. Our village is more bustling than ever." In this sense, the village is "created by us, the workers." In Li's view, this is no theory but a reality. It is just that "those on the top of the coal heap can't find it within themselves to say one kind word to us." For this reason, Li's politics class is merely the setting for the saying aloud of the words that capitalists will not utter. Meanwhile, the workers' response is "Right! What you say is the truth."[15]

Of course I do not deny the political pedagogy in the novel—actually, one of the functions undertaken by the modern novel is precisely to expose the truth, a truth that is always class-based. After all, if politics exposes some sort of clear insight, then literary works have no reason to reject it. The question is how this pedagogy was conveyed artistically or formally.

In light of this pedagogical role, "The Land" nevertheless has a certain narrative aporia. Even if the deserted mountain has been transformed by Old Chang's grandfather and subsequent generations into good soil and now produces rice and this proves that "rice is an exchange for labor power," then where does the legitimacy of the "deserted mountain somewhere" in the old contract reside? "The Land" offers no opinions on the legitimacy of the old contract. That is to say, it still tacitly acknowledges the legitimacy of the old contract. The narrative background of "The Land" is the policy of reduced rent, reduced interest that was pursued in the liberated zones during the War of Resistance against Japan and was in some sense the product of a compromise between the national revolution and the socialist revolution. For this reason, the validity of the old contract is the premise on which the problem of labor is dis-

15. Zhi Xia, *Tiedao youji dui* [Guerrillas on the railways] (Shanghai: Shanghai Wenyi Chubanshe, 1978). Tr.: Page numbers were not provided in Cai's book; we have not located the precise range.

cussed. Also for this reason, the aporia in the narrative is none other than a theoretical one that is a product of the real compromise between the national and socialist revolutions.

After the conclusion of the War of Resistance against Japan, what the Chinese revolution needed to resolve was the residual narrative aporia depicted in "The Land"—precisely the fundamental doubts about the legitimacy of the old contracts possessed by the landlord class. These doubts were not only raised by the civil war of liberation but also were the inevitable result of the progress of social revolution. After the importance of labor was affirmed, the question that immediately followed was about the rights of laborers, including the demand for a transformation in property rights. The land reform movement [of the early 1950s] was the classic expression of the ambiguities embedded in all these questions. While a full discussion of this movement is not my central task here,[16] my main point is to think about what sorts of changes happened in literary and narrative works in the wake of the onset of the land reform movement, including the new definition afforded to labor. It is also possible to say that the relevant narratives are all, in one way or another, revisions of "The Land."

In this regard, what the Chinese revolution overturned was not merely the prevailing systems of political and economic arrangements; more important, it overturned an embedded orthodox mode of thinking about land and labor. For this reason, literature, if it wanted to give expression to this era, could not but touch upon politics; politics could not but be brought and incorporated into the struggle for cultural hegemony.

The first chapter of Liang Bin's *Keep the Red Flag Flying* is not merely the opening of a narrative but a fundamental questioning of the legitimacy of the old contracts. In the narrative, what is demonstrated is not only the illegality of the source of the landlord Feng Laolan's land—for which he commits

16. In October 1947, the Party's Central Committee passed an outline for land reform. In its wake, the land reform movement extended over the country. There are many narratives and studies of this movement, such as William Hinton, *Fanshen: A Documentary of Revolution in a Chinese Village* (New York: Vintage, 1968) and Du Runsheng, *Du Runsheng zishu: Zhongguo nongcun tizhi biange zhongda juece jishi* [Du Runsheng remembers: Memories of the important decisions on China's village structural transformation] (Beijing: Beijing Chubanshe, 2005). A relatively deep discussion of this question can be found in Yang Kuisong, *1946–48 zhonggong zhongyang tugai zhengce biandong de lishi kaocha—youguan zhonggong tugaishi de yige zhenglun wenti* [Considerations on the 1946–1948 Party policy on land reform—debates on Party land reform policy], in Yang Kuisong, *Kaijuan youyi* [Reading is always suspicious] (Nanchang: Jiangxi Renmin Chubanshe, 2007).

murder, among other crimes—but also the original sin of the expropriation of public assets. In the subsequent narrative, this original sin is consistently reinforced. Feng Laolan expropriated not only public assets, but also private property. The process of this expropriation is filled with blood, evil, and cruelty, so much so that even Feng Guitang, who is Feng Laolan's son, expresses disagreement: "Take a little less rent, charge a little less interest; let those who are suffering get by a little better: our days will be far more peaceful and stable. From the evidence of history, how many times have peasants risen up because those above them have lacked humaneness? It is often the cause of the formation and invasion of bandits."[17] Usury, high ground rent, the capturing of the official residences and the monopolization of village power, taking everything there is to take—this is not just the description of Feng Laolan['s actions] in *Keep the Red Flag Flying*, but it is basically the model followed by most literary works of the time. This mode of narrating original sin in fact cancels out the legitimacy of the old contracts.

In such descriptions, labor takes on a very heavy narrative function, which develops at two levels: one is the illegality of the land seizures and the loss of the individual's right to labor; and the second is that at every level of exploitation, the fruits of labor are expropriated by others. In this social milieu, "how can laborers survive?" Li Zheng (in *Guerrillas on the Railways*) describes it thus: "We are those who suffer most in this village and also who work the hardest, and yet all we eat is rubbish, all we wear is rags, our homes aren't even as nice as pigsties. Every day, we have to listen to the complaints of hunger and cold of our wives and children. You see, society is just that unequal."[18] This is a kind of political mobilization, but we cannot deny its legitimacy and reasonable nature.

Clearly, in this sort of society, the meaning of labor is itself questioned. If this world is made through labor, but laborers cannot enjoy the fruits of their labor and cannot even reproduce the basic conditions of life, then where does the meaning of labor reside? As indicated in the *Communist Manifesto*, this is an orthodox Marxist mode of expressing the problem. The doubts engendered about labor do not in any way imply a denial of the centrality of labor; to the contrary, the doubts in this case indicate how labor is situated in a concrete historical context, particularly in concrete class relations as a form of political-economic consideration. Not only does the Marxist concept of labor

17. Liang Bin, *Keep the Red Flag Flying*, trans. Gladys Yang (Beijing: Foreign Language Press, 1961). Tr.: We have not tracked down the exact page numbers for this citation.
18. Zhi Xia, *Tiedao youji dui* [Guerrillas on the railways].

confirm in very common terms the question of who feeds whom, but at the same time it also confirms the necessity of revolution. The point of departure for the Chinese revolution—as a practice and also a theory—clearly involves a deep consideration of labor.

We can now come back to Zhao Shuli's "The Land." The reason I emphasize its importance is because this short story foreshadows some very important political and literary perspectives that subsequently arose. I believe the following two aspects are most important to these perspectives.

First, the liberation of subalterns in the Chinese revolution was not only a political or economic liberation; it also involved the enhancement of dignity. This dignity was gained through the possibilities engendered through the debates on the subjectification of labor. In this sense, dignity means a politics of respect and the affirmation of the centrality of labor. The liberation of subalterns garnered them dignity first in the realm of culture. Without the support of this politics of respect, subaltern society would have no way to affirm its own subjectivity. In this sense, the Chinese revolution was not merely a political revolution; at the same time, it was also a cultural revolution. For this reason, "The Land" in some sense foretold the fierce struggle for cultural hegemony in revolutionary China.

Second, Zhao's discussion of law and reason not only touches upon the problem of the legal subject and the ethical subject, it very specifically expresses the idea that politics is not a topos constituted by the legal redistribution of power alone but also inevitably involves debates on feelings and ethics. The importance of this is not merely to obey power but also to agree with power. This discussion of feeling, reason, and law is thus at the same time expressed in other disciplines, for example in Fei Xiaotong's sociological considerations, that were produced by the encounter between modernity and tradition (subalternity). If we can say that the ordering of China's everyday lifeworld derives from "an order based on a rule of rituals"—what I am calling [sympathy-based] reason—then it inevitably will produce a conflict with "a social order based on a rule of law."[19] Hence, the significance of Zhao's considerations revolves around precisely the following: if the Chinese revolution really wants to root itself in China's subaltern society (the villages), then it must treat the sympathy-based reason that is part of the ordering of everyday life with great respect; that is, it must narrate this sympathy anew, thereby af-

19. Xiaotong Fei, *From the Soil: The Foundations of Chinese Society: A Translation of Fei Xiaotong's "Xiangtu Zhongguo,"* with an introduction and epilogue by Gary G. Hamilton and Wang Zheng (Berkeley: University of California Press, 1992), 106–7.

firming a new perspective on justice. In this sense, Zhao is incredibly modern and even quite radical, because he takes this lifeworld—quotidian lives—and revisions it as a form of politics that can be affirmed.

II. "Reeducation" (*Gaizao*) and Stories of Reeducation

In the third issue of the first volume of *People's Literature* (*Renmin wenxue*) of 1950 a short story by Qin Zhaoyang entitled "Gaizao" ["Reeducation"] was published (in the same issue as Xiao Yemu's "Women fufu zhijian" [My wife and me]).[20] The plot revolves around the reeducation of the landlord Wang Youde and the various stories that occur in the process of this reeducation.

Wang Youde is a small-scale landlord who possesses only a little over one *qing* of land, yet he is an only son and is shared by his own family and his father's two brothers' families, "spoiled to death since his childhood." According to the exaggerated narration in the story, "he relied on his mother to stuff his opened mouth with food; he relied on his mother to put his outstretched arm in his clothing; he relied upon his mother to put his shoes on his feet and make them fit; he relied on his mother to take off his hat if he didn't want to wear it; he relied on his mother to scare away flies if they caused him to feel itchy; he relied on his mother to scratch after mosquitos bit." When he finally grew up, he was not only "very funny-looking," but he also had "a temper that was unbridled": he was, "in short, a complete good-for-nothing incapable of accomplishing any task." This is a narrative mode that clearly derives from folk stories and bears marked traces of those traditions.

The story opens out into a series of humorous sketches. These sketches are told by a number of different narrators from a number of different perspectives. For example, villagers give Wang Youde a nickname: "dictionary of jokes." This "joke dictionary" is actually a compendium of folk stories. Various *xie hou yu* [a two-part saying, of which the first part is descriptive and the second part carries the message], characters, happenings, dialogues, and so on are exaggeratedly woven together one by one into "jokes." By the end, these are summarized by the author to describe Wang Youde's annual "work" to be simply "five words: eating, drinking, pissing, shitting, sleeping." Not only does all of this vividly depict Wang Youde as a character, it also clearly conveys the author's own perspective.

---

20. Tr.: All citations in the text to Qin Zhaoyang's story are from the version in *People's Literature*, and no page numbers are available. Cai mentions Xiao Yemu here because Xiao's story is far more famous and canonical than is Qin's.

The parts of the story that attracted the most controversy were those that described the land reform and the struggle meetings.[21] These descriptions were entirely unlike those more familiar from the mainstream land reform novels—for example, Zhou Libo's *The Hurricane*. Here, the struggle is actually quite mild, even comedic, precisely the kind of description that attracted the dissatisfaction of critics. But if we consider the formal aspects of the story or the story's narrative requirements, then the insertion of a textual fragment (or a scene) often can be seen as a way to get the narrative to a more important point. For this reason, the choice of different texts (or scenes) and their concrete depictions often can be extended into entirely different narrative needs and implications. Clearly, Qin's selection of this type of depiction of a struggle meeting is precisely due to the fact that he had no intention of narrating a land reform story along the lines of *The Hurricane*. That is to say, only in this type of mild narrative of struggle is it possible to extend reeducation into the main topic, which is labor. From the controversy and criticisms aimed at Qin's story, incidentally, we can see how swift, arbitrary, and lacking in attention to specific textual forms political critique could be at the time.

After the land reform, Wang Youde's life became difficult. This difficulty emerged not because he lost the resources [needed] to maintain his life—the village gave him some land, which was one of the provisions of the land reform system of the time. Rather, the difficulty emerges from his refusal to participate in labor. Hence, "when the order came down that the village should not have even one lazy soul not engaged in labor," Wang Youde became the one and only "rotten branch" in the village. "Not one village cadre had any way to cope" with him. It was not that Wang Youde did not want to labor; he actually snuck into the fields. But he "tried it for an hour or so, and he was so exhausted from the effort that he went home and fell into bed." In addition, "he plowed the land no better than a chicken scratching, and even destroyed a good number of wheat stalks." Wang Youde "was disheartened" and even thought "if I die then I die; death would be good." Wang Youde tried to sell fried dough sticks, but he was stopped from so doing in a "humiliating" way by the village cadres as well as the villagers. From this, one can also see that at that time so-called labor did not include commercial activity, but rather was completely limited to the activity of material production. At the time,

21. Tr.: Struggle meetings refers to the practice of putting a perceived or accused criminal—such as a landlord—on a platform and having the exploited peasants "struggle" against him until he admitted his crimes. These were large meetings attended by the entire village and became a form of popular or democratic justice during the land reform period.

that was because of the urgent need to recover productivity; ultimately, it derived from the idea that this recovery was demanded by the needs of modern industrialization. For this reason, there are many novels in which there are sarcastic references to those who engage in petty commerce, and such characters are included in the category of parasite.[22] Thus, "in the end, Wang Youde had no way out."

This very Wang Youde, who had no way out, "suddenly had some angry thoughts" and wished to "set fire to these pitiful days of his." Yet set fire to what? Naturally, set fire to the village wheat. The story describes Wang's thoughts: "At midnight, Youde woke up hungry and heard not a sound coming from anywhere in the village. He thought to himself: 'Everyone says what a piece of crap I am, that I can't do anything at all? Without expending even a bit of energy, I'll go out at this point and it isn't even cold, all I'd need to do is light a small lantern fire, then the wind would blow, and . . .' This is the first time he had such 'heroic' thoughts, and he really did get out of his kang, light a lantern fire and quietly open the door. In the courtyard, he took a stalk of straw."

In this depiction, the author apparently makes a distinction between the individual (quality) and the class (attributes). That is to say, the narrator tends to depict Wang Youde's destructive behavior more as the result of an individual's rage or blindness and not as a conscious opposition entirely born of a class ideology. This type of depiction is not at all uncommon in contemporary Chinese literature; in earlier works, such as Zhao Shuli's novel *Changes in Li Village*, personal characteristics are often the narrative's focus. When class perspective was absolutized, class attributes (attributes that constitute a different kind of generality) substituted for any form of individuality; this came from left-wing (urban-based) intellectual traditions, and in some sense, we can also say that this move was another form of the absolutizing commonality of human nature. The expressive form of this absolutizing was elevating individual attributes into common ones (as, in left-wing intellectual thought, the existence of human nature as such was denied). This resulted in the suppression of individual natures by common natures, and it also gave rise to conflicts between different kinds of commonality. Behind all this was a method of intellectually knowing and grasping the object. For this reason, in discussions of the structuration of contemporary literature and culture, there is still a good deal of latitude for discussion among intellectuals. This latitude indicates how modern new culture [May Fourth] conventions entered the knowledge and

---

22. Tr.: For example, the character Huang Daquan in Chen Dengke's *Feng lei* [Storm].

thought system of left-wing intellectuals; how this system was influenced by revolutionary politics and vice versa; and how this urban intellectual system also came into conflict with nativist ideologies. The critiques of "Reeducation" manifest this point.

Wang Youde's almost comedic destructive behavior is not and indeed could not be completed in the story. This is obvious. However, when he was "handcuffed by the 'wheat protection brigade' and sent to the peasant committee," Wang Youde did not receive particularly harsh punishment ("some favored sending him to the district; some favored thrashing him a bit"). The village cadres' techniques for punishment were unique. One was to "put him in an empty room," where, however, "the walls were very busy with slogans and posters pasted about." These slogans and posters contained such sayings as "Oppose lazy bones!" and "In the new society, it is not permitted to not earn one's own keep!" and "He who does not labor will go hungry!" and "Only through labor will you be able to alter your landlord status!" and "Eradicate parasites!" and so on. In addition, the chairman of the peasant committee, Fan Laogeng, sits at his side and "chain-smokes, chattering away," talking to him about the importance of labor. This basically rehearses the two big functions of ideological disciplining and persuasion. The second technique was having him move three thousand bricks "to the front gate" and allowing him to eat only after the task is completed. In this way, he can experience the principle that without labor there is no food. This expresses a form of coerced labor reeducation. These two forms both come from the experiences of the Yan'an period reeducation campaigns.[23] They gradually became major forms of efforts in subsequent years to reform through labor, whose extreme development would eventually become the policy to reform criminals through labor reeducation.[24]

It is important to note that Wang Youde's opposition to labor is also narrated as a form of ideology. The author uses a host of indirect quotations to indicate the existence of this ideology: "He had always thought that the types of activities that required an expenditure of effort and suffering were not for his type of person, but rather were to be done by certain types of people,

---

23. For example, at the time there had already emerged many methods of reeducation such as oral propaganda, aiding the masses, concentrating the administration, coerced labor, and so on. See Zhu Hongzhao, *Yanan richang shenghuozhong de lishi (1937–1947)* [History of Yan'an's everyday life (1937–1947)] (Guilin: Guangxi Shida Chubanshe, 2007), 57–65.

24. On the existence of such labor camps at the time, see Yang Xianhui, *Jiabiangou jishi* [Memories of Jiabiangou] (Tianjin: Guji Chubanshe, 2002).

those who had been born to suffer, those who had been born disadvantaged. So if he is asked to go do things like they did, he would find it really awful and wouldn't have the courage." It goes without saying that labor or laborism in the Chinese revolutionary discursive world takes on an extremely important narrative function. That is, in addition to helping overthrow traditional social hierarchy both structurally and ideologically, the notion of labor also provides conceptual legitimacy for a genuinely equal society.

Through ideological disciplining and persuasion and especially through the coerced labor reeducation process, Wang Youde eventually does turn over a completely new leaf: "From this time forward, Wang Youde really was transformed: his body became stronger, his complexion was ruddier, he wasn't as afraid of suffering in doing hard labor. If he was made to participate more in labor brigades and collective labor, then perhaps in two or three years, he'd start believing that life without labor wasn't worth living." At this point in the narrative, the main topic of the story, reeducation, is given very clear expression in a line spoken by Fan Laogeng: "It appears if one isn't afraid to expend some energy, then so long as one is not Chiang Kaishek, there is no one who cannot be reeducated."

"Reeducation" is a story of high artistic quality: it borrows the exaggerations and performativity of folk stories to achieve a comedic effect; it also borrows broadly from modern narrative techniques—including those of indirect quoting—which it uses in a masterful manner. At the same time, its narrative attitude is very much akin to the way peasants encounter people and things with generosity, equanimity, and humor. This type of narrative mode does not exactly emerge from China's 1930s radical elite [urban-based] left-wing literary tradition. Rather, one should locate and consider it in the context of the cultural creations of the liberated zones represented by Zhao Shuli. For this reason, this narrative mode could not be fully understood by new culture intellectuals, and nor could they completely adapt themselves to it.[25]

In the second issue of the second volume of *People's Literature*, "two critiques sent in by readers" were published along with an "essay of self-criticism"

25. Tr.: Here is the genealogy Cai is working with: new culture intellectuals were inheritors of an urban-based radical but elite left-wing literary revolution deriving from the May Fourth Movement, and the culture of the liberated zones refers to the Yan'an base area and related spaces in northern China that were ruled by the Communist Party from the mid-1930s through the War of Resistance against Japan and the civil war, up to the 1949 establishment of the People's Republic of China, in which village and mass revolutionary culture became the sine qua non of literary production. The traditions of literature developed by each of these left-wing models were quite different.

by Qin Zhaoyang.[26] At the same time, the editorial board added an editorial note emphasizing that "when readers conscientiously point out the shortcomings of works, it will be beneficial both to the editors and to the authors. We are very grateful." Evidently, on the question of "Reeducation," the attitude of the editorial board of *People's Literature* was not at all clear; indeed, it was rather ambivalent. Of the two letters sent in by readers, one was by Xu Guolun, titled "A review of 'Reeducation'"; the other was by Luo Min, titled "Concealing the Essence of Class Contradiction." Qin himself wrote "A Self-Critique of 'Reeducation'" as a response.

In his piece, Qin told of the origins [of "Reeducation"] and the main thinking that went into the process of writing the story:

> Before the War of Resistance [against Japan], I had witnessed the lives of some parasites leading the lifestyle of the old society. During the struggles in the villages of the liberated zones, I gained some impressions of the life of landlords. Once I left the villages for the city, I came into contact with the lives of various types of urbanites, which also left a deep impression on me. When I thought "love of labor" should become people's new moral compass, it made me want to write a story about parasites embedded in the new society, the shame of them not working for the new society and having no future in that way. I decided to select a small landlord of modest wealth as my protagonist.

Today, when we read the relevant materials again, we can see that the critics of this story concentrated their criticism mainly on the depictions of Wang Youde, a "small landlord of modest wealth." Precisely this fact is alluded to in the title of Luo Min's letter: the concealment of the essence of class contradictions. The concept of the "essence of class" derives from Mao's Yan'an-period Party rectification campaign [1942], during which he had criticized dogmatism and bookishness. Views and works marked by problems supposedly ignoring the essence of class exhibited a complete neglect of the difference between big landlords and medium or small landlords, including their different attitudes toward life and the villagers' very different attitudes toward them; this lack of differentiation basically belonged to the subjective bias and subjective evaluation of urban left-wing intellectuals. On this theoretical premise, the

---

26. Tr.: All quotes from the material discussed here are from this issue of the journal. No page numbers are available.

critic [Luo] accused Qin's story of "conflating the two strands of proper attitude toward class enemies and the bums among poor peasants," thus revealing dissatisfaction with the method of "persuasion, reform" for landlords and emphasizing the necessity for a more radical mode of struggle. This type of perspective actually reveals a certain future potential for political radicalization as it denies any possibility for landlords genuinely to be reeducated.

When critiquing China's [Maoist-era] ultra-left politics [today], we often depict intellectuals as the victims of this politics. Yet we have forgotten that in the process of the formulation of this politics, there was in fact a large group of intellectuals who actively and most likely sincerely participated [in political radicalization]. Determining how to write about these intellectuals, including about their intellectual resources at the time, is an important task.

The critiques written by Xu Guolun and Luo Min mainly focus on the story's narrative attitude toward the landlord, Wang Youde; these critiques did not and indeed could not displace the major subject of "Reeducation," which was that "'love of labor' should become the new moral compass of the masses." To the contrary, this major theme ran through contemporary Chinese literary narration for the entire 1949–66 period. When we discuss the history of the first thirty years of contemporary Chinese literature [1949–79], we tend to focus on the role and function assumed by literary criticism of the time; this is not in dispute. After 1949, contemporary Chinese literature was appropriated into the unity of the Party-state management model, according to which literary criticism not only came to represent political opinion but could also exert influence on this political opinion.[27] For this reason, literary criticism really did exert control over writings in contemporary Chinese literature. At the same time, however, we must not assume that contemporary literature was entirely under the control of criticism. Due to the multiplicity of literary creations and the fact that China's revolutionary politics could not have had the absoluteness that we might now imagine, creative writing could not have been entirely subject to political critical opinion. In this sense, I do not agree with the exaggerated [current] emphasis on the controlling strength of [Party-state-literature] unity. For example, in the midst of the 1957 Anti-

---

27. For a typical example of the mutuality of criticism and politics, see Wang Meng, "A Young Man Arrives at the Organization Department," in *Literature of the Hundred Flowers*, edited and translated by Hualing Nieh (New York: Columbia University Press, 1981). See also Wang Meng, *Wang Meng zizhuan* [Wang Meng's autobiography] (Guangzhou: Huacheng Chubanshe, 2006–7), vol. 1.

Rightist Campaign, there were ill-intentioned critiques such as those penned by Yao Wenyuan[28] for the internal Party circulation, which had very deleterious effects on a number of other works. However, the theme of antibureaucratism and antiprivilege did not completely disappear. To the contrary, this theme continued to be articulated, albeit in a different form.[29] How to identify in detail the real relationship between criticism and writing thus is a very important aspect of how we must write about the literary history of this period.

The narrative subject of the love of labor central to "Reeducation" was not curtailed because of the criticism leveled at the story; rather, it became an extremely important narrative paradigm for contemporary Chinese literature. Of course, there was efficacy in the criticism, so subsequent literary works avoided the kind of moderation and reformism toward landlords depicted in "Reeducation," and this narrative paradigm continued to expand to include not only the reeducation through labor of intellectuals but also that of cadres. It even further strengthened the concept of labor for peasants and workers. We have no evidence that this love of labor narrative theme necessarily derives from the influence of Qin Zhaoyang's "Reeducation." More probably, this subject matter was motivated by a collective unconscious of the era which, to borrow Benjamin Schwartz's concept of "the reign of virtue" represents the "moral tradition" of China's revolutionary politics.[30]

The delineation of an ethical perspective on the love of labor in some sense can be traced back to the Yan'an era reeducation of the lumpen[31] campaign, whose historical context was the border area's military mobilization for "production on a large scale." This "re-education of the *lumpen*" emerged from the material production demands [of the Yan'an period];[32] it also came to take on

---

28. Tr.: Yao Wenyuan was later a member of the Gang of Four in the Cultural Revolution.
29. See chapter 2.
30. Benjamin I. Schwartz, *Chinese Communism and the Rise of Mao* (Cambridge, MA: Harvard University Press, 1996). Tr.: The "reign of virtue" is a major concept developed throughout Schwartz's book.
31. Tr.: Cai uses *erliuzi*, meaning loafers or lazy people, who did not participate properly in productive activities. They are not strictly synonymous with Marx's category of the lumpen proletariat, although they came to be labeled revolutionary enemies later. Cai is pointing here to labor as the standard measure for revolutionary ethicality that emerged in Yan'an and persisted into the narrative literature he is examining from the 1950s and 1960s. For this reason, we translate *erliuzi* as lumpen, since this retains the notion of labor as central.
32. For example, in 1937, Yan'an District was said to have 1,629 lumpen, and by 1941, 1,173 had been successfully reeducated, amounting to 72 percent of the total number [1,629]. At the same time labor power was rapidly increased, and barren land was cultivated while ever more grains were harvested. See Zhu Hongzhao, *Yanan richang shenghuozhong de lishi*, 58.

a far more profound ideological hue. The February 24, 1943, *Liberation Daily* [*Jiefang ribao*] editorial titled "The Reeducation of the Lumpen" summarizes the problem in this way: "In the past years, we've not only engaged in economic, political, and cultural reeducation and construction, but we've also engaged in the reeducation and construction of the 'human (*ren*).' The dregs bequeathed us by the old society—lumpen—have for the most part transformed themselves from their prior mode of being and have mostly become healthy and productive peasants." If we say that this editorial is mostly expressing a political perspective on the desired malleability of humans, then the piece by Bei Qun printed in the May 20, 1943, issue of *Liberation Daily* titled "Gai guo" [Change] offers a different depiction. For example, the lumpen, Zhang Tonghua, with the assistance of the labor hero, Yang Chaochen, opens deserted lands and raises chickens. He labors long and hard and even eschews going to see an opera. When asked, "Old Zhang, why have you transformed into such a good person," Zhang Tonghua gratefully replies: "If not for Brother Old Yang, my life would be over. He woke me from a dream." Another lumpen, Liu Si also says: "If others can learn to be good, why cannot we transform ourselves?" If we eliminate the traces of the intellectual style of narration (for example, "he woke me from a dream"), then "become good" (*bianhao*) and "learn to be good" (*xuehao*) are quite typical examples of rural Chinese speech and tone. Evidently, the author here imported some ethics from everyday rural life that differentiate between good and bad or good and evil.

If we consider the primary distinction in modern politics to be between friends and enemies, then in Chinese villages there exists another even larger and historically more enduring moral principle of good and bad or good and evil. This ethical understanding often transcends modern politics and deeply conditions the lifeworlds of the Chinese people. We could in some sense consider this ethical understanding as a moral politics, or as the moral tradition embedded in Chinese politics. I do not intend to compare this moral political tradition to the natural law of Western political thought. Such a simple comparison is highly likely to lead to many conceptual confusions or redefinitions. To be sure, this type of moral tradition in China's rural village society patently does exist, and people use this type of morality as a political standard of differentiation between good and bad or good and evil in their lifeworlds. In some sense, China's revolutionary politics efficiently mobilized the resources bequeathed it by this moral tradition and ignited the masses' memories of this morality. In other words, the Chinese revolution was not just economic and political; more importantly, it was ethical. For this reason, when the revolution bent its will toward constructing a new society, it inevitably incorporated the futurity of the ability of people to "become good" or to "learn to be good," where goodness is an enduring historical moral tradition.³³

Zhou Libo has called this tradition an "old established practice."³⁴ Meng Yue, in her essay discussing *White-Haired Girl*, calls this the "folk ethical order."³⁵ We can perhaps understand in this way why China's contemporary literary texts are so preoccupied internally with the distribution of moral resources—class enemies are not only antirevolutionary, but more important, they are amoral. For this reason, the first scene of *Keep the Red Flag Flying* inevitably depicts the landlord Feng Laosan's expropriation of common land as the amoral behavior of a bad person, while the father-son pair Zhu Laogong and Zhu Laozhong are determined upholders of morality. This narrative mode reveals the fact that the Chinese revolution is the staunch heir to and protector of rural moral tradition. Indeed, the legitimacy of the Chinese revolution was established upon the basis of this moral tradition, and it even repaired and recovered the enduring promise of this moral tradition, which, at the same time, constitutes the ethical content of the new society (lifeworld). Of course, this moral tradition had no way to saturate the complex content of the Chinese revolution, and the essential modernity of the revolution also inevitably demanded this moral tradition be transformed and redefined.³⁶

33. Yet this morality is a very difficult concept to pin down, as it is loose and dispersed. Exegeses of ancient Chinese texts [*The Book of Rites*] say: "Gain derives from morality" [*De de ye*]. Gain is said to be virtuous, but what is being gained? [The 1930s scholar] Qian Mu believes it is "human nature" (*tianxing*), and he cites Zhu Mu from the Later Han as follows: "Obtaining human nature is what is called 'gaining.'" He also cites a passage from Guo Xiang's *An Explication of the Analects*: "The virtuous or moral one is he who obtains his nature" (quoted in Qian Mu, *Zhongguo sixiang tongsu jianghua* [Popular talks on Chinese thought] [Beijing: Sanlian Shudian, 2002]). According to this specification of nature, it is possible to transcend the modern method of the contract and from there to make one's way back to a more traditional rationality; indeed, this forms part of what overseas new Confucian conservatism is demanding politically. Even if we dispense with that particular notion of nature, we can still understand morality as a form of attitude toward life among Chinese people.

34. Zhou Libo, "*Minjian gushi* xiaoyin" [A small guide to *Folk Stories*], in *Zhou Libo wenji* [Collected Essays of Zhou Libo] (Shanghai: Shanghai Wenyi Chubanshe, 1985), 5:290. On Zhou's notion of "old established practices," see chapter 4.

35. Meng Yue, *Baimaonv yanbian de qishi—jianlun Yan'an wenyi de lishi duo zhixing* [Notes on the evolution of *White-Haired Girl*—A brief discussion of the multiplicity of the history of Yan'an art practices], in *Ershi shiji zhongguo wenxueshi lun* [On the history of twentieth-century Chinese literature], ed. Wang Xiaoming (Shanghai: Dongfang Chuban Zhongxin, 2003), 2:194.

36. While this is a different topic, it is worth pointing out that the very overturning of this moral tradition by the radicalization of modern politics is one main reason for the crisis in Chinese socialism. This type of radicalizating and overturning is typified by the Cultural Revo-

At the same time, however, it is extremely difficult to define moral tradition. Following some of the existing arguments, we can find a way into the task of examining this morality by exploring the areas of overlap between the big (elite) and small (folk) traditions, where the overlapping area could then be called something like a lifeworld. The actual demands of this morality are an ethically and politically ordered lifeworld that not only emphasizes the position of the individual vis-à-vis society and even the natural world, but also emphasizes the positions of power and rights. For these reasons, it includes a strong political content. In my view, what most comprehensively articulates this morality or this moral politics is none other than literature, as literature frequently transmits the strong aspirations of the lifeworld. These aspirations perhaps are utopian and pastoral and are often expressed in terms of wanting to move outside of historical temporality. Yet we ought not understand pastoral poetics as expressions of disillusionment. To the contrary, pastoral poetics genuinely exists among the Chinese and particularly in Chinese rural society. It forms a type of "folk ethical order" (in Meng's terms), and from it can be deduced the ideals of life, while it is also the standard against which good and evil, truth and falsehood, can be measured.

I think that the Chinese revolution resuscitated and enlivened this moral tradition. For this reason, particularly with regard to subalterns, what was most mobilizing and persuasive probably was not the abstract concept of the nation-state but rather that of the new society. The new society was a type of mediating concept between the individual and the state, while at the same time it implied a promise for the lifeworld. This promise in the villages no doubt took on a pastoral utopian hue. For this reason, using nationalism, particularly bourgeois nationalism, to explain the Chinese revolution is not entirely apt. Indeed, even in the historical accounts of the War of Resistance against Japan one can still detect a strong desire for the reconstruction of a new social, political, and revolutionary power. Implied in this kind of pastoral description of life there is a remembered morality, which indicates that this lifeworld is at the same time an ethical society, a good society in which individuals face the important problem of "becoming good" and "learning to be good."

This good society approximates the moral desires and aspirations of the majority of Chinese villagers and peasants. In this sense, Mao's description

---

lution, during which the friend-enemy distinction of modern politics insistently entered into the everyday lifeworlds of the people, which brought about a crisis in trust between the people and the state.

of the ruffians' movement in his 1927 *Report on an Investigation in the Hunan Peasant Movement* never directly entered into the textual norms of modern Chinese literature. Rather, the enthusiastic participants in the peasant movement are all depicted in an orthodox type of peasant imagery, where the real ruffians are identified as those waiting to be struggled against as targets of the revolution. And what controls such narration very possibly derives from the moral tradition in the Chinese revolution. Of course, this tradition incorporates some aspects of the ancient Chinese notion of peasantism and influenced the imaginary of modernization in the Chinese revolution, which included a respect for material production on the one hand and the suppression of consumption on the other hand. The latter tendency included a high degree of vigilance against commercial capitalism, all the way to a radical rejection of the commodity economy.

My task here is not to finish an abstract discussion of this moral politics. Rather, my goal is to use the moral tradition as a framework to discuss how such a politics was contained in the notion of labor. Because there is a status order in traditional society, naturally there is a certain contempt for labor (manual labor), from which derives the Mencian saying, "those who work with their brains rule; those who work with their brawn are ruled." On the other hand, however, because of the essential attributes of rural society it is impossible to completely negate the importance and significance of labor. Especially after the Qin and Han Dynasties, the social status of the literati or gentry gradually came to separate itself from what Mencius had specified: "They are only men of education, who, without a certain livelihood, are able to maintain a fixed heart."[37] That is, they gradually became men of means, and once they became landlords their forms of life underwent huge transformations into, in folk terms, "plough, read, and extend the family." The transformation in their way of life also influenced the theoretical and practical articulations of intellectuals in ancient times, which in turn influenced reforms in local religions.[38] These changes in attitude toward labor exhibit a strong tendency to do things by oneself, which includes the attitude that calls for feeding oneself through one's own labor. This type of thinking about labor was very easily able to strike an alliance with many in China's rural society, so

---

37. Tr.: This comes from the Mencius *Liang Hui Wang* I. What Cai is pointing to here is the long fall of the gentry from an ideal sociological group to an exploiting class.

38. For example, the reforms in the Mahayana religious forms. See Yu Yingshi, *Shi yu Zhongguo wenhua* [The gentry and Chinese culture] (Shanghai: Shanghai Renmin Chubanshe, 1987), 458.

much so that it is quite difficult to even distinguish any sense of a separation between a big (elite) and a small (folk) tradition. The most that can be said is that this concept of labor comprised a murky area of overlap between the big and small traditions, and it became one major factor in the composition of the moral tradition historically.

In reality, in China's rural society labor always has been seen as an individual's virtue. An individual who, through his own labor, obtains the necessities of life not only commands the respect of others but essentially helps maintain "the rule of ritual" theorized by Fei.[39] This is also the moral politics of life symbolized by the rural tradition of "relying on oneself for self-sufficiency." In this rural cultural tradition, labor becomes a standard measure for making distinctions. Indeed, as mentioned above, when it comes to the ruffians' movement, the attitude taken in contemporary literature is extremely scrupulous. For example, Zhou Libo in *The Hurricane* depicts Bai Yushan as someone who does not dislike labor but, rather, as someone who falls into laziness when his right to labor was expropriated by the landlord. The significance of the revolution hence resides in how to turn those whose right to labor has been expropriated back into laborers, which inevitably gives rise to a series of political revolutions. It is worth noting that this type of depiction is not limited to rural novels but also proliferates in novels about the working class.[40]

The Chinese revolution had its own essential quest for sovereignty, and for this reason it had to promise a good and virtuous new society. In this sense, contemporary literature inherited the Chinese traditional perspective on labor or morality. At the same time, as regards the country's modernization, it needed to mobilize a huge amount of legitimate labor power not only for urban industrialization but also for agrarian collectivization. All of this required a reformulation of a modern worker ethic. For this, the traditional Chinese perspective on labor or morality formed an efficient functional resource. This is also why in the image of the old worker or the old peasant we can sense a good deal of virtue. For this reason, even though Qin Zhaoyang's "Reeducation" was roundly criticized, yet the love of labor upheld in this story had to become the new concept of the people—this basic narrative subject not only never was dislodged, but novels written from 1949 to 1966 all used it as a mainstream narrative model.

39. Fei, *From the Soil*, 94.
40. For example, in Ai Mingzhi's *Huozhong* [Kindling] or Luo Dan's *Fengyu de liming* [The storm of dawn] (Beijing: Zhongguo Qingnian Chubanshe, 1959), and so on.

Not only was the emergence of labor as some sort of virtue or morality mobilized for a reformulation of Chinese rural society, but this reformulation articulated the ancestral ties between revolutionary politics and traditional morality. It also enabled the cultural order of rural society to recover from the various destructive blows to which it had been subjected. It was mobilized, in addition, to reeducate the rural people, including landlords. In the early 1950s not only did state politics articulate an aspiration for moral rule, but cultural and spiritual activities, including literature, also harbored such an imaginary. These aspirations played a big role in helping console the masses and even treat the wounds left by many years of war. The social conditions of vigorous political movements attained a measure of calm in these pastoral writings. This is especially the case because, due to the dangers of the disruption of traditional social conditions posed by class struggle, these writings could present an ethical possibility for the re-creation of social structures. The state, because of the deep ethics implied by the establishment of the new socialist society, gained a big boost [from these writings]. If we consider the entirety of Chinese politics and even Chinese literature for the seventeen years (1949–66), the concept of a moral politics could always be an efficient entry into a discussion, as it constitutes a nativized investigative mode.

Of course, labor is not limited to Chinese rural society; it simultaneously includes the reeducation of intellectuals. This reeducation not only included the tendencies toward an epistemology of practice, it also included [class] stand, [class] attitude, [class] passion, and other aspects of "the new emerging from the womb of the old"—those factors to which Mao pointed in his "Talks at the Yenan Forum on Literature and Art" for the "transformation of one class into another."[41] As for the necessary process required for the reformulation of new cadres by the Chinese revolution, labor also was a very important factor. In this sense, labor not only was a functionally efficient mediator between cadres and the masses (that is, fulfilling the requirement to not separate oneself from the masses), but at the same time, it was designed as one way to forestall bureaucratization and the tendency toward the growth of cadre privilege. Novels not only used the sharpest sarcasm to criticize those cadres who separated themselves from productive activities, but in the end they also used such participation as a systemized standard by which to measure cadres.[42]

41. Mao, "Talks at the Yenan Forum on Literature and Art," 3.
42. For the former, see Chen Dengke, *Feng lei* [Storm] (Beijing: Zhongguo Qingnian Chubanshe, 1964); for the latter, one can look at the state regulations and policies of the time that called for what was named the "combination of two participations and one transformation.

The ongoing extension of the meaning of labor and its transformed definition cannot be contained by morality. The fundamental modernity of the Chinese revolution inevitably required that morality, including its labor component, be explored in more modern terms. These terms meant that the goals of the Chinese revolution were never intended to mark a return to tradition. Because of these modern political aspirations, a final rupture was inevitably in the offing between the Chinese revolution and tradition. This rupture not only included social practice but also perspectives on thought itself. For this reason, and especially in the context of collectivized social practice, the concept of labor faced a modern challenge, which was articulated in the following question: how, ultimately, was one to reconcile the two fundamentally different forms of collective and individual labor?

III. *The Builders* and Changes in the Concept of Labor

Liu Qing's *The Builders* uses a narrative of the Hama Tan Village case to epically represent the process of cooperativization in Chinese rural villages. I have already discussed the emergence of this movement in its economic (mode of production), ideological (elimination of difference), ethical (mutual aid and help), political (structures of power), and other aspects. The central political consideration for this movement resided in the attempt by the Chinese revolution to show that its point of departure in equality (land reform) could be deepened into a processual equality that could lead to actual equality. Without this, there would be no substantive distinction between socialism and democracy.[43] However, the significance of the cooperativization movement was not limited to this; in reality, this movement put an end to a thousand years of the individual form of rural labor and the political, economic, moral, and other social cultural systems that were based upon this form of labor. For this reason, the movement really stirred up the entire order of life in the rural villages, which called forth any number of different types of responses, including sharp debates on what should or could be done. When this movement entered literary narrative, it inevitably became symbolic. That is to say, its significance came to transcend any existence in real practice, as these narratives included far more considerations of what should happen—all of which created a certain conflict between the real world and its fabrication and imagination. This is not to say that "the ought" was completely overwhelmed; it

---

43. See the discussion in chapter 1.

is to say that in literary texts there existed a very sharp debate between the ought and reality. The significance of these texts can be found in this debate. Of course, another aspect of this question lies in the blind acceptance of or obedience to the ought (the ideal), which could lead to the obscuring of the real (the actual world) in a given novel. This is where later criticism of such literature finds its foothold. However, the focus on the obscuring was the endpoint of the debate [in the 1980s]. While it is one thing to address reasons why the discussion ended (for example, politics], it is another if one abandons the discussion of the ought altogether [because of the politics].

In the process of cooperativization, labor as a form underwent enormous changes: the thousand-year-old form of individual labor characteristic of the Chinese villages was transformed into a mode of collectivized labor. It is just this transformation—and its socioeconomic and political context along with its corresponding moral-ethical structures—that really called forth an extreme reaction in village society and a correspondingly sharp debate at all levels.

On the very first page of Liu Qing's *The Builders*, there is the following epigraph: "Family properties cause divisions among brothers; labor unites a whole village."[44] It is not clear whether this epigraph is Liu's creation or whether it was collected from folk sayings. The important thing is that, in narratology, the significance of this epigraph can be seen as a type of subtext. The function of a subtext resides in the fact that it is supplementary to and explains the formal text's significance. With this epigraph, the main topic of the *The Builders* is prominently displayed: in the context of collective labor there is embedded a vigilance against and critique of private property. At the same time, it clearly articulates Liu's literary perspective, which is that novels must play an active role in people's imagination of the fate of their own history and community. Actually, this is a common perspective in contemporary literature, although it has often been contained within and under such popular political themes as peasant-worker class consciousness and individual reeducation.

Collective labor does not correspond to the form of mutual aid common in the rural social tradition. Rather, it is a brand-new modern mode of labor. We could say that it is a socialist form of organization borrowed from urban industrialization for the transformation of village life; or we could say that it is China's revolutionary imaginary of socialist practice as an alternative to that of the Soviet rural communes. Most important is not just that the cooperative

---

44. Liu Ching [Liu Qing]. *The Builders*, trans. Sidney Shapiro (Peking: Foreign Language Press, 1964), 1.

form (including the subsequent people's communes) substituted for the family as a productive unit and its corresponding dispersed individual productive mode. But also, at the same time, cooperatives clearly conflicted with the unitary and exclusive mode of production characterized by individual production and private property. It was through this conflict that cooperatives created a practice of collective labor as well as a new collective imaginary. Indeed, in its literary articulation, this collective labor harbored a large number of social and cultural elements.

There is no form other than collective labor that is capable of expressing the importance of the existence of a type of social group.[45] This existence in some sense was strengthened to become a common understanding that "where there are more people, there is strength." Of course, this "more people" had to be fully organized; it thus refers to an organized people. Lu Xun in his 1908 essay "Imbalances in Cultural Development" described his critical target [the unorganized Chinese people] as a "federation of sand," and the phrase "a plate of loose sand" came to be a metaphor for old China. Of course, for Lu Xun, the path toward a "republic of people" had to pass through "the awakening of the people of the nation, the growth of personality"; his emphasis falls on the importance of culture.[46] Somewhat different from Lu Xun, Liang Shuming [in the 1920s and 1930s] paid more attention to "experiments in thought," and like Mao, insisted on focusing on rural China [for transformation]. For Liang, the two aspects most important for China were "group organization and scientific technology." On the question of rural villages, he did not differ too much from Mao: "In order for China to progress, the unorganized, loose countryside had to be organized in some way, for only with organization could advanced science and technology be used. In fact, everyone had to walk this path."[47]

In literature, only through cooperativization as the form of labor could a utopian futurity of life be introduced. That is, a future version of life could

---

45. Tr.: Cai evokes the notion of *qun* here, which is a traditional concept replaced in the twentieth century by the modern category of society or the social. It is not coterminous with either society or the family or village but has a more fluid composition and meaning.

46. Lu Xun, "Wenhua pianzhi lun" [Imbalances in cultural development]. Tr.: We are not clear where Cai got his citations from, although they are easily findable on any Chinese-language Lu Xun website. In addition, "loose plate of sand" was a phrase that was frequently evoked in the 1910s and 1920s by any number of cultural and political figures in China, including Sun Zhongshan.

47. Shuming Liang and Guy S. Alitto, *Has Man a Future? Dialogues with the Last Confucian* (Berlin: Springer, 2013), 66.

only be the product of a collective imaginary. As already discussed in chapter 1, the description in Zhao Shuli's *Sanliwan Village* of three pictures depicting today, next year, and the village under socialism perfectly represents this imaginary utopian futurity. The ensuing sentence is even more important: "It looked very much like one of our present state farms."[48] In fact, in Zhao's works, there is seldom a romantic narrative depiction of village life. Yet it in the midst of this kind of narrative that labor gets transformed into a utopian society of labor. And the possibility of the realization of the utopia lies in the imaginary derived from the promise of the power of collective labor.

In *The Builders* and other related narratives of the time, experiments in re-education are more often than not described as a special moral characteristic of collectivism. Yet in the narrative levels of this collectivism, we can still strongly sense the modern traces of the individual daring to seek individuality. Indeed, it is because of the persistence of these traces that there exists a tendency toward romanticism in these novels' narratives.

If Liu's *The Builders* has a somewhat melancholy narrative tone, then in other literary works, such as Zhou Libo's *Great Changes in the Mountain Village*, there is a much happier disposition associated precisely with the cooperatization movement. This happiness is expressed in the laughter and singing of the young men and women; it is also expressed in the love between Chen Dachun and Sheng Shujun. There are many works that similarly describe collective labor as a location for the production of love; this is not accidental. On the one hand, this extends the old left-wing literary narrative model of "revolution plus love"; on the other hand, the slightly altered narrative of "collective plus love" uses a more in-depth exploration of the collective to deepen its emphasis on where youth and marriage belong. This emphasis makes cooperatization and collective labor a very attractive proposition for young people.

We should note that in the gradual process of the abolition under socialism of private property, the love produced by collective labor is more pure and more carefree. On this point, Ma Feng and Sun Qian's film script, *The Youth in Our Village*, is very clear. It is important to point out that the narrative rendering of collective labor as a form of love or carefree happiness cannot be understood merely as some sort of political tactical move. The politicization of literary works at this time did have to fulfill certain political assignments, yet at the same time we must also recognize that literature also helped create life. This latter aspect is the one that can explain most thoroughly the complex

---

48. Zhao, *Sanliwan Village*, 195.

imbrication of contemporary literature and politics. (The complex imbrication will be discussed further below, when I focus on Zhao Shuli.) For this reason, the happy and carefree depictions should not be seen as entirely fake; rather, they reflect the enthusiasm, daring, and confidence—even a purity and naivete—about creating life in contemporary literature. All this has long since been lost in our times. Yet in this carefree narrative style, the collective, including the strength of the collective, was rendered as happy. Zhou's *Great Changes in the Mountain Village*, in a carefree and happy and even melodramatic fashion, demonstrates through the cooperative and the go it alone (Wang Jusheng) the powerful way in which collective labor could reform its targeted objects.

I think that anyone with even a passing knowledge of literature could point out that in the literary writing of the time the image of nature repeatedly appears. In *The Builders* there is the "green southern mountain," and in *Sanliwan Village* there is the "large Western hollow." In Chen Dengke's *Storm* (*Feng lei*), "green grass lake" continually appears, while there is Bai Wei's *Reclaiming Wasteland* (*Kenhuang qu*) and Huang Tianming's *Frontier Morning Song* (*Bianjiang xiaoge*) [and] all the way through to Lin Yu's *The Geese Fly North*, and so on. All of these turn the effort to clear and open up nature into a major narrative topos. In these narratives, nature is rich and abundant, and for this reason it requires humans to tame and harness it. Nature is also deserted, almost inhuman. For this reason, it becomes a place where man can be put to important tests. All of these descriptions can be traced back to that very important speech by Mao, "The Foolish Old Man Who Removed the Mountain." In this speech, Mao used the metaphors of "old man Yu" and the "Wangwu mountain" to express his strong and somewhat exaggerated affirmation of human (revolutionary) will, which at the same time reconfigured the relationship between man and nature. This relationship is one of man exploiting nature, with exploitation and transformation used to combat the people's superstitions about the mythical wonders of nature. In some sense, it is possible to say that the core thinking of this speech practically formed the basis for a socialist-era philosophy of the environment, a philosophy that also implied a perspective on nature and man's existence.[49]

---

49. Mao Zedong, "Yugong yishan" [The Foolish Old Man Who Removed the Mountain]," delivered June 11, 1945. Tr.: This was subsequently published as an essay, which became extremely popular during the Cultural Revolution because it demonstrated how impossible things could become possible. The translated essay is available in *Selected Works of Mao Tse-tung* (Peking: Foreign Languages Press, 1967), 3: 271–74.

I have no intention of comparing the nature of which I am speaking to subthemes in German romanticism, such as the Schillerian perspective on nature. Clearly, the image of nature in Chinese literature of this period bears little relation to the abstract philosophy of [Friedrich] Schiller. However, two of the most important narrative categories of German romanticism can be found in an alternative way in contemporary Chinese literature. It is in German romanticism that there is the beginning of a subject-object split, where the subject is not only defined through the isolated being as an individual subjectivity, but this subject must also pass through the transcendence and overcoming of the object ("impediment") to have the possibility of self-completion. The overcoming of the object leads to a sort of enthusiasm for and courage about action. And in this action what bursts forth is "that voluntarism that is uninhibited and cannot be restrained," behind which lurks a sort of profound concept—"men throw themselves into things they wish to throw themselves into"[50]—through which a heroism is established. Whether it is Mao's personal attitude toward romanticism (with this attitude emerged the notion of combining "revolutionary realism with revolutionary romanticism") or it is a manifestation of modern Chinese romanticism, we cannot ignore the existence of this romanticism and its influence on Chinese socialism. When we speak of Chinese modernity, romanticism is a very important component, and in researching the multiple elements constituting Chinese romanticism we must also consider German romanticism. This movement not only profoundly influenced all of nineteenth- and twentieth-century Western thought, philosophical concepts, as well as the development of literature, it also came to China in a number of complex ways and entered its modern intellectual history while continuing to influence in various ways Chinese socialism itself. This influence includes revolution and construction, social practice and the cultural imaginary. Actually, this romanticism did not die with the historical end of China's first thirty years [1949–79]; even in the 1980s, whether in novels, literary criticism, or even interpretations of avant-garde literature bearing concepts that dazzled people—uniqueness, genius, difference from the crowd, locality, and so on—in all of these, it is possible to sense the continued influence of German romanticism. But this is a different topic altogether.

  50. For this version of romanticism, see Isaiah Berlin, *The Roots of Romanticism* (Princeton, NJ: Princeton University Press, 2001), and Carl Schmitt, *Political Romanticism*, trans. Guy Oakes (Cambridge, MA: MIT Press, 1986). Tr.: The exact page numbers for these citations are not provided by Cai in his book. They come from Berlin's book.

In the literature of the first thirty years, including its literary criticism, the reason romanticism could receive a new articulation lies in (at least from a certain perspective) the fact that this romanticism had already been transmitted from thought and narrative into a widespread social practice, one form being the mode of collective labor. This mode allowed for the demonstration of a form of human strength in the collective, and this strength was also rendered as a symbolic image of the state or the nation. Even Ba Jin was once quite moved by this huge strength: "The subjugated and oppressed 'sick man of East Asia' in the blink of an eye has begun to build the socialist 'East Asian dragon.'"[51] At the same time, this strength also expressed or offered a sort of modern possibility, which included the wealth and power of the nation, national revitalization, industrialization, and the overall development of science and technology (including agricultural science). Due to the emergence of the conditions of collective labor, especially in rural villages, this strength allowed people to be liberated from every manner of impossibility. From this an extremely ambitious imaginary could be opened, as could an unprecedented form of social practice. This practice had already existed in the various explicit and ambiguous expressions in modern Chinese literature.

Guo Moruo and others of his generation used this strength to reconceive romanticism; even Zhao Shuli, far less prone to romanticism, also uncharacteristically joined in leaving romantic traces in *Sanliwan Village* (for example, the three pictures). In this type of narrative, overcoming nature and transforming the homeland were organically combined. This combining derived from a modern impulse. At the same time, this overcoming and transforming in the end offered an imaginary of human belonging, which rendered the concept of the collective the particularity of socialist narration. For this reason, overcoming and transforming inevitably were transmitted to people's selves, with the self including both the conditions of labor of the individual and the conditions for personal characteristics including conservativism, superstition, laziness, shortsightedness, and unwillingness to change. Thus, the unlimited expansion of the space of nature inevitably brought about the unlimited expansion of people's subjectivity. These modern traces are hidden in the notion of development in socialism.

After the formalization and systematization of collective labor (including the people's communes) in the 1958 Great Leap Forward, this romantic narra-

51. Ba Jin, preface to *Shanghai shinian wenxue xuanji: Duanpian xiaoshuo xuan 1949–1959* [Selected literary works from ten years in Shanghai: Short stories, 1949–1959] (Shanghai: Shanghai Wenyi Chubanshe, 1959).

tion gradually was expanded and soon reached a climactic point. In sociological terms, people often use the term *boastful style* to summarize this period of social practice and its literary expression. To be sure, at that time all over the country there was exposed a modern contagion of dishonesty, bureaucracy, and rigid administrative systems that had nothing to do with concrete ideals. All of this had catastrophic consequences. Aside from this, however, there is another possible path for research. That is that collective labor and the collective strength it demonstrated led to the revival of romanticism—the abolition of superstitions about nature that confirmed superstitions about human capacity. The unlimited expansion of subjectivity produced a blind faith in human will; the power of knowledge chased away the limits to knowledge, which brought about ideals chasing away the empirical. Speed and development were sought in one fell swoop, causing the dizziness of modernity. When Liu Qing or Zhao Shuli saw the influence and the profound changes that collective labor could bring to China, they could not at the same time perceive in their own narratives what unexpected historical consequences romanticism was already exerting. This could be described as a type of schizophrenia.

In this type of romanticized narrative process (and I do not for a moment deny that this narrative conceals a profound aporia), Zhao pioneered a certain oppositional posture not only in his writing but in his practice. In the historical context of the Great Leap Forward,[52] Zhao Shuli published in the fourth issue of *People's Literature* (1961) an article titled "Man of Action: Pan Yongfu." This article is significant not only for the history of contemporary Chinese literature but also for the history of ideas. According to Zhao, this article was a "real story about real people."[53] In fact, Zhao was the type of writer who never really bothered about genre; his writing covers a wide range of genres. In the generic vein of "real stories about real people," he wrote a piece in 1944 called "Meng Yangying Turns a Leaf," and "right after the title, [he] added 'a true story.'"[54] However the fact that Zhao selected to write another "real story about real people" more than fifteen years later undoubtedly was due to some of his own considerations.

52. Tr.: In a 1959 meeting, Zhao was fervently opposed to the bureaucratic covering up of the truth of poor harvests and mass starvation.

53. Zhao Shuli, "Sui 'Xiaxiang ji' jigei nongcun duzhe" [A letter along with "Memories of Going to the Countryside" to my village readers], in *Zhao Shuli quanji* [The complete collection of Zhao Shuli's writings], (Taiyuan: Beiyue Wenyi Chubanshe, 1994), 4:572.

54. Zhao Shuli, "Meng Yangying fanshen" ["Meng Yangying Turns a Leaf" annotated], in *Zhao Shuli quanji* [The complete collection of Zhao Shuli's writings] (Taiyuan: Beiyue Wenyi Chubanshe, 1994), 1:221.

In 1959, Zhao sent letters and several essays to the Central authorities, including "My Views on How Communes Should Lead Production," in which his realist tendency toward the problem of people's livelihood was clearly expressed. In 1961, Zhao used the form of a chronicle to explore the "man of action" spirit of Pan Yongfu to indicate his [Zhao's] profound distaste for the boastful style of the time. We also can see here Zhao's own writing practice as a response to Li Zhun's 1962 query in a forum on rural topics in short stories, in which Li asked whether it was okay to just write an account of one person's life.

In his chronicle, Zhao emphasizes Pan Yongfu's "man of action" spirit. This action is intimately related to Pan's abundant work experience. Stressing experience seems to have been one of Zhao's major concerns in the previous several years, in which he blamed the boastful style on a high-handed lack of experience. Additionally, in Zhao's understanding, experience incorporated deeper meanings, as it really pointed to the increasing separation of cadres from the masses or, put differently, the former's abandonment of the fundamental stance of serving the people. For this, Zhao had the following critique: "Commune cadres are previously all rural cadres, but most cadres of this rank seem now to represent the state with few actually participating in production directly. So-called 'leading production' is really mainly collecting statistics and counting numbers . . . quite distant from on the ground activities. Everybody knows this is not good . . . but every year, reports are sent up this way and no one questions it." He went on to suggest: "Send some of the Commune cadres (those who used to be rural cadres) down to brigades to participate in labor, so as to make room for promoting those who have been in the production brigades."[55] From this, we can understand the following description in Zhaos piece, "Man of Action: Pan Yongfu": "Comrade Pan Yongfu is a man of action who loves to do concrete things and who does not enjoy doing administrative work."

Experience is hence not merely a category of knowledge (an epistemology) but also implies a style of work, political stance, and even a personal quality. The reason Zhao offers a detailed description of Pan's life has to do with wanting to emphasize that Pan "was able long before the revolution to sacrifice himself for others." Here, Zhao once again returns to the spontaneity of the revolution as well as to the problem of morality. Evidently, in Zhao's

---

55. Zhao Shuli, "Letter to Shao," in *Zhao Shuli quanji* [Complete collection of Zhao Shuli's writings] (Taiyuan: Beiyue Wenyi Chubanshe, 1994), 5:310–11.

view, without morality there is no way to talk about "serving the people"; without morality, cadres can only be "quite distant from the reality on the ground." For Zhao Shuli, on the ground reality implies people's livelihood—namely, "do a good job in production first of all, and through education in thought and the arrangement of time, make it possible for the masses to have money to spend, grain to eat, leisure time to take care of themselves, so that they can with a full spirit participate in production."[56] In the conclusion to "Man of Action: Pan Yongfu," Zhao Shuli rectifies in a rational and deliberate way the definition of actual benefits [of production]: "Actually, the most foundational goal of managing production is for actual benefits. Everything that Comrade Pan Yongfu has managed related to production started from the consideration of concrete benefits. If there is anything in contradiction to concrete benefits, he could never let it past him. It is from this that his spirit of action developed; and when he led others he always participated himself."[57]

Bringing the problems of actual benefits or benefits of action into the narrative at the time was not just a result of common sense; rather, it required unusual courage and insight. In such narration, Zhao also drew a definitional border around labor—a demand for control over the unlimited expansion of subjectivity or human will. Actually, in his article "My Views on How Communes Should Lead Production," Zhao had already expressed a similar thought: "Human labor is unlimited, but what that explains is that our country has an unlimited capacity for development in the future; it certainly cannot mean that we can use that for short-term arrangements of production." Clearly, during the Great Leap Forward, Zhao was using his truth and experience to start to challenge the exaggerated romanticist narratives,[58] and he also began to consider new problems raised by collective labor.

56. Zhao Shuli, "Gongshe yinggai ruhe lingdao nongye shengchan zhi wo jian" [My views on how communes should lead production], in *Zhao Shuli quanji* [Complete collection of Zhao Shuli's writings] (Taiyuan: Beiyue Wenyi Chubanshe, 1994), 5:334.

57. Zhao Shuli, "Shiganjia Pan Yongfu" [Man of action: Pan Yongfu], *Renmin wenxue* [People's literature] 1961:4, n.p. (All quotes from this essay are from *Renmin wenxue*.) Tr.: The issue addressed here is how, in the Great Leap Forward, increasing production and boastfully reporting on these increases became the primary style of cadre interaction with the masses. Zhao is pointing out that this style contravenes the revolutionary spirit of serving the people through participation in production, not merely for accumulation and statistics but for real-life benefits. At the time, this was a courageous and unorthodox stance.

58. This narrative is also often understood as being symbolized by science, and it is very hard to say that this was a disguise; it is better to say that it was a type of mythologizing of science. A discussion of the place and significance of science in the ideology of the time is important.

This does not mean that Zhao was a simple empiricist. On the contrary, on some fundamental issues Zhao's stance never budged. Even when Zhao described the problems in collective labor, there was always a fundamental premise: that is, if collective labor "were to end, there would be a redivision in the rural classes after the land reform."[59] Zhao's difference from more shallow romanticists lies in the fact that at the same time as he affirmed the legitimacy of socialism and collective labor, he also thought about how this legitimacy gave rise to all manner of irrationalities; his difference from empiricists lies in the fact that when he critiqued these irrationalities, he never erased the legitimacy of socialism. Even though today his concrete thought cannot be considered particularly deep, nevertheless it is an important path into a serious discussion of socialism.

As I understand it, the debate about collective labor pervades one of the core conflicts of ideas in the sixty years of contemporary literature [1949–2009], a conflict that ultimately led to the end of the collective mode of production in the 1980s, allowing the rural villages to lead the reform of the social economic system. In literary study, the conflict has been manifested in the sharp debate about realism. From 1949 to 1966, contemporary literature functioned as an important tool to provide evidence for the legitimation of collective labor and helped construct a rational imaginary for creating a new world. Indeed, this is what my discussion tries to reveal and demonstrate. However, embedded in this literature were a number of profound crises that were consciously or unconsciously ignored or even covered up. This is precisely one of the unmet challenges of contemporary literature's preoccupation with truthfulness. Nevertheless, in these novels, we can still perceive the emergence of a certain sense of crisis; it is just that these traces or suppressed elements are hidden in the text, or they are roughly dealt with through the topos of class struggle. I believe it is only by grasping the existence of these crises that we can fully understand the 1980s [repudiation of collective labor].

These crises were expressed in the following two ways: one is through memory and one is through distribution (*fenpei*). Memory revolves around the individual and the imaginary of wealth that pertains to individual labor; distribution involves the relationship between the state/collective and the individual/collective, which in the history of ideas has to do with the question of particularity.

59. Zhao Shuli, "Xie gei zhongyang fuze tongzhi de liang feng xin" [Two letters to comrades in the central government], in *Zhao Shuli quanji* [Complete collection of Zhao Shuli's writings] (Taiyuan: Beiyue Wenyi Chubanshe, 1994), 5:323.

In 1959, Li Zhun wrote "The Story of Li Shuangshuang," which was published in the third issue of *People's Literature* [*Renmin wenxue*] in the following year (1960). Not long thereafter, it was made into the movie *Li Shuangshuang* by the Shanghai-based Haiyan Film Studio.[60] From the story to the movie, the narrative subject changed somewhat. The movie *Li Shuangshuang* left viewers with a strong impression of the family relationship between Li Shuangshuang and her husband [Sun] Xiwang, who "first got married and then fell in love." This is one reason this movie has become an important text for gender analysis. What I want to discuss here, however, is one specific detail. In the story, Li Shuangshuang leads the communal kitchen workers in their cleaning tasks; in the process, they find in the old earthen kang in the corner of the dining hall a "liberation-style water wheel." According to the story's explanation, "this water wheel was hidden there by Sun You's family when they joined the commune, and it had been there for several years. When the communal kitchen borrowed the premises [from the Suns], they had thrown things together so quickly, the family hadn't had time to move it."[61] I am uncertain whether this detail of something "deeply buried" actually led to a number of subsequent similar or altered descriptions (such as the landlord's "deeply buried" intention to restore reactionary rule, and so on); however, the behavior of deeply burying implies an individual's dream of disrupting [the collective], while also implying unwillingness to accept the change even while continuing to hope for the restoration [of capitalism], and so on. The narrative element of the deep burying of the item (the water wheel) helps foreground and strengthen certain memories. The formulation of the collective nature of this memory is extremely complex, and it includes the dream of the Sun family to build their family fortune (individual expansion) as well as the emotional attachment to one's land (the private individual form of life). At the same time, there is a certain folk element such as habits of life or attitudes toward life.

In short, at the time, deeply buried individual past ways of life implied various kinds of memory as the new mode of production of collective labor

60. Li Zhun, "Li Shuangshuang xiaozhuan," [The Story of Li Shuangshuang], *Renmin wenxue* [People's literature], March 8, 1960, n.p. All citations from the story derive from this publication. The film version was directed by Lu Ren (Haiyan Film Studio, 1962).

61. Tr.: The implication here is that the Sun family kept some of its private property from collectivization. In the idiom of the time, this indicates the Sun family's intentions to restore capitalism and destroy socialism or communism. As explained in chapter 1, a kang is a brick or earthen platform used as a bed, a table, and so on. Because there is a space under it where a fire was often lit, things could be hidden or stored there.

emerged. The memory traces either intentionally or not became a mode of social conduct, which opened a certain gap and conflict with, even a resistance to, collective production. In "The Story of Li Shuangshuang," the difference between Xiwang [the husband] and Li Shuangshuang is that he continues to resort to the memory of private ownership and repeatedly complains about the dining hall work—work that can be seen as a metaphor for distribution.[62] The existence of such memory traces, and their continuous strengthening, is one of the special characteristics of the gradual formation and systematization of China's cooperatization movement (including the people's communes). This system was not the same as the urban *danwei* [work unit] (including factories), and it was not the same as the Soviet communal farms [*kolkhoz*] (even China's state farms were unlike their Soviet counterparts) as it still preserved a certain element of the private economy (for example, individually cultivated plots). Indeed, as soon as the collective was not able to fulfill the promise of individual happiness, the private economy and those self-cultivated plots came to be major supports for people's daily lives, usually expressed as a form of memory trace. In these expressions, a partial historical truth could be incorporated into memory (for example, the disruption of the dream of building family fortunes or poverty suffered in the past). Hence, collective labor on the one hand produced a collective consciousness, yet on the other hand and at the same time it also produced individualism in the form of individual memory traces. Ultimately, when collective labor encountered problems in reality, this memory and the narrative of this memory would demand the end of this mode of production.

In the 1980s, Chinese fiction gave this memory trace (including the personal aspirations embedded in it) sustained attention, exaggerating it endlessly. This is true of Gao Xiaosheng's *Li Shunda Builds a House* (*Li Shunda zaowu*) all the way to Mo Yan's more recent novel *Life and Death Are Wearing Me Out*. If we say that in the former text, Gao pays a certain historical respect to the legitimacy of land reform (equality at the starting point—for example, the origin of the land where Li Shunda builds his house), then because of doubts about the empirical results of collective labor, he puts aside the very topic that Zhao insists on [raising], which is how, when this mode of production and the land reform end, there will be a redivision of rural classes. Most noticeable as a result of the suspension of this Zhao topic is how, as Mo Yan

62. Tr.: The communes worked on the principle of labor points awarded for particular forms of communal labor in exchange for distributed fruits of that labor (explained in more detail below). Thus "distribution" is the shorthand expression for this exchange.

puts it, one only thinks to work for oneself (as in *Life and Death Are Wearing Me Out*) and the restoration of this type of empty subject matter. This narrative emptying out cuts off a more profound dialogue between the author and history, since whether in history or in the present, the existence of such empty subject matter is always suspect. However, if we decide to follow this line of thinking, I believe we can still engage in a profound consideration of history, which is why, in the end, the appropriateness of collective labor managed to negate the appropriateness of "one only thinks to work for oneself." After all, was not the original point of organization precisely to allow people to really work for themselves? Is there really no compatibility between the individual and the collective? This is one reason why I have never rejected out of hand novels from the 1980s onward. Indeed, exploring the irrationalities that ultimately were produced by collective labor is still a question we must face, except that I would like to approach this issue from a different angle [than Gao or Mo]: that is, from the angle of the mode of distribution.

One of the main topics of Hao Ran's *Sunny Days* is the contradictions and conflicts surrounding the allocation or distribution of grain produced in the high-level cooperative farm of East Mountain. This allocation can be understood on two levels: one is the internal distribution within the collective; one is distribution between the collective and the state. Whether the distribution within the collective is decided according to land and points or labor and points has to do with how the changing structure of the cooperative led to divisions between village and cooperative; distribution between the collective and the state has to do with the question of who gets priority [in allocation]. The author's attitude is very clear: within the collective, one should support labor points; externally, one needs to support the state. This is a very mainstream type of narrative mode.

On the question of the national interest, speaking specifically from the perspective of national modernization, one cannot say that such a stance and its narrative expressions have no legitimacy. Actually, at the time most Chinese writers took the national view in their discussions of the collective, and they viewed the individual from the perspective of the collective. In this context, we have every possibility of entering into a historical discourse and from within it representing the complexity of history. But this entry is problematic because it is still an entry under the guidance of state interest or state intentions. For example, how do we discuss the collective or individual interests of peasants under the heavy weight of the nation? In 1980, it was precisely at this level that the reevaluation of collective labor was undertaken and was thoroughly subverted. It is not possible to say that this reevaluation and subversion were without reason. Yet this kind of extremist historical discourse could simplify history anew.

Actually, even as early as 1962 there were some Chinese writers such as Zhao who were already raising doubts about the mode of allocation between the collective and the state. Zhao unabashedly said: "The accumulation of resources for industry is a bit much." He also said: "In 1952, 1953 when it came to the collective and the individual, we basically relied on the collective for our daily lives. It was not the same afterward: the growth of the collective was not seen to belong to us and only our individually cultivated plots were our own. Cultivating those, we didn't care about volume of production and about points, but just about what we had for ourselves."[63] In 1964, Zhao publicly declared at a meeting that "the contradiction between the interests of the collective and those of the nation are the most intractable. . . . Demands from the state for completing collecting grains were too hard, without enough understanding of the masses." He also said he "hadn't sufficient courage to put yet more ideals into [his] creative work."[64] At the time these types of doubts could not be included directly in novels or in any publishable narratives. Even Hao Ran, many years later, said in an interview that "I knew of the sufferings of the peasantry, I came from the peasantry so I quite understand the peasants' mood. Those years of starvation, I also experienced them. But in those years, could we write of these things in books? Of course not."[65] If we for a moment do not discuss this exclusively from the perspective of telling the truth—there are already plenty of such discussions—then, on the question of distribution, the problem that still needs to be explored is why the state, including the administrative and social planning that resulted from state intentions, was able to ignore local interests and local experiential knowledge.

I think that we can say that after 1949 China had in fact formed a system of "one country, multiple rules." We have to consider that such a one country, multiple rules system expressed itself not only at the level of the territo-

---

63. Zhao Shuli, "Zai Dalian 'nongcun duanpian xiaoshuo chuangzuo zuotanhui' shang de fayan" [A Speech at the Dalian "Forum on Short Stories about Rural Areas"], in *Zhao Shuli quanji* [The complete works of Zhao Shuli] (Taiyuan: Beiyue Wenyi Chubanshe, 1994), 4:509, 511.

64. Zhao Shuli, "A Speech Given at the Chinese Writers' Association, Author and Editor Workshop," in *Zhao Shuli quanji* [The complete collection of Zhao Shuli's writings] (Taiyuan: Beiyue Wenyi Chubanshe, 1994), 4:631.

65. Quoted in Li Jiefei, "Dianxing wentan" [Classical Fora] (Wuhan: Hubei Renmin Chubanshe, 2008), 347.

rial sovereignty of the autonomous regions, but it also expressed itself as an economic element in the combination of a number of newly created economic formations, including the collective economy. This collective economy not only shaped different economic forms of the rural and the urban, it also allowed for, in the urban areas, the existence of differences between enterprises owned by the whole people and those owned as collective property. Hence, from 1949 to 1966, within the modern nation at the level of actual existence, it is possible to say that in some sense there was a pattern of differentiating systems, which received its classical theoretical expression in Mao Zedong's "On the Ten Major Relationships."[66]

However, the first challenge faced by this actually existing pattern of one country, multiple rules was the governing capacity of the state, including its mode of governance. In modern China, to form a highly efficient government has always meant choosing a mode of centralized power to complete the accumulation required for modernization. However, in the model of centralized power, how was one to deal with the pattern of one country, multiple rules? At the level of governance, there turned out to be some very good ideas, such as unified planning with due consideration for all concerned, suitable measures for local conditions, and so on, but the difficulty was in implementation. This was no doubt related to the problem of state versus collective interests, as well as the governance conflicts between the center and the localities, the core and the periphery, and even—in the rural villages—between the commune and the brigade, and so on. One of the expressions of these conflicts was the circulation of political directives, including the circulation of news and information. The explosion of the crisis [in the political and economic situations of the late 1950s] was frequently seen at the level of governance. How to consolidate the interests of the state and the collective, [and] the collective and the individual, among others, often led to contradictions and conflicts in the problem of governance.

Yet an even more profound contradiction lies in the proposition that, if we tend toward the view that at this point China had already begun its transformation to modernity, then one of the characteristics of modernity is universalism and its tendency toward convergence. That is to say, by going through what Anthony Giddens calls "disembedding" among other processes, what modernity seeks to complete is the establishment of a kind of abstract struc-

66. Tr.: Cai is pointing here to the multiplicity of collective forms of urban ownership. Part of Mao's "On the Ten Major Relationships" (1958) theorizes this as a virtue, in contrast to a Stalinist one-size-fits-all version of collectivizing and nationalizing property.

ture, which at the same time also implies the overcoming of differentiation. In the realm of an extreme theory of modernity, one could use a form of planning to even out various types of differentiations, thus arriving at a kind of modern universal.

This type of modern mode encourages the establishment of universality, and it ultimately will create conflict with the actually existing one country, multiple rules [system] and its logic of a pattern of local differentiation. That is to say, the conflict is with the requirement of modernity to complete a convergent transformation. This transformation can deploy socialist reeducation to proceed with its systemic narrative, or it can deploy a "big I, small I" to realize an ethical articulation; it can be expressed in nationalism or the discourse of national ideology, or it can appeal to egalitarian political experiments; and so on. In my view, no matter whether it functions as the real mode of governance or as evidence of the process of convergence, none of this can resolve adequately the creative systemic experiment of one country, multiple rules. For the result of the elimination of differentiation inevitably requires the nation (or the collective) to take on more responsibility for the individual. If the nation has no capacity to take on this responsibility, then it could lead to the real emergence of extreme localism (or individualism). Zhao Shuli forcefully depicted the process of this emergence: "I am now worried about whether collective production can be done well ... the peasants say there is no way and they need to rely upon their individually cultivated plots to resolve the question. Some of the peasant houses in the village are deteriorating and the commune cannot repair them; the peasants rely upon the free market to purchase things to repair their homes. The collective doesn't bother with it, the individual does; the more one relies upon the individual, the more the collective is distrusted."[67]

These are not the only reasons. For example, how do we look at the problem of work points?[68] Work points led to an abstraction of distribution form, yet this abstraction was not expressed in the form of money. Rather, it was based on a year-end calculation of numbers that were then expressed in the

67. Zhao Shuli, "Zai Zhongguo zuoxie zuojia, bianji zuotanhui shang de fayan" [Speech at the Party branch expanded conference of the Writers Association]," in *Zhao Shuli quanji* [Complete collection of Zhao Shuli's writings] (Taiyuan: Beiyue Wenyi Chubanshe, 1994), 5:356.

68. Tr.: Work points were used as a method of allocating the products of labor in the collective or commune. Each member accumulated points based on a system of calculation, which was almost always in dispute and a deep point of contention. Work points determined the amount of food and other goods members and their families received. Cai is making clear that this is, like money, merely another form of abstraction.

form of actual goods (grain). I think that in some sense the introduction of this method led to the emotional distancing of peasants from the land, which in turn made it possible for "deeply buried" memories to reemerge and repeatedly be reproduced.

If we do not limit this problem to the rural villages or to the collective labor mode of the villages, and we locate it in the abstract discursive sphere of thought and discussion, then I think that what it indicates is precisely the question of particularity in socialism, including the problem of how to explain the classification of freedom or the classification of autonomy.[69] Through my framework of discussion, I have argued for the legitimacy of the collective labor mode of production, yet I have also added to that argument a discussion of the irrationalities that were produced by this mode. The emergence of these irrationalities were not necessarily all products of the productive mode of collective labor itself; indeed, to a great extent, the origins lie in the mode of national (or collective) governance or, finally, in how we must regard the modern quest for convergence (or universalism). Placing all these questions in the problem of collective labor was a profound as well as a simplistic reflection that began in the 1980s. In some sense, this development affected how we think of history and how, in a deeper fashion, we think of the future, including the history and future of literature.

IV. *A Riot of Color Is Always Spring* (*Wanzi qianhong zongshi chun*): The Liberation of Women or Gender Reconciliation

Above, I have already touched on how "The Story of Li Shuangshuang" (including the movie *Li Shuangshuang*) became a classic text for gender research into the first thirty years of socialism in China. The story uses a unique characterization to express the liberation of women, which is completely embedded in social movements; it also narrates how, in the process of liberation, labor becomes an extremely potent mediator.

The opening of "The Story of Li Shuangshuang" presents an urgent practical question: "in the beginning of the spring of 1958," Sunzhuang Village, "due to a shortage of labor, has absolutely no way to properly manage its wheat fields." At precisely this moment, Li Shuangshuang has written and posted a big-character poster expressing the desire of women to leave home [to work outside the house]. This poster has attracted the supportive attention of the

---

69. For more on this question, see the conclusion.

township Party secretary, Luo: "If we can liberate housewives and girls from their homes, this Great Leap Forward of ours will grow some wings." Through labor, women leave home and complete their own gender liberation; this type of narrative did not begin with Li Zhun. Already in 1944, Zhao's story "Meng Yangying Turns a Leaf" had a similar theme. Behind this theme we can perhaps sense the existence of some form of national intention or national interest.

In August 1944, Mao wrote in his "Letter to Qin Bangxian" that he disagreed with the slogan of the time to "consolidate the family," because he believed there were "unsuitable aspects." In Mao's view, "peasant families obviously require disruption: when the military enters, or the factory, these are big disruptions and lead in succession to 'leaving the home.'" The reason is: "The foundation of a new democratic society is machinery, not artisanry.... The task of our revolution is to move from [an economy based on] agriculture to one based on industry."[70] However, the entirety of China's socialist experiment and activity did not follow Mao's design; on the contrary, Yan'an's localistic experience with what was called the mass movement to not separate from the family gradually spread to the whole country. This is not to say that Mao's slogan of "leaving the family" and whatever modern content was concealed in this slogan should be ignored, because in China both "consolidate the family" and "leave the family" were mixed up together. That is to say, "consolidate the family" was a way to complete the modern conception of "leaving the family," where the practicable solution was in the creation of a new system of labor. At the same time, this lent any movement for women's liberation in China an "othered" character.

In the villages, the mass movement not to separate from the family was implemented through cooperatization, and it was symbolized in that fashion. In "The Story of Li Shuangshuang" (and in similar types of fiction), cooperatization is not a purely economic productive organizational form; it is at the same time a type of public sphere suffused with politics and infused with the conflict and debate between old and new thinking, ideals, and habits. Among these, naturally there were conflicts and acute debates about the gender question. Because of the special nature of the newly created system of collective labor, there were possibilities for women to "leave the home" and attain economic independence (including the personal independence that follows from this); at the same time, this mode of production made it impos-

---

70. Mao Zedong, "Gei Qin Bangxian de xin" [Letter to Qin Bangxian], in *Mao Zedong wenji* [Collection of Mao Zedong's writings] (Beijing: Renmin Chubanshe, 1996), 3:206.

sible for women to distance themselves from their original village communities (including their families). For this reason, collective labor structured a different path of exploration for Chinese women's liberation, which was how to complete the transformation of the family from within the family, a transformation that included the overturning of male chauvinism and the quest for women's political independence. The ultimate symbolic expression would be the complete establishment of respect for women.

It should be acknowledged that this is a relatively mild literary narrative of women's liberation; it can also be said that it is a form of compromise in gender politics. On the one hand, it represents a compromise with the social quest (naturally including male privilege) for the consolidation of the family;[71] on the other hand, women's independence and liberation was won with state political support. This experiential path in reality indicated that, with the state's political interference, there was a possibility for gender reconciliation. This possibility was expressed only when the family was incorporated as a category of debate into the public sphere, where the process of transformation from respect for men and neglect for women to equality for women and men could be completed within the family. In the movie *Li Shuangshuang* this possibility for gender reconciliation, through debate and reeducation, is most iconically expressed in the famous phrase "first marriage, then love."

Even though Li Shuangshuang and Sun Xiwang inaugurate a large conflict on gender within the family, the background of the conflict is nevertheless public. That is to say, the resolution to the conflict must rely on a public incident. The story uses multiple clues to display the complex intertwining of the family and the public sphere. To express this intertwining, there has first to be a demonstration of how open the public sphere is to women, that women have the right to enter this sphere and participate in it. In the story, through the state's support (in the figure of the township Party Secretary), Li Shuangshuang (the woman) begins to enter the collective as a form of labor and because of her capacity to resolve a public problem [the shortage of labor], she can prove that "women hold up half the sky."[72] In the end, she forces Sun Xiwang (the man) to compromise and respect her. Here, the needs of the public become an important premise of the narrative. This premise not only includes labor power—women becoming labor power—it also implies

---

71. In Chinese villages, the consolidation of the family is in part based on considerations of marriage. See Philip Huang, "Whither Chinese Law?," *Modern China* 33, no. 2 (2007): 163–94.

72. Tr.: This was a major slogan of the socialist era that came to symbolize state support for women's political and social equality with men.

the possibility of freedom. The liberation of labor power comes to simultaneously represent the liberation of women. This is the right to work, which also includes the problem of how to offer the necessary public support for the liberation of labor power (for example, the use of tractors, communal dining halls, and so on). In this sense, we can understand why these types of narratives require the Great Leap Forward as their background.[73] Indeed, entangling the analysis of these narratives with empirical investigations of the Great Leap has little significance. To the contrary, what is true is that the radical public nature of the social experiment that was the Great Leap Forward offered an abundance of resources for the imagination of women's liberation. In the process of this liberation, Li Shuangshuang is extricated from a number of different naming practices: "of the Xiwang family," "Xiwang's wife," "that person inside the home," "Little Tao's mother," "the one who cooks," and so on. To use the narrator's own words: "The year 1958 was the Great Leap Forward, and it was the year when the name Shuangshuang leapt forth." The process of naming is the process of the exercise of power. To cite the historian Harold Isaacs, "a name will seldom itself be the heart of the matter of group identity, but it can often take us to where the heart can be found, leading us deep into the history, the relationships, and the emotions that lie at the center of any such affair."[74]

Using the Great Leap Forward as the narrative background for this gender imaginary is not limited to China's villages. Urban areas offered similar types of storytelling possibilities. Even though the end of the Great Leap Forward was announced for a number of reasons, nevertheless, because of the movement in the urban areas there emerged a variety of public social experiments that did not end, but rather gradually came to be systematized.

In 1960, the Shanghai Literary Publishing House published the cinematic literary script by Shen Fu and others titled *A Riot of Color Is Always Spring* (*Wanzi qianhong zongshi chun*), which also had the 1958 Great Leap Forward as its backdrop. It tells how a Shanghai housewife from a small lane leaves her home in the course of the Great Leap Forward. The movie begins in "the autumn [of 1958], early morning at a small Shanghai vegetable market. Every stall and shop is teeming with a large number of women clutching baskets and

---

73. Tr.: The Great Leap Forward was a time of communal eateries, nurseries, and so on, intended to free women's household labor so as to enable the full deployment of labor power for industrialization and agricultural progress.

74. Harold R. Isaacs, *Idols of the Tribe: Group Identity and Political Change* (Cambridge, MA: Harvard University Press, 1997), 73.

bags."⁷⁵ The use of the "small vegetable market" to enter the everyday lives of Shanghai people as a narrative ploy was revived many years later in an entirely different way by Shanghai writers such as in Wang Anyi. However, in *A Riot of Color*, the clarity, purity, and settledness of everyday life conceal the demand and even the possibility for a profound transformation. This demand in the movie is related in the form of voice. The camera's gaze zooms slowly into the family, passing through every variety of structure (wood house, brick house, one-floor house, apartment), all indicating how everyday life is oppressive for women. Some of this oppressiveness comes from their occupation with housework, some comes from the belching of the mother-in-law, and even more comes from the nonstop demands of chauvinist men, and so on. All these oppressions are narrated orally as a voice-over, as they are shown and reproduced on [the] screen. Patrick Hanan, in his research on modern novels, discusses Gerard Roland's differentiation between narrators: One type of narrator is voice-over, and another is perspectival. If what matters for the perspectival narrator is who sees (the gaze), then what matters for the voice-over is who talks (the voice). Hanan seems to find the voice-over far more important in relation to narrative in Chinese novels, and he calls these "voice-over narratives." These voice-over narratives are represented in vernacular form.⁷⁶ In contemporary Chinese literature, the voice-over narrative form is relatively common (such as in Zhao Shuli's *Good Trumps Evil* (*Xie bu yazheng*). There are many complex factors that have led to the common use of this narrative mode, such as the voice of traditional oral storytelling, among others. However, beyond the formalistic aspects, we have to note the political restrictions. Even though this politics treated the Chinese lower classes as revolutionary subjects, it also demanded that literature take on the task of transmitting the voice of the masses. Finding a truthful way to replicate or represent the voice of the masses consequently became a major narrative technique. I think that while this has to do with the relationship between intellectuals and the masses, it also has to do with the complex intertwining of the goals of the revolution (we could call this modernity) and the spontaneity of the masses' demands (we could call this nativism). The most crucial aspect here was the narrative attitude; what this attitude needed to resolve was how to allow sub-

---

75. Shen Fu, Wanzi qianhong zongshi chun [A Riot of Color is Always Spring]. Filmscript. (Shanghai: Shanghai wenyi chubanshe), 1960, n.p. (All citations in the text are to this filmscript.)

76. Patrick Hanan, *Chinese Fiction of the Late Nineteenth and Early Twentieth Centuries* (New York: Columbia University Press, 2004), 6.

alterns to speak. This is one of the most important legacies of Chinese contemporary literature.

In the replication and representation of oral speech, women's liberation became an important quest for women themselves. In this process, state politics became an important or even the most crucial source of support for women. This liberatory strength is articulated and represented in the speech by Mama Dai [in *A Riot of Color*]: "Everyone has long wanted to contribute to socialist construction; now, we can begin to realize this desire. (Applause.) We need to use the power of the collective to arrange our lives, to arrange housework, and according to the conditions and willingness of individuals, to participate in production, and add to socialism one brick at a time. Sisters, we possess great strength! I believe we absolutely can contribute to socialist construction!" We can see this as a form of political mobilization, which on the one hand uses the collective form to affirm women's own strength while at the same time giving women's liberation a sort of formalized possibility (to organize).

However, on the other hand, this politicized form also included the quest for the rights of women themselves, which is extremely modern: "We women—those of us of a certain older generation—who among us has ever left the stove and kitchen fires? From the time of marriage all the way through our gray-haired years when our eyes have dimmed, when we've become old ladies, what we've been preoccupied with all day is feeding and clothing the old and the young in our families; we know of nothing else. This is really suffering!" Concealed in this formalized (political) articulation is a very strong political quest for women's liberation. This is one reason the politics of the time was so persuasive.

The persuasiveness of state politics included the needs of the state itself (labor power) and to some degree also represented the quest for the rights of women themselves. Complexly intertwined and more important still, this politics produced a mode of re-creating the system that, in the movies (as well as in life) became known as the "neighborhood production teams." These production teams not only took on the task of piecework for state-owned factories, [but] at the same time, to meet the demand to liberate women, they also organized their own nurseries, public dining halls, and so on. These structural forms in "The Story of Li Shuangshuang" also are important plot points in the narrative. The problem clearly comes when these structures are aborted in the villages, while in the urban areas they gradually were systematized and spread. This phenomenon undoubtedly pertains to a sociology of the urban versus the rural forms (for example, the use of currency and forms of exchange, and so on), but it also has to do with a basic question for women's liberation: without systemic support, is it even possible for women to be liberated? Or where could that possibility be located?

The neighborhood production teams offered urban women a mode of labor that allowed them to leave the home, even while being rooted precisely in the home. The neighborhood production teams replicated the labor mode of the cooperatives in the villages; at the very least, women left the home without leaving the neighborhood (the community) just like women in the villages, who left their homes without leaving their villages. This mode of labor on the one hand allowed women to attain the right to work; yet on the other hand, it preserved already existing forms of life. We can acknowledge that this is an extremely mild form of women's liberation that at the same time also assisted in the stabilization of existing social forms. The result was not the wholesale disruption of families or their dissolution.

In his essay "Whither Chinese Law?," Philip Huang has briefly discussed the process of legal concession from the 1931 Chinese Soviet Marriage Regulations through to the 1950s People's Republic of China Marriage Law. In this process, the new law does not accept feudal loveless polygamous marriages, concubines, child brides, or the buying of spouses by matchmakers or parents; the new law demands that the two parties have a strong emotional foundation and not rush into marriage. For this reason, other than for a "breakdown in marital affection," there was a demand that the couple do everything they could to repair the relationship [before seeking a divorce]. In this way the old-style marriages were eliminated, and bourgeois quick marriages followed by rapid divorces were also avoided.[77] On the one hand, the inherent reason for compromise, as Huang says, is that the cost of marriage among the Chinese lower classes was excessive, and thus any demand for divorce by only one side did not suit the realities of life; on the other hand, because China's (especially the subaltern masses') understanding of love in marriage is not entirely similar to that in the West, the tendency was to try to produce the possibility of a couple's marital relationship through mutual respect and mutual compassion. In the 1950s and 1960s, the masses' memories of traditional practices were still not far away and had not much changed. Therefore, the phrase from the film *Li Shuangshuang*—"first marriage, then love"—could become a classic phrase and could be accepted all over the country. Yet the compromise of the law does not mean that there was a fundamental regression in modern

---

77. Huang, "Whither Chinese Law?," 163–94.

conceptualizations; it is just that these conceptualizations gained an alternative possibility for systematization. This possibility appeared in the reform of the family.

In the movie *A Riot of Color*, the array of various conflicts and contradictions among various families represents the environment of women's lives in China; this actually was very difficult to incorporate into the narrative category of class politics. Thus, these contradictions and conflicts were mostly shown to be mild and part of the conditions of everyday life. Among the conflicts, the contradiction in the household of Cai Guizhen is narrated as a form of gender conflict characterized by the oppression of male chauvinism. Cai Guizhen's husband, Zheng Baoqin, is a chauvinist, and thus Cai Guozhen's resistance to him contains within it a good measure of classical feminist narrative particularities. Yet in the process of her resistance, we must add, there is an important role played by the collective.

The establishment of the neighborhood production team socialized the space [of the family], and in the film narratives, this presents the possibility of extricating oneself from fate. Only in this kind of social as well as political and economic space can women's own speech have the possibility to emerge not just from a concern with beauty. If we understand the realm of the aesthetic to reside in the realm of individual emotions, then the endpoint of the process of the universalization of aesthetics in some other sense is the demand for the individual to return to the public sphere and begin to look for political support.[78] Clearly, this political support comes from two sides. First is the demonstration and even complete translation of ability, which often takes the classical form of one's ability to overcome difficulty. Here, in *A Riot of Color*, we can see that these women who used to be housewives not only efficiently overcame the technical problems of toy production, but at the same time they also efficiently overcame the problem of the equipment and design of the padded cotton jacket (including the confidence and ability connected to using the equipment). This type of narrative mode is also evident in *Li Shuangshuang* and other movies.

Here, women, just like men, face the problem of ability—really the capacity to work—in society. Perhaps this can be explained as a form of genderless narrative. However, if we consider the fact that the ability to work had been monopolized by men, then the rights of women can be completely established

---

78. See Schmitt, *Political Romanticism*, 13–18.

only in the course of this type of genderless narrative. Second is that this space [of work] is explained as mass political space. Various female characters take on the narrative task of assisting, educating, and supporting Cai Guizhen in her battle with male chauvinist thought. The internal reform of the family cannot be accomplished in the family alone; rather, social movements enter the family in a complex fashion and help in the completion of the reform.

Likewise, Cai's family begins to enter a condition of struggle, and Cai herself, armed with a confident outlook, demands equal rights in the family. When she courageously demands of her husband "let's talk"—where "talk" is a form of equal negotiation—her husband brushes her off ("what do we have to talk about?"). Faced with Cai's determination ("no, I want to talk"), her husband begins to "feel a sort of amazement." The struggle continues, and the ultimate perspective is concentrated in Cai's demand for divorce. Divorce is merely a form of speech; indeed, the conclusion to the struggle is that Cai returns to the home. It is a victorious return. According to the movie, Cai's husband finally begins to examine his male chauvinist thinking, while Cai's confidence also includes an economic element: "she for the first time received a wage," which she uses to buy a gift for her husband and child.

This type of narrative is not entirely derived either from May Fourth literature or even from left-wing literature; rather, only in the literature of the liberated zones is it possible to find narrative traces that are similar to this one. Generally, the literature of the liberated zones emphasizes the new mode of marriage based upon free love, even while on the question of divorce the attitude was quite careful. In Zhao Shuli's "Meng Yangying Turns a Leaf," the mother-in-law and husband oppress Meng, yet even in the end there is no question of divorce. While this is a true story about real people, nevertheless we can see here Zhao's careful attitude in his treatment of peasants' (or really common people's) marriage.

Women's liberation in the socialist era did not opt for a radical attitude of rupture with men. Liberation most often indicated gender reconciliation. Of course, the premise was the retreat of male centeredness, upon the foundations of which men and women could attain the possibility of a new reconciliation. In *A Riot of Color* it is thus, and in *Li Shuangshuang* it is also thus. The question this leaves is that, if in so many marriages at the level of the relationship, gender reconciliation is emphasized, then the problem of individual emotion and passion tends to be ignored. If the problem stresses too much the issue of facing society as a question of the ability to work, then the problem of gender difference is also ignored. And so on. This is one more reason that the gender question taken up in the 1980s relocated the treatment of aesthetics to the realm of individual passion.

Conclusion

It should be clear that I am not discussing the question of labor merely on the abstract level of social relations. Rather, I am locating labor in contemporary literature to undertake a consideration that must begin from the origins of the revolution, which always requires a presentation of class and the ways in which people's lives are suffused with class, from which we can extrapolate the legitimacy of the revolution. In these narratives, labor not only takes on the task of a legitimizing ethic, it is also a political legitimacy; it not only develops the demands for changes in the property regime, it develops a new imaginary relationship to state power. At the same time and even more important, it also directly indicates dignity: that is, not only individual dignity but class dignity. Moving away from the class embeddedness of the individual (or clan) and merely discussing individual dignity has no real meaning. The Chinese revolution can be said to be a process of practicing a politics of respect. If it had moved away from an engagement with this politics, the Chinese revolution could not have been possible.

For this reason, labor had to be debated in the cultural sphere and inevitably attracted struggles over the power of cultural leadership. These struggles implied that the thousand-year-old cultural and political order symbolized by the adage "those who work with their brains rule; those who work with their brawn are ruled" was challenged and overthrown. This challenge and overturning not only liberated the dignity of the subaltern Chinese masses, it also stimulated their enthusiastic participation in the affairs of the [People's] Republic [of China]. The universal establishment of the concept of love of labor actually was one of the more important properties of the new society. One reason labor could become one of the more important concepts of after-the-revolution China is a question with multiple angles. These angles are intimately caught up with the real economy of China at the time, which included industrialized production. At the same time, the start of the cooperatization movement in the villages even more pointedly augured the intention for a process of establishing equality and the equality of results. Of course, the significance of labor is not limited to this. Labor was not merely a metaphor but also became the ground of social intertwining—for example, of thinking about and experiencing women's liberation.

We can say that labor was an important concept for the whole of the twentieth century. It offered a utopian image of a laboring society, whose rise and fall has profound historical consequences.[79] In China what we really need to consider is how its production of legitimacy also produced irrationalities. In my understanding, this process of production cannot be grasped merely through a rehearsal of logic; to the contrary, there are some very complex factors that enter the problem. For example, validating labor cannot simply be said to exhibit a tendency toward anti-intellectualism. The glorification of labor (particularly of physical labor) might very well have created some sort of oppressive power vis-à-vis the labor of the mind (including the work of intellectuals). The formation of this oppressiveness is also very complex and is bound up with policies toward intellectuals of the period. At the same time, it is also bound up with different attitudes toward a modern society of experts. For this reason, what is required is research of some depth and not some simplified rejection and negative evaluation. I will have more to say on this point in the conclusion of this book.

Most important, in my opinion, is the intimate relation established between this concept of labor and China's subaltern masses. What the changes in the attitude toward the concept of labor relate to is the position of the Chinese subaltern masses, including that period's politics and culture, which was expressed in a relatively unfiltered perspective and even a political ideal. Labor (primarily the physical labor of the production of material goods) did allow the Chinese subaltern masses to attain political subjectivity and a related class dignity, which also created a type of demand for political power. With the advent of new economic forms (the information economy) and the related changes in the situation of labor (immaterial labor), the question of how we can deal anew with this concept of labor along with labor subjectivity gains in importance. In my estimation this new labor mode and situation could produce something like a concept of the intellectual laborer or a cultural proletariat ("white-collar worker" carries more bourgeois middle-class implications). At the same time, in China what we face is a social reality consisting of the combination of multiple forms of labor. For this reason, how to form a new type of labor alliance is a left-wing political possibility required of the future. A core part of this work will be how to deal with the concept of labor.

---

79. Jürgen Habermas, "The New Obscurity: The Crisis of the Welfare State and the Exhaustion of Utopian Energies," trans. Phillip Jacobs, *Philosophy and Social Criticism* 11, no. 2 (1986): 1–18.

6

TECHNOLOGICAL REVOLUTION AND NARRATIVES OF WORKING-CLASS SUBJECTIVITY

To designate the Chinese revolution a peasant revolution is not accurate. Even though modern China lacks a strong industrial foundation and thus does not have a large proletarian base that appears similar to that of Euro-American countries, nevertheless, in the background of the Chinese revolution there was always the concept of the support of the proletariat. That is, the proletariat was always present in the process of the Chinese revolution. The presence of the proletariat determines the modernity of the revolution while absolutely negating the idea of the revolution as some sort of traditional peasant rebellion. Due to the internationalism of the concept of the proletariat, the Chinese revolution also was never merely national but global. Naturally, this concept is often theoretical. But I do not take the importance of theory lightly. Indeed, one of the more important characteristics of the Chinese revolution was its reconstruction of a modern nation with the support of a certain theory.

In literary narratives, of course, no concept can stop at the level of theory; concepts still require images to represent or demonstrate that which is to be represented or demonstrated. After 1949, therefore, in the process through which workers were transformed from slaves to masters, or the reversal of the master-slave relation in the Hegelian sense, how to narrate the worker became an urgent issue confronting contemporary Chinese literature. It was not merely a theoretical issue, but a practical one as well. In this chapter, I wish to discuss the narration of the worker—specifically, the question of how to narrate, and what forces were introduced in the process conditioning such narration.

I. Weapons of the Weak, or the Artisanal Spirit

The establishment of the People's Republic of China in 1949 determined a basic discursive premise for Chinese contemporary literature. This discourse not only implied the end to the large-scale armed resistance phase of the revolution, it also marked the beginning of the transformation of a revolutionary Party into a ruling Party. It is quite impossible to use the concept of *postrevolutionary* to identify this era. But it definitely inaugurated a period that can be called after the revolution.

With regard to the Chinese revolution, we might use the metaphor of entering the cities to think about this period of contemporary literature. In Chinese usage, cities are, on the one hand, the symbol of the suppressive force of the totality that is capitalism: they are counterrevolutionary, corrupt, and degenerate as depicted in Mao Dun's *Midnight* [1933]. Yet from a different perspective, cities also indicate modernization or industrialization, and building a strong and wealthy industrialized modern country was always one of the important political goals of the Chinese revolution. In 1944, Mao Zedong repeatedly emphasized in a speech that "China's backwardness is primarily due to the fact that there is no advanced industry. The reason Japanese imperialists dare to bully China in this way is that China has no strong industry, so they can bully our backwardness." Hence, "to overcome Japanese imperialism, we need industry; the enduring independence of the Chinese nation will be built upon industrialization. Our Chinese Communist Party must work hard for industrialization."[1] It was also in this year that Mao Zedong emphasized in a letter to Qin Bangxian that "the foundation of our New Democratic society is mechanization, it is not artisanal production. We still have few machines, so we have not yet triumphed. If we cannot attain machines, we will never triumph and we will thus perish [as a nation]. The villages are temporarily our base areas, but these cannot be the most important foundations for the entire

---

1. Mao Zedong, "Gongchandang yao nuli yu Zhongguo de gongye hua" [The Chinese Communist Party must work hard for industrialization], in *Mao Zedong wenji* [Collection of Mao Zedong's writings] (Beijing: Renmin Chubanshe, 1996), 3:146.

Chinese democratic social structure. Our revolutionary task is to move China from its agricultural foundations toward industry."[2]

Because of the political desire for industrialization, as early as during the War of Resistance against Japan, Mao Zedong, in the name of the Central Committee, started to require "that the attention of each location be paid to the experience of work in the cities," to the extent that cities began to symbolize the legitimacy of political power.[3] For example, on June 5, 1944, the seventh plenary session of the sixth Party Congress held a special meeting on urban work. At this meeting, Liu Shaoqi hailed the entry into the cities in the following terms: "he who enters first is supreme leader, while he who enters next is only a minister."[4] Meanwhile, Zhou Enlai said: "We enter the cities first, people will elect us, we are thus legitimate; if the Guomingdang [the Nationalist Party] wishes to oppose us, they will be illegitimate."[5] Here, entering the cities implies the beginning of the new after-the-revolution era that was both the accreted product of the Chinese revolution and an extension of the dreams of modernity from the late Qing onward. Yet this entering at the same time brought with it great anxiety centered on the historical process to be completed for the transformation of the revolutionary Party into a ruling Party. Because entering the cities posed a real challenge to the governing capacity of the revolutionary Party, it also posed a real test to the Party's revolutionary intentions. Mao acknowledged the problem. At the second plenary session of the Seventh Party Congress meeting, Mao clearly opposed the method of "accomplishing political and economic tasks in one stroke" because "if the state—particularly the People's Liberation Army and our Party—begin to be corrupted, then the proletariat will be unable to hold on to state power. That will present big problems."[6] In 1944, Mao had already used the example of Li Zicheng to express anxieties over corruption, and he demanded that the Party

---

2. Mao Zedong, "Gei Qin Banxiang de xin" [Letter to Qin Bangxian], in *Mao Zedong wenji* [Collection of Mao Zedong's writings] (Beijing: Renmin Chubanshe, 1996), 3:207.

3. Mao Zedong, "Gedi ying zhuyi zongjie chengshi gongzuo jingyan" [Each location must pay attention to the experience of work in the cities], in *Mao Zedong wenji* [Collection of Mao Zedong's writings] (Beijing: Renmin Chubanshe, 1996), 5:73.

4. Tr.: This proverb, "xiandao weijun, houdao weichen," allegedly comes from the Jiaqing emperor's experience.

5. Quoted in Hu Qiaomu, *Hu Qiaomu huiyi Mao Zedong* [Hu Qiaomu remembers Mao Zedong] (Beijing: Renmin Chubanshe, 1994), 368.

6. Mao Zedong, "Zai zhonggong qijie erzhong quanhui de zongjie" [Summary of the seventh plenary session of the second central committee meeting], in *Mao Zedong wenji* [Collection of Mao Zedong's writings] (Beijing: Renmin Chubanshe, 1996), 5:262.

"take warning from this story."[7] Daniel Bell calls this the problem of the "day after the revolution."

Of course, anxieties about entering the cities found expression beyond these warnings. In the gradual unfolding of the period after the revolution, the renewed debate over identity became an extremely important issue. This debate about identity was not contained only in the self-referential question of whether the Party was a revolutionary or a ruling Party, but it also extended into the question of how to understand the complex relationship between revolutionary China and modern China. This is because the Chinese revolution could not merely achieve the historical task of vigorously industrializing the nation, which would amount to nothing more than establishing a capitalist-like modern China; to the contrary, its task was always to establish a socialist revolutionary China. For this reason, the Chinese revolution should never be seen as equivalent to a bourgeois nationalist revolution. The problem lies in the fact that revolutionary China always had to depend upon modern China; that is to say, once the Chinese revolution clearly determined its political desires for modernization, then ranging from the macro-level issues of constructing a nation-state to micro-level issues such as the bureaucratic management of industrial units, the problems presented by modernity could not but seep into and permeate these endeavors. Under the control of this desire for modernity, then, how was one to guarantee that the pursuit was not merely modernization but also China's continued revolutionariness? I think this was the core anxiety of the first thirty years of China's socialism.

This is not my major question here. Rather, what I want to focus on is the extent to which in this after-the-revolution era, contemporary Chinese literature was shocked into action. This shock, if we recall a previous chapter, was already evident in the discussion of the question of language at the beginning of the 1950s. Xing Gongwan's discussion of the use of dialects and of the national common language in literature and the criticism launched against him by many, for example, were essentially debates pertaining to the important theoretical and practical questions emerging from the historical transition of the period after the revolution. These questions did not exist only in the debate on the national language versus dialects (or local languages) but were

---

7. Mao Tse-tung, "Our Study and the Current Situation, in *Selected Works of Mao Tse-tung* (Peking: Foreign Language Press, 1965), 3:174. Tr.: Li Zicheng was the peasant rebel leader who helped depose the last of Ming emperors (who had been weakened because of vast corruption in the dynasty) in the mid-seventeenth century, paving the way for the Manchu conquest of China that led to the establishment of the Qing dynasty.

also manifested in the theoretical debates over the relationship between the city and the village generated by such fictional work as Xiao Yemu's "Between My Wife and Me" ("Women fufu zhijian").

For this reason, I have decided to use *weapons of the weak* and the *artisanal spirit* to organize my inquiry into the historical transitional process of entering the cities and the corresponding changes in modes of narration and ethical attitudes surrounding the relationship between revolution and production. In 1959 the Chinese Youth Press (Zhongguo Qingnian Chubanshe) published Luo Dan's novel *The Storm of Dawn* (*Fengyu de liming*). The novel's historical backdrop is the 1948 liberation of Anshan,[8] and it essentially tells the story of the Chinese revolution entering the city. In the story, all types of contradictions surrounding this entry are exhibited; or rather, the entry into the city is shown to have stimulated and provoked a number of contradictions. Central among these contradictions is the transition in identity from slave to master.

An important plotline of the novel revolves around one protagonist, Song Zezhou. Through the narrative of Song's decisive action to stop what the novel calls undisciplined acts of dismantling and moving things around in some work units, the role of the master is depicted as synonymous with being a manager, while the role of the slave is portrayed in the image of a rebel who is said to have guerrilla-like habits and is motivated by localism. No matter what kind of legitimation they had received historically, these insurgent and destructive characteristics, once the revolution entered the cities, could inevitably lead to strong opposition on the part of the managers.[9] Song Zezhou and others have already affirmed the concept of nation (including managing), but more importantly, revolutionaries are to become the masters of this newborn nation. For this reason, order must be reaffirmed and all insurgent language must be realigned with the new grammatical system—which, of course, is modern. In the view of the narrator, Song Zezhou and others have rather successfully completed the transition of the revolutionary Party into the ruling Party and have also completed the transformation of their own identities [from insurgent or slave to ruler or master]. That is to say, they are going to as-

8. Tr.: The February 1948 liberation of Anshan City in the Northeast was a major battle in the Civil War between the Chinese Communist Party (CCP) and the GMD. It heralded the liberation of the entire Northeast, a critical moment in turning the tide definitively toward CCP victory and GMD defeat.

9. This type of language of destruction was revived during the Cultural Revolution, when it was expressed as the duality of conservation and destruction rather than of ruler and ruled. Behind this discussion of the continuation of the revolution was a sharp debate about realism and futurism. Of course, this is a different topic altogether.

sume the identity of the new masters to undertake management work for the new nation. However, in this modern order, where is the distinction between new and old?

In the novel, there is a secondary character, Fang Jinfei, who is an engineer and who was also the vice head of Anshan Steelworks during the Guomindang (GMD) period. He did not leave Anshan with the GMD's defeat but rather chose to stay and work with the Chinese Communist Party (CCP). The novel offers a depiction of Fang's choice: "When the Guomindang's leader in the Anshan Steelworks told him to send a telegram, he gathered himself together and dared to respond: 'I am the vice head of the factory, but I do the job of the factory head, earn the salary of a technician, and now I'm supposed to go send a telegram?' This was a form of protest, and at the time it was dangerous to do so." Here, the GMD is shown to be an antimodern destructive force, whereas the CCP is depicted in contrast as the embodiment of modernity. This is assumed to be an important reason for Fang Jinfei's decision to stay in Anshan. What is more, Song Zezhou's attitude toward Fang is not one merely of utility but rather includes a consideration of "how to understand and reform this person, to turn him into an engineer who is firmly one of us." In Song's imagination, technology (science) is not merely some tool but rather constitutes an organic component of the revolutionary process. In this imaginary, revolution and modernity begin to become interchangeable concepts. But in other fictional works, such as Ai Wu's *Steeled and Tempered* (*Bailian cheng'gang*) or Cao Ming's *Riding the Wind* (*Chengfeng polang*) the Song Zezhou–type characters already have begun to face the challenges posed by another kind of revolution. I will discuss this in more detail later in this chapter.

During the transition from revolutionary Party to ruling Party, the position of the proletariat also begins to change subtly. That is to say, the proletariat also faces the problem of a new identity formation. *The Storm of Dawn* begins with the workers resisting the Guomindang; their resistance takes the form of destructive behavior:

> There were some big shots (the workers called all managers and technicians of the Guomindang "big shots") who while never understanding a thing pretended they did. As a result, the workers wouldn't take steel making seriously. Wen Changshan, a worker, referred to "forging steel" as "cooking steel." Sometimes, the top of the furnace burned really hot and really severely so that heated steel emanated from it, like curtains almost, and the workers would remark "it is so beautiful." The bottom of the fur-

nace often had a huge hole underneath, and the workers would say, "oh, the pot is leaking, no more cooking!"¹⁰

At the ceremony to start work, presided over every day by the GMD, the workers are shown to very publicly express a form of destructiveness.

Under the oppression of the political and economic systems, the fact that workers express their dissatisfaction in this destructive attitude ("dismantle the machines; set fire to the factory") was already fully described in exciting prose in [Karl] Marx and [Friedrich] Engels's *Communist Manifesto*. James Scott, for his part, in his consideration of Southeast Asian peasants' oppositional behaviors, also discovered a form of what he called "everyday resistance," often expressed as a type of noncooperation and as a form of resisting the established rules of everyday behavior. This is, for Scott, a form of political resistance. In the course of this resistance, peasants resorted to what he calls the "weapons of the weak": "foot dragging, dissimulation, false compliance, pilfering, feigned ignorance, slander, arson, sabotage, and so forth."¹¹

This form of resistance has happened often in the modern history of China. For example, in the annals of a Shanghai factory, we find that during the War of Resistance against Japan, workers, to prolong the time required for producing military materiel, chose "a number of subtle methods" such as slowdowns, in which everyone often "squatted in small groups at one corner or another, chatting by the side of the lathes, napping, or simply letting the lathes run empty ... They would also deliberately make bad products, either too big, or too small ... parts that did not fit with one another but from the look of them it did not show," and more.¹² Clearly, in these narratives, slowdowns, crude mechanics, and so on were all efficient modes of deploying "weapons of the weak" and received political affirmation and were legitimated as proper modes of resistance. In addition to historical records, contemporary Chinese literature also often depicts such modes of resistance and represents them as a form of revolutionary activity.

10. Luo Dan, *Fengyu de liming* [The storm of dawn] (Beijing: Zhongguo Qingnian Chubanshe, 1959). Tr.: Page numbers not available. Above quotes from this novel are derived from this citation.
11. James Scott, *Weapons of the Weak: Everyday Forms of Peasant Resistance* (New Haven, CT: Yale University Press, 1987). Page number not available.
12. Yin Genxing, ed., *Shanghai Erfangji dangshi dashiji* [Major events in the Shanghai second textile factory party history] (internal publication), 57. Tr.: This is an "internal publication," a form of Party publication that is not disseminated publicly. Historical internal publications are often now accessible to researchers, but they have no publication information attached (as they were not published formally).

If we investigate in detail this type of resistance in the same texts, we will discover that the matter is not always so simple. As in Zhou Libo's novel *The Hurricane* (*Baofeng zhouyu*) [1948] or Ai Mingzhi's novel *Kindling* (*Huozhong*), there are plenty of depictions of the resistance of the weak, but they are often expressed as a form of giving up or hopelessness, and the weapon of this resistance most likely harms only the resister himself. Chinese writers' narrations of these weapons of the weak are quite complex and involve emotional investments. What they most cared about was not the enjoyment that resistance could bring, but rather the political depiction of the exploitation surrounding the necessity to labor for survival. In other words, behind the weapons of the weak were clearly demands for political power. This, I would argue, is where the Chinese revolution differs fundamentally from other types of social movements.

At the same time, because of the early promotion of socialism, the sanctity of labor was not only inscribed in the minds of intellectuals but also was broadly supported by the general population. That is to say, being diligent was a positive image for peasants and workers alike, and the peasant or worker portrayed in this positive image was precisely the moral and aesthetic form required of the cultural production of after-the-revolution China. In historical novels or stories about the Chinese revolution, the resistance of the weak, including the weapons deployed in such resistance—such as slowdowns— must inevitably explain how such resistance was forced, and they must also elaborate on the despair and suffering felt by the resisters themselves. Embedded in such narration was also an inevitable praise and affirmation of labor. Once labor became an abstract notion with an aestheticized quality, we find that at times it helped erase the strict descriptive conventions used for class differentiation. Examples could come from Hao Ran's *Sunny Days* (*Yanyang tian*) or Zhou's *Great Changes in the Mountain Village*. In the paradoxical discursive usage of the revolution/construction type, particularly in the descriptions of new China after the revolution, the weapons of the weak were not only completely appropriated [by the state], but at the same time laziness became an essential target of revolutionary reform.

For this reason, in depicting the opposition to the GMD by the workers at the Anshan Steelworks factory, the author of *The Storm of Dawn* quickly realizes that the unbounded nature of the detailed description can lead to something far more complex. This complexity resides in the fact that, once the factory welcomes the People's Liberation Army's entry into the city, one urgent problem to solve in the era after the revolution is none other than the destructive resisting behaviors of the workers. The issue now is how to transform workers' uncooperative behaviors into genuine cooperation. To complete this transformation, the workers must first be made aware of their own identity—that is, they must become conscious of the fact that they have been transformed from slaves into the factory's (or the nation's) masters. Hence, at the moment when the angry workers, in their desire to express their hatred and loathing of the GMD, hatch a plan to set fire to the "big white building" of the factory, the central character, Wen Changshan, actually now opposes this destructive resistance: "The big white building does not belong to the Guomindang, why in the world would you move heaven and earth to set fire to it? . . . Is not setting fire to the big white building equivalent to burning the factory? There is no circumstance under which that should happen." Of course, the reason given by Wen Changshan is not particularly "political"; he simply believes that "to operate in the wide world out there, how can the Eighth Route Army not need to open this huge steelworks?" In any case, in the narrative context of the novel, Wen's simple belief is enough to indicate a narrative caution against an unbounded destructiveness and resistance.

Relying only on the character of Wen Changshan cannot accomplish the narrative task of completing the transformation of the workers into masters. Of real importance in *The Storm of Dawn* is the character named Xie Niankui. In the novel, we see that Xie is mild and genial. More important is the fact that a great technician of his type in the GMD era is reduced to "selling his skills for petty jobs" on the streets. After the People's Liberation Army enters the city, Xie is able to reenter the factory. The novel describes his mood as he labors in this way: "Formerly, he was on the streets selling his skills for petty jobs. Even though what he does today is still work, somehow or other, he is full of joy in doing today's labor. Maybe it is because he is living out his fantasy dream of returning to the machines at the Angang factory. Xie Niankui felt young again, he felt his body filled with a roaring strength; his hands and feet worked with a renewed agility." In this comparative narrative, the GMD appears as a type of antimodern as well as an antilabor political entity.

However, this does not mean that Xie is just another modern "great technician." To the contrary, he has a plain but clear political consciousness: "the factory, the Eighth Route Army, workers, they are all the same thing." In the perspective of this kind of master, "everything is within one's own reach . . . and all those magnificent buildings are marked with labors' handprints and their blood and toil." Immersed in this poetic depiction is not politics only but also what one could call a neutral laborer's emotions. That may explain why, in various kinds of destructive resistance, we do not see the old man Xie. The concept of politics cannot fully explain this.

Perhaps one detail can help describe the subtlety of Xie Niankui's thinking. Before the People's Liberation Army enters the city, Xie Niankui—with his thirty-five years of work experience as a technician—is forced to "sell contingent labor on the streets of Anshan, repairing people's furnaces, stoves, and brick beds."[13] In a number of detailed depictions of Xie's careful interactions with his clients, the novel highlights Xie's outstanding personal qualities of being kind and warmhearted as well as the honest working habits of a great artisan. We can identify these habits as a sort of artisanal spirit. I think the core of this spirit is that the laborer, in producing his own commodity, expresses his own high degree of responsibility toward society and the public good. Or, put differently, the public nature of the commodity shapes a sense of his own social participation. We could also say that this is an urgently needed ethics for an industrialized society. This is true of capitalism, and socialism is no different. This is why I have emphasized that, in many times and places, there is often not a clear demarcation between [an ethics of] capitalism and [one of] socialism; to the contrary, in many places and times, they can be conflated.

In contemporary Chinese literature, Xie Niankui is a classic symbolic representative of an old worker. However, we have no evidence that as a symbol he influenced how similar characters are represented in other fictional works of the time. That is to say, it is difficult for us to see Xie as a prototype in some narratological sense. A more convincing explanation is that the simultaneity of various representations of an old worker did not rely upon one prototype but rather was rooted in the political unconscious of the era. The so-called artisanal spirit—including the recognition of this spirit and its political affirmation—was one very important aspect of this political unconscious.

As a matter of fact, in contemporary literature of the 1949–66 period, such narration—including the narrative attitude—formed a mainstream mode of writing. In this narrative mode, workers enthusiastically throw themselves into production and engage in a technological revolution, expressing a high degree of responsibility and a selfless work spirit. What is more, this artisanal spirit was not only fashioned through the figure of the old worker, it also extended to the bodies and minds of younger workers. For example, in the important text from 1960s, *Never Forget* (*Qianwan buyao wangji*) [by Congshen], we find the character Ji Youliang. In this play, Ji is a positive character; he is not only a

---

13. Luo, *Fengyu de liming*.

labor model but treats technological renovation as a hobby. In the representation of this idealized modern new man, we can clearly sense the extent to which socialism positively and politically affirmed the artisanal spirit. Even in Cultural Revolutionary literature, such as the Peking opera *On the Docks* (*Haigang*), the old worker Ma Hongliang continues to exhibit the legacy of this old artisanal spirit.

The crux of the issue in *The Storm of Dawn* is not Xie Niankui's virtues, but rather why in the period after the revolution in China, symbols of the old worker, such as Xie, could so quickly emerge from the resistance of the weak narratives. I argue it is because Xie conforms more to the behavioral model demanded by the standardization of the modern factory production process. In other words, when after-the-revolution China chose the path of heavy industrialization [for its modernization model], it inevitably needed the artisanal spirit for the creation of the old worker type such as Xie Niankui or the new worker such as Ji Youliang. According to [the literary scholar] Tang Xiaobing, "the social organizational program for such large-scale industrial production, rather than resulting from an ideological choice, was largely determined by a basic modern industrial logic. The large-scale, high-efficiency factory work relied on a disciplined and organized workforce; and in this sense, an important task for modern industrial production is precisely the preservation of labor power and its reproduction."[14] Tang uses this perspective in his modernist rereading of the text of *Never Forget*.

If we say that literature or culture, by representing the artisanal spirit, just provide an implicit articulation of "the social organizational program for such large-scale industrial production," then a whole series of government documents and laws explicitly expressed the modern demands made of laborers. For example, in 1955 the state formally issued "A Letter from the All-China General Union to Workers on the Guarantees for Completing and Exceeding the First Five Year National Economic Plan." This highly poetic open letter, in addition to reemphasizing the national demand for "socialist industrialization," offers detailed stipulations about the kinds of qualities required of each and every worker:

> We need to let every person, every machine, every coin, and every minute be amply and efficiently engaged and used for the construction tasks iden-

---

14. Tang Xiaobing, [The historical significance of *Never Forget*: Anxiety over everyday life and its modernity], in *Ershi shiji Zhongguo wenxueshi lun* [On the history of twentieth-century Chinese literature], ed. Wang Xiaoming (Shanghai: Dongfang Chuban Zhongxin, 2003), 1:179.

tified in the five-year plan! To reduce waste is the responsibility of each of us! We must conserve natural resources, reduce the production and circulation cost of commodities; we must enhance the quality of our products, reduce and eliminate poor products; we must care for our machines and tools to prolong their lives; in basic construction, we must reduce construction costs; and we must guarantee the quality of construction. We must implement the principle of "good, fast, conserving, safe." We must conscientiously observe all the regulations and constantly and actively strengthen working discipline. Every one of us must assume the attitude and responsibility of the master of the nation and carry out struggle against all forms of wastefulness.[15]

Never Forget and the Peking opera *On the Docks*, in their ideological structure and the scenes of class struggle that propel the dramas, share the artisanal spirit as their core narrative element. In *On the Docks*, while the detail of the dispersed packaging of grain becomes a political event, the real issue the story needs to resolve is the question posed by the character Han Xiaoqiang: "Is your attitude a worker's attitude?" A genuine proletarian, or an idealized one, is really one who resembles the old worker Ma Hongliang who, although he has retired and left Shanghai, "still harbors the docks in his heart." *On the Docks* is a continuation of *Never Forget*; contained in the political exclamation to "never forget class struggle" is the modern political topos that permeated after-the-revolution China—namely, "never forget production and construction." In the discourse of contemporary literature, "the nation" is an extremely important element, as it is precisely the existence of this nation after the revolution that stimulated production as well as the modern demands for workers, including their enthusiastic identification with the artisanal spirit and its political affirmation.

However, when this kind of explanatory has attained the support of modern theory, it is possible, in the historical context of socialism, for people to treat workers reductively as merely a certified example of the labor power required of an industrializing society. Worse still, this kind of explanatory often produces a confused neglect of the important distinction between revolutionary China and modern China.

In this regard, aside from recognizing discipline and organization as the basis for a modern industrial society and its demands for a particular quality

---

15. *Zhonghua Renmin Gongheguo fagui huibian, 1955 nian 7 yue–12 yue* [Compendium of laws of the People's Republic of China, July–December 1955] (Beijing: Falü Chubanshe, 1956), 852.

of laborer, we cannot ignore the concept of the self-consciousness [of the proletariat], as it is precisely this concept that determines the fact that China after the revolution is persistently revolutionary and not merely modern. That is to say, the political quest for revolution was not completely submerged under the political search for the modern; to the contrary, this search for revolution continued to control China after the revolution and, of course, in many ways also determined the fierce conflicts after the revolution in China between revolution and production. The political quest for revolution was not confined just to a principle of equality; it also included positioning the peasants and workers as masters of the nation or society, which is the reason I cited above the open letter and its invocation of "the attitude and resonsibility of the master of the nation." This attitude is not easily confined within the depiction of the artisanal spirit.

To emphasize the peasant-workers as masters of the nation was an important social imaginary to be completed through the ideological work of this period, as well as in literature and art. No matter what distance this ideological imaginary had from reality, it is nevertheless one very important legacy of socialism. In this imaginary, peasants and workers not only attained a certain respect as human beings, but this attainment of respect was the product of politics first and foremost. For this reason, sociopersonal transformation (*fanshen*)[16] was not based only in economics, but more important, it demanded a political transformation. It was only with the establishment of the common feeling of respect that peasants and workers could gain a real sense of their lives having been thoroughly overturned and transformed. In this sense, what socialism needed to challenge was not capitalism only, but also the hierarchical traditions that had persisted from the very beginnings of class society. Hence, in *On the Docks*, for example, what really angers Ma Hongliang is the strong age-old prejudice against "stinking coolie labor."

In a China where illiteracy was still common, depending on the notion of citizen to mobilize the broad masses of the Chinese subalterns to participate in the public affairs of the nation-state was not possible. It was only with the assistance of the concept of masters of the nation that it was possible to form a participatory modern politics. What China at the time most urgently needed was the participation of the whole population, including the subal-

16. Tr.: *Fanshen* is one of those untranslatable words. It carries the meaning of a thorough overturning, and it literally means a turning over of the body. It is more complete than gaizao—transformation through reeducation—insofar as it is not only an attitudinal but also a structural overturning.

terns, in social affairs. This was not only a political necessity but also an economic one. Naturally, during China's socialist period, due to the fact that this participation did not stably form a complete modern political structure and in particular was never really systematized—that is, it was never fully bureaucratized—the political effects of this mobilization-participation structure are still open to doubt.[17] At the level of production, "the attitude and resonsibility of the master of the nation" at various times successfully stimulated the productive enthusiasm of many workers. Yet in the overall context of modernization, including that of the commodity economy, the complete exclusion of the element of individual benefit continued to pose insurmountable challenges to the sustainability of enthusiasm. Still, the imaginary of the master nevertheless contained within it something we might call a structural imagination of people's politics. And this imagination is one of the socialist legacies that we ought to rediscuss and reexamine today.

Of course, this respect could not rely entirely for its affirmation on politics, particularly not on power politics, for its legitimacy already implied the triumph of a common identification. Thus, it needed to find yet more forms, including morality, emotions or feelings, and aesthetics, through which it could be expressed. In this sense, the artisanal spirit came to be articulated simultaneously as an individual's moral character and even as a type of sublime form. This type of sublime beauty is rendered into emotion, whence it becomes the crucial support for the respect due old workers. In this sense, participating in the aesthetic imaginary of the master is not only political but also cultural.

II. "Speaking Cultural Bitterness" and Technological Reform

On July 25, 1952, the *Labor Daily* (*Laodong bao*) published an article titled "We, a Couple" [*Women fufu liang*] by a female worker, Jin Huifang, from a state-owned Shanghai textile factory. In this article, the concept of "speaking cultural bitterness"[18] was raised: "Immediately after the factory set up the

---

17. See chapter 2 for more discussion.

18. Tr.: "Speaking bitterness" was a general method of consciousness-raising for the masses. It required individuals to stand up in village and community meetings to give voice, and thus a language, to the sources of their life's bitterness or suffering. Rather than blame their bad situations on fate, for example, the masses were encouraged to point to landlords, bosses, and others in the exploiting classes—structural factors—as the sources of their bitterness. It thus served the purpose of raising class consciousness and of situating individuals in revolutionary classes. The cultural version of this method took its basic components and elaborated them further.

crash course for literacy, the administration gave me permission to go classes full time. On the first day when we had the speaking cultural bitterness class, I stood up and spoke my bitterness. I started to cry before I finished, as did my classmates. Then I thought that after a month I would be able to learn more than 2,000 characters, so I immediately dried my tears."[19] Through this short description, we can gather that, by the beginning of 1950, a literacy movement was taking place among many Shanghai workers, and that this literacy campaign was somehow connected to the concept of speaking cultural bitterness. This speaking cultural bitterness is clearly an extension of the 1946 speaking bitterness movement carried out in the military and among villagers. In recent years, this speaking bitterness campaign has attracted some scholarly attention, and there has been no small amount of scholarly achievements on the topic. Researchers not only believe that peasants attained some collective identity through individual narrations, but that "as a management technique that transformed people's worldview and a mediation mechanism that helped peasants to form the notion of nation-state," speaking bitterness restructured the relationships between peasants and their surrounding world, including the world of the state.[20]

Yet the speaking cultural bitterness campaign was slightly different from that of the (political or economic) version, as it tended to focus more on the problem of illiteracy and the difficulties that not being able to read brought to workers, including their sense of bafflement and insult. For example, Qian Tongshen was an old worker at the state-owned Shanghai Textile Factory. During the War of Resistance against Japan, the

> Japanese devils in charge of the factory asked him: "what is your name," and he said, "I am Qian Tongsheng." The chief devil was confused and gave him a different surname, writing Qian Tongsheng as Xu Tongsheng. Because Mr. Qian did not know how to read, he hadn't a clue. But afterward, when he heard people calling him Xu instead of Qian, it was as if a knife had gone through his heart. He didn't dare say anything, though, as he was afraid of suffering punishment at the hands of the Japanese devils. This error persisted all the way through the end of the war, after which Mr. Qian

19. Jin Huifang, "Women fufu liang" [We, a couple], *Jiefang ribao* [Liberation daily], July 25, 1952, n.p.
20. Guo Yuhua and Sun Liping, "Suku: Yizhong nongmin guojia guannian xingcheng de zhongjie jizhi" [Speaking bitterness: A form of mediating structure between peasants and the state], *Zhongguo xueshu* [Journal of Chinese Scholarship] (2002): 4, n.p.

was able to heave a sigh of relief, thinking he'd be able to reclaim his real surname. Yet who knew that a flock of black crows would fly over the sky— the Guomindang officials busied themselves with buying bars of gold and Western-style houses, even while workers were unable to buy their daily necessities. Nothing in the factory changed, and on the personnel lists what had been written as Xu Tongsheng remained Xu Tongsheng! Mr. Qian was terribly upset! His left eye was permanently damaged because of all his weeping. Ever since, he's used his one good right eye to see straight through the darkness of the old society, when even the ancestral surnames of workers were stolen away![21]

Of course, speaking cultural bitterness was not limited to the political arena, as it also was related to an individual's everyday life: "When I think of illiteracy, I don't know how much suffering it caused! Let me tell you of a summer day a few years ago when a letter came from my family. At the time, I couldn't find someone to read the letter for me so I put it in a drawer. Three days later, an express letter arrived at which point I took both letters to someone to read. The first letter said that my father had become gravely ill; the second informed me that my father had died. I was incredibly sad when I heard this."[22] It also touched upon ideology:

> I started working when I was little. I lived a hard life and was never educated. When I was fifteen years old, I went with my mother to burn incense at the temple, and I saw that those who were reciting the sutras were all rich ladies of the upper class. My mother said 'they had all earned it in their previous lives. If you want to live a good life, you must learn to cultivate yourself for your next life now.' From then on, I started believing in Buddhism. . . . A while ago, I enrolled in an intensive literacy class and learned 2,000 characters, with which I was able to read the newspaper. One day, I read an article in which it mentioned an airplane pilot, who, when in the air, saw no evidence of palaces or heavenly towers; miners who, after many years working underground in the mines, had never seen evidence of hell; that the clouds in the sky are comprised of condensed water, and that lightning is electricity . . . all of it was quite easily understood. Previously, people had told me not to believe in reincarnation, but I never listened to them and always thought they were just blowing hot air, deliberately

21. "Qian shifu xue wenhua" [Mr. Qian learns some culture], *Laodong bao* [Labor daily], June 12, 1952.
22. Jin Huifang, "Women fufu liang," *Laodong bao* [Labor daily], July 25, 1952.

pouring rain on my parade. Now I've read with my own eyes in books and papers, and I have begun to realize [the truth].[23]

Illiteracy was shown to also bring inconveniences to socialism:

> This year, in March, I was doing a night shift. There was an urgent need to use the cooling pump; I had seen earlier that on the pump switch, there was a note, but I couldn't read it so I just pulled the switch down. All I heard was a clicking sound: the whole safety line snapped in two. My heart beat faster, and I quickly pushed the switch back up. Comrade Zhang saw this and he knew I was illiterate; he read the note to me word by word, at which point I realized I had made a colossal error. The note informed everyone that only a fitter could switch it on or off, and no one else should do that. I opened my eyes wide and was so upset with myself I couldn't even speak.[24]

From the above-cited materials, we can generally sense that the basic content of speaking cultural bitterness did not emanate only from cultural oppression in the political arena, but also from cultural oppression in everyday life; nor only from the ideological arena's blind faith (where blind faith more often was said to be belief in superstition, discussed further below) but also from the question of how to become a genuine worker for the new China, where the new worker needed not only a high level of political consciousness but also a certain degree of cultural and technological training. Hence, this speaking cultural bitterness evokes precisely the three main topics of national education: political education, cultural education, and technological education.

If we take the three-volume *Workers' Culture Textbook*, published in March 1950 by the Proletarian Publishers,[25] as an example, there are lessons on Party politics (such as the ninth lesson of volume 1, "The Communist Party"), on workers' subjectivity (such as the third lesson of volume 1, "The Working Class"), on the nation-state (such as the eleventh lesson of volume 1, "Constructing a New China"), and on everyday life (such as the eighteenth lesson of volume 1, "Vouchers"; the twenty-ninth lesson, "Redeeming Vouchers"; and so on). There are also those on ideology (in volume 2, there are lessons on "The Story of Mao Zedong" and "The Rise of the Taiping Rebellion," and

---

23. "Women de yanjing liangle" [Our eyes are brighter], *Laodong bao* [Labor daily], December 17, 1952.

24. "Wo weishenme yao xue wenhua," [Why I want to study culture], *Laodong bao* [Labor daily], September 24, 1953.

25. Gongren chubanshe, ed., *Gongren wenhua keben* [Textbook for worker culture] (Beijing: Gongren chubanshe, 1950), 3 vols.

in volume 3 "On Self-Criticism," and so on), and there are those on natural science (volume 2 has "The Solar System" and "Lightning," and volume 3 has "The Digestive System," "Blood and Circulation," and so on). This kind of literacy popularization campaign unified in one structure the educational goals of politics, culture, and technology, where science was from the outset a core concept that not only lent legitimacy to ideology but also underpinned modern technological training for workers.

The speaking cultural bitterness and literacy campaigns did not only need to resolve a question at the level of technology. That is to say, these movements undertook the very modern task of training workers (where training is not merely about mechanical skills); at the same time, through literacy, they brought workers into the now of new China's historical making, thus fulfilling Benedict Anderson's posited temporality of simultaneity. In Anderson's view, this simultaneity is achieved when the individual becomes part of the imagined political community of the nation through reading newspapers and novels.[26] Literacy is a basic requirement for entering this historical temporality (the meanwhile), and in this sense the literacy campaigns were eminently modern. However, more important, these campaigns also established the basis for proletarian subjectivity that included the identification of the proletariat with the Party-state and the nation, as well as national and state respect for workers.

Ding Yunliang has conducted a thorough study and collection of materials on the speaking cultural bitterness movement. He notes that "speaking cultural bitterness is a specific product of a specific historical moment. With the establishment of new China, the proletarian class was seen as the leading class, and workers achieved unprecedented political power and personal position. Political transformation led to a society-wide quest for cultural transformation (*fanshen*). Cultural transformation and political transformation were intimately intertwined." Together, these movements "awakened a deeply held desire for collective and personal respect, for social consciousness."[27] Even though the speaking cultural bitterness and literacy campaigns were a form of national political behavior, yet, as with all political movements of the 1949–

26. Benedict Anderson, *Imagined Communities: Reflections on the Origin and Spread of Nationalism* (London: Verso, 1983). See in particular chapters 2 and 3.

27. Ding Yunliang, "Wenhua suku: 1950 niandi Shanghai gongren zhi yanshuo zhengzhi" [Speaking cultural bitterness: 1950s Shanghai workers speech about politics]," in Wang Xiaoming and Cai Xiang, eds., *Refeng Xueshu* [Trends in Scholarship] (Guilin: Guangxi Shida Chubanshe, 2008), 1:115, 125. I want to thank Ding Yunliang for facilitating my collection of some of the materials cited here.

period, at particular historical moments, state political behavior actually dovetailed with individual life imaginaries and individual perceptions of personal benefit. This is a crucial point of entry into any discussion of China's socialism.

The speaking cultural bitterness and literacy campaigns, according to Ding, on the one hand "were [aimed at] individuals who, as a class, shared similar life conditions and who are now occupying the forefront of social construction." Their political consciousness is precisely what constituted the foundational consciousness of being the master. The proletariat under socialism is not merely the modernist figure of productive forces; if it were, we would have no way to understand the problem of self-consciousness. Yet on the other hand, in the interstices of the nation-state's discursive arena we can still sense the importance of culture for workers in their everyday life, which is to say that state political behavior also implies real benefits demanded by workers themselves. It is in such movements that a sort of collective memory is structured, through which a certain collective imaginary of a class is established; simultaneously, these movements were enormously helpful in allowing workers themselves to express "the significance and desires of their own lives." This is one important reason why workers at the time "genuinely participated in voluntary education, studied cultural knowledge with great purpose and diligence, and used this knowledge in their own lives and in their own work practices."[28]

The reason I pay extensive attention to these historical events is not only because they provide background to the literary works I will be discussing momentarily. Rather, what I want to emphasize is that modernity is not our only entry into history. Put differently, when we discuss the specifics of the writings from this period about workers, while industrialization is of course a very important historical element, I argue that the revolutionary and political ideals still functioned to condition the literary or cultural imaginary. Embedded in these ideals were the fundamental principles of transforming workers and peasants, who had been weak social elements, into masters of the nation. This transformation process was not only political but also cultural and even epistemological. The artisanal spirit, therefore, cannot cover the entirety of the complexity of this historical process; otherwise, we could describe this history simply as a process through which the state trained a new labor force suitable for modernization. Perhaps we can say that in this historical process what really needed to be completed was a nonobjectification effort: that is

28. Ibid.

to say, the question posed was how to render the externalities of the nation, factory, and production into constitutive internalities of the worker him- or herself. Here, socialism inevitably had to be described as an internal matter of the worker him- or herself, and this type of description's most appropriate mode was through the concept of the master.

This concept determined that self-consciousness would emerge as a natural state, through which production could easily be politicized. Or we can say that the national search for modernity could be completed through a political identification. This is the alternative modern imaginary offered by socialism. Hence, China after the revolution continuously searched for this type of political identificatory method through which the unification of revolution and production could be completed. This was a highly idealized imaginary method. And to complete this type of idealized political identification required the establishment of a proletarian culture of its own. From another angle, then, the literacy campaigns were also a process of establishing a kind of preparatory knowledge, such as the emergence of worker authors. Of course, this proletarian culture in practice, because it radically rejected and broke from capitalist and extant traditional cultures, was basically a failure. Yet we can nevertheless sense that, particularly in the 1950s, this imaginary stimulated the huge enthusiasm of workers for political identification with the Party-state and socialism.

In 1959, with the ten-year anniversary of the founding of the People's Republic of China as well as the liberation of Shanghai, Shanghai Literary Publishers (Shanghai Wenyi Chubanshe) published *Selected Literary Works from Ten Years in Shanghai: Short Stories, 1949–1959* (*Shanghai shinian wenxue xuanji: Duanpian xiaoshuo xuan 1949–1959*). Because Shanghai was at the time the largest industrial city in China, a majority of the selected stories had an industrial aspect as their main focus, so much so that even the editors wrote: "there are few stories on topics other than industry . . . and this is a big deficiency." However, they continued, "Shanghai is an industrial city, there is very little in the way of agriculture here, so that emphasizing heavy industry is not too biased after all."[29]

This industrial aspect included the huge political enthusiasm unleashed among workers after 1949 as well as the positive character of the political enthusiasm for socialist construction. Ba Jin was quite moved by this positive en-

29. *Shanghai shinian wenxue xuenji: Duanpian xiaoshuo xuan 1949–1959* [Selected literary works from ten years in Shanghai: Short stories, 1949–1959] (Shanghai: Shanghai Wenyi Chubanshe, 1959).

thusiasm: "The subjugated and oppressed 'sick man of East Asia' in the blink of an eye has begun to build the socialist 'East Asian dragon,'" and "people's spirits and faces have been transformed from 'every man for himself' to 'being pleased to work for the happiness of our descendants.'"[30] This transformation implied a certain consciousness of the attainment of the position of master.

The industrial aspect thus also implied a rewriting of the self by the workers: this rewriting no longer stressed resistance of the weak but rather, now located in a new historical discourse, spoke of how a new master consciousness would be politically structured and ultimately internalized as the proletariat's own subjectivity. In the process of this rewriting, the importance of the author is of particular note. Wei Jinzhi, in his preface to the above-mentioned book of literary selections, specifically emphasized:

> In this short space of a decade, a large number of young proletarian writers have already been quickly and successfully raised to maturity under the Party's guidance. Here, there are Hu Wanchun, Fei Liwen, Tang Kexing, Zhang Ying, and others. Among them, there were those who, before liberation, were half-illiterate and could not have written an even half-decent letter. Some, right after liberation, were able to write only a several-hundred-character report on the factory's chalkboard. Yet now we can see from the works collected in this anthology—particularly in Comrade Hu Wanchun's "A Man with a Special Character," Comrade Fei Liwen's "Tides of the Huangpu River," and Comrade Zhang Ying's "The Elderly Shock Team"—the settings, the magnificent boldness, the liveliness, the clarity of the prose, the spirit of struggle that suffuses every detail of these works.[31]

This flowery praise was obviously the result of the constraints and influence of the discourse of the time, yet through this description we can still perceive the collective face of the proletarian writer and his or her basic narrative strategy. Naturally, this [type of] writing collective, because of the limitations in their knowledge, their overly politicized nature, and so on, disappeared with the later huge historical transformations. From their initial flourishing to their disappearance, these proletarian authors index the successes and failures of

---

30. Ba Jin, preface to *Shanghai shinian wenxue xuanji: Duanpian xiaoshuo xuan 1949–1959* [Selected literary works from ten years in Shanghai: Short stories, 1949–1959] (Shanghai: Shanghai Wenyi Chubanshe, 1959), 1:n.p.

31. Wei Jinzhi, preface to *Shanghai shinian wenxue xuanji*, n.p. Tr.: All subsequent references to Wei Jinzhi are to this preface, for which pagination is unavailable.

proletarian culture; the lessons of this flourishing and disappearance can help us revisit and rethink the very concept of proletarian culture.

At the time, because of their strong political backgrounds, proletarian authors constituted a newly arising cultural force that introduced a new element into the contemporary cultural writing genealogy, particularly the industrial aspect. We should say that this introduction more strictly speaking can be understood as a wedge that, while not changing the overall structure of contemporary Chinese literature, nevertheless stimulated a whole series of tremors. These tremors included the renewed raising of the issue of identity, where identity was not just about the degree of familiarity with one's life circumstances. As Wei Jinzhi said, "they assume a worker's identity and apply a burning enthusiasm along with a sharp eye and acute sense to describe the life, work, thoughts, and fighting spirit of workers at their jobs; they describe the active, optimistic, and uncompromising attitude and spirit of the Great Leap Forward movement." Whether these beautiful words are appropriate or not is another matter; what matters here is the fact that worker identity included a high degree of political identification that at the same time was also a self-identification. In my view the significance of this self-identification is not just about creating and shoring up respect for workers but also represents a process of nonobjectification. In this process, politics included the nation-state, production, the factory, machines, and so on, all of which were internalized as one's own business by the workers. This led to an affirmation of an identity as a master.

On January 3, 1954, the *Liberation Daily* published a short story by a proletarian writer, Tang Kexin, titled "Gu Xiaoju he tade jiemei" ("Gu Xiaoju and Her Sisters").[32] Previously, on August 23, 1953, the same newspaper had published Tang's short story "Wode shifu" ("My Mentor"). The latter story is more of a literary sketch. Written from the first-person perspective, it tells of the protagonist's *shifu* at work [*shifu* refers to an apprentice's master], Tan Yirong, "an over-fifty-year-old worker, Communist Party member," who also has worked "for thirty years [and has] abundant work experience, [and is] warm and enthusiastic about teaching others technology and skills." Tan Yirong here has two identities: Party member and technician, through which are implied the two important concepts of politics and technology. The unity of these two constitutes the artisanal spirit of socialism, in which technology

---

32. Tang Kexin, "Gu Xiaoju he tade jiemei" ["Gu Xiaoju and Her Sisters"], *Jiefang ribao* [Liberation daily], January 3, 1954.

is very important. The story is about how "enthusiastic about teaching" Tan Yirong is, and how seriously "I" learn from him the requisite skills. In the 1950s, standing behind technology is the importance of culture and knowledge, all of which are affirmed by modern heavy industry. At the same time, the modernity of technology inevitably links it internally to a totality, which means any individual's technological skills must be supported by a spirit of heavy industry and by a consciousness of totality. Tan Yirong teaches "me": "Your work is related to the quantity and quality produced by the entire cloth workshop; it is a big responsibility. If one person wishes to grasp the entirety of the workshop, then you must understand that one person's job is related to those of hundreds in that workshop, and if your work is lacking even ever so slightly, it will influence the work of hundreds of others."[33] In the discourse of modern heavy industry, on the one hand, there is a high degree of labor division and specification that gives rise to a high degree of divided expertise; yet on the other hand, the relations among expertises must structure a tight totality. Hence, an intimate relationship has to be forged among individuals between division and cooperation, while at the same time and even more important, a macro-level perspective must be affirmed. This macro-level perspective must be articulated as a simple and straightforward concept: an individual's sense of responsibility.

Here, we can already sense that the ideology of socialism and the social formation demanded of heavy industrialization in modernization are linked to one another in various ways; that is to say, socialism's ideology itself is built upon the social formation demanded by modernization and heavy industrialization. Both demand that individuals become individuated, from which a free market in labor power is formed; yet both oppose an absolute atomization of individual persons, as this would prevent the formation of a consciousness of the totality. Yet the difference between the two lies in the following: industrial capitalism organizes individuals through a very hierarchically formed system of management whose order always possesses a logic of objectification. Through this objectification, a model depending upon a high level of concentration of power is achieved. Clearly, this objectification method is in sharp conflict with the master ideological consciousness for the proletariat encouraged by socialism. Hence, the tendency in socialism is toward the transformation of the proletariat as master to form a nonobjectified, internal-

---

33. Tang Kexin, "Wode shifu" [My mentor], *Jiefang ribao* [Liberation Daily], August 23, 1953.

ized, and highly politicized identity. This identity is both political and ethical, and hence the sense of responsibility contains a high political consciousness and a high degree of moral imperative. This is why, in the story "My Mentor," Tan Yirong must be depicted as an old worker who has a high degree of political awareness and not merely as a great artisan who exhibits no political consciousness whatsoever.

Yet this kind of political unconscious about being a master would inevitably come into conflict with the extant industrial social formation of the time, including the system of bureaucratic management. I will have more to say on this point below. Here, I just want to point out that among Shanghai proletarian authors of the 1950s, this aspect did not receive deeper treatment. It may have had to do with the limitations of the short story genre, but more importantly, it may have had to do with the limited knowledge level and depth of thought of the totality of these writers as a whole. Hence, even though "My Mentor" deploys a large amount of political language—for example, Tan Yirong is described as being a Communist Party member with a history of heroic struggle—nevertheless, what stands out in the narrative's articulation is what was called in political discourse the theme of "respect your mentor and love your apprentice." That is to say, revolving around the issue of becoming the master may be a whole series of confused and complex conflicts, which could become simplified or submerged into a simplistic notion of the artisanal spirit. Actually, the form of writing in "My Mentor" structured a rather common model of writing at the time, many examples of which also were collected in the anthology published celebrating the tenth anniversary of the liberation of Shanghai. Interestingly, the editors of the volume on the one hand affirmed the positive aspects of these works, but on the other hand also expressed a certain difference of opinion. For example, Wei Jinzhi, in a comparison of two works by Hu Wanchun, said: "If we compare these two works, the former was published in August 1958, whereas the latter was published a year earlier. In the former, the author's choice of material is slightly different from the more normal 'respect your mentor and love your apprentice' type, but it is still limfited to this theme and to the old materials upon which this theme is based. The latter piece escapes the confines of that theme and uses new materials and themes. It tries to reach more deeply into the characters' spirit and portrays characters with clearer characteristics."

Why, though, cannot the theme of "respect your mentor and love your apprentice" reach into the deepest recesses of a person's spirit? Aside from the cultural theory of the time that maintained "materials determine the work," are there other factors at play? Wei continues with an analysis of Fei Liwen's "One Year" and "The Tides of the Huangpu River," along with Ren Gan's "Eternal Progress" and "Kindred Spirits." In this kind of comparative discussion, we can see the basic points include hopes for the writers to move beyond simple "'locational or mechanical descriptions" so as "to stand on a higher point of view," and to "convey a depiction of an individual, . . . his innermost heartfelt changes and his interactions with others," and so on. Even though this type of articulation is unspecific and murky, nevertheless we can consider the fact that in the critic's mind, the Great Leap Forward was a very important concept. That is to say that for the critic, it was precisely because of the Great Leap Forward that writers changed their writing tactics, enabling them to "stand on a higher point of view," as it was called in the discourse of the time, from which they would be able "genuinely to reach the deepest recesses of people's spirit." In this sense, the critic was not arguing about artistic techniques in creative writing but rather about how to raise the level of thought.[34] So Wei repeatedly emphasized, with comparisons, the changes in these works. In this, there was political constraint, but it also had to do with the new political and aesthetic demands made by the Great Leap Forward.

If we temporarily put aside the sociological analyses of the Great Leap Forward and treat it mainly as a cultural symbol, then at the time, we can see that this symbol caused a number of political, cultural, and even aesthetic tremors. One aspect of these tremors was that the Great Leap became a mediator between the individual and the state; that is to say that the Great Leap as a symbol effectively internalized the state in the individual's subjectivity. Hence, in articulation, the Great Leap needed a macroperspective. "Standing on a high point of view" means to see further: height and distance require a type of new vision. This vision in reality required a high degree of abstraction in writing. Yet in the dogmatic training of the revolutionary realism of the time, this abstraction could be expressed only through the depiction of an individual's personality. This is perhaps why Wei was so taken with Hu Wanchun's "A Person of Special Characteristics." A highly abstracted aesthetic requires a high degree of politicization behind it, which requires individuals to be liberated from trivial aspects of their lives. The individual can thus assume

---

34. Tr.: These were requirements as set forth in Mao's "Talks at the Yan'an Forum on Literature and Art." See Translator's introduction for the importance of these "Talks."

the position of the master and enter the realm of national (political) affairs. Here, not only was a conflict created between being red and being expert,[35] there was also a narrative conflict created between being far and being near. Very possibly, to the critics, certain features (such as descriptions of locations or machines) were not enough to fulfill the new abstract political and aesthetic requirements. What all of that resulted in was an aesthetic conflict between abstraction and particular features.

As mentioned above, because of the constraints of revolutionary realism, this abstracted political and aesthetic requirement never found a completely appropriate expressive mode in the 1949–66 period. It sought to articulate abstract political and aesthetic sensibilities through the method of particularizing features, and this is perhaps the reason why personality became one of the most common descriptive modes of the period. Actually, this aesthetic conflict was not confined to the representations of industry. The debate, after 1958, about "household work, children's emotions" as represented in Ru Zhijuan's creative work can also be seen as a reaction to this aesthetic conflict. The question is whether particular features can support the abstracted requirements of politics and aesthetics. That is to say, in the actual process of representation, there was a rupture between particular features and abstraction that rendered the particular (character or personal characteristics) a suspect realm; this is one reason some of the works of the time strike us as rather fake. This point, in actuality, was already exposed to some degree in Hu Wanchun's piece, yet his "A Person of Special Characteristics" was considered more suitable to the new political and aesthetic demands of the time.

I think that one big reason for the failure of proletarian culture is related to its choice of form. It was quite difficult for so-called realism to take on the burdens of this more and more radical cultural and ever more abstract political and aesthetic demand.[36] Of course, behind the crisis in form, a more profound reason for failure may have to do with the preference for "distance" over proximity. What happened is that, in the process of the high degree of interiorization of political and aesthetic demands, the individual's subjectivity faced the danger of being hollowed out, which instigated a strong backlash

---

35. Tr.: "Red" means Communist or radical; "expert" means technologically adept and educated. The ideal was to be red and expert, although there were ongoing debates about what that actually meant and how to achieve it.

36. A different type of abstraction emerged in the early Cultural Revolutionary period with such novels as *History of Line Struggles in Hong Nan, Niu Tianyang*, and so on. Yet this choice of form also could not escape the fate of failure. A discussion of this could perhaps open a wider space for the consideration of contemporary Chinese literature.

from individuals, including among workers. The crisis instigated by this high degree of interiorization was articulated most clearly in the course of cultural narratives of the 1960s.

However, in the 1950s, particularly before the Great Leap Forward, new political and aesthetic demands had not completely formed. For this reason, in literary descriptions of the industrial aspect, what was called in cultural discourse "life's matters close to hand" remained an important narrative resource. Those "life's matters" are mostly set in a factory (or workshop) and focused on interpersonal conflicts and relations between man and machine, centering around industrial production. This representational mode actually was quite similar to that used during and in the wake of the Great Leap Forward in works by such writers as Hu Wanchun. The choice of narrative setting, in addition, was intimately related to Marxism. Marx's labor theory of value was established precisely on the basis of production, where all value is intricately concealed in the process of production. Hence, whether exposing the essence of capitalism, emphasizing the modernizationist desires of socialism, or establishing the consciousness among workers of their position as masters, all such literature would, consciously or unconsciously, choose the factory as a space for narrative representation.[37] However, in this relatively simple space of production, to really deepen the articulation of complex political conflicts became a genuine difficulty at the level of narrative. That is, in the factory environment where production was key, the position of workers, including all the conflicts that this position entailed, also became subject to the logic of production. Naturally, a difference persists: after the Great Leap Forward began and with it, the increasing radicalization of narration, conflict was highly politicized and was repeatedly resignified and dealt with by exaggeration. Such treatment, needless to say, left behind narrative traces of generalization.

In some sense, Tang Kexin's "Gu Xiaoju and Her Sisters" can be seen as marking a point between "My Mentor" and "A Person of Special Characteristics," as a somewhat neutral narrative. "Gu Xiaoju and Her Sisters" selects for its major narrative space the textile factory with which the author is familiar. What is different is that the short story begins with Gu Xiaoju and her sisters going to visit a neighboring factory, a visit that sets in motion a number of different conflicts. The significance of the irruption of the neighboring factory

---

37. In the 1960s, because of the new importance of the concept of consumption, the choice of spatial form experienced a certain alteration. I discuss this further in chapter 7.

into the narrative lies in the fact that it effectively disrupts some sort of natural habitat. There, the factory is located in a broader discursive space indicating not just one type of industry, but rather the political form of the nation-state. In this narrative mode, the short story's protagonist travels outside—such traveling taking the form of visiting or inspecting—and what she learns is an important aspect of the traveler's own maturation process.

This type of writing not only draws upon the industrial aspect; it is also visible in any number of short stories about agriculture. What traveling offers is a national geographical imaginary, even if it is often restricted to one particular industry or one particular region. Nevertheless, in this traveling, the gap between places and their respective situations is effectively disrupted, and different places are reattached to one another by way of national identification. Traveling in this sense is essentially politicized. Yet it is precisely with this type of politicized traveling that the worker (or peasant) can struggle free of a naturalized status as mere labor power and acquire the master consciousness through identification with the nation. Hence, visiting a neighboring factory represents the expansion of an individual's spatial horizons; it also represents the irruption into the narrative space of a national or master consciousness.

At the same time, this travel to learn or obtain information can also bring anxiety to the protagonist, an anxiety whose origins reside in the contrast between being advanced and backward. At the neighboring factory, Gu Xiaoju senses the pressure of new work methods. This suggests that the labor competitions that took place during the 1950s did not just exist as bureaucratically organized activities; they were simultaneously internalized as a certain discourse and even a form of culture. However, these competitions also included the rankings (and awards) that resulted from them. In this sense, they betrayed a certain way of ordering hierarchy in the industrial worlds, in which the higher ranking (award-winning) laborers would tend to exert a certain oppressive pressure on the lower ranking ones. The hope was for such pressure to result in the lower ranking factories desiring to change their situation for the better by making new efforts, thereby creating a positive atmosphere for competitiveness. Such competitions, however, could always produce an opposite [result], a certain remnant that at the time was fictionally represented as a form of backwardness. For this reason, competition, especially the resulting differentiation between advancement and backwardness, tended to generate a series of psychological confusions among the masses.

Today, when we read Tang Kexin's short story through this lens, what draws our attention is no longer what new work model Gu Xiaoju manages to come up with, but what kind of psychological reaction Gu's advanced quality causes among her coworkers. According to the story, Gu hears some "unfavorable comments," and it relates the comments via another character, Yu Fang, in this way: "We workers have organization and discipline; everyone does their work in this way, and only you do it some other way. Are you not separating yourself from the masses?" "Guiying has the most critical views on this. She says that 'if we do things that way, and one person finishes thirty units in one day, then we'll have no free time at all.'" "But people say that increasing production and decreasing waste is not about intensifying labor. How much could it cost to reduce [our product to] 2–3 reels of silk?"

To the charge that there will be "no free time," Gu responds that "when those girls are free, they don't do anything at all; aren't they just playing?" This rejection of play represents the intention of public temporality to appropriate fully the time of the individual, an intention whose source derives from a master standing on a higher ground with an elevated self-consciousness and moral imaginary. Of course, the regulative principle of this ideology cannot completely eliminate the stubborn desires of the individual, which includes the individual's desire to control her own time. Of course, in Gu's period, this contradiction was deeply buried in the unconscious of the text, and only in the 1960s would play again float to the surface of texts (such as in *Never Forget*).

The idea that Gu is separating herself from the masses is more complex. "Does this way of doing things mean I disregard organization and discipline? I don't get it," Gu says. This "unfathoming" makes Gu Xiaoju feel "very isolated, like a lonely flagpole." And yet, in the midst of her isolation, Gu Xiaoju thought of Cailan in the third platoon, the number A work group; Lingling from the neighboring factory; and Hu Jinxiu, the secretary of the Youth League branch. In the end, "she smiled with satisfaction. . . . Aren't the Party and the Youth League like the closest and warmest of all families?!" Here, the proletarian again becomes a mode of imagination: the individual transcends the concrete identity of a worker and reattaches herself more closely to the proletariat class and the nation. Still, this reattachment cannot solve the problem of her "separation from the masses." For the more crucial question is how seriously to consider the challenges from the masses and their desires. At that time, it was impossible for this question properly to enter the narrator's point of view.[38]

38. Tang, "Gu Xiaoju he tade jiemei."

As mentioned earlier, "Gu Xiaoju and Her Sisters" treats one's working position as a neutral mediating space between the individual and the nation, thus effectively representing the elevated spirit of the working class of the 1950s in assuming the position of masters of the nation. However, in such narratives, we can still, either murkily or clearly, sense the presence of a certain latent crisis.

With the speaking cultural bitterness and literacy campaigns, workers entered into the imaginary mode of the proletariat via culture and knowledge. This imaginary both demanded that workers become the masters of the state and demanded that they measure themselves against this standard. This was a process of interiorization, or a process of deobjectification. But the explicit moralized disposition of this process (it was not to be for individual interests) inevitably butted up against stubborn individual desires and their oppositions, which were themselves produced through and by the widespread industrialization and modernization of society. That is to say, the social formation of industrialized society (including its mode of remuneration) is a continuous objectification of the individual, from which the goals of modernized management can be achieved. This managerialism includes the stimulation of desire for material goods. Hence, in this industrialized social formation, it is precisely individual desire that is difficult to deobjectify, and in face of this desire the elevated position in actuality occupied a certain position of oppression and pressure. So at the same time as deobjectification, there was actually a need to reobjectify. In the 1950s, this [re]objectification was quite mild. Regardless of whether they were narrating industry or agriculture, the focus tended to be mainly on conflicts between new person or new issues and old person or old issues. In the 1960s, however, due to the ever sharpening conflicts between distribution and consumption, this [re]objectification process underwent a fundamental alteration. In *Never Forget*, for example, the conflict between the advanced and the backward was elevated to the level of a class struggle (still largely in the realm of ideology). By the time of *On the Docks* in the Cultural Revolution, it had become a motivating aspect of the melodramatic action. Regardless, these treatments manifest the various crises the aforementioned interiorization encountered.

Even though this 1950s crisis underwent a continuous reevaluation, one of the main sources of the crisis remained the acute conflict between the modernized and industrialized formations and the proletariat as masters of the state. This conflict was not only represented in the contradiction between the advanced and the backward, but even more so in the inevitable multifaceted conflicts between the imaginary mode of the masters and the modern bureaucratic order.

III. Anti-Intellectualism or Anti-Expertism?

In the *Selected Literary Works from Ten Years in Shanghai*, there is one piece by Yang Bo titled "Promotion" ("Tiba"). The story revolves around an "ordinary worker" at a textile factory, Jin Rumei, who is promoted "in unprecedented fashion" to become the head of her workshop. The proximate reason for Jin Rumei's promotion, according to the short story, is "so that we can prepare well for tomorrow's tasks. As the nation's large-scale economic construction begins, old factories will support new factories and we will need to transfer sets of cadres to those factories."[39]

In the 1950s, a lack of managerial talent was one of major difficulties facing the "large-scale economic reconstruction" in after-the-revolution China. Promoting ordinary workers to management positions was intended to address such difficulties. But of course there was a deeper reason for pursuing this path. Politics was clearly the most important factor. This politics involved a continued suspicion of intellectuals, but it also included a contradiction between the discourse of proletarians as masters and bureaucracy. If in actual work and life the masters in effect occupied a position of being managed or controlled, then how could one establish the leading cultural parameters of the master discourse? Of course, aside from this political consideration, the epistemological basis of work experience was also proffered as an important element in promotions: in the short story, the positive character, Zhang Hongchun, is described not only as someone who knows technology, but who also has abundant experience in production. Here, genuine technological know-how is not about theoretical knowledge but knowledge situated within the "abundant experience in production"—namely, knowledge in practice. Once one incorporates practical experience into the definition of knowledge, not only is the system of knowledge expanded, but even more importantly, it underpins the knowledge of production of someone like Jin Rumei in the story, thus legitimizing her promotion.

39. Yang Bo, "Tiba" [Promotion], in *Shanghai shinian wenxue xuanji: Duanpian xiaoshuo xuan 1949–1959* [Selected literary works from ten years in Shanghai: Short stories, 1949–1959] (Shanghai: Shanghai Wenyi Chubanshe, 1959), 1:242.

Yet the basic content of China's actual industrialization was none other than modern, and for this reason one of its fundamental elements was technology. Even with technology being appropriated as practical knowledge of production, modern theories about technology remained unchallengeable. The impossibility of challenging these theories inevitably demanded positive response from the narrator. Hence, in "Promotion" even though Jin Rumei is dissatisfied with her superior, Xu Qinglian, this does not stop her from making a careful study of technology: "From this time forward, Jin Rumei went to the workshop to work with Zhang Hongchun, and whenever she had questions, she'd ask. At night when she returned home, no matter how tired she was, she'd spend at least an hour reading technology books and [she] began a study of the principles of textile production, the structure of spools and looms, how to manage various aspects, and so on. But because she had little education, the parts she didn't understand, she traced out with a pencil and asked Xu Qinglian."[40]

From speaking cultural bitterness to literacy campaigns all the way to Jin Rumei's efforts to study technology or theory, there is one logical trajectory—namely, for peasants and workers to become the masters of the state, they must be in possession of corresponding cultural knowledge. This logic also implies a very important political topos. To wit: political participation is at the same time participation in knowledge. On this point, describing Chinese socialism simplistically as anti-intellectual is obviously inaccurate. In reality, from 1949 to 1966, science was always a very crucial concept; it effectively permeated the national ideological formation. On this, one need note only one of the three component parts of Marxism: scientific socialism. Hence, to go from social science to natural science was not at all an odd turn to take. Because of this emphasis on science, there naturally developed a great respect for scientific knowledge and a corresponding demand for the popularization of scientific knowledge. In many of the lessons included in the *Textbook of Culture for Workers* I discussed earlier, we can already get a good sense of the intention to popularize this kind of knowledge. On the one hand, this popularization was part of the struggle against what was called feudal superstition (in effect, cultural conflicts in the realm of knowledge); and on the other hand, this popularization was evidence of the central position that science occupied in national ideology. On this point—that is, in attitudes toward science—the Chinese revolution exhibits its modernity and its antifeudalism.

40. Ibid., 1:249.

What is quite interesting and worth noting is that one basic motivation for Jin Rumei to study theory comes from a kind of depressing force embodied in Xu Qinglian. From Jin's perspective, the story describes the vice director of the workshop, Xu, as "cynical, pretentious, and condescending toward others." In Zhang Hongchun's words, Xu's "technological knowledge is okay," but "he's unwilling to teach others" and "everyone calls him 'sticky candy' because he works lackadaisically; when he encounters something urgent, he would always say slow down and there's no hurry."[41]

The portrayal of Xu is largely typical of its time, the caricatured image of technological intellectuals: arrogant, self-important, conservative, stubborn, knowledgeable, technologically trained, but not willing to teach others, and so on. This image is not only familiar from fiction; it also appeared in dramas and operas, such as the one-act drama *Class Love* [Jieji zhi ai].[42] *Class Love* and the short story "Promotion" both concern themselves with the question of how to break the monopoly of knowledge so as to allow more common workers and ordinary intellectuals to participate in the construction of the nation and modernization. Also important is that standing behind this participation in knowledge is the even more profound demand to participate in politics. In essence, it was an expression of political democracy as articulated in the realm of knowledge. In this type of political democracy where the consciousness of the master controls all political participation, there is an inevitable acute conflict with the modern system of scientific expertise, along with the systems of ideology and professionalism that support the monopoly of the expert. The significance of this lies in the fact that, at that time in China—or at least for some radical thinkers of the time—there was no point in establishing an expert society, strictly speaking. Their efforts were focused on encouraging the participation of a large number of common people in the reconstruction of the nation and society. For this reason, it was absolutely necessary to disrupt the monopoly on knowledge by experts and, on the basis of the modern division of labor, emphasize common cooperative relations and, therewith, the consciousness of workers as masters. From this there would arise a strong motivation for participation and a strong sense of responsibility and self-awareness. Against such thinking, some technological experts (absolutely not all) often had to be situated as representatives of experts and powermongers who exhibited a certain conservatism and selfishness in their ideological

---

41. Ibid., 1:235.
42. Wu Yijian, "Class Love" (Hankou: Xinhua Shudian Zhongnan Zongfendian, 1950).

dispositions. The negative implications of such depictions have been shown by history, but history still needs to show the latent possibilities—positive, albeit crude—for liberation in this negativity. More important still, this type of narrative implicitly indicated the conflict between the Yan'an way and the Soviet model, and the eventual rupture of China from the Soviet technocratic model.

In the story "Promotion" there is the following description: under the glass desktop of Engineer Zhou there is a piece of paper with a motto citing Stalin, "The pioneer here is the technological intellectual because he is intimately involved with the process of production." In the beginning of the 1950s, Stalin's theories in effect functioned as a textual authority on [how to represent] technological intellectuals. In quoting Stalin, the story attempts to point to a certain positive and correct view on intellectuals. Or, in so doing, the story reasserts the political quest for national modernization, stressing the shared goal between the state and intellectuals in the search for modernity. Ironically, however, the story puts more emphasis, first, on how technological intellectuals must be led by a correct political view, and second, on how the monopoly of expertise is to be disrupted so as to allow more common workers to participate in the management of the factory. In some sense, these considerations structure a large portion of the 1950s fictional themes that took up the industrial sphere. What clarified and ultimately systematized all these considerations was the subsequent appearance of the famous Angang Constitution.

The Angang Constitution refers to the March 11, 1960, "Report of the Anshan City Committee Regarding the Beginning of the Movement for Technological Reform and Technological Revolution."[43] On March 22 of the same year, the Party's Central Committee approved this document and sent it on to the Shanghai Bureau, the Committees of the Cooperative Zones, Provincial Committees, Committees of the Autonomous Regions, and so on. It was designated by Mao as the Angang Constitution. The Angang Constitution was issued as a challenge to the Soviet Ma'anshan Constitution (named for a Soviet metallurgy factory in Magnitogorsk whose model Angang had been following until then), which had a complete set of management techniques, rules, and standards, and even laws. The Ma'anshan Constitution is based upon the po-

---

43. Tr.: The Chinese name of this Report is "Anshan shiwei guanyu gongye zhanxianshang de jishu gemxin he jishu geming yundong kaizhan qingkuang de baogao." Cai does not indicate where he obtained the original Report from, although it is available in Chinese online. We are unable to verify which version Cai used to cite from here or elsewhere in the text below.

litical principle of "experts in charge of the factory," which implies acknowledgment of the power of experts over production. In that model, there was also a very strict system of factory control under the director. In Mao's view, what the Ma'anshan Constitutional model led to was not only "opposition to the leading role of the Party in the factory directorship's responsibility," but also an "antipolitical line, where trust is placed in a minority who carry out their tasks without enthusiasm." In contrast, the Angang Constitution promoted the factory director (manager) responsibility system under the leadership of the Party Committee for State-Owned Enterprises, which on the one hand strengthened the leadership role of the Party in enterprise work while also [on the other hand] promoting the mass line and the fuller development of mass democracy, and helping to avoid all sorts of deficiencies introduced by the system of factory control under one director. Another important aspect of the Angang Constitution for Mao was its "two participations, the one reform, and three combinations,"[44] which was an extremely important and unique experiment in the China of that time in its efforts to promote democratic and scientific management in enterprises. In the 1960s, this constitution played an enormous role in the readjustment of the relationships among various personnel within the enterprises and the mobilization of the enthusiasm and creativity of the workers.[45]

Even though the promotion of the Angang Constitution betrays a clear political goal of critiquing rightist opportunism in the shadow of the Sino-Soviet debates, the democratic thought implied in it is still worth discussing even today. This democracy does not only point to economic democracy. Indeed, economic democracy—including, for example, democratic policy making, democratic labor participation, democratic use of technology, and more—is not merely a political democracy that seeks its fulfillment in the economic arena. Indeed, a few years later, even the non-Marxist scholar Robert Dahl argued: "If there is no economic democracy and there is economic inequality, then political democracy is always empty and fake; it has no real significance. A politically democratic society must have as its basis economic equality and economic democracy." An economic democracy indicates "where all interest

---

44. The participations are cadre participation in collective productive labor and worker participation in enterprise management; the reform refers to the elimination of unreasonable regulations; and the combinations refer to cadre, technological personnel, and workers in participating in the reforms and improvements in production, technology, and management.

45. See Cui Zhiyuan, "Angang xianfa yu hou futezhuyi" [Angang Constitution and post-Fordism], *Dushu* [Readings] 1996, 3, n.p.

groups within an economic system enjoy equality of participation and the power to decide, no matter whether these interest groups are or are not owners of the property itself."[46] At the time of the Angang Constitution, standing behind this disposition toward economic democracy was a profound consideration of politics. Actually, from December 1959 to February 1960, Mao, in his *Reading Notes on the Soviet Critique of Political Economy*, already had touched on the "two participations, one reform, and three combinations." As he said, "in the productive process, interpersonal relations are also relations of production. Here, for example, in the attitude that emerges from the relation between the leaders and common laborers, it must be implemented with equality so that the regulatory system is advanced, cadres participate in production, workers participate in management, and there is a tripartite unification among leaders, workers, and technological personnel, and so on. There is much to be said about this."[47] Yet the most crucial thing is [that] "we must talk about the right of laborers to manage the state, the military, various enterprises, and culture and education. This is the most fundamental right of the laborers under socialism. Without this power and right, there can be no guarantee of laborers' right to labor, to leisure, to educate themselves, and so on."[48]

If we exclude from consideration some of the more radical political vocabulary included in the Angang Constitution, then this constitution actually implies the kinds of managerial rights over enterprise sought by intellectuals and workers. It also affirms the value of human beings (and especially the creativity of workers and progressive capacities of scientific technology for social production). In this way, it marks a clear difference from the ossified Soviet system of management and bureaucratism as congealed in the Ma'anshan Constitution.

Mao's annotations on the Angang Constitution include three main components: (1) the ruling ideas for enterprises (politics in command, massification of the technological revolution); (2) the leadership system of enterprises (the factory director responsibility system under Party leadership, which is different from the system of one director); and (3) the management system

---

46. Quoted in Wang Shaoguang, *Minzhu sijiang* [Four lectures on democracy] (Beijing: Sanlian Chubanshe, 2008), 252–53.

47. Mao Zedong, "Du Sulian 'zhengzhi jingjixue jiaokeshu' de tanhua" [Talks on reading the Soviet textbook on political economy], in *Mao Zedong wenji* [Collection of Mao Zedong's writings] (Beijing: Renmin Chubanshe, 1999), 8:134.

48. Ibid., 8:129.

of the enterprises (the two participations, one reform, and three combinations). Of course, in practice, because of the constraints of leftist radicalism, the Angang Constitution exhibited the following problems: the biased critique of the technological bureaucracy led to the emergence of political bureaucracy; the emphasis on politics in command became a panpolitics [which paradoxically depoliticized everything]; emphasizing the leadership positions of workers alienated the criticized intellectuals and became entirely exclusionary; emphasizing participation led to a neglect of systemic management or the importance of regulations; promoting massification of the technological revolution led to a comparative neglect of the utility of experts and expert knowledge. All of this eventually rendered the Angang Constitution empty and indirectly led to the restoration in the reform literature in 1980s of the Ma'anshan Constitution.

Still, at the time, the emergence of the Angang Constitution strongly encouraged the active and creative spirit of workers and ordinary intellectuals. In some sense, the emergence of the Angang Constitution was not arbitrary; it was the inevitable expression of the ideology of the peasantry and proletariat as masters as exhibited in the sphere of industry. It was also the expression of the quest for the right of mass participation in all spheres of society, including the economic sphere. Some of the basic designs and thinking included in this constitution had already been broached in the early 1950s in certain kinds of literary texts. Naturally, more profound and more complete expressions of this thinking could be accomplished only in the longer form of novels, such as Ai Wu's *Steeled and Tempered* and Cao Ming's *Braving the Wind and Waves* (*Chengfeng polang*). These two novels and their publication are related to Angang, but both were published before the document's formal designation as the Angang Constitution. From a different angle, this fact can prove that the Angang Constitution was not an isolated event. The literature written at the time that we study now (such as the previously cited worker literature from Shanghai) does not reflect the practice only of one place either.

In 1952, Ai Wu participated in a national literary writing group and traveled to Angang to experience life there. He lived at the factory for one and a half years, during which time he wrote "New Home" [Xinde jia] and other short stories. In 1953, he used the lives and work of steelworkers as his materials and completed the first draft of his novel *Steeled and Tempered*, which, after many revisions, was published in *Harvest* [*Shouhuo*] in 1957. The next year, May 1958, after the Literary Publishers published the novel as a book, the favorable reviews flowed in, although there were also some critical opinions that emerged. The novel revolves around the technological revolution taking place at Furnace No. 9 (called the rapid steelmaking methods).

From 1949 to 1966, in fiction taking up the industrial sphere, technological revolution is one of the most commonly seen themes or plot devices. This technological revolution, of course, is never restricted to the level of technology; rather, it includes various complex imaginaries of modernity and many acute contradictions and their conflicts. For example, these contradictions or conflicts could be staged between workers' desire to participate in the affairs of the factory and the state; the disruption of the monopoly of knowledge [by experts] and [mass] technology; demands for changes in the bureaucratic system; anti-expertism and antibureaucratism; advanced and backward thinking, including even moral conflicts; the political and emotive mobilization by the state of workers; and so on. The Angang Constitution's high degree of approval for the technological revolution and reform was of major importance, as was its recognition that the enthusiasm of the masses needed to be fomented and harnessed.

In its treatment of the technological revolution, the attitude exhibited by Ai Wu in his novel *Steeled and Tempered* is not as politicized as the Angang Constitution was later to be. Still, it did already contain the radical political vocabulary later included in the Angang Constitution and the core thinking that this vocabulary indicates. For example, there is repeated emphasis, as in the Angang Constitution, on "the unification of self-sufficiency and big-style cooperation," while demanding "the use of one type of education for the majority of the masses and workers, to promote the spirit of communist cooperation, to make others' difficulties into your own difficulties, to use your own leaping forward to assist others to leap forward." The idea of big-style cooperation is based upon the characteristic foundations of modern industry: "because of the continuous nature of modern production, unified standards are required, as is unified leadership, so as to proceed with the technological revolution and reform in each relevant sphere of production. Practice proves that realizing self-sufficiency as the basis, while also organizing big-style cooperation and big-style mutual aid, is the key to all progress, to break through technological difficulties and to realize the Great Leap Forward in all arenas. This is the Great Leap's most basic and common experience of success." The spirit of this "big-style cooperation" is socialist China's contribution to an alternative imaginary of modernization and its practical methods.

In *Steeled and Tempered*, this spirit focuses on the contradiction and conflicts between individual interests and collective interests. In the novel's narrative, we get the general sense that Furnace No. 9 is divided into A, B, and C shifts, and to make one batch of steel requires all three shifts to work in concert. At the time, the steelmaking factory is in the midst of promoting the "method of speedy steelmaking" so as to shorten the time of production. Aside from political mobilization, there are also systems of incentivization. However, this system of incentivization provokes the acute contradictions and conflicts at Furnace No. 9. These conflicts concern the presence of individual interests as well as struggle in the ideological sphere. At the same time, these extend into the arena of the bureaucratic system of factory management and even into the family, love, and various other arenas of everyday life. It should be said that among the novels of the time taking up the industrial realm, *Steeled and Tempered* is particularly noteworthy.

Qin Degui, Yuan Tingfa, and Zhang Fuquan are the three shift leaders of A, B, and C shifts of Furnace No. 9. The origin of the conflict is this: one day, Qin Degui produced 7.5 units of steel, thus setting a new factory record; yet at the same time he also provoked the jealousy and even hatred of Yuan Tingfa and Zhang Fuquan. This jealously or hatred touches on, again, the advancement versus backwardness issue, its structural oppressiveness and the negative reaction from the masses to its oppressiveness, and conflicts of interest. What needs to be noted is that at the time, the designation of advancement [in the sense of progressiveness] could often translate into a certain political or cultural capital of a given individual. Hence, competing for advancement often could be mixed with individual interests. What this really indicates is that socialism, including the labor competition practices of socialism, in the absence of political or cultural regulatory systems can still lead to hierarchization in the ranks of the workers, and even to opening a gulf between them. Yet in the works taking up the industrial sphere, including *Steeled and Tempered*, there is not much profound thinking on this matter. Instead, they quickly turn that contradiction into a conflict between the interests of the collective and those of the individual. This conflict is concretely represented in the record-setting production of steel by Qin Degui, who, at the same time as he produces so much steel, also leads to the "weakening of the furnace." According to the newly adopted regulations of the factory: "Whenever a furnace is newly repaired, if it can be maintained without melting for thirty or more operations, bonuses will be awarded. If it does not reach thirty without melting, not only will there be no bonuses but the leaders in charge will be punished and fined." Thus, the reason for the anger of Yuan Tingfa and Zhang Fuquan is: "It really was easy to maintain the furnace through the twenty-fifth usage; but on the twenty-sixth, it was all used up by Qin Degui. So upsetting!" The origins of this "upset" are many, yet the revocation of bonuses is certainly among them, as it pertains to Yuan's wife as well as to the love prospects of Zhang. As a result, they both consider Qin to be "selfishly concerned only with himself and not with others."[49] The lack of big-style cooperative spirit among the shift leaders is evident, not to mention other elements of socialist spirit. From the very beginning, writers did not stop at the level of technology alone when they discussed the problem of technological revolution and reform; rather, for them the human element was crucial, and it was this element that the Angang Constitution centrally addressed.

Yuan Tingfa is the best-wrought of the characters in this novel. In some ways, we can see him as a revised version of those great artisan or old worker characters such as Xie Niankui [in *The Storm of Dawn*]. According to the novel, Yuan is someone who particularly loves technology: "During the Manchukuo period, steelmaking factories were introduced." However, at that time, Yuan was doing odd jobs in a workshop, and under the circumstances of the Japanese grip on technology, he learned the techniques of steelmaking on the sly (after the Japanese discovered this, they moved him to work in the canteen). During the Guomindang period, he "thought he could expend his energy working for his country, only to find himself mistreated with frequent insults and sneers." Only with "the advent of the Communist Party's liberation of the city was he able to demonstrate his steelmaking knowledge. From this time forward, he led an unprecedentedly happy life. He felt that his life was entirely entwined with the fate of steelmaking; there was no longer any possibility of separating them." Hence, even on vacation or rest days, he would ride his bike over to the factory "to have a look at the steelmaking." If it rained, he would stay home and watch the factory's chimneys: "From the amount of smoke emanating from the chimney, he could tell whether the day's work was going smoothly or not."[50] This depiction is a very typical one for a great artisan type. For this reason, in the novel he is most trusted and liked by the factory director, Zhao Liming. Yet at the same time, he also emphasizes the hierarchical order, and he often keeps some technological know-how to himself.

49. Ai Wu, *Bailian cheng'gang* [Steeled and tempered], new ed. (Beijing: Renmin Wenxue Chubanshe, 1983). Tr.: The pages for this passage could not be verified.
50. Ibid.

It should be said that Ai's depiction of Yuan Tingfa is relatively balanced. For example, in describing Yuan's individual interests, the question of money is not very important (in this, he is differentiated from Zhang Fuquan). However, Yuan is far more interested in rewards, position, and the recognition he gets from the factory management. Precisely because of this deep "excavation" (in Lu Xun's words), the writer is able to magnify the two shortcomings of Yuan, which are issues that would later be part of what the Angang Constitution aimed to address. In any case, in the plot structure of the novel, we can say that Yuan is the mass support for the factory director Zhao Liming's management bureaucracy; that is, this management system, including the bureaucratism to which it gave rise, is established on the basis of some form of hierarchical order and concept as well as the unconscious identification with hierarchy on the part of the masses. The problem is that this concept of hierarchy often suppressed the participatory desires of the masses as well as their enthusiasm. Because of this, the novel deliberately makes comparisons between Yuan Tingfa's ambitious arrogance and Qin Degui's easygoing nature, including the management outcomes produced by each personality.

As for Yuan's keeping some know-how to himself, the novel gives a more clear critique (despite a few sympathetic passages). Ai actually already discovered the relationship between rewards and position, and hence, although Yuan is not particularly interested in money, nevertheless his pursuit of rewards and position is also a form of individualism. If we recall, a central contradiction in socialism is, on the one hand, in order to stress big-style cooperation, a certain selflessness is required of each person; this sacrifice is narrativized as a sort of communist spirit; yet on the other hand, socialism also chooses the Marxist slogan, "from each according to his abilities, to each according to his needs," which in turn legitimizes a certain pursuit of self-interest. Ai himself theorized the difference between self-interest and individualism in the following terms: "self-interest is objectively extant, it is impossible to oppose; and yet obstructing collectivism in the pursuit of self-interest develops into individualism." The problem, however, is that "self-interest and individualism are sometimes quite proximate to one another: sometimes the gap between them is as thin as a piece of paper."[51] Thus, what is this paper, and under what circumstances would this piece of paper tear? And how can one prevent self-interest from developing into individualism?

51. Ai Wu, "Aiwu tongzhi guanyu *Bailian cheng'gang* yu Huang Zuliang tongzhi de tongxin" [Comrade Ai Wu's letters to Comrade Huang Zuliang on *Bailian cheng'gang*], in Ai Wu, *Bailian Cheng'gang* [Steeled and tempered], new ed. (Beijing: Renmin Wenxue Chubanshe, 1983), 351.

We could say that from 1949 to 1966, contemporary Chinese literature did a huge amount of narrative work to clarify the moral imagination in this regard. If 1950s narration on the issue was still relatively mild—insofar as it retained the legitimacy of self-interest—then in the 1960s, not only individualism but also self-interest encountered a legitimacy problem and were completely rejected. Here, if for a moment we do not speak of the radical ideological and political implications, we can see that socialism left behind a difficult topic in its theorization of distribution. That is, in the principle of "from each according to his abilities, to each according to his needs," there is an element of bourgeois capitalist rights, and the debate on these rights in fact permeated the entire socialist period. Returning to the novel, the issue with Yuan Tingfa has to do with intellectual property rights. That is, if Yuan demands that the more you labor, the more you get, then he must keep some know-how to himself so as to maintain his status. But in doing so, he would also negatively affect collective interests. This is in no way, of course, a question of Yuan's personal quality, but rather a crisis produced precisely by the socialist system itself. In order to overcome this crisis, Ai Wu repeatedly emphasizes that "in socialist society, self-interest and the collective interest are one." Thus, "an individual does not need to keep track of his own self-interest."[52]

This type of idealism, which was not entirely a form of moralistic description in the 1950s, was employed as a major method to overcome crisis. So at the end of the novel, the narrator especially emphasizes that, after Yuan Tingfa publicly reveals the secret of the technology, the spontaneous participation of the masses (strongly supported by the intellectuals and technological personnel) achieves a new steelmaking record, thus seemingly closing the circle of self-interest and collective interest. Of course, in actual social practices, this crisis could not be completely overcome. The remnants of capitalist bourgeois rights continued to encourage and produce individual desires and ambition, even while the radical leftist suppression of this self-interest stimulated its further growth. Both constituted the root of the subversive return of self-interest in the 1980s. Still, at the time, the criticism of Yuan Tingfa actually exhibited the demands to overturn hierarchical order (bureaucracy) and the monopoly on knowledge (technological conservatism). It was only with the actual overturning of bureaucracy and the monopoly on knowledge that widespread mass participation could be realized and that genuine big-style cooperation could be achieved in modern enterprises. We should acknowl-

52. Ibid., 352.

edge the fact that this ideal exerted a huge influence on the socialism of the time, while also giving rise to the special characteristics of modern enterprise management methods in China.

In the novel in question, all such positive imaginaries are turned into beautiful attributes, and the narrator in turn piles all of them onto the Qin Degui character. Qin is a socialist new person, and as such he is portrayed as having the ability to overcome all the possible crises of socialism. That is, all problems ultimately were reduced to political or moral ones, in essence pertaining to the question of socialist self-consciousness. Such a new person had already been represented by Liu Qing's protagonist, Liang Shengbao, in *The Builders*. In some sense, we can say that Qin Degui is Liang Shengbao transposed from agriculture to the industrial sphere. If we suspend discussion of the significance of this new person in the sphere of everyday life, we can see that its fundamental significance does not exist only at the level of the system but also in the question of what it means to be human. Even today, when we reconsider issues of the system, this is still a possible question for us to discuss and debate anew.

All socialist new persons to one extent or another possess what Pavel Korchagin[53] once described as the "saint-like demeanor of a communist." Thus, they need to continuously overcome various worldly desires, from which they can attain a certain religious-like grace. At the time, the various worldly desires were explained as a tendency toward individualism, so even Qin Degui is said to still "have certain traces of individualism. In some situations, he still could not properly unite the individual with the collective."[54] By extension, the critics' praise for Qin Degui is mostly because this character ultimately defeats these traces of individualism. Evidently, the new person still faced the task of reforming himself. But the problem remains that, on the one hand, socialism strove to rely on the sacredness of these new persons in pursuit of an ideal society of the future, yet on the other hand, the modern characteristics of socialism overdetermined its secular tendencies, which continuously produced the stubborn lure of individual desire. In some sense, this is where the internal crisis of socialism lies: the continuous development of a modern secular tendency led to the challenge to, and even defeat of, certain kinds of collective

---

53. Tr.: Korgachin was the Soviet author of the famous novel *How Steel Is Forged*.
54. Sun Changyi, "Shengchan zhanxianshang de yingxiong, gongren jieji de mofan—shilun Ai Wu zhu *Bailian Cheng'gang* zhong de Qin Degui" [Heroes on the front lines of production and proletarian models—a discussion of Qin Degui in Ai Wu's *Steeled and Tempered*], *Wenshi zhe* [Literature, history, philosophy] (1958), 10.

goals. This contradictory conflict was concentrated in the debates of the 1960s on a number of fictional works. And because of these contradictions, the new person became more and more abstract and more and more subservient to political demands, even though at the time critics also believed that Qin Degui's "level of thinking is still not elevated enough" because "he did not dare to uphold the principles so as to open a salvo in thought struggles," and so on. Of course, the author himself did not think much of such critiques.[55]

We should note that Ai Wu's description of Qin Degui is not monochromatic. Rather, Ai writes about the different layers of Qin's personality, including his love life (Qin Degui has the right to look for love); this is because Ai believes that "self-interest objectively exists and we may not oppose it."[56] However, once self-interest comes into conflict with the collective interest, then this self-interest could develop into individualism, which then necessitates a struggle. This is what the novel writes of Qin Degui's struggle for collectivism and his painful abandonment of his love interest, even though he is crazily in love with Sun Yufen. The novel's description of love is not particularly notable; however, worth noting is that the modern revolution plus love tradition in contemporary literature exhibits a certain tendency toward separation (even though the ending of the novel provides a scene of great unity). This type of separation had already emerged in the love story between Liang Shengbao and Xu Gaixia in *The Builders*. In this kind of narrative, revolution and love are not united from beginning to end; to the contrary, as soon as there is some divisiveness between them, revolution inevitably must be victorious over love and becomes the representative emotive mode of overcoming self-interest. Thus, if in Zhao Shuli's and others' works, the theme of great unity becomes the mode for dealing with love so as to express the passionate aspect of politics and its tendency toward naturalism, and thus to reaffirm the legitimacy of revolution in everyday life,[57] then here the separation of revolution from love expresses a certain uneasiness. This atmosphere of unease manifests a gradual radicalization of reason and emotion in revolutionary narratives, even to the point of certain rupture. Once revolution retreats from the emotive sphere of the individual, its legitimacy will become a suspect in that domain. This, incidentally, explains why in the 1980s what was called re-

55. The critics' words and Ai's own reaction both in Ai, "Ai Wu tongzhi guanyu *Bailian cheng'gang* yu Huang Zhuliang tongzhi de tongxin." Tr: Page number unclear here.
56. Ibid.
57. See chapter 3 for more on this topic.

flection literature problemtized the legitimacy of revolution precisely in the emotive sphere of love. But this is a separate issue.

In some sense, Qin Degui, this socialist new person, is closely related to the artisanal spirit symbolized by Yuan Tingfa. Hence, as soon as Yuan Tingfa is able to overcome his own individualistic tendencies, he could become another Qin Degui. In other words, in the novel's structure, Qin Degui and Yuan Tingfa have a mutually representative function. By contrast, Zhang Fuquan becomes the stereotype of an individualist, and the author focuses on how this character's self-interest is transformed into individualism. To be sure, such characterization is heavily symbolic. But the question is, if we enter the world by way of a theory and if we do not stop at interpreting the world with it, but rather we want to change the world, then some kind of symbolized narration is inevitable. Therefore, at issue is not symbolism, but rather how this symbolism can be transmitted in a more artistic fashion. On this point, leftist literature of the 1930s, because of its overreliance on realism, suffers from the problem of typification. This issue as a whole exceeds the scope of this discussion, so let us just take a look at the character Zhang Fuquan. The representation of this character in effect signifies the author's thinking on the problem of self-interest or individualism. While his thinking is not necessarily profound, it is genuine. Ai Wu, on the one hand, emphasizes that in the phase of socialism, and particularly under the condition of socialist distribution, self-interest is legitimate. At the same time on the other hand, he firmly opposes the transformation of self-interest into individualism, an attitude on his part that most probably is not dictated by the Party politics of the time. In fact, this topic had already been broached by Ai in his earlier works.

Perhaps in Ai Wu's view the possibility for self-interest to transform itself into individualism can be located where the individual, in seeking his own interest, chooses a strategic method, at which point there is a great danger for this interest to become individualistic in tendency. Thus, Ai and those like him tend to favor a big-style cooperation, which, in the discursive arena of coordination, somehow allows an individual to attain benefits from within the collective. Authors of the time may not have been so consciously deliberate in their choices, but their worries about individualism may well have had to do with their experiences of life in preliberation society. This perhaps led them to affirm a form of collectivism (whether ideological or systemic). Ai had already broached the topic of how the principles of socialist distribution could lead to profound differences in thinking, yet he also passed over it with a swipe of his pen by turning this conflict of ideas into class struggle. This is manifested in his depiction of Li Jiming, an alien in class terms, who is truly a stereotyped or caricatured figure.

In the 1950s, particularly toward the end of the decade, and into the early 1960s, using class struggle as a way to solve certain social conflicts was a popular strategy of fictional narration. This mode of narration essentially revolved around a unified structure of new and old class enemies who collude to cause destruction. Once their conspiracy is uncovered, victory is achieved. Such a narrative structure seemed to suggest that the social crisis could also be easily overcome by discovering conspiracies. This is not an insignificant structure, and it clearly manifests the paradox of the era: on the one hand, authors sensed social crisis (or contradictions), and on the other hand, perhaps because of limitations in perspectives or because of the contraints of Party politics, they were unable to recognize this crisis as the result of the alienation in socialism itself. All they could do was confine the crisis within the narrative of the intentions of the new or old class enemy toward evil destruction, or narratives of the representatives of this class enemy hiding in the midst of the Party itself.[58] Thus, using class struggle to overcome crisis became a popular political expressive structure. *Steeled and Tempered* was no exception.

Of course, in China of the time the depiction of the CCP is important to these issues. At a general level, the CCP was understood to be the representative of the interests of the majority of the Chinese masses. For this reason, the politics of the Party represented the highest and most correct principle. In addition, whether this Party politics contained within it the possibility of alienation was an extremely important subject in Chinese socialist thought, even while it was banished from most discussions. Thus, in the novel, when the factory director is put under the supervision of the Party committee, the question of who supervises the Party committee could not really be broached in the space of the narrative. As mentioned above, then, when strong one-sided criticism of the technology bureaucracy led to the growth of a certain kind of political bureaucracy (bureaucrats who did not understand technology, issued wrong directives, and so on), it further led to the revival of Ma'anshan Constitution in 1980s reform literature.

In September 1959, one year after *Steeled and Tempered* had appeared, the Writers Publishers put out Cao Ming's novel, *Braving the Wind and Waves*. This

---

58. See chapter 2 for more on this topic.

novel is quite similar in some regards to *Steeled and Tempered*. Cao Ming, like Ai Wu, had lived at Angang for a long period, and for this reason the novel takes a steelmaking factory as its narrative space. It also concerns workers and their pursuit of a technological revolution, as well as the contradictions and conflicts between a Party secretary and the factory director. I have no intention of arguing that Cao Ming's novel was influenced by Ai Wu's; in my structure of argument, this kind of supposition has no meaning whatsoever. I am more interested in putting these two novels in a coextensive temporal structure.

One example of this coextensive structure is the fact that both Qin Degui in *Steeled and Tempered* and Li Shaoxiang of *Braving the Wind and Waves* are more advanced than other workers; they both come originally from the villages and were tempered in the course of the War of Resistance against Japan; they both also became adherents of Party education relatively early. This type of narrative arrangement is not accidental; what it demonstrates is precisely the way in which the Chinese revolution defined the concept of proletariat. In understanding the concept of the Chinese-style proletariat, there is emphasis not on its social attributes (such as industrial worker), but rather on its class consciousness, which is attained through the teachings of the Party and its politics of class subjectivity. This type of understanding expands the class category of the proletariat, which becomes rather capacious and, at the same time, relatively flexible. This allows the Chinese revolution to resolve the problem of the fundamental weakness of the industrial working class in China. However, more important still is that this also explains why the workers had no naturalized political legitimacy and why they thus had to prove themselves through revolutionary tempering and self-reform. While this helped consolidate the authority of the Party theoretically, from a different angle, it also emphasized the importance of cultural hegemony, including its power over workers.

Although *Steeled and Tempered* and *Braving the Wind and the Waves* are similar in many ways, their differences are also quite glaring. Compared to *Steeled and Tempered*, in *Braving the Wind and the Waves* the political flavor is much more pronounced: the inner-Party struggle of criticizing right opportunism becomes an important backdrop to the novel's narrative as well as structuring central plot conflicts within the narrative. If in *Steeled and Tempered* the conflict between the Party secretary, Liang Jingchun, and the factory director, Zhao Liming, is a secondary plotline, then *Braving the Wind and the Waves* essentially revolves around Song Zifeng's series of criticisms against the one director system (the Magang Constitution system) and the expertism that supports this system. Clearly, this accords well with the fundamental content of the Angang Constitution, and perhaps that is the reason why the novel went through so many editions after it was first published.[59]

Some of the thinking that is encapsulated in the advent of the Angang Constitution was abundantly represented in the industrial fiction of the 1949–66 era. This imaginary went much farther and was far more complex than the Angang Constitution itself, yet its basic idea was still the critique of the system and ideology of experts, [with] an emphasis on disrupting the monopoly on knowledge and allowing workers to attain the possibility of participation in multiple arenas: politics, management, and knowledge production. It was only with this expanded and radical massification of participation that the consciousness of the master could genuinely be situated within the political and economic structures of society. In some sense, it was the radical echo of political democracy in the sphere of the economy. And it was fiction that took on the task of promoting in enthusiastic and bold literary fashion this theoretical imaginary.

Conclusion

I want to return now to the questions with which I began this chapter: how did the after-the-revolution context produce certain paradoxical themes, and how were these paradoxical themes overcome in literary form?

From the very outset, the national demands for modernization in the sphere of industry controlled the politics of this era, including the literary imagination and cultural activity. The control of modernity inevitably demanded that workers become certified modern labor power. For this reason, the resistance of the weak inevitably had to be transformed into some sort of constructive artisanal spirit—or the establishment anew of a modern work ethic. In this regard, modernity was always an effective entry into discussion. As regards self-consciousness in this framework, one can also see it as a relatively less difficult method of accruing social capital that yields high productive returns. However, the potential danger in all of this is that revolutionary China could just be equated to modern China, and socialism then confused with capitalism, despite the fact that, yes, the boundaries between socialism and capitalism were not as sharp as we might like to think. Still, there are fundamental

---

59. For example, by April 1964, the novel had already been reprinted six times and had sold over 198,000 copies.

differences between the two. One major one is that the core political ideal of socialism is to promote the peasantry and proletariat into the position of master of the nation-state and, borrowing from this master identity, it intends to complete the restructuring of its social system. This type of idealized society is impossible to realize using only the artisanal spirit.

For this reason, in the historical context of after the revolution, an acute conflict developed between the Marxist political symbolic and capitalist modern identity indicated by the category of worker-master. One representative aspect of this conflict can be found in the fact that it is very difficult to subsume the problem of the modern production and management bureaucracy into this worker-master category. Yet for the political pursuit of the state as well as its ideological needs, it was only through the political symbol of worker-master that the imaginary of the proletariat could genuinely be realized. In this completion, the leadership role of intellectuals and the cultural realm had to be reappropriated and significantly radicalized. From speaking cultural bitterness to the literacy campaigns, from anti-expertism to the two participations, one reform, and three combinations [of the Angang Constitution]—all of these were intended to allow workers to participate fully in the political goal of attaining leadership power. In this process, literature took on the task of narrating the master imaginary. At the same time, of course, this narration also brought with it tremendous social dreams.

To give an overall evaluation of these works is not my task here. For example, I have not concerned myself with what the experience of actual workers might have been—in these kinds of works there is very little that takes up the concrete difficulties and complex challenges actual workers faced in their everyday lives. There are many reasons for this type of narrative tendency, among which possibly the most important was the grip of [Mao's] injunction to generalize. This generalizing tendency was aimed at producing a historically strong class consciousness. Using the abundance of particularities and complexities to evaluate literature has already become a commonsensical way of critiquing literary works; it is quite boring by now, so I will add no more on this here. In my research framework, by contrast, what I find more interesting is how this generalizing trend promoted and possibly even romanticized working-class subjectivity and its imaginary of the future.

An important method of this imaginary is precisely what I have discussed throughout this chapter, which is a type of interiorization process. This process led to two types of possibilities: on the one hand, working-class subjectivity grew exponentially through interiorization and, in the process, it was emptied out. This process turned ideology into heroic words. At the same time and from another angle, on the other hand, there was an inevitable othering contained in this process of interiorization. That is, this process produced its remnants, and this was the condition for the production of a crisis. Transforming these remnants into others was a major effort undertaken to overcome this crisis. I will discuss this further in the next chapter.

Despite all of this, we can nevertheless still sense in these narratives an effort to produce a politics of respect for the working class. This is not merely a literary or ideological imaginary; at the very least, this politics of respect at the time had already been transformed into a type of social practice. In my view, respect is always about politics. Simply speaking of personal respect is of no significance here. Any type of individual respect is related to the fate and position of one's class or social group in society, and it is related as well to class consciousness. I personally witnessed and experienced the ebb and flow of the historical fate of the working class, including the ultimate collapse of class consciousness that has led to the complete loss of respect for individuals of that class.

7

CULTURAL POLITICS, OR POLITICAL CULTURAL CONFLICTS, IN THE 1960s

At the Tenth Plenary Session of the Eighth Central Committee of the Chinese Communist Party (CCP), held in September 1962, Mao Zedong reissued the theory of class struggle. He unequivocally stated that, during the socialist period, "there exists class struggle between the proletariat and bourgeoisie, and the struggle between the socialist road and the capitalist road."[1] In May 1963, in "Changes Made to the 'Chinese Communist Party's Resolution (Draft) on a Few Issues Regarding Work in the Countryside'" ("Dui 'zhonggong zhongyang guanyu muqian nongcun gongzuo ruogan wenti de dueding [cao an] gao' de xiugai")], Mao put it simply: "Once the theory of class struggle is grasped, any problem can be solved (*jieji douzheng, yi zhua jiu ling*)."[2]

---

1. Mao Zedong, "Dui zhonggong bajie shizhong quanhui gongbao gao de piyu he xiugai" [Remarks and changes made to the draft of the resolution of the tenth committee meeting of the Party's eighth central congress], in *Jianguan yilai Mao Zedong wengao* [Mao Zedong's manuscripts since 1949] (Beijing: Zhongyang Wenxian Chubanshe, 1996), 10:196–97.

2. Mao Zedong, "Dui 'zhonggong zhongyang guanyu muqian nongcun gongzuo ruogan wenti de dueding (cao an) gao' de xiugai" [Changes made to the "Chinese Communist Party's resolution (draft) on a few issues regarding work in the countryside"], in *Jianguan yilai Mao Zedong wengao* [Mao Zedong's manuscripts since 1949] (Beijing: Zhongyang Wenxian Chubanshe, 1996), 10:304.

In the political context of the 1960s, Mao's class struggle theory focused on two levels of the issue. One had to do with society, where a severe class struggle was believed to be occurring, and where only by way of socialist education (*shehuizhuyi jiaoyu*) could revisionism be stopped in its tracks. The other had to do with the Communist Party itself, where a class of bureaucrats was believed to have formed. This class "has become or is becoming bourgeois, sucking the blood of the workers"; and because of that, they also had become the "objects of struggle and of revolution."[3] Corresponding to this class struggle theory was not only a series of political movements in the 1960s (such as the five antis [*wu fan*] and the four cleanups [*si qing*] that were part of the socialist education movement), its influence was also found in literature. It is hard to say that it affected all literature of the time, but it did give rise to certain radical ideas. This explains why, in some recent studies of that period, critics tend to treat it as the prelude to the Cultural Revolution and argue that symptoms of the Cultural Revolution already existed in the first half of the 1960s.[4]

On a different level, however, these symptoms can also be seen as symptomatic of the crisis in socialism. In my analytical framework, I do not treat socialism as an abstract concept. Rather, I interpret it as a historical process, or a historical context, in which various complex forces took part and played their role; the interaction between these forces constituted what I identify as a productive installation (*shengchan xing de "zhuangzhi"*). This installation is both socialist and modern, both revolutionary and postrevolutionary,[5] both international and national. As such, this installation produced not only the concept of equality but also new social differences: not only the collective but also the individual, not only a revolutionary urge (or drive) to challenge and subvert but also loyalty and submission to the postrevolutionary state and its needs. These contradictions coexisted in Chinese socialism, constituting different levels of challenges to both the socialist system and socialist theory. When these contradictions deepened or radicalized, crises began to surface. What is more important to understand, therefore, is not just how the class

3. Hu Angang, *Mao Zedong he wenge* [Mao Zedong and cultural revolution] (Hong Kong: Dafeng Chubanshe, 2008), 41–42.

4. See Hu, *Mao Zedong he wenge*, for example.

5. Tr.: Here "postrevolution" comes from the term *geming hou*, which Cai theorizes as "after the revolution" in other parts of the book. Used in this sense, it ought not to be confused with *hou geming*. which is also translated as postrevolution in English but denotes the economic reform era after 1978.

struggle theory came about and was practiced, but what kind of social reality, along with its crisis form (*weiji xingtai*), the theory faced in the 1960s.⁶

To date, there have been different scholarly interpretations of the existence of this crisis and its different forms of expression.⁷ I believe that in the 1960s crises had already occurred and expressed themselves at least in two areas—namely, distribution and consumption. Issues of distribution not only exposed conflicts between different social levels but also revealed and radicalized the contradictions among the state, the collective, and the individual. Some literary works of the 1960s, such as *Sunny Days* (*Yanyang tian*) [by Hao Ran] and *Seize the Seal* (*Duo yin*) were in effect addressing these issues. There, the antibureaucratic theme was supported by the class struggle theory. Issues of consumption, in contrast, gave rise to the notion of the individual, which not only made it possible for the individual to drift outside the state collective but also began to threaten, theoretically, the formal framework of socialist political society.⁸ In such works as *Never Forget* (*Qianwan buyao wangji*), *The Young Generation* (*Nianqing de yidai*)⁹ and *Sentinels under the Neon Lights* (*Nihongdeng xia de shaobing*)¹⁰, the narratives unfold mainly around this theme, not only for the purpose of reestablishing the relationship between the individual and the state (read: revolution) based on the class struggle theory, but also clearly pointing out the importance of educating the next generation.

As a result, literary works during this period not only leaned heavily on interpreting the political intent of the state, but at the same time also conveyed very complex information on ideas, some of which extended into the Cultural Revolution and received radical treatment, such as [Yu Luoke's] "Chushen lun" (On family origins). However, despite these earlier symptoms, I do not see this period as the prelude to the Cultural Revolution. On the contrary, the Cultural Revolution was an overcoming or subversion of some of the themes

6. For a discussion of the socialist crisis, see the conclusion.

7. For example, Hu interprets it as an "illusion of crisis" (*weiji huanjue*), by which he means that "when there is a disconnect between subject understanding and social reality, policy makers have a tendency to twist (or misrecognize) external phenomena; such misrecognition (or illusion) can lead to underestimation, overestimation, or misjudgment" (Hu, *Mao Zedong he wenge*, 75).

8. The concept of political society I employ here differs from that of Partha Chatterjee in *The Politics of the Governed* (New York: Columbia University Press, 2004). It comes from Lenin's discussions of political society, which I will elaborate later in the chapter.

9. *Nianqing de yidai* [The young generation], dir. Zhao Ming (1965).

10. Shen Ximeng et al., "Nihongdeng xia de shaobing" [Sentinels under the neon lights], *Juben* [Drama scripts] (1963), 2:2–43. It was then adapted into a film of the same title, dir. Wang Ping (1964). Tr.: Subsequently, the film became far better known than the original script.

and concepts of the earlier period. In some ways, the first and second half of the 1960s (the second half being the Cultural Revolution) witnessed extremely complex, even contradictory, ideas and practices. Those contradictions were often manifested as drifting or ambiguous narrative details in many of the works of the early 1960s.

Even though the problems of distribution and consumption are closely related, due to the fact that I have discussed the issue of distribution in several of my other writings, in this chapter, I will focus on the issue of consumption. My discussion takes the Cultural Revolution as an implicit point of reference but focuses more on explaining (1) the extent to which the problem of consumption produced a crisis in socialism; (2) how consumption itself was also produced by socialism; (3) what kind of narrative function, if any, the class struggle theory performed; and (4) the paradoxes (or contradictions) that existed in revolutionary and postrevolutionary theories.

I. Material Abundance and Anxiety about It

In 1963, the playwright Cong Shen published *Wish You Good Health* (*Zhu ni jiankang*) (the title was later changed to *Never Forget*) in the November–December issue of *Juben* [Drama scripts]. More than thirty years later, this work reentered the horizon of literary studies, in part thanks to an excellent discussion by Tang Xiaobing titled "Qianwan buyao wangji de lishi yiyi: guanyu richang shenghuo de jiaolü jiqi lishi yiyi" (The Historical Significance of *Never Forget*: Anxiety over Everyday Life and Its Historical Significance).[11] In this essay, Tang creatively interpreted the deep historical implications in the concept of "anxiety over everyday life." Together with other essays included in [Tang's] *Reinterpretation* (*Zai jiedu*),[12] Tang and other authors began to bring Chinese socialism into the framework of modernity for further examination. These reinterpretations must be applauded because they provide a kind of revolutionary insight into not only the contemporary history of Chinese literature but also the contemporary history of ideas. They help

---

11. Tang Xiaobing, "Qianwan buyao wangji de lishi yiyi: guanyu richang shenghuo de jiaolü jiqi xiandaixing" [The historical significance of *Never Forget*: Anxiety over everyday life and its modernity], in *Ershi shiji Zhongguo wenxueshi lun* [On the history of twentieth-century Chinese literature], ed. Wang Xiaoming (Shanghai: Dongfang Chuban Zhongxin, 2003), 2:176–84.

12. Tang Xiaobing, *Zai jiedu: Dazhong wenyi yu yishi xingtai* [Reinterpretation: Ideology and popular literature and art] (Beijing: Beida Chubanshe, 2007).

free the Chinese revolution from the once prevalent interpretative framework of feudalism and open a new space for interpretation. Of course, in Tang's discussion, modernity is closely related to the form of industrial production. Before discussing the text (of the aforementioned drama), I would like to turn to the historical context of the 1960s, to see if further discussion can provide new interpretation.

In 1963, *Red Flag* (*Hongqi*) magazine published an article by Yu Tingying titled "Strengthen Political Education for Youth" ("Jiaqiang dui qingshaonian de zhengzhi jiaoyu").[13] The article clearly states the importance of "educating the next generation of revolutionaries": "Youth are our future. It is central to the great socialist and communist causes that we bring up our youth as reliable successors to the proletarian revolutionary mission, forever upholding the proletarian revolutionary red flags and insisting on the direction of communism." To do so, the article continues, "the first task is to strengthen political education for youth" and to struggle against "old ideas and old consciousness."[14] What is worth noting in this article is how the author foregrounds the idea of mediums (*meijie*) by borrowing the image of Mama Chang [Chang Mama] from Lu Xun.[15] Yu states that "it is via the 'medium' like Mama Chang that old ideas and old consciousness seamlessly influence our youth," and therefore "it is the responsibility of the teachers and parents to instill in our youth the ability to discern and resist the temptation of reactionary ideas, and to ensure that they carry on the revolution and never change."[16] Crucial in the author's use of Mama Chang as a metaphor is the concretization or personalization of such abstract notions as discern and resist. The use of this rhetorical motif not only influenced literary narratives (think of the use of certain characters in dramas like Mother Yao in *Never Forget* and Xiao Wu in *The Young Generation*) but also helped redirect the struggle over cultural leadership from the domain of ideas to social and political arenas. It also made

13. Yu Tingying, "Jiaqiang dui qingshaonian de zhengzhi jiaoyu" [Strengthen political education for youth], *Hongqi* [Red flag], 1963, 9:5–7.

14. Ibid., 6.

15. Tr.: "Mama Chang" is a character found in some of Lu Xun's autobiographical essays. Known in real life as Ah Chang, she was Lu Xun's childhood nanny. In China there have been scholarly discussions about how to make sense of Lu Xun's depiction of her. One of the interpretations is foregrounded in the article that Cai cites here: Mama Chang as representative of the past that resists the new and progressive.

16. Yu Tingying, "Jiaqiang dui qingshaonian de zhengzhi jiaoyu" [Strengthen political education for youth], 9:7.

it possible for class struggle theory to acquire concrete objects of its own, which, I might add, deeply influenced the form that the Cultural Revolution would take.

To some extent, the promotion of educating the next revolutionary generation was closely related to the idea of peaceful evolution (*heping yanbian*) that was circulated in the 1960s in the West as part of America's Cold War strategy (propaganda that was aimed at the socialist countries in promoting bourgeois lifestyle, culture, and ideology, for the purpose of causing a peaceful evolution in those socialist countries toward freedom). Articles about this capitalist world strategy were being circulated among the top leaders of the CCP, generating worries and anxiety. Examples include an article written by An Ziwen titled "Fostering Revolutionary Successors is a Strategic Task for the Party" ("Peiyang geming jiebanren shi dang de yixiang zhanlüe renwu").[17] In the article, the author quotes a speech made by [U.S. Secretary of State John Foster] Dulles at a press conference on October 28, 1958. Dulles is quoted as saying that peaceful evolution in China was "absolutely possible in a few hundred years, but perhaps just a matter of a few decades."[18] An Ziwen also quoted from an article by Lieberman that appeared in the *New York Herald Tribune* on April 10, 1964, which apparently said: "What can we see about the future through the fog? We can see that Communist China can (in ten to twenty years) become a country like today's Soviet Union."[19] It so happened that during this same period, the CCP had itself begun to see the Soviet Union as an example of peaceful evolution, which became a point of contention in the Sino-Soviet debates of the later 1950s and into the 1960s.[20]

But what exactly did peaceful evolution entail? What did it intend to change? In his piece titled "Zhenzheng geming, chedi geming de yingxiong" (Real and complete revolutionary heroes) included in *Stories of Young Heroes* (*Qingnian yingxiong de gushi*), which based on the stories of eleven young heroes and published in 1965, Luo Ruiqing offered a summary of core values that he believed it was most important to uphold: "dedication to arduous struggle," "selfless devotion to the public," "doing extraordinary things in ordinary work," "class hatred" (*jieji chouhen*) and "class feelings" (*jieji ganqing*), being "a nail

17. An Ziwen, "Peiyang geming jiebanren shi dang de yixiang zhanlüe renwu" [Fostering revolutionary successors is a strategic task for the Party], *Hongqi* [Red flag], 1964, 17 and 18:1–13.
18. Ibid., 18:5.
19. Ibid.
20. See, for example, "Guanyu Heluxiaofu de jia gongchanzhuyi jiqi zai shijie lishi shang de jiaoxun" [On Khrushchev's phony communism and its lesson for world history], *Renmin ribao*, July 14, 1964.

that never rusts," "protecting national interests," and "bringing glory to the country and the people."²¹ Obviously, what peaceful evolution threatened was the legitimacy of these ideas. Meanwhile, forces for peaceful evolution did not come from the outside only. They were mostly entangled with traditional old ideas and old consciousness, including such mediating elements as Mama Chang.

While these aforementioned political expressions essentially informed the core value standards in literary writing of the time, they did not however indicate the possibility of crisis produced by socialism itself. For example, in Luo, "peaceful evolution" was metaphorically referred to as "sugar-coated bombs" (*tangyi paodan*).²² But what was the "sugar coat"? In corresponding political expressions and literary narratives, we find it to be associated with bourgeois lifestyle, one manifestation being the individual's pursuit of material enjoyment. But is pursuing or constructing a materially abundant society not the modernization goal of socialism?

Some recent studies have noted the economic conditions of China in the 1960s. China was emerging from the so-called three-year natural disaster period and was in the middle of the second five-year-plan period. The economy was beginning to recover and on its way to faster development and the production of more material goods. In the literature of that period, one major theme was to emphasize the importance of socialist construction. We find this theme not only in films like Women cunli de nianqingren (*Young People in Our Village*)²³ but also in novels that ostensibly emphasize class struggle, such as Sunny Days and In Praise of the Longjiang (*Longjiang Song*).²⁴ Maurice Meisner argues that improved material life could very well undermine people's faith in communism, an issue that in turn became a major concern for the CCP leadership. "For Mao," Meisner states, "on the other hand, the combination of rapid economic development and a continuous process of increasingly radical social and ideological transformations was necessary to fully release the latent productive energies of the masses and to prevent the ever-present dan-

21. Luo Ruiqing, "Zhenzheng geming, chedi geming de yingxiong" [Real and complete revolutionary heroes], in Qingnian yingxiong de gushi [Stories of young heroes] (Beijing: Zhongguo Qingnian Chubanshe, 1965), 2:1–3.
22. Ibid.
23. *Women cunli de nianqingren* [Young people in our village] I and II, dir. Su Li, 1959 and 1963.
24. Chen Ye, "Taiqian, muhou" [On stage and back stage], MA thesis, Shanghai University, 2009. I would like to thank Chen for her research and for providing me with information related to my book.

ger of backsliding into capitalism."[25] In that postrevolutionary context, there seemed to exist a natural contradiction between revolution and construction. On the one hand, [the goal of] revolution lies in the construction of a materially well-off society. On the other hand, this materially well-off society may also destroy the revolution itself or at least cause it to stop. Similar to the title of the drama "After the Success" ("Chenggong yihou"),[26] the question that most preoccupied [people in] the period was how to continue the revolution after the "success" of the revolution, or the harvest. The corresponding "anxiety over everyday life" at the time was in many ways an anxiety about material things. What we still need to further explore, however, is why material things would necessarily undermine people's faith in communism. That is to say, did the cause of anxiety come from material things themselves or from other, more historically complex reasons, including a lack of sufficient theoretical readiness?

According to the author Feng Deying, he began to prepare for the novel *Bitter Flowers* (*Ku cai hua*) in 1953, finished the first draft in 1955, and published it in 1958.[27] In this novel about revolutionary history, there is a seemingly insignificant narrative moment: when one of its characters, Feng Deqiang, is about to join the army, a woman, Xingli, has some things to give to him. Among the items "there is a white towel, a brown-colored knitted scarf that Xingli herself has often used, and a colorfully made 'hygiene bag.'" According to the novel, "a 'hygiene bag' is a small rectangular bag, made of cloth of different colors, for things like toothpowder, toothbrush, and soap. It is a special present that women gave to men who joined the [revolutionary] army."[28] For its part, the novel *Behind the Enemy Lines* (*Dihou wugongdui*) also contains a narrative moment related to issues of hygiene. In emphasizing how to avoid the attention of the Japanese troops, Yang Zizeng, the commander of the armed work team, specifically mentions a few details and points out that "things like ink drops on tables and walls, using paper in peasants' outhouses . . . are all some of the little things that would draw suspicion from the enemy's frontline soldiers." A team leader named Wei Qiang, meanwhile, confesses that after joining the

---

25. Maurice J. Meisner, *Mao's China and After: A History of the People's Republic*, 3rd ed. (New York: Free Press, 1999), 195.

26. Su Shigui and Qiu Shi, "Chenggong yihou" [After the success], *Juben* [Drama scripts], 1964, 8:71–86.

27. Feng Deying, "Xie zai xinban 'san hua' qianmian" [Preface to the new publications of the "three flowers"] (Shenyang: Chunfeng Wenyi Chubanshe, 2003).

28. Feng Deying, *Ku cai hua* [Bitter flowers] (Beijing: Jiefangjun Wenyishe, 1958), 133.

[revolutionary] army "one of the most difficult things to get used to was to use bricks or pieces of roof tiles to wipe myself."[29]

In the historical context of the Chinese revolution, the army (Red Army, Eighth Route Army, People's Liberation Army) was never simply a military force. On the contrary, it simultaneously shouldered the political responsibilities of organizing, mobilizing, and educating the masses. Along with political reforms in the army (by establishing a Party branch at the company level [*zhibu jianzai lianshang*]), the military in effect functioned like the mobile embodiment of the Party (including its politics). This may help explain why in China, where there was a weak industrial base, a proletarian party was nevertheless able to develop and gain strength. In those narratives, the mention of such objects as hygiene bags and [toilet] paper in effect functioned to demarcate the difference between ancient and modern civilization. According to Ruth Rogaski, since the mid-nineteenth century, "with the arrival of armed imperialism, some of the most fundamental debates about how China and the Chinese could achieve a modern existence began to coalesce strongly around this word [*weisheng*, or hygiene]. Its meaning shifted away from Chinese cosmology and moved to encompass state power, scientific standards of progress, the cleanliness of bodies, and the fitness of races."[30] Rogaski identifies all of this as "hygienic modernity."

To be sure, these narrative details are not representative of the major themes of those novels, but they nevertheless reveal, subconsciously, a kind of longing for what was considered to be modern. Such longing helps explain the readiness to integrate what was considered to be (modern) civilized material elements into the genealogy of "revolutionary modernity. Even though my main task here is not to analyze these narrative details, I still want to point out that the narrators in these stories are particularly concerned about the modern nature (*xiandai shuxing*)—such as the civilized culture (*wenming*), science, and technology—of those material elements. What is more, the presence of these material objects in many literary works was meant not only to demonstrate the modernity of the Chinese revolution, it was also meant to help construct the revolution's metanarrative, including establishing its own exclusivity as a modern revolution marked by the use of things related to modern science and technology.

29. Feng Zhi, *Dihou wugongdui* [Behind the enemy lines] (Beijing: Jiefangjun Wenyi Chubanshe, 1979), 41, 42.

30. Ruth Rogaski, *Hygienic Modernity: Meanings of Health and Disease of Treaty-Port China* (Berkeley: University of California Press, 2004), 1.

So underpinning narratives that address issues of material abundance is the logic of modernity. In Xu Huaizhong's 1957 novel, *Women bozhong aiqing* [We sow our love], for example, what opposes the agriculture station that handles agricultural machinery, seeds, and so on is the backward and decadent Tibetan serfdom system.[31] There, "we" not only sow [seeds of] love but also [seeds of] modernity. Another example is found in Bai Wei's 1963 novel *Reclaiming Wasteland* (*Kenhuang qu*): the arrival of tractors symbolizes the modern future for rural villages.[32] The barging in of this future (symbolized by tractors) resolutely expresses a modern rupture of the traditional (which is also a material) order in rural China. I must quickly add that the introduction of modern things was aimed at constructing a type of public narration. When the individuals were shown to be effectively organized around such things and a public-oriented idealism was thus upheld by science (and technology), the narrative not only helped promote the collective as the legitimate public form but also helped legitimize the control of individual desires as part of being modern. The danger of such narration, however, lies not only in interpreting history in a historicist manner as a linear process of [developing] self-sufficiency in the arena of technology (*jishu lingyu zizhuhua*) but also in the possibility of blurring the necessary boundaries between revolution and the modern. My discussion below will focus on the question of what kinds of conflict occur when material things enter individuals' everyday life. If, according to [Jean] Baudrillard, the context of everyday life is in fact still a system of abstraction,[33] rather than interpreting the conflicts as between things and everyday life, then, we are better served to recognize the conflicts as those between different ideas.

Historically speaking, narrative themes and representations about anxiety over material things and corresponding conflicts did not begin in the 1960s. It had already emerged in the 1950s. The most representative [work] was Xiao Yemu's "Between My Wife and Me" ("Women fufu zhijian"). The story was published in *People's Literature* (*Renmin wenxue*) in 1950.[34] In more than one

---

31. Xu Huaizhong, *Women bozhong aiqing* [We sow our love] (Beijing: Zhongguo Qingnian Chubanshe, 1957).

32. Bai Wei, *Kenhuang qu* [Reclaiming wasteland], 2 vols. (Beijing: Zuojia Chubanshe, 1963).

33. Jean Baudrillard, *The System of Objects*, trans. James Benedict (London and New York: Verso, 1996).

34. Xiao Yemu, "Women fufu zhijian" [Between my wife and me], *Renmin wenxue* [People's literature], 1950, 1:37–45.

way, narratively, this story anticipated the works that would appear in the 1960s, including *Never Forget, Sentinels under the Neon Lights, Jiating wenti* [Family Problems][35], and *The Young Generation*.

In "Between My Wife and Me," we see two types of things: one consists of things that belong to one's self or family—such as a woolen vest, cotton padded jacket, or sesame leaves (*da zhima ye*)—all things that carry memories and have histories of their own. In the context of the story, they denote the revolution's history. The other type contains things that are city related, including silk curtains, a patterned rug, a sofa, neon lights, cigarettes, and leather shoes. For the wife in the story, the latter represent a kind of alien force, or another abstract system, and causes her discomfort in relation to the environment (abstract system). For the narrator, on the other hand, these particular things "feel familiar, comfortable ... with a strong power of deduction," so much so that he walks "with a delight in my steps ... quietly thinking to myself that a new life has just begun."[36] This representation, or characterization, already anticipates that of a character named Chen Xi found in the drama [and the film] *Sentinels under the Neon Lights* (for example, Chen Xi "feels that the breeze on Nanjing Road is fragrant"). The only difference between the two is that Chen Xi comes from the countryside while "I" [the narrator in "Between My Wife and Me"] originally comes from the city ("having left the city for twelve years"). What they have in common, however, is that they both subconsciously begin to take leave of their own history and try to capture the moment at which to enter another kind of history.

"I" looks for justification by saying that the "situation is different now." He begins to feel that his wife's "rural points of view" are incompatible with the city but believes that "she can be slowly reformed." His wife, on the other hand, feels strongly the need to "thoroughly reform the city." In essence, the question of who reforms (and transforms) whom becomes the most important narrative theme in the story.

Unlike the way in which this theme would be played out in works of the 1960s like *Sentinels under the Neon Lights*, in the 1950s, transformation was mutual. On the one hand, the wife successfully reforms "I" by helping him reestablish revolutionary ideals (including the spirit of endurance and suffering; concern for the masses; and control over one's own desires). On the

---

35. *Jiating wenti* [Family problems], dir. Fu Chaowu, 1964.
36. Xiao Yemu, "Women fufu zhijian" [Between my wife and me], *Renmin wenxue* [People's literature], 1950, 1:38.

other hand, "I" also successfully reforms the wife, who changes from rejecting "material things" (such as lipsticks and permed hair) to appreciating how to "dress up presentably"! She stops using words like "tamade" [fuck] and "jiba" [cock] and even "buys herself a pair of used leather shoes."[37] In defending these changes of hers, the wife points out that "even among ordinary female workers, there are those who use lipstick and have permed hair.... Therefore one should not judge others based on appearance and habits." She even goes so far as to criticize her own previous zeal, saying that such judgments were due to her "low cultural and theoretical level, and an inability to well comprehend government policies."[38]

When the story was published, it immediately met with criticism. For example, Chen Yong criticized "Between My Wife and Me" for observing and depicting life based on a bourgeois point of view and for making a female revolutionary appear vulgar and ugly.[39] Shortly afterward, the *Newspaper of Literature and Arts* (*Wenyi bao*) followed with a reader's letter titled "Fandui wannong renmin de taidu, fandui xin de diji quwei" (Against toying with people's attitude, and against new vulgar taste). The author criticized Xiao Yemu for "a lack of real love and warmth toward our people" and for his portrayal of the wife in a playful manner that showed no respect! An editorial of the newspaper praised the author of the letter, Li Dingzhong, in that "his sharp criticism points out the dangerous tendency in Xiao Yemu's creative work. It further supplements Chen Yong's criticism. We believe this is good."[40] On August 25, the same paper published an open letter to Xiao by [the well-known woman writer] Ding Ling, in which the latter expressed her further concerns about having "smelled a bad tendency in literature and art."[41]

It is not a pleasant thing to recall that such literary criticism once existed. And our difficulty lies precisely in how to renarrate the literariness of the literature in question while simultaneously recounting its unpleasant history. Still,

37. Ibid.
38. Ibid., 43.
39. Chen Yong, "Xiao Yemu chuangzuo de yixie qingxiang" [Some tendencies in Xiao Yemu's creative work], *Renmin ribao* [People's daily], June 10, 1951.
40. Li Dingzhong, "Fandui wannong renmin de taidu, fandui xin de diji quwei" [Against toying with people, against new vulgar taste], *Wenyi bao* [Newspaper of literature and arts], June 25, 1951.
41. Ding Ling, "Zuowei yizhong qinxiang laikan—gei Xiao Yemu tongzhi de yifengxin" [Seen as a tendency: A letter to Xiao Yemu], *Wenyi bao* [Newspaper of literature and arts], August 25, 1951.

there are complex issues to explore. In my view, objects or things in "Between My Wife and Me" are in effect neutralized. This neutralization makes visible the possibility of communication between people from different social levels. That is, a mutual sharing of things (such as lipstick that "many women workers also use") demonstrates the existence of a kind of cultural community. Actually, this observation is right on target: human communities are formed not just for political and economic reasons; there are also cultural norms; besides political or economic communities, there are cultural and subcultural communities. Literary works with such an understanding represent the complexity of human groups. Such an understanding came from a certain kind of political (and cultural) self-confidence in the 1950s. This confidence stemmed not only from the theoretical support for the new democratic community but also had to do with the fact that socialist political and cultural practices were not yet being fully implemented. Moreover, it was a time of shortage in material things, which nevertheless fostered a positive imagination about objects related to science and technology. As a result, in the 1950s, there existed an optimistic spirit in various types of public expressions.

At the same time, however, a neutralization of (the meaning of) material things is not enough when faced with practical and theoretical challenges. This has to do with the fact that we cannot deny there are structural relationships between things and the monetary sign, and it is precisely these relationships that underscore the symbolic function of material things. It is in this sense that we understand Baudrillard's thinking over conflicts between things and the environment of everyday life. Or, as Stuart Hall puts it, it is through our use of things that we give them meaning and, moreover, give meaning to other people, objects, and events based on our own framework of interpretations, which further explains the stories and narratives (including fantasies) that we make up based on all of this. As Hall states, "it is through culture and language in this sense that the production and circulation of meaning takes place."[42] And "culture, in this sense, permeates all in society."[43] In other words, behind the anxiety over material objects is none other than a struggle over cultural leadership.

In this sense, we can see that, in the 1960s, the neutralized meaning of material objects in narratives began to be replaced by narratives that emphasized

---

42. Stuart Hall, introduction to *Representation: Cultural Representations and Signifying Practices*, ed. Stuart Hall (London: Sage, 1997), 5.

43. Ibid., 3.

the symbolic meaning of such objects. Material things, tastes, aesthetic feelings, and lifestyles came to be treated in a compartmentalized manner. Coexisting within such treatment were attempts at structuring an imagined socialist way of life and its related system of things. Certain concrete objects came to be seen as obstacles to the establishment of this way of life and system of things.

The opening scene of *Never Forget* goes as follows: Ding Shaochun comes onto the stage wearing a borrowed leather jacket. His mother-in-law remarks that he looks like a "technician" in this jacket. Then his wife Yao Yujuan asks him to try on a woolen jacket that Dr. Xu from the clinic has just bought. After Ding puts on the woolen jacket, his mother-in-law remarks that he looks like a "big-shot engineer." The dramatic conflicts in this play begin right from that moment, which turns out to be a common narrative construction found in many other works from that period. In *Sentinels under the Neon Lights*, for example, the story of saving Chen Xi centers on a pair of nylon socks. Similarly, in *The Young Generation*, what triggers tensions between Lin Yusheng and Xia Qianru are "such expensive things" as "a few canned foods and some snacks plus a dress," those "Western type of things," as Xia puts it.

A closer look helps us further realize that these objects are mostly borrowed, in that, instead of coming directly from a genuine proletarian life style, they come from a different system of things. Such borrowing implies the possibility of emulating a different social class ("technicians" or "engineers") and a different way of life. So if in the 1950s, the imaginary of a materially abundant modernity was a governing force for society as a whole (which legitimized production), in the 1960s, production (related to material abundance) nevertheless generated anxiety about the role of the revolution. That is, if in the 1950s, modernization successfully juxtaposed revolution and production, this juxtaposition came to be questioned in the 1960s. According to the critic Cong Shen, in his "The Subject Matter of *Never Forget*" ("'Qianwan buyao wangji' zhuti de xingcheng"), tensions between different lifestyles were directly related to the "struggle between proletarian and bourgeois ideas."[44] If we borrow a term from Baudrillard, as I will discuss below, we can say that what happened in the 1960s was none other than a movement against "deterritorialization" combined with endeavors to "reterritorialize."

44. Cong Shen, "'Qianwan buyao wangji' zhuti de xingcheng" [The subject matter of *Never Forget*], *Xiju bao* [Drama news], 1964, 4: 27–28.

II. Deterritorialization versus Reterritorialization

In [Gilles] Deleuze and [Félix] Guattari's *What Is Philosophy?*, the word *territoriality* is one of the most frequently used terms.[45] It also frequently appears in their discussion of [Franz] Kafka.[46] In their discussions (especially of Kafka), the meaning of territory appears undeterminable, and the word more often than not functions like a metaphor. Sometimes, territory or territorialization is described as one of "the cares of daily life," while other times it refers to "the names of history—Jews, Czechs, Germans, Prague, city-county," all symbolizing "territory."[47] Apparently, in Deleuze and Guattari's interpretation, "Kafka moves from a classic Oedipus of the neurotic sort, where the beloved father is hated, accused, and declared to be guilty, to a much more perverse Oedipus who falls for the hypothesis of the father's innocence, of a 'distress' shared by father and son alike."[48] The two critics do not want to give Kafka a Freudian interpretation and prefer to understand territory in terms of political philosophy. It goes without saying that territory implies symbolically one's birthplace; it also denotes control over the birthplace.

When it comes to territory and the movement of deterritorialization, the two critics state rather vividly and metaphorically: "Rich or poor, each language always implies a deterritorialization of the mouth, the tongue, and the teeth. The mouth, tongue, and teeth find their primitive territoriality in food. In giving themselves over to the articulation of sounds, the mouth, tongue, and teeth deterritorialize."[49] The question is what force (or forces) lead to such deterritorialization. To Deleuze and Guattari, it is the force "strengthening desire instead of cramping it, displacing it in time, deterritorializing it, proliferating its connections, linking it to other intensities."[50]

Of course I do not intend to simplistically compare Chinese literature of the 1960s with Kafka, which would no doubt be absurd. The two differ fundamentally in their narrative perspectives. The former narrates from the point of the father, which is quite different from Kafka's perspective. This difference

---

45. Gilles Deleuze and Félix Guattari, *What Is Philosophy?*, trans. Hugh Tomlinson and Graham Burchell (New York: Columbia University Press, 1994).
46. Gilles Deleuze and Félix Guattari, *Kafka: Toward a Minor Literature*, trans. Dana Polan (Minneapolis: University of Minnesota Press, 1986).
47. Ibid., 9.
48. Ibid., 12.
49. Ibid., 19.
50. Ibid., 4.

also affects how narratives develop. Chinese narratives focus on the conflict between the father and the youth, in which the former tries to prevent the latter's deterritorializing movement. Still, I find the concept of territory useful and hope to borrow it to explore the following: (1) what was the original territory of socialism in the 1960s in China; (2) what factors generated the deterritorialization of the young generation (represented by such characters as Ding Shaochun in *Never Forget* and Lin Yusheng in *The Young Generation*); and (3) what forces [were involved], and why did the father resort to or mobilize them in opposition to and in efforts to try to stop the deterritorialization.

Works like *Never Forget*, *The Young Generation*, and Hu Wanchun's story "Family Problems" all took family as their narrative setting for dramatic conflicts, and the characters are clearly marked with their familial origin. Ding Shaochun is from a worker's family; Lin Yusheng is from a family of revolutionaries; the new soldier Tong A'nan in *Sentinels under the Neon Lights* is from a poor urban family; Chen Xi, the platoon leader in *Sentinels*, is a soldier who has gone through the revolutionary wars. Telling stories of familial origin was a rather common narrative practice of the 1960s, even though there were different types of family (for example, the Beijing opera *Red Lantern* [*Hongdeng ji*] is structured around a family whose members are not biologically related).[51] In works like these, family or family origin is portrayed as the original territory that young people like Ding Shaochun come from. The question is why in the 1960s it was family that was chosen, narratively, to represent original territory?

Before I proceed, I would like to take a detour in first discussing Lenin's concept of political life and the Chinese interpretation and practice of this concept. In April 1940, Xie Juezai published an article titled "The Actuality of Democratic Politics" ("Minzhu zhengzhi de shiji").[52] In the fourth section of the article, titled "What does democracy mean?," Xie focuses on Lenin's definition. He states that

> Lenin defines the soviet as an avant-garde group. "It is an organization consisting of the most conscientious, hardworking, and progressive from the oppressed working and peasant classes. The majority of the oppressed

---

51. For a detailed analysis of *Hongdeng ji*'s use of such a family, see Li Yang, *50–70 niandai Zhongguo wenxue zai jiedu* [Rereading 1950s–1970s Chinese literature] (Jinan: Shandong Jiaoyu Chubanshe, 2003), 233–45.

52. Xie Juezai, "Minzhu zhengzhi de shiji" [The actuality of democratic politics], in *Yanan minzhu moshi yanjiu ziliao xuanbian* [Selected materials for researching the Yan'an democratic model] (Xian: Xibei Daxue Chubanshe, 2004).

people still exist outside history and political life today. The soviet can function as an avant-garde organization to educate, train, and lead them." Democracy is for "those who have always existed outside history and political life" to facilitate entry into history and political life. In the play *At a Checkpoint* (*Cha lutiao*), Auntie Liu (*Liu dama*), as a representative of those who exist outside history and political life, takes up political responsibility when she states that "even if Commander Zhu comes, he must also show his permit [to pass the checkpoint]!" "Who told you so?" "The commander himself in his public notice." If we still have not yet let those like Auntie Liu participate in political life, democracy has not been fully achieved. If every Auntie Liu–like individual participates in politics, who knows what power that will be like? That will be the full effect of democracy.[53]

As he further notes, in the political imaginary of Yan'an, "turning over people's life (*fanshen*) does not just mean for them to be able to eat and be clothed; it is also a change from being slaves to being masters."[54] In debating democracy in Yan'an, Xie specifically points out that "for some comrades, democracy only means people electing officials. To be sure, elections are a major form of democracy. But if there is nothing else, how is it different from elections in modern capitalist countries? There, people still cannot be free from the control of the bourgeois dictatorship."[55] Wang Shaoguang has jokingly called democracy simply "electing masters" (*xuan zhu*).[56] Obviously, Xie has a politically inflected interpretation of democracy as [a system in which] "the affairs of all are decided by all, and conducted by all. Under conditions accepted by all (the minority follows the majority, the individual follows the whole, and so on), everyone can express their opinions, and good ideas will definitely be adopted; everyone has the duty and right to manage [public] affairs. This is the essence of democracy."[57] It is because of this that Auntie Liu in *At a Checkpoint* would have attracted such a high level of attention from Xie Juezai (and the Yan'an political scene in general), who viewed her as representing "let-

53. Ibid., 42.
54. Xie Juezai, "Minzhu zhengzhi shi jiu renmin de, fan minzhu zhengzhi shi duansong renmin de" [Democracy saves people, antidemocracy sacrifices people], in *Yanan minzhu moshi yanjiu ziliao xuanbian* [Selected materials for researching the Yan'an democratic model] (Xian: Xibei Daxue Chubanshe, 2004), 34.
55. Xie, "Minzhu zhengzhi de shiji," 42.
56. Wang Shaoguang, *Minzhu sijiang* [Four lectures on democracy] (Beijing: Sanlian Chubanshe, 2008).
57. Xie, "Minzhu zhengzhi de shiji," 41.

ting those who are outside history and political life enter history and political life." Xie viewed this process of letting people enter history as the actuality (or essence) of democracy. The actuality of democracy is none other than the political, while history is none other than the temporal form of political life. From all of this, we can sense that the socialist ideals and social imaginary already existed in the debates on democracy in 1940s Yan'an.

I identify this imaginary as the structural form of a certain political society. This structural form [re]channeled those who were "outside history and political life" into the public domain of politics, thereby constructing the general form of a political society. The central key to [the success of] this [political] social form lies in "how to help the masses learn to understand the big picture and long-term issues based on an understanding of their own experiences."[58] In other words, this structural form must on the one hand rely on the Party and its political education to establish a utopian vision of the big and long-term picture, and on the other hand it must also connect the big and long-term picture with people's own interests or things that concern them most. Only in this way can there be a political society in which everyone participates.

This political society, I must point out, differs from Partha Chatterjee's notion of political society, which is based on his interpretation of Indian experiences.[59] This (Chinese) political society is in effect a public one in which a certain public event often becomes the social and representational form of its political life. Sometimes only public events can form the condition of such political society. In the 1940s, for example, it was the war that made it possible for Auntie Liu to enter the public domain ("history and political life"). After 1949, it would be a series of public events such as the patriotic hygienic movement, the Great Leap Forward, and so on. All of this may be explained as the extension of the logic of such a political society based on rational support, as opposed to some kind of irrational social engineering.

Meanwhile, throughout the long history of the revolution, this political society was also imagined as a moral one; every individual was not only a political subject but also a moral one (as in Mao's poetic line, "six hundred

---

58. Ibid., 42.

59. Tr.: Partha Chatterjee's notion of political society presents a separation between the public and the private, so that the private remains untouched or relatively insulated from the public arena of politics. Cai here maintains that political society is both public and private simultaneously. See, for example, Partha Chatterjee, *Politics of the Governed: Reflections on Popular Politics in Most of the World* (New York: Columbia University Press, 2004).

million in this land all equal Yao and Shun" [*liuyi shenzhou jin shunyao*]).⁶⁰ Within this moral vision, the emphasis was on individuals' responsibility, exercise of self-control, willingness to give and to sacrifice themselves, with the goal of collective development. According to Henri Lefebvre, "production in a socialist society is defined by Marx as production for social needs. These social needs, in great part, concern space: housing, equipment, transportation, reorganization of urban space, and so forth. These extend the capitalist tendency to produce space while radically modifying the product. This is what contributes to the transformation of daily life, to the definition of development more in social than in individual terms, without the exclusion of the latter."⁶¹ Based on this theoretical and historical exploration, we can now explain the extent to which this political society was a kind of original territory of socialism.

In the postrevolutionary historical context, political society would very likely face challenges from two fronts, one being the bureaucratic form of modern management. Such bureaucraticization can not only dilute political life but can also thereby once again refuse the masses' entry into history and political life. Hence, we see the challenge of the Magnitogorsk Constitution from the Angang Constitution.⁶² The other challenge comes from everyday life itself, which can produce privacy via individual narratives through which the masses may themselves refuse to enter history and political life and even express lack of interest in political or public life. In the 1960s, it is precisely the growing narratives of the private around everyday life, which were strengthened by the concept of consumption (*xiaofei*), that appeared to be poised to disintegrate the political society.

To be sure, not all activities of consumption naturally produce privacy or individuality; privacy is largely produced by excesses in consumption. Discussions about overconsumption led to the formation of modern theories on consumerism. According to Jukka Gronow, discussions on the "surplus part of consumption" largely concentrate on three areas: "First, consumption can be understood in terms of an expanding capitalist commodity production:

---

60. Mao Tse-tung, "Farewell to the God of Plague," July 1, 1958, Marxists.org, accessed April 4, 2015, http://www.marxists.org/reference/archive/mao/selected-works/poems/poems 25.htm.

61. Henri Lefebvre, "Space: Social Product and Use Value," in *Critical Sociology: European Perspectives*, ed. J. W. Frieberg (New York: Halsted, 1979), 285–95.

62. See chapter 6 for an extensive discussion of this point.

consumption is functional to the demands of economy. The second approach is mainly interested in the different ways in which people use goods in order to create social bonds or distinctions. The third perspective is concerned with the emotional pleasures of consumption, with the dreams and desires associated with the world of goods."[63]

I do not want to suggest that China in the 1960s was in an era of consumerism. At the same time, I believe that in a time when material things grew to be relatively abundant especially in cities, the symptoms of consumerism did begin to appear. It is precisely the appearance of such symptoms that simultaneously generated a quiet deterritorialization among the young generation and an anxiety about and vigilance against (material) objects. In addition, it is this anxiety that hastened the start of a movement to fight against deterritorialization, and this movement would be carried out under the banner of never forget class struggle. The struggle here was in essence between two different political cultures or cultures of politics. At the same time, it also projected signals of a quiet transformation from an industrial age to that of consumerist one.

To simply apply Western theory on consumerism in the discussion of the 1960s China is surely problematic, but I still hold that this theory can help explain aspects of the issues at hand. After all, even in the 1960s, China and the West both existed in a modern global context. Gronow's summary of the three areas of debate, therefore, can help us enter our discussion of the 1960s.

Since consumption—in Gronow's discussion, the first area—never received legitimacy in the socialist period, the major conflicts concentrated on the second and third areas he identifies. Here I move directly to the second area he summarizes—namely, "the different ways in which people use goods in order to create social bonds or distinctions." Such individuals are identified as status seekers. In the 1960s in China, what did such status seeking mean? Why would it lead to a kind of imitation that would further lead to the impulse to deterritorialize? Additionally, in "the emotional pleasures of consumption, with the dreams and desires associated with the world of goods" there is bound to exist hedonism and corresponding narcissism, but the question is why such narcissism would be in strong conflict with the original territory (political society). As for pleasure, there is the corresponding issue of taste, around which there can be intense struggle over cultural leadership.

63. Jukka Gronow, *The Sociology of Taste* (New York: Routledge, 1997), 4.

To fully address these questions, I would like to return to the texts themselves or, in effect, to the historical logic of the literature of the 1960s.

The central event that constitutes the dramatic conflict in *Never Forget* is the "wild-duck shooting" (*da yeyazi*) by Ding Shaochun. Out of this incident three issues present themselves: (1) Ding Shaochun enjoys hunting, and as such it is a matter of taste; (2) Ding hunts wild ducks after work, which is therefore a leisure-related activity;, and (3) the purpose of Ding's duck hunting changes over time [from enjoyment] to some kind of imitation. As such, it is related to status seeking. Taste, leisure, and imitation thus in effect constitute three extremely important issues and concerns for the play (and other similar works), despite the fact that they were in the end quite crudely handled under the central theme of never forget class struggle.

Among the three issues, the most important has to do with certain imitation-related acts. Such acts were interpreted as originating from the corrosive impact of bourgeois ideology. This interpretation was simplistic and crude, to be sure, but it was directly related to one of the most important issues in the Chinese socialist period—namely, issues regarding cultural leadership.

Never Forget begins with the appearance of Ding Shaochun's mother-in-law, Mother Yao (Yao Mu). The depiction in the script goes as follows: "There [are] more than ten packs of newly purchased cigarettes on the table. Mother Yao is sitting next to the table, holding three cigarettes in two hands and slowly puffing them one after another. If it had been in the past, she would be considered a 'wealthy-looking' old lady. What 'wealthy looking' means has to do with two characteristics: a fair complexion and a somewhat plump but not necessarily healthy body, and dressed in 'old style' silk clothing and wearing two golden earrings." This scene is followed by the appearance of Ding Shaochun, who, wearing his engineer-like "borrowed leather jacket," enters from the left. The significance of this engineer-related element is further extended by Mother Yao in her depiction of Ding's second oldest brother-in-law's lifestyle: "Just see how they use gas to cook; 'puff,' the fire comes on—so clean and convenient. . . . And look the way your brother-in-law is dressed, just like the important engineer that he is! That morning when we saw him off at the airport, he was wearing a suit that cost more than two hundred yuan! A woolen windbreaker on top of that! And those imported leather shoes." However, when the brother-in-law Shao Yongbin appears in the third act, the way he is dressed appears to dispel the myth about him: "he wears an ordinary blue colored working outfit, trousers rolled up, a cloth cap on his head, an army-green canvas bag across his shoulder with a white towel tied to the bag's strap, and holds a raincoat. He looks like a vegetable seller who is often on work-related trips." The actual appearance of the brother-in-law suggests that Mother Yao's earlier depiction is fictional. And the fictitious nature of her depiction also seems to suggest that what Ding Shaochun imitates is based on bourgeois ideals and does not belong to a particular existing social class (*shehui jieceng*). But this does not explain the petty individualism displayed by Shao Yongbin's younger son—"My father is more powerful than your father! My father has studied abroad! He is an important engineer"—even though one may suggest that he merely repeats what he hears from Mother Yao.

In this seemingly rather confusing narrative structure, we can in fact recognize the existence of a degree of social stratification. It is such stratification that allows Mother Yao to hierarchically situate those social levels and to ideologize the difference. Meanwhile, in the face of such social stratification, the playwright obviously lacked the readiness to further explore the issue (or deliberately avoided it). As a result, he was able only to adopt a narrative method that would deflect this social reality—that is, not only placing Shao Yongbin in the family history of Ding Shaochun, but also emphasizing the simple way he looks (like a vegetable seller).

It is without question that socialism produced its own bureaucratic class, a factor directly related to the outbreak of the Cultural Revolution. At the same time, socialism also produced its own middle class or "middle social level." This social level mainly consisted of factory managers, experts, and technicians. The city became the major space in which they existed. As such, they were part of the so-called three big differences (*san da chabie*) identified by Mao (between workers and peasants, between city and countryside, and between mental and manual labor). Because of the existence of these differences, due to which the new urban middle level was able to enjoy a relatively comfortable life and working environment, this social level in turn became the object of envy and imitation (in pursuit of social status). Hence, we have Lin Yusheng in *The Young Generation* and his insistence on staying in the city, and we have in *Never Forget* Ding Shaochun's taste in imitating an engineer.

Ordinary people in a given society tend to imitate and even aspire to become like those at a social level not too far out of their own reach. As a result, the middle-class way of life tends to become the dignified or presentable dream for most people in a given society; the middle class not only makes popular pursuits seem attainable but also provides a lifestyle to be imitated. This is the case largely due to the fact that those from that social level tend to enjoy a relatively comfortable life and working environment (the latter includes their knowledge structure), tend to be respected by society at large, and as a result their lifestyle (including taste and classiness) tends to command a level of dominance culturally as well. This is the case even in a socialist society.

The power of cultural leadership, therefore, is not just at a political level. It must include an everyday lifestyle and corresponding taste criteria for the society. Taste produces a hierarchy between high and low, as well as between elegance and vulgarity. Individuals define themselves accordingly and are also defined by others accordingly. Gronow quotes [Hans-Georg] Gadamer in pointing out that "taste was basically a *Bildungsbegriff*, and as such an ideal of education and emancipation."[64] A more radical argument, according to Gronow, comes from [Pierre] Bourdieu, who "adopted one possible empiricist solution to the antinomy of taste by claiming that the taste of the ruling class is always the legitimate taste of a society. But in his opinion this legitimate taste is not genuine good taste: in fact, there could not possibly be any genuine good taste. Legitimate taste pretends to be the universally valid and disinterested good taste, whereas in reality it is nothing more than the taste of one particular class, the ruling class."[65] Regardless, both Gadamer and Bourdieu identify the (social) differentiating function of taste, and the production of difference between social groups in the name of self-cultivation.

If we agree with Bourdieu that socially legitimate taste is always the taste of the ruling class, China in the 1960s was nevertheless quite a bit more complex than this. Whether in *Never Forget* or *The Young Generation*, the taste that prompted imitation impulses was obviously not from the political ruling class but the taste that governed everyday life, even if in the guise of elegance. Bourdieu correctly points out there are power mechanisms behind taste, but that power does not always come from the political ruling class. It goes without saying that a society's sense of elegant taste and its criteria come from a variety of sources, including tradition, demands for cultivation, ideas, ideology, education, customs, even the various standards [used] to measure the quality of objects. Thinking along this line about 1960s China, we find a rather unclear socially legitimate taste. For both Ding Shaochun and Lin Yusheng, the taste they imitate belongs to a nonruling class, while at the same time this taste actually constitutes the dominant legitimate taste (as elegant taste) that governs people's private lives.

64. Ibid., 11.
65. Ibid.

In *The Young Generation*, what Lin Yusheng imitates is some "Western/foreign stuff" like "canned food, pastry, birthday parties" and so on. His taste is influenced by a character named Xiao Wu. According to Xia Shujuan, another character in the play, Xiao Wu, is someone who "refused the job assigned to him and depends on his wealthy family to provide a parasite-like lifestyle through which he readily shows off his family's wealth," and "there is something Western in the way he carries himself around." It goes without saying that all of this is related to the characteristics of the issue of peaceful transition (*heping guodu*) in the socialist period. For that transition, the urban industrial capitalist class was completely retained, not only in terms of their economic condition ("those families that have money") but also in terms of their way of life, taste, and cultural preferences (all in a Western way). What is worth noting is that what Ding Shaochun imitates, such as the leather jacket and Western suit, are signs symbolic of a Western lifestyle. On the other hand, Mother Yao's taste, although being placed in a position to be criticized (as shown in her old-style silk clothing and her wearing two golden earrings) does not belong to what Ding would imitate. This is not due to gender difference but more due to the nature of Mother Yao's social status as being that of a so-called lower-class city dweller (petty urbanite). After the cleansing (*saodang*) of the May Fourth New Culture Movement and subsequent revolutionary culture, this social class was unable to embody socially legitimate taste. Indeed, after more than a hundred years of social changes, any type of traditional taste including the one that belonged to the traditional ruling class had lost the ability to command future cultural development. In this sense, we can say that the role Mother Yao performs in the play is more like that of Mama Chang—namely, to help [as a medium] those like Ding Shaochun find the opening for their desire to deterritorialize.

In the 1960s, China had become increasingly modernized, not only in terms of the establishment of a basic modern industrial system, but also in terms of the establishment of an urban-centered socialist culture. This culture led certain fashions in the 1960s, which means that the newly emerging middle class was interested in finding a more modern lifestyle to imitate or [in which] to locate socially legitimate taste. In their observations of the lifestyle of the rising middle class ("a rapidly growing group of 'privileged' people consisting of educated specialists and top workers")[66] in the Soviet Union of the 1960s, some

66. Ibid., 50.

Western scholars discovered that such a lifestyle did not originate from homemade Soviet culture: "These new luxuries and the production of modern consumer goods mostly imitated in a rather crude manner the life and consumption model of the middle classes which had become common in the USA and the most prosperous countries of Western Europe after the Second World War."[67] If we take into consideration the semicolonial tradition in China, we can say that the newly emerging middle class in 1960s China quickly located Western resources on its own soil. These resources were scattered throughout the [retained] industrial capitalist class whose Western lifestyle was admired by individuals such as Lin Yusheng, Ding Shaochun, and even Mother Yao. In this sense, the party politics of the 1960s, in its vigilance against peaceful evolution and sugar-coated bombs, was obviously not baseless or groundless.

Lifestyle (including corresponding material objects and taste) is not a value-neutral aesthetic concept, especially when a particular lifestyle is being imitated in which the imitator unavoidably identifies with the values of the imitated. In China, incidentally, the impact of this relationship would not become obvious until the 1980s, when value identification with the West was mediated precisely via lifestyle (objects or taste) at the level of ordinary people's everyday life.[68] When lifestyle is expressed by way of material objects and taste, it is also at the same time an expression of social hierarchy and ideology; behind the elegance or classiness exists arrogance toward vulgarity or bad taste. In this sense, conflicts between different lifestyles often become conflicts between different ideologies. In the 1960s, the conflict between different lifestyles directly threatened the overall imaginary of a political society. For example, in *The Young Generation*, the desire for a good life makes Lin Yusheng reject the "political interpellation" [Althusser's words] of the time and try every means possible to be able to stay in the city. In *Never Forget*, Ding Shaochun's imitation is expressed via consumption (a Western suit) that brings him pleasure. If Ding's grandfather still insists on guarding social (territorial) boundaries when he asks "What kind of family is ours? . . . for you to buy such expensive clothes," Mother Yao's reply ironically and rather pointedly exposes the ideological and fantasy nature of consumption: "Well, Uncle, the stores will sell things to whoever can pay regardless of what family they're from." The implications are twofold. On the one hand, consumption renders class

---

67. Ibid., 51.
68. Tr.: For an extensive discussion of this issue, see Cai Xiang, "1970: Modai huiyi" [1970: End of an era of memories], *Jintian* [Today], fall 2008.

background invisible, thereby creating an ideological illusion of equality. On the other hand, what makes consumption possible is the consumer's ability to pay; the differences between such abilities in turn reveal the ideologically illusionary nature of that equality. For example, to be able to afford a suit, Ding Shaochun must hunt wild ducks to exchange for money ("two more hunting trips and I will be able to pay for that smart suit; how wonderful!"). This further makes him feel that "money is everything" ("What problems? If you have money, nothing is a problem"). It goes without saying that consumption contributed to the production of individual consciousness in China's socialism and also to the production of the consumerist-oriented aesthetic value that more expensive equals more beautiful. It is precisely this individual consciousness that further contributed to the desire of the young generation to deterritorialize. If we consider as the original territory the very political society that emphasizes that "the affairs of all are decided by all, and conducted by all," what was being threatened at that time was none other than the notion of everybody in all [literally, the big family (*dajia*)]. In a specific situation like *Never Forget*, it becomes a sharp conflict between the individual worker and his factory. More important, however, is not what lies in the dramatic conflicts on the surface, but rather the fact that consumerism embodies what Zygmunt Bauman would later identify as the condition in which "individual freedom" coexists with "collective impotence." Bauman states: "The growth of individual freedom may coincide with the growth of collective impotence in as far as the bridges between private and public life are dismantled or were never built to start with; or, to put it differently, in as far as there is no easy and obvious way to translate private worries into public issues and, conversely, to discern and pinpoint public issues in private troubles."[69] In some sense, in the face of consumption, both socialism and capitalism can experience the threat of the erosion of the public sphere.

Even though works like *Never Forget* unequivocally objected to the deterritorializing movement and resorted to the method of class struggle as a way to solve the various kinds of problems generated by [desires for] consumption, the so-called proletarian culture did not necessarily retain an unequivocal upper hand in the conflict. Resorting to political methods for solving cultural problems was no doubt arbitrary, but the real problem lies in the fact that, in the name of class struggle, not only did these individual issues fail

---

69. Zygmunt Bauman, *In Search of Politics* (Stanford, CA: Stanford University Press, 1999), 2.

to be included in the public sphere, they were also simplistically pushed beyond the horizon of the history of ideas. It is precisely through this rather crude way of addressing the issues that the crisis in everyday life in the 1980s was manifested. Of course, the historical conditions of the 1960s would not have made it possible for these issues to be fully addressed at that time. Or, rather, the historical situation of the time could not have provided the conditions through which to overcome such a crisis in lifestyle, consumption, class struggle, or signification. Let us further consider the following issues.

First, under the Chinese socialist system, the state (or the collective) was responsible for meeting people's needs for livelihood. When it comes to addressing needs on the level of basic everyday necessities, egalitarian principles tended to allow socialism to be particularly competitive. But as soon as people's needs increased and diversified, the state (or the collective) had difficulty satisfying those needs. In the 1960s, Zhao Shuli began to notice this problem in his considerations of rural issues. "Money," he states, "is still something that peasants want, to buy things.... They want to live a decent life." He continues:

> Peasants' active participation is based on the profits obtained from exchanges between industrial and agricultural products.... But if there is no guarantee of material gain, ideological education alone is not enough.... Industrial capital has been rather over accumulated.... In 1952 and 1953, most people depended on the collective to get by. But as time goes on, however, things are different. What the collective has accumulated does not belong to him [the peasant]. Only the family plot is his. So whether it is [collective] production or grain purchases by the state, the peasant takes care of his family plot first.[70]

Western scholars like Bauman argue that a socialist society with massive consumption is self-contradictory, due to the incompatibility between socialism and modern consumption.[71] Leaving aside whether or not such an argument is correct, it does touch upon some essential issues regarding socialism. For example, the socialist planned economy is based on the logic of necessity, while modern consumer society follows the logic of want/desire. In a

---

70. Zhao Shuli, "Zai Dalian 'nongcun duanpian xiaoshuo chuangzuo zuotanhui' shang de fayan" [Speech at the "Forum on the Rural-Themed Short Story" in Dalian] in *Zhao Shuli quanji* [The complete works of Zhao Shuli] (Taiyuan: Beiyue Wenyi Chubanshe, 1999), 4:509–11.

71. Zygmunt Bauman, "Introduction," in *In Search of Politics* (Stanford, CA: Stanford University Press, 1999), 2.

"socialist society with massive consumption," then, any failure or disappointment in people's "desire" [to consume] can be turned into the problem of the state, which, by extension, can lead to a deterritorialization movement. In this sense, socialist society cannot always be politically stable. Indeed, some of the fiction from the 1980s—such as *Li Shunda Builds a House* (*Li Shunda zaowu*) by Gao Xiaosheng—are historical reflections on the issue of desire [in the socialist period] (what kinds of narratives in China in the last thirty years the logic of wants or desire has resulted in is a topic for another day).

Second, if socialism did follow the logic of needs, this logic could itself produce the logic of wants or desire, due to the fact that, to a certain extent, needs and wants are not always clearly distinguishable. If by needs we refer to certain kinds of collective needs or some basic everyday needs, such needs cannot nevertheless remain unchanged. For one thing, if one of the modern pursuits after the revolution was to construct a materially abundant society, material production could simultaneously produce personal desires. We cannot deny the fact that modern technology has greatly changed people's form of existence, which at the same time has also changed the way desire is produced. For example, when society produces the city as a materialized form of space, it simultaneously produces forms of expression about people's desire for such space. Such desire, if we recall, is expressed in the conflict between Lin Yusheng and Xiao Jiye in *The Young Generation*. Also, socialism as a modern social form not only produces its working time (*laodong shijian*) but also its leisure time. In cities, along with the establishment of eight-hour workdays and with technological development, leisure hours also increase. Desire and its various cultural expressions, such as aesthetics, emotional life, and taste, are all related to leisure time. We can even argue that it is leisure time that produces desires in modern societies. Cong Shen clearly recognized the importance of "time" in this sense. In his article "The Subject Matter of *Never Forget*," he reports that "one evening, I talked about this issue with a Youth League branch secretary who shared a room with me (before becoming the secretary, he was a worker). He said that every day, a worker only spends eight hours in his or her factory, working. If there's a meeting, at most two more hours. But there are twenty-four hours in a day." Instead of asking about how workers spend the rest of the hours, the author immediately brings up an ideological point: "How do their families educate the young workers? Who are their relatives and friends? These are all difficult questions. There are all kinds of people, all kinds of ideas. While we conduct socialist education, there are also those who spread bourgeois ideas.... Thus, what education the young workers receive during the day in their factory can be instantly overwritten at home in the evening."⁷² While desires can be understood, or explained, as ideological issues, leisure time as a productive installation that produces desires nevertheless does not disappear on account of an ideological understanding.

The third point has to do with another discovery in Cong Shen's aforementioned article. He mentions a young worker "whose father is an old worker with both excellent technical skills and a revolutionary consciousness" and "who himself has the desire to improve himself [politically]." What Cong Shen discovers is that this young worker "not only does not dislike a young fellow worker who has developed bourgeois ideas, but feels somewhat envious of him." This discovery was later incorporated into or developed in the relationship between Ding Shaochun and Mother Yao in his play. Similar depictions also exist in the relationship between Lin Yusheng and Xiao Wu. Cong Shen interprets this as the young worker "lacking a clear sense of right and wrong," but such an interpretation is obviously not insightful enough. If, as Bourdieu argues, "socially legitimate taste is the taste of the ruling class," the question is why, for individuals like Ding Shaochun and Lin Yusheng, the "taste of the ruling class" (original territory) does not become the socially legitimate taste that they want to imitate? Why, on the contrary, is it the taste of a nonruling class that functions like the taste of the ruling class? We can certainly explain this along the lines of the power of traditional customs, or the power of the so-called ocean of petit bourgeoisies, but we must also acknowledge the fact that political and ideological conflicts cannot completely replace conflicts between tastes. Thus, the real question is whether or not as the ruling class, the proletarian class is able to offer a socially legitimate taste of its own.

On this issue, the play *Never Forget* is somewhat ambiguous. For example, Ding Haikuan and [his son] Ding Shaochun have a debate about "woolen cloth" and "gunnysack cloth" (*madai pian*). The former states: "Woolen cloth is good stuff. It's better than the twill that I am wearing, better than serge. It's something that working people in the past didn't dare to want. Today, you not only dare to want it but many are already wearing [clothes made of] it. This is a good thing; it is the accomplishment of the revolution and construction! We will one day let people in all China and throughout the world wear the best clothes! But right now, there are millions of people in the world who

---

72. Cong Shen, "'Qianwan buyao wangji' zhuti de xingcheng" [The subject matter of *Never Forget*].

are unable to wear even the worst clothes! . . . If all you think about now is woolen cloth or hunting more wild ducks, then you'll forget to shut off electric switches, forget to go to work, forget that our country is still struggling to become strong, and forget the world revolution."[73] In this ideologically clear speech, interestingly enough, the fact that woolen cloth still dominates the ruling taste is tacitly accepted, even if it is being postponed to the future. Cong Shen in the aforementioned article also mentions this issue. He admits that the objection expressed in the original script against the "woolen-cloth suit" was somewhat one-sided and later underwent changes after being criticized by some comrade officials (*lingdao tongzhi*). This shows, incidentally, that the 1960s was not all tense and rigid as we have imagined.

The real issue, however, lies elsewhere. It has to do with the following: if socialism cannot offer a good form of life with a corresponding system of things of its own, it will inevitably face whatever kind of future to become reality and the debate between woolen cloth and gunnysack cloth will also continue. Therefore, if political conflicts are not transformed into conflicts between tastes, thus establishing an alternative socially legitimate taste, relying only on ideological persuasion or training (including class struggle) for effective transformation would be of quite dubious efficacy. Furthermore, I would argue that to some extent, political legitimacy must also come from the support of taste (lifestyle). As a matter of fact, on the level of the social life of the time, taste for woolen cloth was not left hanging as it was in the play *Never Forget*. Wang Anyi, for example, in her *The Enlightened Era* (*Qimeng shidai*), somewhat gently portrays the conflict of taste during the Cultural Revolution: "Names of streets and shops were changed. The new names sounded somewhat naive (*youzhi*), such as *fanxiu* [antirevisionism], *hong taiyang* [red sun], or *zhandou* [fighting]. So straightforward that they lay bare the width of the mind. Shop windows became simple looking with almost no decoration, and commodities were also mainly a few basic necessities."[74] The problem is that the ruling class's taste, established as it is based on power or even violence, cannot necessarily become the socially legitimate taste, and even the ruling class itself may not subscribe to its own taste. Dominant taste, in addition to the support of the power of the ruling class, must also contain a level of cultural content, or even just some measure of a technological component. Years later, after the Cultural Revolution, for example, Wang Shuo in his "To

---

73. Cong Shen, "Qianwan buyao wangji" [Never forget], *Juben* [Drama scripts], 1963, 10/11:36.
74. Wang Anyi, *Qimeng shidai* [The enlightened era] (Beijing: Renmin Wenxue Chubanshe, 2007), 1–2.

Play Is Heart-throbbing" ("Wan jiushi xintiao") dismisses the taste of the [revolutionary] "ruling class," to which he once belonged: "all that clumsy-looking furniture issued by the state." Indeed, in the 1980s, one of the most serious challenges that traditional Chinese socialism encountered came from issues related to taste [lifestyle]. Today, in rediscussing socialism, we must reach deeper into these issues. Otherwise, problems already present in the 1960s will not be fully overcome.

In my view, the proletarian class did not in fact win an upper hand in the cultural conflicts over taste in the 1960s. When socialism was unable to offer a unique and good lifestyle and relied on power to turn conflicts between [different] tastes (lifestyle) into political ones (in terms of class struggle), in effect a kind of anxiety was manifested. This anxiety, of course, is not one about everyday life, but more of a political one. When, in following the logic of desire (*yuwang de luoji*), the young generation produced an urge to deterritorialize, socialist political society inevitably faced the danger of disintegration. It is only in this sense that can we understand why, in the 1960s, the positions of the young and the old were dramatically reversed. That is, if after the May Fourth Movement, youth always symbolized a young China while old people (*laoren*) were made to symbolize the conservative, in the 1960s, youth came to be placed in the awkward position as those needing to be educated.[75] At the same time, the old generation, who were the educators, did not have a powerful confidence of their own; there was, in other words, anxiety or impotence behind (a seeming) confidence.

There are several manifestations of this political anxiety.

First, with regard to characters such as Mother Yao and Xiao Wu in the aforementioned plays: they are like Mama Chang, as emphasized by the critic Yu Tingying in the article "Strengthen Political Education for Youth." As mentioned earlier, Yu states: "It is via the 'medium' like 'Mama Chang'" that such old ideas and consciousness are mediated. In face of these Mama Changs, writers all appeared to express anxiety over whom the young associated themselves with. In *Never Forget*, the character Ding Shaochun is to move out of his own big family, via marriage, to live with his wife (Yao Yujuan) and his mother-in-law (Mother Yao) in a nuclear family. We can understand this move as symbolizing deterritorialization and reterritorialization. In the process from deterritorializing to reterritorializing, Mother Yao functions like a private tutor, an instructor for Ding's private life. In the play, her instruction is

---

75. For an extensive discussion of this point, see chapter 3.

interpreted as the major cause for Ding's change: "it's all this old woman's fault that the kid was misled." In *The Young Generation*, similarly, Xiao Wu, a character who never appears on stage, also functions as Lin Yusheng's "personal instructor," which prompts Lin Jian of the old generation to anxiously caution that Lin should "be careful whom you befriend." Issues of consumption and desire produced by socialism itself were simplistically attributed to the influence of bourgeois ideology, an attribution that further generated anxiety over association (*jiaowang*). To be sure, writers of these works were clearly aware that anxiety over association could not be eased simply by forcefully disrupting the association. That is, they understood that you "cannot place the young generation in a safety box/safe." Nevertheless, when such association could so easily produce the young generation's desire to deterritorialize, it signifies a lack of confidence, albeit a subconscious one, in 1960s culture, despite the fact that it was expressed in a highly confident manner.

Second, as characters, Mother Yao and Xiao Wu are designated with specific class positions (the former being the owner of a mom-and-pop store and the latter the offspring of a bourgeois family), but we can also understand them as symbols representing a particular ideology or the "traditional customs shared by millions of people." According to Lenin, "it is in fact far easier to defeat the powerful and centralized bourgeois ideas than to 'defeat' tens of millions of small business owners. The everyday, trivial, and invisible activities of the latter are the very corrosive ones that can lead to restoration of bourgeois class."[76] This quote from Lenin became one of the major theoretical sources for Cong's creation *Never Forget* and was in effect a common source of theory for all such works of the time. To some extent, what the 1960s faced was precisely this kind of ideology, idea, or habit of being (*xiguan shili*) that is "everyday, trivial, and invisible." The problem is that, in the historical context of the 1960s, such an idea or habit of being was prematurely and hurriedly formalized into a discourse of class struggle. When that happened, the trend was to divide people up into political categories that may have in fact prevented true cultural conflicts from further unfolding and deepening. Meanwhile, due to the serious cultural implications in this new form of class struggle, writers of the aforementioned works knew quite well that, in face of mediating figures like Mother Yao and Xiao Wu, what they were confronting was not so much a specific class as ideas or habits of being permeating everyday life, [as] trivial

76. Lenin, "Gongchan zhuyi yundong zhong de 'zuopai youzhibing'" ["Left-wing" communism: an infantile disorder], in *Lienin xuanji* [Selected works of Lenin] (Beijing: Renmin Chubanshe, 1972), 4:200–201.

and invisible. But when old habits of being were perceived as powerful and boundless and when the revolution began to retreat from imagining a political society to the setting of a proletarian family, such a retreat signaled a degree of helplessness. In fact, it is precisely during the 1960s that familial revolutionary history was rehashed and brought to the fore. In the process, revolutionary history was represented as family history, and individuals began to be identified with different family backgrounds. Whether the poor-peasant-to-worker genealogy of the Ding family in *Never Forget*, or Lin Yusheng in *The Young Generation* being an orphaned son of a revolutionary martyr (*lieshi yigu*), both emphasize a political orthodoxy or purity of revolutionary successors. This emphasis on political genealogy subsequently produced the bloodline theory during the Cultural Revolution. It also helped define the legitimacy of the speakers who narrate family history, through which the legitimacy of the relationship between the old and the young as that of educator and educated was reestablished. It also conditioned the ways in which family, as a form, was used to fight against deterritorialization and reterritorialization. Unfortunately, in the process of reterritorialization, as we can see in hindsight, by the 1960s, the political society imagined in the 1940s and 1950s—as in "the affairs of all are decided by all, and conducted by all," so as to "let those who are outside history and political life enter history and political life"—and the corresponding political confidence disappeared. In its place came the family-oriented narratives of reterritorialization tinted with a subconscious implication of the bloodline theory. This cultural phenomenon manifested a degree of political anxiety and a certain lack of cultural confidence.

The third point has to with the production of the new socialist person for the purpose of overcoming the anxiety mentioned above. Production of the new socialist person did not begin with the 1960s. Earlier examples include Liang Baosheng in *The Builders* and Xiao Changchun in *Sunny Days*. In comparison, in addition to their shared political position, the new person from the 1960s carried with him certain characteristics unique to that period. In *The Young Generation*, for example, the triangular relationship between Xiao Jiye, Xia Qianru, and Lin Yusheng can be seen as a rehashing of the triangular relationship between Lu Jiachuan, Lin Daojing, and Yu Yongze in *The Song of Youth*. However, without the component of romantic love as in *The Song of Youth*, the narrative of the former story demonstrates something fundamentally different, in that Xiao Jiye [in *The Young Generation*] is represented as someone without desire for sexual or romantic love. Similar characteristics can be found in Ji Youliang in *Never Forget*. Ji is altruistic and devotes himself to all things public, but when it comes to love, he appears uninitiated. Such a narrative model led to what Huang Ziping eventually satirized as "Cultural Revolution literature about the sexless human body."[77] But I prefer not to view such narratives simply as absurd. On the contrary, there was actually rational thinking underlying such narratives, in that if desire was understood as the opening for deterritorialization, then to control desire would be the precondition for reterritorialization or returning to the territory. Obviously in this kind of narrative, desire (including romantic love, sex, family, and so on) was understood as an obstacle (due to its banality) to individuals' socialization. The question is that, whether in the 1960s or after, when society kept producing desires via consumption, was it possible to depend on the control of desire as a form of resistance to establish [a different kind of] society and community? A minor literature (*ruoshi wenxue*) that does not or cannot deal with trivial private matters does not have much of a future.

The so-called minor literature is a concept found in Deleuze and Guattari's discussion of Kafka, which can also be understood as minority literature or peripheral literature. Such literature challenges Western mainstream literature (about individuals or private life) with three characteristics of its own: (1) [there is] a strong tendency to deterritorialize, (2) everything is politically related, and (3) all is communal.[78] However, if we approached Chinese literature of the 1960s from this perspective, we would find that in fact it is not particularly applicable.

For one thing, the proletarian literature of the 1960s in China had already become the dominant literature. As such, it tended to use [established] political power to fight again any deterritorializing movement. In terms of narrative structure and discourse, it retained the pedagogic characteristics of persuasion and training.

For another thing, however, because the original territory that proletarian literature tried to strengthen was strongly communal, such literature would at the same time tend to exclude trivial private matters. More significantly, even though the proletarian class had absolute political and economic power in the socialist state, in the cultural domain, especially in terms of everyday life, it did not acquire absolute power. Because of that, it had to resort to political and collective or communal narrative forms to reexamine the existing

---

77. Huang Ziping, "Geming, xing, changpian xiaoshuo" [Revolution, sex, and the novel] in *"Huilan zhong" de xushu* [Narration in the "Chalk Circle"] (Shanghai: Shanghai Wenyi Chubanshe, 2001), 63.

78. See Deleuze and Guattari, *What Is Philosophy?*

cultural order. So long as the reexamination is about the existing world order, it is bound to be political.

This particular situation regarding the narratives of the time indicates the awkward position occupied by proletarian literature in China's socialist period: politically strong while culturally weak. What cultural conflicts existed were aided by the political power that ironically prevented cultural politics from being further carried out. The deeper difficulty about this awkward position still has to do with the question of how socialism deals with the class differences and individual desires that it itself produces.

III. Trivial Private Matters and Important State Affairs

If we take political society as symbolizing a certain kind of socialist original territory, Auntie Liu in *At a Checkpoint* is an example of what such a society strives for: so that "those who are outside history and political life" can become part of them. Indeed, in the Yan'an political imaginary, the turning over in people's lives (*fanshen*) was not just from having no food and clothing to having them, but also moving from the position of slave to that of the master. It was a politics of dignity in practice that at the same time advocated a democratic imaginary that, once again, promoted the idea that "the affairs of all are decided by all, and conducted by all." This imaginary, I might add, continues to encourage us to imagine a path for a better future society.

At the same time, however, this imagined political society must depend on an organizational form that is highly politicized or event-oriented, in which both important state affairs and trivial private matters have a possibility to coexist in a unified way. In Xie Juezai's words, the key is "how to help the masses learn to understand the big picture and long-term issues based on an understanding of their own personal experiences." If to a certain extent war as a "state of exception"[79] enfolds everyone in a state of political life and history, important state affairs would also incorporate everyone's trivial private issues." Through war, individuals profoundly experience the "the big picture and long-term issues" that are closely related to their personal lives, including the interests of the state. Auntie Liu at a checkpoint thus becomes a classic symbol of wartime political society.

---

79. "State of exception" is a term that derives originally from Carl Schmitt (*Political Romanticism* and *The Concept of the Political*) and that is further theorized most recently and widely by Giorgio Agamben (*Homo Sacer: Sovereign Power and Bare Life* and *State of Exception*).

The problem of course is how to successfully transform the state of exception due to war into a postrevolutionary normalcy. As mentioned earlier, in postrevolutionary normalcy, political society could face two kinds of challenge: One is from modern bureaucracy, which cannot only dissolve political life but can also prevent the masses from entering history and political life. The other challenge can come from everyday life itself, which can involuntarily produce privacy-oriented individual narratives and cause the masses to refuse to enter history and political life by becoming uninterested in the political or public. In the 1960s, this is exactly what was happening when the individual-oriented narratives about everyday life, made attractive via consumption, began to threaten political society with the possibility of being dissolved.

In face of such a threat came the refocus on class struggle. It was a highly political or event-based way of reorganizing society, aimed at redirecting the masses into history and political life while also commanding them to overcome various personal desires. Meanwhile, it was not enough to rely on class struggle to overcome personal desires. There had to be a form of life politics (*shenghuo zhengzhi*). In his *Modernity and Self-Identity*, Anthony Giddens explains that so-called life politics is "a politics of lifestyle."[80] The narratives of Chinese literature in the 1960s were indeed highly political, but when never forget class struggle was practiced at the level of "educating the next generation of revolutionaries," it both was an imposition from the state and had embedded in it a narrative form (*xushi xingtai*) of life politics. The aim of the rise of this life politics was none other than to address the gap (or fissure) that had occurred between trivial private issues and important state affairs.

Between 1963 and 1965, the magazine *Youth of China* (*Zhongguo qingnian*) organized a two-year-long discussion on "what kind of view of happiness young people should have." The discussion originated with a letter by Hu Dongyuan, a reader from Jiangsu Province. In the letter, Hu explained his perplexities about the question "what is happiness," which arose during the process of "learning from Lei Feng."[81] He was puzzled over such issues as the relationship between material life and spiritual life, the relationship between

---

80. Anthony Giddens, *Modernity and Self-Identity* (Stanford, CA: Stanford University Press, 1991), 214.

81. Tr.: Lei Feng (1940–1962) was a PLA soldier killed in the line of duty. Before his death, he had already often been praised for the various good things he did for his fellow soldiers and for ordinary people in the surrounding area where his troop was stationed. After his death, Mao Zedong called upon people nationwide to "learn from Lei Feng" (*xiang Lei Feng tongzhi xuexi*) (in 1963), thereby turning Lei Feng into a national hero.

the individual and the collective, and more. These perplexities manifested a kind of tension over cultural values that, by extension, manifested a certain kind of tension within socialism itself. If, for example, "when the correct view of happiness means that someone puts their spiritual life first, how then do we explain the fact that, when someone is able to buy whatever they want to eat, they feel pleasure and happiness?" Perplexity, then, concerns the issue of "pleasure." The letter's author states further: "There are also those who argue that to pursue a better material life not only will not lead to a 'loss of will' but most likely will help 'strengthen the will,' because the more urgent the hope for a better material life is, the harder one will struggle for the realization of communism."[82] Is it not true that the goal of socialism is to build a materially abundant society? Furthermore, "if one lives so that others will live better, then, so long as that person does not shamelessly harm others for their own gain, isn't it true that living like this also means living for oneself? Our revolutionary goal is for everyone to live a better life which should also include ourselves . . . and which is also in keeping with the spirit of 'from each according to his ability, and to each according to his work.'"[83]

Incidentally, we can see Hu's letter and the perplexities mentioned within as the prehistory to Pan Xiao's letter "Rensheng de daolu weishenme yue zou yue zhai" (Why is life's path becoming narrower and narrower?) published in 1980.[84] We can also see it as the conceptual expression of the views represented by such characters as Ding Shaochun and Lin Yusheng. I argue that these are expressions of crises (*weiji xingshi*) produced by socialism itself.

If the correct view of happiness emphasizes putting spiritual life first, how should one explain the pleasure derived from material enjoyment? At the same time, if one puts emphasis on material-oriented happiness, how does one solve the social differences [or social stratification] caused by the [uneven] distribution between those who have more money and those who have less? It is precisely the newly produced distribution differences that could lead to a reconstruction of the relationship between material things and monetary signs which, in turn, generated deterritorialization impulses in Ding Shaochun and the like in their pursuits of individual (material-oriented) happiness. There was also a new contradiction between [living] for others and [liv-

---

82. Hu Dongyuan, "Qingnian yinggai you shenme yang de xingfuguan" [What kind of view of happiness should young people have?] *Zhongguo qingnian* [Youth of China], 1963, 7:15–17.
83. Ibid.
84. Pan Xiao, "Rensheng de daolu weishenme yue zou yue zhai" [Why is life's path becoming narrower and narrower?], *Zhongguo qingnian* [Youth of China], 1980.

ing] for the self. If, in the imaginary of a political society, self and the other are highly identified with one another, in the postrevolutionary context, the socialist principle of "from each according to his ability, and to each according to his work" in effect expedited new stratification of different social levels. If acts of putting others in harm's way can be prevented or controlled, there does not seem to be a legitimate boundary for [living] for one's self. Outside of any social level, the individual is an empty word; and there always exists a tenacious sense of belonging between the individual and the social. With the emergence of new social level(s) came a new sense of belonging, including [social] imitation. Such imitation, as mentioned earlier, tended to take the form of taste or lifestyle.

Politics then assumed the form of life politics in trying to solve the conflicts between taste and the value system (*jiazhi guan*) and to also establish the view of happiness acceptable to the ruling class, in this case the various interpretations surrounding Lei Feng. The first challenge for such interpretations lies in how to redefine the spiritual life of revolutionaries.[85] To revitalize the concept of revolutionary was to restore the utopian vision of the bigger and future vision, thereby reestablishing meaning and a purpose to living. The bigger and future vision can be either the nation (as in "people's living condition in one's own country is still relatively low") or the world (as in "a majority of people in the world are struggling on the verge of starvation and death").[86] In my view, reestablishing Utopia was precisely the central characteristic of 1960s China: to rebuild a political society as the socialist original territory; to revitalize such big concepts as revolution, nation, world, and people; and to redefine individual values and lifestyle.

This reestablishment of Utopia was also related to the production of the concept of the Third World. The latter not only significantly expanded the spatial dimension of Utopia, but on a temporal level also made it possible for the revolution never to end. In this context, to once again promote the significance of revolution and its urgency and, accordingly, to reorganize society and everyday life so as to keep individual desires under control, managed to gain a new kind of legitimacy. Even though all public expressions affirmed material life, they nevertheless emphasized the importance of taking a stand against bourgeois hedonism, including the bourgeois view of happiness oriented around satisfying the pleasure of the senses. The correct view toward

---

85. Wei Wei, "Qi yanque zhizhi, mu honghu er gaoxiang" [In admiration of the high-flying swans] *Zhongguo qingnian* [Youth of China], 1963, 20/21:8.

86. Ibid., 6.

material life should therefore be: (1) first and foremost, improve the lives of all laboring people, as opposed to the lives of oneself and small groups of people; (2) prioritize developing production; (3) realize that there are poor and oppressed people all over the world and that, in addition to political and moral support, there should be economic support [for them]; and (4) keep in mind an important principle in one's personal life—namely, to feel content about one's own living condition.[87] The points of the author, Gan Feng, here represented the mainstream values of the time. By 1965, these views were further expressed as "hedonism is the core of the bourgeois view of happiness," and "the proletarian view of happiness is to fight for the revolution."[88] These publicly presented views indicated the tensions between spiritual life and material life, and it is this tension that governed the creation of works like *Never Forget* and *The Young Generation*.

Within the postrevolutionary [socialist] context, however, the difficulty became how the big and far-reaching task of reestablishing Utopia could become part of an individual life's trivial matters. In relation to all of this, in 1964, there was also a debate about "how should revolutionary youths understand ideals and contribution?" Questions explored included: what should the youth base their ideals on, whether or not participating in agricultural production constituted an ideal, how to deal with differences in people's ability to contribute, how to understand the relationship between being a cog and being a pillar [of the nation], how to realize far-reaching ideals in everyday life, and how to combine ideals with reality.[89] By now, the discussions had apparently once again returned to the relationship between life's trivial matters and big affairs of the state. And efforts were made to close the gaps between the two aspects. Positive answers often heard were "my ideal is to completely transform saline-alkaline land," or "big experts can come from practice in production," or "work wholeheartedly to transform barren mountains into mountains of flowers and fruits."[90] In short, the image of the socialist new person of

---

87. Gan Feng, "He zichanjieji xianglezhuyi huaqing jiexian" [Take a stand against bourgeois hedonism], *Zhongguo qingnian* [Youth of China], 1963, 16:11–13.

88. Gao Zehong, "Xiangle zhishang shi zichanjieji xingfuguan de hexin" [Hedonism is the core of bourgeois view of happiness], *Zhongguo qingnian* [Youth of China], 1965, 3:24–25.

89. Chen Yiqun, "Geming qingnian yinggai zenyang kandai lixiang he gongxian" [How should revolutionary youths understand ideals and contribution?], *Zhongguo qingnian* [Youth of China], 1964, 5:16.

90. See "'Geming qingnian yinggai zenyang kandai lixiang he gongxian' wenti taolun" [On discussions regarding "how revolutionary youths should understand ideals and contribution"], *Zhongguo qingnian* [Youth of China], 1964, 7:27–29.

1960s China was symbolized by the qualities echoed in such discussions: keep the whole country in mind and the whole world in view; keep one's mind on one's work and be assiduous and self-disciplined; work hard, live plainly, and actively improve one's self. The classic image of this socialist new person at the time of course was Lei Feng. In *Never Forget*, it is the character Ji Youliang who represents the new person and who is best interpreted with the metaphor of cog. Indeed, from any perspective, Ji Youliang fits the criteria of the socialist new person, and it goes without saying that his characteristics were based on Lei Feng, especially on how the latter's story was constructed.

Ji Youliang also comes from a worker's family, but in comparison to Ding Shaochun, he has never had the impulse to deterritorialize. He has not only persisted in his loyalty to the original territory but is also clear about his own position [identity] as its master. He is a guardian of sorts of this territory, which in the discourse of the time would be called revolutionary successor (*jiebanren*). In Ji Youliang, we do not see father-son conflicts; he is the natural extension, or the staunch defender of and heir to, or a replica of the father. As such, he cannot tolerate any betrayal or attempt at deterritorialization. Ji's characterization is also seen in Xiao Jiye in *The Young Generation*, along with similar new person characters in other works. In essence Ji forms a "rescuer—to-be-rescued" relationship with Ding Shaochun, a relationship also found in many other works, including between Xiao Jiye and Lin Yusheng in *The Young Generation*, or Lu Dacheng and Chen Xi in *Sentinels under the Neon Lights*.

Such loyalty comes first from a kind of political consciousness that is based on an unshaken faith in the larger and long-term revolutionary goals set forth by the state. During the 1960s, however, it also came from a consciousness of family background—that is, a sense of historical continuity based on political blood ties. This sense of continuity seemed to suggest that the relationship between the individual and revolution was not from faith or historical consciousness only, but also from a sense of belonging to a certain social status. An emphasis on this sense of belonging at once represented an awareness of one's identity (*shenfen zijue*) and an anxiety about such identity, and also at once manifested the political impulse to reestablish a Utopia and the start of an ongoing shrinking of the socialist original territory in the postrevolutionary [socialist] context surrounded by multitude of customary practices. At least such a sense of crisis had occurred in the self-consciousness of the state politics of the time. Ji Youliang, then, was an awkward product of this historical moment, signaling an attempt to overcome the crisis.

To ensure Ji's purity as a guardian or successor, he not only must have [correct] consciousness but he must also, first of all, have [correct] associations. Among the individuals that Ji (and those like him) associates with, we do not find any dissidents on the list. That is, Ji's associations are confined within the blood ties of a certain social level. As I mentioned above, in the 1960s there was anxiety, even fear, about [social] associations. The confidence in the power of the revolutionary interpolations that once had existed (for example, in the novel *The Song of Youth*, Lu Jiachuan's call to Lin Daojing) began to appear not as strong as it once was. As a result, the emphasis shifted to the reliability of associations. In addition to the issue of association, secondly, there is the issue of [self-]control. In Ji Youliang, we recognize a level of loftiness, which exerts great pressure on individuals like Ding Shaochun and which is also based on the control or exclusion of desire. In the narratives before the 1960s, revolution (including socialism) was often narrated as the mode of production for romantic love, whereas in the 1960s, producing that kind of romantic love became part of the narrative anxiety.

Within this narrative mode, for Ji Youliang, work becomes the major content of his life. At the same time, the concept of revolution was changed to the concept of construction, one that also denotes the production of material goods. But this concept of construction indicated that the reterritorialization in the 1960s was taking place in a postrevolutionary context. In this sense, Tang's analysis of the industrialization logic and its organizational discipline behind the anxiety over everyday life is quite enlightening.[91] Only in a modern industrial context would there be a discussion of the relationship between cog and pillar. High technology, high specialization, and high division of labor in modern industrialization inevitably produce demands for cogs, or a sense of one's positionality.[92] At the same time, to overcome the decentralization of responsibilities due to specialization and division of labor, there is also a requirement for workers to have a sense of responsibility and to cooperate with one another. All of this constitutes the narrative theme in the representation of Ji Youliang. There, we find a transformation in terms of the identity of youth in the postrevolutionary context: they have been transformed from opponents shaped in a confrontational politics to images of producers who are now masters. Hence, the focus of discussion became how to realize large and

91. See Tang, "'Qianwan buyao wangji' de lishi yiyi: guanyu richang shenghuo de jiaolü jiqi xiandaixing."
92. For a further discussion of this point, see chapter 6.

far-reaching ideals in day-to-day life. Meanwhile, the large and far-reaching ideals would also be assumed in the mode of production due to the realization that "in addition to political and moral support," the "poor and oppressed people all over the world" need "economic support."[93] Also, when the notion of original territory was transformed to symbolize the political society of the nation, the latter's postrevolutionary [socialist] context would also inevitably condition the state to find itself in need of management. What we find in all of this, therefore, is that the 1960s promotion of the image of the new person was in fact informed by a complex historical condition and a multitude of social or historical demands. At the same time, the powerful promotion of obedience and loyalty often extended from the political to the moral domains— for example, the discourse about Lei Feng was mixed with layered narrative implications, but the image of Lei Feng was mostly understood in terms of its moralistic meanings (*daode yiyi*). It is in this sense that all the representations of the new person such as Ji Youliang, and to some extent even the entire political context of the 1960s, were oriented around the call to never forget class struggle, and in fact focused on producing a social morality emphasizing being obedient. This particular morality emphasizes cultivation of the heart and a moralization of everyday life; it stipulated that a good citizen of revolutionary China must be both a good revolutionary and a good producer.

However, mixed into the image of such a perfect new person, there existed elements of crisis. First, despite the introduction of the utopian vision of the Third World revolution aimed at overcoming the contradiction between material production and material enjoyment, this vision still was not able, either theoretically or in practice, to solve the problem with regard to issues of distribution and consumption in socialism, except to temporarily push it aside. In actuality, these issues and the desires stemming from them continued to exist, indeed all the way to the 1980s—when they reemerged as a major social and narrative drive.

Second, although the notion of master was meant to help turn the young generation from opponents to producers, the question is, in the historical context of industrialization, can machines, resultant alienation, and impulses to break out of alienation be made to disappear just because there is a change in the system of ownership? This, I might add, not only constituted the difficulty in narrating industry-related subject matter during the socialist period but was also manifested in some of the narrative concerns in the 1980s.

93. See Gan, "He zichanjieji xianglezhuyi huaqing jiexian."

Third, in the Yan'an period, the imaginary of political society was essentially established in a rural space, within which everyone was concerned with everyone else's business. In the increasingly modernized society of the city, the introduction of bureaucracy, especially of specialization and divisions of labor, created different positionalities that in turn made impossible a direct dialogue between trivial private matters and large state affairs. In what ways, then, were authors to reconnect the [once] close relationship between trivial private matters and big and far-reaching matters? Is it possible to just rely on ideological indoctrination?

Fourth, the big and far-reaching utopian ideals tend to stimulate a kind of romantic impulse. But when it comes to everyday life and its trivial matters, what is needed is often a realistic attitude. Yet in various narratives, romantic impulses are in fact often repressed by realism. The question, then, is in what ways can romantic impulses be released?

Finally and most important, if the emphasis in the 1960s was placed on cultivating obedience as the citizen's morality (despite the fact that such morality was hidden under the cloak of class struggle), how do we explain [the emphasis on] revolution and class struggle that belong to the category of confrontational and oppositional politics? That is, if the emphasis was transformed from producing examples of perfect [obedient] individuals from workers who occupy specific positions, to producing opponents for confrontational politics, then political decisions would need to be made on a general and grand scale. In October 1965, Mao emphatically stated in a speech that "if revisionism occurred in the central government, [people] should rebel."[94] But the question is: can the new mission to rebel be shouldered by a new person like Ji Youliang?

The point of these questions lies in the following set of tensions: as long as there is a need for continuous revolution under socialism, there are bound to be confrontational politics and demands for producers to resume the position of opponents, for corresponding political decisions, for a political vision that is totalizing and grand in scale, and more. All of this constitutes the awkward identification of opponents with producers. To some extent, we can say that the outbreak of the Cultural Revolution was in part to overcome the obedience fostered during the first part of the 1960s—even though the confrontational politics then assumed a different kind of obedience.

94. Quoted in *Mao Zedong zhuan* [Biography of Mao Zedong], ed. Pang Xianzhi and Jin Chongji (Beijing: Zhongyang Wenxian Chubanshe, 2003), 1395.

Conclusion: Why Did Literary Youth Reappear?

There is a character by the name Lin Lan in *The Young Generation*. She seems to function as a footnote for explaining Xiao Jiye to us: someone who was once young, pure, full of life, and even somewhat immature as a revolutionary. Indeed, in Lin Lan, we find numerous elements uniquely reminiscent of the 1960s: a young woman who is pure, kind, sincere, honest, and willing to help others and at the same time is also full of dreams and prepared to travel far at a moment's notice. She seems to be naturally against a vulgar philistine existence and is unwilling to settle for a quiet and comfortable life. At the same time, she has a strong will, loyalty, and faith, and an ability to make political judgments. I call such an image literary youth (*wenxue qingnian*).

In his discussion of Tsuge Yoshiharu's works, Sato Masao offers a description of Japanese literary youth as follows:

> In modern Japanese society, there was a group of writers identified as "literary youth." For a long period of time, these writers occupied a unique position. Simply put, "literary youth" were those young people who worked hard in their aspiration to become writers, poets, or playwrights. At the same time, in the Meiji period, it was widely accepted that one could not make a living from writing novels or poetry. For those with literary aspirations, therefore, economic success would not be part of their dreams. Socially, they were seen as individuals who cared only about their own desires—self-expression and pursuit of social and human truth—as superfluous beings who buried themselves in their own pursuits. From the point of view of social conventions, they were naturally objects of contempt, but from the point of view of anticonvention, they were strong men worthy of respect. They once constituted a special group of individuals in Japanese society. In this sense, "literary youth" refers to none other than those "who search for the way."[95]

Of course, Lin Lan is not a "literary youth" as defined by Sato Masao, nor is it my intention here to trace the historical trajectory of literary youth as defined and developed in China. However, with this notion, I want to highlight the kind of quality in Lin Lan in terms of literary youth, which can be briefly described as romantic, willing to imagine, free, self-expressive, extraverted or

---

95. Sato Masao, "Guanyu weixiao—Tuozhi Yichun he ta de zuoping" [About smiles: Tsuge Yoshiharu and his works], *Refeng Xueshu* [Warm wind scholarship], trans. Sakai Hirobumi (Shanghai: Shanghai Renmin Chubanshe, 2010), vol. 5.

aggressive, against conventions, and in pursuit of ideals or the way (*dao*). In modern Chinese history, these qualities—especially the passions associated with them—have been effective resources for revolutionary or confrontational politics. At the same time, of course, these qualities have often been in conflict with revolution, especially with institutionalized revolution. For example, in his discussion of Ding Ling's story "Zai yiyuan zhong" (In the Hospital), Huang Ziping clearly notices such qualities in the character Lu Ping: "[in her], such love of literature is undoubtedly mixed with other elements such as passion, ideals, dissatisfaction with the status quo, and a determination and participation in struggles to change a weak/ill society."[96]

To a certain extent, we can see that Xiao Lin, a character in Wang Meng's story "A Young Man Arrives at the Organization Department," signaled that the genealogy of this kind of literary youth was coming to an end in 1957. There are a number of reasons for such an end, one of which may have had to do with, to echo discussions above, the fact that after socialism was institutionalized, what socialism needed was producers not opponents, as well the reestablishment of public morality and social order. Under the pressure of institutionalization, literary youth would come to be identified as part of the petit bourgeoisie. At the same time, as long as socialism still finds continuous revolution and confrontational politics necessary, it will still need oppositional forces.

The appearance of a character such as Lin Lan manifested another political need for 1960s China: this character offers both the possibility of liberating romanticism from trivial private matters of the everyday and a capability for political judgment. Additionally, we must also note the amateur nature of Lin Lan's position, which, unleashed from the control of specialization, is represented as one that is full of passion, ideals, determination, and participation. In the literature of the 1980s, incidentally, we encounter a character with similar qualities in Zhang Chengzhi's *River in the North* (*Beifang de he*);[97] perhaps only in narrating those who are not professionals can the qualities or characteristics of professional revolutionaries be represented.

The difficulty that the decade of the 1960s faced was that, under the banner of class struggle, different crises—generated by issues of distribution and

---

96. Huang Ziping, "Bing de yingyu yu wenxue shengchan—Ding Ling 'Zai yiyuan zhong' ji qita" [The metaphoric use of illness and literary production: On Ding Ling's "In the Hospital"], in *Ershi shiji zhongguo wenxueshi lun* [On the history of twentieth-century Chinese literature], ed. Wang Xiaoming (Shanghai: Dongfang Chuban Zhongxin, 2003), 66.

97. Zhang Chengzhi, "Beifang de he" [Rivers in the north], *Shi Yue* [October], 1984, 1.

consumption and methods of dealing with such crises—were not clearly differentiated and were mixed together. If issues in distribution might give rise to a kind of confrontational politics and oppositional forces, desires produced by consumption and ways to control them would require the establishment of public morality and order so as to suppress individuals' impulse to deterritorialize. Meanwhile, the cultivation of personal ethics was geared toward being obedient. The contradictions between these two impulses in China paradoxically coexisted in the narratives of the 1960s.

Finally, I would like to end this discussion in a nonacademic fashion. Let us imagine how Ding Shaochun, Ji Youliang, Xiao Jiye, Lin Yusheng, and Lin Lan might enter the Cultural Revolution that was about to happen; what roles they might play; and what positions they might occupy as the Cultural Revolution unfolds. In our dramatic imagination about the fate of these characters, we may be able to better discern the entanglement of the layered logics of the 1960s. We can also further imagine a perhaps more paradoxical reencounter between Lin Lan and Lin Yusheng in the 1980s, to ponder how in that era oppositional politics effectively made use of the individual's desire for consumption and how the latter also used the form of oppositional politics. Of course, this would be a different story from a different historical era.

CONCLUSION
The Crisis of Socialism and Efforts to Overcome It

I prefer to understand crisis as a productive concept. In a certain sense, any social structure is at the same time a crisis production mechanism. When a crisis is produced, the questions of whether society can overcome it and what resources society uses to overcome it are extremely important and must be confronted by all of society. Yet dealing with crisis often provides the possibility for a new revolution. Chinese socialism likewise has produced its own crisis, including the means to overcome the crisis. In this sense, I prefer to think that socialism is not the end of revolution; on the contrary, it births a new revolution—of course, the internal structural elements of this new revolution are incredibly complicated.

However, today *the crisis of socialism* perhaps carries another meaning. The last thirty years, or the so-called post-thirty years (*hou sanshinian*), have produced a new interpretation of the previous thirty years of socialism. This interpretation consists of two aspects: on the one hand, the entirety of socialism has been demonized and vilified; but on the other hand, especially in the past decade, with the start of the great debate between the New Left and liberalism, socialism has in a certain sense been idealized and utopianized. The issue here is that, if we completely idealize and utopianize the thirty years of socialism that came before the 1980s, how do we explain the 1980s? What is the significance of the 1980s? Additionally, a more serious problem is that if we completely idealize that period of history, then what is the reason for the failure of those thirty years of socialism? Instead of increasing our understanding of socialism, this idealization might, on the contrary, obscure the issue. Therefore, to debate the crisis of socialism again and in conjunction with these circumstances may help us delve more deeply into the history of Chinese socialism.

I. What Is the Crisis of Socialism?

I always refer to contemporary China with the concept of revolution—"Revolutionary China"—but this is only a general or metaphorical way of speaking. If we understand revolution as a large-scale mass movement (or political practice), especially one characterized by the seizing of political power through military force, then revolution took a vacation after 1949. This is not to say, of course, that the concept of revolution ceased to function; rather, it continues to function but merely manifests [itself] in a different form. For this reason, we can call the post-1949 period "after the revolution" (*geming zhihou*). Since the 1990s, some scholars have liked to use the term *postrevolutionary*, or *postsocialist*, to indicate that we have entered another historical context. However, I prefer to call the period from 1949 to the 1980s—the second half of the twentieth century—the after-the-revolution era.

This era has two characteristics. One is an emphasis on construction, [both] political construction and economic construction, which differentiates it from the previous large-scale revolutionary movements aimed at resistance and overthrow. Thus we often discuss Yan'an, because the Yan'an period included some concepts and institutional planning for this post-1949 construction. The other characteristic is that the After Revolution era, aside from construction, also emphasized governance. This is to say that it clearly highlighted the importance of the state. The original revolution challenged and overthrew the existing form of the state, but after 1949 a society undergoing reconstruction required governing, and because it required governing, the concept of governance (*zhili*) became the second main characteristic of the After Revolution era. Talk of governance highlights the importance of the state. Without a state, there can be no governance. These problems are all related to Leninism, especially the idea of "realizing socialism within one country."

Since we have entered the historical context of the After Revolution era, the concept of revolution inevitably came into conflict with the concepts of construction and governance. The core of this conflict is still an issue in and of modernity. How can this contradiction be resolved? Do we have the ability to resolve it? When it cannot be resolved, it can develop into a form of crisis and produce elements of crisis in Chinese society.

Based on this, I summarize the contradictions of the socialist period—that is, the After Revolution historical context, into five categories: (1) the contradiction between egalitarianism and social class differentiation, (2) the contradiction between bureaucratic hierarchy and mass participation, (3) the contradiction between political society and the world of (everyday) life, (4) the contradiction between internalization (*neizai hua*) and objectification (*duixiang hua*), and (5) the contradiction between maintaining the status quo and facing the future.

Of course there are many other areas of contradiction. But through analysis of only these five categories of contradiction, we can see that, when modernity entered the historical picture, it produced a structural conflict between the ideals of revolution and the historical context of the After Revolution era. This structural conflict forms the crisis of socialism.

1. EGALITARIANISM AND SOCIAL CLASS DIFFERENTIATION

The Chinese revolution fundamentally included a political appeal for egalitarianism. Such an appeal inevitably led to a revolutionary change in the distribution of wealth and ownership throughout society. But modernity cannot tolerate absolute egalitarianism. As a result, even the supply system of the Yan'an period included a certain amount of difference between ranks, which [as mentioned in chapter 2] was criticized by Wang Shiwei at the time, as the "peasants are divided into three colors; food is divided into five levels." If there had not been such an egalitarian ideal, the radical literary youth (*wenxue qingnian*) at the time would not have harbored such strong resistance against the internal ranking differences of the supply system.[1]

But the ranking distinction in the supply system served two purposes: to guarantee the working needs of the leading cadres and to entice higher-level knowledgeable talents [talented people] into the system. Therefore, the

---

1. Tr.: That is to say, during the Yan'an period and after, basic supplies were lacking and thus rationed. The supply system was intended to distribute goods equitably, but clearly some people got more than others.

supply system already included the two fundamentally modern characteristics of the post-1949 period: specialization and division of labor. These characteristics of modernity inevitably influence the system of wealth distribution in society. And we are familiar with the 1950s transition from the supply system to the salary system based on occupational levels.[2] This transition actually presaged the possibility of the redifferentiation of social classes.

In this sense, After Revolution socialism is actually a very complex concept. On the one hand, it emphasizes equality, yet on the other hand, it redifferentiates social classes under the conditions of modernity. This differentiation of social classes in fact included three aspects: (1) the distinction between cadres and the masses, (2) the distinction between intellectual labor and manual labor, and (3) the distinction between urban and rural. A society without distinctions cannot exist in reality—socialism is not an exception to this. However, if distinctions are expanded limitlessly, then socialism not only can produce a new bureaucratic class, it can also produce a new bourgeoisie. And that is what actually happened. In the Chinese literature of the first thirty years of socialism, there in fact existed contradictions between intellectual labor and manual labor and between urban and rural, but they were not openly or clearly represented. More often than not, literary works concealed or obscured these contradictions by resorting to such notions as individualism or bourgeois thought. We see this in many texts. For example, in *Never Forget* (*Qianwan buyao wangji*), the criticism of Ding Shaochun overshadows the contradictions. Ding's desire for a leather jacket and a suit in effect reveals a distinction of status between intellectual and manual labor. But to overcome this distinction the play merely defines the desire for higher status as individualism or bourgeois ideas of fame and profit. Another kind of narration seeks to overcome the distinction between urban and rural—for example, in *Sunny Days* (*Yanyang tian*). In this novel, there is an emphasis on do not forget the nation at the moment of bumper harvest (*fengshou buwang guojia*).[3] This emphasis suggests a high degree of identification with the nation, which at the same time overshadows the existence of the contradiction between urban and

---

2. For details, see Yang Kuisong, "Cong gonggei zhi dao zhiwu dengji gongzi zhi: Xin Zhongguo jianli qianhou dangzheng renyuan shouru fenpei zhidu de yanbian" [From the provision system to the salary system based on occupational level: Changes in the income distribution system of party members around the establishment of new China]," *Lishi yanjiu* [History research] 4 (2007): 111–37.

3. Tr.: As Cai explains elsewhere in this book, this emphasis was important because previously, peasants would keep the bumper crop for themselves; under socialism, they were exhorted to hand over the correct proportion to the state for nationwide redistribution.

rural. This repressed or concealed contradiction led to retaliatory narratives in the 1980s. The irony is that the retaliatory narratives not only did not stop the trend of social class differentiation; they actually caused such social division to gain legitimating support.

However, the division between cadres and the masses became a particularly strong symbol of the contradiction between egalitarianism and social class differentiation. The widening of social differences and the emergence of a new bureaucratic class inevitably led to a challenge to the notion of egalitarianism, which was an important revolutionary ideal. Therefore, antibureaucracy and anti–special privileges was always an important theme of Chinese literature during the first thirty years of socialism. This narrative theme has stubbornly persisted to this day; indeed, despite political interference and regardless of the many changes in how it is expressed, we can still sense its existence. Moreover, this theme has always enjoyed the support of none other than the revolutionary concept of egalitarianism. This support constitutes a sort of internal narrative impetus as well as an in-depth reflection on reality. For example, in the process of land reform, some cadres used their power to obtain, during resource distribution, more of the fruits of victory than normal peasants, be it land or other property. Today when discussing history, people tend to do so from [the point of view of] the results of history, such as the problems brought about by the formation of cooperatives. But if cooperatives had not been organized at the time, the cadres who had gained more resources than the masses during land reforms might have quickly turned themselves into a new oppressive class. Zhao Shuli in *Evil Does Not Oppress Good* (*Xie bu ya zheng*) and *Sanliwan Village* (*Sanli wan*), Liu Qing in *The Builders*, and others all touched on this issue. Furthermore, this new class would have been stronger than the previous landlord class in one respect: they [members of the new class] would simultaneously hold the resources of political power and wealth. This would be a terrible prospect. This is why, as early as in the 1950s, literature was already proactively responding to the emergence of such elements of crisis. These were all new problems arising from the process of social wealth distribution. If the contradictions were not well addressed and dealt with, they would produce crisis.

2. BUREAUCRATIC HIERARCHY AND MASS PARTICIPATION

In the After Revolution socialist context, China had to walk the road of high specialization and division of labor to construct a modernized society. In other words, institutionally, China unavoidably had to implement a hierarchical mode of management. This management mode simultaneously produced a so-called bureaucracy. Wang Meng in his "A Young Man Arrives at the Organization Department" discussed this problem relatively early in the process. At the same time, however, the Chinese revolution always emphasized mass participation as one of its key characteristics. So when it comes to the management model of bureaucratic hierarchy, can the masses still participate? In what ways can they participate? The contradiction between the two—bureaucracy and the masses—led to the appearance of the following several issues.

First, a modern enterprise must satisfy two conditions: a high level of specialization, and a large and qualified modern labor force. Socialism was faced with these two issues. Mao Zedong described in positive terms the ruffian movement (*pizi yundong*) in his [1927] "Hunan nongmin yundong kaocha baogao" [Report of the investigation of the Hunan peasant movement], but so-called ruffians were never positively represented in contemporary Chinese literature.[4] Rather, promoting a qualified modern laborer always entailed upholding the value of (traditional) craftsmanship—that is, representing someone expressing a strong sense of social responsibility through producing good products. Most of contemporary literature thus contains the notion of production. Even in the slogan "grasp revolution, promote production," the ultimate goal of the revolution was to resolve the problem of production. This problem is none other than that of modernity. Yet in addressing the issue, contemporary Chinese literature resorted to many traditional resources. For example, in his articles, Zhao Shuli repeatedly used the word "upright and decent" (*zhengpai*), saying that cadres must be upright and decent, and peasants must also be upright and decent. What was "upright and decent"? In the literature of the first thirty years of Chinese socialism, there are many images of old workers and peasants whose representations leave one with an impression of morality. The fact that this traditional resource was adopted in After Revolution socialism actually has to do with the needs of modernity. But if we stop short at this point, we would easily muddle the boundaries between revolutionary China and modern China. Because the real question is: what sort of society does a high level of specialization intend to construct?

---

4. Mao Tse-tung, "Hunan nongmin yundong kaocha baogao" [Report on the investigation of Hunan peasant movement], *Selected Works of Mao Tse-tung* (Peking: Foreign Language Press, 1965), 1.

Anthony Giddens in *The Consequences of Modernity* especially emphasizes the abstract nature of modern society.[5] This highly abstract system involves many aspects: concepts, institutions, economics, and so on. But this highly abstract system necessarily relies on the support of technology. Without technological support, such a highly abstract system could in fact not be established. This explains the important function of specialization, and how modern expert society is formed. At the same time, however, a highly abstract society is also one with a high level of risk. To overcome crises that stem from high risk, a system of trust must be established between the individual and society. In a modern society, (technical or knowledgeable) experts often act as the medium of this trust.

In the first thirty years of Chinese socialism, this highly abstract system was not necessarily formed entirely by experts. That is to say, after 1949 the Chinese revolution was not interested in establishing an expert society. But we cannot say that this [new] society did not have a high level of abstraction. Its abstract system was realized through the [Chinese Communist] Party and politics, especially through the personal charisma of the Party leader, Mao. When discussing the Chinese Cultural Revolution (1966–76), Benjamin Schwartz observes that the situation was chaotic and the Party [Central] Committee actually ceased to function, but that Chinese society did not fall into chaos, production did not stop, and the order of life did not completely dissolve. To explain this anomaly, he employs the notion of "reign of virtue" to suggest that what governed Chinese society was not some kind of a superficial institutional system.[6] This "reign of virtue" in effect formed the highly abstract [Chinese] system and gained a high level of trust from members of society. It was not until the 1980s that this trust ran into problems, generating what is now known as the trust crisis of the 1980s. We must realize, therefore, that in the historical context of After Revolution China, the governing system was different from that of the Soviet Union, which was largely an expert society, because the Chinese model first had to confront challenges of mass participation.

It goes without saying that, if we emphasize in a biased manner the expert society, the so-called masses of workers can only be seen as nothing more

---

5. Anthony Giddens, *The Consequences of Modernity* (Stanford, CA: Stanford University Press, 1990).

6. Benjamin I. Schwartz, "The Reign of Virtue: Some Broad Perspectives on Leader and Party in the Cultural Revolution," *China Quarterly* 35 (September 1968): 1–17.

than a modern labor force. Such a perception would be in sharp conflict with revolutionary ideals. What is more, how do we understand the notion of "people?" What does democracy really mean? Will it be possible for people to yield their rights to experts? Max Weber in his essay "Politics as a Vocation" already showed a political anxiety about "expert society."[7] A more important question, in my view, is how to maintain the subaltern's sense of dignity in an expert society. Between expert society and mass participation, there are often very difficult challenges and choices, including choices of necessary institutional innovation.

Second, Chinese society, especially in the process of the revolution, gradually formed its own structure of mobilization despite the fact that this structure was not institutionalized. Such a structure would inevitably come into conflict with expert society. James Townsend and Brantly Womack in *Politics in China* discuss in particular the characteristics of "mobilized society" and touch on its difference from totalitarianism.[8] They argue that totalitarianism is impenetrable due to the fact that totalitarianism is composed of (techno) bureaucrats and therefore is a highly specialized expert society. A mobilized society, in contrast, is characterized by constant mobilization; it is diverse and constantly changing. Indeed, a highly specialized expert society would have great difficulty tolerating all-out participation of the masses.

Third, another reason China did not immediately establish a highly specialized expert society after 1949 has to do with the lack of experts and the low literacy rate of the masses. Without enough experts, many issues and problems had to be solved through mass participation. This method of mass participation was conducted on two levels. First, from the Yan'an period through the 1950s, there existed a widespread and large-scale literacy movement; second, an emphasis on intellectual participation did not mean that knowledge would be concentrated in the hands of a few. Knowledge was to be popularized; this was very important at the time, hence the opening of knowledge and technology to the masses and promotion of technology innovation. All of this—the opening of knowledge and technology to the masses—was in effect a challenge to the notion of intellectual property. In the literature of the seventeen years [1949–66], such as Ai Wu's *Steeled and Tempered* (*Bailian cheng'gang*), the severest criticism often concerns an individual's refusal

7. Max Weber, "Politics as Vocation," *Essays in Sociology* (New York: Oxford University Press, 1958), 77–128.
8. See James R. Townsend and Brantly Womack, *Politics in China*, 3rd ed. (Boston: Little, Brown, 1986).

to share his [or her] technological knowledge with others. In this sense, such mass participation does seem to have an antimodernity dimension; it emphasizes that the construction of modern Chinese society should not depend on a small number of experts only, and it should also have universal mass participation. And for universal participation to be possible, there had to be open knowledge and technology. It is in this sense that there existed at the time the conflict between "red" and "expert." In essence, however, this was quintessentially an issue in and of modernity: it sought to solve, on an institutional level, the tension between bureaucratic hierarchy and (mass) democracy, which was essentially an issue of political democratization in the realm of economics. Such an intent found expression in the 1960s through the Anshan Steel Charter [of the later 1950s].

Of course, the issue was not nearly as simple as this. For example, in the 1980s there was criticism and analysis of the so-called work units; critics argued that work units had taken on many social functions that they should not have. Needless to say, such criticism was based on the belief that modernity entailed a high level of division of labor and specialization. Yet when, throughout the socialist period, work units bore many social functions, and even many family functions—such as [making] bathhouses open to workers' families—the work unit model also bred strong solidarity and had an affective appeal to the workers.[9] This kind of quasi-kinship relationship between work units and workers cannot be easily explained away by division of labor and specialization.

Still, however, we recognize the existence of contradictions between bureaucratic hierarchy and mass participation, which on the one hand made it less possible for an elite group of experts to emerge, and on the other hand also led to politically erroneous policies toward intellectuals.

3. POLITICAL SOCIETY AND THE WORLD OF EVERYDAY LIFE

As discussed in chapter 7, Xie Juezai viewed the process of letting people enter history as the actuality (or essence) of democracy. The actuality of democracy is none other than the political, while history is none other than the

---

[9]. Tr.: The social functions of the work units were in part mandated by the lack of individual amenities in the housing stock of the units. For example, it was rare for people to have running hot water in their apartments, so bathhouses were a practical way for people to take hot showers. Furnaces that helped boil water, where people would go to fill thermoses with boiled (thus drinkable) water helped save people from using coal to boil their own water. In other words, it was a method of social collectivized living that was rejected with the privatizations of the 1980s and beyond.

temporal form of political life. From all of this, we can sense that the socialist ideals and social imaginary already existed in the debates on democracy in 1940s Yan'an. I identify this imaginary as the structural form of a certain political society.

The structural form of this political society emphasizes the important function of political parties and upholds the principle that only through the party's political life can the masses who have existed "outside history and political life" be brought into history and political life. But on the other hand, we must also note that the formation of this particular political society was closely related to the war environment, the "state of exception," of the time. The question, then, is this: in the After Revolution historical context—namely, the normal state of Chinese socialism—what is the nature of the relationship between this political society and the lifeworld of the masses (especially of the urban masses)?

One possibility for this political society is an unlimited expansion of political space that leads to intense conflicts between it [political society] and the [everyday] lifeworld. I certainly do not affirm the narrative model that sets political society and the everyday lifeworld as complete opposites; such a narrative model can lead only to a simplistic narration of history. In this simplistic narrative mode, the individual's lifeworld cannot tolerate encroachment from the outside and is absolutely self-sufficient. The implication lies in a caution against and a rejection of public political power. The lifeworld certainly does have relative autonomy, but it also has an intimate relationship to politics. Not only does politics permeate and control the individual's lifeworld, the latter can also assert influence on politics. But again the lifeworld does have dimensions of autonomy; therefore, if political space gets expanded without limit, it can generate annoyance and dissatisfaction from the lifeworld, especially when it infringes on individuals' benefits, desires, interests, and so forth.

What is more, even if the lifeworld is not completely autonomous and self-sufficient, there always exists a desire for self-sufficiency, which in turn helps construct a corresponding fantasy. We must confront the importance of this fantasy head on. It contains potentials for opposition, especially in literature. In a certain sense, what literature deals with is precisely this kind of fantasy, including the contradictions and conflicts between this fantasy and practices of everyday life.

In the early 1960s, conflicts between political society and lifeworld grew especially intense. One reason for the intensification was the development of urbanization. Individual desires, issues of time, tastes, and lifestyles were expressed in a variety of ways and tended toward dispersion. In turn, how to confront the city and the issues produced within it constituted one of the biggest challenges of the first thirty years of Chinese socialism. In a certain sense, we can say that the Chinese revolution did not deal well in its relationship with the lifeworld of urbanites. This relationship ultimately headed toward a rupture (*polie*), which, on the level of everyday life, resulted in people responding positively to the thought liberation movement of the 1980s.

4. INTERNALIZATION AND OBJECTIFICATION

In the first thirty years of Chinese socialist practice, there was an extremely important concept: master (*zhuren*). In the words of Xie Juezai, "turning over people's life (*fanshen*) does not just mean for them to be able to eat and be clothed; it is also a change from being slaves to being masters." This means that the concept of socialism contains the extraordinarily important politics of respect and dignity. The system of wealth distribution is not the only thing important to a society; equality among and respect for members of society is also important. That the concept of master produced great political energy and identification with the nation-state needs no further argument. What requires further discussion are the theoretical and practical challenges faced by this concept.

In my view, [the concept of] master implies an internalization process. For example, machines originally were objectified vis-à-vis the workers. In the socialist period, neither the machines nor the factories are objectified vis-à-vis workers, but they have all now become part of "us" and found embodied expressions through us. In 1955, the state formally issued "Zhonghua quanguo zonggonghui wei baozheng wancheng he chao'e wancheng guomin jingji de diyige wunianjihua gao quanguo zhigong shu" (A Letter from the All-China General Union to Workers on the Guarantees for Completing and Exceeding the First Five Year National Economic Plan). While repeatedly emphasizing the quest for or pursuit of the socialist industrialization of the state, it also stipulated in detail the labor qualities that every laborer must possess:

> We need to let every person, every machine, every coin, and every minute be amply and efficiently engaged and used for the construction tasks identified in the five-year plan! To reduce waste is the responsibility of each of us! We must conserve natural resources, reduce the production and circulation cost of commodities; we must enhance the quality of our products,

reduce and eliminate defective products; we must care for our machines and tools to prolong their lives; in basic construction, we must reduce construction costs; and we must guarantee the quality of construction. We must implement the principle of "good, fast, conserving, and safe." We must conscientiously observe all the regulations and constantly and actively strenghten working discipline. Every one of us must assume the attitude and responsibility of the master of the nation and carry out struggle against all forms of wastefulness."[10]

Clearly, what upholds this modern craftsman spirit is not just the ideals of modernization. Also involved is a Marxism-informed political attitude of the proletariat being the master of the country. However, will the problem of alienation disappear as a result of this process of internalization? Can machines, the state, institutions, officials, and so forth be reobjectified and even alienated? In debating socialism, therefore, it may be more important to delve deep into the question of socialist alienation. The alienation issue did not receive in-depth theoretical treatment during the first thirty years of Chinese socialism. On the contrary, in the process of internalizing the master narrative, the subject (*zhuti*) expanded uncontrollably. The limitless expansion of the subject in turn generated the following question for narration: in what language or discourse can this limitlessly expanding subject be expressed? Grand slogans were thus produced! But in another sense, what this limitlessly expanding subject managed to weaken may well have been none other than class consciousness.

Moreover, the internalization could not have been completely thorough. There were always some things and some people who could not be internalized. The process of internalization would inevitably produce remainders, which would in turn be reobjectified. For example, labor competition. Labor competition emphasizes mass participation and stimulates enthusiasm for participation. This enthusiasm is then formalized through good reputation, but the good reputation inevitably differentiates between those who charge ahead and those who fall behind; and those who are advanced inevitably produce a sense of oppression on those who fall behind. There is repression in every society; the key is how to deal with it. Of course, the essence of repression varies. Mao repeatedly emphasized the need to correctly deal with

---

10. *Zhonghua Renmin Gongheguo fagui huibian, 1955 nian 7 yue–12 yue* [Compendium of laws of the People's Republic of China, July–December 1955] (Beijing: Falü Chubanshe, 1956), 852.

two different kinds of contradictions (the contradiction between the self and the enemy, and the internal contradictions of the people). However, with the expansion of class struggle, not only did the boundaries between these two contradictions at times grow rather unclear, [but] even among the people, the frequently used criticism and self-criticism method of correcting mistakes often caused face-to-face confrontation and conflict. As a result, while socialism produced its own supporters, it also produced its own opposition. Once such opposition was given a name, such as liberalism, it would be turned into an ideology. And this was precisely one important factor that constituted the challenge to traditional socialism in the 1980s.

Another important issue is how to deal with the master-slave relationship in a class society. This problem manifested itself in the first thirty years of Chinese socialism as the issue of class background. When this issue came into conflict with the ideal of rights equality, it offered significance to Yu Luoke's *On Family Origins*. When he wrote *On Family Origins*, Yu did not demand acknowledgment of those with bad family background; rather, he insisted that they also had the rights to participate in the revolution. A strong memory of class oppression [animated by the Cultural Revolution era of class discrimination against those with bad family backgrounds] continues to exist to this day and has functioned as an important factor in the last thirty years of economic reforms. This requires careful analysis.

Today, a paradox that confronts us is that, on the one hand, this memory of class oppression continues to exist, while on the other hand, despite emphasis on the working class in the first thirty years, the subjectivity of the working class gradually disappeared from the concept of master.

5. MAINTAINING THE STATUS QUO AND FACING THE FUTURE

If we consider the first thirty years of Chinese socialism to be a historical movement full of self-negation, then what this movement may have produced are none other than contradictions and conflicts between maintaining the societal status quo and confronting the future. Once China entered the historical context of the After Revolution—that is, [the need] to build socialism within one country—it had to emphasize governance, norms, production, rectification, and the establishment of a [political, social, and economic] order. This order at the same time included a moral and ethical dimension. In this sense, it inevitably affirmed reality by emphasizing that this reality was the result of the historical movement [of the revolution]. As a result, the legacy issue and successor issue were all related to the maintenance of reality.[11] At the same time, however, in the revolutionary ideals, there always existed a foundational attitude regarding the future. This attitude was constituted of two aspects. First, the so-called reality had to be in a certain sense the result of compromise; yet how to break the situation of compromise was in turn forever central to the question of reliberating the future. Second, the future, or the envisaging of communism was a utopian ideal of the Chinese revolution, and therefore Chinese socialism could never stop at or be content with the After Revolution compromised historical condition. These two factors could each cause the formation of radical politics or radical cultural ideas. Such radicalism existed not only at the highest social levels, but in every level of society; together, such ideals formed a radical antisystemic force critical of reality. And within such confrontations and conflicts, youth were always an important symbol for repeated struggles and renarration. If we say that in the long process of the Chinese revolution, youth once were the symbol of facing the future (such as [in Liang Qichao's early twentieth-century story] "Young China" ["Shaonian Zhongguo shuo"]) and functioned as an affective production mechanism, which as a result produced a narrative mode in which the young educate the old—then in the After Revolution context, youth came to exist in the narrative mode of being educated. In the early 1960s this narrative mode was solidified. Of course, in a more concrete sense youth mainly signified literary youth. However, once the Chinese revolution remobilized the future, this literary youth could immediately be reenlisted as a narrative object. This reenlistment happened in the late 1960s during the Cultural Revolution, during which time youth came to constitute the main antisystemic force, simultaneously extending the ideas of rebellion and conservatism. What must be pointed out here is that this self-negating historical movement caused instability in society. Once the instability spun out of control, it generated strong discontent among people. Only when we fully recognize this point can we understand why the 1980s slogan of "stability and unity" had such great resonant force.

---

11. Tr.: The successor and legacy issues were bound up with the question of who the next leaders of the revolution, and thus of China, would be, and how they would be found: were the future leaders to be those whose families were already leaders (the legacy or bloodline view), or would they be created from among the youth (the successors or antibloodline view). Again, this issue reached an apotheosis in the Cultural Revolution.

These issues, being the core issues of modernity, constituted the main contradictions and the main elements of the crisis in socialism. When they could not be overcome, social crisis erupted, compelling socialism to find different means to overcome the crisis.

II. Efforts to Overcome the Crisis

In the 1950s, these contradictions had not yet manifested themselves very strongly. On the one hand, the transformation of socialism had just begun, and its internal contradictions and crises had not yet completely unfolded. On the other hand, socialism in its competition with capitalism showed a great self-confidence. For example, novels of the time had episodes of settling accounts. Zhou Libo's *Great Changes in a Mountain Village* describes Liu Yusheng settling accounts with Sheng Jiaxiu to mobilize her to join the cooperative. He confidently shows her the costs and earnings of working alone as compared to the costs and earnings of working in the cooperative. But this does not mean that literature in the 1950s lacked the courage and strength for self-criticism. For example, *Flowers Reblooming* (*Chong fang de xianhua*), which was published in 1979 by the Shanghai Literature and Arts Publishing House, contains twenty short stories that were severely criticized during the 1957 Anti-Rightist Campaign. Among them, twelve involve the relationship between cadres and the masses. One can say that the subject of antibureaucracy was in fact a shared topic in these stories. The 1957 Anti-Rightist Campaign was a complex historical event, but among the many rightist groups, there were some who could actually be called young leftists. As I have mentioned elsewhere in this book, in the socialist period, the boundaries of the so-called politics of resistance were very difficult to define. On one hand, the system sought to use resistance politics to overcome the defects of the system itself, but on the other hand, if the resistance politics exceeded defined limits, the system would move to suppress mass movements: the Anti-Rightist Campaign, the Cultural Revolution, and so on, were all like that. What happened from "the hundred flowers blooming and contending" [1956] to the Anti-Rightist Campaign [1957] demonstrated the awkward position and even tragic fate of resistance politics in China. With the further unfolding of the contradictions and crises within socialism, this resistance politics would repeatedly be enlisted for use, yet the forms of its expressions nevertheless grew increasingly enigmatic.

In my view, in the early 1960s China began to see symptoms of a transition from an era of accumulation to an era of consumption. These symptoms further inflamed the elements of crisis within socialism. This crisis was manifested through the two aspects of distribution and consumption.

Issues of distribution led not only to class opposition after the redifferentiation of social classes, it also included conflicts of interest between rural villages and cities. Issues of consumption led to the increasing production of individual desires, which gradually produced an impulse to separate from state politics. Clearly, the appearance of these elements of crisis led to the "never forget class struggle" idea of the period.

Behind the concept of class struggle lies a new differentiation of the enemy-self relationship and the desire to overcome elements of crisis in socialism. Thus, it is necessarily highly politicized. In this highly politicized effort to overcome crisis, there appeared such terms as *bureaucratic bourgeois class* and *special privileges class*. These notions constitute the most important intellectual legacies of the 1960s. But I wish to point out the problems embedded in the form of class struggle that was intended to overcome the crisis.

If we understand class struggle as a mode of dealing with the enemy-self relationship, then trying to use this mode to address all internal contradictions of socialism is inevitably simplistic. For example, both *Sunny Days* (*Yanyang tian*) [by Hao Ran] and *Seize the Seal* (*Duo yin*) contain the distribution contradiction between villages and cities. When this contradiction is fully brought into the mode of class struggle, it ends up concealing true conflicts of interest. Merely relying on identification with the nation clearly cannot truly resolve such contradictions. These conflicts gained a retaliatory narrative possibility in the 1980s, when, for example, Zhang Yigong in "The Story of the Prisoner Li Tongzhong" ("Fanren Li Tongzhong de gushi") sought to rewrite this type of work. Likewise, the contradictions and conflicts expressed conceptually clearly cannot be resolved by resorting to the mode of class struggle between enemy and self. On the contrary, this mode obscured or confused the distinction between real politics [realpolitik] and cultural politics.

During this period, class struggle was understood via the model of internal or external collaboration, treating the traditional enemy classes (such as landlords or merchant capitalists) as part of the newly arisen special privileges class and as the class basis of individualistic thoughts. The problem with this model lies in the fact that, in the process of its concrete practice, various interfering forces could easily turn the focus to the outside of socialism, attributing the problems to the corrupting and tempting power of external class enemies.

As a result, certain elements of crisis within socialism—such as alienation—were bypassed. What is more, unconstrained representations of this enemy-self relationship constituted another major factor behind the expansion of class struggle. In a certain sense, the exaggerated narration of the residual power of traditional enemy classes promoted in the 1960s allowed discriminatory violence (especially toward children of bad family backgrounds) to exist. This was one social reason for Yu's *On Family Origins*. With the expansion of class struggle, the phrase *digging deep* floated to the surface and became one of the most popularly circulated concepts of the Cultural Revolution. The direct consequence of digging deep was that all people felt themselves in danger. As this class struggle mode grew increasingly political—in terms of focusing on people's political positions and attitudes—it became manipulatable by power politics. Consequently, this class struggle not only did not overcome the crisis of socialism, [but] in fact it accelerated the production of oppositional forces within socialism while suppressing the genuine antisystemic forces and preventing the formation of a true resistance politics.

I do not mean to fundamentally negate the legitimacy of class struggle. On the contrary, I think that the problems of the 1960s reveal an overreliance on the traditional mode of class struggle and a lack of formal innovation. What transpired not only concealed the complexity of the issues, it was also crude and violent. The more serious resulting problem was that this violent form generated the retaliatory narration of the 1980s, which often targeted this form of class struggle consciously or unconsciously, without paying attention to the real problems concealed within the issue of class itself.

There have been many academic works on the Cultural Revolution. Even though not all of them are satisfactory, at least they have uncovered the tip of the iceberg. The problem is that much of the scenic view is limited by the height of the fences erected by the Party, which direct our focus mainly on narrating power struggles. Such a focus and narratives have so far taken the place of substantive analyses of all the complex factors of this historic time.

Even though description of this historic time is not my major concern in this research project, nevertheless I think that in a certain sense we can still view the movement that erupted in 1966 as a temporal continuation of the overcoming of the crisis in socialism. In what follows I will briefly review the New Thought Trend (otherwise known as the "heretical thought trend" [*yiduan sichao*]) that occurred during the Cultural Revolution. I do so mainly because the New Thought Trend debate in many aspects touched on elements of crisis within socialism that had already appeared in the early 1960s and offered its own way of solving the crisis. What is more, the New Thought Trend debate had a relatively strong theoretical orientation, and its spread during the Cultural Revolution presaged the debates of the 1980s.

Much of what constituted the New Thought Trend remains debated today. One broad interpretation includes many heretical views from the early Cultural Revolution, including not only Yu's *On Family Origins* but also the bloodline theory of Tan Lifu and more.[12] But here I focus on the trend represented by the 1967 "On the New Thought Trend: 'Declaration of the April Third Faction,'" which includes Yang Xiguang's (Yang Xiaokai's) "Whither China?"; "Declaration of the Beidou School," "How to Understand Proletarian Political Revolution," and "Declaration of the Bei, Jue, and Yang Faction"—*bei* refers to the Beidou School; *jue* means "determination" from "Juexin ba wuchan jieji wenhuadageming jinxing daodi de wuchan jieji gemingpai lianluozhan" (Network Outpost of Proletarian Revolution Determined to Fully Implement Proletarian Cultural Revolution); and *yang* is an abbreviation for "Yangzijiang pinglun" (*Yangzijiang Review*) [which published the aforementioned "Declaration" and a few other pieces]—as well as the "Yiqie weile jiuda" (All for the Ninth Congress) produced by the "Shanghai zhongxuesheng chuanlian hui" (Shanghai's Zhongchuan Association or the Shanghai Middle School Movement Association).[13] Li Yizhe's 1974 "Guayu shehuizhuyi de minzhu yu fazhi" (On the Democracy and Legal System of Socialism) can be seen as the conclusion of this trend of thought. Even though this so-called New Thought Trend had different perspectives that were not always expressed very clearly, we can still tease out a trajectory of the change in thought and orientation from a radical Paris Commune–style idea of democracy to an idea focused on legal democratic systems with hints of liberalism. The evolution of thought in this process remains an extremely important area of research.

One relatively evident characteristic of the New Thought Trend lies in its direct reaction to 1967. In that year, with the establishment of the Revolutionary Committees (*geming weiyuanhui*), society began to see traces of the

---

12. For example, Song Yongyi and Sun Dajin, eds., *Wenhuadageming he ta de yiduan sichao* [The Great Cultural Revolution and its heretical thought trend] (Hong Kong: Tianyuan Shuwu, 1997). The various New Thought Trend materials cited in the present chapter all come from the resources collected in this book.

13. Tr.: All of these essays and posters were extremely important mass intellectual and political statements that were part of the huge public debates of the time. They often were mimeographed and passed from hand to hand, posted on billboards, torn down, reposted, and so on. The situation was chaotic but also quite intellectually lively. Most of the authors paid dearly for their intellectual participation.

reemergence of institutions. But the anti-institutional radicalism that had formed in 1966 had not yet abated; on the contrary, it came into intense conflict with this turn toward reinstitutionalization. Some relatively vague ideas became clearer and began to be expressed through various means. Today, the reason why the declaration of the Beijing April Third Faction [in 1967] has received attention from researchers is largely because, first, it used the term *new thought trend*, and second, it points out in no uncertain terms the acute conflict between "people with special privileges and the [ordinary] people" (*tequan renwu he renmin*). It also applied Marxism in its analysis: "Socialist society is born out of capitalist society. The traces of capitalist society's distribution system and legal system cannot be eliminated immediately." Meanwhile, they [members of the April Third Faction] argued that power could corrupt the leading class of socialist society. Therefore, they further argued that the Cultural Revolution struggle ought to center on the redistribution of power and that this struggle ought to be continual and enduring. Because the appearance of the April Third Faction was to a large extent a challenge to the "Associative" (*liandong*) thought trend (whose advocates supported the bloodline theory), some researchers believe that this political manifesto of the April Third Faction is in effect a continuation of the anti–special privileges idea of Yu's *On Family Origins*, and that it later influenced Yang Xiguang's "Whither China?"[14]

Anti–special privileges thought sparked much consideration of the nature of power and even of the state, constituting an important arena of thinking by folk intellectual groups. For example, in a big-character poster written by "Cao Sixin" (a name that mimics in reverse the pronunciation of New Thought Trend: *xin sichao*) titled "A Perspective That Should Be Made Clear," the author quoted extensively from Marxist state theory and stressed that "the state is merely a disaster that the proletariat must inherit after seizing government power" ([Friedrich] Engels), "the state is a force produced out of society that stands above society and daily grows distant from it. Consequently, the proletariat not only must seize state power, it also must eliminate the organs that manifest this distanced power of the state" ([Vladimir] Lenin), and so on. The article then further emphasized the importance of the oversight of state power by the masses, indicating that "the state institutions during the seventeen years, due to a lack of effective oversight by the revolutionary masses, allowed the most dangerous class enemies of the proletariat

14. Song Yongyi and Sun Dajin, eds., *Wenhuadageming he ta de yiduan sichao*, 244.

to hide within the government structure." Even the "revolutionary committee," a "new-born thing of the Great Proletarian Cultural Revolution," "still carries traces of the old because it was born of the old form." More important, "who gives the revolutionary committee its power? The working class gives it; the poor and middle peasants give it; the working people who are more than 90 percent of the population give it." In another article, "Guanyu gongdaihui jiandu geweihui de kouhao bao" (Report on Workers' Committee Oversight of the Revolutionary Committee's Slogans), the same author [Cao Sixin] notes more clearly: "We must not only overthrow the capitalist roaders, we must also eliminate the conditions that produce capitalist roaders. Continually reforming state structure and gradually guaranteeing mass oversight in its organization, and making the state structure connect closely with the masses, is an important measure at present to counter and guard against revisionism."[15] In a certain sense, one could even say that this was a kind of continuation of the Anshan Steel Charter. If we say the Anshan Steel Charter emphasized the legitimacy of [the factory's] Party committee's oversight of the power of the factory manager (the single leader system), in these articles it was the legitimacy of the masses' oversight of the political party that was stressed. Here, the thinking about power began to extend to the level of the Party-state.

At the time, these ideas of Cao Sixin were not unique. They permeated the entire New Thought Trend. Yang Xiguang's "Whither China?" was and is [still] considered a representative work of the New Thought Trend. In it, Yang not only criticized the "'bureaucratic' class that was formed during the seventeen years," he also argued that the "revolutionary committee" was merely a "fake 'commune' usurped by the bourgeoisie"; all its formation did was "fire individuals, while not overthrowing the special privilege class, and not smashing the rotten old state apparatus." Even more radically, he proposed the need for "a military force organized by the revolutionary people themselves . . . relying on military force to seize government power and relying on internal revolution for war."

Yet simply understanding the New Thought Trend as a theory of anarchism is not at all accurate. To the contrary, Paris Commune–style democracy

---

15. Quoted in Xiao Fan, "Guoqu yu sixiang: 'Wenge' huiyi lu (jiexuan)" [The past and thought: Reminiscences of the 'Cultural Revolution' (selections)," in *Juannian de yipie: Mengmeng jinian wenji* [A stroke of longing: Collection commemorating Mengmeng] (internal publication), 249, 252. Tr.: As explained in chapter 6, "internal publications" are Party publications that are not disseminated publicly. Historical internal publications are often now accessible to researchers, but they are rarely paginated and have no publication information attached.

supports this so-called New Thought Trend. And the New Thought Trend criticized the revolutionary committee established in 1967 precisely because it betrayed the commune principle. Thus those thinkers wanted to establish a Chinese People's Commune—a new democratic government body styled after the Paris Commune.

As mentioned in chapter 2, in 1926, Mao had published "The Importance of Commemorating the Paris Commune" ("Jinian bali gongshe de zhongyao yiyi"). In the article, he concluded that there were two reasons for the failure of the Paris Commune. One was that it did not have a united, focused, and disciplined party to lead it. The other was that it was too accommodating and benevolent toward its enemies.[16] In this we can see clearly the influence of Leninism. But in commemorating the ninety-fifth anniversary of the Paris Commune uprising in March 1966, greater emphasis was placed on the election system of the commune (for example, the principle that the people have the right to elect, to oversee, and to relieve officials of their duties), the pioneering revolutionary spirit exhibited by the masses (for example, "one liberates oneself"), and so forth. The "Chinese Communist Party Central Committee Decision on the Great Proletarian Cultural Revolution," abbreviated as the "Sixteen Points," which was passed on August 8, 1966, clearly noted that "the Cultural Revolution Subcommittee, the members of the Cultural Revolution Committee, and the birth of the Cultural Revolution Congress should be like the Paris Commune. They must enact a comprehensive election system ... representatives elected to the Cultural Revolution subcommittee, the Cultural Revolution committee, and the Cultural Revolution Congress can be criticized at any time by the masses. If one does not live up to his duties, then through mass debate representatives can be reelected or removed." Clearly, the "Sixteen Points," the New Thought Trend, and the Paris Commune all share a common ideal [which is radical democracy]. The problem lies in why the initiators of the movement based on this concept of commune did not carry through with it, especially in the institutional arrangement of the Revolutionary Committee. This is one reason why [advocates of] the New Thought Trend believed that the leaders of the Cultural Revolution had betrayed the Cultural Revolution. While there are complex reasons for this that await further research, speaking generally, the gradual retreat of the commune [political] ideal exposed the paradox and split between Mao's personal

16. Mao Zedong, "Jinian bali gongshe de zhongyao yiyi" [The importance of commemorating the Paris Commune], in *Mao Zedong wenji* [Collected writings of Mao Zedong] (Beijing: Renmin Chubanshe, 1993), 1:35.

theoretical ideas and his political practices. This paradox and split was classically represented in the "January Storm" in Shanghai in 1967. The establishment of the Shanghai People's Commune rapidly caused ripples at the highest levels of the state. One reason for this was that it touched on the question of the state system. One researcher has pointed out that, pressured by the majority in the Politburo of the Central Committee and considering the complexity of state system reform, [the top leaders] thought it would be better to call the People's Commune a Revolutionary Committee. This Revolutionary Committee followed the principle of the three-in-one system, which referred to an organizational form consisting of the revolutionary masses, the revolutionary cadres, and the revolutionary army. Instead of the Paris Commune's universal voting system, this system readopted the appointment system.[17] Clearly, the issue of the state system became a key problem, but the problem was not that simple, for it also touched on how to govern the state, including the model that involved bureaucratic hierarchy. At the same time, a more important point was that the introduction of this Paris Commune principle implied a challenge to Leninism. That is, it opposed ceding individual power to the political party and insisted that people participate in direct elections and liberate themselves and their pioneering revolutionary spirit. This explains why, after 1968, the New Thought Trend was destined to be severely suppressed.

Clearly, during the Cultural Revolution, resources for overcoming the crisis of socialism gradually turned to the organizational mode and political notions of the Paris Commune. However, the possibility of enacting all of that remained extremely slim. The radical democratic tendency, including total negation of specialization, not only could not easily overcome the international or geopolitics of the time, it also faced many institutional hurdles within the country. However, its clearly articulated idea of antibureaucracy and anti–special privileges, including the various imagined institutional arrangements such as oversight of power, was extended into the 1980s. From this we can see that the Cultural Revolution is not devoid of theoretical content, as some people think.

More worthy of our attention is perhaps Li Yizhe's "On the Democracy and Legal System of Socialism" big-character poster that appeared in 1974. In it, he on the one hand inherited the New Thought Trend idea of antibureaucracy and anti–special privileges, yet on the other hand he proposed for the first

---

17. Hu Angang, *Mao Zedong he wenge* [Mao Zedong and cultural revolution] (Hong Kong: Dafeng Chubanshe, 2008), 216.

time the concept of "democracy and [a] legal system." This concept demanded the elimination of speech crimes, relying on the law to protect the material interests of workers and peasants, and emphasized opposition to feudalism, the rule of rites, and the rule of men.[18] These three points in essence constituted the thought of the 1980s. Li's article summarized the significance of the Cultural Revolution as "training the people to liberate themselves with their own revolutionary democratic spirits," where there were "constitutionally guaranteed freedoms of speech . . . as well as the constitutionally not-yet-recognized but nevertheless practiced freedom of association." The theoretical sources of Li's big-character poster are mixed and complex, incorporating democratic ideas of the Paris Commune and ideas of legalism. It is difficult to say that Li's poster demonstrated a kind of liberal constitutional democracy, but its ideas are certainly quite different from those of the 1967–68 New Thought Trend.

If we say that the theoretical resources of the 1967–68 New Thought Trend originated from the Paris Commune and Marx's and Engels's descriptions of it, then Li's poster in contrast turned more toward sources external to socialism. Even though at present I am not entirely clear on Li's theoretical background, there are evident traces that explain the change in ideology. I point this out because I wish to indicate that [events in] the decade of the 1980s did not happen out of the blue. Rather, it was the result and consequence of the crisis of socialism and the ideas and practices that emerged to overcome these crises. This result and consequence make evident the social efforts to overcome the crisis and at the same time also indicate the difficulties in finding resources to overcome the crises from within existing socialist theory. On the one hand, the 1980s demonstrated a society's vital energy for self-rejuvenation, but on the other hand, it [the decade] also manifested many historical contingencies, when [those leading] the efforts to find resources to resolve the socialist crisis turned to the West. The 1980s implied the birth of a new and greater crisis.

III. The Intellectual Transition of the 1980s

A detailed discussion of the 1980s is not my task here; it is one of my other research projects. Yet the decade of the 1980s has already become an important narrative realm whose importance lies in the fact that if we do not understand the complex evolution of the prior thirty years, we have no way to truly

---

18. Tr.: The point here is that Li's article began to argue for the "rule of law" rather than Party or charismatic rule. The rule of law was understood to be less capricious than the rule of one man or the Party.

understand the 1980s. By the same token, if we do not understand the 1980s, then we similarly cannot understand the many-layered logic connecting the historical movements of the earlier thirty years with the later thirty. Therefore, in the sixty years of contemporary Chinese history, the 1980s was an extremely important era of transition. It presages the gradual entrance of China into the world system, and the end of the 1980s also signified the end of the twentieth century because, in the words of certain theorists [such as Li Zehou and Liu Zaifu], it bade "farewell to revolution" (*gaobie geming*).[19]

In a multilayered narrative perspective, the 1980s seems muddled and even chaotic, which precisely indicates the richness of the decade. What I must point out here, however, is that the temporality of the 1980s is equally important, both regarding the time within the decade—including how we interpret the significance of the first three years (1976–79)—and regarding the time outside the decade, such as how we understand the historical connections between the 1980s and other decades. Some materials touch on the historical origins of the 1980s, origins that obviously are not necessarily all based on the same logic. For example, in the narratives of some researchers, we can see that the mainstream domestic trend in 1975 was thorough rectification [of the Party and state]. But in fact, Mao had earlier already said that "the Great Proletarian Cultural Revolution has already lasted eight years. Now, stability and unity are the best. The Party and the military must unite." Some coincidental political occurrences also happened at this time. Following the 1972 Shanghai Communiqué, U.S. President Gerald Ford visited China in 1975 to talk about the establishment of diplomatic relations between the United States and China. It was also in this year that Chiang Kai-shek passed away in Taiwan, and Chiang Ching-kuo succeeded him as chairman of the Nationalist Party. It was these developments in both international and domestic affairs that led the Communist central government to release detained ranking party, government, military, and special members of the Nationalist Party. According to one researcher, Mao also wrote on the Public Security Bureau's report "Instructional Report on Dealing with Provincial and Commanding Level Party, Government, Military, and Special Persons" that "[I] suggest releasing them all." Deng Xiaoping further instructed the Public Security Bureau to act according to Mao's instructions. In the process of releasing these prisoners, large meetings were held, and all were given citizenship rights, their release

---

19. Liu Zaifu and Li Zehou, *Gaobie geming* [Farewell to revolution] (Hong Kong: Tiandi Tushu Gongsi, 1995).

papers, a set of winter clothing and underwear, a blanket and hat, shoes and socks, one hundred yuan, and so on. At the same time it was made clear that anyone who wished to return to Taiwan could go and would be offered the means to do so.[20] What can these trivial historical materials explain? Perhaps we can see the political origin of stability and unity, one of the most important concepts of the 1980s. Perhaps we can also identify some signs of the thawing of relations between the two shores (*liang an*) [of the Taiwan Strait] that would happen in the 1980s. This is not insignificant. Even though the 1980s rectification of order changed into the restoration of order, the importance of order was nonetheless repeatedly stressed, and this emphasis necessarily leaned heavily toward the construction of a modern society. Likewise, in the 1980s the political notion of reducing conflicts within the nation gradually turned into a theorized illusion of class harmony. However, it was precisely this modern illusion of great harmony that led to the 1980s pursuit of so-called universality (humanity, shared aesthetics, and so on).[21] Obviously, the decade of the 1980s was not without origins.

Similarly, some scholars have also noticed the historical connections to the 1980s in relation to bildungsroman. For example, in the "Editorial Note on the 1970s Special Issue" ("'Qishi niandai zhuanhao' bianzhe an") of the magazine *Today* (*Jintian*), Bei Dao and Li Tuo emphasize the significance of the 1970s: "the 'generation' that we speak of here is fairly specific, mainly referring to the generation of people who were youth and teenagers in the 1970s. The unique historical environment in which they grew up produced a unique generation of youth, which played a very important and particular role in Chinese history after the Cultural Revolution."[22]

The historical connections remind us of why, after 1976, China did not return to traditional socialism (that of the seventeen years, 1949–66), even though the desire to return to the seventeen years had once been expressed by the mainstream ideology (the "seventeen years" I refer to here are the seventeen years that were repressed by the radicalized political practices [of the continual revolution of the Cultural Revolution decade]). Historical continu-

20. Yu Zhen, "Nie Gannu xingshi dangan" [Criminal case file of Nie Gannu], *Zhongguo zuojia* (2009), 4:6–83.
21. See Cai Xiang, Luo Gang, and Ni Wenjian, "Wenxue: Wuneng de liliang ruhe keneng" [Literature: How the power of the powerless is possible], June 25, 2009, accessed August 10, 2012. http://www.douban.com/group/topic/7075717/.
22. Bei Dao and Li Tuo, "'Qishi niandai zhuanhao' bianzhe an" [Editorial note on the 1970s special issue), *Jintian* 3 (2008).

ity also lies in the fact that, after 1976, China inherited the historical process of the crisis of socialism and efforts to overcome it.

We can consider on many levels why the 1980s refused the possibility of returning to traditional socialism—a refusal that contributed to the intense conflict between the reform faction and the conservative faction. The logical starting point is none other than the concept of reform and opening. For instance, "Banzhuren" (Class Supervisor)[23] [a short story written by Liu Xinwu] stresses a kind of opening of knowledge, even though this opening in the story is limited to reading works like *Niu Mang* (*The Gadfly*) [by Ethel Lilian Voyvich, popular in the Soviet era]. This opening necessarily generated an intense demand for book reading. In Li Honglin's article "Reading Books without Prohibited Areas" ("Dushu wu jingqu"), which was published in the inaugural issue of the magazine *Dushu* (Reading) in early 1979, reading books is extended into a demand for the political rights of democracy:

> In the realm of books, the main issues at present are: good books are scarce, the thinking of some comrades is not yet liberated enough, and the masses still lack the democratic right to read books and are not allowed to drift freely. To adjust to the demands of the [four] modernizations, we urgently want to see more and better books. We should dismantle prohibited areas. As long as they nourish us and assist in the realization of the four modernizations, all books, whether Chinese, foreign, ancient, or modern, should be liberated and made available and be tested in practice.[24]

The political appeal for democracy in the 1980s, especially in the first three years, carried that era's intense demand for reform. In a certain sense, we can see it as an intellectual continuation of Li Yizhe's (1974) big-character poster "On the Democracy and Legal System of Socialism." Replacing the rule of men with the rule of law and autocracy with democracy was one of the most important expressions of thought of the 1980s. In contrast, *feudal* (no matter how imprecise the word may be) became a metaphor for the previous thirty years and thus marked the boundary between the two periods. On the one hand, this distinction drove intellectual innovation in the 1980s, but on the other hand it also produced a new prohibited area of thought—namely, how to discuss the intellectual legacy of socialism.

23. Liu Xinwu, "Banzhuren" [Class supervisor], *Renmin wenxue* [People's literature], 1977, 10:17–30.

24. Li Honglin, "Dushu wu jigqu" [Reading Books without Prohibited Areas], *Dushu* [Reading], 1979, 1:4–9.

More important still may be the understanding of modernization. It was in the 1980s that modernization became a kind of self-evident metadiscourse and gained its authoritative nature. The problem is that a merely technological understanding of modernity can lead to a different logical development—a development from technology worship to institution worship [and then] to ideology worship. The internal force of this logic, no matter how it is theoretically rendered and corrected, makes it very difficult to stop the movement of this logic, a movement that is geared toward imitating the West—from institutional or structural design to cultural production.

Meanwhile, the emotional structure of this society also quietly changed. Through the repeated narration of scar literature, everyone became a victim, from intellectuals to ordinary people; resentment and fear became the most direct emotional reaction to the previous thirty years of Chinese socialism. Meanwhile, the topic of the future was repeatedly brought up—this time the future was clearly defined as Western-style modernity [and modernization]. Even though the state ideology has continued to resort to its old language, under the direct attack of modernity, this ideology has been torn to pieces. From politics to economics, and in the realms of intellectual and everyday life and even of the unconscious, seemingly everywhere impelled by a great force, there was a demand for China to return to the world, despite the fact that China once sought to struggle free of this world and tried to create a different one.

The changes that took place in the 1980s were profound. The newly enlisted intellectual resources formed a powerful force to overcome the crisis of traditional socialism, an overcoming that cannot be called ineffective. And this overcoming was on multiple levels, including the recognition of individual interests and an adjustment of intellectual policy, an adjustment that implied respect for specialization, free space for thought, and so on. But a greater crisis was also produced at the same time. The de facto exiling of egalitarianism has since led to the legitimization of social class differentiation and hence caused more severe polarization. The emphasis on bureaucratic hierarchy in fact eliminated the possibility of mass participation, which led to the disappearance of the politics of respect for the [working] masses. The legitimatization of the lifeworld of the individual was simultaneously accompanied by the withering of the public sphere. Aside from the kind of politics that prevent the masses from entering the public sphere, unbridled personal desires—directly produced by the strong forces of commodity capitalism—in addition to producing a zeal for [meeting] the individual's own needs, produces only apathy toward public affairs. The concept of the [proletariat as] master has died, leaving the subaltern masses to once again become no more than a qualified modern labor force. Labor, once again, entered a state of alienation. The future has been lost, while the West has become China's future. Any kind of innovative thought [in opposition] is labeled a restoration of leftist thought. And so on and so forth.

It goes without saying that the retreat of socialism means the disappearance of the most important counterbalancing power to this kind of modern development. Once the logic of capital becomes the primary force that controls us, it leads to the accumulation and explosion of a different kind of crisis. Thirty years later, we can already feel this crisis acutely.

Of course I do not mean to blame this crisis on the 1980s. Even today I still have great feeling for that era, and moreover it created many historic opportunities and opened us to a wide horizon. The issue is that we must rethink the 1980s. The 1980s cannot become merely a memorial hall for the generation of the 1980s. Rather it must become a library of history that allows us to read repeatedly. What we must also repeatedly read are the first thirty years of Chinese socialism, not only to see why its legitimacy produced its irrationality but also to examine its theoretical limitations. As I have mentioned above, the changes from the Paris Commune–style radical democracy of the early Cultural Revolution to the later legal democracy of Li Yizhe are themselves important research topics.

Concluding Remarks

I think that for any serious thinker, discussing and studying Chinese socialism does not imply that he or she desires to return to that era—that would be too simplistic. But we still need this kind of debate and discussion, because we not only need to respond to Chinese socialism as a period of history, but more important, we need to respond to the ideals of that history. In responding to the ideals of revolution, we debate not only their legitimacy but also how the legitimacy produced its irrationality. We not only debate its great success but also its failures and lessons—of course, failures in a relative sense. As long as we still support the ideals—that aim at liberating labor and the working class from a state of alienation—then we must treat our own history seriously, including the literary history of this period. In this sense, history has already become a living library, available for us to read anytime and use repeatedly.

In this library, the most fundamental theme remains: what should the world be? The importance of imagination is highlighted with this question. If we are not satisfied with the arrangement of the current order, then we should confront the same question again: how do we want the world to be? As soon as we seek to revisit the issues regarding the world order, we will advance again toward politics. In this sense, I believe that behind the literary always lurks the political. Or perhaps the political itself already constitutes the literary.

BIBLIOGRAPHY

Ai Wu. *Bailian cheng'gang* [Steeled and tempered]. New ed. Beijing: Renmin Wenxue Chubanshe, 1983.
———. [Comrade Ai Wu's letters to Comrade Huang Zuliang on *Bailian cheng'gang*]. In Ai Wu, *Bailian Cheng'gang* [Steeled and tempered]. New ed. Beijing: Renmin Wenxue Chubanshe, 1983.
An Ziwen. "Peiyang geming jiebanren shi dang de yixiang zhanlue renwu" [Fostering revolutionary successors is a strategic task for the Party]. *Hongqi* [Red flag], no. 17 and 18 (1964): 1–13.
Anderson, Benedict. *Imagined Communities: Reflections on the Origin and Spread of Nationalism*. London: Verso, 1983.
"Anshan shiwei guanyu gongye zhanxianshang de jishu geming he jishu geming yundong kaizhan qingkuang de baogao" [Report of the Anshan City Committee regarding the beginning of the movement for technological reform and technological revolution].
Arendt, Hannah. *On Revolution*. New York: Penguin, 1990.
Ba Jin. *Jia* [Family]. Shanghai: Shanghai Kaiming Shudian, 1933.
———. Preface to *Shanghai shinian wenxue xuanji: Duanpian xiaoshuo xuan 1949–1959* [Selected literary works from ten years in Shanghai: Short stories, 1949–1959]. Shanghai: Shanghai Wenyi Chubanshe, 1959.
Badiou, Alain. "The Communist Hypothesis." *New Left Review* 49 (January–February 2008): 29–42.
Bai Wei. *Kenhuang qu* [Reclaiming wasteland]. 2 vols. Beijing: Zuojia Chubanshe, 1963.

Baudrillard, Jean. *The Consumer Society: Myths and Structures.* London: Sage, 1998.
———. *The System of Objects.* Translated by James Benedict. New York and London: Verso, 1996.
Bauman, Zygmunt. *In Search of Politics.* Stanford, CA: Stanford University Press, 1999.
———. *Liquid Modernity.* Cambridge, UK: Polity, 2000.
Bei Dao and Li Tuo. "'Qishi niandai zhuanhao' bianzhe an" [Editorial note on the 1970s special issue]. *Jintian* [Today] (2008).
Bell, Daniel. *The Cultural Contradictions of Capitalism.* New York: Basic, 1976.
Berlin, Isaiah. *The Roots of Romanticism.* Princeton, NJ: Princeton University Press, 2001.
Berman, Marshall. *All That Is Solid Melts into Air.* New York: Simon and Schuster, 1982.
"Bianzhe de hua" [Editor's statement], *Hongqi piaopiao* [Red flags flying]. Beijing: Zhongguo Qingnian Chubanshe, 1957, 1.
Bo Yibo. *Ruogan zhongda juece yu shijian de huigu* [Remembering a few major decisions and incidents]. Beijing: Zhonggong Zhongyang Dangxiao Chubanshe, 1991.
Button, Peter. *Configurations of the Real in Chinese Literary and Aesthetic Modernity.* Leiden: Brill, 2009.
Cai Rongtian, ed. *Shanxi wenxue wushinian zongheng lun* [A comprehensive discussion of fifty years of Shanxi literature]. Taiyuan: Shanxi Renmin Chubanshe, 2000.
Cai Xiang. "1970: Modai huiyi" [1970: End of an era of memories]. *Jintian* [Today], fall 2008.
———. *Xia yu yi—wuxia xiaoshuo yu Zhongguo wenhua* [Knight-errant and meaning—stories of knights-errant and Chinese culture]. Beijing: Shiyue Wenyi Chubanshe, 1993.
Cai Xiang, Luo Gang, and Ni Wenjian. "Wenxue: Wuneng de liliang ruhe keneng" [Literature: How the power of the powerless is possible]. June 25, 2009. Accessed August 10, 2012. http://www.douban.com/group/topic/7075717/.
Cai Yuanpei. "Laogong shensheng" [The sacredness of labor]. In *Wusi yundong de wenxuan* [Selected essays from the May Fourth Movement]. Beijing: Sanlian Shudian, 1979.
Cao Ming. *Chengfeng polang* [Riding the Winds and Waves]. Beijing: Zuojia Chubanshe, 1959.
Cao Yu. *Richu* [The sun rises]. *Wenxue yuekan*, vol. 1, no. 4 (1936).
Castoriadis, Cornelius. "Mao zhuyi yu faguo zhishi fenzi" [Maoism and French intellectuals]. *Ershiyi shiji pinglun* [Twenty-first century review], no. 36 (August 1996).
Chatterjee, Partha. "Community in the East." *Economic and Political Weekly* 33, no. 6 (1998): 277–82.
———. *The Politics of the Governed.* New York: Columbia University Press, 2004.
Chen Dengke. *Feng lei* [Storm]. Beijing: Zhongguo Qingnian Chubanshe, 1964.
———. "Tongzhi, laoshi, zhanyou—yi Qian Yi" [Comrade, teacher, comrade in arms—remembering Qian Yi]. In *Hongqi iaopiao* [Red flags flying], 1. Beijing: Zhongguo Qingnian Chubanshe, 1957.
Chen Duxiu. "Laodongzhe de juewu" [The awakening of laborers]. In *Wusi yundong de wenxuan* [Selected essays from the May Fourth Movement]. Beijing: Sanlian Shudian, 1979.
Chen Jianhua. *Geming yu xingshi: Mao Dun zaoqi xiaoshuo de xiandaixing zhankai* [Revolution and form: The depiction of modernity in Mao Dun's early writing]. Shanghai: Fudan Daxue Chubanshe, 2007.
Chen Lide. *Qianqu* [Pioneer]. Beijing: Zuojia Chubanshe, 1964.

Chen Sihe. "Minjian de chenfu: cong kangzhan dao wenge wenxueshi de yige jieshi" [The ups and downs of the folk: An explanation of the literary history from the War of Resistance to the Cultural Revolution]. In *Ershi shiji Zhongguo wenxueshi lun* [On the history of twentieth-century Chinese literature], edited by Wang Xiaoming. Shanghai: Dongfang Chuban Zhongxin, 2003.

Chen Ye. *Taiqian, muhou* [On stage and back stage]. Unpublished MA thesis, Shanghai University, 2009.

Chen Yinque. "Feng Youlan Zhexueshi shangce shencha baogao" [Review report on Feng Youlan's *History of Chinese Philosophy*]. In *Chen Yinque ji: jinmingguan conggao erbian* [Collected writings of Chen Yinque: second volume of the jinmingguan collection]. Beijing: Sanlian Shudian, 2001.

Chen Yiqun. "Geming qingnian yinggai zenyang kandai lixiang he gongxian" [How should revolutionary youths understand ideals and contribution?]. *Zhongguo qingnian* [Chinese youth], no. 5 (1964): 16.

Chen Yong. "Xiao Yemu chuangzuo de yixie qingxiang" [Some tendencies in Xiao Yemu's creative work]. *Renmin ribao*, June 10, 1951.

Chen Yun. *Nianqing de yidai* [The young generation]. *Juben*, no. 8 (1963): 2–32.

Chou, Li-po [Zhou Libo]. *Great Changes in the Mountain Village*. Translated by Derek Bryan. 2 vols. Peking: Foreign Language Press, 1961.

Chu Po [Qu Bo]. *Tracks in the Snowy Forest*, translated by Sidney Shapiro. Peking: Foreign Language Press, 1962.

Cong Shen. "'Qianwan buyao wangji' zhuti de xingcheng" [The subject matter of *Never Forget*]. *Xiju bao*, 4, 1964.

———. "Zhu ni jiankang" [Wish you good health]. *Juben*, no. 10/11 (1963): 4–45.

Cook, Alexander, ed. *Mao's Little Red Book: A Global History*. Cambridge: Cambridge University Press, 2014.

Cui Zhiyuan. "Angang xianfa yu hou futezhuyi" [Angang Constitution and post-Fordism]. *Dushu* [Readings], no. 3 (1996): 13–23.

Deleuze, Gilles, and Félix Guattari. *Kafka: Toward a Minor Literature*. Translated by Dana Polan. Minneapolis: University of Minnesota Press, 1986.

———. *What Is Philosophy?* Translated by Hugh Tomlinson and Graham Burchell. New York: Columbia University Press, 1994.

Deng Youmei. "Zai xuanya shang" [On cliff]. *Wenyi xuexi*, 1 (1957).

Ding Ling. "Kuadao xinde shidai lai—tan zhishifenzi de jiu xingqu yu gongnongbing wenyi" [Stepping into the new era: On the old interests of intellectuals and worker-peasant-soldier culture]. *Wenyi bao* 2, no. 11 (1950).

———. *The Sun Shines Over the Sanggan River*. Translated by Gladys Yang and Yang Xianyi. Beijing: Foreign Languages Press, 1984.

———. "Zuowei yizhong qingxiang laikan—gei Xiao Yemu tongzhi de yifengxin" [Seen as a tendency: A letter to Xiao Yemu]. *Wenyi bao*, August 25, 1951.

Ding Yi. "Bai Mao Nü Zaiban Qianyan" [Introduction to the republication of *White-Haired Girl*]. *Bai Mao Nü* [White Haired Girl]. Huadong Xinhua Shudian, 1949.

Ding Yunliang. "Wenhua suku: 1950 niandai shanghai gongren zhi yanshuo zhengzhi" [Speaking cultural bitterness: 1950s Shanghai workers speech about politics]. In *Refeng xueshu* [Scholarly Trends], edited by Wang Xiaoming and Cai Xiang, 1:112–30. Guilin: Guangxi Shida Chubanshe, 2008.

Dirlik, Arif. *Anarchism in the Chinese Revolution*. Berkeley: University of California Press, 1992.

———. *Origins of Chinese Communism*. New York: Oxford University Press, 1989.
Dong Zhilin. *Jiu meng xin zhi: "Shiqinian" xiaoshuo lungao* [Old dream, new knowledge: Writings on the "seventeen-year" fiction]. Guilin: Guangxi Shifan Daxue Chubanshe, 2004.
Du Pu. "'Zuoqing lilun yu shehui zhuyi quzhe renshi de guanxi" [The relationship between "left-leaning" theory and the complex understanding of socialism]. In *Huishou "wenge": Zhongguo shinian "wenge" fenxi yu fansi* [Reexamining the "Cultural Revolution": Analyses of and reflections on China's ten-year "Cultural Revolution"]. Beijing: Zhonggong Dangshi Chubanshe, 2000.
Du Runsheng. *Du Runsheng zishu: Zhongguo nongcun tizhi biange zhongda juece jishi* [Du Runsheng remembers: Memories of the important decisions on China's village structural transformation]. Beijing: Renmin Chubanshe, 2005.
Duara, Prasenjit. *Culture, Power, and the State: Rural North China, 1900–1942*. Stanford, CA: Stanford University Press, 1988.
Fei, Xiaotong. *From the Soil: The Foundations of Chinese Society: A Translation of Fei Xiatong's "Xiangtu Zhongguo."* With an introduction and epilogue by Gary G. Hamilton and Wang Zheng. Berkeley: University of California Press, 1992.
Feng Deying. *Ku cai hua* [Bitter flowers]. Beijing: Jiefangjun Wenyishe, 1958.
———. "Xie zai xinban 'sanhua' qianmian" [Preface to the new editions of the "three flowers"]. Shenyang: Chunfeng Wenyi Chubanshe, 2003.
Feng Zhi. *Dihou wugongdui* [Behind the enemy lines]. Beijing: Jiefangjun Wenyi Chubanshe, 1979.
Fitzgerald, John. *Awakening China: Politics, Culture, and Class in the Nationalist Revolution*. Stanford, CA: Stanford University Press, 1996.
Foucault, Michel. "What Is Enlightenment?" In *The Foucault Reader*, edited by Paul Rabinow, 32–50. New York: Pantheon, 1984.
Fu Chaowu, dir. *Jiating wenti* [Family problems], 1964.
Gan Feng. "He zichanjieji xianglezhuyi huaqing jiexian" [Take a stand against bourgeois hedonism], *Zhongguo qingnian*, no. 16 (1963): 12–13.
Gao Jie, ed. *Ma Feng, Xi Rong yanjiu ziliao* [Ma Feng, Xi Rong research materials]. Taiyuan: Shanxi Renmin Chubanshe, 1985.
Gao Zehong. "Wuchanjieji de xingfuguan jiushi wei geming er douzheng" [Proletarian view of happiness stems from struggle for the revolution]. *Zhongguo qingnian*, 4 (1965): 20–21.
———. "Xiangle zhishang shi zichanjieji xingfuguan de hexin" [Hedonism is the core of bourgeois view of happiness]. *Zhongguo qingnian*, no. 3 (1965): 24–25.
Gaoji xiaoxue keben: yuwen [Advanced elementary school textbook: Chinese]. Vol. 3. Beijing: Renmin Jiaoyu Chubanshe, 1958.
Geertz, Clifford. *The Interpretation of Cultures*. New York: Basic, 1973.
Gellner, Ernest. *Nations and Nationalism*. Ithaca, NY: Cornell University Press, 1983.
"'Geming qingnian yinggai zenyang kandai lixiang he gongxian' wenti taolun" [On discussions regarding "how revolutionary youths should understand ideals and contribution"]. *Zhongguo qingnian*, no. 7 (1964): 27–29.
Giddens, Anthony. *The Consequences of Modernity*. Stanford, CA: Stanford University Press, 1990.
———. *Modernity and Self-Identity*. Stanford, CA: Stanford University Press, 1991.
Gong Pengcheng. *Da xia* [The great knight-errant]. Taipei: Taiwan Jinguan Chunbanshe, 1987.

Gongren Chubanshe, ed. *Gongren wenhua keben* [Textbook for worker culture], 3 volumes. Beijing: Gongren Chubanshe, 1950.

Gouldner, Alvin Ward. *The Future of Intellectuals and the Rise of the New Class*. New York: Seabury, 1979.

Gronow, Jukka. *The Sociology of Taste*. London, New York: Routledge, 1997.

"Guanyu Heluxiaofu de jia gongchanzhuyi jiqi zai shijie lishi shang de jiaoxun" [On Khrushchev's phony communism and its lesson for world history]. *Renmin ribao* [People's daily], July 14, 1964.

Guo Moruo. "Chi fandong wenyi" [Denounce antirevolutionary culture]. In *Zhongguo dangdai wenxueshi: shiliao xuan* (shang) [History of contemporary Chinese literature: original historical materials, volume one], edited by Hong Zicheng. Wuhan: Changjiang Wenyi Chubanshe, 2002.

———. "'Xin ernü yingxiong zhuan' xu" [Preface to New heroic sons and daughters], Beijing: Renmin Chubanshe, 1956.

Guo Yuhua and Sun Liping. "Suku: yizhong guojia guannian xingcheng de zhongjie jizhi" [Speaking bitterness: A form of mediating mechanism for the formation of peasants' national consciousness]. *Zhongguo xueshu* [Chinese scholarship] no. 4 (2002).

"Guowuyuan guanyu chuli fandongde, yinhuide, huangdande shukan tuhua de zhishi" [State Council instructions on how to deal with antirevolutionary, obscene, and preposterous books, magazines, and pictures]. In *Zhongguo dangdai wenxueshi. shiliao xuan* [Contemporary Chinese literature, selected materials], edited by Hong Zicheng, vol. 1. Wuhan: Changjiang Wenyi chubanshe, 2002.

Habermas, Jürgen. "The New Obscurity: The Crisis of the Welfare State and the Exhaustion of Utopian Energies." Translated by Phillip Jacobs. *Philosophy and Social Criticism* 11, no. 2 (1986): 1–18.

Hall, Stuart. Introduction to *Representation: Cultural Representations and Signifying Practices*, edited by Stuart Hall. London: Sage, 1997.

———, ed. *Representation: Cultural Representations and Signifying Practices* London: Sage, 1997.

Hanan, Patrick. *Chinese Fiction of the Late Nineteenth and Early Twentieth Centuries*. New York: Columbia University Press, 2004.

Hang, Krista Van Fleit. *Literature the People Love: Reading Chinese Texts from the Early Maoist Period (1949–1966)*. New York: Palgrave MacMillan, 2013.

Hao Ran. *Yanyang tian* [Sunny days]. Beijing: Zuojia Chubanshe, 1964.

He Qifang. *He Qifang wenji* [Collected writings of He Qifang], vo1. 2. Shijiazhuang: Hebei Renmin Chubanshe, 2000.

Hinton, William. *Fanshen: A Documentary of Revolution in a Chinese Village*. New York: Vintage, 1968.

Hong Zicheng. *Wenti yu fangfa* [Issues and Methods]. Beijing: Sanlian Shudian, 2002.

———, ed. *Zhongguo dangdai wenxueshi: shiliao xuan* (shang) [History of contemporary Chinese literature: original historical materials, volume 1]. Wuhan: Changjiang Wenyi Chubanshe, 2002.

Hook, Sidney. *The Hero in History: A Study in Limitation and Possibility*. New York: John Day, 1943.

Hu Angang. *Mao Zedong he wenge* [Mao Zedong and the Cultural Revolution]. Hong Kong: Dafeng Chubanshe, 2008.

Hu Dongyuan. "Qingnian yinggai you shenmeyang de xingfuguan" [What kind of view of happiness should young people have?], *Zhongguo qingnian*, no. 7 (1963): 15–17.

Hu Qiaomu. "Hu Qiaomu huiyi Mao Zedong" [Hu Qiaomu remembers Mao Zedong]. Beijing: Renmin Chubanshe, 1994.

Huang, Philip. "Whither Chinese Law?" *Modern China* 33, no. 2 (2007): 163–94.

Huang Ziping. "Bing de yinyu yu wenxue shengchan—Ding Ling de 'Zai yiyuan zhong' ji qita" [The metaphoric use of illness and literary production: On Ding Ling's "In the Hospital"]. In *Ershi shiji zhongguo wenxueshi lun* [On the history of twentieth-century Chinese literature], edited by Wang Xiaoming, 2: 65–77. Shanghai: Dongfang Chuban Zhongxin, 2003.

———. *Geming, lishi, xiaoshuo* [Revolution, history, fiction]. Hong Kong: Oxford University Press, 1996.

———. "Geming, xing, changpian xiaoshuo" [Revolution, sex, and the novel]. In *"Huilan zhong" de xushu* [Narration in the "Chalk Circle"]. Shanghai: Shanghai Wenyi Chubanshe, 2001.

———. "Mingyun san chongzou: Jia yu 'jia' yu 'jia zhong ren'" [Life's ensemble of three: *Family*, family, and family members]. In *Geming, lishi, xiaoshuo* [Revolution, history, fiction]. Hong Kong: Oxford University Press, 1996.

Isaacs, Harold R. *Idols of the Tribe: Group Identity and Political Change*. Cambridge, MA: Harvard University Press, 1997.

Jiang Shan, ed. *Gongheguo dang'an* [Archives of the republic]. Beijing: Tuanjie Chubanshe, 1997.

Jin Huifang. "Women fufu liang" [We, a couple]. *Jiefang ribao* [Liberation daily], July 25, 1952.

Kang Zhai. *Kang Zhai xiaoshuo xuan* [Selected stories of Kang Zhai]. Changsha: Hunan Renmin Chubanshe, 1984.

Karatani, Kōjin. *Origins of Modern Japanese Literature*. Translation edited by Brett de Bary. Durham, NC: Duke University Press, 1993.

Kau, Michael Y. M., and John K. Leung, eds. *The Writings of Mao Zedong 1949–1976*. Armonk, NY: M. E. Sharpe, 1986.

King, Richard. *Milestones on a Golden Road: Writing for Chinese Socialism*. Vancouver: University of British Columbia Press, 2013.

Kuang Xinnian. "Minzu zhuyi, guojia xiangxiang yu xiandai wenxue" [Nationalism, nationalist imaginaries and modern literature], *Shanghai wenlun*, 2007, 2.

———. "People's Literature: An Unfinished Historical Project." In *Debating the Socialist Legacy and Capitalist Globalization in China*, edited by Xueping Zhong and Ban Wang, 253–72. New York: Palgrave Macmillan, 2014.

Larson, Wendy. *From Ah-Q to Lei Feng: Freud and Revolutionary Spirit in 20th Century China*. Stanford, CA: Stanford University Press, 2009.

Lefebvre, Henri. "Space: Social Product and Use Value." In *Critical Sociology: European Perspectives*, edited by J. W. Frieberg, 285–95. New York: Halsted, 1979.

Lenin, V. I. "Gongchan zhuyi yundong zhong de 'zuopai youzhibing'" ["Left-wing" communism: an infantile disorder]. In *Lienin xuanji* [Selected works of Lenin], 4. Beijing: Renmin Chubanshe, 1972.

Li Dazhao. "Shumin de shengli" [Victory of the common people]. In *Wusi yundong de wenxuan* [Selected essays from the May Fourth Movement]. Beijing: Sanlian Shudian, 1979.

Li, Gucheng, ed. *A Glossary of Political Terms of the People's Republic of China*. Hong Kong: Chinese University of Hong Kong Press, 1995.

Li Honglin. "Dushu wu jinqu" [Reading books without prohibited areas]. *Dushu*, no. 1 (1979): 4–9.

Li Hui, ed. *Ba da yangbanxi* [Eight model plays]. Beijing: Guanming Ribao Chubanshe, 1995.

Li Jiefei. *Dianxing wentan* [Classical fora]. Wuhan: Hubei Renmin Chubanshe, 2008.

Li Liuru. *Liushinian de bianqian* [Sixty years of transformation]. Revised edition. Vol. 3. Beijing: Renmin Chubanshe, 2005.

Li, Oufan [Leo Oufan Lee]. "Wan Qing wenhua, wenxue yu xiandai xing" [Late Qing culture, literature, and modernity]. In *Liwa he pan lun wenxue* [Discussing literature by Liwa River], edited by Chen Zishan and Luo Gang. Shanghai: Huadong Shifan Daxue Chubanshe, 2006.

Li Tuo. "1985." *Jintian* [Today], nos. 3 and 4 (1991).

Li Xifan. "Geming yingxiong dianxing de xunli" [Overview of revolutionary hero types]. *Wenxue pinglun*, no. 1 (1961): 33–47.

Li Yang. *50–70 niandai Zhongguo wenxue zai jiedu* [Rereading 1950s–1970s Chinese literature]. Jinan: Shandong Jiaoyu Chubanshe, 2003.

Li Yaru, et al. *Duo yin* [Seize the seal]. *Juben* [Drama scripts], no. 3 (1963): 4–37.

Li Zhun. "Li Shuangshuang xiaozhuan" [The story of Li Shuangshuang]. *Renmin wenxue* [People's literature], March 8, 1960.

Liang Bin. *Bo huo ji* [Spreading the fire]. Tianjin: Baihua Wenyi Chubanshe, 1963.

———. *Keep the Red Flag Flying*. Translated by Gladys Yang. Beijing: Foreign Language Press, 1961.

———. "Mantan *Hongqi pu* de chuangzuo." *Renmin wenxue*, no. 6 (1959): 15–26.

Liang Qichao. "Shaonian Zhongguo shuo" [The young China]. In *Liang Qichao xuanji* [Selected works of Liang Qichao], edited by Wu Jiaxun and Li Huanxing. Shanghai: Shanghai Renmin Chubanshe, 1984.

———. "Xin shixue" [New historiography]. In *Qingdai xueshu gailun* [An overview of Qing Dynasty scholarship], edited by Xia Xiaohong. Beijing: Renmin Daxue Chubanshe, 2004.

Liang, Shuming, and Guy S. Alitto. *Has Man a Future? Dialogues with the Last Confucian*. Berlin: Springer, 2013.

Lin, Chun. "The Language of Class in China." In *Transforming Classes: Socialist Register 2015*, edited by Leo Panitch and Gregory Albo, 24–53. London: Merlin, 2014.

———. *The Transformation of Chinese Socialism*. Durham, NC: Duke University Press, 2006.

Liu Ching [Liu Qing]. *The Builders*. Translated by Sidney Shapiro. Peking: Foreign Language Press, 1964.

———. *Chuangye shi* [The builders]. Beijing: Zhongguo Qingnian Chubanshe, 2009.

Liu Xinwu. "Banzhuren" [Class supervisor]. *Renmin wenxue*, no. 10 (1977): 17–30.

Liu Zaifu and Li Zehou. *Gaobie geming* [Farewell to revolution]. Hong Kong: Tiandi Tushu Gongsi, 1995.

Lu Ren, dir. *Li Shuangshuang* (film). Shanghai Film Studio, 1962.

Lu Xun. *Diary of a Madman and Other Stories*. Translated by William A. Lyell. Honolulu: University of Hawaii Press, 1990.

———. "San Xian Ji xuyan" [Introduction to *San xian ji*]. In *Lu Xun quanji* [Complete collection of Lu Xun's works], 4:5. Beijing: Renmin Chubanshe, 2005.

———. "Women xianzai zenyang zuo fuqin" [How can we be fathers today?], in *Lu Xun quanji* [Complete collection of Lu Xun's works], 1:135. Beijing: Renmin Chubanshe, 2005.

Luo Dan. *Fengyu de liming* [The storm of dawn]. Beijing: Zhongguo Qingnian Chubanshe, 1959.

Luo Pinghan. *Dangdai lishi wenti zhaji* [Records of contemporary historical issues]. Vol. 2. Guilin: Guangxi Shida Chubanshe, 2006.

"Luo Ruiqing: Zhenzheng geming, chedi geming de yingxiong" [Real and complete revolutionary heroes]. In *Qingnian yingxiong de gushi* [Stories of young heroes], 2. Beijing: Zhongguo Qingnian Chubanshe, 1965.

Ma Feng, Xi Rong. *Lüliang Yingxiong Zhuan* [Chronicles of the Lüliang heroes]. Beijing: Renmin Wenxue Chubanshe, 1952.

Mao Dun. "'Geming jia 'lian'ai' de gongshi" [The "revolution" plus "love" formula]. In *Mao Dun quanji* [Complete collection of Mao Dun's works], 20: 317–52. Beijing: Renmin Chubanshe, 1990.

———. "Guanyu 'lüliang yingxiong zhun'" [Concerning *Chronicles of the Lüliang Heroes*]. In *Ma Feng, Xi Rong yanjiu ziliao* [Research materials on Ma Feng, Xi Rong], edited by Gao Jie. Taiyuan: Shanxi Renmin Chubanshe, 1985.

———. "Guanyu yishu de jiqiao: zai quanguo qingnian wenxue chuangzuozhe huiyi shang de baogao" [On the techniques of art—Speech at the all-China young literary writers' conference." In *Ershi shiji Zhongguo xiaoshuo lilun ziliao* [Documents on twentieth-century Chinese theories of the novel], edited by Hong Zicheng. Beijing: Beijing Daxue Chubanshe, 1997.

———. *Ziye* [Midnight]. Shanghai: Shanghai Kaiming Shudian, 1933.

Mao Tse-tung [Mao Zedong]. *Selected Works of Mao Tse-tung*, 5 volumes. Peking: Foreign Language Press, 1961.

Mao Zedong. "Farewell to the God of Plague." July 1, 1958. Marxists.org. Accessed April 4, 2015. http://www.marxists.org/reference/archive/mao/selected-works/poems/poems25.htm.

———. *Jianguo yilai Mao Zedong wengao* [Mao Zedong's manuscripts since 1949], 10. Beijing: Zhongyang Wenxian Chubanshe, 1996.

———. *Mao Zedong Wenji* [Collected writings of Mao Zedong], 8 volumes. Beijing: Renmin Chubanshe, 1996.

———. *Mao Zedong xuanji* [Selected writings of Mao Zedong], vols. 1–4, 1966.

Marx, Karl. "Falanxi neizhan" [The civil war in France], *Makesi Engesi xuanji* [Selected works of Marx and Engles], vol. 3. Beijing: Renmin Chubanshe, 1995.

Masao, Sato. "Guanyu weixiao—Tuozhi Yichun he ta de zuoping" [About smiles: Tsuge Yoshiharu and his works]. In *Refeng Xueshu* [Scholarly trends], translated by Sakai Hirobumi [from Japanese to Chinese], vol. 5. Shanghai: Shanghai Renmin Chubanshe, 2010.

Meisner, Maurice J. *Mao's China and After: A History of the People's Republic*. 3rd ed. New York: Free Press, 1999.

———. *Marxism, Maoism, and Utopianism*. Madison: University of Wisconsin Press, 1982.

Meng Yue. "'Baimaonü' yanbian de qishi: jianlun yanan wenyi de lishi duozhixing" [On the evolution of *White-Haired Girl*—A brief discussion of the multiplicity of the history of Yan'an art]. In *Ershi shiji Zhongguo wenxueshi lun* [On the history of twentieth-century Chinese literature], edited by Wang Xiaoming, 2: 185–203. Shanghai: Dongfang Chuban Zhongxin, 2003.

———. *Lishi yu xushu* [History and narrative]. Xi'an: Shaanxi Renmin Jiaoyu Chubanshe, 1988.

———. "Zhongguo wenxue de 'xiandaixing' yu Zhang Ailing" [The "modernity" of Chinese literature and Zhang Ailing]. In *Ershi shiji Zhongguo wenxueshi lun* [On the history of twentieth-century Chinese literature], edited by Wang Xiaoming, 2: 94–111. Shanghai: Dongfang Chuban Zhongxin, 2003.

Mittler, Barbara. *A Continuous Revolution: Making Sense of Cultural Revolution Culture*. Cambridge, MA: Harvard Asia Center Publications, 2012.

Nan Fan. *Hou geming de zhuanyi* [Postrevolution transference]. Beijing: Beijing Daxue Chubanshe, 2005.

Pan Xiao, "Rensheng de daolu weishenme yue zou yue zhai" [Why is life's path becoming narrower and narrower?], *Zhongguo qingnian*, no. 5 (1980): 3–5.

Pang Xianzhi and Jin Chongji, eds. *Mao Zedong zhuan* [Biography of Mao Zedong]. Beijing: Zhongyang Wenxian Chubanshe, 2003.

Qian Liqun. *Wo de jingshen zizhuan* [An autobiography of my spiritual life]. Guilin: Guangxi Shida Chubanshe, 2007.

Qian Mu. *Zhongguo sixiang tongsu jianghua* [Popular talks on Chinese thought]. Beijing: Sanlian Shudian, 2002.

"Qian shifu xue wenhua" [Mr. Qian learns some culture]. *Laodong bao*, June 12, 1952.

Qin Zhaoyang, "Gaizao" ["Re-Education"]. *Renmin wenxue* [People's literature], vol. 3, 1950.

Qiu Chi. "Yu Chen Bo zhi shu" [Letter to Chen Bo]. In *Guwen guanzhi xinbian* [Guwen guanzhi newly edited], edited by Qian Bocheng. Shanghai: Shanghai Guji Chubanshe, 1988.

Qu Bo. *Linhai xueyuan* [Tracks in the snowy forest]. Beijing: Renmin Wenxue Chubanshe, 2005.

Robertson, James Oliver. *American Myth, American Reality*. New York: Hill and Wang, 1981.

Rogaski, Ruth. *Hygienic Modernity: Meanings of Health and Disease of Treaty-Port China*. Berkeley: University of California Press, 2004.

Said, Edward W. *Culture and Imperialism*. New York: A. A. Knopf, 1993.

Schmitt, Carl. *Political Romanticism*. Translated by Guy Oakes. Cambridge, MA: MIT Press, 1986.

Schram, Stuart, ed. *Mao's Road to Power*. Armonk, NY: M. E. Sharpe, 1997.

Schwarcz, Vera. *The Chinese Enlightenment: Intellectuals and the Legacy of the May Fourth Movement of 1919*. Berkeley: University of California Press, 1986.

Schwartz, Benjamin I. *Chinese Communism and the Rise of Mao*. Cambridge, MA: Harvard University Press, 1996.

———. "The Reign of Virtue: Some Broad Perspectives on Leader and Party in the Cultural Revolution." *China Quarterly* 35 (September 1968): 1–17.

Scott, James. *Weapons of the Weak: Everyday Forms of Peasant Resistance*. New Haven, CT: Yale University Press, 1987.

Selden, Mark. *China in Revolution: The Yenan Way*. Cambridge, MA: Harvard University Press, 1971.

———. *China in Revolution: The Yenan Way Revisited*. Armonk, NY: M. E. Sharpe, 1995.

Shao Quanling. "Zai dalian 'nongcun ticai duanpian xiaoshuo chuangzuo zuotanhui' shang de jianghua" [Speech at the "Forum on the rural-themed short story" in Dalian]. In *Zhongguo dangdai wenxue shi: shiliaoxuan* [History of contemporary Chinese literature], edited by Hong Zicheng, 2: 501–11. Wuhan: Changjiang Wenyi Chubanshe, 2002.

Shen Dali. "Bali 'gongshe qiang' kaobian" [Investigations on the Paris Commune Wall]. In Shen Dali, *Bali Shengying* [*Voices and Traces of Paris*]. Beijing: Beijing Press, 1989.

Shen Fu. *Wanzi qianhong zongshi chun* [A riot of color is always spring]. Filmscript. Shanghai: Shanghai Wenyi Chubanshe, 1960.

Shen Ximeng, et al. "Nihongdeng xia de shaobing" [Sentinels under the neon lights]. *Juben*, no. 2 (1963): 2–43.

Shintani Akinoku, ed. *Sulian shi shehuizhuyi guojia ma?* [Is the Soviet Union a socialist country?]. Translated from Japanese by Yu Yiqian. Hong Kong: Xianggang Sanlian Chubanshe, 1970.

Song Yongyi and Sun Dajin, eds. *Wenhuadageming he ta de yiduan sichao* [The Great Cultural Revolution and its heretical thought trend]. Hong Kong: Tianyuan Shuwu, 1997.

Su Li [1]. *Fazhi yu qi bentu ziyuan* [Rule by law and its native resources]. Beijing: Zhongguo Fashi Daxue Chubanshe, 1996.

Su Li [2], dir. *Women cunli de nianqingren* [Young people in our village] I and II, 1959 and 1963.

Su Shigui and Qiu Shi. "Chenggong yihou" [After the success]. *Juben*, no. 8 (1964): 71–86.

Sun Changxi. "Shengchan zhanxianshang de yingxiong, gongren jieji de mofan—shilun Ai Wu zhu *Bailian Cheng'gang* zhong de Qin Degui" [Hero on the production line and model of the working class: a tentative discussion of the character Qin Degui in Ai Wu's *Steeled and Tempered*]. *Wenshi zhe*, no. 10 (1958): 42–46.

Sun Jingrui, *Hongqi chashang Damendao* [Planting the red flag on Damen Island]. Shanghai: Wenyi Chubanshe, 1958.

Sun Li. "Lotus creek." *Lotus Creek and Other Stories*. Beijing: Foreign Language Press, 1982.

———. *Stormy Years*. Translated by Gladys Yang. Beijing: Foreign Language Press, 1982.

Sun Qian. "Qiyi de lihun gushi" [A strange divorce story]. *Changjiang wenyi*, 1956, 1.

Sun Zhongshan. *Sun Zhongshan wenji* [Collected writings of Sun Zhongshan]. Edited by Meng Qingpeng. Beijing: Tuanjie Chubanshe, 1997.

Tang Kexin. "Gu Xiaoju he tade jiemei" [Gu Xiaoju and her sisters]. *Jiefang ribao* [Liberation daily], January 3, 1954.

———. "Wode shifu" [My mentor]. *Jiefang ribao* [Liberation daily], August 23, 1953.

Tang Tao. "Guanyu wenxue yuyan" [On literary language]. *Wenyi yuebao*, no. 8 (1959).

Tang Xiaobing. "'Qianwan buyao wangji' de lishi yiyi: guanyu richang shenghuo de jiaolü jiqi xiandaixing" [The historical significance of "*Never Forget*": Anxiety over everyday life and its modernity]. In *Ershi shiji Zhongguo wenxueshi lun* [On the history of twentieth-century Chinese literature], edited by Wang Xiaoming. Shanghai: Dongfang Chuban Zhongxin, 2003, 2: 176–84.

———. *Zai jiedu: Dazhong wenyi yu yishi xingtai* [Reinterpretation: Ideology and popular literature and art]. 2nd ed. Beijing: Beida Chubanshe, 2007.

Taylor, Charles. "The Politics of Recognition." In *New Contexts of Canadian Criticism*, edited by Ajay Heble, Donna Palmateer Pennee, and J. R. (Tim) Struthers, 98–131. Peterborough, ON: Broadview, 1997.

Townsend, James R., and Brantly Womack. *Politics in China*. 3rd ed. Boston: Little, Brown, 1986.

Viswanathan, Gauri, ed. *Power, Politics and Culture: Interviews with Edward W. Said*. New York: Vintage, 2002.

Vukovich, Daniel. *China and Orientalism: Western Knowledge Production and the P.R.C.* London: Routledge, 2012.

———. "From Charting the Revolution to Charter 2008." In *Culture and Social Transformations: Theoretical Framework and Chinese Context*, edited by Cao Tianyu, Zhong Xueping, Liao Kebin, and Ban Wang. Leiden, the Netherlands: Brill, 2014.

Wallerstein, Immanuel. "Northeast Asia and the World-System." *Korean Journal of Defense Analysis* 19, no. 3 (2007): 7–25.

Wang Anyi. *Qimeng shidai* [The enlightened era]. Beijing: Renmin Wenxue Chubanshe, 2007.

Wang, David Der-wei. *The Monster That Is History*. Berkeley: University of California Press, 2004.

Wang Hongsheng. "Shirun de xushu: Bo'er yu Chen Yingsong" [Humid Narratives: Bauer and Chen Yingsong]. *Shucheng Zazhi* [Journal of book city], no. 11 (2007): 15–16.

Wang Hui. *The End of the Revolution: China and the Limits of Modernity*. London: Verso, 2009.

Wang Jing. *High Culture Fever: Politics, Aesthetics, and Ideology in Deng's China*. Berkeley: University of California Press, 1996.

Wang Meng. *Qinchun wansui* [Long live youth]. Beijing: Renmin Chubanshe, 1979.

———. *Wang Meng zizhuan* [Wang Meng's autobiography]. 2 vols. Guangzhou: Huacheng Chubanshe, 2006–7.

———. "A Young Man Arrives at the Organization Department." In *Literature of the Hundred Flowers*, edited and translated by Hualing Nieh. New York: Columbia University Press, 1981.

Wang Ping, dir. *Nihongdeng xia de shaobing* [Sentinels under the neon lights], 1964.

Wang Shaoguang. *Minzhu sijiang* [Four lectures on democracy]. Beijing: Sanlian Shudian Chubanshe, 2008.

Wang Wenshi. *Heifeng* [Hei Feng]. Beijing: Zhongguo Qingnian Chubanshe, 1963.

———. "The Master Carpenter." *The Night of the Snowstorm*. Translated by Gladys Yang. Peking: Foreign Language Press, 1961.

Wang Xiaoming, ed. *Ershi shiji zhongguo wenxueshi lun* [On the history of twentieth-century Chinese literature]. 2 vols. Shanghai: Dongfang Chuban Zhongxin, 2003.

Wang Yao. "Zhongguo xin wenxue daxi (1937–1949), xu" [Preface to the encyclopedia of new Chinese literature (1937–1949)], 9–10. Shanghai: Shanghai Wenyi Chubanshe, 1990.

Weber, Max. *From Max Weber: Essays in Sociology*. Translated, edited, and with an introduction by H. H. Gerth and C. Wright Mills. New York: Oxford University Press, 1946.

Wei Wei. "Qi yanque zhizhi, mu honghu er gaoxiang" [In admiration of the high-flying swans]. *Zhongguo qingnian*, no. 20/21 (1963): 5–13.

"Wo de yanjing liang le" [My eyes are brighter]. *Laodong bao*, December 17, 1952.

"Women fufu liang" [We, a couple]. *Laodong bao* [Workers daily], July 25, 1953.

"Wo weishenme yao xue wenhua" [Why I want to study culture]. *Laodong bao*, September 24, 1953.

Xiao Fan. "Guoqu yu sixiang: 'Wenge' huiyi lu (jiexuan)" [The past and thought: Reminiscences of the "Cultural Revolution" (selections)]. In *Juannian de yipie: Mengmeng jinian wenji* [A stroke of longing: Collection commemorating Mengmeng]. Internal publication.

Xiao Yemu. "Women fufu zhijian" [Between my wife and me]. *Renmin wenxue*, no. 1 (1950): 37–45.

Xie Juezai. "Minzhu zhengzhi de shiji" [The actuality of democratic politics]. In *Yanan minzhu moshi yanjiu ziliao xuanbian* [Selected materials for researching the Yan'an democratic model]. Xian: Xibei Daxue Chubanshe, 2004.

———. "Minzhu zhengzhi shi jiu renmin de, fan minzhu zhengzhi shi duansong renmin de" [Democracy saves people, antidemocracy sacrifices people]. In *Yanan minzhu moshi yanjiu ziliao xuanbian* [Selected materials for researching the Yan'an democratic model]. Xian: Xibei Daxue Chubanshe, 2004.

Xing Gongwan. "Guanyu 'fangyan wenxue' de buchong yijian" [Additional views on "literature written in dialects"]. *Wenyi Bao* 3, no. 7, 1951.

Xiong Yuezhi and Zhou Wu, eds. *Shanghai: yizuo xiandaihua dushi de biannianshi* [Shanghai—A chronicle history of a modern metropolis]. Shanghai: Shanghai Shudian Chubanshe, 2007.

Xu Huaizhong. *Women bozhong aiqing* [We sow our love]. Beijing: Zhongguo Qingnian Chubanshe, 1957.

———. *Women bozhong aiqing* [We sow our love]. Beijing: Renmin Wenxue Chubanshe, 1960.

Xu Qingquan. *Wentan boluan fanzhen shilu* [Documenting bringing order out of chaos in cultural domains]. Hangzhou: Zhejiang Renmin Chubanshe, 2004.

Xue Ke. *Zhandou de qingchun* [The spring of battle]. Beijing: Renmin Wenxue Chubanshe, 2005.

Yan, Yunxiang. *Private Life under Socialism: Love, Intimacy, and Family Change in a Chinese Village, 1949–1999*. Stanford, CA: Stanford University Press, 2003.

Yang Kuisong. "Cong gongjizhi dao zhiwu dengji gongzi zhi—xin zhongguo jianli qianhou dangzheng renyuan shouru fenpei zhidu de yanbian" [From the provision system to the salary system based on occupational level: Changes in the income distribution system of party members around the establishment of new China]. *Lishi yanjiu*, no. 4 (2007): 111–37.

———. *Kai juan you yi* [Reading is always suspicious]. Nanchang: Jiangxi Renmin Chubanshe, 2007.

———. "1946–48 zhonggong zhongyang tugai zhengce biandong de lishi kaocha—youguan zhonggong tugaishi de yige zhenglun wenti" [Considerations on the 1946–1948 Party policy on land reform—debates on Party land reform policy]. Nanchang: Jiangxi Renmin Chubanshe, 2007.

Yang Mo. *Qingchun zhi ge* [Song of youth]. Beijing: Renmin Chubanshe, 1960.

———. *The Song of Youth*. Translated by Nan Ying. Peking: Foreign Language Press, 1964.

———. "Zibai—Wo de riji" [Confession: My diaries]. In *Yang Mo wenji* [Collected writings of Yang Mo] vol. 6. Beijing: Beijing Shiyue Wenyi Chubanshe, 1994.

Yang Xianhui. *Jiabiangou jishi* [Memories of Jiabiangou]. Tianjin: Guji Chubanshe, 2002.
Yao Wenyuan. "Wenxue shang de xiuzheng zhuyi he chuangzuo qingxiang" [On revisionism in some cultural and creative tendencies]. *Remin wenxue*, no. 11 (1957):109–26.
———. "Zhaoxiangguan li chu meixue" [Aesthetics in a photo shop]. *Wenhui bao*, May 8, 1958.
Ye Hongshen. *Shushan jianxia pingzhuan* [A critical biography of shushan jianxia]. Taipei: Taiwan Yuanjing Chuban Gongsi, 1982.
Yu Tingying. "Jiaqiang dui qingshaonian de zhengzhi sixiang jiaoyu" [Strengthen political education for the young]. *Hongqi*, no. 9 (1963): 5–7.
Yu Yingshi. *Shi yu Zhongguo wenhua* [The gentry and Chinese culture]. Shanghai: Shanghai Renmin Chubanshe, 1987.
Yu Zhen. "Nie Gannu xingshi dang'an" [Criminal case file of Nie Gannu]. *Zhongguo zuojia* no. 4 (2009): 6–83.
Yuan Jing, and Kong Jue. *Xin ernü yingxiong zhuan* [New heroic sons and daughters]. Beijing: Beijing Wenxue Chubanshe, 1978.
Zhang Chengzhi. "Beifang de he" [Rivers in the north], *Shi Yue*, no. 1 (1984): 4–115.
Zhang Jing. *Xiandai gonggong guize yu xiangcun shehui* [Modern public rules and rural society]. Shanghai: Shanghai Shudian Chubanshe, 2006.
Zhang Yigong. "Fanren Li Tongzhong de gushi" [The story of the prisoner Li Tongzhong]. *Shouhuo*, no. 1 (1980): 93–115.
Zhang Zhongxing. *Liu nian sui ying* [Fleeting years and fragmented shadows]. Beijing: Zhongguo Shehui Kexue Chubanshe, 1997.
Zhao Ming, dir. *Nianqing de yidai* [The young generation]. Shanghai: Dianying Zhipian Chang, 1965.
Zhao Shuli. *Sanliwan Village*. Translated by Gladys Yang. Peking: Foreign Language Press, 1957.
———. *Zhao Shuli quanji* [Complete collection of Zhao Shuli's writings], vols. 1–5. Taiyuan: Beiyue Wenyi Chubanshe, 1994.
———. *Zhao Shuli wenji* [Collected writings of Zhao Shuli], vols. 1–4. Beijing: Gongren Chubanshe, 1980.
Zheng Chaolin. *Zheng Chaolin huiyilu* [Zheng Chaolin's memoir]. Vol. 2. Beijing: Dongfang Chubanshe, 2004.
Zheng Qian. "Dangdai shehui zhuyi gaige yu zhongguo de 'wenhua dageming'" [Contemporary socialist reform and the "Cultural Revolution"]. In *Huishou "wenge": Zhongguo shinian "wenge" fenxi yu fansi* [Reexamining the "Cultural Revolution": Analyses of and reflections on China's ten-year "Cultural Revolution"]. Beijing: Zhonggong Dangshi Chubanshe, 2000.
Zhi Xia. *Tiedao youjidui* [Guerrillas on the railways]. Shanghai: Shanghai Wenyi Chubanshe, 1978.
———. "'Tiedao youjidui' de chuangzuo jingguo" [The creative process behind Guerrillas on the railways]. In *Tiedao youjidui*. Shanghai: Shanghai Wenyi Chubanshe, 1978.
———. "'Tiedao youjidui' houji" [Afterword to Guerrillas on the railways]. In *Tiedao youjidui*. Shanghai: Shanghai Wenyi Chubanshe, 1978.
Zhonghua Renmin Gongheguo fagui huibian, 1955 nian 7 yue–12 yue [Compendium of laws of the People's Republic of China, July–December 1955]. Beijing: Falü Chubanshe, 1956.

Zhou Erfu. *Shanghai de zaocheng* [Morning of Shanghai]. Vols. 1–3. Beijing: Renmin Chubanshe, 1980.

Zhou Hangsheng. "Ta ba shufa xie shang tiananmen hongqiang—yu zhumin shufajia, yishujia Zhong Ling duihua" [He brought calligraphy to the red walls of Tiananmen: A conversation with the famous calligrapher and artist Zhong Ling]. *Dangan chunqiu*, no. 5 (2006).

Zhou Libo. [Discussing "dialect literature"]. *Wenyi bao*, March 10, 1951.

———. *Great Changes in the Mountain Village*. Translated by Derek Bryan. Peking: Foreign Language Press, 1961.

———. *The Hurricane*. Beijing: Foreign Language Press, 1981.

———. *Shanxiang jubian* [Great changes in the mountain village]. Beijing: Renmin Wenxue Chubanshe, 2005.

———. *Zhou Libo wenji* [Collected writings of Zhou Libo], vol. 5. Shanghai: Shanghai Wenyi Chubanshe, 1985.

Zhou Yang. "Fayang 'wusi' wenxue geming de douzheng chuantong." *Renmin wenxue*, no. 5 (1954): 7–12.

———. "Lun Zhao Shuli de chuangzuo" [A discussion of Zhao Shuli's creative writings]. In *Zhongguo xin wenxue daxi (1937–1949)* [The encyclopedia of new Chinese literature (1937–1949)], 1. Shanghai: Shanghai Wenyi Chubanshe, 1990.

Zhu Hongzhao. *Yanan richang shenghuozhong de lishi (1937–1947)* [History of Yan'an's everyday life (1937–1947)]. Guilin: Guangxi Shida Chubanshe, 2007.

Žižek, Slavoj. *The Sublime Object of Ideology*. London: Verso, 1989.

INDEX

Ai Wu, 200, 343, 350–51, 353; and *Bailian cheng'gang* [Steeled and tempered], 100, 312, 343–44, 346–48, 410
Anderson, Benedict, xiv, 91, 324; and *Imagined Communities*, 29, 38, 68, 222, 238
Angang Constitution, 340–47, 354, 375
Anti-Rightist Campaign [1957], 9, 24, 99, 101, 123, 417
An Ziwen: "Peiyang geming jiebanren shi dang de yixiang zhanlue renwu" [Fostering revolutionary successors is a strategic task for the Party], 362
Arendt, Hannah, 167

Ba Jin, 147–48, 227, 285, 326–27; and *Family* [*jia*], 147
Badiou, Alan, 2–4, 7, 25
Bai Wei: *Kenhuang qu* [Reclaiming wasteland], 56, 283, 366
Baudrillard, Jean, 237, 366, 369–70
Bauman, Zygmunt, 4–5, 65, 382–83
Bell, Daniel, 310; and *The Cultural Contradictions of Capitalism*, 13, 99n31
Berman, Marshall, 56

Cao Ming: *Chengfeng polang* [Riding the Wind and Waves], 100, 312, 343, 352–53
Chatterjee, Partha, 29, 60, 66, 374
Chen Dengke, 136; and *Feng lei* [Storm], 43–44, 283; and "Tongzhi, laoshi, zhanyou—yi Qian Yi" [Comrade, teacher, comrade in arms—remembering Qian Yi], 136–37
"Chenggong yihou" [After the success], 364
Chen Yinque, xxvi; and "Feng Youlan Zhexueshi shangce shencha baogao" [Review report on Feng Youlan's *History of Chinese Philosophy*], 2–3
Cold War, xix, 15, 362
Cong Shen, 164, 360, 384, 386; and "Zhu ni jiankang" [Wish you good health], 163, 360; and "'Qianwan buyao wangji' zhuti de xingcheng" [The subject matter of *Never Forget*], 370, 385
the Cultural Revolution, xiv, xix–xx, xxviii, 9–10, 23–24, 63, 68n97, 85, 95, 97, 100, 112, 127, 143, 160, 164, 255, 336, 358–60, 362, 378, 386, 389, 399, 402, 415–17, 419–25

Deleuze, Gilles, 17–18, 371, 390
Ding Ling, 153, 226–27, 368, 401; and *The Sun Shines over the Sanggan River*, 49, 86, 89

Du Runsheng: *Du Runsheng zishu: Zhongguo nongcun tizhi biange zhongda juece jishi* [Du Runsheng remembers: Memories of the important decisions on China's village structural transformation], 11, 52, 172, 262

Fei Xiaotong, 27, 75, 172, 264
Feng Deying, 364; and *Kucai hua* [Bitter flowers], 183, 364
Foucault, Michel, 148

Gaizao [reeducation or self-remolding], 34, 43–44, 265; and alteration, 198; and the mobilization reform (*dongyuangaizao*), 85–86; and reform, 95, 107, 197
Gellner, Ernest, 38–39
Giddens, Antony, 64–65, 167, 294–95, 392, 409
Gramsci, Antonio, 14, 100, 156
the Great Leap Forward, 63, 286, 288, 299, 328, 331, 333, 344, 374
Gronow, Jukka, 375–76, 379
Guo Moruo, 162, 225, 285; and "'Xin ernu yingxiong zhun' xu" [Preface to New heroic sons and daughters], 201, 209

Hao Ran, 54, 125, 293; and *Yanyang tian* [Sunny days], 54, 68–70, 87, 111, 125, 292, 314, 359, 418
Hong Zicheng, 10, 34
Hook, Sidney, 202
Huang Ziping, 155; and "Bing de yinyu yu wenxue shengchan—Ding Ling de 'Zai yiyuan zhong'ji qita" [The metaphoric use of illness and literary production: On Ding Ling's "In the Hospital"], 401; and *Geming, lishi, xiaoshuo* [Revolution, history, fiction], 148, 186, 190, 233; and "Geming, xing, changpian xiaoshuo" [Revolution, sex, and the novel], 390

Jiang Guangci, 165–66
Juben [Drama scripts], 126, 163–64, 359–60, 364, 386

Karatani, Kojin: and *Origins of Modern Japanese Literature*, 29–32, 37, 77, 200
Kuang Xinnian, xx–xxi

Lefebvre, Henri, 375
Leninism, 20, 38, 87, 96–97, 106, 127, 129, 138, 260, 404, 423–24; and Lenin, V. I., 13, 46, 97, 100, 136, 372, 388, 421
Li, Oufan [Leo Oufan Lee], 170, 217, 222
Liang Bin, 246; and *Bo huo ji* [Spreading the fire], 40–41, 230; and *Hongqi Pu* [Keep the Red Flag Flying], 262–63; and "Mantan *Hongqi pu* de chuangzuo" [Speaking of the creative process for *Keep the Red Flag Flying*], 243–45
Liang Qichao, 29, 165; and "Shaonian Zhongguo shuo" [Young China], 61, 146–47, 416; and "Xin shixue" [New historiography], 6, 248
Li Dazhao, 230, 252–53
Lin Chun, xxiv, xxvi–xxvii
the literature of the seventeen years, xii, 18, 410–11
Li Tuo, 189, 427
Liu Ching. *See* Liu Qing
Liu Qing, 286; and *Chuangye shi* [The builders], 44, 54, 56, 66, 75, 87,109, 117, 121–22, 161, 255, 279–80, 349, 407
Liu Zaifu, xx–xxii, 426
Liu Zuocong: "Wo dui 'fangyan wenxue' de yidian yijian" [Some more comments on "dialect literature"], 77
Li Yang: *50–70 niandai Zhongguo wenxue zai jiedu* [Rereading 1950s–1970s Chinese literature], 71–72, 82, 158, 177, 189, 217, 241
Li Zehou, 426
Li Zhun, 278, 297; and "Li Shuangshuang xiaozhuan" [The story of Li Shuangshuang], 290
Luo Dan, and *Fengyu de liming* [The storm of dawn], 117–18, 277, 311–13
Luo Ruiqing, 239–40, 262–63
Lu Xun, 29–30, 38, 77, 93, 123, 140–41, 178, 243, 281, 347, 361; and "San Xian Ji xuyan" [Introduction to *San xian ji*], 155; and "Women xianzai zenyang zuo fuqin" [How can we be fathers today?], 155; and "Wenhua pianzhi lun" [Imbalances in cultural development], 281

Ma'anshan [Magnitogorsk] Constitution, 341–43, 375
Ma Feng, 195–96n14, 198–99, 212, 282–83; and Ma Feng, Xi Rong, *Lüliang Yingxiong Zhuan* [Chronicles of the Lüliang heroes], 201–2, 204, 207–8, 210
Mao Dun: and "'Geming' jia 'lianai' de gongshi" [The "revolution" plus "love" formula], 165; and "Guanyu 'luliang yingxiong zhun' " [Concerning *Chronicles of the Lüliang Heroes*], 208; and "Guanyu yishu de jiqiao: zai quanguo qingnian wenxue chuangzuozhe huiyi shang de baogao" [On the techniques of art—Speech at the all-China young literary writers' conference"], 79–80; and the "Mao Dun tradition," 76, 81, 165–66, 168, 177, 209, 243–44; and *Ziye* [Midnight], 184, 308

Maoism, 94, 96–98, 100, 106, 271
Mao Zedong (Mao Tse-tung), 9, 12, 15, 43, 45–48, 50, 54, 76, 86, 95, 101–2, 108, 127–59, 161, 163–64, 180–81, 230, 235, 238, 248, 253–54, 275–76, 281, 283–84, 294, 297, 323, 340–43, 355, 357–59, 363–64, 374–75, 378, 399, 408, 414–15, 426; and *Mao Zedong Wenji* [Collected writings of Mao Zedong], 6, 88, 97, 103, 113, 116, 134–37,151, 155, 180–81, 203, 229, 248, 297, 308–310, 342, 423–24; and *Mao Zedong zhuan* [Biography of Mao Zedong], 399; and *Mao Zhuxi zai sulian de yanlun* [Chairman Mao's speeches in the Soviet Union], 164; and "On Agriculture Co-Operation" ("Guanyu nongye hezuohua wenti"), 96, 98; and "The Question of Love—Young People and Old People," 149, 166; and "Talks at the Yan'an Forum on Literature and Art" (or "Talks" or "Talks at the Yenan Forum on Literature and Art"), xiii–xix, 79, 136, 138, 157–58, 189, 191, 194, 217, 221, 278
Marx, Karl, 76, 97, 100, 128–31, 252, 333, 375, 425; 252, 333, 375, 425; and *Communist Manifesto*, 65; 313; and Marxism, 2, 7, 21, 37–38, 76, 90, 131–32, 137–38, 183, 186, 247, 252–54, 259–60, 263, 333, 338, 347, 355, 414, 421
Masao, Sato, 95, 400
May Fourth (or the May Fourth Movement), xiii, xx, 42, 48, 51, 62, 66, 76, 149, 151, 155, 162, 166, 168, 180, 182, 192, 195, 197–98, 222, 243–45; and May Fourth literature, xx–xxi, 51, 162, 169, 193, 242, 304; and the May Fourth New Culture Movement, xxi, 6, 49, 93, 149, 187, 194, 196–98, 200–201, 208, 233, 242, 246, 267, 380
Meisner, Maurice J., xxii–xxiii, 90, 97–98, 363–64; and the "Yan'an Spirit," xxi–xxiii
Meng Yue, 33, 36, 41, 45, 59, 200, 215, 247, 274; and *Lishi yu xushu* [History and narrative], 51; and "Zhongguo wenxue de 'xiandaixing' yu Zhang Ailing" [The "modernity" of Chinese literature and Zhang Ailing], 190, 214

Nan Fan, 133
Nianqing de yidai [The young generation], 164, 359

Qian Liqun: and *Wo de jingshen zizhuan* [An autobiography of my spiritual life], 139
Qin Zhaoyang, 265, 270
Qiu Chi, also "Yu Chen Bo zhi shu" [Letter to Chen Bo], 39
Qu, Bo [Chu, Po], also *Linhai xueyuan* [Tracks in the snowy forest], 105, 189, 211–12, 215

Rogaski, Ruth, 365

Said, Edward W., 156–57
Schmitt, Carl, 284, 303, 391
Schwartz, Benjamin I., 94, 100, 272, 409
Scott, James, 313
Selden, Mark, 45, 47–48, 61, 145n1, 229–30n86
Shen Fu: *Wanzi qianhong zongshi chun* [A riot of color is always spring], 299–300
the Soviet model, 96, 130–31, 340
Su Li: *Women cunli de nianqingren* [Young people in our village], 174, 363
Sun Jingrui: *Hongqi chashang Damendao* [Planting the red flag on Damen Island], 239
Sun Li, 35–36; and *Fengyun chuji* [Stormy Years], 35–36, 40; and "Hehua dian" ["Lotus creek"], 35, 39–40
Sun Qian: "Qiyi de lihun gushi" [A strange divorce story], 182

Tang Tao, 79
Tang Xiaobing, 360–61, 397; and *Zai jiedu: Dazhong wenyi yu yishi xingtai* [Reinterpretation: Ideology and popular literature and art], 5, 360; and "'Qianwan buyao wangji' de lishi yiyi: guanyu richang shenghuo de jiaolü jiqi xiandaixing" [The historical significance of "Never Forget": Anxiety over everyday life and its modernity], 317, 360
Taylor, Charles: and "The Politics of Recognition," 150–52, 159
Townsend, James R., and Brantly Womack: also *Politics in China*, 49–50, 87–88, 410

Vukovich, Daniel, xiii–xiv, xix

Wallerstein, Immanuel, 15
Wang, David Der-wei, 146, 165–67, 169
Wang Anyi, 300; and *Qimeng shidai* [The enlightened era], 67n97, 386
Wang Hongsheng, 219
Wang Hui, 7, 81, 83, 243
Wang Meng, 100, 119, 121; and "A Young Man Arrives at the Organization Department," 153, 162, 401, 408; and *Qinchun wansui* [Long live youth], 161, 164; and *Wang Meng zizhuan* [Wang Meng's autobiography], 163–65, 219
Wang Shaoguang: *Minzhu sijiang* [Four lectures on democracy], 373
Wang Wenshi: *Heifeng* [Hei Feng], 60–62, 69, 161; "The Master Carpenter," 70–71
Wang Yao, 192–93, 197

Weber, Max, 1; and "Politics as a Vocation," 410
Wenyi bao [Culture News, Newspaper of Literature and Art, Literature and Art Newspaper], 76–79, 226–27, 368
"Womende yanjing liangle" [Our eyes are brighter], 323
"Women fufu liang" [We, a couple], 320–22
"Wo weishenme yao xue wenhua" [Why I want to study culture], 323

Xiao Yemu, 368; and "Women fufu zhijian" [Between my wife and me], 160, 224, 265, 311, 366–67
Xie Juezai, 12, 373–74, 391, 411–13; and "Minzhu zhengzhi de shiji" [The actuality of democratic politics], 372–73
Xing Gongwan, 76–77, 80–81, 310–11; and "Guanyu 'fangyan wenxue' de buchong yijian" [Additional views on "literature written in dialects"], 77–78
Xue Ke: *Zhandou de qingchun* [The spring of battle], 91–92, 113, 182
Xu Huaizhong: *Women bozhong aiqing* [We sow our love], 56, 174, 366

Yan, Yunxiang, 171–72
the Yan'an Path, 96–97, 137
Yang Kuisong, 129–30
Yang Mo, xvii, 179; and *Qingchun zhi ge* [The Song of youth], 62, 158, 177–78, 185
Yao Wenyuan, 120–121, 271–72; and "Wenxue shang de xiuzheng zhuyi he chuangzuo qingxiang" [On revisionism in some cultural and creative tendencies], 119–20; and "Zhaoxiangguan li chu meixue" [Aesthetics in a photo shop], 179
Yuan Jing, and Kong Jue: *Xin ernü yingxiong zhuan* [New heroic sons and daughters], 36, 201, 205
Yu Luoke: "Chushen lun" [On family origins], 12, 112, 359, 415
Yu Tingying: "Jiaqiang dui qingshaonian de zhengzhi sixiang jiaoyu" [Strengthen political education for the young], 361, 387

Zhang Chengzhi: "Beifang de he" [Rivers in the north], 401

Zhang Yigong: "Fanren Li Tongzhong de gushi" [The story of the prisoner Li Tongzhong], 418
Zhang Zhongxing, 179
Zhao Shuli, xvii, xxv, 14–15, 17–19, 22, 175, 191n7, 195–96, 198–200, 226, 245, 267, 269, 283, 286–89, 291–93, 295, 300, 350, 383, 407; and "Dengji" [Registration], 171–72; and *Diban* [The land], 254–62, 264; and "Meng Xiangying fanshen" [Meng Xiangying stands up], 92–93, 304; and "Meng Yangying fanshen" ["Meng Yangying Turns a Leaf" annotated], 286; and "My Views on How Communes Should Lead Production," 287–88; and *Sanliwan Village*, 50–54, 121–22, 161, 173, 282, 285; and "Shiganjia Pan Yongfu" [Man of action: Pan Yongfu], 286–88; and "Xiao Erhei jiehun" [Xiao Erhei gets married], 169–173, 196, 254; and the Zhao Shuli path, 19, 191, 193
Zheng Chaolin: *Zheng Chaolin huiyilu* [Zheng Chaolin's memoir], 28–29
Zhi Xia: *Tiedao youji dui* [Guerrillas on the railways], 202, 211–12, 214–21, 223, 260–61, 263; *Zhonghua Renmin Gongheguo fagui huibian, 1955 nian 7 yue–12 yue* [Compendium of laws of the People's Republic of China, July–December 1955], 317–18, 413–14
Zhou, Libo [Chou, Li-po], 110, 116, 154, 247; and *Baofeng zhouyu* [The Hurricane], 89, 116, 266, 277, 314; and *Shanxiang jubian* [Great changes in the mountain village], 51, 95, 110, 116, 161, 173, 255, 417; and "Tan 'fangyan' wenti" [Discussing "dialect literature"], 78–9, 86; and *Zhou Libo wenji* [Collected writings of Zhou Libo], 207, 246, 274
Zhou Erfu: *Shanghai de zaocheng* [Morning of Shanghai], 92, 117
Zhou Hangsheng: "Ta ba shufa xie shang tiananmen hongqiang—yu zhumin shufajia, yishujia Zhong Ling duihua" [He brought calligraphy to the red walls of Tiananmen: A conversation with the famous calligrapher and artist Zhong Ling], 135
Zhou Yang, 169, 177, 191–92, 197, 199–200, 242–43
Zhu Hongzhao, 222–23
Žižek, Slavoj, 220

www.ingramcontent.com/pod-product-compliance
Lightning Source LLC
Chambersburg PA
CBHW070745020526
44116CB00032B/1931